FROMMER'S
IRELAND ON $25 A DAY

by Susan Poole

DONALD + MARLA
        McMANARA

RiveRSDALe House,
DRiPSey, Co. CORK
PH No. 334188

1985-86 Edition

Published by Frommer/Pasmantier Publishers
A Division of Simon & Schuster, Inc.
1230 Avenue of the Americas
New York, New York 10020

ISBN 0-671-52472-0

Manufactured in the United States of America

*Although every effort was made to ensure the accuracy
of price information appearing in this book,
it should be kept in mind that prices
can and do fluctuate in the course of time.*

CONTENTS

Introduction   **IRELAND ON $25 A DAY**   **1**
- 1. Ireland & the Irish   **2**
  - The Lay of the Land   **3**
  - The Weather   **3**
  - The Flora and Fauna   **3**
  - Geographic Divisions   **4**
  - The Irish   **4**
- 2. A Brief History   **6**
- 3. Ireland with this Book   **18**
  - Region by Region   **18**
  - Towns, Villages and Cities   **19**
- 4. Basics of Budgeting   **22**
- 5. $25-A-Day Travel Club   **25**

Chapter I   **THE PRACTICALITIES**   **29**
- 1. The Currency   **29**
- 2. Preparing for Your Trip   **30**
  - Travel Documents   **30**
  - What Clothes to Bring   **30**
  - Tourist Information   **32**
  - When to Book Ahead   **34**
  - Read Before You Go   **35**
- 3. Discounts for Students   **36**
  - Before You Come   **36**
  - When You Arrive   **37**
  - Transportation Savings   **37**
  - Study in Ireland   **38**
- 4. Where to Stay   **39**
  - Campgrounds   **40**
  - Hostels   **40**

	Town and Country Homes	41
	Farmhouses	43
	Guesthouses	43
	Hotels	44
	Self-Catering	45
	5. Where to Eat	46
	Picnics	48
	Pubs	48
	Tourist Meals	48
	Budget Restaurants	48
	Guesthouse Meals	49
	Irish Recipes	49
	6. Big Splurges	50
	7. Shopping	51
	Shopping Basics	51
	Shannon Duty Free	
	Shopping	52
	Other Shops	53
	Aran Sweaters	53
	Woolens and Tweeds	54
	Waterford Glass	54
	Irish Lace	54
	Crafts	55
	Books	55
	Ireland by Mail	56
	Miscellaneous	56
Chapter II	GETTING TO AND AROUND IRELAND	57
	1. From America	57
	Air Fares to Ireland	57
	European Connections	
	from Ireland	58
	Your Choice of Airline	58
	Package Tours	59
	2. From Britain	60
	By Air	60
	By Sea	60

3. From the Continent 61
   By Air 61
   By Sea 61
4. Getting Around Ireland 62
   By Foot and Bike 62
   By Horse-Drawn Caravan 62
   By Bus and Train 64
      Rail and Bus Passes 65
      Local Buses 65
      Sightseeing Tours 65
   By Car 66
      Car Rentals 67
      A Discount Rate 68
      Other Car Hire Firms 69
5. Suggested Itineraries 69

Chapter III   **IRELAND, A TOURIST'S SURVEY** 74
1. Things to See and Do 74
   Special Events 74
   Historic Places 76
   Art Galleries 76
   Museums 77
   State Forests 77
   Cruising 77
   Sports 78
2. Ireland After Dark 80
   Irish Pubs 80
   Musical Nights 82
   Banquets and Cabarets 84
   Theater 84
3. Tracing Your Irish Roots 84
4. Meet the Irish 85

Chapter IV   **DUBLIN AND THE EASTERN REGION** 86
1. Introduction to Counties
   Dublin, Wicklow, Louth,
   Kildare, and Meath 86

2. Dublin   87
    Orientation   87
    Useful Information   88
    Accommodations   90
    Where to Eat   101
    Things to See and Do   107
      Seeing the City   107
      Points of Interest   108
      Museums and Art
        Galleries   111
      The Guinness Brewery   112
      Parks and the Zoo   113
      In Search of Literary
        Greats   113
    Dublin After Dark   114
      The Pubs   114
      Traditional Irish Music   118
      Theater   119
      Concerts   120
      Cabaret   120
      Dancing   120
    Special Events   121
    Shopping   122
3. Around the Eastern Region   123
    Accommodations by
      County   123
    Where to Eat by County   125
    Things to See and Do
      by County   126

Chapter V   **WEXFORD, WATERFORD, AND THE SOUTHEAST**   131
    1. Introducing Counties
      Wexford, Waterford,
      Kilkenny, Carlow, and
      South Tipperary   131

        2. Wexford   **132**
             Orientation   **132**
             Useful Information   **134**
             Accommodations   **134**
             Where to Eat   **135**
             Things to See and Do   **137**
             Wexford's Pubs   **138**
             Wexford Opera Festival   **138**
        3. Waterford   **139**
             Orientation   **140**
             Useful Information   **140**
             Accommodations   **141**
             Where to Eat   **143**
             Things to See and Do   **144**
        4. Around the Southeast   **148**
             Accommodations   **148**
             Where to Eat   **155**
             Things to See and Do   **158**

Chapter VI   **CORK, KILLARNEY, AND THE
                 SOUTHWEST**   **166**
        1. Introduction to the Southwest   **166**
        2. Cork City   **167**
             Orientation   **168**
             Useful Information   **168**
             Accommodations   **169**
             Where to Eat   **173**
             Things to See and Do   **174**
             Cork After Dark   **176**
             The Pubs of Cork   **177**
             Special Events   **178**
        3. Killarney and Its Lakes   **179**
             Orientation   **180**
             Useful Information   **180**
             Accommodations   **181**
             Where to Eat   **185**

Things to See and Do   **186**
Crafts and Other
   Shopping   **188**
Killarney After Dark   **189**
Special Events   **191**
4. Around Counties Cork and
   Kerry   **191**
Accommodations   **191**
Where to Eat   **199**
Things to See and Do   **201**

Chapter VII   **LIMERICK AND THE SHANNONSIDE**   **212**
1. Introducing Shannonside   **212**
2. Shannon Airport   **212**
3. Limerick   **213**
Orientation   **213**
Useful Information   **215**
Accommodations   **215**
Where to Eat   **217**
Things to See and Do   **218**
In the City   **219**
Limerick Lace   **219**
Bunratty Castle and
   Folk Park   **219**
Limerick's Pubs   **220**
Limerick After Dark   **221**
Medieval Banquets   **222**
The Captain's Table   **223**
4. Around Counties Limerick,
   Clare, and North Tipperary   **223**
Accommodations   **223**
Where to Eat   **227**
Things to See and Do   **229**
Lough Gur   **229**
Irish Dresden   **229**
Lough Derg and
   Killaloe   **229**

	The Craggaunowen Project	229
	Clare Heritage Centre	230
	Ennis	230
	Cliffs of Moher	230
	Loop Head Peninsula	230
	Doolin	231
	The Pubs of County Clare	231
	The Burren	231
	Holy Cross Abbey	232
	Roscrea	232
Chapter VIII	**GALWAY AND THE WESTERN REGION**	**233**
	1. Introducing the Western Region	233
	2. Galway	234
	Orientation	234
	Useful Information	234
	Accommodations	235
	Where to Eat	238
	Things to See and Do	240
	In the City	240
	The Aran Islands	241
	Galway After Dark	242
	A Literary Banquet	242
	Theater	242
	Traditional Music	243
	Special Events	243
	Shopping	244
	3. Around Counties Galway and Mayo	245
	Accommodations	245

	Where to Eat by County	**250**
	Things to See and Do	**252**
	Connemara	**252**
	Cong, Ashford Castle and *The Quiet Man*	**254**
	Knock	**255**
	Ballintubber Abbey	**255**
	Croagh Patrick and Westport	**256**
	Achill Island	**256**
Chapter IX	**SLIGO, DONEGAL, AND THE NORTHWEST**	**258**
	1. Introducing the Northwest	**258**
	2. Sligo Town and Yeats Country	**259**
	Orientation	**259**
	Useful Information	**259**
	Accommodations	**259**
	Where to Eat	**262**
	Things to See and Do	**263**
	Sligo Town	**263**
	Yeats Country	**264**
	Prehistoric Sligo	**264**
	Sligo After Dark	**265**
	Special Events	**266**
	3. Donegal Town	**266**
	Useful Information	**266**
	Accommodations	**266**
	Where to Eat	**267**
	Things to See and Do	**267**
	Donegal After Dark	**268**
	4. Around Counties Sligo, Donegal, and Leitrim	**268**
	Accommodations	**268**
	Where to Eat	**273**
	Things to See and Do	**274**

Chapter X **THE MIDLANDS** **278**
        1. Introducing the Midlands **278**
        2. Around Counties Cavan,
           Laois, Longford,
           Monaghan, Offaly,
           Roscommon, and
           Westmeath **278**
           Accommodations **278**
           Where to Eat **281**
           Things to See and Do **282**

Chapter XI **INTRODUCING NORTHERN IRELAND** **285**
        1. The Practicalities **287**
        2. A Suggested Itinerary **289**

Chapter XII **BELFAST AND LONDONDERRY** **290**
        1. Belfast **290**
           Accommodations **290**
           Where to Eat **293**
           Things to See and Do **294**
        2. Londonderry **295**
           Accommodations **296**
           Where to Eat **297**
           Things to See and Do **297**

Chapter XIII **AROUND NORTHERN IRELAND** **298**
        1. County Antrim **298**
           Accommodations **298**
           Where to Eat **299**
           Things to See and Do **299**
              The Carrickfergus
                Castle **299**
              The Glens of Antrim **300**
              The Giant's Causeway **300**
              Carrick-a-Rede Rope
                Bridge **300**
              Dunluce Castle **300**
              Bushmills Distillery **300**

Chester Arthur
  Ancestral Home **301**
  Round Tower of Antrim **301**
2. County Armagh **301**
  Accommodations **301**
  Where to Eat **301**
  Things to See and Do **302**
  Cathedrals **302**
  Derrymore House **302**
3. County Down **302**
  Accommodations **302**
  Where to Eat **303**
  Things to See and Do **304**
  Ards Peninsula **304**
  St. Patrick's Grave **304**
4. County Fermanagh **305**
  Accommodations **305**
  Where to Eat **305**
  Things to See and Do **306**
  Belleek **306**
5. County Londonderry **306**
  Bellarena Fish Smokery **306**
6. County Tyrone **307**
  Accommodations **307**
  Where to Eat **307**
  Things to See and Do **307**
  Ulster-American Folk
  Park **307**

Chapter XIV **THE ABC'S OF IRELAND** **309**
Chapter XV **P.S.—MORE BIG SPLURGES** **313**
Eastern Region **313**
  1. County Dublin **313**
  2. County Wicklow **317**
  3. County Louth **318**

    4. County Kildare   **318**
The Southeast   **319**
    1. County Wexford   **319**
    2. County Waterford   **320**
    3. County Kilkenny   **321**
    4. South Tipperary   **321**
The Southern Region   **322**
    1. County Cork   **322**
    2. County Kerry   **324**
Shannonside   **325**
    1. County Clare   **325**
    2. County Limerick   **327**
The Western Region   **327**
    1. County Galway   **327**
    2. County Mayo   **329**
The Northwestern Region   **331**
    1. County Sligo   **331**
    2. County Donegal   **332**
    3. County Leitrim   **332**
The Midlands   **333**
    1. County Monaghan   **333**
Northern Ireland   **333**
    1. County Antrim   **333**
    2. County Londonderry   **334**
    3. County Down   **335**

MAPS

Ireland 20–21
Dublin 88
Downtown Dublin 91
Wexford 133
Waterford 139
Cork 170
Killarney Lakes 179
Killarney Town 181
Limerick 214
Galway/Salthill 235
Sligo 260
Belfast 291

*To Dee, who has found her own special
love for Ireland.*

INFLATION ALERT: Ireland—for all its magic—is not immune to the ravages of inflation. Also, currency exchanges continue to fluctuate with international monetary trends.

While we have made every effort to quote the most reliable prices and price forecasts, in today's world conditions change so rapidly that during the second year of this edition—1986—the wise traveler will *add about 20%* to the prices quoted in Irish pounds throughout and will carefully *check the exchange rate* at the time of travel.

A DISCLAIMER: We have personally checked the recommendations contained in the main body of this book. You should note, however, that those establishments described under the title "Readers' Suggestions" have *not* in many cases been inspected by the author and are the opinions of individual readers only. They do not in any way represent the opinions of the publisher or author of this book.

ABOUT THIS BOOK

Having bought this book, you no doubt already *know* what it's about. Simply stated, it's about saving you money.

If you've already decided you're going to Ireland, let me say that *you* have taken the first step toward that money-saving goal. If you haven't yet made up your mind, I'll do my very best in the following chapters to convince you that you should—for the traveler with a keen eye on the budget, there are few places in this inflation-ridden world that so happily offer so magical an experience at anywhere near the bargain prices you'll find in the Emerald Isle. We'll deal with the magic on almost every page, but for now, let's get down to basics: value-for-dollar.

Basics are what you'll buy for the $25 in our title. A place to sleep and three meals a day can easily be budgeted for that amount without sacrificing comfort, diet, or enjoyment. In fact—and this is a big part of the magic—in Ireland, your room will be clean, comfortable, and more often than not include an enchanting view plus (for not one cent extra) some of the most charming and entertaining hosts you're likely to find anywhere on the face of the earth.

The key is to go the bed-and-breakfast, farmhouse, guesthouse route. The only thing you'll forego is a private bathroom, although in more and more cases a toilet and shower *will* be available at only slightly more than the cost of just a room.

For a maximum of $11 a day, you'll be welcomed into an Irish family home and overwhelmed each morning with a breakfast so ample you'll be hard pressed to eat another bite until dinnertime. That by no means implies you'll be giving up your midday meal: the $14 balance in our budget will easily cover a pub lunch (which runs about $4) and a more-than-adequate dinner (about $10).

Of course, if you're a hostel devotee or eligible for student discounts, you'll have money left over. While researching this book, I met a young American student just ending a three-week stay at an average cost of $11 a day. And she did *not* look malnourished!

Above our basics, you'll have to figure additional costs for travel, entertainment, shopping, and the like. But, since our purpose is to save you money in *every* area, you will find in these pages reports on the best bargains we could find in each of these categories. We've quoted prices in both Irish pounds and American dollars to save you some mental arithmetic (be sure to read the Inflation Alert carefully, however, and keep an eagle eye on the current exchange rate when you travel).

Because Ireland is chock-a-block with special places—and not *all* come at budget prices—you'll also find "Big Splurges" in almost every region. You might consider our budget recommendations as the meat-and-potatoes of this book, while Big Splurges are like the out-of-season strawberries you treat yourself to no matter what they cost. Whether or not you indulge will be up to you, your personal inclinations and your budget. They are *not* included in our $25-a-day: they *are* worth a thought or two.

One last word about that magic. In all the years I've been visiting Ireland, I've found it in places as disparate as big, luxury hotels (so impersonal most other places), B&Bs with just one or two bedrooms, and casual pub encounters. Most of all, though, it exists in stumbled-on, out-of-the-way places, be they accommodations, eateries, or scenic spots. You have my personal guarantee that, as a budget traveler lodging with Irish families, you'll be steered to many a favorite pub or local attraction or unforgettable character by your hosts, and that's the *best* bargain you'll find for your $25-A-Day!

Enjoy!

ACKNOWLEDGMENTS

MY HEARTFELT THANKS to the people of Ireland, who have—from the moment I first set foot in their country—made me very welcomed. Very special thanks to Bord Failte, whose marvelous staff should serve as a model for all other tourism organizations around the globe; to Aer Lingus, all that an Irish airline should be; and to good Irish friends like the John Flynns, Frank Lewis, Micheal Macgiobuin, John B. Keane, Mary and Noel McLoughlin, Angela and Tony Muckley, Brenda Weir, Philomena Morin, Pat Mackey, and scores of others who have joined in the researching of this book with typical Irish wit, good humor and helpfulness. To Pat Tunison Preston, in New York, my undying gratitude for special support and unfailing aid.

IRELAND ON $25 A DAY

1. Ireland and the Irish
2. A Brief History
3. Ireland with this Book
4. The Basics of Budgeting
5. The $25-A-Day Travel Club— How to Save Money on All Your Travels

YOU KNOW ABOUT IRELAND, of course—it's that lovely isle that appeared when "a little bit of heaven dropped from out the sky one day!" Skeptical? Well, look around for the most hard-nosed skeptic you know who's *been* to Ireland and then get set to listen to hours of rapturous memories!

Ireland has that affect on people. All people. For me, it began back in 1973, when I first encountered the incredible beauty of this small country's landscape and learned with amazement that the magnificent sum of $2.40 would make me an instant member of warm Irish families who were anxious to share their fireside, friends, favorite pub, innumerable cups of tea, and the most enormous breakfasts I'd ever seen.

I stayed three weeks that year, and haven't missed going back for a part of every year since. That's been possible for me—a confirmed budget traveler—because Ireland is so *affordable*. Oh, prices have risen there quite as fast as they have everywhere else in the world (in 1984 I paid anywhere from $7 to $11 for that same bed-and-breakfast), but Ireland is still one of the best travel buys I've come across.

But there's much, much more to it than that. There are some things that would be cheap at *any* price, and Ireland has more than its fair share of those priceless commodities. Each visit has brought fresh discoveries and new friends. There are always new tales to bring home; still more witty one-liners that spring so naturally to Irish lips to try to remember; more memories of nights of unplanned music and song that somehow just happened; still more miles of unbelievably beautiful coastline or mountains or rolling green fields suddenly unfolding around corners I'd not turned before; new Irish names to add to my Christmas list.

Perhaps even more important is the glow I bring back each year after spending a little time with people who have managed to hold on to basic values that in other parts of the world these days seem as elusive as a dream.

Blarney Stone blather? Not so. Just wait until you hear the ravings of your plane mates on the flight back home! I am just *one* of the Americans who every year head off to Ireland—almost 300,000 in 1983. We're joined by thousands of enthusiastic English, French, Dutch, Germans, and a good number from countries as far away as Japan, New Zealand, and Australia, who send the total number of foreign visitors over the two million mark. Many Europeans return year after year for superb fishing or golfing or biking or horse racing or theater or music—or simply to soak up the unique atmosphere of this little country and the extraordinary personality of its people. And each of us leaves Ireland filled with its special kind of magic, eager to spread the word to all and sundry. I'm willing to wager you'll do the same.

It's a formidable task to write about Ireland and the Irish. Back in 1842, William Makepeace Thackeray wrote an English friend: "I am beginning to find out now that a man ought to be forty years in this country instead of three months, and *then* he wouldn't be able to write about it!" Far be it from me even to attempt to beat Thackeray—I can only try to tell you about the Ireland *I* have discovered in several years of exhaustive research, pass along the finds of other travelers who have been kind enough to write, and tell you how it is not only *possible* to visit Ireland on our $25 a day—it's the *best* way to go!

1. Ireland and the Irish

Before diving into a detailed discussion of what you can expect to find in Ireland, let's talk about what you *won't* find. First of all, you won't find the stereotyped "stage Irish" of so many comedy skits. Nor will you find a land peopled entirely by saints and scholars (although, Lord knows, there's a plentiful supply of both). Or a land ravaged by violence, as the news media would sometimes lead you to believe—sure, it *does* exist, but it does *not* pervade the country. And, as the Irish are the first to point out, you won't find a telephone system that works with anything like the efficiency you're used to at home (which can, I suppose, drive you a little dotty if you're in a hurry, but which can also, I *know*, lead to some pretty interesting telephone conversations with operators while you both wait to get your call through). One thing more: you won't find a populace out to take you for every cent in your holiday purse—in my experience, the phrase "what the traffic will bear" just doesn't exist in Ireland.

Today's Ireland is a land still covered with small farms in unspoiled countryside but moving away from an economy wholly dependent on agriculture, with more and more hi-tech industries moving in and making scarcely a ripple on the smooth waters of the world's most relaxed way of life.

It's a land of cities whose antiquities live quite comfortably, elbow-to-elbow, with modern luxury hotels and an increasing number of sophisticated cabarets and nightclubs. A land filled with social centers that go by the name of pubs. Whose Tidy Towns competition each year rates even the tiniest hamlet on its success—or lack of it—in the ongoing battle against litter. Where there's never sweltering heat or bone-chilling cold, and a rainy day really *is* a soft day.

Ireland is where the word "friendly" probably originated. Where stopping to ask directions can land you in a family kitchen swapping tales over a "cuppa." Where the answer to every question is a short story. Where you may—as I once did—wind up as the Dublin house guest of an Irish lady you meet quite casually over breakfast at a B&B in Kerry.

Today's Ireland will take over your heart the minute you land and send you away looking back over your shoulder with a head full of plans to come right back.

THE LAY OF THE LAND: To get the statistics out of the way: Ireland covers 32,524 square miles, stretched out 302 miles at its longest and 189 miles at its widest points. It's the "last parish before America," i.e., the most westerly island of Europe, and its bowl-shaped contours are formed by a great limestone plain surrounded by mountains (Kerry's Carrantuohill is the highest at 3,414 feet).

Its coastline is so indented by jagged peninsulas that the sea is never more than 70 miles distant. That glorious coastline measures more than 3,000 miles and encircles 9,000 miles of meandering rivers (the 230-mile Shannon is the longest) and some 800 lakes, the largest of which is Lough Neagh (153 square miles).

To the east, Great Britain lies across the Irish Sea; to the south, France is on the other side of the Celtic Sea; and the Atlantic Ocean wraps around the southwest, west, and northern coasts.

THE WEATHER: The Atlantic brings along with it the Gulf Stream's warming currents to create a friendly climate that deals in moderation rather than extremes—seldom more than 65° in July or August, 40° in January or February.

Rave to the Irish about their glorious country, and nine times out of ten the response will be, "Sure, it's nice enough, if it only weren't for the weather." It's no use trying to convince them that the weather really isn't *that* bad —they're apparently born with an apology complex about their climate, and that's that! However, that famous (or infamous) rainfall is heaviest and most frequent in the mountains of the west, and frequent enough in the rest of the country to keep at *least* forty shades of green glowing. Showers come and go—sometimes several times in one day—but for the most part, they consist of a misty, almost ethereal sort of rain, nothing like the savage, slashing onslaught you might expect, one that adds an extra dimension to the landscape. If you want to see more sun than rain, you'll generally find it in May everywhere except in the midlands and southeast, where June is apt to be sunnier.

THE FLORA AND FAUNA: As for the flora of Ireland, the vast majority of trees today are imports. That's because back in Neolithic times large areas of the oak, ash, and rowan forests that covered much of the central limestone plain were cleared for cultivation or grazing. English landowners of the past few centuries can be faulted for many sins against Ireland, but one of the positive things they brought across the Irish Sea was their passion for planting exotic trees and gardens, which went a long way toward the re-greening of the countryside. Since the beginning of this century, reforestation efforts concentrated on large plantings of conifers and other evergreens, many in more than 400 national forests and other wooded areas open to the public. In addition to the verdant forest areas, you'll find the lovely heathers of the bogs and the unique wildflower population of Co. Clare's Burren.

One of the everlasting joys of Ireland's environment for me, personally, is that I can walk through woodlands, bogs, or Burren without watching every step for fear of snakes! The experts say that's because the country was cut off from mainland Europe during the retreat of the Ice Age before the serpents could make their venomous way across; any Irishman worth his salt will insist the good St. Patrick is solely responsible for this blessing. As far as *I* am concerned—me, with my deathly fear of the reptiles!—it matters not one whit who or what brought it about: I'll take a snake-free environment any way I can get it! As for other fauna, no life-threatening species roam the countryside (thanks, again, to the last Ice Age), although fossils of several gigantic examples of same have been unearthed by archeologists. The quite harmless fox, hare, and stoat are about all you're likely to find around today.

GEOGRAPHIC DIVISIONS: From its early history, Ireland's 32 counties have been divided into four provinces (those "Four Green Fields" of song and story). To the north, **Ulster** is now divided into the six counties that from Northern Ireland—Derry, Antrim, Armagh, Down, Fermanagh, and Tyrone—and three which lie in the Republic—Donegal, Monaghan, and Cavan. In the east, **Leinster** is composed of the twelve counties of Dublin, Wicklow, Wexford, Kilkenny, Carlow, Kildare, Laois, Offaly, Westmeath, Longford, Meath, and Louth. **Munster,** in the south, consists of counties Waterford, Cork, Kerry, Limerick, Clare, and Tipperary. And the west's **Connaught—** of Cromwell's slanderous "To hell or . . ." remark—is made up of Roscommon, Leitrim, Sligo, Galway, and Mayo.

TO SUM UP: There, then, are the bare facts of Ireland—and, believe me, they are *bare.*

It's only when you see the delicate play of light and shade on the mountains while driving from Glengarriff in Co. Cork to Kenmare in Co. Kerry, or ride through the lush greenness of Co. Waterford byways, or stand and drink in the mystical moonscape of Co. Clare's Burren, or watch a grassy hillside go from the brightest hue of green to silver-gray in the changing light, or gaze at a cloud-studded sky so enormous it makes eternity seem small, or stand on the rocky Dingle Peninsula shore at Ventry where legend says the King of the World went down to defeat at the hands of Fionn MacCumhaill and his Fianna warrior band—it's only then that the face of Ireland comes truly alive. Around every bend, that luminous, ever-changing landscape cries out for the poet, and many a poet has answered its call. Poor Thackeray—no *wonder* he was so frustrated!

George Bernard Shaw, however, put it quite simply:

> There is no magic like that of
>   Ireland.
> There are no skies like Irish
>   skies.
> There is no air like Irish air . . .
> The Irish climate will make the stiffest
>   and slowest mind flexible for life.

Amen!

THE IRISH: If it's hard to find words for Ireland, itself, it's well nigh *impossible* to capture the personality of the people who live there. Flexible they most certainly are, to the point of a complexity that simply defies description. Warmhearted, witty, sometimes devious, filled with curiosity about visitors, deeply religious at Sunday's mass but the very devil in the pub on Saturday night, great talkers and even greater listeners, sometimes argumentative to the point of combativeness—and with it all, *friendly*. That's the Irish, all right. But it's the *style* in which they are all of the above that so delights when you visit them at home.

There's a certain panache about the Irish. Take, for example, the time I walked into a store in Cork and asked for a certain address, confessing that I was lost. With a smiling, sweeping bow, the owner allowed as how, "You're lost no more, darlin', come with me." Whereupon he walked me to the building I was looking for several blocks away, chatting a steady stream and asking questions all the way. Now, *that's* panache!

Which is not to say, however, that you're going to be greeted at the airport by Irishmen rushing to bowl you over with all that chatter and charm. If there's anything they're not, it's intrusive—yours will have to be the first conversational move. But ask the first question, make the first comment, and you're off and running, your American accent an open invitation for the inevitable, "And where in America would you be from?" followed up by the equally inevitable "Well, now, and didn't my own uncle Pat (or brother Joe or great aunt Mary), go out to Chicago (or New York or Savannah or wherever it is you hail from)." And you're taken over by stories of the wandering relatives, more often than not over a pint or a cuppa with this perfect stranger who will, in his own good time, get around to what it was you wanted to know in the first place.

If it's directions you're after and there's more than one person present, the general discussion that erupts will enlighten you about all the alternative routes, the advantages and disadvantages of each, and a good many thumbnail sketches of the folks who live along the various ways. When everyone has had his say (and not until then!), you'll be sent on your way—if, that is, you don't accept a warm invitation to "stay over for the night and we'll have a bit of a singsong"—with detailed instructions on where *not* to go as well as the right route. Many's the time a stern "you'll come to a crossroad with a church, but pay no mind to it and keep to the road straight ahead" has kept me from making a wrong turn.

If the whole thing gets too complicated, don't be surprised if someone hops eagerly into the car to show you the way, brushing aside his return with an easy "And wasn't I wanting to go to the next town, anyway." And he won't think a thing about hitching all the way back home, for he was raised in a tradition that says if you've a roof over your head, a fire at your hearth, and a potato in the pot, it's very close to a mortal sin not to share them all with a stranger in need. More than that, he'll welcome the chance of a bit of conversation with someone from other parts—and he'll take the time for both the help and the "crack."

All the foregoing takes place, of course, in English. But it's the most melodic, lilting rendition of the language you'll ever hear. "Sure, the English gave us their language," say the Irish with a grin, "then we showed them how to use it." And they did, with writers like Jonathan Swift, Edmund Burke, Oscar Wilde, George Bernard Shaw, William Butler Yeats, James Joyce, and a host of others pouring out masterpieces of English prose as easily as most men tip the whiskey jar. They're still at it today—I'll tell you about some of my favorite modern writers in the next chapter. But your average Irishman—*or* woman—embellishes everyday conversation with all the eloquence of the greatest writers and colorful, image-making phrases that would make any writer weep with envy. And they string them together in yarns that may be wildly fanciful, but are never dull.

Tim Pat Coogan, in his excellent book *Ireland and the Arts,* suggests that the Irish have used their words as both a sly release from and effective weapon against cruel oppression suffered over long centuries of invasion and foreign rule. There's truth in that, for in today's Ireland—as another Irish writer in an *Inside Ireland* article stated categorically—"Exaggeration and lighthearted blasphemy are national pastimes."

There's more to the Irish, of course, than talk. There's the strong religious influence that passed from Celtic to Catholic rites without a hitch. And the fascinating mix of Celt, Viking, Norman and Saxon blood that has melded into an "Irish" race of brunettes, blonds and redheads. And the paradoxical nature that led Chesterton to write, "All their wars are merry, and all their songs are sad."

Mary Moran, up in Castlebar, Co. Mayo, passed along to me (and to other guests at her Lakeview House B&B) an unsigned poem that probably comes as close as anyone can to describing the Irish in these lines:

> He's wild and he's gentle,
> He's good and he's bad,
> He's proud and he's humble,
> He's happy and sad.
> He's in love with the ocean,
>   the earth and the skies,
> He's enamored with beauty
>   wherever it lies.
> He's victor and victim, a star and a clod,
> But mostly he's Irish,
> In love with his God.

As I said, that's *close*. But it's a safe bet you'll go home thinking of "the Irish" in terms of John or Kitty or Suibhan or Michael—and you'll be as close as any poet can ever come!

2. A Brief History

The landscape of Ireland is haunted by its history. Its ghosts lurk along every road, around every bend, behind every bush.

Stone Age Irish move eerily behind the mists of prehistory that cloak dolmens left in their wake. Visit the reconstructed crannog at Craggaunowen in Co. Clare and Bronze Age men and women almost materalize before your eyes. Iron Age forts make a quiet day ring with the sounds, just beyond your ears, of those who sheltered there. Great monastic crosses and ruined abbeys accent the tremendous influence of early Christians, while round towers tell of the dangers they faced from Viking raiders. Listen carefully in Dublin and Waterford and you may hear the echoing footsteps of their Viking founders. Norman spirits inhabit ruined castles that squat along riverbanks, atop lofty cliffs, and in lonely fields.

The multifaceted history that shaped the fascinating Irish character we know today travels with you wherever you go in Ireland.

IN THE BEGINNING: When the world's last Ice Age retreated, it left Ireland with multitudes of scooped out lakes and tumbled mountains plus a land bridge that connected it to Great Britain. Sometime around 6,000 B.C., a race of Stone

Age settlers crossed over that land bridge to Ireland—we don't know where they originally came from, only that they clustered around the seashore and along inland riverbanks, fashioning crude flint tools, and surviving by fishing and hunting.

Long after the land link to Britain disappeared and Ireland had become an island—about 2000 B.C.—newcomers brought with them cows and other domesticated animals. They also brought the skill to clear the land and plant crops, thus beginning Ireland's long tradition of farming and cattle raising. It was this Neolithic race who cremated their dead and created communal burial chambers beneath stone cairns or inside earthen, tunnel-filled mounds. Newgrange, in Co. Meath, a full acre in size, is the best known of the surviving tumuli and the most accessible to visitors.

THE METAL WORKERS: While the farmers in Ireland were tending their fields, European tribes were beginning to work with metals, which led to an ever-widening search for copper to be used in fashioning bronze weapons and tools and gold for making exquisitely crafted ornaments and jewelry. The search eventually reached to Ireland and its rich deposits of both metals. The Bronze Age had begun, an age which was to see this remote, primitive little island add to its agricultural population the artisans, merchants, and peddlers who roamed all over western Europe, leaving examples of their arts and crafts scattered around the continent.

Those who came to Ireland during this period are thought to be of Mediterranean origin. They were short, dark-haired, and swarthy-skinned and may have been Picts. The Romans knew them as the *Iberni,* but they were called the *Uib-Ernai* in Ireland, where they were believed to be descendants of the fertility goddess Eire, whose name means "noble." The island country was very soon known by that noble name, and today it is the oldest existing national name in the world (never mind that it's been corrupted by dropping the initial letter and tacking on "land"—*officially,* the country is still "Eire").

As beautifully crafted as are the metal objects created by these early Irish settlers, they fade in significance when compared to the most important legacy of this period. A wealth of megalithic stone structures still stand in solid, silent testimony of incredible scientific knowledge and engineering skill. Great pillars and huge standing stones bear mute witness to feats of construction that must have required great organization, hundreds of workers, and a dedication that defies belief. The megaliths of Ireland are among her most valuable treasures, and to the traveler's delight, they stand in solitary splendor in the green fields and atop rocky hilltops with nary a neon sign or souvenir stand in sight!

AND THEN CAME THE CELTS: Tall, fair-skinned, and red-haired, the Celts were fierce, warlike people who roamed the face of Europe before migrating to Ireland in the fourth century B.C. They came with iron weapons and a military prowess that soon established them—and their language—as rulers of the land.

Some 100 tribes spread across the country, setting up small kingdoms under petty lords, or chieftains. Those smaller units, in turn, paid allegiance (at least in theory) to regional kings, and in time a High King of Ireland sat at Tara. The five regional kingdoms were known as Ulster, Munster, Leinster, Meath, and Connaught, which became the four provinces of Ireland as we know it when the Kingdom of Meath merged with Leinster.

Hot-blooded Celts were not, however, *about* to let any of those titles and divisions go unchallenged. The countryside rang with the sounds of battle as petty king fought petty king, regional kings embarked on expansionary expeditions, and the High King of the moment never sat easy on his honorary throne. Peasants and bondsmen toiled for whichever chieftain was in power at the moment, and the free farmer anted up both tribute and loyalty, while craftily throwing up a sturdy earthen ring-fort (also called a "rath" or "lis") as protection against roaming marauders. Lismore, in Co. Waterford, takes its name from the large lis on its outskirts.

As for any sort of unity, it existed in the strong bonds of a common culture and traditions bound together by the common language. Petty kingdoms might be at war, but all paid strict obeyance to the traditional laws of the Brehons (lawyers), who traveled freely from one kingdom to another. Learned men in all professions were honored throughout the land and established schools that set intricate graded scales of achievement. Traveling bards who recited long, epic poems of past heroic deeds were much revered and richly rewarded when they came up with new compositions that put a poetic purpose behind the latest exploits of whichever chieftain might be offering hospitality at the moment. Only slightly less homage was paid to the most skilled of the many artists and craftsmen who labored for each chieftain and often shared his table. Above everyone, the Druids were heralded as *all* tribes' wisest men and conducted or prescribed the most sacred of their ceremonies.

It was this strange mixture of barbarous warring and a highly developed culture that greeted the arrival of Christianity in the fifth century A.D. And all the foregoing is the story of how it evolved—at least, that's the way archeologists and historians *think* it evolved, based on their best assumptions from carbon datings, artifacts, and educated guesses.

But listen to another version of the same story.

THE LEGENDS: Those early bards and the *seanachies* (storytellers) who followed also tell of three distinct racial groups involved in Ireland's beginnings. Their story, however, is a delightful blend of fact, fancy, and mysticism and has nothing whatsoever to do with carbon dating.

There were, they say, the "men of the quiver"—the *Fir Bolg*, the "men of the territory"—the *Fir Domhnann,* and the *Fir Gaileoin*—the "men of Gaul." In one of the oldest legends, telling of the coming of the Celts, the bards explained that it was their iron-bladed spears (*laighens*) that gave Leinster its name. From that point, the stories go on to speak of the brave deeds of Conaire Mor, King of Ireland in the second century B.C. The hero we know as Finn Mac Cool was born as Fionn MacCumhail in a blaze of glorified chivalry and courage as gigantic as the fictitious man himself. His faithful Fianna warrior band matched their leader in feats of bravery and daring. There were tales of the Knights of the Red Branch in the north and of the Ulstero hero, Cuchulainn. Queen Maeve, who ruled Connaught, and the tragic Diedre of the Sorrows were chief among the heroines who figured in song and story.

Later on, the seanachies, in a fit of revisionist history, came up with a quite satisfactory rationale for the shared traits of Irish and Scottish Celts. All were, they reckoned, descended from one man, Mileadh (Milesius), and they could look back in their lineage to one Gadelius and a lady known as Scota!

Which version holds the most truth, archeologists' or that of the seanachies? Take your pick. But I can tell you that to my Irish friends, those legendary heroes are as alive and well in their minds and hearts today as when the bards of old spun their tales. Which version would *I* choose? Why, both, of course—with, perhaps just the slightest leaning toward Finn Mac Cool and Cuchulainn.

SAINTS AND SCHOLARS: The Romans, rampaging in southern Britain, never did get around to conquering Ireland, but in the mid-fifth century A.D., a conquest of quite another nature took place. A pagan religion that had flourished for centuries surprisingly embraced quickly and with enthusiasm the doctrines and rites of Christianity that landed on Irish shores along with St. Patrick. A Roman by birth, in his youth the budding saint had tended swine in Ulster as a slave, escaped, and made his way back to the continent, where he entered religious life, returning to his former captors as a missionary in 432 A.D.

Those early years among people who were to become his devout followers may well have given St. Patrick the insight to convert many pagan *practices* as well as pagan people, thus making it easier for them to make the switch than it might otherwise have been. Retaining just enough pagan roots to avoid hostile resistance, he managed to transplant rites and superstitions into Christian soil without a murmur—the healing powers of many Irish "holy wells," for example, are those attributed to them by ancient Celts long before St. Patrick arrived on the scene. His firsthand knowledge of Celtic love of the mystical—especially when applied to the natural world—perhaps inspired him to use the native shamrock to symbolize the Holy Trinity, Ireland's most enduring national symbol.

Irish king after Irish king listened to the missionary and led his subjects into the new religion, although never abandoning such distinctly Celtic pastimes as intrakingdom warfare and riotous revelry within his own court. In homage to their new God (or maybe in penance for their more unchristian practices?) kings and other large landowners endowed His earthly representatives with lavish gifts of precious metals, land on which to build churches and monasteries, and other valuables which helped fund St. Patrick's work.

With the coming of Christianity, Celtic culture took a giant step forward. Already deeply respectful of learning in its higher forms, in the hundreds the Irish devoted themselves to a cloistered life within great monasteries that taught all the learning of their time, both Celtic and Roman. As Europe entered its culturally barren Dark Ages, Ireland's monastic universities kept the lights of philosophy, theology, astronomy, literature, poetry, and most of the known sciences brightly burning, attracting thousands of students who fled the continent during those centuries. Artistic achievement hit new heights inside their walls, as the exquisitely illustrated *Book of Kells* demonstrates. Until the end of the eighth century, Ireland's Golden Age was the brightest beacon in the then-known world.

Away from these seats of learning, monks of a more mystical leaning moved out to more remote parts of the country and to rocky, misty islands just offshore. There they lived austere lives of meditation, building the beehive-shaped stone dwellings still intact today and marvelously engineered little stone churches like Dingle's Gallarus Oratory, constructed entirely without mortar and watertight for the past 1500 years. The impressive stone Celtic crosses that dot the landscape had their origins in the seventh century.

Eventually, Europe's age of darkness was forced into retreat, helped mightily by returning European scholars and Irish monks and scholars who left home to carry their teachings into cathedrals, royal courts, and great universities they helped establish.

VIKING INVADERS: The first invaders of Ireland's recorded history were terrifying Viking raiders who came by sea in A.D. 795 to launch fierce, lightening-fast strikes along the coastline, taking away hordes of plunder and captives and leaving behind only smoking ruins. Their superior mail battle dress and heavy arms made easy victims of even the most stout-hearted, battle-loving Irish, and their raids moved farther and farther inland, with rich monastic settlements yielding the most valuable prizes. Churchmen found an answer to the danger in tall, round towers with their only entrance high above the ground (they stored their most precious treasures there, then pulled up long ladders to make access impossible). I have, incidentally, run across more than one seanachie whose story is that Finn Mac Cool built the first of these and the doorway was simply put at his natural entry-level—the monks just latched on to what turned out to be a perfect protective device. You'll find one of the best preserved at the Rock of Cashel, in Co. Tipperary.

As the years went by, raiders turned into settlers, establishing the first of a string of coastal cities at Dublin in 841, followed by Wexford, Waterford, Cork, and Limerick. Vestiges of city walls, gates, and fortifications remain to this day —Reginald's Tower, in Waterford, is one of the most perfect examples. Former raiders turned to peaceful trading and—in a pattern to be followed by subsequent "conquerors"—they were soon intermarrying with natives and becoming as Irish as the Irish themselves.

Not a few resident Irish chieftains, after disastrous defeats, began to take note of successful Viking battle methods and turn them back against the victors. But it wasn't until 1014 that Brian Boru—the High King of Ireland at the time—engaged his enemies at Clontarf, just outside Dublin, and won a decisive victory after a full day of battle. Interestingly, so intermixed had the two races become by that time that while a large part of the Viking forces consisted of "Irish" allies, Brian Boru's loyal "Norse" warriors were among the most valiant on the field! Boru was mortally wounded in the fray and ascended into the rarefied stratosphere of Ireland's most revered heroes.

THE NORMANS MOVE IN: Brian Boru's death was followed by a century and a half of kingly tug-of-war to establish one central authority figure. It was one of those ambitious combatants who took the first step on Ireland's long path of involvement with the British. His name was Dermot MacMurrough, King of Leinster, and he made the fatal mistake of stealing the beautiful wife of O'Rourke, the King of Breffni, who promptly stirred up Leinster's minor chieftains and hounded MacMurrough out of Leinster.

MacMurrough crossed the Irish Sea to Britain, then under the rule of Norman counquerors from France for a little over a century, and convinced King Henry II to give him a volunteer army to help win back his lost throne. It arrived in 1169 and landed in Waterford under the command of the Earl of Pembroke, popularly known as Strongbow. By marrying MacMurrough's daughter in Reginald's Tower, the Norman became King of Leinster when his father-in-law died the very next year.

Strongbow's military prowess quickly brought most of Leinster and Munster under his domination. He defeated Rory O'Connor (buried at Conmacnois, Co. Offaly), the last High King of Ireland, and appeared to be well on his way to achieving power to rival that of King Henry II. Needless to say, from Henry's point of view, something had to be done. Espousing a sudden interest in the religious eccentricities of Irish Catholics (who sometimes showed faint regard for the edicts of Rome—their Easter fell on a date different from that proclaimed by the Pope, for instance), Henry rushed to Ireland clutching a document from the Pope (Adrian IV, the only *English* pope in the Church's history!) giving him feudal lordship over all of Ireland, Strongbow notwithstanding.

Under the guise of a religious reformer, Henry was able to win the support of most Irish bishops, and the papal authority gave him a potent lever to gain the submission of Irish kings, lords, and large landowners. Stating that he held absolute ownership of all lands, it granted him the undisputed right to rent it to such nobles as professed loyalty and withhold it from those who refused to do so. Many of the Irish kings, anxious to hold on to their territories even if it meant fealty to the English king, traveled to Dublin to make the required submission.

But that feudal lordship flew squarely in the face of long-established Irish law, which had insisted since the days of the Brehons that no king or lord had the right to take lands owned by individuals or groups and that any attempt to do so should be resisted, by force if necessary. That basic precept kept Norman and Irish lords growling at each other across a legal chasm for the next 350 years. Although every English monarch who followed Henry laid claim to the Lordship of Ireland, each was too busy with civil wars and foreign conquest to send armies to enforce that claim. Normans acquired title to more than half the country, building most of those sturdy castles in which you'll sightsee, banquet, or even spend the night during your visit.

All the while, however, the same thing that happened to the Vikings was happening to the Normans. Quickly adapting to their new homeland, they intermarried with the Irish and strayed so far from their sacred loyalty to the English throne and all things English that laws had to be passed in Parliament against their use of Irish dress, manners, and the native language—to my knowledge, the only time in the world's history that a *language* has been banished! Those laws turned out to be about as useless as the armed forces that never arrived—Norman families evolved into *Irish*-Norman families, with more loyalty to their own land holdings than to either Irish or English rulers.

As for those Irish chieftains and kings who refused to recognize English rights to their land, they just couldn't get their act together to oppose English claims with a united front. Instead, each Irish faction battled independently, with no central authority. Incessant warfare *did,* however, serve to concentrate the beleaguered English crown forces in a heavily fortified area around Dublin known as "The Pale" and a few garrison towns around the country. Had not a pervasive religious dimension been thrown into the Irish stew, the Irish might have eventually managed to wrest control of their ancient land from British rulers. But King Henry VIII and the Reformation changed all that in the late sixteenth century.

AN ENGLISH "KING OF IRELAND" AND THE FLIGHT OF THE EARLS: Henry VIII brought to the throne of England a new approach to English rule in Ireland. Breaking with Rome, in 1541 he proclaimed himself King of Ireland by right of conquest rather than by papal decree. To convince those troublesome Irish and their Anglo-Irish cohorts of the legitimacy of his claim, he dubbed all opposition open rebellion against "their" king and set about driving rebel leaders from their lands, so that he might grant the properties to his loyal followers, be they English or Irish.

Enter religion on the scene in full battle array. By the time Elizabeth became queen, the Reformation was firmly entrenched in England and the staunchly Catholic Irish found themselves fighting for their religion with even more fervor than they had fought for their lands. The great chieftains led uprising after uprising and, when English forces proved too great, appealed to Spain for help in 1601 to make a decisive stand at Kinsale, in Co. Cork. The Spanish arrived and joined Irish forces to occupy the town, which was quickly surrounded by English troops. From up north, however, Irish chieftains O'Neill and O'Donnell mounted an epic winter march to come upon the British from behind. Hopes were high for an Irish victory, but it just wasn't in the cards.

As luck would have it, a drunken Irish soldier wandered into English hands and spilled the whole plan, enabling the English to win the day and send the brightest and best of the native chieftains into hiding, their lands in Ulster now confiscated *in toto* by the Crown and resettled by loyal—and Protestant—English and Scots. In 1608, the surviving Irish chieftains met in Rathmullen, Co. Donegal, and decided to set sail for the Continent as a body, vowing to return to fight another day—a vow never fulfilled. That Flight of the Earls marked the end of any effective organized resistance to English rule for generations.

Organized or not, the ornery Irish continued to harass the British with bloody attacks, always followed by even bloodier reprisals. Finally, in 1641, they mounted a long-planned offensive to retake the lands of Ulster, and thus brought down on the land one of the bloodiest episodes in Irish history, one mirrored across its landscape even today.

TO HELL OR CONNAUGHT: By 1649, Irish incursions into Ulster and the massacre of hundreds of its Protestant settlers had so ravaged the land that Puritan general Oliver Cromwell arrived in force to squelch the rebellious Irish once and for all. Driven by religious fervor as well as political motives, Cromwell embarked on a campaign of devastation kicked off by the brutal slaying of more than 30,000 Irish men, women, and children at Drogheda.

From there, his trail of blood and destruction led to Wexford and thence across the country, leaving in its wake thousands dead, churches and castles and homes demolished, forests burned, and a degree of horror greater than any the Irish had known. Irish who escaped with their lives were shipped in the hundreds to work as slave labor on English plantations in the Sugar Islands—banishment to a virtual "hell"—or driven to the bleak, stone-strewn hills of Connaught.

To his loyal soldiers and their commanding officers, Cromwell awarded vast estates in the choice and fertile counties of the country. In the end, less than one-ninth of Irish soil remained in the hands of natives.

KING BILLY, THE TREATY OF LIMERICK, AND THE PENAL LAWS: Irish spirits rose once more when a Catholic, James II, ascended to the English throne in 1688, and when he was deposed by supporters of William of Orange—King Billy—and fled to Ireland in 1689, they took up arms in his defense. In Ulster, Londonderry and Enniskillen became the major refuge for Protestants loyal to William, and the stout walls of Londonderry held against a 105-day siege by Jacobite forces. King Billy, himself, arrived in 1690 to lead his army to a resounding victory in the Battle of the Boyne, after which James once more took flight, leaving his Irish supporters to their own devices. Hoping to get the best possible terms of surrender, the Irish fought on under the leadership of Patrick Sarsfield until October of 1691, when they signed the Treaty of Limerick, which allegedly allowed them to retain both their religion and their land. Parliament, however, had no intention of sanctioning any sort of threat to the Protestant Ascendancy, and refused to ratify the treaty, instituting instead a series of measures so oppressive they became known as the Penal Laws.

Catholics, under the Penal Laws, were stripped of all civil and political rights—they could neither vote nor hold office; enter any of the professions, especially law; educate their children; own a horse valued at more than £5; bear arms; or (the origin of Ireland's tiny farmlands of today) will their land to only one son, being required instead to divide it into smaller plots for all male heirs. Forced to work the estates of absentee English landlords, Irish farmers paid enormous rents for the privilege of throwing up rude huts and using a small plot of ground to raise the potatoes that kept their families from starving.

It was a sorry state of affairs for the proud descendants of heroic kings and chieftains, and it was to last a full century.

UNITED IRISHMEN, UNION, FAMINE, AND EMIGRATION: In the time-honored pattern of earlier Irish rulers, Anglo-Irish Protestants gradually came to feel a stronger allegiance to Ireland than to England, and in the late 1700s, Henry Grattan led a Protestant Patriot party in demanding greater independence. What they got was a token Irish Parliament in 1782, which sat in Dublin but was controlled from London. Things seemed to be taking an upward turn as Penal Laws were gradually relaxed and trade began to flourish. Dublin's streets blossomed with the Georgian mansions and gracious squares that are still its most distinctive features.

Like a little learning, a little independence turned out to be a dangerous thing. With a newly independent France as a model, a group of Irishmen led by Protestant Wolfe Tone formed the Society of United Irishmen in 1791 to work for the establishment of a totally independent Irish republic. Enlisting military aid from France, Tone led a full-fledged insurrection in 1798 that ended in pure disaster on the battlefield and even greater disaster in the halls of the English Parliament.

British leaders now had the ammunition they needed to insist on ending any semblance of Irish parliamentary rule. Even so, it took considerable bribery, promises of seats in the London parliament and threats to get the Dublin MPs to vote the end of their supposed legislative power. But in 1800, the Act of Union passed and Ireland became an extension of British soil. That should have put Ireland in her proper place—again—but in 1803, the Irish were at it once more, and with Robert Emmet urging them on, they launched yet another uprising. It was the same old story, however, and ended with Emmet gallantly declaring from the gallows, "When my country takes her place among the nations of the earth, then, and not till then, let my epitaph be written."

In the 1820s, a young Catholic named Daniel O'Connell started to make noises about Catholic Emancipation—a total repeal of the Penal Laws and the restoration of all Catholic civil rights. Elected to Parliament in 1828, he accomplished that goal the following year and embarked on a campaign for repeal of the Act of Union. About all he got for his efforts in that direction was the affectionate title of "The Liberator," and just as members of the Young Ireland movement were beginning to be heard on that score, tragedy struck and the Irish goal became one of simple survival.

It was in 1846 that a disastrous potato blight spread throughout the country, destroying the one food crop of most Irish families. Until 1849, crop after crop failed, and a population of nearly 9 million was reduced to a little over 6 million. Hundreds of thousands died of pure starvation—it became a common sight to see roadside ditches filled with bodies of famine victims who had nowhere else to die simply because they had been evicted from their wretched homes by landlords who continued to demand exorbitant rents from tenants who no longer had the means to pay them. Well over a million turned their backs on Ireland and set out for the United States and Canada on ships so overcrowded and filthy and disease-infested they were little more than floating coffins.

THE LAND LEAGUE, HOME RULE, AND SINN FEIN: By 1879, the Irish tenant farmers were so fed up with the oppressive rentals that some had literally paid with their lives during the four years of famine that they eagerly joined with Charles Stewart Parnell and Michael Davitt in forming a union known as the Land League. They enlisted farmers around the country to strike back at any landlord who evicted tenants by the simple, but deadly effective, method of "boycott" (so called for the Captain Boycott against whom it was used for the first time). With their families shunned by an entire community and services of any kind cut off, landlords began to rethink their policies and to reduce rents to a fair level, grant some degree of guaranteed occupancy to tenants and, eventualy, to allow tenants to purchase their own acreage.

Far from being grateful for such small favors, the Irish continued to fan the flame of their inherited zeal for freedom from English rule. Parnell for years led an energetic campaign for Home Rule which would grant limited independence, but it wasn't until the eve of World War I that such a measure was adopted by the British. Even then, there was strong and vocal opposition by loyal Unionists in Ulster, Protestants all, who were determined to keep Ireland a part of the mother country. Outnumbered by Catholics, they feared Home Rule would become Rome Rule, and the Ulster Volunteers were formed to put up armed resistance against the equally determined Irish Republican Army, the military arm of Sinn Fein, a republican political party whose name is pronounced "shin fain" and means "ourselves alone." With the British Army already firmly ensconced, the country fairly bristled with arms when everything was put on "hold" by the urgency of world conflict.

"A TERRIBLE BEAUTY" IS BORN: To the astonishment of almost everyone—most of all, the Irish people—Easter Monday of 1916 put the whole question of Irish independence right back on a *very* hot front burner. Leading a scruffy, badly outfitted and poorly armed little band of less than 200 patriots, Patrick Pearse and James Connolly marched up Dublin's O'Connell Street to the General Post Office and proceeded to occupy it in the name of a Provisional Government. Standing between the front pillars of the impressive building, Pearse read in stirring tones "The Proclamation of the Irish Republic to the People of Ireland." Behind him, his valiant little "army" prepared to dig in and hold their position as long as was humanly possible. Hopelessly small contingents were stationed at St. Stephen's Green and one or two other strategic points.

For six days following Pearse's proclamation, the Post Office stood embattled under the ancient symbol of Ireland (a golden harp on a pennant of brilliant green) and the Sinn Fein banner of green, white, and orange. The rebels numbered only about 1,000 all told, and their remarkable courage as they faced overwhelming British military might is the stuff of heroic legends —and, indeed, the very stuff of which Ireland's history is made!

It was a bloody, but unbowed, band that finally surrendered and was marched back down O'Connell Street to a future of prison or execution. Dubliners, many of them uncertain of where their loyalties lay, watched and waited to learn their fate. When Pearse, Connolly, and fourteen others were executed by a firing squad and hundreds of others were imprisoned or exiled, Irish loyalties united behind their new Republic and world opinion stood solidly behind the ideal of Irish independence.

It was at that moment—as the gunsmoke cleared in Kilmainham Jail's yard—that Yeats was to proclaim "A terrible beauty was born."

In the years between 1916 and 1921, Britain tried every means at her disposal—including sending the ruthless Black and Tan mercenaries to terrorize the citizenry as well as rebels—to quell the rebellion, which continued to rumble even in defeat. In 1919, when Sinn Fein won a huge majority of parliamentary seats, they refused to go to London, but set up the National Parliament of Ireland in Dublin, which they christened the Dail (pronounced "dawl"). From then on, guerrilla warfare raged, replete with atrocities, ambush tactics, and assassinations. After two years of bitter bloodshed, a truce was finally called and negotiations began which ended in December of 1921 with the signing of the Anglo-Irish Treaty that named 26 counties as the Irish Free State. Still within the British Empire, it was to be self-governing in the same manner as Canada and other British dominions. Six counties in Ulster would remain—as they wished—an integral part of Great Britain and be ruled from London.

A Free State under the treaty terms was not, however, what many Irish believed they had been fighting for, and civil war raged until 1923. Eamon de Valera, at the head of the I.R.A., stood solidly against pro-treaty forces led by William Cosgrave in the conviction that only a united Ireland which included all 32 counties was acceptable. Cosgrave and the newly formed government felt that the treaty terms were preferable to continued war with Britain and that in time the six counties of Northern Ireland would join the other 26 by constitutional means. The question still throws its devisive shadow over Ireland today.

Fighting between the two factions was made more bitter because it often pitted brother against brother and there was wholesale destruction of property. As it became clear that the Dublin government would endure, de Valera threw in the towel militarily and in three years' time had formed the Fianna Fail ("feena foil") party. When that party took office in 1932, the oath of allegiance to the British Crown was finally abolished, and in 1948, Great Britain formally declared Ireland outside the Commonwealth when a coalition government headed by John A. Costello declared that "the description of the State shall be the Republic of Ireland."

ONWARD AND UPWARD: Since the proud day it became truly independent, Ireland has set about catching up with the progress so long held at bay by her fight to become her own master. Efforts to develop Irish industry resulted in state companies such as Bord na Mona building a thriving business from one of the country's greatest natural resources, peat (or turf). Aer Lingus, the national airline, was established, and the Shannon Free Airport Development Company has developed one of the world's leading airports along with an industrial complex that attracts companies from all over the world. The Industrial Development Authority has assisted firms from the United States, Germany, Japan, Great Britain, and a score of other countries in setting up factories and processing plants (most of them remarkably *clean* industries) and providing employment opportunities for a new generation. From the United States alone, more than 200 electronics companies have expanded into Ireland, employing some 17,000 people.

Along with all these developments, there have also been some interesting changes in demographics. In 1926, still feeling the decimation of its population by starvation and emigration that spanned a century following the famine of the 1840s, Ireland counted only 2.972 million inhabitants in its first official census. The vast majority lived in rural areas and looked to farming for a living.

A decline in population continued as recently as 1961, when the figures showed 2.818 million. Every census since then, however, has shown a slight increase, with a 2.2% jump in the short period of 1979/81. The latest (1981) report shows a population of 3.443 million and a shift in distribution. For example, Ireland now has one of Europe's youngest populations, with more than one-half under the age of 21. And more and more, the Irish are moving to towns and cities—or, to be more precise, to the metropolitan suburbs, since most Irish still cling to the notion of a private house with its own garden. Back in 1966, urban and rural populations were just about even, but in 1981, some 1.915 million lived in urban areas compared to 1.529 million in rural localities.

Luckily for you and me, along with industry, successive Irish governments have recognized the potential for tourism in this gloriously beautiful land. And why not, since they've been hosts to "visitors" in one form or another since the dawn of history! Bord Fáilte (the "board of welcomes") has worked closely with hoteliers, bed-and-breakfast ladies, restaurateurs, and entertainment facilities to see that we're well taken care of. And they've wisely insisted that the *character* of the country is as much an attraction for us as are the natural beauties and ancient relics we come to see.

On the cultural scene, the lilting Gaelic language was reinstated as the official tongue, reclaiming an Irish identity very nearly lost during long years of suppression. Called "Irish" to distinguish it from other forms of Gaelic, the language takes first place on street signs, city and town name signs, and in governmental titles such as Taoiseach ("tee-shuck") for the Prime Minister or gardai ("guardee") for police or guards. Aer Lingus (Gaelic for "air fleet") welcomes you aboard in rhythmic Irish, and news broadcasts sign off in the native tongue on both radio and television. Until 1973, every school child was required to study Irish in an attempt to revive its day-to-day use, and although the vast majority now use English as their first tongue, there are some 40,000 Irish speakers who use English only occasionally. Most live in closely knit communities called the Gaeltacht ("Gale-tuck-ta"), often in rural, rather isolated locations in the west. Dingle and Connemara are both part of the Gaeltacht, where natives will readily converse to you in English, with asides in Irish to their friends and neighbors.

Irish arts—theater, literature, painting, music—have also seen a heartwarming revival, and ancient Irish crafts are now producing works of beauty and utility to rival any in the world.

On the political front, Ireland steadfastly held on to its neutrality during World War II, even in the face of tremendous pressures from both Britain and America. Nevertheless, hundreds of Irishmen volunteered in the armed forces of both countries. Since 1955, Ireland has been a member of the United Nations and has sent peace-keeping forces to Cyprus, the Congo, the Sinai Desert, and Lebanon. As long as Northern Ireland remains under British rule, however, no Irish government has authorized NATO membership, since NATO is pledged to guarantee the territorial integrity of its members. As a member of the European Economic Community, Ireland shares in the joys and woes of that controversial alliance. (If you want to get a good "crack" going almost anywhere in Ireland, just bring up the subject of EEC membership—there are as many views on its results as there are Irish to discuss it!)

NORTHERN IRELAND: It's always a temptation to oversimplify the underlying reasons for the tensions that have troubled Northern Ireland since that 1921 treaty set it apart from the rest of the country.

Certainly, all that history we've just gone through is *really* at the root of things, for it created an environment in which injustices of the past live in the memories of a Catholic minority who see themselves as victims of inequities of the present. Their strong yearning for a united Ireland that would improve their status takes the form of support for Irish nationalism. Protestants who now have centuries of family history firmly rooted in Ireland must contend with a status quo not of their making, yet one they are fearful of changing. Despite all this, the majority in each population segment live side by side, somewhat warily, but more interested in making a living and raising decent, law-abiding families than in having to profess loyalty to extremists on *either* side.

The tangled threads of political events in Northern Ireland over the years of its separation from the south weave a pattern almost too complex to follow. There was the Civil Rights movement that began in 1968, only to bog down as the current "troubles" erupted and the British Army was called in to keep a peace that still eludes them. In 1973, hopes were raised when a Northern Ireland Assembly held out the promise of active participation in government by the minority, only to be dashed when it was violently opposed by extreme factions of both loyalists and nationalists. There was the Women's Peace Movement of 1976 which for a time looked as though it might bring an end to violence and let men of peace get on with a solution—and while it was useful to show the depth of revulsion on all sides for terrorism, it, too, bogged down and faded away. In 1974, there was an effort made to set up a power-sharing Executive, but it was too short-lived to make any headway. Today, a Secretary of State for Northern Ireland is the chief administrator and reports directly to Parliament in London.

In May of 1984, a report was issued by the All Ireland Forum which may hold out more real hope of an eventual solution than any other development thus far. The Forum consisted of leaders from all political sectors both north and south of the Border, and it met nearly 100 times over the course of a full year. Its final report contains detailed, well-thought-out discussions of several acceptable compromises. Only time will tell if this, too, will be but another step along the long road to a free and peaceful Ireland.

In the meantime, sporadic outbreaks of violence continue to grab international headlines while long spells of nonviolence go unnoticed. And Americans all too often cut out of their Irish itinerary a corner of the country that has a unique dimension to add to any Irish visit. Travel north of the Border presents no real problem for the tourist, and I highly recommend that you read more about it in the chapter titled "Introduction to Northern Ireland" before you make that same mistake.

3. Ireland with this Book

An Irish friend once said to me, "Whenever I am with visitors, I always wish there were some way to show them all the nooks and crannies of Ireland as well as the highlights tourists usually see." It was a wistful, heartfelt wish, and one I heartily echo.

Ireland's highlights are, of course, numerous and spectacular. And because you and I are limited by the amount of time we have to travel, it is simply not possible to take in all of the country's charms on one trip. Add to that limitation the fact that even those who live there are constantly stumbling onto new nooks and crannies, and my friend's wish becomes even more wistful.

What this book will do is point you to those highlights you just must *not* miss and throw in a nook or cranny wherever I have found one. It's a safe bet, however, that you'll come home with fond memories of more than a few you've found on your own—it's the *unexpected* that will charm you most and send you home warbling "Danny Boy" in the closest thing you can manage to a brogue!

IRELAND REGION BY REGION: Historically, Ireland is divided into the four provinces of Leinster, Munster, Connaught, and Ulster. For the modern-day traveler, however, its geography falls naturally into somewhat different divisions. Bord Fáilte recognizes eight regions, and to make it as easy as possible to correlate what you'll find in this book and Bord Fáilte information you'll pick up on your travels, I have followed their lead. The map on pages 20 and 21 gives you an overview, and set out below are the regions and the counties encompassed by each.

Eastern	**Southeast**	**Southern**
Dublin	Waterford	Cork
Wicklow	Wexford	Kerry
Louth	South Tipperary	
Kildare	Kilkenny	
Meath	Carlow	

Shannonside	**Western**	**Northwestern**
Clare	Galway	Donegal
Limerick	Mayo	Sligo
North Tipperary		Leitrim

Midland	**Northern Ireland**
Cavan	Antrim
Laois	Derry
Longford	Tyrone
Monaghan	Fermanagh
Offaly	Armagh
Roscommon	Down
Westmeath	

Rather than follow a predetermined itinerary, this book is designed to give you the highlights (and *my* nooks and crannies) of each region, county by county. In Chapter II, there are several suggested itineraries, including the two-week circular route favored by many first-time visitors to Ireland. It's a good way to catch a glimpse of highlights, but it doesn't allow very much time for the unexpected. So, if you should find yourself bewitched by a particular area—or if you're going to be based in one town with Aunt Mary and Uncle Sean—you'll find in-depth information about the close environs and those within easy day-trip range. Add a few overnight trips, use day-trip itineraries from your overnight destination, and you'll get in an amazing amount of sightseeing without dashing around the country at breakneck speed—a travel method, incidentally, that I highly recommend even if you're *not* staying with Aunt Mary and Uncle Sean!

TOWNS, VILLAGES, AND CITIES: No matter how you get around Ireland, take time to savor at least some of those small villages and towns you'll pass through. Almost all have a square, or mall, or green around which shops and homes cluster. Although not as numerous as they once were, you'll still find some wonderful examples of handcarved storefronts with ornately painted signs. Many towns have canals or rivers flowing right through the center of town and are crossed by lovely old stone bridges. Still others boast sturdy old towers or town halls or gracefully spired churches. Look for the local courthouse, market house, or tholsel, many of which are early nineteenth-century structures of fine cut limestone.

You might make it a point to park the car in one town each day to walk the streets, call into a pub, or purchase fresh baked bread from the local baker and a hunk of good Irish cheese from the local grocer for picnic makings to be rounded out by a bottled lager or stout from the pub. You won't be charged for the friendly conversation that comes with each purchase, and you'll pick up a wealth of information about the locality.

What I'm trying to say is that Irish towns and villages, as well as cities, are for *loitering,* not rushing through!

One of the first things you'll notice in Ireland is that each village, town, and city name is signposted in both its Anglicized spelling and the original Gaelic. As noted earlier, the Irish language is not an easy one to get your tongue around, and since a fractured-Irish pronunciation is both awkward and embarrassing, I'll give you the correct pronunciation along with the original meaning of major place names. That way, when you're down in Co. Cork, you'll never once say "You-gal" for a town whose name is spelled Youghal, pronounced "Yawl," and means "Yew Wood."

All place names, of course, have some meaning, and in Ireland they often refer to a natural or man-made feature of the locality or to clans and leading families. Some of the Gaelic words used in place names that will tip you off as to the history, setting, or appearance of the village or town are:

Gaelic Word	Meaning
ard	height
áugh *(au)*	ford
bally or baile *(balla)*	town, place or farm
béarna *(barna)*	gap between hills
boher *(bo-her)*	road
cashel	castle
carn	heap of stones
carraig or corrig	boulder
cahir *(care)*	castle
cnoc or knock	hill

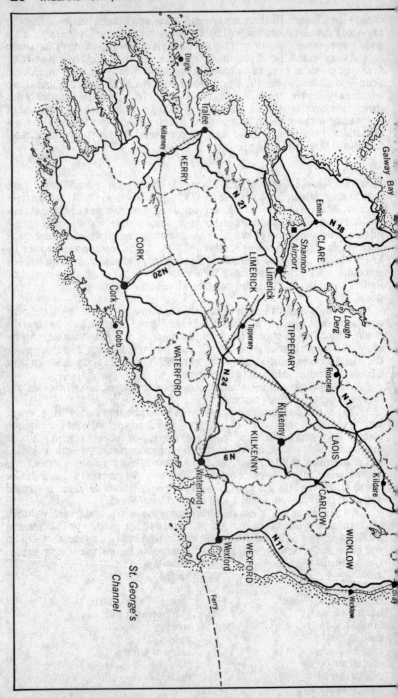

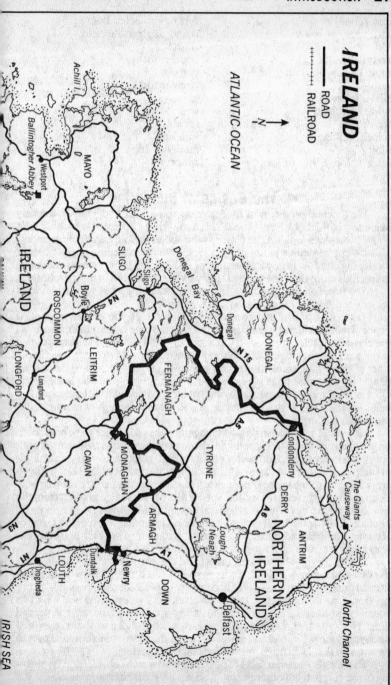

IRELAND

—— ROAD
+++++ RAILROAD

dun *(done)*	fort or protected house
inis, inch, or ennis	island or riverside field
kill	church
lios *(lis)* or lis	circular fort
moin or moyne *(mine)*	bog
rath	circular fort
slieve *(sleeve)*	hill
tobar or tubber	well
trá or tray	beach
tulach, tullow, or tully	small hill
uibh *(iv)*	family or tribe
uisce *(ish-ca),* isk, or isky	water

4. The Basics of Budgeting

We touched on the most fundamental "basic" for budgeting in the very beginning of this book (see "About This Book"), i.e., a place to lay your head at night. Now, let's look a little closer at the subject. No moaning or groaning, please—you're definitely *not* in for a lecture here on pulling in your belt or sacrificing comfort in any way, shape, or fashion. On the contrary, budgeting in Ireland, more than any other country I've encountered in my travels, turns out to be fun, and lots of it! It's all a matter of knowing what's available, what *you* are looking for, and how to go about finding it.

Take, first of all, that roof over your head. If you're *really* counting pence, Ireland will put you up in hostels that in some cases outshine some of the classiest hotels in the country. There's one in Killarney, for instance, that is the sort of magnificent old country mansion most travelers only glimpse from afar, wishing vainly they could step inside for a look at how the Ascendancy lived in those huge piles of stone. As a hosteler, *you'll* be living there. Others, on a more "plain folks living" plane, provide all the necessaries, albeit sans the gigantic marble fireplaces and soaring ceilings of mansions like the one in Killarney.

Now, don't get me wrong—as magnificent as some are to behold, both inside and out, no hostel is going to give you the luxurious modern conveniences of a fancy hotel. But, neither is any hostel going to have you roughing it in such spartan fashion that you'll be aching for a decent night's sleep. If you are willing to purchase real savings at the expense of a private room, you'll sleep in comfort in dormitory-like space. More hostel savings come from the fact that you can buy dinner at the local grocer's and prepare it in a communal kitchen. In Chapter I, I'll give you details on just what to expect in terms of accommodations and prices, but for now, suffice it to say that hosteling is a very pleasant, rock-bottom-priced way to base your budgeting.

Before leaving the subject, I must add that there are intangible benefits to traveling around Ireland via its hostels. You'll meet fellow budgeteers from around the world, all eager to compare experiences and pass along budget tips. One of the neatest Irish conversations I've ever had was with two young Australian girls who were hosteling around Ireland for the second time. Not only had they a load of money-saving advice to share, they had discovered more "nooks and crannies" leads than most of us could expect to encounter, thanks in large part to their fellow hostelers.

There's also another facet of hosteling well worth considering. By sleeping in the company of other penny-pinchers *most* of the time, you can use the money saved to live it up for the one or two truly "Big Splurges" that would not be possible if your funds had to be averaged out over the entire trip. A night, say, in Dromoland Castle (not to be considered by most budgeteers!) would certainly counterbalance any sense of deprivation brought on by a week of dormitory living.

For those of us whose budgets stretch to include a room of our own, however, Ireland's biggest bargain is its plethora of bed-and-breakfast home (in town and country) and farmhouse offerings. I simply cannot sing their praises enough! So addicted to them have I become that even if they *didn't* provide attractive, comfortable sleeping accommodations, I'd suffer a less-than-perfect bed just to indulge in the friendly family life so graciously shared in all. Now, that's a *personal* bias, and I know many, many travelers who could care less about meeting and getting to know an Irish family and insist (in all too many cases!) on hotel amenities at budget prices—until, that is, they experience firsthand a couple of B&B overnights, after which wild horses couldn't drag them back to the hotel route, amenities or no amenities! And I hasten to say that you won't be asked to make that exchange of a good bed for friendly hospitality—at least, not in the B&Bs listed in this book.

Let me say, right up front, that you can forget about hotel amenities unless you're also willing to forget about the budget. No B&B *I* know of is going to have a telephone in your room or offer room service or—in the vast majority of cases—give you your own private bathroom. No, if you are serious about budgeting, the cardinal rule is: *private baths are something you have at home, not when you're saving money on the road.* A sacrifice, you say? Well, let me ask you this: When was the last time you stayed in a friend's home and were given your own bathroom? Point made. Chances are ninety-nine out of a hundred that before you leave your first B&B, you'll know you've stayed with *friends,* shared bath and all!

Having said all that, I must confess that while researching this edition, I became aware of a very curious phenomenon: all around the country, I found B&B hostesses installing private toilets and shower stalls in guestrooms, all available on a first-come, first-served basis at no additional cost. I don't know if this is a trend or simply an extension of the very Irish wish to make guests as comfortable as possible (and every Irishman or Irishwoman knows without doubt that all Americans want a private bath!). Also, I must tell you that in many cases, you'll be charged an extra IR£1 ($1.20) per night for a private bath. And if private facilities are that important to you, you're bound to view that as a very minimal charge. However, if you're willing to share the bath down the hall in order to save the IR£1, but in your heart of hearts would prefer private facilities, it's worth asking about when you book.

Another budget-stretching device is to base yourself at one B&B or farmhouse for an entire week and take advantage of the half-board rate which includes bed, breakfast, and dinner each night at a good reduction. I've already mentioned my own preference to settling in for a few days in one place rather than moving every night. Well, if you book in for a solid week in or near, say, Waterford, using that as a base to explore the eastern and southeastern regions, then book for another week in the west, you'll realize not only the traveling benefits I spoke of, but a much healthier budget as well.

The next "basic" when traveling is eating three squares a day. The first of those will be more than adequately taken care of in your B&B. An Irish breakfast is, simply put, overwhelming. If you're not a breakfast person at home, I'll wager that when in Ireland you won't be able to resist the repast spread before your eyes every morning. Coffee and toast only, you say? I *defy* you to pass up the juice, cereal, bacon (not your shriveled up, fried-to-a-crisp pork, but a meaty, succulent offering much like what we call Canadian bacon in the U.S.), sausage, broiled tomato, brown bread, and golden butter set before you in an Irish B&B! If, in addition, black pudding (I won't tell you what it's made of) appears on your plate, my best advice is, try it, you'll probably like it.

As for the remaining two meals of the day, there are two approaches. Traditionally, the Irish have always had their heartiest meal at midday. That's primarily because as an agricultural nation, those working in the fields felt the need for sustenance to see them through a long afternoon. Travelers could, by making lunch their main meal of the day, save considerably. That still holds true today—a full lunch will provide as much to eat as most dinners, at several punts less in cost. That's the first option.

However, as more and more Irish have become urbanized, eating habits have changed. And I, personally, welcome that change. I simply am not *ready* for a full meal at midday after that sumptuous breakfast. Indeed, there are days on end when breakfast and dinner constitute my full diet because I cannot accommodate more food. If that's not the case with you, however, just look for the nearest pub offering pub grub, relish hearty soup and a sandwich or salad plate (at a "peanuts" price), and save your main meal for late afternoon or the evening. Even better, stop in a town or village, chat with the local grocer as you shop for picnic makings, then head for the country and lunch under the trees or at the shore.

Another option is to choose high tea instead of a dinner menu. In days gone by, because of the national eating habits described above, high tea *was* the evening meal. It was, for all intents and purposes, a "mini-dinner" that would, to most of us, constitute a full meal, especially following an ample midday repast. Nowadays, however, high tea is a rather ambiguous term. I have had a high tea (at about IR£4—$4.80—less than a dinner menu) that was more nourishment than I could comfortably handle; and, on the other side of the coin, I've had a high tea that consisted of one or two skimpy sandwiches, and maybe a sweet, that most certainly would not see me through the night. My best advice is, if your B&B or a local restaurant offers high tea, *ask* what it consists of. High tea can save you as much as 50% of your dinner costs, but you *must* know what "high tea" means to those offering it.

On a more positive note, however, you'll find restaurants listed in this book in every region that offer dinner menus for $10 or under that are full dinners. Most offer the special Tourist Menu, which in 1984 consisted of a three-course meal at either IR£4.65 ($5.58) or IR£6.40 ($7.68). Prices have not been set for 1985 as we go to press, but you may be sure they'll remain under $10. For a complete listing of all restaurants offering these specials, pick up the "Special Value Tourist Menu" booklet from any Bord Fáilte office.

As for transportation costs, there are several money-saving ways to get around, all spelled out in detail in Chapter II. Train and bus travel comes cheap and will get you most places you want to go, although perhaps not at the exact time you want to go. Cycling is one of the cheapest and most popular ways to get around; shank's mare (hiking) is, it goes without saying, the least expensive; and hitchhiking is an accepted and time-honored mode of transportation. Using one, or a combination, of these methods will save pence that quickly add up to punts.

DROP A LINE: As is the practice with all Frommer's guides, you are invited to participate in future editions. All the judgments, opinions, and comments in the text of this edition are based on personal inspections and experiences, except for those listed under the heading "Readers' Suggestions." Change is the very nature of the travel world, however: accommodations and restaurants appear and disappear, change managements, ownership and chefs, improve or go to pot. Should you find any of these conditions, please do let me know about it.

Most of all, don't be shy about sharing with me any especially good discoveries of your own. Some of the best listings in this edition have come from Readers' Suggestions I have looked into.

You have my word that each and every letter will be read by me, personally, although I find it well nigh impossible to *answer* each and every one. Just write: Susan Poole, Frommer/Pasmantier Publishers, 1230 Avenue of the Americas, New York, NY 10020. You can rest assured I'll be listening to what you have to say!

5. The $25-A-Day Travel Club—How to Save Money on All Your Travels

In this book we'll be looking at how to get your money's worth in Ireland, but there is a "device" for saving money and determining value on *all* your trips. It's the popular, international $25-A-Day Travel Club, now in its 22nd successful year of operation. The Club was formed at the urging of numerreaders of the $$$-A-Day and Dollarwise Guides, who felt that such an organization could provide continuing travel information and a sense of community to value-minded travelers in all parts of the world. And so it does!

In keeping with the budget concept, the annual membership fee is low and is immediately exceeded by the value of your benefits. Upon receipt of $15 (U.S. residents), or $18 U.S. by check drawn on a U.S. bank or via international postal money order in U.S. funds (Canadian, Mexican and other foreign residents) to cover one year's membership, we will send all new members the following items.

(1) *Any two* of the following books
Please designate in your letter which two you wish to receive:

> **Europe on $25 a Day**
> **Australia on $25 a Day**
> **England and Scotland on $25 a Day**
> **Greece on $25 a Day**
> **Hawaii on $35 a Day**
> **Ireland on $25 a Day**
> **India on $15 & $25 a Day**
> **Israel on $30 & $35 a Day**
> **Mexico on $20 a Day**

New York on $35 a Day
New Zealand on $20 & $25 a Day
Scandinavia on $35 a Day
South America on $25 a Day
Spain and Morocco (plus the Canary Is.) on $35 a Day
Washington, D.C. on $35 a Day

Dollarwise Guide to Austria and Hungary
Dollarwise Guide to Canada
Dollarwise Guide to the Caribbean (including Bermuda and the Bahamas)
Dollarwise Guide to Egypt
Dollarwise Guide to England and Scotland
Dollarwise Guide to France
Dollarwise Guide to Germany
Dollarwise Guide to Italy
Dollarwise Guide to Portugal (plus Madeira and the Azores)
Dollarwise Guide to Switzerland
Dollarwise Guide to California and Las Vegas
Dollarwise Guide to Florida
Dollarwise Guide to New England
Dollarwise Guide to the Northwest
Dollarwise Guide to Southeast and New Orleans
Dollarwise Guide to the Southwest
(Dollarwise Guides discuss accommodations and facilities in all price ranges, with emphasis on the medium-priced.)

Dollarwise Guide to Cruises
(This complete guide covers all the basics of cruising—ports of call, costs, fly-cruise package bargains, cabin selection booking, embarkation and debarkation and describes in detail over 60 or so ships cruising in Alaska, the Caribbean, Mexico, Hawaii, Panama, Canada, and the United States.)

How to Beat the High Cost of Travel
(This practical guide details how to save money on absolutely all travel items—accommodations, transportation, dining, sightseeing, shopping, taxes, and more. Includes special budget information for seniors, students, singles, and families.)

The New York Urban Athlete
(The ultimate guide to all the sports facilities in New York City for jocks and novices.)

Museums in New York
(A complete guide to all the museums, historic houses, gardens, zoos, and more in the five boroughs. Illustrated with over 200 photographs.)

The Fast 'n' Easy Phrase Book
(The four most useful languages—French, German, Spanish, and Italian—all in one convenient, easy-to-use phrase guide.)

Where to Stay USA
(By the Council on International Educational Exchange, this extraordinary

guide is the first to list accommodations in all 50 states that cost anywhere from $3 to $25 per night.)

A Guide for the Disabled Traveler
(A guide to the best destinations for wheelchair travelers and other disabled vacationers in Europe, the United States, and Canada by an experienced wheelchair traveler. Includes detailed information about accommodations, restaurants, sights, transportation, and their accessibility.)

Marilyn Wood's Wonderful Weekends
(This very selective guide covers the best mini-vacation destinations within a 175-mile radius of New York City. It describes special country inns and other accommodations, restaurants, picnic spots, sights, and activities—all the information needed for a two- or three-day stay.)

Bed & Breakfast—North America
(This guide contains a directory of over 150 organizations that offer bed & breakfast referrals and reservations throughout North America. The scenic attractions, businesses, and major schools and universities near the homes of each are also listed.)

(2) A one-year subscription to *The Wonderful World of Budget Travel*

This quarterly eight-page tabloid newspaper keeps you up to date on fast-breaking developments in low-cost travel in all parts of the world bringing you the latest money-saving information—the kind of information you'd have to pay $25 a year to obtain elsewhere. This consumer-conscious publication also features columns of special interest to readers. **The Traveler's Directory** (members all over the world who are willing to provide hospitality to other members as they pass through their home cities); **Share-a-Trip** (offers and requests from members for travel companions who can share costs and help avoid the burdensome single supplement); and **Readers Ask . . . Readers Reply** (travel questions from members to which other members reply with authentic firsthand information).

(3) A copy of *Arthur Frommer's Guide to New York*

This is a pocket-size guide to hotels, restaurants, nightspots, and sightseeing attractions in all price ranges throughout the New York area.

(4) Your personal membership card

Membership entitles you to purchase through the Club all Arthur Frommer publications for a third to a half off their regular retail prices during the term of your membership.

So why not join this hardy band of international budgeteers and participate in its exchange of travel information and hospitality? Simply send your name and address, together with your annual membership fee of $15 (U.S. residents) or $18 U.S. (Canadian, Mexican, and other foreign residents), by check drawn on a U.S. bank or via international postal money order in U.S. funds to: $25-a-Day Travel Club, Inc., Frommer/Pasmantier Publishers, 1230 Avenue of the Americas, New York, NY 10020. And please remember to specify which *two* of the books in section (1) above you wish to receive in your initial package of members' benefits. Or, if you prefer, use the last page of this book, simply checking off the two books you select and enclosing $15 or $18 in U.S. currency.

During the term of your membership, no books will be mailed to you unless you specifically request them. There are "no strings attached" to your membership.

Chapter I

IRELAND: THE PRACTICALITIES

1. The Currency
2. Preparing for Your Trip
3. Discounts for Students
4. Where to Stay
5. Where to Eat
6. Big Splurges
7. Shopping

THIS CHAPTER MAY WELL CONTAIN the most important words between the book's covers. Not the most exciting, perhaps, but certainly careful reading of this part of your "homework" can make all the difference in whether you get back home bubbling over with happy memories unmarred by uninformed mistakes (budgetary *and* trip-planning) or slightly bewildered that you never *did* get to do and see the things you really wanted to.

We'll talk about details you should know *before you leave home* if your trip is to be a carefree one. It is absolutely essential that you know about such things as currency, the rate of exchange, and travel documents. And it is equally desirable that you be well informed on what to expect by way of accommodations, restaurants, shopping, sightseeing and a host of other activities.

Since finances are the bottom line for any budget traveler, let's begin with an examination of Ireland's currency.

1. The Currency

The 1970s saw two significant changes in Irish currency. First, in 1971, the country went on the decimal system; that is, the Irish pound was divided into 100 pence. It was certainly a step toward simplification for those accustomed to such arithmetic, but even in 1985 you'll hear references in Ireland to the "old money" system of pounds, shillings, and "old pence." Since the Irish pound maintained parity with the pound sterling, English notes and coins were interchangeable with Irish money (although the reverse was never true and Irish currency was not accepted in England).

In 1979, however, the second currency change occurred when, as a member of the European Monetary System, the Irish government linked its monetary values to those of major EEC currencies and the Irish pound officially became the "punt." As a result, although English notes are now accepted on the same basis as any other foreign currency by many shops, restaurants, hotels, etc., life is simpler for the traveler if all transactions are in Irish punts (often still referred to as the "Irish pound").

The punt is still divided into 100 pence, and coins come in denominations of 1/2 pence, 1 pence, 2 pence, 5 pence, 10 pence, and 50 pence. All banks make exchanges on the basis of daily quotations, and it is wise to change your money always at a bank or an American Express office. It is true that some of the larger shops and hotels also work on daily quotations, but many more simply take a weekly average when figuring exchange rates, which can sometimes cost you more when changing notes. Bear in mind, too, that *you'll get a better rate with travelers checks than with cash.*

The conversion chart below is based on an exchange rate of IR£1 = $1.20, the rate in effect at press time. Fluctuations have been almost daily in recent months, however, and these figures should be taken only as a guide. *Be sure to check with a bank at the time you travel for the current rate.*

IR£	$	IR£	$
1p	1¢	IR£1	$1.20
5p	6¢	IR£2.50	$3.00
25p	30¢	IR£3	$3.60
50p	60¢	IR£4.50	$5.40
75p	90¢	IR£10.00	$12.00

2. Preparing for Your Trip

Now, down to the nitty-gritty. There are the things you *must* do ahead, such as arming yourself with the necessary documents and wardrobe, and the things you will *want* to know and do in order to get every last bit of enjoyment from your trip.

TRAVEL DOCUMENTS: All United States citizens need to travel in Ireland is a valid passport. It is no longer necessary even to show proof of smallpox vaccination when returning to this country. If you're a British citizen, you can travel freely in Ireland without a passport, but I'd strongly advise bringing it along if you have one, since on some occasions it may be the only acceptable form of identification (for picking up money orders sent from abroad, etc.). If you're a citizen of any other country, be sure to check with the Irish Embassy in your area as to what additional documents you may need.

WHAT CLOTHES TO BRING: You can really put off the final decision on what to pack until you have pretty firmly in mind just what sort of Irish holiday you plan on, but there is one item that is an absolute *must,* no matter what time of year you come or what you plan on doing. You guessed it, it's a raincoat.

Ireland's capricious weather can—and often does—skip from a drizzly morning to a sparkling, sunny afternoon to evening showers all in the space of one day. Mind you, the rain truly *is* a soft rain and you'll seldom, if ever, encounter a slashing, unfriendly onslaught of the sort that often attacks you here in the U.S. However, soft or not, Irish rain can be as *wet* as any other— and more unexpected than most. Also, I find that a lightweight raincoat comes in handy not only to keep dry, but as a wrap on chilly spring or fall evenings, as well.

As for the rest of your packing, keep in mind that Ireland is basically a very *casual* country. Even if you're planning to spend most of your time traipsing around the countryside, but refuse to leave the country without at least one night of Dublin theater or cabaret, you won't need to bring along a separate evening wardrobe. Women will find that a semi-dressy blouse to go with the same pants that traveled quite comfortably around the Ring of Kerry will see them through almost any Dublin evening. Personally, I like to take along an "old-faithful" long skirt for any unexpected invitation to a more formal function, but a simple skirt and dressy top does just as well. For men, a sports jacket and a tie will serve for any "dressy" occasion in the city. There are a few "Big Splurge" restaurants you may want to budget for in which you'll also be more comfortable with this type of attire.

There's just one exception to the above, however, and it probably goes without saying. I'll say it anyway: even though almost anything goes for after-dark Dublin, the theater, a dinner cabaret, or a posh restaurant are definitely *not* places for jeans! So, if you're a jeans-and-tee-shirt traveler, stick in one outfit for your big-city night out.

One word of caution: All of the above holds true for any Irish holiday unless you plan to take in Dublin's swank Horse Show Week or Wexford's Opera Festival. In that case, women will want to have along a cocktail dress and appropriate shoes for the round of parties and receptions that are so much a part of those scenes. And their male escorts will be more comfortable with a dark suit for those occasions.

For traveling around the rest of the country, stick to every veteran traveler's tried-and-true formula of packing sensibly and *light*. No matter how much you'd love to take along that smashing pure cotton outfit or linen jacket, if it won't drip-dry or must be ironed every time you unpack, *leave it at home*. Interchangeable tops and bottoms (pants or skirts, depending on your personal preference—either is perfectly acceptable these days in Ireland) will lighten your load.

You may want to put in a lightweight sweater or shawl, since nights can sometimes be cool even in summer months, although my trusty raincoat usually sees me through and leaves room for another shirt or two in the suitcase. Remember, too, that unless you're steel-willed enough to resist those gorgeous Irish hand-knit sweaters, you'll no doubt acquire one during your travels, and it might as well begin its long years of service right on its own home turf.

You may or may not want to include a dressing gown for those trips down the hall to your B&B bathroom—again, if space is at a premium, I often use that same trusty old raincoat. However, if there's room in the suitcase, the robe goes in.

The mix-and-match principle applies to shoes as well as other clothing. Now, I'm not suggesting that your stout walking shoes will go waltzing out to dinner or the theater, but sandals or pumps that match a dressy top as well as a sports outfit do double duty easily. One more word about shoes: stick in one pair more than you think you'll need. No, I'm not violating that pack-light principle, I'm just advising you to be practical. Those unexpected showers can leave your feet pretty soggy, and it's best to have along a spare pair. An inexpensive can of waterproofing spray to treat your shoes before leaving home is a good investment.

One of the most awkward items to pack is always my toiletries case, and I've learned to carry along only an initial supply of such things as toothpaste, shampoo, etc., and buy replacements as I go along. Ireland's pharmacies and department stores are well stocked with many of the same brands you'll be used to at home. As for medications, in addition to your anticipated needs, it's a good idea to bring along prescriptions (for eyeglasses, as well) from your local doctor just in case you need refills.

Far be it from me to set down a strict "how to pack" formula, but I do have some suggestions for a method that I've evolved over the years that works pretty well. First of all, the pack-light theme begins with my suitcase. A sturdy duffle bag or one of the marvelous lightweight (and flexible) nylon bags now on the market add almost no weight and seem to have endless space in which to fit one more item. Zippers are all-important with this kind of luggage, so be sure you conduct a careful inspection before leaving home.

Bulky items like shoes or hairdryers or the toiletries case go in first and provide a firm bottom layer. Underwear and tee-shirts go in next, followed by layers of blouses, shirts, trousers, and skirts. A commodious shoulder bag carries the items I'll need en route and traveling around the country (and I find it handy to stick in a traveling toothbrush and small tube of toothpaste for those times it's inconvenient to go scrounging around the suitcase).

There's one more thing I never leave home without—an extra nylon bag that folds into a tiny envelope cover. That's for all the things that I inevitably pick up along the way and for those things that just won't go back into their original place in the bag I brought over. I pack that at home simply because I happen to have one that has seen yeoman's service, but if you don't already have one, you can easily pick up an inexpensive nylon duffle bag or folding bag in one of the department stores in the larger cities of Ireland. Just thought I'd warn you that you'll probably be needing one.

TOURIST INFORMATION: The native hospitality of the Irish begins long before you embark on your visit to their shores, and few countries send you off as well prepared as Ireland. The friendly folk at any branch of the Irish Tourist Board (Bord Fáilte, in Ireland) take their literal name, Board of Welcomes, quite seriously. They're an official government agency that somehow seems to escape the impersonal, don't-care attitude that so often pervades bureaucratic institutions. My best advice (even if you're in the beginning stages of just *thinking* about an Irish holiday) is to hie yourself down to the nearest ITB office (or contact them by mail or telephone) and plug in to one of the most helpful organizations in the ranks of international tourism.

On this side of the Atlantic, they'll supply you with literature to help with your initial planning, answer any questions that may come up, advise you on tracing your Irish ancestry, arrange for you to meet Irish families, and generally see to it that you're off to a good start.

You'll find Irish Tourist Board offices located at these addresses in the United States:

590 Fifth Ave.
New York, NY 10036
Tel. 212/869-5500

230 N. Michigan Ave.
Chicago, IL 60601
Tel. 312/726-9356

681 Market St.
San Francisco, CA 94105
Tel. 415/781-5688

There are also offices in London, Paris, Frankfurt-am-Main, Amsterdam, Brussels, Milan, Manchester, Birmingham, Glasgow, Belfast, and Toronto. In the South Pacific, you'll find representatives in both Sydney and Auckland.

Study carefully the following list of their informative publications to request either at any one of the United States offices or when you're in Ireland.

Ireland—The Unexpected Pleasures (holiday planner that incorporates a Traveler's Guide with specific information on vacationing in Ireland).

Irish Homes (a complete listing of approved accommodations in town and country homes and farmhouses).

Town and Country Homes Association Guest Accommodation (listing, with photos, of association member homes—small charge).

Farm Holidays in Ireland (descriptions and photos of members of Farm Holidays Association—small charge).

Ireland—Self-Catering (holidays in cottages, castles, houses, bungalows, chalets, flats, and apartments).

Hotels and Guesthouses (a comprehensive list of hotels and guesthouses with gradings of all properties and photos of many).

Dining in Ireland (listings of all categories of restaurants).

Special Value Tourist Menu (listing of restaurants around the country offering inexpensive meals—a must for budgeteers!).

Map of Ireland (detailed road map with scenic routes outlined—indispensable, even if you're not driving!).

Ireland's Heritage (castles, houses, and gardens open to the public).

Craft Hunter's Guide (details on where to find Irish crafts around the country).

Irish Tourist Board Offices (listing of all locations in Ireland and their opening times).

Discover Young Ireland (a guide to learning and leisure opportunities for students).

Calendar of Events (dates and venues of happenings around the country all through the year).

Golf Guide (details on courses around the country).

Equestrian Guide (where to ride in Ireland).

That's a long list, but it is by no means complete. If you don't see a publication for your special interest, ask about Information Sheets on that aspect. Information Sheets are concise, detailed reports on everything from sailing schools to hiking to museums to folk music, and you'll almost certainly find that one has been issued on the subject in which you are interested.

Tourist Offices in Ireland

Irish Tourist Board headquarters are at Baggot Street Bridge, Dublin 2 (tel. 01-765871); there are eight regional offices open year round whose addresses will be listed in the appropriate chapters of this book; and all told there are over seventy local offices around the country (some open only during the high season).

If you carry along the official listing (see above), you'll never be at a loss to find a tourist information office, no matter where you find yourself. However, even without that list, they are easily spotted if you look for the green "i" sign that is posted in such diverse locations as a pub or grocer's out in the boondocks or along the Quay in Waterford or in the handsome modern quarters at 14 Upper O'Connell St. in Dublin. Wherever you find that sign, rest assured there are friendly, knowledgeable people who seem to exist for no other reason than to point you to the accommodations, restaurants, sightseeing attractions, local pubs, or sporting events that will make your holiday a pleasant one.

Hours vary according to location and season, but you can count on year-round offices being staffed from 10 a.m. to 5 p.m. weekdays during winter months, with weekend and longer evening hours during the summer season.

Room Reservation Service

One of the most used of all Irish Tourist Board services is their accommodations booking service. It allows a flexibility of movement that frees you and me to move about as our fancy dictates, secure in the knowledge that, having rambled far off our intended itinerary, we have only to call into the nearest ITB office when we're ready to move on and they'll happily telephone ahead for the next night's lodgings. Not only that, they'll stick to the room rate we specify without a grumble or groan (always provided, of course, that we ask for a *reasonable* rate). I have yet to hear a tourist office person attempt to pressure anyone into opting for a higher-priced accommodation than the limit specified just because that limit may be in short supply. They'll phone around until they have you settled in at the price you want to pay.

If you stray so far from a set travel plan (the best thing I could hope for you in Ireland!) that you arrive in town with no place to lay your head that night, the local tourist office will perform the same service in their own locality.

In every case, you'll be asked to pay the telephone charges, plus 50p (60¢) for local bookings, IR£1 ($1.20) for those out of town. Caution: If you're booking ahead, be sure to get to the tourist office in time to wait up to a half-hour for the office at your next stop to find your room and get back to the office making the request.

WHEN TO BOOK AHEAD: By now, you must know that Ireland invites a delightful, spur-of-the-moment travel plan. That, in my opinion, leads to gloriously unpredictable holidays and treasured memories. I am *not,* however, enamored of stumbling off a trans-Atlantic plane, numb with jet lag and faced with the prospect of having to hunt for a room, even with the helpful ITB crew. Nor, having done it once or twice, am I inclined to hop behind the wheel of a car and head off into the country before my body adjusts to the time change or my mind is clear enough to cope with left-side-of-the-road driving. Even less desirable would be to arrive in the country, present myself to the nearest car rental agency and find there's no car available! Or plan on seeing a play at the Abbey Theater and find it booked out for the only night I'm in Dublin.

To put it succinctly, there are some advance reservations that are absolutely vital to a happy holiday, even for the most haphazard traveler! If you're of a temperament that gets very, very nervous if you don't know where you'll be sleeping a night or two down the road, then prearranged reservations become a must. With all that in mind, may I suggest the following minimal advance bookings.

At the top of the list is your first night's accommodation. Whether you're flying into Shannon or Dublin, I strongly recommend that you plan to spend the first day and night right there. Jet lag (yes, Virginia, there *is* such a thing as genuine jet lag—it is *not* a question of mind over matter!) is one strong reason for that recommendation, but there are others.

In the case of Shannon, for example, far too many visitors rush right through the Limerick area and miss one of Ireland's richest sightseeing spots. But, if you're booked into a B&B and can catch a few hours' sleep soon after you arrive, you'll be refreshed and ready for Bunratty's medieval banquet that night (also booked ahead), a perfect introduction to the country. Or you might want to while away the evening at Durty Nellie's or one of Limerick's other great pubs. The next day could see you on your way around the country after short detours by the Cliffs of Moher, just a short drive away, or some of Shannonside's other outstanding attractions. For Dublin arrivals, what better first night (after that catnap to get your body straightened out) than a cabaret or pub crawl.

You can book your first night's stay either through **Central Reservations Service,** 14 Upper O'Connell St., Dublin 1 (tel. 01-747733) or by writing directly to one of the accommodations listed in this book. If you choose the latter, you'll save time by enclosing a deposit and an international reply coupon for postage. The same applies if you're especially anxious to stay at any of the accommodations listed in this book and you're certain of the dates for each—during summer months you could be disappointed otherwise.

Then, there's the matter of a car rental. Ireland is a small country, with most of its visitors descending during summer months, and there simply is not an inexhaustible supply of automobiles. Especially if you plan to come during the high season, it is absolutely essential to book your car as far in advance as possible. For more specialized holidays, such as horse caravans or cabin cruisers, it is even more important that you get your reservation in early. Reserve through travel agents or by writing the rental company direct at addresses listed in Chapter II.

As for special events, such as a castle banquet, hotel cabaret, Dublin theater, etc., Irish Tourist Board offices can make those bookings for you, but it is much more direct to write to each separately, enclose the international reply coupon for postage and a deposit (or the full price), and ask for immediate confirmation.

As I said at the beginning of this section, *some* advance bookings just must be made. But, I want to end this section by stressing again that if you schedule your Irish stay *too* rigidly, you'll miss half the fun of Ireland!

READ BEFORE YOU GO: In the introductory pages to this book, I have tried to give some indication of the uniqueness of the Irish people and the country in which they live. But, the characters of both are best illuminated by native writers, those luminary figures who have cast a glow across the world's literary scene for centuries. Their names are legion, and I would not even *attempt* to give you a definitive list of writings that would lend the most insight and color to your Irish experience.

I have always found that reading is a very personal choice, but I would like to share with you a few of the writings which have been most meaningful to me—personally—as I have come to know Ireland and its people. Beyond that, I can only say that such reading has always enriched *any* travel for me, and I hope you will take the time—either before or after your visit to Ireland —to explore the Irish dimensions available only through the country's literature.

There are, of course, the greats: Synge, O'Casey, Joyce, *ad infinitum*. For me, to capture the sheer poetry of the country, almost anything by Yeats can be recommended; the gutsy, gusty irreverence of Brendan Behan (I have especially enjoyed *Brendan Behan's Island—an Irish Sketchbook)* brings a sense of poignant hilarity to the Irish scene that I've found nowhere else; James Plunket's *Strumpet City* paints a rich, full portrait of Dublin that encompasses Dublin's multilayered society in the years leading up to World War I; and John B. Keane's writings—be they essays or plays—bare the soul of the Irish countryman in an honest, telling, and affectionate manner that lends understanding and depth to many an Irish encounter.

Further, I have a recommendation you won't find listed anywhere under Ireland's great writers, but which represents some of my most enjoyable and instructive Irish reading. Walter Macken, a native of Galway, was only 51 when he died in 1967, leaving a trilogy of Irish historical novels which have quite literally brought the country's history alive for me through characters and events that throb with reality. *Seek the Fair Land* is set in 1649, the Cromwell era; *The Silent People* tells of the famine years and British oppression; and *The Scorching Wind* is a tale of Ireland's Civil War. You'll find them in most Irish bookshops and at Shannon and Dublin airports, and I urge you to read any or all of them for the simple pleasure of a good story well told and for a sort of "instant history" lesson.

3. Discounts for Students

For students, Ireland has so much going for it that I sometimes think it should be a compulsory part of any first-rate school curriculum. First of all, as pointed out in the Introduction, with half its population aged twenty-five and under, it is truly a haven for the young *(Tir na nog,* the ancient Celts called their version of heaven, and the Gaelic name translates to "land of youth"). Sports, music, dancing, and a host of other activities are geared for the young and available wherever you go in the country.

Not only are recreational and leisure pursuits at your fingertips in Ireland, but the ancient tradition and reverence for learning continue to this day, with all sorts of interesting educational experiences available.

BEFORE YOU COME: Any student traveling to Ireland will be literally missing the boat without an **International Student Identity Card,** which opens doors to marvelous events and activities aimed only at students as well as substantial discounts on almost every facet of travel. You must, however, arm yourself with this valuable document *before you leave home.* The cost in 1984 was $8, and you can obtain your card through **CIEE** (the Council on International Educational Exchange), 205 E. 42nd St., New York, NY 10017 (tel. 212/661-1414). With the card in hand, you'll be entitled to participate in all the listings below, as well as many, many more happenings you'll discover once you arrive on Irish soil.

For anyone between the ages of 15 and 26, CIE's **Youth/Student Rambler Ticket** is a budget godsend. It allows you unlimited travel on bus and rail services, standard class, for a cost of $58 for eight days, $76 for 15 days, or $100 for 30 days. It must, however, be purchased *before* your arrival in Ireland. Available through travel agents or from CIE Tours International, 590 Fifth Ave., New York, NY 10036 (tel. 212/944-8828).

You should also obtain, well in advance, the Irish Tourist Board publication, **Discover Young Ireland: A Guide to Learning and Leisure Opportunities.** In its pages, you'll find full descriptions of budget holidays, whether of the just-for-fun or more studious variety. You should also request their **Student Group Accommodation List,** which is especially useful during school holiday periods (Easter and July and August) for student residence halls that offer accommodations at reduced rates to students.

WHEN YOU ARRIVE: The student's best friend in Ireland is the **Irish Student Travel Service (USIT).** If you deplane at Shannon, your very first Irish stop should be the Limerick office at 31 Upper Cecil St. (tel. 061-45064 or 48925). Hours are 10 a.m. to 2 p.m. and 3:15 to 5 p.m. on weekdays, 10 a.m. to 1 p.m. on Saturdays. The head office is in Dublin at 7 Anglesea St. (off Dame St., tel. 01-778117), with hours of 9:30 a.m. to 5:30 p.m. on weekdays, 10 a.m. to 1 p.m. on Saturdays. Elsewhere, there are USIT offices (with varying hours) in Waterford (33 O'Connell St., tel. 051-72601), Belfast (68 Donegal St., tel. 0232-224073), Coleraine, Co. Derry (New University of Ulster, tel. Coleraine 52161), Cork (University College, Cork, tel. 021-23901), Galway (University College, tel. 091-24601), and Maynooth, Co. Kildare (St. Patrick's College, tel. 01-2860035).

USIT will arrange cut-rate travel between Ireland and other European destinations, help you plan itineraries both inside the country and beyond, advise you about accommodations, camping, summer jobs, and student values in every area you can think of.

TRANSPORTATION SAVINGS: One of USIT's most valuable services is the **Travelsave Stamp** which, affixed to your International Student Identity Card, entitles you to such benefits as a month's unlimited travel on Dublin buses and trains for about IR£20 ($24); IR£18 ($21.60) in Cork; and IR£14 ($16.80) in Galway, Limerick, and Waterford. In addition, you'll be given a 50% reduction in train and bus travel, as well as ferry service to the Aran Islands and the UK. Any USIT office can furnish the stamp, or you can apply by mail to the Dublin Head Office. In 1984, the cost was IR£4.50 ($5.40), and it is valid for a calendar year.

Another transportation bargain available through USIT (to those under the age of 26) is the **Inter-Rail Card,** which is good for one month's unlimited rail travel in most of continental Europe, as well as half-fare bus, train, and ferry travel in Ireland, Northern Ireland, and Great Britain. The 1984 price was IR£25.75 ($30.90), and the card can be purchased at any USIT office upon presentation of your passport (student ID card is not necessary for this one).

In Dublin, you can purchase an **Educational Travel Concession Ticket** through the Tourist Information Office, 14 Upper O'Connell St. (tel. 01-747733), that permits unlimited travel on Dublin bus and train services at a cost of IR£14 ($16.80) for two weeks or IR£20 ($24) for four weeks.

Of course, cycling, hiking, or hitchhiking are the three cheapest—and, to my mind, the most fun—means of transportation for the young or young-at-heart. Through the **Raleigh Rent-A-Bike Scheme** (details from any Irish Tourist Board office), you can rent bikes at more than 100 locations around the country for rates of about IR£4 ($4.80) per day or IR£22 ($26.40) per week. USIT also operates a **Rent-A-Bike program,** with offices at main Dublin bus, rail, and air terminals and (in June/September only) at Rosslare Harbor. Prices run about IR£3 ($3.60) per day, IR£17 ($20.40) per week, and you can get full information from: USIT Rent-A-Bike, 58 Lower Gardiner St., Dublin 1 (tel. 01-725399 or 725931).

STUDY IN IRELAND: The aforementioned *Discover Young Ireland: A Guide to Learning and Leisure Opportunities,* published by the Irish Tourist Board, is a cornucopia of study possibilities in Ireland, many of which include accommodations in Irish homes, weekend travel, and cultural events. Subjects are as varied as Irish literature, drama, music, archeology, crafts, and the Irish language. Bookings for every course should be made as far in advance as possible, so you should write for the booklet and make your decision early (see ITB addresses listed in Section 2 of this chapter, or contact the Youth and Education Department, Irish Tourist Board, 590 Fifth Ave., New York, NY 10036, tel. 212/869-5500).

There are two excellent study programs in Ireland sponsored by U.S. organizations. The Council on International Educational Exchange (CIEE) offers **Encounter Ireland** to any full-time student of an American college or university. For four weeks, participants spend three weeks with an Irish family in Dublin and attend lectures, concerts, art exhibits, and other cultural events and visiting the sightseeing highlights of the city and its environs. A fourth week is left free for you to travel around the country independently, using the rail pass which is included in the price. To qualify, you must send them a 500-word essay on your reasons for wanting to go to Ireland, two passport-type photos, a reference from one of your professors, and a completed application form. The price in 1984 (1985 costs are not available as we go to press), including round-trip airfare from New York, was $995, or $595 without airfare, and dates are mid-June and mid-July. For full details and an application, contact CIEE, Encounter Ireland Program, 205 E. 42nd St., New York, NY 10017 (tel. 212/661-1414).

The second program is sponsored by the Irish American Cultural Institute and is called the **Irish Way.** This, too, gives you four full weeks in Ireland, all at Gormanston College in Co. Meath, some 25 miles north of Dublin. Studies during that time range from mythology, history, archeology, and drama to literature, folk music, and balladry. There are interesting and entertaining field trips, and for spare time recreation, there's an indoor swimming pool, tennis courts, and facilities for golf, handball, and soccer. The estimated cost for 1985 is $1295 plus airfare, and some partial scholarships are available. The program begins in early July and runs into early August. For details, write: The Irish Way, Irish American Cultural Institute, 683 Osceola Ave., St. Paul, MN 55105.

4. Where to Stay

The most amazing single fact about Ireland's budget accommodations is that there just *isn't* one *single* category of budget accommodations! Oh, I know I've sung the praises of the town and country B&Bs, and I'll keep right on doing that. But, they are by no means the only budget accommodations on the Irish market. If your notion of budget travel is camping, there are good campgrounds located in just about every scenic section of the country; backpackers will find a marvelous supply of hostels at dirt-cheap rates; next up on the cost scale come those wonderful Irish family B&Bs; then there are the farmhouses, which range from modern bungalows to great Georgian mansions, all on working farms; if you lean towards the "small inn" type of home-away-from-home, there are the guesthouses a little (but very little) higher up the price range; and for families or small groups traveling together, self-catering cottages may prove to be the most economical way of all to enjoy an Irish visit. There's even a country-wide holiday program that includes some very nice hotels with special midweek and weekend package rates that can only be called budget.

The selection within those ranges that you'll find in these pages have all been personally inspected, but you'll never be buying a pig in a poke even if you book into a place that *isn't* in our book. The ever-vigilant Bord Fáilte staff keeps a sharp eye on every accommodation they approve, with annual, unannounced inspections. That green shamrock approval sign is so highly coveted among Irish housewives that new wallpaper goes up at the first sign of wear and you may well find your hostess slapping a brand new paint job on woodwork with a vengeance. I sometimes think Irish women *paint* their woodwork far more frequently than I get around to *washing* mine! And a quirk of the Irish vocabulary you're bound to notice is that every vacuum cleaner is known as a "hoover"; equally quirky is the fact that "hoovering" seems to take place several times a day—just let one speck of dirt or dust appear on the carpet, and out comes the hoover.

What I'm trying to say is that wherever you see the Bord Fáilte approved sign, you'll find *clean* premises. Not only that, but each approved accommodation is required to register its rate for the year with the Bord and cannot charge more than that unless higher rates for holidays or special events are also registered and appear in the Bord Fáilte listings. They also certify that you'll get the exact accommodation you bargained for when you booked and that you'll never be asked to share a room with a stranger. If, by chance, you run into what you think is a violation of these rules, you are expected to make your complaint known—first to the hostess, and failing satisfaction, to Bord Fáilte, Baggot Street Bridge, Dublin 2. If you think you've been overcharged, be sure to get a receipt to send on to Dublin.

Now, not all B&Bs, guesthouses, and hotels are approved, which isn't to say there aren't some very good unapproved accommodations out there. It's just that if you book into one that isn't, you're strictly on your own unless—as is the case in a very few listed herein—we've been there, tested facilities and hostess for you, and found them more than just adequate. Some of the warmest, most hospitable places I've stayed in Ireland have not been on Bord Fáilte's list, and to be honest, I have run into only one or two that were perfect horrors. All the same, it's a good rule of thumb to stick to the approved places unless you have a recommendation from someone whose judgment you trust.

CAMPGROUNDS: If the great outdoors holds such appeal for you that tenting is the only way to go in your book, then the very first item in your backpack should be Bord Fáilte's **Caravan & Camping Parks** booklet. It's available for a small charge from the Irish Tourist Board, 590 Fifth Ave., New York, NY 10036, and it lists approved campgrounds, camping equipment hirers, and (for the less hardy) caravan—we know them as vans or recreational vehicles—hirers.

To be approved, campgrounds must provide good toilet facilities, water supply points, rubbish disposal facilities, and properly spaced sites for tents and caravans. Many offer far more than these minimum requirements, with laundry and recreation facilities, a shop, or sometimes even a restaurant on the premises. Charges vary according to location and season, and can range from IR£2.50 ($3) to IR£5 ($6) per night for caravans or tents, with a small per-person additional charge; weekly rates offer a considerable savings over daily rates.

HOSTELS: The first thing to be said about hostels is that, although they're called *youth* hostels, you'll be welcomed if you're six or sixty. The second thing to be said is that in order to use them, you must have an **International Youth Hostel Card,** which *must be purchased before you leave home.* They are available from **American Youth Hostels, Inc.,** 1331 "I" St. NW, Suite 800, Washington, DC 20005, and cost $10 for those under 18 or over 59, and $20 ages 18 to 59. For another $7.50, you can purchase their *International Youth Hostel Handbook* (Vol. I—Europe and North Africa) in which you'll find Irish hostels listed.

An Oige is the Irish Youth Hostel Association's official name, and they're a voluntary organization dedicated to helping residents and visitors take full advantage of Ireland's outdoor offerings and to providing hostel accommodations at minimum rates. They also put together such holiday bargain packages as the Rambler/Hostelling Holiday, which cost IR£69 ($82.80) in 1984 for an eight-day bus/train ticket plus eight overnights in hostels for those under 21, IR£73 ($87.60) for those over 21. There are cycling holidays and combination rail/cycling holidays, as well. For full details, write them at: An Oige, Irish Youth Hostel Association, 39 Mountjoy Sq., Dublin 1 (tel. 01-745734). Other offices are in Cork (2 Redclyffe, Western Rd., tel. 021-432891), Limerick (1 Pery Sq., tel. 061-314672), Galway (75 Lower Salthill, tel. 091-22185) and Waterford (c/o Farrells Travel Agency, The Quay, tel. 051-74959).

Any office can furnish their *An Oige—Irish Youth Hostel Handbook* for less than IR£1 ($1.20), which details every one of the 53 hostels throughout the country, along with information on making reservations, rules and regulations to be observed, and such extras as travel discounts on certain ferry services available to hostel card holders.

As for the hostels, you'll find them in locations convenient to all sightseeing and ideal for short hikes, bike day trips, swimming and other sports activities. They come in all shapes and sizes, from Georgian mansions like the one in Killarney I mentioned earlier to hunting lodges, converted coast guard cottages, old farmhouses, and former schoolhouses. All have separate sleeping and washing facilities for men and women, a self-catering kitchen, dining room, and common room. A warden is on duty at each, and the hostels are in use between the hours of 5 p.m. and 10:30 a.m.

Pillows, blankets, cooking utensils, and dishes are provided, but you'll need to bring your own sheet bag or sleeping bag, cutlery, and tea and bath towel. Overnight charges are based on age, season, and location, and in 1984 ranged from IR£2.20 ($2.64) to IR£3.10 for Seniors (over 20); IR£1.65 ($1.98) to IR£2.40 ($2.88) for Juniors (18–20); IR£1.45 ($1.74) to IR£1.75 ($2.10) for Juniors (16–17); and 90p ($1.08) to IR£1.10 ($1.32) for Juveniles (under 16). There will undoubtedly be slight increases in 1985 and 1986.

TOWN AND COUNTRY HOMES: Absolutely *the* best travel buy in Ireland! It isn't only that the rates in Irish B&Bs stretch your budget so far; even more, it's that they offer the best possible way to get to know the Irish as they live in their own homes. It's that you become an integral part of those homes, sharing family life as a young daughter—or son—brings your breakfast or offers the loan of a bike or volunteers to show you the way to a very special local attraction you won't find in guidebooks (one of those nooks and crannies I talked about earlier), or explains how easy it is to rent a boat for a day's fishing on the lake. It's relaxing in a pretty, individually decorated room that has all the comforts, but not a smidgin of the "sameness" of a motel room. It's starting off the day with a breakfast to end all breakfasts and a friendly chat with your hostess, who really *is* interested in your plans for the day and eager to offer suggestions, directions, or whatever else you may need. It's coming in from an evening out to find a fire lit and the tea table set or, if your evening has been really late, a pot of tea in your room. In short, although it's budget prices you'll be paying, you'll be extended a brand of hospitality no amount of money could buy.

One of the most delightful features of traveling via B&Bs is that no two are alike. One night you may stay in a gorgeous city townhouse, the next in a seaside bungalow, the next in an idyllic country home. Many have only three or four rooms to rent, while others have added extensions to accommodate their guests (my personal preference is for those smaller, homier places, although the extensions generally have been designed especially with the traveler in mind and sometimes have more amenities). Nor are any two hostesses alike except in their friendliness. You'll be staying with bustling mothers of a large brood, whose offspring wait tables, make beds, do the "hoovering," polish furniture, and help in the kitchen. Then, there will be the lovely widow whose children have all grown up and fled the nest and who will tell you she gets far more from your company than she can ever repay. You'll be treated to a look at family life far different from our own, where the telly may draw an audience, but it is a fickle one that will switch it off in a second if there's the prospect of a good "crack" with someone from America. You'll be shown the cards that came last Christmas from guests of the previous season (with the not-so-subtle hint that your hostess would *love* to hear from you from time to time when you go back home).

As for the practicalities, your room may be so spacious you'd call it a mini-suite in the U.S., or it may be small and cozy. In most cases, you'll share the bathroom with other guests and sometimes with the family. In others, you'll have your own toilet and/or shower or bathtub, and there will probably be a charge of about IR£1 ($1.20) for that luxury, although I encountered many while researching this edition in which all rooms cost the same, private facilities or not. Some B&Bs charge a small additional sum for hot baths (that's because running the hot water heater is quite expensive in Ireland), in which case you'll be on the honor system to report how many baths you've had and pay when you leave. Stay out as late as you please in the evening—you'll have your own front door key. In fact, in some rural areas that won't even be necessary, for they still follow the tradition of leaving the key in the door all night.

I should add here a word about central heating: not all B&Bs have it, and you must remember that even where you do find it, Irish central heating is not like that at home. Where it doesn't exist, there's almost always a small heater in your room to take the chill off, if not exactly heat it up. What that means is that your room may tend to be chilly around the edges at times. My own solution is to throw on a light sweater, usually enough to keep me comfortable. And there's not a B&B lady in the whole of Ireland who won't gladly furnish a hot-water bottle to make your bed warm and toasty when you retire.

If you'd like to have dinner at your B&B, most will accommodate you if you let them know by noon, and you'll be served a wholesome, well-prepared meal for about the same price as your room rate. There's never any charge, however, for the endless cups of tea that appear magically when you drag in from a day's sightseeing or return from an evening out. Likely as not, the evening cuppa will come with hot scones or a bit of cake, and you'll share it in the lounge with the entire family. It is then that a spontaneous singing or storytelling session is apt to break out that often lasts until the wee hours and send you to bed glowing with a new, heart-expanding Irish experience.

Babysitters can usually be arranged at very modest fees, and almost all B&Bs offer reductions for children sharing a room with parents. Single travelers may have a problem finding a single room—there just aren't very many, and if you're given a double room, there may be a small supplementary charge. Another thing to keep in mind is that many of these homes are two and three stories high, so if you're elderly, handicapped, or just plain don't like to climb stairs, it will pay you to ask about a ground-floor room (not a "first-floor" room, since the Irish consider that to be what we would call the second floor).

For all the above, you'll pay anywhere from IR£6 ($7.20) to IR£9 ($10.80) in the country and smaller towns, slightly more in cities. In Dublin, prices in the few B&Bs in the inner city are quite a bit higher, but there's a multitude of accommodations within easy suburban bus rides. Most B&Bs also offer a Partial Board rate, a weekly charge for bed-and-breakfast plus the evening meal, that is a real money-saver.

For a list of all approved town and country homes, plus farmhouses (see next section), pick up or send for the Irish Tourist Board's booklet *Irish Homes in the Town and Country and on the Farm,* available for a small charge at any ITB office or by mail from the Irish Tourist Board, 590 Fifth Ave., New York, NY 10036. Also, the Town & Country Homes Association publishes a *Guest Accommodation* booklet with pictures of all member homes. It's available for a small charge from any Irish Tourist Board office. The Association is nationwide, and its members can book you ahead to your next destination with any other member. I find standards exceptionally high in these homes and have yet to find one I couldn't recommend, both for facilities and friendly hospitality.

If you plan to book before leaving home *(especially* for that first night), you can do so through your travel agent; the Central Reservations Service, 14 Upper O'Connell St., Dublin 1 (tel. 01-747733); or directly with one of the B&Bs listed in this book. If you choose the last option, be sure to write well in advance, state the exact dates you want to book, and enclose a deposit of one night's charge and an International Reply Coupon. If you book by telephone, have all the information right in front of you before you call, and then confirm by letter.

FARMHOUSES: You'll find the very same sort of hospitality in Irish farmhouses. And there's more: for an equally modest price range, they throw in country settings that can make you almost weep from the beauty of it all, the enchantment of a working farmyard, vegetables fresh from their own gardens, lamb and beef that not long ago was hoofing it around their own fields, fish caught that very morning in the river that flows through their land, perhaps a pony or horse to ride, and a day of sharing farm chores if you'd like to know what it's like to be a farmer. I can't imagine a more heavenly vacation for a child—or grownup—than one on an Irish farm.

Farm breakfasts are, if anything, even more massive than those in town and country homes, and very often there's the bonus of fresh fruit or berries, homemade butter, and homemade jams. Dinner is likely to be a whopper, with four courses and desserts swimming in rich, fresh cream. As with town and country homes, you'll have to let your hostess know by noon if you want to dine with her that evening.

The one essential for a farmhouse holiday is a car, since almost all are off the beaten track and cannot be reached by public transportation. A happy—and inexpensive—way to arrange both is through **Johnson & Perrott's Irish Farmhouse Holiday Program.** It combines a Ford Fiesta with unlimited mileage with farmhouse accommodation at any of the 38 participating locations around the country for seven nights for IR£185 ($222) per person from July through mid-September, IR£155 ($186) other months. That's for two people traveling together, and if you want a larger car, there's a supplementary charge. For details, contact Johnson & Perrott, Ltd., Emmet Place, Cork (tel. 021-23295). Even if you don't go for the combination package, remember that Johnson & Perrott discounts basic car rentals by 15% for our readers (see Chapter II).

Prices for farmhouse accommodations usually run one or two punts higher than town and country homes, and they offer those budget-stretching Partial Board weekly rates, as well. As stated above, they're listed in the ITB publication, and there's also an **Irish Farm Holidays Association (Fáilte Tuaithe)** publication (small charge) with pictures and a brief description of each member farmhouse. Standards seem to be just that little bit higher in Association farmhouses, and they, too, will gladly book you with a fellow member along your itinerary.

Booking procedures for farmhouses are the same as in the town and country section above.

GUESTHOUSES: I don't really know how to describe a "guesthouse" accurately —it always seems to me they fit the pattern of a traditional small inn. Suffice it to say that they combine many of the services you expect in hotels (some, for instance, have telephones in guestrooms) with the personalized service and informality of a B&B. Some have been built for this specific purpose, others are in period residences, others have just sort of grown into being as a popular B&B expanded to meet the demand.

There are several advantages to staying in a guesthouse, even though you'll be paying a higher rate than in the B&Bs. For example, many have a restaurant right on the premises, which can be a real convenience. They are also allowed to sell wine (but not spirits) to guests. Ariel House, in Dublin, adds such personal conveniences as a hair dryer in every room.

Rates are based on both single-person occupancy as well as per-person-sharing. In the disadvantage column, all guesthouse rates are subject to an 18% Value Added Tax (VAT) for accommodation, 23% for food, drink, and other services. For all that, there are some guesthouses in Ireland whose sheer attractiveness, convenience, and charm make the added tax seem a small price to pay. The ones you'll find in these pages are those I consider exceptional and look forward to visiting again and again. Whether you're addicted to those extra little creature comforts or just plan to treat yourself to an occasional guesthouse stay, I can assure you of one thing: some of the intimacy of a B&B may be missing, but you'll find exactly the same brand of hospitality in both.

Guesthouse rates range all over the place, depending on facilities, location, and season, from a low of IR£10 ($12) to as high as IR£40 ($48) per-person-sharing. Not really budget, but good value, all the same. The Irish Tourist board publishes a list of all approved guesthouses in their *Hotels & Guesthouses* booklet, available for a small charge. The front section has pictures of some locations, as well as a listing of special package offerings that can turn out to be real bargains. Also, through a Discover Ireland program, designed to encourage the Irish to explore their own country (you'd be surprised how many set off for foreign shores without a thought, but never venture beyond their own country's borders at home!), guesthouses, B&Bs, and hotels in some of the most scenic locations in the country offer astonishingly low midweek and weekend specials. Pick up the *Discover Ireland* booklet in any Tourist Office in Ireland (you won't find it outside the country), and you'll be as welcomed as any native to take advantage of these savings and enjoy the luxury of accommodations well outside the budget at their usual rates.

HOTELS: Don't jump to any hasty conclusions—I'm not about to suggest that you can hotel it around Ireland on our $25-a-day budget. But, because Ireland's hotels have gotten a rather bad press (largely deserved) in recent years, I want to bring you up to date just in case you opt for a hotel night or two.

It is true that for many years most of the country's hotels were low- to sub-standard, with only a few Dublin shining examples along with the luxury castle hotels. In the past five years or so, however, that situation has changed drastically, and for the better. Today, there are small, owner-operated hotels all around the country that feature clean, attractive guestrooms, good dining rooms, and service just one step away from being as personal as guesthouse or B&B hospitality. Surprisingly, I've even experienced that same friendliness in some of the largest luxury establishments, where you'd expect the hustle and bustle of coach tour traffic to make any sort of personal contact impossible. On second thought, given the ebullient Irish nature, that probably isn't surprising at all!

About those luxury hotels: they vary in style from long-established, comfortably "clubbiness" to sophisticated elegance that can hold its own on an international scale. If you do consider treating yourself to an overnight in one, you'll have a choice of decor and atmosphere. A good way to shop around for one that suits you is to go into the ones that catch your fancy and have a drink at the bar and look around the public rooms. And, although the desk clerk may think you a bit "bold," he or she will be happy to show you a guestroom if there are vacancies and you ask nicely—after all, this is *your* big moment, and you don't want to be disappointed.

As for prices, see the "Big Splurge" section later in this chapter for just what you can expect to pay for luxury hotels. Overnight in a good, small hotel such as the Blue Haven in Kinsale, Co. Cork, will run you about IR£32 ($38.40) for a double room, IR£20 ($24) single.

SELF-CATERING: One of the most effective—and increasingly popular—money-saving devices is to rent your own "home" and eat in when it suits you. That doesn't necessarily mean that your travels are restricted, for it is quite possible to rent a self-catering premises in a central location on Ireland's east coast for your first week, make easy day trips from that home base, then shift to another on the west coast for your second week. While you're trading in that lovely B&B hospitality for economy's sake, you'll be given a wonderful excuse to shop in the small markets, chat with local housewives doing the same, pop into the local pub on a regular basis, and—wonder of wonders!—have your own hearth around which to serve your own tea to the new friends you're bound to acquire.

Self-catering accommodations come in all guises, from inner-city townhouses and flats to free-standing houses in small towns, country and seaside bungalows, thatched cottages, and chalets. In off-season months, it is possible in some locations to rent for a few midweek days or weekends only, but most rental periods run from Saturday (beginning 4 p.m.) to the following Saturday (ending before 12 noon). There are three price periods: April, May, June, September (mid-range prices); July and August (peak prices); and all other months (lowest price). Rates can range from about IR£80 ($96) in the mid-price range to IR£100 ($120) in the high season for a cottage that accommodates seven. More luxurious accommodations run higher, but are still a very good buy. As you can see, if you're traveling with a gaggle of children or friends, your per-person costs can be cut to the very bone by self-catering.

Your basic rate will usually include all linens, and if not, they can almost always be rented for a small charge. Kitchens come fully equipped, and some premises even have central heating. In addition, you can expect extra charges for electricity, heating oil and cooking fuels, telephone and, in some cases, television. In projecting your costs, be sure to count those extras in. If you're uncertain about what they will be, ask at the time you book for an estimate by the landlord based on the number of people sharing the premises.

The Irish Tourist Board has compiled a book listing all approved self-catering accommodations except inner-city Dublin flats and the cottages listed below, entitled simply *Self-Catering,* and it's available for a small charge. For Dublin flats available, write to Dublin Tourism, 14 Upper O'Connell St., Dublin 1 (tel. 01-747733). This should be another part of your "homework" before catching that outward-bound plane. Study carefully the descriptions, terms and photographs, book directly with your choice as far ahead as you possibly can, and you'll arrive fully prepared to be a temporary Irish resident.

All the above applies to privately owned self-catering accommodations, but there is one, very special widespread scheme you should know about, especially if you get all dreamy-eyed at the thought of a traditional thatched cottage. Known as **Rent an Irish Cottage Ltd.,** the organization has put together small villages of rental cottages in the west of Ireland that combine the traditional hearth, half-door, and raftered ceilings you've dreamed about with modern conveniences like central heating (when you really don't want to bother with a turf fire), electric kitchens (no wood to chop or heavy pots to hang over an open fire), and shiny bathrooms with showers. The Irish lady who once lived in a thatched cottage *without* all those comforts would go all dreamy-eyed with wonder if she could see these!

The cottages are arranged in a circle surrounding a green, just as in most Irish villages, and they're all located close to some of the country's most splendid scenic spots, never far from facilities for recreational activities like fishing, swimming, golfing, pony-trekking, or long hikes through gorgeous countryside. Needless to say, what with grocery shopping, pubbing, etc., it won't take long for you to become a part of the local scene.

There are four types of cottage design, all hand-thatched, with accommodations for from five to eight. During peak season, weekly rentals range from IR£110 ($132) to IR£206 ($247.20), but they descend to a low of IR£82 ($98.40) in other months, when you can book the cottages for as little as IR£65 ($78) on weekends.

A brief rundown on the thirteen locations follows:

Corofin, Co. Clare (close to lakes, castles, the Burren, and underground caves).

Feakle, Co. Clare (24 miles from Shannon Airport, near woodlands, rivers, lakes, and the Cliffs of Moher).

Puckane, Co. Tipperary (two miles from the Shannon River in North Tipperary, with watersports, boating, and fishing nearby).

Kilfinane, Co. Limerick (27 miles from Limerick City near the Ballyhoura Mountains, with horseback riding and fishing available).

Ballyvaughan, Co. Clare (close to the shores of beautiful Galway Bay, with an ocean beach just three miles away).

Carrigaholt, Co. Clare (set at the mouth of the Shannon, with historic ruins and majestic cliff scenery close by).

Holycross, Co. Tipperary (Holy Cross Abbey, dating from the 12th century, is a stone's throw away, as is excellent fishing).

Murroe, Co. Limerick (just seven miles from the city, near historic castles and wooded glens).

Broadford, Co. Clare (Shannon Airport is only 14 miles away, near all Shannonside castle banquets and sightseeing attractions).

Renvyle, Co. Galway (right on the edge of Connemara's stark beauty, only a mile from the Atlantic).

Louisburg, Co. Mayo (a lovely little fishing village and a good jumping-off place for touring the Northwest).

Terryglass, Co. Tipperary (on the shores of lovely Lough Derg).

Ballycastle, Co. Mayo (on Mayo's northern coast, alongside a sandy beach, good fishing, and an excellent base for touring north to Sligo and beyond).

For complete details and booking information, contact Rent an Irish Cottage Ltd., Shannon Airport House, Shannon, Co. Clare (tel. 061-61588).

5. Where to Eat

For centuries, the Irish—sometimes by choice, sometimes from necessity—seemed to eat simply to exist, without much thought to anything beyond a basic diet of little more than tons of boiled potatoes and gallons of buttermilk.

Before you begin to pity them *too* much, however, wait until you've tasted a real Irish potato—its mealy innards have a taste far superior to any grown on this side of the Atlantic, and when slathered with rich, golden butter, there just isn't much better eating. I must confess *I* could make a meal of them any day.

Be that as it may, however, while most of my Irish friends still make the potato a main part of their daily diet, these days the old spud comes to the table roasted, baked, mashed, or in the form of french fries. And far from being the main dish, it is strictly an accompaniment to homegrown veal, beef, lamb, or salmon (fresh and or smoked), prawns, plaice, or trout from Ireland's abundant waters. Tender, sweet lettuce, tomatoes that taste of the sun, and cucumbers the size of our squash go into fresh salads, and vegetables both homegrown and from the gardens of Spain or Israel complete the heaping plates of "mains." Bread? It's that famous soda or brown bread, freshly baked and many times still warm, just waiting to be spread with pure, golden butter. Starters can be thick, tasty barley, beef, or vegetable soup or shrimp cocktail or homemade pâté or small portions of that wonderful smoked salmon. Desserts tend to be apple or rhubarb tart or sherry trifle, all topped with lashings of sweet, rich fresh cream. Tea, of course, comes in a bottomless pot to pour endless cups. All pretty plain foods, all wholesome, and all in *gigantic* portions.

That's in Irish homes. As for Irish restaurants, they've come a long way from the times when "chefs" were simply cooks who had moved from the hearth into hotel dining rooms, small tea rooms, or the few fancy eateries concentrated mostly in Dublin. Today's chefs are likely to have been trained in leading culinary schools on the continent or in one of Ireland's excellent hotel training institutions. Menus are more varied than I ever thought I'd see in this land of plain-food eaters. International cuisine is available not only in Dublin, but in all the larger cities and small villages tucked away beside the sea or in the basement of a mansion on the grounds of Bunratty Castle. French, Italian, Chinese, and even Russian restaurants are to be found, along with some very good ones which serve wonderfully prepared native dishes. It is even possible nowadays to get a decent cup of perked coffee in many restaurants, although I find (even as a confirmed coffeehound at home) the tea so much better that I seldom long for coffee.

There are several native foods you should be sure not to miss while you're in Ireland. For me, dairy products top the list: never have I tasted butter or cream to compare with Ireland's. And if you're a cheese lover, you'll find some excellent cheddars made by creamery co-ops as well as commercial firms (I make it a practice to ask the locals about cheeses made in their locality, and I've struck real gold in Kerry's mountains as well as Waterford's fertile fields). Smoked salmon is not only a delicacy, it's *affordable* in Ireland, and you can gorge yourself to your heart's content. Dublin Bay prawns are a "don't miss," as is plaice, a freshwater fish served all over the country. Small town bakeries often have soda bread for sale fresh from the oven, as well as some cream-filled pastries that are as light as a feather and as sweet as heaven itself.

But, as pennypinchers, our main interest is in satisfying each day's hunger on the budget we've set for ourselves, and believe me, you'll do that and eat *well*. So well, in fact, that I'll wager you'll be able to treat yourself to at least one pricey meal in the Big Splurge restaurant of your choice. Remember, you're going to begin every day with a mammoth breakfast that will either carry you over all the way to dinner or at the very least call for only a light midday repast. Remember, too, that if you're staying in B&Bs, it is probable that you'll be served tea and scones or cake along about ten o'clock in the evening, and it won't cost you a cent!

PICNICS: One of the most joyous dining experiences in Ireland is a picnic in that glorious outdoors. In the more than 400 forest areas open to the public you'll find picnic sites galore, many with tables and benches provided for your comfort. There are very good booklets available giving directions to all 400, and I always keep a publication called *The Open Forest: A Guide to Areas Open to the Public* in the car—that way, I can locate the nearest forest park quickly, no matter where I happen to be. That, plus several leaflets on nature trails, are available for a very small charge from the Amenity Section, Forest and Wildlife Service, Leeson Lane, Dublin 2. Pick up some fresh bread, a good Irish cheese, a bottle or two of lager or stout, and you're in business. If you're not near one of the forest parks, there's always the seashore or a riverbank or just a spot alongside the road (unless you're on one of the main highways, you won't be bothered by traffic). Need I add that you should leave the countryside as rubbish free and beautiful as you found it?

PUBS: Not all pubs serve food, and almost none serve it in the evening. But some of my best Irish lunches have been pub grub that has varied from soup and sandwiches to a heaping plate of hot roast beef, mashed potatoes, vegetables, and rolls, depending on my appetite at the moment. Some pubs also serve marvelous salad plates of chicken, beef, or salmon. A cup of hearty soup and rolls or a sandwich will run you about IR£2 ($2.40), and that hot meal will cost under IR£4 ($4.80). If you're not in the mood for an alcoholic brew, you'll almost always be able to get a pot of tea. One note of caution: Irish sandwiches, for the most part, are skimpy little things compared to those we're accustomed to in the U.S., so be sure you aren't really hungry before you settle for them. If the pub serves soup, brown bread and butter, it's a much better choice—tasty and filling.

TOURIST MEALS: Ah, here's the heart of our dining budget. The Irish Tourist Board—God bless 'em—has organized a Tourist Menu program with restaurants all around the country. Sometimes called "special value meals," these menus offer a full three-course lunch or dinner at bargain prices. There are, in fact, two price levels: for IR£5 ($6), you may be restricted to a limited choice of main course meats; for IR£7 ($8.40), the selections will be more varied. Either way, the food is the same the restaurant serves on its pricier menu and portions are never skimpy. You can identify those eateries serving these meals by a distinctive sign displaying a smiling Irish chef. However, you must be sure to ask specifically for the Tourist Menu, or you may wind up being surprised when the check is presented. In almost any Tourist Office you can pick up a free Tourist Menu booklet which lists all participating establishments.

BUDGET RESTAURANTS: There are many restaurants, pubs, tea rooms, and department store cafeterias, some of which do not offer the Tourist Menu, but do serve very good food at budget prices. You'll find many listed in this book, but a good IR£1 ($1.20) investment is the Irish Tourist Board's booklet, *Dining* *in Ireland,* which gives details on eateries in all regions, including a brief description of the cuisine, hours, and prices. It has been a lifesaver in my travels, and I never have any difficulty in finding dinner for under $10.

GUESTHOUSE MEALS: A happy way to dine inexpensively is to book for dinner with your B&B, farmhouse, or guesthouse hostess. As I've said several times before, you must let her know by noon or shortly thereafter that you want the evening meal. What you're almost certain to get is a version of the meal described at the beginning of this section, with such huge portions you'll roll away from the table and head for an outdoor stroll to walk off some of the pounds you can feel piling up around your hips. Not a bad way to end the day, now is it? As a rule of thumb, you can count on the price of dinner being the same as your overnight B&B rate, but to be safe, ask the cost when you book for dinner.

IRISH RECIPES: Guaranteed not to taste exactly the same back home, but set down here anyway for all you good cooks out there are the following traditional Irish recipes, each given to me by one tried and true Irish friend who is a terrific cook, a delightful widow lady who runs a small-town bakery that's been in business over two hundred years, and a publican whose expertise behind the bar is legendary.

Irish Stew:

    3 lbs. neck of lamb
    3 onions
    8 potatoes
    Salt and pepper to taste
    2 cups water
    1 teaspoon chopped mixed herbs
    2 tablespoons chopped fresh parsley (for garnish)

Trim excess fat from meat and cut into small pieces. Peel and slice onions and potatoes (make thick slices). Layer sliced potatoes on bottom of casserole, add layer of lamb and layer of onions. Sprinkle seasonings and herbs over all and top with sliced potatoes. Add water, cover and cook in medium oven (350°) for 1½ hours, or until lamb is tender. Sprinkle parsley on top just before serving.

Irish Brown Bread:

    1 cup wholewheat flour
    1 cup white flour
    4 tablespoons (½ stick) butter
    ½ tsp. bicarbonate of soda
    ½ tsp. cream of tartar
    Pinch of salt
    Dash of sugar (if desired)
    Milk (just enough to wet and mix dough)

Mix flour, soda, salt, cream of tartar, and sugar thoroughly in a large bowl. With fingers, crumble butter into dry ingredients and mix well. Add just enough milk to form a soft pasty dough easy to handle, but not sticky. Turn soft dough onto a floured board and knead it smooth. Shape into a round (not too flat) cake and cut an X across top (don't omit this step—the X is not just for ornament, but to help in the rising). Bake in a preheated 350° oven for about an hour, or until brown and firm. *Note:* For a tasty preview of this recipe, stop in to Barron's Bakery in Cappoquin, Co. Waterford, and pick up one of Mrs. Barron's freshly baked cakes.

Irish Coffee:

Fill a large, stemmed glass with hot water, then empty when glass is warm. Pour in one full jigger of Irish whiskey and add at least one teaspoon sugar (the more sugar, the more the cream rises to the top). Add hot black coffee (the hotter, the better) to about an inch from the top and stir. Top it off with lightly whipped cream—there's an art to doing that: just sort of float it off over the back of a spoon.

6. Big Splurges

All through this book, you'll find "Big Splurge" accommodations and restaurants listed. For example, no budgeteer in his or her right mind would contemplate a night in one of Ireland's luxury hotels or the romantic castles now open to guests. Yet, where and when else are you and I going to indulge our fantasies? And what better time and place than in Ireland? So, while I don't exactly advocate that you go all out and bust the budget, I'm not exactly dead set against at least one "bust-out" overnight in a dream setting!

I'll give you two examples of Big Splurges that I'll save for all year. The first is Dromoland Castle, in Newmarket-on-Fergus, Co. Clare. For me, its crenelated turrets, massive entrance hall, and tower rooms are the stuff dreams are made of. Add to those charms a staff who greet me as warmly as the wealthiest of their upper-strata guests, and I'll dine on peanut butter sandwiches for a month just to have an overnight there! The other is Fitzpatrick's Castle Hotel, in Killiney, just outside Dublin, where I revel in the friendliness of a family-run establishment that pampers my budget-ridden soul.

For that kind of luxury, I must pay IR£65 ($78) at Dromoland (but it does include a gorgeous breakfast!)—doubles run IR£42 ($50.40) per person. At Fitzpatrick's, singles pay IR£37 ($44.40), doubles IR£23 ($27.60) per person, and breakfast is extra. That's a lot of peanut butter sandwiches!

You'll find all hotels listed in the Irish Tourist Board's *Hotels & Guesthouses* book. For the crème-de-la-crème of country houses (also well above our travel budget), pick up a copy of *Irish Country Houses and Restaurants* from any ITB office. In its pages you'll find pictures and full descriptions of such special places as Ard na Greine Inn, in Schull, Co. Cork, and Longueville House, in Mallow, Co. Cork, and Rathmullan House up in Rathmullan, Co. Donegal.

Luxury country houses will cost between IR£25 ($30) and IR£35 ($42) per person, and most rates include breakfast.

The above are just two of the Big Splurges listed in the chapters to follow, but there are scores more around the country, each special in one way or another—and unless you break out in hives at the mere thought of peanut butter sandwiches, I heartily recommend that you include at least one in your plans for an Irish holiday.

All of the above applies equally to posh restaurants. My personal favorites are in the following pages; almost any listed in the *Irish Country Houses and Restaurants* are worthy of your "bust out" dollars; and if you feel the urge for a super—and expensive—dinner out but haven't a clue where to find one, just ask around, everyone in the neighborhood will know where your hoarded wealth will be well spent.

7. Shopping

Most of Ireland's shopping bargains are variations of arts or crafts carried down from ages past, from those wonderful Aran sweaters to soft Donegal wools to drawings in the Celtic style to the incomparable Waterford glass. You'll find many still done in their traditional forms, but there's much excitement in seeing how they've been adapted to modern times. Woolens come in highly sophisticated styles, and contemporary crafts carry the imprint of today combined with the skills of ancient days.

SHOPPING BASICS: In the following chapters, I'll tell you about the best buys I've located in each locality. But first, there are some ground rules you should know before you set foot in any shop.

Customs

Customs regulations of both Ireland and the U.S. will determine what you bring into Ireland and what you may take home with you. Citizens of non-EEC countries may bring the following into the country: if you're over the age of 17, 400 cigarettes, 100 cigars, 18 ounces of tobacco and 1 liter of distilled beverages and spirits exceeding 38.5° proof or 2 liters of other spirits; all ages may bring other dutiable goods valued at up to IR£ 27 ($32.40); and as much currency as you wish—or have! On leaving, there are no restrictions on any Irish purchase you carry with you, but you may not take out of the country more than IR£100 ($120) in Irish currency (if you wind up with a surplus, be sure to have notes converted to travelers checks—on which there is no restriction—at a bank prior to departure).

Upon reentering the U.S., you'll be allowed to bring back purchases valued up to $400 without paying customs or filling out a declaration form. Anything in excess of that amount will be assessed a flat 10 percent on the next $1,000 and an average of 12% for all over $1,400. Antiques that are over 100 years old come in duty-free, but you must have an authentication of age from the dealer from whom you bought them to present to U.S. Customs.

The very detailed, 15-page booklet *Know Before You Go* (Publication No. 512) is available without charge from the U.S. Customs Service, Box 7407, Washington, DC 20044, and if you plan to do a lot of shopping, be sure you have it before leaving home.

Value Added Tax

It has been true for many years that no items mailed or shipped out of the country were subject to the Value Added Tax (VAT), but in May of 1984, that relief was extended to those things you carry back home in your luggage. That is a big break and can make a whopping difference—as much as 18 to 35 percent! —in the cost of your Irish purchases.

When making your purchase, you must prove to the merchant that you are a nonresident of Ireland by presenting your passport or other documentation (U.S. driver's license, etc.). You'll be issued an invoice which must be stamped by Irish Customs to prove that you did, indeed, take the merchandise out of the country. That invoice *must be returned to the vendor,* whether he allows you the VAT exemption on the spot or sends you a refund upon receipt of the stamped invoice.

When you get the exemption is strictly up to the vendor (I know, you'd rather have those extra percents to spend in Ireland instead of after you're home—so would I, and the Irish government is probably missing out by not putting it in our hot-to-buy hands right then and there). Any shop is liable for the amount of the tax if it makes the deduction and you don't return that stamped invoice. So, don't hassle your salesperson—just try to be as charming and as reliable-looking as you can, then *be sure to return the invoice.* The whole refund procedure is simplified if you use credit cards instead of cash, of course, when it's a simple matter of issuing a credit to your account. Another good reason for using plastic money as often as you can (see below).

Credit Cards

Aside from the obvious convenience of buying now and paying later, thus giving you more cash for immediate needs and pleasures, and the advantage pointed out above, you'll usually save a dollar or two when you use American Express or VISA credit cards (the two most widely accepted, along with Diners Club and Access). Your billing will be at each company's exchange rate, which almost always averages several cents better per dollar than banks.

You won't be able to use your credit cards in many small shops, but you'll find they're accepted in all major department stores, many souvenir shops, car rental companies, hotels, some restaurants, and all duty-free shops.

SHANNON DUTY-FREE SHOPPING: Back in the 1950s, the world's first duty-free shop opened at Shannon Airport, and today it has grown into a super supermarket offering an incredible array of international products plus—best of all—a wide selection of the best of Irish-made goods. You'll save a bundle on Aynsley, Wedgwood, and Royal Worcester bone china from England, perfumes from France, cameras and Hummel porcelain figures from Germany, watches from Switzerland, and even cigarettes from the U.S. From Ireland itself, there are bargains in hand-knit sweaters, woolens and tweeds, fine Belleek china, Waterford glass (as well as that from Galway and Cavan), Irish linens, jewelry and other items of Connemara marble jewelry, records and books, and a host of craft items.

As for prices, they're far lower on *all* items than you'd pay at home, not too much lower, if any, on *Irish* goods than those in Irish shops, since the object is not to compete with the home market. Prices are marked in both Irish punts and U.S. dollars, and I find this a good place to use up any leftover punts as I leave for home, as well as a convenience when I'm down to only U.S. currency. Credit cards are also accepted.

In view of all this, should you save your shopping for Shannon just before departure? Well, that depends. You could have your heart set on taking home that special piece of Waterford glass, only to find that it happens to be the one item missing from the large stock at that particular time. Or you may remember with regret a lower price on an Aran sweater that you passed up somewhere on your rambles through the west and wind up paying a bit more at Shannon.

These are really considerations of the past, however, for just recently the Duty-Free Shop at Shannon inaugurated a new policy that lets you browse through its aisles *as you arrive.* So, you can start out knowing just what's available and the price ranges—a great base for comparative shopping as you move around the country. Any purchases you make on arrival will be held for your departure flight, but it isn't necessary to buy anything at all then. No matter what your shopping plans, I strongly advise taking a half-hour or so to see what's there. While you're at it, pick up a copy of the pamphlet *Shannon Shopping Guide* for ready reference when you're shopping elsewhere.

You can, in fact, get your duty-free shopping off to a good start even before leaving home by ordering the very good catalog that illustrates a representative selection, with prices shown in U.S. dollars, plus shipping charges by surface or air. Send $2 to Shannon Mail Order Stores, Shannon International Free Airport, Ireland. If you order by mail (a foot- and time-saving device), you'll pay any customs duty directly to your postman upon delivery, but you'll still come out way ahead of U.S. prices. Incidentally, you can request a catalog while you're at the airport, and it will be mailed to your home address. The $2 is deductible from your first mail order.

OTHER SHOPS: The one absolute for me in Ireland is to *buy it when I see it*. Never mind comparative shopping. There isn't really a big difference in prices around the country, as a rule, and I've found just the right woolly sweater in a little shop in Glengarriff, a beaten brass plaque depicting St. Brendan's epic voyage in a Donegal shop, and a few other items I might never have been able to call my own had I waited to find a better price elsewhere, since I never came across them again. For that reason, I hesitate to tout one shop over any other. There are, however, the following which I have found to be reliable for both variety, quality, service, and price, and I can recommend each without any hesitation. You'll find them detailed in the appropriate regional chapters.

In Dublin, my first stop is always the **House of Ireland**, where I've found several unusual Irish-made products (they have a good mail-order service, as well); in Killarney, **Hilliard's** carries on a long tradition of large stocks and good value, plus one of the friendliest, most helpful staffs in the country (they also have a mail-order service); **Padraic O Maille's** is excellent for woolens, and just outside Galway, **Mairtin Standun's** can be depended on for bargain prices on a variety of items.

ARAN SWEATERS: At the top of most visitors' shopping list is one of Ireland's famed Aran knit sweaters. They are as much a part of the Irish landscape as stone walls and green fields, and they're perfect to buy early and use for chilly weather during your stay. They've been made in Ireland as far back as the ninth century, and originated with fishermen along the west coast (especially in the Aran Islands, hence the name), who valued their water resistance as well as their warmth. Today, most of the heavy natural oil has been removed from the wool from which they're made, and they're much softer than they used to be.

Designs, however, have changed not one whit. And for good reason. Long ago, each stitch depicted a different part of Irish life: the cable stitch stood for the fisherman's strong rope (it's also supposed to bring good luck) and the trellis stitch represented familiar stone walls. Using a combination of many such symbolic stitches, fishing villages designed patterns unique to each community, making it possible to return any drowning victim to his hometown for burial. Interestingly, in the beginning the sweaters were knit by men—women were relegated to the spinning of the wool.

The vast majority of Aran sweaters are knit in creamy, off-white bainin ("bawneen") wool, but you'll also find them in soft browns or mottled grays that are undyed, just as they came from the sheep. Their making is still very much a cottage industry (although all the knitters are women these days), and a fast worker can produce about two sweaters a week. A delightful touch is the little slip of paper placed in a pocket of each finished sweater that tells you which Irish lady is responsible for keeping you warm. Most are handwritten, and it's amazing the instant link you feel between maker and wearer.

A word of caution is in order about these sweaters (called "jerseys" in Ireland), since not all the creamy, off-white, cable-stitched sweaters you see are handmade. More and more machine-knits are appearing in shops, and if price is the primary consideration or you prefer a lighter weight garment, you may be just as happy with one of these. They will *not*, however, have anything like the wearing qualities of the real thing. Hand-knits wear like iron, and I have one I'm sure will be passed on for several generations when I'm long gone! You should be able to tell the difference by the sheer weight of a hand-knit (or by that little slip of paper in the pocket), but if you have any doubt, be sure to ask the salesperson.

You can expect to pay something like $48 to $65 for an adult hand-knit pullover, slightly more for cardigans, and anywhere from one-half to one-third less for children's sizes. **Standun's,** in Galway, and **Kathleen's,** in Donegal, both have good stocks and prices, but if you find the one you like elsewhere, buy it when you see it!

WOOLENS AND TWEEDS: For centuries, Donegal homes came complete with looms from which poured the lovely tweeds and other woolens which are known all over the world. It is rare, however, to find a home loom today, because most of the weaving is done in small factories concentrated in Donegal and a few spotted around the country. You can watch a weaver at work if you call in to **Donal Houlihan's Handcraft Shop** in Glengarriff, Co. Cork, or at **Avoca Handweavers,** in Co. Wicklow. All department stores carry woolens both by the yard and made up into coats, suits, capes, and skirts, but some of the best buys are to be found at **Gillespi Brothers** in the little Co. Donegal town of Mountcharles, **Magee** of Donegal, and **Padraic O Maille's** in Galway. The **House of Ireland,** in Dublin, has a stylish selection of woolen garments.

WATERFORD GLASS: Actually, Waterford "glass" is crystal, earning that distinction by the addition of 33% lead oxide to basic ingredients of silica sand and potash (crystal must contain no less than 22%, no more than 33½%). It has been around for two centuries (although actually produced for only one), and it is both beautiful beyond words and expensive.

You can tour the factory in Waterford (see Chapter V), and buy its products in many shops and department stores all around Ireland. And, if Waterford glass is your shopper's heart's desire, best buy it here, for prices virtually double when it's imported. You won't be able to buy any items at the factory, and prices vary only slightly in shops. **Shannon Duty-Free Shops** carry a pretty good selection, and you'll find extensive stocks and good prices at **Joyce's** in Wexford and the **House of Ireland** in Dublin.

IRISH LACE: There is no purchase more evocative of long ago elegance and a more gracious age than Ireland's handmade lace from Limerick or Carrickmacross. Supplies are becoming more and more limited each year as the younger generation becomes less and less willing to spend their days doing the tedious, time-consuming, and exquisite handwork. You can, however, still purchase examples of both from the convents which have kept the art alive.

In Carrickmacross, Co. Monaghan (15 miles west of Dundalk, just off the road from Dublin to Belfast), it's **St. Louis Lace Center** (see Chapter V), where a lovely collar and cuffs set will run about IR£26 ($32.20). In Limerick, a lace handkerchief will cost IR£35 ($42) and upwards at the **Good Shepard Convent** on Clare St. (see Chapter VII).

CRAFTS: Back in the 12th century, a traveler to Ireland waxed lyrical about the country's fine craftsmen in these words, "Fine craftsmanship is all around you. . . . Look carefully at it, and you will penetrate to the very shrine of art. You will make out intricacies so delicate and subtle, so exact and compact, with colors so fresh and vivid that you might say all this was the work of an angel, not of a man." I'm happy to tell you that things haven't changed all that much over the intervening centuries. There are over 800 craftspeople working full time and more than 1,000 part-time craft workers throughout Ireland. There are over 44 craft guilds, associations, and organizations affiliated with the Crafts Council of Ireland, which in turn is a member of the World Crafts Council and the Crafts Council of Europe. And there is now a Minister for State responsible for crafts in the country.

What all the above means to you and me is that Ireland is, indeed, a happy hunting ground for superb workmanship demonstrated in one of the most widely varied range of crafts in any one country in the world. To those skills we've already discussed above, you can add beautiful woodwork, leathers, pottery, ceramics, artistic metalwork, and many, many others. They're scattered all over the face of Ireland, working in small workshops usually, but maintaining standards that would make their legendary Celtic ancestors—themselves no slouches when it came to gold and bronze!—beam with pride.

By all means obtain a free copy of the *Crafthunter's Pocket Guide* from one of the Irish Tourist Board's U.S. offices, and failing that, plunk down the small charge for a copy at any Tourist Office within Ireland itself. It tells you exactly where to find which craftsmen, and it is indispensable in searching out those particular crafts in which you are interested.

BOOKS: What better memento to carry home from Ireland than the printed word! After all, words have been pouring from those agile Irish minds to the printed page in a veritable flood since the beginning of recorded history. Any booklover is quite likely to go a bit mad at the sight of such a wealth of bookshops, and the bargain hunter will happily spend hours sifting through used-book stalls and bookstore basements with their tables of reduced volumes.

Dublin has lost a few of its oldest, most revered bookshops, which fell victim to increased taxes, rentals, and traffic. You'll still, however, find one or two family-run shops along the Liffey quays, and both **Greene's Bookshop** in Clare St. and **Parson's** in Baggot St. are havens to which I could repair for weeks on end. In addition to these traditional shops, there are bright, new, and *large* bookshops galore. In Galway, **Kenny's Bookshop** is virtually a national treasure, and a treat not to be missed. You'll find details on these and some others in the chapters that follow. Use them as a *beginning* in your quest for books to take home, but keep your eyes open as you travel around—bookshops are tucked away in some of the most amazing places, and the Irish who run them are kindred spirits who'll wrap some memorable conversations with the book you end up buying.

IRELAND BY MAIL: I don't rightly know if these two suggestions belong under the "shopping" heading, but it occurs to me that they both represent an ongoing connection with the country you'll have lost your heart to during your two weeks' stay, and at bargain prices.

The first is *Inside Ireland,* a quarterly newsletter written especially for the likes of you and me who live somewhere else but want to keep up with what's going on over there. It's published by two Dubliners, Brenda Weir and Gill Bowler, who are experts on such far-ranging subjects as politics, cooking, and travel and who have an enthusiastic and intense interest in everything else! The newsletter is an eclectic collection of witty and informative tidbits, in-depth articles, humor, services such as restaurant and accommodation reviews, answers to subscribers' queries on costs of an Irish visit, procedures for buying a home or retiring to Ireland, and genealogy research. There's never any advertising in its pages, and all reports are totally unbiased and fully researched. You can get a sample copy by sending $1, or subscribe for a year for $30, to *Inside Ireland,* Rookwood, Ballyboden, Dublin 16 (tel. 01-931906).

The second publication that will keep your Irish memories fresh is *Ireland of the Welcomes,* a travel magazine published bimonthly by the Irish Tourist Board. It's beautifully produced and illustrated and each issue has writing by some of the country's leading writers, as well as those of other nationalities, but always on a subject intimately connected with Ireland. You might learn about postmen who go their appointed rounds via bike in one issue, the brave men of the Coast Guard in another, and an especially notable art collection in yet another. It's a grand way to transport yourself back to Ireland while sitting in America, and the cost is a mere $12 for a year's subscription. Write: Irish Tourist Board, Baggot Street Bridge, Dublin.

MISCELLANEOUS: Ireland has such an embarrassment of riches when it comes to gifts and souvenirs that we can only touch on a few in this book. Among those things to look for: **Connemara marble** in anything from bookends to letter openers to ashtrays to jewelry; **Owen Irish Turf Crafts** pressed and molded turf that comes in inexpensive pendants and paperweights and pricier wall plaques, all adorned with Celtic designs; the **Claddagh ring,** with its traditional folk design of two hands clasping a heart which wears a crown (it was originally the Claddagh, Co. Galway, wedding ring) that comes in moderately priced silver versions as well as more costly gold; records of Irish traditional music groups (what a great way to ease the heart when it grows homesick for Ireland once you're back home!); authentically dressed character dolls depicting such historical figures as the lady emigrant dressed in bonnet and shawl, or Molly Malone, with her wheelbarrow of cockles and mussels (look for them at the House of Ireland in Dublin).

Chapter II

GETTING TO AND AROUND IRELAND

1. From America
2. From Britain
3. From the Continent
4. Getting Around Ireland
5. Suggested Itineraries

FROM NEW YORK TO SHANNON is a five-hour flight; from Shannon back to the States takes six hours; and there's a five-hour time difference, so you can count on having at least a touch of jet lag.

1. From America

In these days of fierce airline competition and fares that change almost daily, you'll have to take the following figures as *guidelines* only. I can promise that you'll get different quotations, but about the same categories, when you set out to book your Irish flights.

No matter *what* the figures, however, before you settle on a fare, be sure and ask about any current specials or packages available—from time to time, Aer Lingus runs short-term, promotional fares that can put considerably more money in your pocket to be spent on *being* there instead of *getting* there.

AIR FARES TO IRELAND: Because of those fluctuating fares, it is impossible to give you even projected 1985–86 fares. We can, however, tell you those filed through 1984, and they serve as a pretty good basis for comparison between the different fare types. My best advice is to work with a tried and true travel agent. If you don't know of one, ask around or look for the Certified Travel Counselor certification (it means the agent has had specialized training and met rather high requirements). It will cost you no more and save a lot of time and mental strain. Having said that, I must add that *you* should be as well informed as possible before you sit down to talk to an agent—the more you know about what's available, the more intelligently you can assess what's best for the budget. In other words, if you're serious about this budget business, you'll get the best results by combining your own, informed, judgment with that of a good agent.

When you travel to Ireland is a very important money-saving factor. For example, travel from mid-September to mid-May eastbound, or mid-October to mid-June westbound, is considerably cheaper (it's called the Basic Season in airline jargon) than if you go during Peak Season (all other months). Specific dates for season changes can vary from one year to the next, so you should check with the airline before setting your departure date. You should be aware, too, of any restrictions concerning advance booking, stopovers, etc., that apply to some of the less expensive fares (they change!).

Also, a Boston departure will cost you less than a New York departure, and flying on to Dublin rather than deplaning at Shannon will add extra dollars to your fare. Fares quoted below are the 1984 round-trip costs between New York and Shannon.

First Class

$2,200 year round. Certainly not in the budget class, but it gives a very good idea of the savings available by making another choice!

Economy Class

$886 during Basic Season, $1,078 in Peak. Ticket is good for one year, and there are no advance purchase requirements.

APEX

$489 during Basic, $599 in Peak. This one's good for six months only and must be booked 21 days in advance.

Green Saver

$489 in Basic, $599 in Peak. Also good for only six months, must be booked at least seven days in advance, and is many times lowered for special promotional fares. You should always inquire about the current Green Saver fares when booking.

EUROPEAN CONNECTIONS FROM IRELAND: Aer Lingus can either fly you on their planes or hook you up with other airlines to reach any European destination on either end of your Irish visit. For the budgeteer, a good plan is to book a one-way Economy flight to Ireland, use a Eurailpass or Eurail Youthpass (purchased on *this* side of the Atlantic) to travel around Ireland and some 16 other countries on the Continent, then fly back Economy Class from your final destination city. Details on the rail passes are given later in this chapter. If you're visiting only Ireland and Great Britain, Aer Lingus will book you for arrival in Shannon and departure from London, or the reverse, at the regular round-trip fare.

YOUR CHOICE OF AIRLINE: "I believe our greatest achievement lies in the fact that we have captured the hearts and minds of the public." Those words were spoken in 1957 about the spirit of the **Aer Lingus** staff on the airline's twenty-first anniversary of its founding, by a man who had been general manager for fourteen years. Well, I don't know about the *rest* of the flying public, but almost thirty years after Jerry Dempsey made that statement, I'm here to testify that Aer Lingus and its staff have certainly captured *my* heart and mind!

As far as I'm concerned, my Irish arrival begins at Kennedy Airport in New York the minute I walk up to the Aer Lingus check-in counter and am greeted by a smile and a lilt straight from the "auld sod." And if the lovely green and blue Boeing 747 proudly sporting a shamrock won't exactly provide a "flight of angels," at least it bears the name of a saint—now, I ask you, could any such vehicle fail to be blessed? As a matter of fact, for years there's been an annual blessing of the fleet. Something comforting in that tradition.

But, it's not the aircraft that engages my affection, it's the lovely people who fly it. The pretty Irish colleens in their snappy green uniforms who walk a million miles up and down the aisles to keep me and my fellow passengers happy. And the little group of black-clad nuns giggling away at the prospect of getting back home for a visit. And the sons and daughters of Ireland with *their* sons and daughters in tow headed back to report to the Mam and Da on their life in America. And the slightly inebriated footballer who joshes with the stewardess about his exploits on the field up at Gaelic Park in the Bronx. And the scores of excited Americans—like me—who smile and smile and smile with the contentment of being, if not quite in Ireland, at least being surrounded by the Irish. Never mind that this is Ireland's state-owned airline and earns a bit of loyalty on that score—as the man said, it's the *spirit* that gets you!

It's a spirit that first reared its head back in May of 1936, when most European countries already had established airlines in full operation. The best Ireland could do (she was, after all, still struggling to be a nation in her own right) was to send a little wood-and-canvas De Haviland 84 Dragon biplane named *Iolar* from a galvanized hut at Baldonnel's military aerodrome to Bristol and back. The five passengers weighed in on huge scales, and the airline's entire stock of spare parts went along in a biscuit tin. It was a small, brave, and spirited beginning, but by 1951, one million passengers had flown with the saints and shamrocks. I couldn't tell you how many passengers now fly with Aer Lingus every year—I can only tell you I count myself lucky to be among them.

Sentiment aside, Aer Lingus also offers the most frequent service from the U.S. to Ireland and can fly you on to any place in Europe from Copenhagen to Rome. Reason enough to choose the country's national airline.

PACKAGE TOURS: Dedicated budget watchers have long known that when it comes to travel, some of the best bargains going are chartered flights or tours (escorted or unescorted). Once upon a time, that meant you were herded around with a group of other Americans, with little opportunity to break out on your own and freewheel it through a country, the only *real* way to get to know it, in my humble opinion. That is no longer true, and you can now realize enormous savings on airfare and accommodations and never see those other American faces except in the airplane going over and coming back. Not that I have anything against my countrymen, you understand; it's just that I don't go to *Ireland* to be with *Americans*.

Aer Lingus offers a wide selection of such bargains under their **Discover Ireland** program. You can choose only the fly/drive combination and take care of your own accommodations; the fly/drive/farmhouse, B&B combination, which covers your room each night from a choice of over 800 accommodations; or one of the most popular, the Irish Heritage package that covers air and land arrangements plus the services of the Irish Genealogical Research Society, who will do the groundwork in finding your ancestors, then give you a map showing those places important in your family's history. All can be tailored to your particular needs, time available, and budget. Book through Aer Lingus or travel agents.

Round Tower Travel, Suite 1507, 745 Fifth Ave., New York, NY 10151 (tel. 212/371-1064 or 1-800-221-4611) is one of the oldest and most reliable travel agencies specializing in tours to Ireland. With offices also in Boston, Philadelphia, Washington D.C., and Chicago, they can organize almost any kind of Irish holiday to suit your fancy. In 1984, for example, their one-week **Meet the Irish Tour** provided seven days and six nights at a farmhouse or B&B (with the freedom to book as you go, choosing from more than 500 accommodations all over the country), a car with unlimited mileage and your first or last night pre-booked in a Limerick hotel, all at a cost of $258 plus airfares of $399 or $449, depending on date. Having used their service to book an Irish holiday for myself and my 85-year-old aunt, I can highly recommend them.

2. From Britain

A holiday combination of Great Britain and Ireland is a simple matter, with good links between the two countries by both air and sea.

BY AIR: Fares from London are calculated in pounds sterling, not Irish punts, since you will, of course, be paying with English currency. As we go to press, 1985 prices are not available, and although the following figures will undoubtedly be different when you travel, the categories and savings will be the same.

The regular **Aer Lingus** one-way airfare between London and Dublin in 1984 was £72 ($94.32). By booking two weeks ahead, however, you could take advantage of the APEX fare and pay only £47.50 ($62.23). The PEX fare, which requires no advance booking, was £53.50 ($70.09).

BY SEA: Sealink operates daily car ferry service from Pembroke to Rosslare, Holyhead to Dun Laoghaire (Dublin), Fishguard to Rosslare, and Stranraer to Larne (Northern Ireland). In 1984, one-way fares (pounds sterling) for passengers without cars traveling to any of the Republic of Ireland ports were £21 ($27.51) in summer months, dropping to £14 ($18.43) other months. A car with driver paid £82 ($107.42) or £50 ($65.55). There are bargain round-trip specials offered at certain times of the year, known as **Motoring Money Savers,** which can save you a considerable amount if you're coming to Ireland for weekends or short stays of up to five days. Fares for the Northern Ireland service ranged from £16 ($20.96) to £9 ($11.79) for foot passengers (depending on season and first or second class travel), and drivers paid an additional £46 ($60.26) to £43 ($56.33) for their car.

In the U.S., you can get current Sealink sailing schedules and rate information by contacting: Sealink, c/o Britrail, 630 Third Ave., New York, NY 10017 (tel. 212/599-5400).

B+I Line sails between Holyhead and Dublin and Liverpool and Dublin on a daily basis, and in 1984, one-way fares ranged from £22 ($20.69) to £48 ($62.88). For current rates and schedules when you travel, contact: B+I

Line, c/o Lynott Tours, 117 East 36th St., New York, NY 10016 (tel. 212/684-6207).

READER'S SUGGESTION: "For those under 26, **Transalpino** (24 Talbot St., Dublin 1; tel. 01-723825/742382) offers discounted fares good for two months to eight European destinations, with as many en-route breaks as you please. In 1984, I paid only IR£17 ($20) for the Dublin/London Sealink train ferry, when the regular fare was IR£34 ($40.80)" (P. Scully, Sharpsville, Pa.).

3. From the Continent

You can begin or end a European holiday in Ireland, with easy access either way by air or by ship.

BY AIR: Again, the fares quoted here are those in effect in 1984 and are quoted in French francs.

Aer Lingus, in 1984, would fly you from Paris to Dublin for a regular one-way fare of 1,470 French francs ($167.62). If you choose the Super APEX fare, you'd have paid 944 francs ($107.63), and the PEX fare was 1,122 francs ($127).

BY SEA: Most travel agents can make ferry bookings for you before you leave home, and you'll find listings below for each company's U.S. representatives, who will be glad to furnish details to help in your holiday planning.

Irish Continental Line lets you extend your Irish holiday into Europe, with frequent sailings from Rosslare (near Wexford) to Le Havre, Rosslare to Cherbourg, and—from June 21 to September 7 only—from Cork to Le Havre. Two ships, the *St. Patrick II* and the *St. Killian II*, operate alternately, and both can accommodate cars as well as foot passengers. On board, you'll find restaurants, cafeterias, lounge bars, discothèques, duty-free shops, a movie theater, and a delightful mixture of nationalities and ages.

The ships do not sail on a daily basis, so best check on current schedules before you make final plans. In 1984, fares began at IR£52 ($62.40) for a foot passenger in a six-berth cabin, IR£161 ($193.20) for car and driver. Sailing time is 22 hours to Le Havre and 18 hours to Cherbourg.

The line also has some terrific holiday package plans that can mean real savings for a European holiday. For example, in 1984, their two-week Villa Holiday provided a three-bedroom villa in a Brittany beach resort, with prices starting at IR£118 per person in low season, and a seven-day "Drive as You Please" plan offered bed-and-breakfast plus dinner, with a choice of over 170 good hotels around the country and prices beginning at IR£131 ($157.20). There are similar plans covering Spain and Jersey Island. These packages change from year to year, but they offer very good value and are well worth looking into. (Ask for their *Ferrytours* booklet, which describes all current plans.)

For advance information on current schedules, fares and holiday plans, contact: Irish Continental Line, c/o O'Shea Tours, 195 South Broadway, Hicksville, NY 11801, or Irish Continental Line, 19/21 Aston Quay, Dublin 2 (tel. 01-774331).

There is also one-day-a-week, year-round service from Ringaskiddy (just south of Cork city) to Roscoff (Brittany) via Brittany Ferries. The spacious *Quiberon* is a car as well as passenger ferry and has a restaurant, lounge, gaming area, and duty-free shop. Roscoff is a popular seaside resort without the traffic congestion of Le Havre or Cherbourg, an important consideration for drivers. The 14-hour crossing begins in Ringaskiddy on Saturday afternoons, and arrival is early Sunday mornings. Fares in 1984 ranged from a high of IR£76 ($91.20) for a deluxe cabin to IR£43 ($51.60) for a berth in a four-berth cabin to IR£35 ($42) for passenger without sleeping accommodations. Brittany Ferries also offers excellent continental holiday plans (ask for their holiday planner booklet). In the U.S., you can get full details from: Brittany Ferries, c/o Express Int'l. Inc., Main St., Saltillo, Pa. (tel. 814/448-3945).

4. Getting Around Ireland

Whether you come for a day or two, a week, two weeks or longer, you'll find it easy to get around Ireland. If you're here for only a few days, you'll want to settle in to one city (or B&B in the country) and take day-trips only, perhaps using the excellent CIE (Irish Transport System) coach tours to save the expense of renting a car. For longer visits, you have a multitude of choices via hiking, biking, escorted coach tours, rail and bus travel with an unlimited travel ticket, or a rental car with unlimited mileage. Or, you may decide to work out a combination of more than one means of transportation—for example, renting a bike to carry along in your rental car can pay off when you suddenly discover a nook or cranny that's inaccessible by car.

In the following sections, I'll tell you about several Information Sheets issued by the Irish Tourist Board on specific modes of transportation. It's a good idea to write in advance for those you'd like to have, since not all ITB offices in Ireland have complete stocks at all times.

BY FOOT OR BIKE: Hiking, hitchhiking, and cycling are all quite acceptable and very popular ways to get around Ireland. My only caution would be against hitchhiking alone. If you team up with a companion, however, there is certainly no risk.

If you are a hiker, you'll be drawn to off-the-main-thoroughfare spots of incredible beauty—and I'll have to warn you that they're numerous and frequent! The Irish Tourist Board issues an Information Sheet on Hill Walking and Rock Climbing (No. 31) that highlights many of these spectacular climbs. As for biking, there are more than 100 Raleigh Rent-a-Bike dealers around the country that rent bikes at rates of IR£4 ($4.80) per day or IR£22 ($26.40) per week. You'll be asked for a deposit of IR£30 ($36) when you book. And, speaking of booking, that is virtually a requirement if you plan a long bike trip during the months of July and August. Students can rent at a discount through USIT (see Chapter I). Information Sheet No. 52 lists all dealers and details on conditions of hire.

The following Information Sheets will be particularly helpful in planning your cycling itinerary: No. 44, A Cycling Tour of Ireland; No. 45, Cycling Dublin and Ireland East; No. 46, Cycling the South East; No. 47, Cycling Cork and Kerry; No. 48, Cycling Shannonside; No. 49, Cycling Donegal/Leitrim/Sligo; No. 50, Cycling the Lakelands; No. 51, Cycling Ireland West.

BY HORSE-DRAWN CARAVAN: Ireland is one of the few places left in the world where you can pamper the gypsy in your soul (breathes there a soul among us so dead it hasn't dreamed of gypsy caravans and campfires? I think not.) The gaily painted caravans are comfortably fitted out to accommodate up to four—in fact, you probably should have at least four in your party to travel this way—and your leisurely pace give you many opportunities to drink in details of Ireland's gorgeous landscape that those traveling by car will never see.

You've never handled a horse? Well, unless you're just plain scared to death of the dear creatures, that's no problem at all. The caravan operator will give you a quick course in harnessing and unharnessing, as well as the care and upkeep of your animal companion. If you wish, he'll also take you for a test drive to be sure you and your horse are compatible. Also, the farmers along your route who are appointed to provide feed and give you a parking site for the night will be all too happy to help you with any questions that come up after you've hit the road.

With a caravan, you're not really free to ramble just any old where—some roads are too steep or too heavily traveled to be suitable for your slow conveyance. Instead, you'll be offered a choice of carefully selected routes to follow, with overnight stopping places clearly marked. At some, you'll find showers, and almost all have sanitary facilities. You probably won't average more than about 15 kilometers a day, which allows plenty of time for chatting with the locals as you plod along, stopping for a pint in a friendly pub and just dreaming away the time. Time, did I say? You won't know the meaning of the word after a day or two of gypsying.

Come dinner time, you'll have the option of eating in (you'll have cooking facilities, utensils, eating ware, and a sink) or sprucing up for a meal in the best local eatery. As a caravaner, you'll have an instant conversation-opener, and you're more likely than not to be the last one out of restaurant or pub, with the crack still going strong.

What this idyllic journey will cost you depends on the season. In 1984, high-season charges for a four-berther ranged from IR£180 ($216) to IR£300 ($360) per week, while they dropped to lows of IR£100 ($120) to IR£145 ($174) April through May—cheap enough on a per-person basis! Add to that an average of about IR£4 ($4.80) per night for overnight stops.

Information Sheet No. 14 details the delights of traveling in a horse-drawn caravan, and the following are operators with whom you can book directly:

Mr. Joe O'Reilly
Blarney Romany Caravans
Blarney, Co. Cork
Tel. 021-85700
(for travel from Blarney through West Cork)

Mr. Jerry Desmond
Ocean Breeze Horse Caravans
Harbour View
Kilbrittain, Co. Cork
Tel. 023-49731/49626
(West Cork coast and river routes)

Mr. David Slattery
Slattery's Horse-Drawn Caravans
Slattery's Travel Agency
Tralee, Co. Kerry
Tel. 066-21722
(the Dingle Peninsula and Killarney)

Mr. Dieter Clissmann
Dieter Clissmann Horse-Drawn Caravan Holidays
Carrigmore, Co. Wicklow
Tel. 0404-8188
(Wicklow mountains and coast)

BY BUS AND TRAIN: One of the best buys in the travel market is the **Eurailpass,** good for unlimited rail travel in Ireland and on the Continent (but not in Great Britain or Northern Ireland), as well as on Irish Continental Lines ferries between Ireland and France. The good news is that it can now be used on Ireland's Expressway Bus Network, which means you can get to virtually any city, town, or village with your pass. They're available to any non-European resident, and should be bought before you leave home. Costs for 1985 are: $260 for 15 days, $330 for 21 days, $410 for one month, $560 for two months, and $680 for six months. Those between the ages of 14 and 26 are eligible for the **Eurail Youthpass,** which costs $290 for one month, $370 for two. Purchase through travel agents or write: Trains, P.O. Box M, Staten Island, NY 10305 (tel. 212/586-0091).

You won't be long in the Republic before "bus and train" disappear from your vocabulary, to be surplanted by **"CIE."** It's used universally to refer to **Coras Iompair Eireann** (Irish Transport System), which operates all bus services, trains, and the Aran Islands ferry from Galway.

Somehow, that bald statement just doesn't convey the essence of CIE. It is, literally, the lifeline of the country, transporting Irish housewives from Cappoquin to Cork for a day's shopping, businessmen from Killarney to Dublin for the day, university students home for weekends, commuters from Bray or Howth to and from work each day in Dublin, and travelers like you and me to just about anywhere we want to go in the country. Natives and visitors alike take CIE day-trips to Ireland's most scenic spots at bargain prices, and for those addicted to escorted coach tours as a means of seeing a country with the least amount of personal planning, CIE provides some of the best.

CIE's home office is at Heuston Station, Dublin 8, and the central number for schedule and fare information is 01-787777. Timetables and other travel information are available at the main Booking Office at 59 O'Connell St., Dublin 1, as well as at bus and train depots around the country. There's also a pamphlet (not available at all depots) entitled *List of Rail Fares with CIE Mainline Stations* that will help you compute rail fares from one point to another. Second Class travel is best for the budget, but you can go First Class for a small supplement. Children under 15 go for half-fare, and ages 15 to 21 pay less than two-thirds of the adult fare. One thing more: CIE is constantly offering special fares—weekends, midweek, etc.—so whenever you travel, be sure to ask about the cheapest fare available at the time.

Armed with a **Train Timetable** and a **Provincial and Expressway Bus Timetable,** there are few places you won't be able to reach in Ireland. The country's not that large (Galway is just three hours from Dublin by train!), both buses and trains are modern and comfortable, and your only inconvenience may be schedules for remote places, some of which don't have daily service. Of course, all those things are not all there is to public transportation. Rubbing elbows with the Irish as they go about their daily business is an added bonus for which CIE doesn't charge you a cent extra, and I must confess that some of my most memorable Irish experiences (and eavesdropping) have come from bus or train trips. Like everything else in Ireland, this kind of travel is so informal you'll think you're riding along with friends and neighbors by the time you reach your destination.

Rail and Bus Passes

If you're not using a Eurailpass, CIE will sell you a money-saving **Rambler Pass** for unlimited travel on rail or bus. Prices in 1984 were: IR£63 ($75.60) for 15 days, IR£43 ($51.60) for eight days. A combination rail and bus Rambler Pass cost: IR£78 ($93.60) for 15 days, IR£54 ($64.80) for eight. Students are eligible for the **Youth Student Pass** (see Chapter I). All passes are available from mainline railway stations in Ireland, or you may purchase them through travel agents in the States or CIE Tours International, 590 Fifth Ave., New York, NY 10036 (tel. 212/944-8828).

Local Buses

In Dublin, Cork, Waterford, Limerick and Galway, CIE operates doubledecker buses in the inner city and outlying areas, as well as frequent service from Shannon Airport into Limerick and Dublin Airport into that city. Fares are computed on the distance you travel and are surprisingly low (they start at 42p—50¢—and a five-mile journey costs only 58p—70¢). There are special **shopping fares** available in Dublin (see Chapter IV), and students are eligible for weekly discount tickets (see Chapter I). If you're going to be in Dublin a few days, you'll want to pick up a **Dublin District Timetable**, available at most newsstands for a small charge.

You won't pay as you board a local bus. Just get aboard (usually through the back door) and find a seat—the conductor will be along to collect your fare based on how far you're going. Those big doubledeckers will usually accommodate everyone, so there's no need for the pushing and shoving and elbowing we so often encounter at home—the Irish simply queue up politely and everyone boards in turn. Very civilized.

Sightseeing Tours

You can fill every day of your visit with CIE sightseeing tours around the country at prices that are better than bargain. For instance, city sightseeing excursions cost about IR£6 ($7.20); seven-hour trips are IR£7 ($8.40); a 12-hour, all-day tour goes for IR£12 ($14.40); and there are scenic drives for as little as IR£4 ($4.80).

The tours operate from tourist centers all around the country, and there are few scenic spots they miss. I sometimes think it's worth the price just to listen to the patter of your driver/narrator—he not only knows the terrain and everything about it, but also throws in an Irish tale or two you're not likely to forget. Brochures entitled "Day Trips" detailing tours available in a particular area are available from Tourist Offices and local bus and train stations.

In addition to day trips, CIE operates first-rate escorted coach tours, as well as two self-drive, go-as-you-please tours using either hotel or B&B accommodations. They represent exceptional value (in 1984, per person land cost for a seven-day self-drive tour was $99 per person for a car, accommodations and several sightseeing and shopping extras; and a seven-day escorted Irish Heritage tour loaded with cabaret, medieval banquet, and other bonuses, ranged from $399 to $529, depending on season). Every coach tour passenger has a chance to engage in an intriguing CIE Treasure Hunt, which could net you another Irish holiday at CIE's expense. You're given a list of rhymed clues to ten questions (example: name two towns in the U.S. named for Irish towns, giving the U.S.

state and the Irish county), and half the fun is getting the Irish you meet in your travels to help you unravel the answers.

BY CAR: Budget or no budget, there's just no better way to travel around Ireland than by car. Total freedom comes with the keys. You can loiter over an afternoon pint; extend a B&B overnight to three days when the place starts to feel like "home"; pull over into a layby (we'd call it an overlook) for an hour or two to steep yourself in Irish skies, mountains, coastline, fields, and rivers; stop to give a hitchhiker a lift (he'd call it a spin) to the next town and gain yet another Irish friend; seek out the perfect picnic spot and stay as long as you please; and wander as your fancy dictates, with no regard for schedules of any sort.

About that budget: this is where this book can earn its cost many times over, for with it, you'll be given a 15% discount on car rentals that have escalated greatly in the past few years. In fact, if you're traveling with a party of three or four, that discount could well bring the cost down into near-budget range. Details are spelled out in the section which follows, so have your trusty calculator handy.

You probably don't need me to tell you that driving is on the left in Ireland, but I'll pass along a few tips garnered from my ten years or so of driving on the "wrong" side of the road. First, before you even turn the ignition key, take time to check the rear-view and side mirrors to be sure they'll give you a clear view of the road behind. Check your luggage to be sure it's secure and won't come tumbling down if you make a sudden stop. Go over the gear system to be sure you understand it (every other rental car seems to have a different position for reverse!), then check the light dimmer and windshield wiper. Elementary details, to be sure, but while you're doing all this, you'll be adjusting to the transition from plane to customs to car. If your arrival is an early morning one, it's a good idea to stop for a nice hot cuppa in the airport to help that transition along. Remember, this is Ireland—you don't have to rush.

You'll be reminded of the drive-on-the-left edict by frequent signs between Shannon and Limerick and the Dublin Airport and that city. Still, the very first time you make a sharp turn, your inclination is going to be to head for the right-hand side of the road. Also, when you stop for gas, a pint, or a meal, it's very, very easy to pull off on the right side (which is the wrong side in Ireland, of course). I make it a practice to stop the car headed in the direction in which I'll be going, which somehow makes it easier to pull off on the left side. No matter what precautions you take, however, you're bound to feel awkward the first day —and maybe the second. So, try to set a little tape recorder up there in your head to play and replay "Drive left" until it becomes second nature.

Speed limits in towns and cities will be 30 or 40 miles per hour (they're prominently posted), and it's 55 on the open road. Mileage is signposted in both kilometers and miles (if it's green and white, it's kilometers; black and white, miles). If you're into conversions, one kilometer equals .62 miles, and an easy conversion method is to divide kilometers by 8 and multiply the result by 5. Gas will cost anywhere from IR£2.85 ($3.42) a gallon up, and you'll find the cheapest prices at Jet stations. Those are Imperial gallons—larger by volume than ours— and in a small car, you'll cover remarkable distances on a tankful of gas.

You'll learn a whole new automotive vocabulary: your luggage will go into the boot, not the trunk; the hood is now the bonnet; the windshield becomes a windscreen; you'll park in a car park, not a parking lot; those are lorries, not trucks, you pass; and you're driving a car-for-hire, not a rental car, that runs on petrol, not gas. And those signs with bold Gaelic lettering reading "Geill Sli" mean "Give Way," and mean precisely that! Got it?

Now, about Irish roads—quite simply, I think they're wonderful! You may disagree. But, you see, I have an active dislike for huge, speedy double-laned highways (another new phrase, dual carriageways), and in spite of the fact that only about 3% of Ireland's roadways fall into that category, I grumble every time I see the bulldozers hard at it widening and straightening one of my beloved little country lanes. And they seem to be even harder at it with every visit. Of course, when you're trying to pass one of those gigantic trucks (excuse me, lorries), the wider roads do come in handy. But, if you take my heartfelt advice, most of the roads you travel will fall into the 90% that are small, sometimes bumpy, and a hundredfold more interesting than the National Primary Routes. They always make me feel that I'm traveling right inside the landscape, not whizzing by it.

There are some things you ought to know about those little roads. Like the fact that in early mornings and evenings, you're sure to meet at least one farmer and his hardworking dog driving the cows to or from the fields—right down the middle of the road. Don't panic, just stop like everybody else, relax, give your man a nod or a wave, and let the sea of cattle wash right around you. Also, you're probably going to get lost at least once. That's because road signs sometimes mysteriously get turned around (leprechauns?), or you come to a junction with no signs. But, let me tell you that getting lost in Ireland is a pleasant adventure. Stop at a pub to ask directions, and you're in for some delightful conversation, especially if things are a little slow. An Irish friend tells me that the classic answer to such a request is "Well, if I were going there, I wouldn't be starting from here"—I'm still waiting to hear that one for myself!

Your car-hire company will provide you with a map, of course (not that it will keep you from getting lost), but most are not all that easy to follow. I highly recommend the **Holiday Maps** (regional, as well as for the entire country), which are much more detailed, have city maps (you'll need them), and give you a wealth of useful tourist information. They sell for IR£2.25 ($2.70) and can be bought at most news agents.

One last suggestion. **Comprehensive Communications, Inc. (CCI),** has put together three **Auto-Tape Tours of Ireland** which follow a circular route around the country, beginning at Shannon. Commentators are both American and Irish, and along with a very good narration on the localities you're passing through, they throw in bits of folklore and music and odd bits of information that add color to your trip. They come with a map, and the tapes are timed for your probable rate of speed, but make suggestions for deviating from the prescribed itinerary to explore a nook or cranny or two. You don't have to buy all three if you're going to be in one section of the country only. Tape 1 takes you from Shannon to Sligo via Limerick, the cliffs of Moher, Galway, Yeats Country, and the prehistoric sites that dot this landscape. Tape 2 carries you on from Sligo through Dublin, Wicklow, Wexford, and Waterford to Cork. And Tape 3 completes the circle back to Shannon by way of West Cork's beautiful coastline and tiny villages, Kerry's mountains, Killarney, and Tralee. Actually, you'll enjoy your trip much more if you order these tapes ahead and listen to them before you leave for Ireland; when you return home, they're a lasting memento of your visit. Order from CCI, P.O. Box 385, Scarsdale, NY 10583 (tel. 914/472-5133); each tape costs $10.95 plus 75¢ for postage and handling.

Car Rentals

The first thing you must know about renting a car in Ireland is that it is absolutely necessary to book ahead. That's especially true from the first of July through the end of September, but in this small country, a run on the stock available can develop suddenly if there's a special event of some kind that draws lots of visitors. You should also know that you must be between the ages of 23 and 70 (top age with some companies is 65).

The rate you pay will depend on the size of the car and the season of the year. Seasonal dates may vary slightly from one company to another, but generally you'll find the highest charges July through September, a more moderate rate in May, June, and October, and the lowest from November through April. Prices for the smaller, stick-shift cars are the best value: larger vehicles (the only ones available with automatic transmission) can run as much as a third more.

The rates quoted will include third-party and passenger liability insurance, but unless you add on collision damage waiver insurance, you'll be responsible for the full cost of repairs should you be involved in an accident. Even though that can add as much as IR£30 ($36) to your weekly costs, I strongly advise you to take it—otherwise, you'll be required by most companies to make a refundable payment of as much as IR£150 ($180). You may also be asked for a deposit at the time you book, but this is many times waived if you present a recognized credit card. Almost every company allows pickup at one airport and dropoff at another if you wish.

A Discount Rate

Jerry O'Riordan, General Manager of **Johnson & Perrott, Ltd.,** Emmet Place, Cork (tel. 021-23295), has for years given readers of this book a 15% discount on basic car rentals when they mention it when booking and have it with them when they pick up the car. That's a nice saving, but even nicer is the fact that it will get you to one of the most reliable, efficient, and helpful car-hire companies in Ireland. To illustrate, let me tell you about my experience with J&P on my very first visit to Ireland back in 1973. I had requested a certain make car, which didn't happen to be available when I checked in with them at Shannon. However, a pretty colleen behind the desk—Maureen—assured me that one was due to be checked in later that afternoon and sure, wouldn't she be glad to drive me in to Limerick to my B&B for a bit of rest, then bring the car I wanted when it arrived. And sure, didn't she do it! The trip in included a running string of tips about where to go and what to do in the Shannonside area, as well as a lot of places around the country (that's how I first learned about Durty Nellie's)—places I might otherwise have missed. Came the late afternoon and came Maureen with my car, followed by a second J&P car to deliver her back to Shannon so I wouldn't have to drive her myself. At the time, I was overwhelmed by such consideration, but in the ensuing years, I've become almost blasé about that kind of courtesy—it seems to come naturally to the entire staff. They've helped me plan itineraries and choose the best routes all over Ireland, all the while as gracious and friendly as if they weren't putting themselves out at all.

Johnson & Perrott have pickup points at all air and sea ports, and in Dublin, Cork, and Limerick, with desks at the Dublin, Cork, and Shannon airports. In those cities, they'll even deliver the car to your accommodation at no extra charge. There's no drop-off charge either at Shannon, Dublin, and Cork airports (or they'll arrange to pick the car up at your guesthouse in those cities). Like all car-hire firms, they charge more during the high season, but it's a remarkably short one, July 1 to September 15, and the same Ford Fiesta that goes for IR£165 ($198) per week during that period drops to IR£147 ($176.40) other months. Both rates include unlimited mileage, as does the daily rate of IR£28 ($33.60).

There are several money-saving specials available at Johnson & Perrott: I've already detailed their farmhouse holiday program (see Chapter I); there's a special "Businessman's Discount" for people coming to Ireland on a regular basis for business purposes; and you'll be given one free day in May and October if you rent the car for six days or more. Be sure and inquire when you book about any specials in effect at the time. When booking, enclose a minimum $60 deposit. You can book through travel agents or with J&P directly.

Other Car Hire Firms

The Irish representative for National Car Rental and Europcar is **Murray's Rent-A-Car,** Baggot Street Bridge, Dublin 4 (tel. 01-681777). You'll find their offices at Dublin, Shannon, and Cork airports, with city desks also in Dublin, Cork, Galway, Rosslare, and Wexford. There are free pickup and drop-off privileges at all offices, and rates start at IR£60 ($72) for a Ford Fiesta with unlimited mileage for three days. Special "Passport" rates may be booked in advance in the U.S. from National Car Rental (tel. toll-free, 800/328-4567).

Both **Avis** and **Hertz** are represented in Ireland, each with offices around the country and free drop-off privileges from one office to the other. You can book through travel agents, but rates are considerably higher than either Johnson & Perrott or Murray's.

5. Suggested Itineraries

Set itineraries present a very real danger in Ireland. A fifteen-minute pub break in an afternoon's drive can easily turn into a two-day layover, all because your man behind the bar insists you'll be very welcomed at the evening's singsong with such conviction that it is suddenly very clear that the Blarney Stone can wait another day—which turns into yet *another* day when you fall in with such convivial company at the sing-song that nothing will do but that you stay over for the next night! Now, don't misunderstand me: it *is* possible to "do" a very good, circular tour of Ireland in two weeks. But whether or not you get all the way around will depend entirely on how determined you are to stay on that schedule.

Bearing all that in mind, you'll find some recommended tours set out below. The first, and longest, takes you around the outer rim of Ireland's cuplike terrain (see map on page 20). This tour encompasses only the Republic: add another three to five days if you intend to visit Northern Ireland. Remember, this swing around the country will only touch the highlights, some of which you may wish to skip in favor of spending more time at a spot you find especially intriguing.

It's important to remember, too, that although mileages may *appear* short, these are *Irish* miles—distances, road conditions, and the usual driving considerations have absolutely nothing to do with how long it takes you to cover them.

There's an old Irish saying, "An Irish mile is long, but easy traveled." After one or two stops, you'll know the truth in that! Every pub or lunch or sightseeing stop will make it clearer, and you won't want to miss the photo "musts" that lurk around almost every bend.

Right here, I'd like to make a suggestion based purely on my personal choice of how to travel. The first of our suggested itineraries is a circular tour which anticipates that you will move from place to place almost every night.

Well, I don't know about you, but I don't particularly enjoy packing and unpacking every single night. To avoid that, it is quite possible to select several major destinations along the route, settle in for a day or so and make longish day trips, returning to the same homey B&B in the evening. Besides, while Irish pubs are notoriously hospitable to visitors, if you return the *second* night, you're an instant "regular"—lots more fun! Of course, such a plan means longer stretches of driving when you do move along, but you will have taken in a lot of the sights along the way on your day trips, making those Irish miles go more quickly.

Shorter, regional itineraries can be incorporated into the circular route or taken on their own, depending on the time you have to spend and your own inclinations. To help you make any such adjustments, you will find full details for each region in the chapters that follow. One last time, I want to point out that these are *suggested* itineraries, and they are by no means cast in stone. Do as the Irish do and just "go with it," whatever "it" turns out to be, and you'll have a happy holiday.

TWO WEEKS—A CIRCULAR TOUR: The suggested starting point is Dublin. If you deplane at Shannon, however, you can simply begin with the Day 9 itinerary and follow our route to the north or south, ending up again at Shannon for your flight home.

Days 1–2: Allow arrival day for settling into your Dublin digs and getting the feel of the city. Devote the second day to exploring Dublin's fine historic buildings and Georgian squares, ending with a hotel cabaret or an evening's pub crawl.

Day 3: *Dublin to Waterford (or Tramore).* Get an early start and drive south to Enniskerry to visit the Powerscourt estate and gardens. Then on through Roundwood to Glendalough with its early-Christian ruins in a spectacular setting of mountains and lakes. Avoca is next, where Thomas Moore wrote his melodic "The Meeting of the Waters." South through Arklow to Enniscorthy, with time out to visit its small museum, and on straight through to Waterford, or detour over to historic Wexford's narrow, charming streets before continuing on to Waterford's Reginald's Tower (built in 1003) and its remarkable collection of city charters and other artifacts. Stop for the night in the city itself, or drive on to the seaside resort of Tramore with its three miles of sandy beaches.

Day 4: *Waterford to Cork.* Drive south through the old market town of Dungarvan, then westward to Youghal. Stop at the clock tower in the middle of town to visit its interesting museum, allowing ample time for the walking tour described in a brochure available there, which will take you along some of Ireland's oldest surviving city walls. On to Cork, where you can play the famous Shandon Bells at St. Mary's, visit the city's many historic sites, and enjoy an evening meal in one of its fine restaurants.

Day 5: *Cork to Killarney.* Stop by Blarney Castle to kiss the legendary stone, then head for Macroom, Ballingeary, and the Pass of Keimaneigh (you may want to make the short detour to Goughane Barra National Park). On to the lovely holiday resort of Glengarriff, then turn north through rugged mountain terrain to Kenmare and on to Killarney.

Days 6–7: *Killarney.* You'll want to spend one day visiting the famous lakes, islands, and ancient abbeys. On your second day, Killarney is the ideal base from which to make either the 109-mile Ring of Kerry drive or a 93-mile circuit of the bewitching Dingle Peninsula.

Day 8: *Killarney to Limerick.* If you opted for the Ring of Kerry on Day

7, you can swing around Dingle en route to Limerick (but it makes for a *long* day of driving—Dingle is, in fact, a perfect place for one of those itinerary adjustments to allow for an overnight stop). Then back through Rathkeal, Newcastle West, and the beautiful village of Adare to Limerick (only 16 miles from Shannon Airport). Save this evening for the Bunratty or Knappogue castle medieval banquet (which must be booked ahead).

Day 9: *Limerick to Galway.* Take time to explore Limerick's St. Mary's Cathedral before heading north, then add a few extra miles to take in the stunning Cliffs of Moher. Lisdoonvarna, the popular spa resort, is next, then the barren beauty of the Burren's limestone hills, Ballyvaughan, Clarinbridge, and Galway. Traditional music in a pub in Galway or nearby Salthill makes for a memorable evening.

Day 10: *Galway to Donegal.* A full day's drive will take you through Connemara to Moycullen, Oughterard, Recess, Clifden, Leenane, and along Clew Bay (with over 100 islands) into Westport. Not far away is Westport House, with its magnificent interior, beautiful gardens, and zoo park. Then head north through Castlebar, Pontoon, Ballina, and Enniscrone, a charming family seaside resort (stop for a swim or a walk along the strand). Then drive on to Sligo to see the 13th-century Franciscan Friary and the county library museum or just walk the narrow old streets and soak up the atmosphere so dear to Yeats' heart. You'll find the poet's burial place at nearby Drumcliff, then on to Bundoran, Ballyshannon, and Donegal.

Day 11: *Donegal.* Early in the day, explore Donegal town, with its Franciscan Friary and castle. Then head off for a circular tour of Co. Donegal by driving west through Mountcharles, Killybegs, Ardara, Glenties, Maas, and Kincasslagh (Donegal tweed country). Push farther north through Annagry, Crolly, Bunbeg, Bloody Foreland, Gortahork, and into Dunfanaghy, nestled at the foot of steep cliffs along the shores of Sheephaven Bay. Drive south to Letterkenny (and if you've an extra day, I strongly recommend the 120-mile loop around the Inishowen Peninsula to Buncrana, Malin Head, and Moville—the scenery is truly spectacular and well worth the drive), then through the picturesque Finn Valley back to Donegal Town.

Day 12: *Donegal to Carrick-on-Shannon.* Make this a leisurely driving day, south through Ballyshannon and Bundoran, then southeast to Manorhamilton (look for the ruins of a 1638 castle brooding over the town). Continue south through Drumkeeran and along the shores of lovely Lough Allen (a good day and place for a picnic lunch) to Drumshabo and Leitrim and into Carrick-on-Shannon, with its fleet of cruise boats bobbing at the wharves.

Day 13: *Carrick-on-Shannon to Dublin.* Drive through lake country to Cavan town by way of Mohill, Carrigallen, Killeshandra, and Crossdoney. On through Bailieborough and Carrickmacross to Drogheda. From Drogheda, visit prehistoric tombs at Newgrange, Knowth, and Dowth, then drive on through Slane into Navan. A further six miles will bring you to the Hill of Tara, home of ancient Irish high kings. From there, it's back to Dublin via historic Trim, Black Bull, Clonee, Blanchardstown, and the Phoenix Park.

Day 14: *Dublin.* A day for odds-and-ends and departure.

ONE WEEK—EAST COAST AND LAKELAND: Starting point for this tour is also Dublin, and **Day 1** is reserved for your arrival, settling in and perhaps a cabaret in the evening.

Day 2: Drive south through Dun Laoghaire, Dalkey, and Killiney along the Vico Road, with its spectacular views of Dublin Bay, into the seaside resort of Bray (leave the main road to detour along the seafront). Then on to Enniskerry beneath Sugarloaf Mountain. Visit nearby Powerscourt Estate and Gardens. Glendalough and its timeless ruins are next along the scenic mountain drive, then on to Rathdrum, Avoca, and Woodenbridge into Arklow. On to Co. Wexford's Gorey, Enniscorthy (stop in the museum), and into Wexford town, where an overnight stop will give you time to walk its narrow streets and relive its gallant history.

Day 3: From Wexford, head southwest to Ballyhack to catch the ferry across Waterford Harbor to Passage East in Co. Waterford (if you're enamored of tiny seaside villages, make the short detour to Dunmore East). See Waterford's 1003 Reginald's Tower and remnants of its Viking-built city walls. Kilkenny is next, where you should stop to see Kilkenny Castle, Rothe House, and the Kilkenny Design Workshops. Then it's on through Tullamore (home of the famous Tullamore Dew) to Athlone, "capital" of the midlands. Make this your overnight stop.

Day 4: Drive northwest to Roscommon to have a look at Roscommon Abbey, then on to the market town of Longford, with its 19th-century cathedral. Head southeast to Edgeworthstown (where you may want to visit the museum dedicated to novelist Maria Edgeworth) and through the angling center of Castlepollard to see nearby Tullynally Castle. Lough Derravaragh, in the immediate vicinity is the setting of the Irish legend of the *Children of Lir*. Detour to Fore to see its Benedictine Abbey and ancient crosses, then back to Castlepollard and south to Mullingar to spend the night.

Day 5: From Mullingar, drive through Kinnegad to Trim, with its impressive Norman castle, then head for Navan, where a short detour onto the Dublin road will bring you to the royal Hill of Tara. Back to Navan and on to Donaghmore and Slane. Look for Bronze Age cemeteries at Brugh na Boinne and visit Mellifonte Abbey and Monasterboice, then on north to Dunleer, Castlebellingham, and Dundalk. If there's time, drive a bit farther north to the rugged little Carlingford Peninsula, then back to Dundalk and along the coast through Clogher, Termonfeckin, Baltray, Drogheda, Balbriggan, Skerries, Rush, Swords, and Howth (where there are marvelous views of the bay) and on to Dublin by way of Sutton.

Day 6: Spend this day exploring the city.

Day 7: Departure.

ONE WEEK—WEST COAST: A good tour for those deplaning at Shannon. Spend Day 1 in Limerick, visit Bunratty Folk Park, and take in a castle banquet in the evening (must be booked ahead).

Day 2: Drive to Ennis, then southwest to the picturesque seaside resort towns of Kilrush and Kilkee. North to Lahinch and skirt Liscannor Bay to the mystical Cliffs of Moher. On to Lisdoonvarna, through the bleakly beautiful Burren to Black Head, Ballyvaughan, Kinvara, and Clarinbridge into Galway, where you'll spend the night.

Day 3: Head for Connemara by way of Spiddal, Costello, Screeb, Derryrush, Carna, Toombeola, Ballynahinch, and Clifden. Head northward to Letterfrack and Leenane, where a turn to the southeast will take you through Maam, Cong (setting of *The Quiet Man* movie), Ballinrobe, Patry, Ballintubber (stop to see the abbey) and in to Castlebar. Visit Clonalis House, and make Castlebar your overnight stop.

Day 4: Drive to Westport and visit impressive Westport House with its magnificent mansion and zoo park. Take the road to Newport and travel through Mulrany to the Curraun Peninsula, Achill Sound and on to the breathtaking views of Achill Island (reached by a causeway). Allow time to drive as far out as Keel and Dooagh. Stay overnight on Achill or return to Westport.

Day 5: Turn inland through a changing landscape to Castlebar, Claremorris (Knock and its celebrated shrine are a short detour away), Ballyhaunis, Castlerea, and Roscommon (visit its famous abbey) to Athlone for the night.

Day 6: Heading south from Athlone, drive to Birr and stop to visit the gardens at Birr Castle. Farther south, Nenagh's fine castle dates from about 1200. Turn due west for Portroe and drive along the shores of Lough Derg to Killaloe. From here, it's a short drive, via O'Brien's Bridge and Ardnacrusha, into Limerick.

Day 7: Departure.

THREE DAYS—SOUTHWEST: On **Day 1,** starting from Cork (but only after you've had time to visit some of the city's highlights), drive the five miles to Blarney Castle for the obligatory kiss of that magical stone, then back through Cork and south to the charming fishing town of Kinsale. Continue southwest through Timoleague, Clonakilty, Rosscarbery, Glandore, and Union Hall to the old town of Skibbereen. The route on through Ballydehob, Schull, Toormore, Durrus, and Bantry into Glengarriff is one of the loveliest in the country. In Glengarriff, visit Garnish Island, then climb through rugged mountains via the Tunnel Road to Kenmare and on to Killarney for the night.

Day 2: Allow the entire day to drive the Ring of Kerry (110 miles), since you won't want to rush through some of Ireland's most spectacular sea and mountain landscape. Retrace your steps to Kenmare, then west to Sneem, Castlecove, Derrynane, Waterville, Cahirciveen, Glenbeigh, and Killorglin before returning to Killarney for the night.

Day 3: Devote this day to Dingle Peninsula's very special charms. From Killarney, drive to Killorglin, then north to Castlemaine, west to Inch (where much of *Ryan's Daughter* was filmed), Annascaul, Dingle, Ventry, Slea Head, Dunquin, Ballyferriter, Murreagh, and back to Dingle. Cross Connor's Pass to the north side of the peninsula and Stradbally, Camp, and Tralee before heading back to Killarney. Alternatively, stay the night in one of the lovely B&Bs on the peninsula.

Chapter III

IRELAND, A TOURIST'S SURVEY

1. Things to See and Do
2. Ireland After Dark
3. Tracing Your Irish Roots
4. Meet the Irish

OUR SURVEY OF IRELAND'S TOURIST TREASURES must, of necessity, be somewhat abbreviated—entire books have been written on each of the topics we'll cover in this chapter—but we'll talk about some of the highlights and point you in the direction of more complete details on the subjects that most take your individual fancy.

As I've said so many times already in the preceding chapters, if you give yourself up to Irish fate and just "go with it," you'll be ready to write a book or two yourself on the things you've discovered on your own that *aren't* covered in this book! For example, if you have always been fascinated by lighthouses and the people who man them, you might want to visit one of Ireland's 22 manned lighthouses. Well, you can do that by contacting the Irish Lights Office, 16 Lower Pembroke St., Dublin 2. Intrigued? That's just a sample of unique travel experiences waiting for you on your Irish visit in addition to those we have space for below.

1. Things to See and Do

The Irish Tourist Board issues Information Sheet No. 40, listing more than 80 free attractions throughout Ireland, and in the regional sections that follow, you'll find our choices of things to see and do in almost every county. For now, though, we'll talk about generalities.

Special Events

It may be a *slight* exaggeration to say there's a "special event" of one sort or another every other day in Ireland, but it's been my experience that the simplest, most ordinary occurrence can take on that air if two or more natives are present.

If you're lucky enough to arrive in a small town or village when its own special festival (sometimes called "pattern day") is in progress, you'll be in for a real treat. There is always at least one day, usually several, filled with the likes of fancy dress parades, donkey races, traditional music and dance contests, and ending with a dance that draws locals from miles away. By all means stop, mingle with the Irish, and let the itinerary take care of itself. As far as I know, no one has ever compiled a list of these festivals and their dates, so you'll just have to be on the lookout for the homemade signs on the outskirts of town as you travel around.

From March through November, however, there are enough more formal, organized special events to set you thinking about an extended visit to take in more than one. Any Irish Tourist Board office can furnish a complete *Calendar of Events* to help you plan your travel dates around the ones most appealing. Some of the most outstanding and the months in which they usually fall are:

March
St. Patrick's Week (his day is the 17th, of course)

April
Dublin Arts Festival

May
Spring Show (Dublin)
Pan Celtic Week (Killarney, Co. Kerry)
Fleadh Nua (Ennis, Co. Clare; the national traditional music, song, and dance festival)

June
Writers' Week (Listowel, Co. Kerry; Irish literature workshops, lectures, plays, etc.—you don't have to be a writer to attend)
Festival of Music in Great Irish Houses (Dublin)

August
Dublin Horse Show *(the* social event of the year—requires booking far in advance for accommodations in Dublin)
Rose of Tralee (Killarney, Co. Kerry; sometimes held in early September)

September
Waterford Festival of Light Opera (Waterford)
Gaelic Football and Hurling Finals (sometimes fall in late August)
Galway Oyster Festival (Galway)

October
Dublin Theater Festival (future is uncertain—be sure to check if it's on the year you visit)
Wexford Opera (Wexford)
Cork Jazz International Festival (Cork City)
Dublin City Marathon (Dublin)

In 1985, Cork City will be celebrating its 800th anniversary (11850–1985) with a year-long program of special activities (details from any Irish Tourist Board office), and Ireland will be participating in several international celebrations. For the European International Music Year, concerts, exhibitions, workshops, and conferences will span the musical scale from formal orchestral concerts to informal folk groups. For full details, contact Marion Creely, Executive Secretary, Irish Committee, European Music Year 1985, 70 Merrion Sq., Dublin 2 (tel. 01-764685) or any Irish Tourist Board office.

A major scouting jamboree in Tuam, Co. Galway, as well as a wide range of cultural events, is just part of Ireland's observance of the United Nations International Year of Youth in 1985 (details from National Youth Council of Ireland, 6 Waterloo Rd., Dublin 4; tel. 01-685379 or 685386).

Historic Places

There are more than 800 reminders of Ireland's antiquity scattered around the countryside that are labeled State Monuments, 100 high crosses, 120 round towers and *30,000* earthen ring forts! It's anybody's guess how many exist in unofficial splendor in green fields, on mountainsides and along coastal indentations. Information Sheet No. 6, published by the Irish Tourist Board, gives a good overall view of what to look for and how they came to be there. I also recommend for history and archeology buffs, Peter Harbison's excellent *Guide to the National Monuments of Ireland* (Gill and Macmillan Publishers), available in most Irish bookshops.

To breathe life into the ancient times that left all those relics in their wake, the Irish have gone to great pains to preserve some in their state of ruin and restore others. The secluded full-scale Bronze Age lake dwelling on the grounds of **Craggaunowen Castle** in Co. Clare will send your imagination spinning right back to those dim and hazy days of Ireland's past. **Blarney Castle,** any one of the castle medieval banquets, **Bunratty Folk Park** in Co. Clare and **Glencolumbkille** in Co. Donegal bring you closer to modern times, and **Muckross House** in Killarney, Co. Kerry, re-creates the life of a still later period.

In Dublin, look for those marvelous 18th-century Georgian mansions, as well as the gracious squares and crescents that give it such unique character. Outside of Dublin (many within easy reach of the city), there are splendid residences built by wealthy Anglo-Irish aristocrats to indulge their luxurious tastes and lifestyles. You can visit many of these castles and stately homes, as well as some of the most beautifully landscaped gardens in the world, for surprisingly small fees. There's **Malahide Castle,** Malahide, Co. Dublin; **Bantry House** in Bantry, Co. Cork; **Muckross House** in Killarney, Co. Kerry; **Clonalis House** in Castlerea, Co. Roscommon; and **Knappogue Castle** in Quin, Co. Clare, to name a few. Among the gardens you won't want to miss are those at **Mount Usher,** Ashford, Co. Wicklow; **Powerscourt,** Enniskerry, Co. Wicklow; and **Abbey Leix,** Abbeyleix, Co. Laois. Check at Tourist Offices and bookshops for the illustrated booklet on those maintained by the **Historic Irish Tourist Houses and Gardens Association (HITHA),** or contact The Secretary, HITHA, 3A Castle St., Dalkey, Co. Dublin (tel. 01-801185), for full details.

You can pare your costs to visit these magnificent homes and gardens even further by means of one of Ireland's best sightseeing bargains, the **Passport to Ireland's Heritage & Culture.** It's a glossy, beautifully illustrated booklet describing 18 such attractions and containing coupons entitling you to a 50% discount at each. You can obtain a copy through Tourist Offices for a small fee which you'll recoup (in savings) after only one or two visits.

Art Galleries

There are quite good art collections in galleries, some large and impressive, others small but still impressive. Dublin's **National Gallery,** Merrion Square West, and **Hugh Lane Municipal Gallery of Modern Art,** Parnell Square, are both on the "don't miss" list; **Malahide Castle,** Malahide, Co. Dublin, has an outstanding portrait collection; in Kilkenny, it's the **Kilkenny Castle Art Gallery;** in Waterford, the newly opened (1984) **Waterford Arts Center;** the

Cork Arts Society Gallery is at 16 Lavitt's Quay; the **Fota Estate,** Carrigtwohill, Co. Cork, houses an extensive private collection of Irish landscape paintings; Limerick's **Belltable Arts Center,** in O'Connell St., has regular shows by local artists; **Kenny's Bookshop and Art Gallery,** High St., Galway, also exhibits works by local artists; and in Sligo, nearly 100 paintings by John and Jack Yeats, as well as other Irish artists, are shown at the **Sligo Art Gallery,** Stephen St.

Check with the Irish Tourist Board (Information Sheet No. 37 is devoted to art galleries) and The Arts Council, 70 Merrion Sq., Dublin 2 (tel. 01-764685), for further details about these and the many other galleries around the country.

Museums

Allow yourself plenty of time to visit the **National Museum** in Kildare St. in Dublin, **Kilmainham Jail Museum** in the Kilmainham section of Dublin, and the **James Joyce Museum** in the tower at Sandycove, Co. Dublin. And as you drive around the country, don't miss museums like **Reginald's Tower** in Waterford, **Rothe House** in Kilkenny, the **Clock Tower Museum** in Youghal, Co. Cork, the **museum at Craggaunowen,** Co. Clare (where Tim Severin's replica of St. Brendan's boat has found a permanent home), or **Glencolumbkille Folk Museum** in Co. Donegal.

If you're really into museum hopping, you can obtain an illustrated guide to the 150 museums in Ireland (including Northern Ireland) from many bookshops or direct from **The Irish Museums Trust,** Gardiner House, Ballsbridge, Dublin 4. It sells for IR£3.95 ($4.74), plus postage if you order by mail.

State Forests

Ireland's state forests—more than 300 of them—are for the most part small and undeveloped havens of nature trails, bird songs, and tranquility. Many have picnic sites, inviting the nice notion of an outdoor lunch in a different woodland every day. You can do that—or just plot a peaceful half-hour break each day—with the help of *The Open Forest, A Guide to Areas Open to the Public,* a publication of the **Forest and Wildlife Service,** 22 Upper Merrion St., Dublin 2 (tel. 01-789211). They can also furnish a whole bevy of detailed pamphlets on individual state forests.

You'll find the state forests well cared for and rubbish-free—you'll be on your honor to help keep them that way.

Cruising

Ireland's hundreds of miles of inland waterways offer an ideal escape from the rigors of driving and one of the most peaceful travel experiences you could dream of. Cruising along the magnificent Shannon or from Belturbet to Belleek by way of Lower and Upper Lough Erne and its connecting river or on the Grand Canal from Dublin all the way to the Shannon or Barrow invokes a tranquility that just doesn't exist behind the wheel of an automobile. Add to that the delight of a unique view of the Irish countryside and stopovers at waterside towns and villages, and you have the holiday of a lifetime.

The beauty of such a holiday is that you don't have to be a seasoned sailor to hire a cabin cruiser from one of the eleven companies approved by the Irish Tourist Board. You'll be given free instruction on handling the craft, reading charts, etc., and I'm told most people are fully confident and ready to set sail after little more than an hour (if you're the least bit timid, however, your instructor will stay with you until your qualms have disappeared). It's a comfort, too, to know that especially during peak holiday seasons the waterways are constantly patrolled by professionals to keep an eye out for any holiday sailor who *might* get into difficulty. There's no license involved, but you must be over 21 years old and there must be one person other than the "Captain" who understands the controls and charts.

Cruisers range in size from two to eight berths and are fully outfitted with all the comforts of home (full kitchen, showers, hot water, etc.). For budget travelers, the savings from doing your own cooking and sharing the costs with a full passenger load make cruising a viable option.

The Tourist Board can furnish a full list of companies that rent cabin cruisers. Booking is done directly with the firm of your choice. As for costs, in 1984, those listed below charged rates of IR£88 ($105.60) to IR£950 ($1140) depending on the size of the cruiser, the season, and the length of rental (they're available for weekends and one or two weeks):

Carrick Craft, Carrick-on-Shannon, Co. Leitrim (tel. 078-20236)
Emerald Star Line, St. James's Gate, Dublin (tel. 01-720244)
Flagline (1972) Ltd., Rosebank Marina, Carrick-on-Shannon, Co. Leitrim (tel. 078-20172)
Athlone Cruisers Ltd., Jolly Mariner Marina, Athlone, Co. Westmeath (tel. 0902-72892)
Shannon Castle Line, Ringsend, Dublin 4 (tel. 01-600964)

Sports

For the sports-minded, Ireland is a veritable banquet table loaded with goodies! **Golfers** will be welcomed guests at more than 180 courses (over 50 are championship class) around the county, be they professionals or bumbling amateurs who just like to whack the ball around. Green fees run from around IR£5 ($6) to IR£8 ($9.60) per day. Courses range from 18-holers with such extras as a pro shop, resident pro to give instruction, and tea room to windswept greens overlooking the sea. *The Visitors' Guide to Irish Golf Courses,* available from Tourist Offices in Ireland, lists them all and gives specific information on what's available to visitors at each.

Caddies are not generally available (although they can be booked ahead at some of the larger courses), and don't look for a golfmobile—the closest you'll come to that is a lightweight pull cart. Some courses have clubs for rent at about IR£3 ($3.60) per set per round, but most do not, so you'll be well advised to bring your own unless you have an Irish golfing buddy or two who's good for the loan of a set.

Irish Golfing Holidays can be arranged to include accommodations, golf clinics, and special golfing weekends with groups and societies. For full particulars—or for help in setting up a golf holiday itinerary on your own— contact: J. P. Murray, Golf Promotion Executive, Irish Tourist Board, Baggot Street Bridge, Dublin 2.

If there's such a thing as a **fisherman's** heaven, it must be located in the Emerald Isle! You can go after such freshwater fish (coarse fishing) as bream, dace, pike, perch, and various hybrids in all those rivers, streams, and lakes, and never have to worry about a license or permit. Or stalk the famous Irish salmon from January 1 to September 30 in coastal rivers, their stillwaters and headwaters. Sea trout and brown trout are among the other challenging game fish. One license covers both salmon and sea trout (IR£5—$6—all districts, seven days; IR£7—$8.40—for a single district, full season; and IR£15 —$18—for all districts, full season). Sea anglers will find plentiful supplies of bass, whiting, mullet, flounders, plaice, pollack, and coalfish to be had from shore casting on rocks, piers, beaches, and promontories. Deep-sea angling for shark, skate, dogfish, pollack, ling, and conger is yours for the incredibly low cost of IR£8 ($9.60) to IR£16 ($19.20) per person for a six-hour day.

For help in planning a fishing holiday, contact the **Angler's Information Service,** Irish Tourist Board, Baggot Street Bridge, Dublin 2. You will no doubt want to send for one or all of the helpful angling guides published by the Tourist Board at a cost of IR£1 ($1.20) each, which includes postage. Entitled *Sea Angling in Ireland, Freshwater Coarse Angling,* and *Salmon and Sea Trout Fishing,* they point you to the best fishing locations, boat rentals, fishing competitions, bait stockists, and even provide angling maps. Available from: Irish Tourist Board Literature Dept., P.O. Box 1083, Dublin 8.

Other water sports include **surfing** (for full information, contact Brian V. Britton, Chairman, **Irish Surfing Association,** 266 Sutton Park, Sutton, Dublin 13—tel. 042-73170); **water skiing** (contact Sean Kennedy, President, **Irish Water Ski Association,** 7 Upper Beaumont Drive, Ballintemple, Co. Cork—tel. 021-292411); and **boardsailing** (contact Vincent Mulrooney, Secretary, **Irish Boardsailing Association,** 79 Mount Anvile, Dublin 14—tel. 01-726204). And, of course, there are all those lovely beaches for swimmers who don't demand summer temperatures much above 70. Personally, I find walking the sandy strands and deserted coves more fun than braving the waves—it is positively restorative to commune with sea and sun on long stretches when there's not another soul in sight. Seaside *resorts* can also be fun, from the lively, crowded Tramore in Co. Waterford to the quieter Kilkee in Co. Clare.

As for spectator sports, Irish **horseracing** has got to be close to the top of the list. A day at a race meet is very like a day at a country fair, with bookmakers vying for punters (bettors) while shouting out odds that change momentarily and punters shopping around to get their bets down when the odds are at their best. If your horse comes up a winner, you'll be paid from a big satchel at the bookmaker's stand at the odds in existence at the time you placed your bet (so timing can be important, and it *pays* to do a little shopping around). Irish horses, of course, are world famous, and it's a thrilling sight to see them round the last bend of a grass course against a backdrop of mountains or seashore or rolling green fields.

There are over 250 race meets each year, the Big Five being the **Irish Grand National** at Fairyhouse on Easter Monday, the **Leopardstown Steeplechase** in February, **Punchestown Steeplechases** in April, the **Irish Derby** in the Curragh at the end of June or beginning of July, and (probably the most popular of all with the Irish) the **Galway Races** in July. Tourist Board offices can furnish exact dates, and if you should happen on a meet somewhere else in the course of your travels, there goes another itinerary change (one of the happiest Irish times in my personal memory was an evening race meet at Clonmel in Co. Tipperary when *my* itinerary called for me to be en route to Killarney!)

Gaelic football is a century old in its present, organized form, but it must have roots way back in the days of fierce tribal rivalries when encroaching civilization undoubtedly shoved all that competitive spirit from battleground to football pitch. None of the fervor of either participants or spectators has been lost in the shift, however, and for sheer excitement nothing quite matches that of sharing the stands at Croke Park in Dublin with upwards of 90,000 fans roaring support for their county teams in the All Ireland finals.

Hurling is unique to Ireland, and I sometimes think it takes the Irish to figure out its two-level scoring. There are goals and points (depending on whether the little leather ball is hit past the goaltender and over the goal line or over the goaltender's head between the upright goalposts. And right there ends my personal knowledge of the game's scoring. My ignorance notwithstanding, I find a Sunday afternoon match irresistible—the skill and speed of agile athletes wielding hurleys (wooden sticks not unlike our hockey sticks) are wondrous to behold!

READER'S SUGGESTION: "Irish foot races are different from those in the U.S., although the fun and enjoyment are the same. You can find out about upcoming races in Ireland by looking in any current copy of the Irish *Runner* magazine, sold at any newsstand and most sports stores or you can look in the telephone directory for the local chapter of the BLE (Bond Luthcleas Na H Eireann), the runners' association of Ireland. Registration can be made through the mail or by telephone, and you pay a small registration fee at the race. This can be an excellent way for amateur runners to keep the waistline in shape and enjoy meeting Irish runners" (D. Imholte, Milpitas, Ca.).

2. Ireland After Dark

Because the Irish summer day is a long one, many of the "after dark" activities described in this section actually take place while the sky is still light, so you may take that heading to mean evening hours, dark or not dark. You can also extend almost any of your daytime activities into the evening (except, of course, where sightseeing attractions are not open then), playing a round of golf, fishing, etc., after dinner until 9:30 or 10 p.m.

What we'll do here, however, is talk about those things you can do only in the evening hours. With one notable exception. You'll notice that pubbing tops the list below, but that's not to suggest—or even *hint*—that this particular activity should be limited to after dinner. Perish the thought that you miss Irish pubs in the afternoon! Things are slower then, with Dublin pubs catering mostly to footsore tourists, housewives taking a break from shopping (often with a tot or two in tow), and a few freewheeling Dubliners whose lifestyle does not confine them to an office. The publican is more relaxed, and the crack flows smoothly, ebbing around you, taking you in, and playing hob with a big chunk of your afternoon. In rural pubs, this is when you're likely to encounter those craggy oldtimers just itching for you to pose a question or otherwise open up a dialogue so they can proffer their philosophy and local expertise without being bold. So my reason for discussing pubs right up front is that no matter what *else* you plan of an evening, a pub stop is the very best way to begin and/or end it.

Irish Pubs

A wise man once said that "a pub is the poor man's university." That it certainly is in Ireland! And it's an ongoing education as you encounter pubgoers from different walks of life and regions, each with an outlook on life, politics, religion, and any other subject as individual as his looks and a highly developed personal way with the words to expound on any of the above.

There's more to it than just that, however. Out in rural areas, the local pub is the social center around which everything revolves. What gossip and news isn't picked up at the creamery is dispensed as freely as a pint in the pub. Personal decisions which must be weighed and finally taken are a topic of general conversation in which everyone present lights up the problem with his own particular perspective. I once spent the better part of an afternoon in a small Co. Waterford pub absolutely fascinated by the dilemma posed by the fact that a wedding and a funeral were both scheduled for the following day—after about two hours of wrestling with the problem of which to attend, my fellow imbibers *still* hadn't reached a conclusion when I reluctantly picked myself up and moved on. But, I can tell you that there are aspects to that agonizing decision I'd never dreamed of before that afternoon!

Pubs are, by and large, also where you're most likely to find traditional music and song in the "singing pubs" that bring in leading musical groups or give performing space to the local lads aiming in that direction. It must be added that you're just as likely to find the familiar twang of Country and Western hits as the impassioned lyrics of Ireland's native music. Even if a pub is *not* known for music, however, the lyrical Irish spirit frequently bursts its bounds in the country's drinking places, especially towards the end of the evening, when a fiddle or tin whistle suddenly appears and song just sort of erupts—along with reams of poetry that can be from the classics or entirely spontaneous, depending on the clientele.

The pubs themselves range over a wide spectrum of decor. In cities like Dublin and Belfast you can have a jar in an ornate, Victorian-style drinking establishment; a glitzed up chrome-and-mirrored abyss of pseudo sophistication; an oldtime pub replete with time-worn wood, etched glass, and touches of brass; an elegant hotel bar that is considered a pub despite its fancy getup; or a bare bones drinking place which depends on its colorful "regulars" for whatever decor might exist. Out in the country, a pub might well be one half of a grocery or hardware store; a traditional style pub that's been dispensing drink and hospitality since the days of coaching inns; a cozy, wallpapered, and carpeted appendage to a guesthouse or small hotel; or a large, barnlike room with linoleum on the floor and telly behind the bar.

There are still pubs around with little blocked off private rooms called "snugs" and lovely old etched-glass partitions along the bar to afford a bit of privacy. In some pubs, the dart board stays busy; in others, there's almost always a card game in progress; some keep the fireplace glowing. Most will have a main bar and an attached "lounge," which once was the only place you'd ever catch a female in what was exclusively a man's domain. Nowadays, the lounges are filled with couples of all ages, as well as singles (even males who, for one reason or another, prefer not to elbow it at the bar).

Pub etiquette is a delicate and complex matter, and your awareness of some of its intricacies can spell the difference between a night of unsurpassed conviviality and one of cool isolation that leaves you wondering where all that famed Irish pub joviality is to be found. Novelist and radio newscaster David Hanly once laid down the one vital ground rule that should see you safely through those first few minutes when you enter what many Irishmen consider their own personal club. He was writing about Dublin pubs, but the rule applies across the board: "If you are to be accompanied on this jaunt, choose a partner who is loud neither in dress nor in voice. Dubliners abominate strange noises in their pubs, and high, demanding voices—no matter what the accent—carry deadly imperial echoes." Need I comment that his reference to "partner" was a typically Irish, backdoor, way of saying that *you* should tread softly?

So, keeping your voice and manners suitably moderated, you take your place at the bar, order your brew (*never* a fancy mixed cocktail unless you're in one of those city hotel bars mentioned above) and gradually—oh, so gradually—drift into conversation by way of a question. You're on your own as far as the question is concerned; it doesn't really matter so long as you project a real need for assistance that only a local can provide. Inquiries about the best place to eat, the best traditional music group around, etc., will do just fine and open up a general conversation likely to run the length of the bar, with everyone in attendance anxious to lend a hand to a visiting Yank.

The times and economic pressures are slowly eroding one facet of Irish drinking etiquette that was once inviolate, that of "buying the round." That ritual consisted of each member in a drinking group picking up the tab for a round of drinks for everybody. It was (still *is* in many places) as deadly a breach of manners to leave *after* you'd paid for your round as before your turn rolled around. Everybody drank until everybody had bought his round. Keep that in mind should you run into drinking companions, however casual your acquaintance, who insist that you'll not be permitted to pay for your first drink at all; the round-buying tradition requires that you hang in there until your check-paying turn arrives and stay the course.

The only exception to the above routine concerns women. In all my years of visiting Ireland, I've only insisted on buying my round once, and my male drinking companions were so uncomfortable with the whole thing that I've resolved to relax and go with local custom without the slightest twinge of guilt. As I said, however, what with the high price of the pint these days, round-buying is disappearing from the Irish pub scene, with everyone buying his own more often than not.

About prices: in some city bars you can pay as much as IR£1.20 ($1.44) for a pint of black, satiny smooth Guinness topped off with a creamy white head (that, in the well-pulled pint, lasts all the way to the bottom of that 20-ounce Imperial pint). By New York or Los Angeles standards, that's still a bargain, but many an Irishman nurses the one pint or orders by the glass (half-pint) to stretch things out through most of the evening for no other reason than the state of his purse. In suburban and rural pubs, you'll pay anywhere from IR£1.17 ($1.40) up. A "drop" of whiskey will run a little less than a pint, and you should know that an Irish "drop" is a big one. Drinks in the lounge rather than at the bar generally cost around 2p more.

Pubs are open from 10 a.m. to 11 p.m. in the Republic during the winter, until 11:30 p.m. in summer months. Sundays, it's 12:30 to 2 p.m. and 4 to 10 p.m. year round. You're out of luck if you develop a terrible thirst in Cork or Dublin on a weekday between 2:30 and 3:30 p.m.—pubs are closed up tight in observance of what is uniformly known as the "Holy Hour," which also means you shouldn't plan on a late pub lunch in those two cities.

One last word to the ladies: you'll be very welcome in Irish pubs, whether you're on your own, one of a bunch of females, or with a male escort. You may, however, be more comfortable in the lounge than at the bar (that varies from pub to pub, so try to size the place up when you first come in). Even being a nondrinker is no reason for missing out on pub sociability: all Irish pub stock soft drinks (try the light, fizzy white lemonade) and nobody is going to look askance if you stick to those.

Musical Nights

Since the pre-Christian days when they revered their bards, the Irish have celebrated, mourned, exalted, damned, and lamented everything in their lives through music. Until the 1690s and Cromwell, songs and ballads were composed entirely in Irish; after that, English was the language meant to help erase any remaining traces of nationalism. Even the penal laws were unable to do that, however, for the wily Irish praised their country under the guise of singing about their sweethearts: "Roisin Dubh," "Kathleen Huallachain," and "Grainne Uail" speak of loved ones, but every Irishman knew they really were odes to Ireland herself. Those traditional songs and airs are still played frequently today, and if you listen closely to modern Irish ballads, you'll notice that a good few still concern themselves with celebrating, mourning, exalting, etc., etc., some facet of Ireland or Irish life.

The tones that spring from the harp, uilleann (elbow) pipes (played sitting down and developed to get around English law, which forbad the playing of any instrument while standing to prevent the pipes from playing troops into battle), the bodhran (a sort of drum made of goatskin stretched tightly over a round wooden frame), the tin whistle, fiddle, and accordion mix in a unique harmony that can break your heart or send your spirits (and your feet!) soaring. We've heard them on this side of the Atlantic in recent years most often from groups such as the Chieftains, and despite complaints to the contrary by American tourists in the past, they're to be found almost everywhere in Ireland, itself.

The trick, of course, is to know where to look for them. Actually, it isn't much of a trick at all, for there's a central organization whose sole purpose is the promotion of traditional music, song and dance. **Comhaltas Ceoltoiri Eireann** (universally known as "coalthus") is based in the Dublin suburb on Monkstown, but has branches in every county. It organizes traditional entertainment in hotels, pubs, and at local branch meetings, all of which are open to the public, and you'll be very welcome as a visiting American.

At the Monkstown headquarters, there are traditional music sessions on weekends all year round, with admission a paltry IR£1.50 ($1.80). During summer months, they organize other events, like the **Fonntrai** (a folk theater show featuring traditional music and dance), a **ceili** ("kay-lee," traditional set dancing as done in Irish homes in years gone by), and the **cois teallaigh** (musicians, singers, and dancers talk about and demonstrate their various arts). Admissions range from IR£1.50 ($1.80) to IR£3.50 ($4.20), and scheduled nights vary. You can usually enjoy a pre-show dinner of traditional, homecooked recipes, in their traditional kitchen/restaurant by calling 01-800295 to book. Prices are moderate to cheap.

To learn what's on during your visit, both in Monkstown and around the country, contact: Comhaltas Ceoltoiri Eireann, Belgrave Square, Monkstown Co., Dublin (tel. 01-800195).

During the last weekend in August, look for the **All-Ireland Fleadh** ("flah"). It's a three-day traditional music and song festival held each year in a different town, and music lovers from around the world congregate in the pubs, hotels, private houses, and even in the streets to play, sing, and just listen to this music in a completely informal setting. A word of warning: accommodations are generally booked for miles around once the venue is announced, so be prepared to book ahead, camp out, or stay up all night (not unheard of, I might add).

The **Fleadh Nua,** always held in Ennis, Co. Clare, on the last weekend in May, is another showcase for the best in traditional music. The caution mentioned above applies here as well.

No visit to the west of Ireland will be complete without taking in a performance of **Siamsa** ("sheemsa"), the national folk theater of Ireland. It is based in Tralee, but performs regularly during summer months in Killarney and occasionally in other towns. Talented performers demonstrate such traditional Irish folk ways as thrashing and tatching the roof through music and dance. Information on performance schedules and the low admission charges (around IR£4—$4.80) is available at most Tourist Offices (the Killarney office always has Siamsa information).

Another place to look for traditional Irish entertainment is **Seoda** ("shoda"), a dramatic and musical evening held in Galway's Gaelic theater, **Taibhdhearc** ("thive-yark"), on selected evenings during the summer.

Banquets and Cabarets

An absolute standout among nighttime activities is any one of the medieval banquets held in **Bunratty** and **Knappogue** castles in Co. Clare and **Dunguaire** castle in Co. Galway. Each begins with a meal that harks back to the days when these were residences as well as fortifications, and each ends with superb entertainment that includes music, dance, song, and a bit of pageantry. Prices (about $30) are well above "budget," but this is the *one* Big Splurge I implore you not to miss.

For a different sort of musical evening that combines traditional and modern music, song, dance and "stage Irish" comedy, look for the popular cabaret shows in leading city hotels. They're a bit sophisticated, a bit hokey, and loads of fun. Many include a pre-show dinner if you wish, although you can come usually along for the show alone if you prefer. A mark of the quality of these shows is the smattering of Irish you'll see in the audience (along with busloads of visiting tourists like ourselves). Prices are about $20 for the dinner/show combination, $12 for just the show.

Theater

Think of Ireland and one of your first thoughts is of the theater. Think of Irish theater, and you immediately think of Dublin's **Abbey Theater.** It should be high on every visitor's "don't miss" list, and prices are so affordable even those of us who keep a tight rein on the budget can work in at least one performance. Admission at the better-known theaters will run from IR£5 ($6) to Ir£7 ($8.40), and many smaller theaters charge even less.

Don't make the mistake of thinking that theater is to be found *only* in Dublin, however. There are good productions all around the country, some on a regular basis (like Cork's **Opera House**), others on a periodic basis. Look in local newspapers for productions, then go along, and for a pittance enjoy a night of good theater and—many times, though not always—a chat in the lobby after the show with the cast.

One of the best things to happen to Irish theater, and one that can reduce your costs even more, is the **Theatre-Go-Round** pass that discounts tickets to some eighteen theaters throughout Ireland by 10%. For certain Monday Night specials, the savings can be as high as 25%. The pass is available through Tourist Offices.

3. Tracing your Irish Roots

If you're one of the more than forty million Americans whose forebears were Irish, it's a good bet you'll want to look into your family tree while in Ireland. What with some fourteen of our presidents claiming Irish ancestry, our White House having been designed by Irishman James Hoban, and one of our states (Pennsylvania) bearing the name of a Corkman (William Penn), you're in very good company, indeed.

Tracking down your Irish roots may not prove to be such a simple matter. More than 1000 basic family names were established in Ireland between the 12th and 19th centuries, with each of *those* having several variations. Not to be discouraged, however: there are descendants of families described in a 1201 account of Cathal O'Conor's inauguration as King of Connaught *still living on the same lands as their ancestors!*

To find your particular branch of a particular family, you'll want to know all you possibly can about your family history before you leave home. Search any and all records (letters, Bibles, relatives' memories, etc.) for the mention of specific townlands, villages, or counties from which your folks went out to America. The more you know about what they did, who they married, when they left home, and the like, the easier your job will be.

In Dublin, present yourself and your records to the **General Register Office of Births, Marriages, and Deaths** at 8/11 Lombard St. East, Dublin 2 (tel. 01-711000). Charges range from a low IR£2.50 ($3) for a Search Certificate (IR£1.50—$1.80—for each extra copy) when you go through the records yourself for a five-year period in search of an individual. For six hours of unrestricted research, the charge is IR£11 ($13.20).

For genealogical and land tenure records dating as far back as the 17th century, check with the **Public Record Office;** land transactions back to 1708 are recorded with the **Registry of Deeds,** in Henrietta St.; there is a wealth of all manner of family information at the **Genealogical Office** in Dublin Castle; and the **National Library** in Kildare St. holds journals and directories relating to Irish families.

Once you have basic data, it's off to the locality of your ancestors, where **parochial registers** often hold exactly what you're looking for and a talk with the parish priest may well send you off to shake the hand of a distant cousin or two still living in the neighborhood.

For Northern Ireland roots, consult the **Public Record Office of Northern Ireland,** 66 Balmoral Ave., Belfast and the **Presbyterian Historical Society,** Church House, Fisherwick Place, Belfast.

Of course, the fastest way to get the search done is to join an Aer Lingus Irish Heritage Holiday tour (see Chapter II). They'll do the groundwork and furnish a list of local historians who can many times fill in the gaps.

4. Meet the Irish

Of course, you'll be meeting the Irish from the moment you touch foot on Irish soil. But, I want to tell you about a special **Meet the Irish Program** that the Tourist Board runs from April through September each year that puts you in touch with those Irish who have interests similar to yours, be they professional, occupational, or cultural. It's a great way, for instance, for American farmers to meet Irish farmers and compare notes.

To set this up before you leave home, write for the Meet the Irish Program form to: Irish Tourist Board, Baggot Street Bridge, Dublin 2, then return it with all pertinent information filled in—at least a month before your departure—to that same address. You'll hear from the Tourist Board or the hosts they've selected to spend an afternoon, dinner, or whatever with you during your visit.

All is not lost, however, if you arrive without those prior arrangements: stop into any Tourist Board office around the country and they'll most likely be able to arrange much the same, even on short notice.

Chapter IV

DUBLIN AND THE EASTERN REGION

1. Introduction to Counties Dublin, Wicklow, Louth, Kildare, and Meath
2. Dublin
3. Around the Eastern Region

THE CITY OF DUBLIN IS, OF COURSE, the centerpiece of Ireland's Eastern Region. And a sparkling centerpiece it is, strung out along the banks of the River Liffey with a lively mix of history nudging modernism, Georgian architecture nestling alongside the glass and steel of today, and a population happily convinced their city is not only the center of *Ireland*, but the universe as well (and just as happily skipping off to "the country" at the merest hint of an excuse!).

1. Introduction to Counties Dublin, Wicklow, Louth, Kildare, and Meath

While the city itself could keep you busy and thoroughly entertained for as long as your visit lasts, outside its boundaries the rest of the region is rich with attractions that will draw you like a magnet. The *county* of Dublin is blessed with a coastline sometimes soft and gentle, sometimes wild and rugged—the majestic curve of Dublin Bay from Howth on its rocky perch in the north to Dalky and its island at the crescent's southern tip, scenic fishing villages and pleasure-ridden seashore resorts north and south of the Bay all beckon invitingly to the visitor. Then there are the mountains that form a verdant, dramatic backdrop for bustling city, sleepy villages, and that enchanting seascape.

Wicklow glows with the greens and blues of a landscape often dubbed the "Garden of Ireland." Kildare's flat fields and bogs have seen historic figures come and go and today hold stables which have bred racehorses of international fame and the world-famous Curragh racecourse where modern-day sports-world history is written by homegrown champions of the sport. Counties Louth and Meath together hold enough historic sites to fill an entire book on their own—one the setting for Tara's home of Irish royalty, the other the scene of one of Cromwell's most devastating assault on the Irish people.

In the sections that follow, we'll take an in-depth look at Dublin and the Eastern Region, and I can only add a word of warning: you're likely to be so beguiled by this part of Ireland that you may forget there's a mother lode of treasures just as beguiling beyond its borders—it's easy to loiter too long around here, so read on before you even begin to draft an itinerary.

2. Dublin

Baile Atha Cliath ("the town of the ford of the hurdles") is its ancient Irish name (that ford was probably where the Father Matthew Bridge long ago replaced a frail wicker bridge—the "hurdles"—that once spanned the river); Norsemen called it *Dubh-Linn* ("black pool") when they founded the present city on the banks of the Liffey in 837; and a modern writer has called it "the most instantly talkative city in Europe."

By any name, Dublin is one of Europe's loveliest capital cities, with proud old Georgian buildings, elegantly groomed squares of greenery (Fitzwilliam, Parnell, Merrion, etc.), and acres of shaded leisure space (St. Stephen's Green and the Phoenix Park). Its heart beats to the rhythm of the Liffey, and its horizons extend to craggy Howth Head to the north, the softly curving shores of Dublin Bay to the east, and the slopes of the Dublin Mountains to the south. This sheltered setting along a natural transportation route has been the focal point of a long, rich, and complex history that has left its mark on the face of its landscape as well as its people.

Little remains nowadays of medieval Dublin, but it's easy to trace its outlines and see how the modern city has grown around it. Just stand on O'Connell Bridge looking west up the river. On the south bank of the Liffey, you'll see Christ Church Cathedral's square tower—that was almost the exact center of the original city. To the east, Grattan Bridge stands near the "black pool" that marked its eastern boundary. Little Ship Street follows the course of the River Poddle (now underground), once a city boundary on the south bank of the river, and the quays along the north bank marked another outpost of the ancient city.

ORIENTATION: Today, as at its birth, Dublin is delineated by the brown waters of the **Liffey,** which flows from west to east, passing beneath some ten bridges en route. **O'Connell Bridge** is probably the most important for you and me, since it connects those sections of the mile-long city center "north of the Liffey" (to Parnell Square at the northern end of O'Connell Street) and "south of the Liffey" (to St. Stephen's Green at Grafton Street's southern end). Keep that firmly in mind, since Dubliners locate *everything* by its relation to the river—"north of" and "south of" are a part of the city's vocabulary you'll soon adopt as part of your own.

The main thoroughfare north of the river is **O'Connell Street,** an extension of the bridge. That's where you'll find the historic **General Post Office,** statues of Parnell, Father Matthew, and (who else!) Daniel O'Connell. At the base of his statue, look for the heroic "Victories," representing Fidelity, Eloquence, Courage, and Patriotism. The **Dublin Tourism Visitor Center** is also on O'Connell Street, along with several good hotels, shopping in one large department store and a jumble of smaller establishments, quick food eateries and a number of important office buildings.

To the south of O'Connell Bridge, **Westmoreland Street** extends for only one block to the wide, statue-filled intersection known as **College Green,** which sprawls before the entrance to Trinity College. College Green, in turn, funnels into Dublin's most fashionable shopping thoroughfare, **Grafton Street,** so narrow that it is at times blocked off for pedestrian traffic only. If

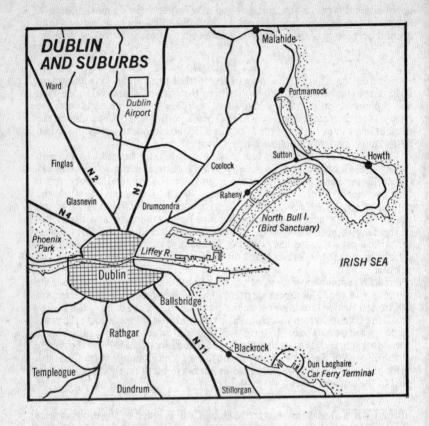

DUBLIN AND SUBURBS

Ward

Dublin Airport

Malahide

Portmarnock

Finglas

N 2

Coolock

Sutton

Howth

N 1

Raheny

Glasnevin

N 4

Drumcondra

North Bull I. (Bird Sanctuary)

Phoenix Park

Liffey R.

IRISH SEA

Dublin

Ballsbridge

Rathgar

N 11

Blackrock

Dun Laoghaire Car Ferry Terminal

Templeogue

Dundrum

Stillorgan

you've walked that city-center mile, by the time you reach the end of Grafton, you'll sigh with gratitude for the beautifully landscaped, restful refuge of **St. Stephen's Green.**

USEFUL INFORMATION: You'll find the **Dublin Tourism Visitor Center and Room Reservation Service** at 14 Upper O'Connell St. (tel. 01-747733), just across from the General Post Office. It's open Monday through Friday from late September to mid-March, 9:15 a.m. to 5:15 p.m.; Monday through Saturday from mid-March to late May, 9 a.m. to 5 p.m.; and Monday through Saturday from late May to late September, 8:30 a.m. to 6 p.m.; closed New Year's Day, St. Patrick's Day, Easter Monday, October Public Holiday, and St. Stephen's Day (December 26). . . . National headquarters for all bus and rail transportation (including sightseeing tours) is the **CIE** office at 59 Upper O'Connell St. For all bus and rail information, call the **CIE Information Bureau** (01-787777) 9 a.m. to 9 p.m. . . . The **Central Bus Station** (Busaras) is in Store St., north of the Liffey (tel. 01-742941). . . . The three major **CIE railway stations** are Connolly Station (Amiens St. near Busaras), Heuston Station near the Guinness Brewery on St. John's Road, and Pearse Station on Westland Row (serves suburban rail lines). CIE trains meet all ferries arriving at Dun Laoghaire ("Dun Leary") and the seven-mile ride into Dublin is included in the boat fare. . . . **Taxis** operate from ranks at all bus and rail stations, in the center of O'Connell Street, in College Green, at St. Stephen's Green, and at several leading hotels (they're listed in the telephone directory under "Taxi-cab ranks"). You can telephone 761111, 772222, 766666, or 507777 for a taxi, but an extra service charge will be added to the fare. Minimum fare is IR£1.45 ($1.74) for the first mile, 10p (12¢) for each additional one-seventh of a mile or 1.3 minutes of waiting time. All taxis are metered, with a charge of 40p (48¢) for each additional passenger and each piece of luggage and 60p (72¢) on bank holidays and between 8 p.m. and 8 a.m. . . . The **General Post Office** is on O'Connell Street (across from the Dublin Tourist Center) and is open from 8 a.m. to 11 p.m. weekdays (to 7 p.m. only for mailing or receiving parcels, from 9 a.m. on Sundays and Bank Holidays). General Delivery mail can be picked up at the **Post Restante** desk until 8 p.m. Telegraph service is available at the GPO, as well as coin telephones. . . . Local telephone calls from coin phones cost 10p (12¢). For emergency calls, dial 999. . . . Shopping hours are 9 a.m. to 5:30 p.m., Monday to Saturday, with major shopping areas on Grafton Street, Henry Street, O'Connell Street, and South Great Georges Street. . . . The telephone prefix for Dublin is 01.

Local Buses and Trains

There's excellent bus service to all parts of Dublin and outlying suburbs, making it easy to search out accommodations beyond the city center, where prices are considerably lower. Any bus marked **An Lar** (it means "the center") will be headed for the city center. Buses run from 7 a.m. (10 a.m. on Sundays) to 11:30 p.m., and that's 11:30 p.m. sharp to catch the last bus leaving the city center—if you're planning a late night in the city, better plan on taking a taxi to any outlying accommodation. Most buses depart from O'Connell Bridge, but you can check on your particular bus line by calling the CIE Information Bureau (01-787777) from 9 a.m. to 9 p.m. or by picking up a copy of the Dublin District Bus and Rail Timetable from any CIE office or almost any newsstand. Fares are graduated according to distance, with children under 16 traveling for half-fare.

Bus discounts are offered during certain hours on certain lines, and one of the most useful is the **shopping fare** offered between 10 a.m. and 4:30 p.m. within center-city boundaries. Students can purchase discount tickets on a weekly basis from the Tourist Office at 14 Upper O'Connell St. by showing their I.D.

New in 1984 is the **electric train suburban service** that runs from Howth to Bray, with stops at some 25 stations en route. Operated by Dublin Area Rapid Transit (DART), the service is fast, silent, and convenient, since departures will be every five minutes during peak hours, every fifteen minutes other times. Service will begin at 7 a.m. and end at midnight, making it possible to stay in your favorite city pub until last call and still make the last train to a suburban accommodation (a great boon for budgeteers!). Both the frequency and the speed now make it feasible to make your base at a resort like Bray or Dalkey and have easy access to all city attractions—a terrific, as well as money-saving, idea, since you'll be able to enjoy the seashore and the city equally. Some nineteen feeder bus lines link up with the rail system, which stops at the following stations: Howth, Sutton, Bayside, Howth Junction, Kilbarrack, Raheny, Harmonstown, Killester, Connolly Station, Tara Street Station, Pearse Station, Landsdowne Roade, Sandymount, Sydney Parade,

Booterstown, Blackrock, Monkstown, Salthill, Dun Laoghaire, Sandycove, Glengeary, Dalkey, Killiney, Shankill, and Bray. Timetables can be obtained at most of these stations.

If You're Driving

A word about driving in Dublin: Don't! Public transportation is so efficient and so frequent, traffic can be so heavy (especially in early morning and late afternoon hours) and Dublin's one-way streets can be so confusing that I urge you to drive directly to your accommodation, park the car, and leave it there until you're headed out of town! Parking can also present a real problem, since most spaces are metered for only two hours. All that is not to say, however, that it's impossible to drive around the city—it's just that even if you have to spring for a taxi occasionally (and I, for one, would opt for at least one taxi ride just for the conversation—Dublin taxi drivers are the most knowledgeable and entertaining in the world), you'll come out better and save both time and nerves if you leave the driving to someone else. Actually, once you reach the city center, most places are going to be within easy walking distance—and there's no better walking city than Dublin.

Dublin Airport

Just seven miles north of the city center, Dublin Airport is in Collinstown. There's an ample supple of free luggage carts, so you won't need a porter (no tipping!). Should you land without a place to lay your weary head, help is at hand at the **Tourist Information Desk** located in the **Arrival Terminal**. It's open every day from 9 a.m. to 6 p.m. during winter months, from 8:30 a.m. to 10:30 p.m. during the summer.

On the mezzanine, there's an inexpensive **cafeteria** for hot or cold snacks, as well as a **Grill Bar** for more substantial fare (a light meal for about IR£4—$4.80; a four-course dinner for under IR£8—$9.60). You'll also find bars and snackbars in both the Arrival and Departure halls. The **Bank of Ireland** is on hand in both halls to change your money, closed only on Christmas Day. For those flying on to Britain or the continent, there's a duty-free shop selling liquor, cigarettes, and perfume; those headed to North America will be given a 45-minute shopping stopover at Shannon Airport (see Chapter I) to browse through the well-stocked duty-free shop there. There's also an Aer Lingus booking office in the airport.

Airport Bus fares into the Central Bus Station will run IR£2.50 ($3) for adults, half that for children. The regular Dublin **city bus no. 41A** (which runs much less frequently than the Airport Bus) will take you into Lower Abbey Street for about 50p (60¢); check with the Tourist Office desk or **Airport Information Desk** for a timetable. A **taxi** into town will run about IR£8 ($9.60).

ACCOMMODATIONS: You'll probably pay your highest accommodation rate in Dublin, which is not as intimidating as it may sound, for "highest" can still keep you within the daily budget limit of this book. However, you should know in advance that as distance from Dublin increases, prices decrease.

Accommodations in Dublin and its immediate environs are so numerous it's possible to stay in almost any section you like and in almost any price range you prefer (keeping in mind that the bottom range here is likely to be higher than elsewhere). There are good hostels, bed-and-breakfast homes, guesthouses, self-catering flats, small, intimate hotels, and large, luxury hotels. No problems, then, right? Not exactly. The greatest problem is that price range and

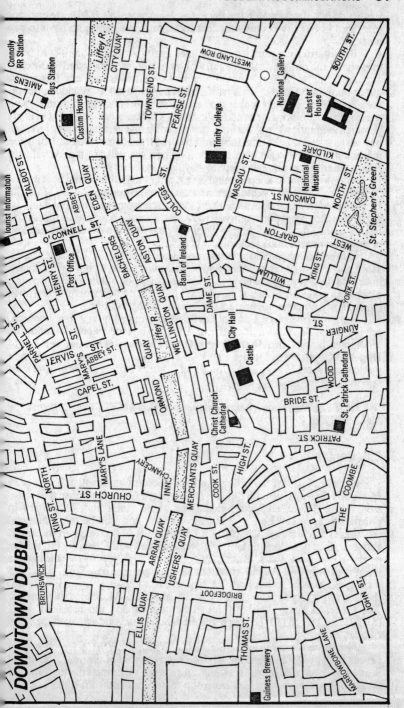

DOWNTOWN DUBLIN

locality do not *always* match up. For example, inexpensive B&Bs are not concentrated in the city center—for that location, you're going to have to pay more.

The alternative—and it is sometimes a very attractive one—is to book into one of the outlying suburbs (all with excellent transportation to the city) and enjoy the two different environments as you travel back and forth. You might book into Howth, Dalkey, Killiney, or Bray (in Co. Wicklow, but on the new rail service that makes it an easy commute) and spend mornings on the beach, afternoons or evenings in town. On the other hand, if (as is my personal inclination) you're a little lazy about all that getting about or want to be able to stay out later than those last bus and train departures with only the minimum taxi fare to get back to your lodgings, you will find it good value to skimp other places and pay more to stay right in the city.

Another thing to keep in mind is that prices in Dublin often soar during holidays and special events such as Easter, the Spring Show in May, the Horse Show in August, All-Ireland Finals in September, and international rugby matches. Best plan your visit to Dublin around those events unless you have a special interest in them—if you do plan to come during one of these periods, be sure to book well in advance.

In the recommendations below, you'll find a smattering of all the accommodation categories mentioned above, including some higher-priced guest-houses in the city proper who give readers of this book a substantial discount, along with one "Big Splurge" hotel that I have found well worth the extravagance. For your convenience, I have listed them by location.

Dublin is one place I do not advocate arriving without a firm booking, but if you should arrive in that state and not find a place among the following recommendations, turn to the **Tourist Office Central Reservation Service**, 14 Upper O'Connell St., Dublin 1 (tel. 01-747733), or arm yourself with their publication *Irish Homes in the Town and Country and on the Farm* and start telephoning around.

NOTE: Prices shown below are those in effect in 1985—expect them to be higher in 1986.

City Center

Hostels: North of the Liffey, An Oige operates an excellent **hostel** at 39 Mountjoy Sq. S., Dublin 1 (tel. 01-745734), in a Georgian house that dates from 1798. There are accommodations for 22 men and 40 women in dormitory rooms. There's a common room and completely equipped communal kitchen (see Chapter I for what you will be expected to bring). City bus lines run along nearby O'Connell Street, and Connolly rail station is just 10 minutes away. Hours are 5 p.m. to 11:30 p.m., but during the months of July and August, you may deposit luggage here from noon to 5 p.m. It is essential to book ahead, and you must claim your bed by 9 p.m. the first night of your stay. Book directly with Mrs. M. Sheridan, Warden. The hostel is open April 1 through September 30, and rates are IR£1 ($1.20) to IR£3.10 ($3.72) per night, depending on your age and when you come.

Just three blocks from St. Stephen's Green, the **YWCA Hostel** is at 64 Lower Baggot St., Dublin (tel. 01-766273). For most of the year, the hostel is open only to college students, but tourists are welcomed during July and August. Rooms are very like those of a motel (hot and cold water in each) and accommodate either two or three, for a total of 22. The door is locked at midnight, but you'll be given a key if you must be out later, although they prefer all guests to observe the closing hour. City buses nos. 4 and 10 provide convenient transportation. Bed-and-breakfast rates are IR£6 ($7.20).

A little farther out, a popular privately run hostel is **The Young Traveller,** St. Mary's Pl., Dublin 7 (tel. 01-305000). There are 12 four-bedded rooms and one two-bedded room, each with its own shower. Amenities include an attractive lounge, TV lounge, launderette, and a self-service restaurant. Rates for bed-and-breakfast are IR£7.50 ($9).

Guesthouses: The two guesthouses listed here are both north of the Liffey on a street of Georgian mansions that were once quite elegant, and both have brought enthusiastic letters from readers who have stayed there. I must add that the neighborhood is not what it once was, but is safe enough and just a short walk from buses on O'Connell Street. At the end of this section, you will find center-city guesthouses in choice locations which discount their higher rates for our readers.

Harvey's, 11 Upper Gardiner St., Dublin 1 (tel. 01-748384), is one of those four-storied Georgian homes, built in 1785. Mr. and Mrs. Harvey are pleasant and very helpful to guests, and their guesthouse is especially popular with young Americans. There are some interesting antiques mixed in with comfortable modern furnishings, and central heating has been installed. Drivers have the use of a private car park at no extra cost. Bed-and-breakfast rates are IR£10 ($12) single, IR£17 ($20.40) double.

Mr. and Mrs. Smyth, your hosts at **Stella Maris,** 13 Upper Gardiner St., Dublin 1 (tel. 01-740835), always extend a warm welcome to Americans, as do their four charming children, ranging in age from six to fourteen. Theirs is another of those large Georgian houses with high ceilings and an interesting mixture of old and new furnishings. You'll have your breakfast in a dining room dominated by an impressive antique sideboard and beneath red deer antlers with a six-foot span. Bedtime cups of tea and homemade cookies make a nice ending to the day here. Rates for bed-and-breakfast are IR£12 ($14.40) single, IR£20 ($24) double or twin. One-third reduction for children.

Hotels: I know budgeteers don't usually head for hotels, but two of Dublin's older hotels are both so centrally located, with so much character and so relatively inexpensive that I think you should know about them. While they're definitely not in the budget range, neither are they "Big Splurges," and their convenience and comfort make them well worth breaking over budget bounds.

The **Clarence Hotel,** Wellington Quay, Dublin 2 (tel. 01-776178), has for many years been a favorite with the Irish when they come to Dublin for business or pleasure, and it combines Grade A facilities with moderate prices, a comfortable and homey atmosphere, and a friendly staff. Its central location on the south bank of the Liffey puts you within walking distance of the entire center city, and the lounge (a gathering place for Dubliners as well as guests) is a haven of low-key conviviality when the day is done. The Grill Room (also favored by businesspeople, especially at lunch) serves delicious, inexpensive meals, while its pretty dining room is reputed to serve the best steaks in the city. Rooms are attractive and comfortable, and if you ask for one on the river side, you'll have a great view of port activity along the Liffey (others look down on city streets and the view can be just as fascinating). Rates run from IR£21 ($25.20) to IR£23 ($27.60) for singles, IR£33 ($39.60) to IR£37 ($44.40) for doubles, plus a 15% service charge. There are attractive weekend and off-season specials.

Across the river on the Liffey's north bank, **Wynn's Hotel**, 35/39 Lower Abbey St., Dublin 1 (tel. 01-745131), has the same ownership as the Clarence, and is just as well loved by the Irish. In fact, my first afternoon tea at Wynn's was in the company of Dublin housewives taking a break from shopping, Irish families obviously in from the country, and a fair smattering of priests and nuns, all happily at home in the lounge. There was a friendly, relaxed air about the place that invited conversation, and my fellow tourists who had also discovered this charming place were nearly all chatting away with someone Irish. It's that kind of hotel, and later that evening the teak and mahogany bar in the lounge bar was lined with young couples, theatergoers, and contented guests. Meals in the ultra-modern Grill Room are positively bargain priced. Rooms are nicely furnished and attractively decorated, with rates the same as those at the Clarence. Here also there are special rates during off-season and on weekends.

Ballsbridge

Just a few blocks south of the city center, Ballsbridge is a residential neighborhood that holds several luxury hotels, the American Embassy, and rows of well-tended old homes. It is in this area that you'll find some of the nicest guesthouses that offer you, our readers, substantial discounts on rates. You will also find here the very good guesthouse listed below.

Guesthouse: In the vicinity of the American Embassy, **Montrose House,** 16 Pembroke Park, Dublin 4 (tel. 01-684286), is just off Herbert Park. It's a two-story red-brick house fronted by a flower garden, furnished with antiques and lots of mahogany pieces, and presided over by Mrs. Catherine Ryan. The pretty, white-walled dining room looks out onto the garden through a bay window. All eight rooms are attractively done up and comfortable, and there's central heating. Depending on season, bed-and-breakfast rates are IR£11.50 ($13.80) to IR£13.50 ($16.20) per person. Take bus no. 10, 46A, or 64A to the Herbert Park stop.

Sandymount

Sandymount is right on Dublin Bay, just a little to the east of Ballsbridge.

YWCA: Just two blocks from the sea, the **YWCA Radcliff Hall,** St. John's Road, Sandymount, Dublin 4 (tel. 01-694521), used to be a convent, and its renovation has retained the chapel as well as the well-tended 2½ acres of flower gardens, lawn, and fruit trees. There are some 40 high-ceilinged rooms in the main building which once housed nuns, and 20 more recently built chalets in the rear, all of which have twin beds and private baths. While the decor is simple, the rooms are attractive and comfortable. The light and airy modern dining room opens onto a patio, where meals are sometimes served in summer. There's a laundry room with irons, a TV and recreation room, and a library for guests' use. So you shouldn't feel too pampered in a setting of such beauty and comfort, you're required to make your bed in the morning. As you can imagine, Radcliff Hall is very popular with tourists. Also, this is the site of many conferences and it caters mainly to students during winter months, which simply means that advance booking (with a IR£8, $9.60, deposit) is an absolute must, especially if you'd like a room with a private bath. Bed-and-breakfast rates of IR£10 ($12) per person for a twin-bedded chalet with bath and IR£8 ($9.60) per person for a single or double room in the main house without bath (add 10% to all rates) make this one of Dublin's best bargains. If you're staying an entire week, there's a half-board (breakfast and dinner) rate of IR£80 ($96) per person. City bus no. 3 passes the door, and you can also reach it on buses nos. 52, 6, 7A, 8, and 18.

Bed-and-Breakfast: Dolores and Tony Murphy are the delightful hosts at 14 Castle Park (off Guilford Park), Sandymount, Dublin 4 (tel. 01-698413). Their modern, semi-detached house is brightly decorated and neat as a pin, and guests are welcome to sit in the sun in the small garden out back. There are three rooms with built-in wardrobes and sinks. You'll meet at least one or two of the Murphy offspring (two boys and two girls), who often help serve meals, and the entire family seems dedicated to making guests feel at home. Dolores will be glad to prepare the evening meal if you give her sufficient advance notice. Rates for bed-and-breakfast are IR£8.50 ($10.20) per person, and they're open May through September. City bus nos. 2 or 3 will get you to the city center in ten minutes.

Donnybrook

Hostel: One of An Oige's better hostels is **Morehampton House,** 78 Morehampton Rd., Donnybrook, Dublin 4 (tel. 01-680325). There are dormitory accommodations for 44 men and 38 women, a completely equipped communal kitchen, and common room. Hours are 5 p.m. to midnight, but during July and August, you can deposit luggage from noon until 5 p.m. Rates range from IR£1 ($1.20) to IR£3.10 ($3.72) per person, depending on your age and the season. See Chapter I for the few items you'll be expected to furnish. City bus no. 10 will get you to and from the city center; no. 46A from Dun Laoghaire.

Rathgar

To the southwest of the city, Rathgar is a residential section with exceptionally good bus transportation into the city center, about a ten-minute ride.

Guesthouse: Phyllis McGhee, a long-time nurse, presides over **St. Aidan's Guest House,** 32 Brighton Rd., Rathgar, Dublin 6 (tel. 01-970559), and her natural interest in people has made this a very popular place with many of our readers. Located on a tree-lined street, St. Aidan's is a large Victorian house that Phyllis has modernized and decorated in good taste. The lovely drawing room, complete with TV, has a tea and coffee trolly for the use of guests at any time of the day or night. The 12 bedrooms are done up in Laura Ashley decorator fabrics, have sinks, and are centrally heated. Three have TV, and there's a portable TV you can borrow for a short time. One is a large double bedsitter with a bay window, and four are singles. Amenities include laundry and ironing facilities, hair dryers, a playroom for small children, and a covered car park. Dinners are said to be of gourmet quality. Bed-and-breakfast rates are IR£12.50 ($15) to IR£20 ($24), for doubles, depending on season. Discount for children is 20%. Take bus nos. 15A, 15B, 15C or 47.

Dun Laoghaire

This is where car ferries arrive and depart for Great Britain, and with the new train service, as well as numerous bus lines, it offers great value as a Dublin area base.

Bed-and-Breakfast: Annesgrove, 28 Rosmeen Gardens, Dun Laoghaire, Co. Dublin (tel. 01-809801), is a pretty, two-story home in a cul-de-sac close to train and bus transportation, and a short walk from the car ferry. Mrs. Anne D'alton is the gracious hostess here, and she is happy to provide an early breakfast for those with an early morning departure. There are three nicely appointed bedrooms, and the evening meal is available if you give sufficient notice. For bed-and-breakfast, rates are IR£9.50 ($11.40); dinner is IR£10.50 ($12.60); and there's a 20% reduction for children. Open March to October. Take bus 7, 7A, or 8.

In central Dun Laoghaire, Mrs. Doris Pittman presides over **Scarsdale,** 4 Tivoli Rd., Dun Laoghaire, Co. Dublin (tel. 01-806258). The modern house is nicely decorated and has three rooms, all with clock radios as well as sinks. Meals are served in a pleasant dining room looking out onto the garden, where Mrs. Pittman grows both flowers and vegetables. She'll furnish the evening meal with adequate notice, and gives an early breakfast for ferry passengers. Rates are IR£8.50 ($10.20) for bed-and-breakfast, IR£6.50 ($7.80) for dinner, and there's a 20% reduction for children.

Dalkey

Another scenic seaside spot, Dalkey is seven miles outside town, but with easy bus and train access to the inner city.

Bed-and-Breakfast: Rockview, Coliemore Road, Dalkey, Co. Dublin (tel. 01-858205), is in a quiet residential section. The car ferry at Dun Laoghaire is just two miles away. Mrs. Seaver has four bedrooms. all with sinks. She doesn't serve evening meals, but does provide a nice high tea at IR£6.50 ($7.80). Bed-and-breakfast rates are IR£8.50 ($10.20) per person, with a 25% reduction for children. Bus no. 8 and the train run into town.

Hotel: At rates just slightly above those at guesthouses, the **Dalkey Island Hotel,** Coliemor Harbour, Dalkey, Co. Dublin (tel. 01-850377), sits on the very edge of Dublin Bay looking out to Dalkey Island (boats are available right next door to take you out for an idyllic day on the uninhabited and very scenic island). The hotel is charm itself, with an Island Lounge featuring nightly entertainment in the summer and sea views all year long. The Sorrento Restaurant specializes in fresh seafood dishes at moderate prices and also has views of the sea. Both the lounge and restaurant are popular local gathering places. All guestrooms have private bath, telephone, color TV and radio, and there are eight that front on the sea, most with terraces (five are glassed in for all-weather comfort). Rates, which include breakfast, run from IR£17 ($20.40) to IR£29 ($34.80) for singles, IR£20 ($24) to IR£35 ($42) for doubles, depending on season.

There's a 12½% service charge, and a 25% reduction for children. Dalkey is on the Dublin train route, and is also served by bus no. 8.

Bray, Co. Wicklow

By rights, the seaside resort of Bray should be listed in the next section of this book. However, with the new electric train service into Dublin, it has moved into the "suburb" category and makes an ideal base if you want a little of both seashore and inner city. It is also convenient to Co. Wicklow sightseeing such as Glendalough and Powerscourt.

Bed-and-Breakfast: Strand House, Seafront, Bray, Co. Wicklow (tel. 01-868920), is a two-story, neo-Georgian house which faces the sea from its own set-back grounds (with convenient off-street parking). Mrs. Maeve O'Loughlin is the charming, helpful hostess, and her home is nicely decorated throughout. She keeps tourist literature on hand for guests and is quite knowledgeable about local restaurants as well as sightseeing highlights. Breakfast comes atop linen tablecloths, with a selection of dishes and perfect little butter curls, all of which probably reflect her long hotel experience. There are five bedrooms, all with sinks, one with private bath, and one rather small, cozy room overlooking the sea. Bed-and-breakfast costs IR£8.50 ($10.20), with IR£1 ($1.20) more per person for the room with private bath.

Glasnevin

Northwest of the city center, the Glasnevin section is close to the Botanic Gardens, with several city bus lines providing frequent service.

Bed-and-Breakfast: Mrs. Lambert, 8 Ballymun Rd., Glasnevin, Dublin 9 (tel. 01-376125), has been called "the perfect Irish mother" by one of our readers, and she does indeed make guests feel very much at home. Students who have stayed with her find her advice and information about the city especially helpful. Her two-story home has rather plain but comfortable furnishings, and there are four bedrooms, two of which have sinks, one double with a bay window. Bed-and-breakfast rates are a low IR£7.50 ($9), and she can provide high tea for IR£6 ($7.20). Take bus no. 11, 11A, 13, 13A, 19, 19A, 34, or 34A.

Clontarf

To the northeast of the city, Clontarf is a pleasant residential section with several very good budget-priced accommodations.

Bed-and-Breakfast: Wavemount, 264 Clontarf Rd., Clontarf, Dublin 3 (tel. 01-331744), is a pretty, two-story home overlooking Dublin Bay. Pixie-faced Maura O'Driscoll and her husband, Raymond, have earned glowing accolades from our readers over the years, and when I called in on them, it was easy to see why. The house itself was spotless and shining, but even more impressive was the warmth with which this couple greet their guests. Breakfasts (featuring homemade bread) are overly generous and, to quote one reader, "magnificently presented" in a bright front room with a bay window looking out to the sea. There are three bedrooms (one with a bay window and that marvelous sea view), one with private bath, and one with shower. No extra charge for the private facilities and there's central heating. Bed-and-breakfast rates are IR£9 ($10.80), with a 20% reduction for children. Mrs. O'Driscoll will also provide the evening meal with sufficient notice. Open February to October. City bus no. 30 gets you into town in a quick ten minutes. Highly recommended.

Joe and Mary Mooney are hosts at **Aisling,** 20 St. Lawrence Rd., Clontarf, Dublin 3 (tel. 01-339097). Their graciousness is matched only by the beauty of their home, which is a period residence on a quiet street just off the Clontarf/Howth road. Furnishings include antiques such as the grandfather clock in the entrance hall, and the lovely dining room is lit by a Waterford glass chandelier. Breakfast comes on beautiful china set on linen tablecloths, with Galway crystal stemware and sterling flatware. In short, the Mooneys and their two teen-aged daughters have a very special home which they happily share with guests. The four bedrooms are spacious and attractively decorated; all have sinks, one comes with private bath, and there's a family room with shower. Central heating. Rates for bed-and-breakfast are IR£9 ($10.80), with IR£1 ($1.20) per person extra for private facilities and a 10% reduction for children.

Padua, 3 Hollybrook Park, Clontarf, Dublin 3 (tel. 01-333597), is a small, pleasant house presided over by the bubbly Mrs. McDonagh. There are four bedrooms, two of them triples and all with sinks. Although the house is not centrally heated, there are electric heaters for the bedrooms. A lovely flower garden blooms out back. Rates are IR£8.50 ($10.20) for bed-and-breakfast, and Mrs. McDonagh will furnish the evening meal with advance notice. Discount for children is 10%. Bus service is via nos. 28, 29, 31, 32, or 54 from Abbey Street.

About Those Discounts

The following guesthouses are all exceptional; all have especially good value-for-dollar rates, but are somewhat above our budget range; and all extend a 10% discount to readers of this book who *mention it when booking*. The reduction is on *room rate only*, and such expenses as taxes, service charges, and meals (except breakfast) will be charged at the full rate. Advance reservations are necessary at each one. All have my highest recommendation and are well worth "busting the budget."

Ariel House, 52 Landsdowne Rd., Ballsbridge, Dublin 4 (tel. 01-685512), is one of Dublin's most popular guesthouses—and you can give the credit for *that* to Michael O'Brien, its genial owner/manager, who has a unique ability to put himself in the traveler's shoes, understand what will make traveling easier, more comfortable, and more fun, then proceed to furnish exactly that! He worked in some of San Francisco's leading hotels for several years and has done a fair bit of traveling himself, and his attitude towards his guests goes far beyond mere hospitality.

Ariel House's location is only five minutes from the city center and both major bus routes and a rail stop are just a few steps from the house. Landsdowne Football Stadium is just next door, and within easy walking distance are the American Embassy, the Royal Dublin Society, Chester Beatty Library, and the Berkeley Court and Jury's hotels (convenient if you want to take in an evening cabaret). The century-old red-brick house and its modern garden extension out back combine the graciousness of age with all the modern comforts you could possibly dream up. Guestrooms are models of good planning (the best designed clothes-and-luggage space I've come across) and thoughtfulness—all have a built-in hair dryer, TV, telephone (soon to be direct-dial), and a private bath. Those in the main house have modern furnishings and high ceilings and are reached via a lovely old staircase. The garden extension rooms are ground level, and there's a ramp for wheelchairs. All rooms have either twin beds or one double and one single, and there are two large family rooms in the main house.

The pleasant dining room (also accessible by wheelchair) overlooks the garden, and in the evening, it becomes a first-rate restaurant open to residents and nonresidents alike (see "Where to Eat"). If you're planning a cabaret or theater evening, dinners are available from 5 to 7 p.m. to get you there in time.

Seasonal rates for room with private bath and full Irish breakfast range from IR£20 ($24) to IR£25 ($30) single, IR£33 ($39.60) to IR£40 ($48) double, and there's a 10% service charge, as well as a one-third reduction for children. Be sure to mention the name of this book when you reserve in order to get the 10% discount.

Just a ten-minute walk from St. Stephen's Green, **Kilronan House,** 70 Adelaide Rd., Dublin 2 (tel. 01-755266), is a four-story townhouse with 11 guestrooms. Mrs. Josephine Murray, its gracious owner/manager, has years of hotel experience which are very evident in the smooth running of her attractive home. Tea and cookies are served each evening in the lounge, which has a TV and is a gathering point for guests, and breakfasts are highlighted by homemade brown bread and Mrs. Murray's homemade preserves. All guestrooms have telephones, and many have private baths with shower. Two family rooms with private facilities cost IR£45 ($54); two double-bedded and two twin-bedded rooms with private facilities are IR£34 ($40.80); three with double beds and no bath are IR£30 ($36); and there's one single without bath for IR£18 ($21.60). Reduction for children is 25%. A full Irish breakfast costs an additional IR£3.50 ($4.20). City buses nos. 14, 15, 19, 20, and 46A are nearby. Be sure to ask for the 10% discount to readers of this book when you reserve.

Iona House, 5 Iona Park, Glasnevin, Dublin 9 (tel. 01-306855, 306217, and 306473), is in a charming Victorian section and is a lovely old red-brick house built around the turn of the century. Karen and Jack Shouldice provide such extras as perked coffee and American-style bacon (crisp, rather than thick, like the Irish bacon) to make visiting Yanks feel at home. There's a homey lounge and a private garden. Guestrooms (which tend to be on the small side due to the installation of private baths) are attractive and comfortable, with private shower, color TV, radio, and telephone. Central heating. Both German and French are spoken here. Seasonal rates range from IR£12.50 ($15) to IR£16 ($19.20) single, IR£25 ($30) to IR£32 ($38.40) double, with a 25% reduction for children. The 10% discount is forthcoming if you mention this book when reserving.

Big Splurge

This one *is* a "Big Splurge," and there's no discount involved. However, it is such a special place that I'll just let you know about it and you can let your conscience (and your budget) be your guide.

Fitzpatrick's Castle Hotel, Killiney, Co. Dublin (tel. 01-851533), is one of Dublin's finest luxury hotels, and is about a 20-minute drive from the city center on the outskirts of an ancient and charming village. It was built in 1740 as a manor house and sits on 9 landscaped acres and occupies the site of a much older building, whose huge 15th-century stone fireplace is now the dominant feature of the Dungeon Bar (which has nightly entertainment during summer months). The house, with its three turreted towers and white battlements, was pretty much a wreck when Paddy Fitzpatrick bought it and set about its transformation. These days, the entire Fitzpatrick family is involved in running the place, which probably accounts for the graciousness and warmth that seems to extend to every member of the staff.

The fifty bedrooms all have private baths (tub *and* shower), TV, telephone, and radio. Those facing the front have little walk-on balconies set with a table and chairs, and those on the back all boast lovely canopied beds. There's an indoor swimming pool, indoor squash courts, saunas, hairdressing salon, and a very good giftshop. The popular bar is a gathering place for Killiney locals, and the dining room is a favorite of Dublin businessmen for lunch and families in the evening. In fact, you'll probably see as many Irish faces as tourists, since many make this their Dublin headquarters when coming from other parts of the country.

Adjoining the Castle is a block of modern, luxury time-sharing holiday homes which are often available for weekly rentals, providing self-catering facilities along with all the amenities of the hotel (contact the hotel for rates and availability if you're interested).

Rates range from IR£35 ($42) to IR£56 ($67.20) single, IR£50 ($60) to IR£80 ($96) double, plus a 12½% service charge.

READERS' SELECTIONS: Space will not permit us to publish all the good Dublin recommendations from our readers, but these appear to be outstanding. Remember, however, that we have not personally inspected any of the following.

"It would be hard to surpass **Mrs. Eileen Kelly's** house at 17 Seacourt, St. Gabriel's Rd., Clontarf (tel. 01-332547). Rooms, all centrally heated, are large and tastefully furnished and guests are encouraged to use the family's own living room, with comfortable lounge chairs and cozy open fire. Mrs. Kelly is a superb cook, and I found her knowledge of Ireland and places to see very useful before setting off to see the country" (D. O'Brien, Lorn, Australia). . . . "We enjoyed five days at **St. Dunstan's,** 25a Oakley Rd., Ranelagh, Dublin 6 (tel. 01-972286), the home of Mrs. Bird. She has a brick Edwardian house, newly decorated, with central heating, spotlessly clean. South of the Liffey, Ranelagh is a district of lovely homes, near shopping centers, restaurants and good pubs" (Meg and Alex Rowley, Calgary, Canada). . . . "I want to enthusiastically recommend **Mrs. P. Doody,** 286 Clontarf Dr. (tel. 01-333470). The family was gracious and generous and the lodgings very comfortable" (S. Connell, Oakland, Calif.). . . . "I cannot recommend a better place than Mrs. Irene Blowers' **'Jimire,'** 19 Woodlawn Park, Mounttown, Dun Laoghaire (tel. 01-808228). Not only were we treated to an early breakfast (in order to catch an early ferry) that was hot, tasty and hearty, but Mrs. Blowers set a beautiful table with lovely silver and china in her charming dining room. But that is only half the story. She and her husband helped us retrieve two Aran sweaters we had left on a bus in Waterford by tracking down the bus driver, who had them for us the next morning when he delivered passengers to the ferry. Then, Mr. Blowers drove us to the ferry because our taxi was late and wouldn't accept any money, saying only that it was his pleasure" (P. Vena, Lawrenceville, N.J.). . . . "We found the best Dublin choice for B&B is **Mrs. M. Murphy's,** 13 Marlborough Rd., N. Circular Rd. (tel. 01-308039). Her hospitality was one of the highlights of our trip. Her location is within walking distance to the Phoenix Park, and there's bus service to the center city and parking is available" (Michael and Jacki Willette, Tahoe City, Calif.). . . . "**Mrs. Colette O'Brien,** Arus Mhuire, 8 Old Bridge Rd., Templeogue, Dublin 16 (tel. 01-944281), is four miles from the city center, but five different bus routes are nearby. There's a TV lounge for guests and five comfortable bedrooms, with a bath and shower in one. Mrs. O'Brien is hospitable and friendly" (P. Rogers, New York, N.Y.). . . . "A new B&B we came across in Dun Laoghaire was run by **Mrs. Mary Lehane,** 5 Tivoli Rd. (tel 01-807355). Although we arrived early in the afternoon, she and her husband greeted us warmly and set us up in their lounge with tea and the TV to watch the Wimbledon tennis matches. Their house in new and clean and convenient to the ferry, as well as within walking distance of the beach." (J.V.R. Kaufman, Washington Depot, Conn.). . . . "**Mrs. O'Connell,** San

Vista, 237 Clontarf Rd. (tel. 01-339582), is full of fun, a wonderful listener, kind, full of good information on where to go in Dublin, and the warm, friendly, caring kind of person I went to Ireland to meet. I highly recommend her clean, neat and happy home. Excellent breakfasts served when you get up!" (R. Cantrell, Yamhill, Ore.). . . . "**Mrs. M. Kennedy,** Abrae Court, 9 Zion Rd., Rathgar, Dublin 6 (tel. 01-979944), gave us one of our nicest tastes of Irish hospitality, with warmth, friendliness and information. In addition—and quite important for those requiring it—this B&B is in the Terenure section, which is the only real Orthodox Jewish area in all of Ireland and is just one block from the Chief Rabbinate's office and within easy walking distance of the Terenure Synagogue" (M. Gelfenstein, Teaneck, N.J.). "We were delighted with our stay at **Hillcrest,** 13 Marlborough Rd., N. Circular Rd. (tel. 308039). Mrs. Murphy was a gracious and helpful hostess, the house is lovely, and the location is convenient to Phoenix Park and Heuston Railway Station. You just couldn't do better in Dublin" (G. Shore, Minneapolis, Minn.).

WHERE TO EAT: From picnics in St. Stephen's Green to pub grub to Tourist Menu meals to elegant Big Splurges, Dublin offers wide variety in cuisine as well as price. For convenience, the listings below are by both category and location, i.e. south or north of the Liffey.

South of the Liffey

Pub Grub: Both hot and cold light meals are available in some of Dublin's most atmospheric pubs at midday—a good way to save money and do a little pub hopping at the same time.

The **Stag's Head,** 1 Dame Court, is a real beauty. Built in 1770, its last "modernization" was in 1894. Lots of gleaming wood, wrought-iron chandeliers, stained-glass skylights, huge mirrors, and (need I say it?) mounted stags' heads. Between 12:15 and 2:15 p.m. you can have soup and toasted sandwiches for about IR£1.50 ($1.80), or heaping hot platters of bacon, beef, or chicken plus two vegetables for IR£3.50 ($4.20), or—if you're ravenous—sirloin steak with chips (french fries) and onions for just IR£7.50 ($9).

The **Old Stand,** Exchequer St. (tel. 987123), is a Dublin tradition, especially among sports figures. A century and a half ago, this was a forge, but today, you'll find outstanding figures of the sporting world gathered to engage in "the crack" and exceptionally good pub grub. From 12:30 to 2:30 p.m., there are sandwiches and snacks for around IR£1.50 ($1.80), a daily special of soup, meat, vegetables, and tea or coffee for IR£4.50 ($5.40), omelettes or salad plates for under IR£4 ($4.80), and hot platters of chicken, steak, or fish for IR£4 ($4.80) to IR£8.50 ($10.20).

In the Liberties section, near Christchurch, the **Lord Edward,** 23 Christchurch Pl., has a genuine old-world atmosphere, complete with stone fireplaces, beamed ceiling, and white stucco walls in the ground-floor pub. Upstairs is one of the city's finest (expensive, but well worth a splurge) seafood restaurants, but the same high-quality food and excellent service comes at modest prices in the pub during lunch hours. You'll lunch well for IR£2.75 ($3.30) to IR£5 ($6).

Foley's Lounge Bars, Merrion Row (across from O'Donoghue's) serves excellent pub grub from noon to 2:30 p.m. for well under IR£5 ($6) Monday through Friday.

The **Dubliner Bar,** in Jurys Hotel, Ballsbridge, serves up a Carvery Lunch ample enough to be your main meal of the day. The chef carves from a joint of beef and you help yourself to as much as you want from a wide variety of salads. Hours are 12:30 to 2 p.m., Monday through Friday, and best come early, since the place gets packed with Dubliners.

Restaurants: Place of honor among "south of" eateries would have to go to **Bewley's Café** for longevity, if nothing else. But never fear, the quality of food is never in doubt (nor has it ever been in the chain's 140-year history) at any of the five locations: 11/12 Westmoreland St., 78 Grafton St., 12 S. Great George's St., and the Dundrum and Stillorgan shopping centers. The devoutly Quaker Bewley family has, since 1972, shared ownership with all employees, which probably explains the courtesy and friendliness of the staff. Interiors are much like old-time tea shops, and indeed you can purchase teas, coffees, fresh baked breads, and terrific pastries (for a St. Stephen's Green picnic, perhaps) to take away. A good three-course lunch will run you about IR£3.25 ($3.90) from the à la carte menu, and although lunch hours are noon to 3 p.m., you can get a full Irish breakfast starting at 8:15 a.m., and coffee, tea, and snacks right up to 6 p.m.

Good budget-priced meals are also available at six center-city eateries operated by the **Regency Fare** group. They stress "freshness, variety, and quality," and you'll find everything from traditional Irish dishes at the upstairs P.J.'s to take-away or eat-in salads, sandwiches in the deli-style Only Natural down below. This is a very popular, rapidly expanding group, so you may find even more than these locations in existence as we go to press: Regency Fare, 28 South Anne St. (8:30 a.m. to 6 p.m.); Graham O'Sullivan, 52 Dawson St. (8:30 a.m. to 5:30 p.m.); Graham O'Sullivan, 11 Duke St. (9 a.m. to 5:30 p.m.); Only Natural, 12 Duke St. (10 a.m. to 6 p.m.). There are two other locations, both under the Graham O'Sullivan name, in the Dun Laoghaire Shopping Center. In all, you can eat well for IR£3 ($3.60) to IR£5 ($6).

At the National Gallery of Ireland, Merrion Square, you'll dine against a background of classical music, at prices that give "budget" a good name. It's self-service and offers as many as five fish selections, six meat or poultry dishes, and a couple of vegetarian choices. Prices run about IR£4 ($4.80) for a main dish with side salads, less for vegetarian selections. Hours are 10 a.m. to 6 p.m. Monday through Saturday (until 9 p.m. on Thursdays), and 2 to 5 p.m. on Sundays.

One of my personal favorites for the evening meal is actually the dining room of **Ariel House,** 52 Lansdowne Rd. (tel. 685512), open to the public from 5 to 9 p.m., Tuesday through Saturday. It's an intimate room overlooking the guesthouse rose garden, and candles on the wooden tables wear wreathes of colorful blooms from out back. Chef Marian Gary's experience in leading hotels of Ireland and Scotland shows up here in the guise of specialties like pork escalopes in mushroom sauce, plaice in dill and cucumber, and rack of lamb persillé, as well as starters such as mushroom beignets and French ham crêpes. Everything is cooked to order, and both Marian and owner Michael O'Brien are always on hand to assure friendly, polite, and efficient service. For the handicapped, there's wheelchair access both at the front entrance and in restrooms. There's pre-theater/cabaret service from 5 to 7 p.m. (Jurys cabaret is an easy walk away), and the menu is a la carte. Best reserve ahead.

A longtime favorite with Dubliners is the **Unicorn Restaurant,** 11 Merrion Court (a lane just off Merrion Row, tel. 762182/688552). Not far from St. Stephen's Green, the Unicorn is owned and operated by Mr. and Mrs. Renato Sidoli, who came to Dublin from Bardi, Italy, some 25 years ago. Cuisine is, of course, Italian, with everything from traditional veal dishes to pastas to pizza. Italian wines are served (and also on sale to take away), and there's marvelous espresso and cappuccino. This is a cozy place with white walls, booths, and tables, and when the weather is fine, tables set outside in the sun. You can drop in here any time you feel the onset of hunger pangs—hours are 10 a.m. to 10 p.m. on weekdays, noon to 2:30 p.m. and 6 to 10 p.m. on Saturdays. Closed Sundays and bank holidays.

Two choice restaurants south of the Liffey (and another on the north bank) are actually owned and run by American-born brothers of Irish descent. The two O'Driscolls have combined some of their Yankee knowhow with Celtic and American dishes to come up with a surefire restaurant formula (recipe?) that keeps all their eateries jammed with locals as well as visitors. They have, in fact, consistently won the Tourist Board's Award of Excellence. They also accept all major credit cards. **Beefeaters** (formerly Murph's), 100 Lower Baggot St. (tel. 760784/681205), is right in the heart of Georgian Dublin in the old wine cellars of two handsome mansions. Arches, cozy nooks, and small, partitioned spaces give it an intimate air, and house specialties (as you might guess from the name) are steaks, roast prime ribs of beef, and a wide variety of other beef dishes. Non-beef lovers can choose chicken Kiev or a Catch-of-the-Day fish selection, and for smaller appetites, there are hamburgers and steak sandwiches. Prices range from IR£4 ($4.80) to IR£9.50 ($11.40). Hours are noon to 2:30 p.m. for lunch, 6 to 10 p.m. for dinner, closed Sundays.

Casper & Giumbini's Food & Drink Emporium, Wicklow St., also an O'Driscoll enterprise, is just across from Switzer's side entrance and has been a gathering place for some of Dublin's most attractive younger set (executives, students, office workers, etc.) since it opened in the basement of what was once the old Wicklow Hotel, replete with hand-carved mahogany, burnished brass, Tiffany lamps, and stained-glass windows on multi-level floors. This combination pub and restaurant is always lively with conversation, and it's one of the few places you can order a drink right through the "Holy Hour" (2:30–3:30 p.m.). At lunch and on weekends, there's a resident pianist. At the handsome old bar (from the Wicklow), you can order any one of a dozen imported beers (including American brands) and soup, sandwiches, smoked salmon, bangers-and-mash, and other pub grub. Table service includes such full-meal items as seafood, chicken, veal, lamb, and steaks, as well as lighter fare like quiche, pizza, omelettes, hamburgers, etc. Sunday brunch is a standout here, with two free drinks accompanying your selection of eggs benedict; eggs with sausage, bacon, hash browns, black pudding, grilled tomatoes, and brown bread; smoked salmon and scrambled eggs with croissant; or steak and eggs with hashbrowns—all for IR£5 ($6). Bar prices are in the IR£1.25 ($1.50) to IR£3.75 ($4.50) range; à la carte selections, IR£3.50 ($4.20) to IR£6.95 ($8.34); and there's a table d'hôte menu at IR£7.95 ($9.54). Hours are noon to midnight seven days a week, and all major credit cards are honored.

Note: The O'Driscolls also operate **Murphy Doodles** (downstairs at 18 Suffolk St. off Grafton St.), where deli-style sandwiches, meat and fish salad plates, and pizzas are priced from IR£1.50 ($1.80) to IR£3.50 ($4.20). During summer months, the Tourist Menu is available.

Rajdoot Tandoori, 26/28 Clarendon St. (tel. 791122, ext. 132), is Dublin's newest Indian restaurant, and Mr. Sarda, its owner, opened his first restaurant in London's Chelsea back in 1966. You enter the elegant restaurant beneath a glittering 200-year-old crystal chandelier from a maharajah's palace in India. Inside, subdued lighting, brass tables, statues, and Indian prints provide a proper setting for excellent North Indian specialties. Tandoori dishes such as pigeon breast, lamb, and fish appear along with curries and kebabs. Nan, roti/shapat, paratha, and other Indian breads are also delicious. The five-course set lunch is priced at IR£7.50 ($9), and à la carte main courses for lunch and dinner run from IR£6 ($7.20) to IR£10 ($12). The Rajdoot is just off Grafton St. in the Westbury Centre; hours are noon to 2:30 p.m. for lunch (except Sunday), 6:30 to 11:30 p.m. for dinner. Open seven days.

The **Berni Inn**, 45 Nassau St. (tel. 772109), is just off Grafton St. and is a handsome complex of three separate restaurants, each with a different specialty of steak, fish, chicken, or duck. All feature lots of polished wood and dark red plush upholstery. It is fully licensed and serves sherry "off the wood," i.e., from the barrel. Hours are 12:30 to 10:45 p.m. weekdays, 5 to 10:30 p.m. Sundays, and menus are posted outside giving hours, prices, and directions to the different rooms inside.

Kilmartin's Wine Bar, 19 Upper Baggot St. (tel. 686674), is a small, intimate restaurant located in a former bookmaker's shop. Mementos of that activity are displayed on exposed brick walls. The wine list here is excellent, and there's a good menu selection of lasagne, moussaka, fish, steak, veal, and chicken. Prices in this friendly place range from IR£7 ($8.40) to IR£9 ($10.80). Open noon to midnight (to 10 p.m. on Sundays), seven days a week.

Through the South William Street entrance to Powerscourt Town House Centre, you'll find **Timmermans Wine Cellar,** ensconced in the original cellars of the mansion. Cozy alcoves hold hand-carved wooden booths brought in from an old chapel and these are also used in the courtyard area open to a parade of shoppers. There are more than 50 wines from which to choose (French, German, Italian, Spanish, Greek, and Californian, among others), as well as several sherries and ports. Food here is excellent, with salad platters and hot plates running from IR£3 ($3.60) to IR£4 ($4.80). Brown bread and a very good pâtè cost IR£1.50 ($1.80). As if that weren't enough, there's lunchtime piano music and nighttime entertainment featuring jazz, ballads, or folk music on different days of the week. Hours are 10:30 a.m. to 11 p.m., seven days.

Also in the Powerscourt Town House Centre, on the ground floor near the South William St. exit, is the **Periwinkle Seafood Bar,** which serves a terrific selection of hot and cold seafood dishes from noon to 5 p.m., Monday through Saturday, at minimal prices.

Best go to **Shrimps Wine Bar**, 1 Anne's Lane (tel. 713143), at an off hour, since this has become one of the city's most popular gathering places with locals and it gets really jammed during the usual lunch and dinner hours. It's not surprising that this tiny place, with its marble-top tables, bentwood chairs, and dark green walls, has caught the fancy of Dubliners— food is outstanding, service pleasant and efficient, and the Italian, French, and German wines are of the finest. The extensive menu features at least ten salads, from seafood to Westphalian ham and melon to smoked trout to chicken Caribbean, and hot dishes that include such exotic choices as lamb's liver in orange and brandy. Desserts are equally good, and there's a superlative cheeseboard. In fact, I find Shrimps a great place for a mid- or late-afternoon stop for cheese and wine, as well as for regular meals. Hours are noon to 11 p.m. every day except Sundays and bank holidays.

Dublin has one—and only one—23-hour restaurant (closed 5 to 6 a.m.), a handy place to know about at the end of a late evening or the early beginning of a day. The **Coffee Dock Grill**, in Jurys Hotel, Ballsbridge (tel.

605000), is also very much in the budget price range, with seafoods, salads, mixed grills, omelets, sandwiches, ravioli, and spaghetti available along with snacks and sweets at nominal prices—none over IR£6 ($7.20). Also, a good wine list.

Note: If you're staying out in or near Dalkey, an excellent choice for dinner is **Nieve's,** 26 Castle St., Dalkey (tel. 956156). It's a family-run restaurant with personal service in a cozy, intimate setting and has a resident pianist. The menu consists mainly of traditional Irish dishes, with outstanding seafood and a very good wine list. Dinner will run from IR£8 ($9.60) to IR£12 ($14). Hours are 6:30 p.m. to midnight, and it's closed only on Christmas Day and Good Friday. Very popular with the locals, so be sure to book.

North of the Liffey

Pub Grub: Patrick Conway's, 70 Parnell St., is just across from the Gate Theatre and dates from 1754. You'll often find theatrical people bending an elbow here before and after a show in the evening. At lunchtime, however, there's very good pub grub on offer (they're especially known for their hot apple tart). It's a large, rambling place, but do take notice (you can't really miss it!) of the huge circular bar just inside the entrance which encloses a carved wooden structure of Gothic proportions.

Daly's Lounge and Grill, 10 Eden Quay, is right on the Liffey. Downstairs is an old-time pub, often lively with the chatter of newspaper people. Upstairs, you'll find lunches that go a bit beyond the usual pub grub, with several hot dishes as well as cold salad plates. Evening meals, too, are good and inexpensive (around IR£5—$6). Lunch runs from 12:30 to 2:30 p.m., dinner from 5:30 to 11 p.m. every day except Sunday.

Restaurants: The O'Driscoll Brothers have crossed the Liffey with **Murph's,** 21 Bachelors Walk (tel. 731420/731122), just along the quay from O'Connell St. They've converted a 300-year-old warehouse into an airy, attractive restaurant. Lots of greenery swings from high roof trusses, a skylight lightens the scene, and exposed-brick walls are hung with huge gilt-framed mirrors. Lunch, including beverage, will run no more than IR£3.50 ($4.20), with a menu of quiche, hamburger, lasagne, pizza, chili, etc. A three-course dinner can be put together from the à la carte menu, featuring chicken Kiev, scampi, fresh fish, and steaks, for IR£4 ($4.80) to IR£9.50 ($11.40). Salad plates, omelettes, hamburgers, and other light-meal selections are available on their "Snacks that Aren't" menu, and from May to September they serve the Special Value Tourist Menu. Wine is available by the glass or bottle at reasonable prices. Open every day but Sunday from noon to midnight.

Another very good place to eat north of the Liffey is the **self-service restaurant** downstairs at the Municipal Gallery of Modern Art, Parnell Square (tel. 788238). For well under IR£5 ($6), you can choose from curries with rice, beef carbonnade with vegetables, a selection of salad plates, and desserts that include chocolate roulade, apple pie, and ice cream. There's wine by the glass. On Sundays, the popular lunch is a set IR£6 ($7.20) for adults, IR£4 ($4.80) for children. Hours are 10 a.m. to 5 p.m. Tuesday through Saturday, 12:30 a.m. to 4:30 p.m. Sunday.

À la carte prices at **The Pancake H.Q.,** 5 Beresford Pl. (tel. 744657), are in the IR£4 ($4.80) to IR£6.50 ($7.80) range for a nice selection of salads, steaks, seafood, and hamburgers. Definitely the star here—at least, for me—are the dessert pancakes. The gigantic crêpes are overflowing with fruits and other fillings and topped with luscious fresh cream—a meal in themselves! Prices for these divine creations run from IR£1 ($1.20) to IR£2.50 ($3), and I highly recommend the strawberry crêpe as a sinfully delicious lunch. Hours are noon to 11 p.m., Monday through Saturday. This management has recently opened a similar place in Dun Laoghaire, called **The Wishbone.**

Big Splurge: Dublin has a host of elegant restaurants, any one of which merits one of those memorable, kick-over-the-budget-traces splurges. The two following, however, are my personal favorites that have stood the test of time. If your traces are just too tight to kick over for dinner, lunch at either will be sumptuous at about half the cost.

Snaffles, 47 Lower Leeson St. (tel. 760790/762227), is in the basement of a 19th-century brick mansion and has been beloved by Dubliners for years. And for good reason! Not only is the interior one of understated, unpretentious elegance and the green-aproned waiters the very soul of helpfulness, but the food is both interesting and superbly prepared. Where else in Ireland could you find, for example, pheasant en croûte or breast of pigeon in port or ox tongue in paprika sauce? Less exotic dishes of fish, fowl, beef, veal, and ham are usually represented on the menu also. Starters and desserts are dazzling as well. To accompany all this, their wines and clarets are exceptional. A meal at Snaffles, be it lunch or dinner, is an experience you'll long remember. Lunch will run about IR£9 ($10.80) without wine, dinner about IR£16 ($19.20). Hours are 12:30 to 2 p.m. and 6:30 to 11 p.m., and reservations are an absolute must.

The Grey Door, 23 Upper Pembroke St. (tel. 766890), has two faces, an informal bistro for lunch or pre-theater light supper and an elegant restaurant which owner Barry Wyse has created in the drawing room of a Dublin townhouse. On the ground floor, the bistro is a charming setting of arched alcoves and nicely spaced tables. Prices here are in the moderate range: a three-course lunch runs about IR£6.50 ($7.80) as compared with IR£9 ($10.80) for the executive lunch in the upstairs dining room. That dining room has been beautifully furnished in the Georgian manner, and on cool evenings the fireplace is ablaze. Candlelight adds to the romantic atmosphere and fresh flowers at each table complete the scene. Cuisine is that of Northern Europe, with emphasis on Finnish and Russian dishes such as solyanka, borscht, blini, salmon severnaya, and chicken Kiev. Service is as elegant as the setting, and often there's a Russian guitarist on hand softly strumming his native folk music. Dinner, without wine, will run about IR£16 ($19.20), and you should book as far in advance as possible at this popular place. All major credit cards are accepted. Hours are 12:15 to 2:30 p.m. and 6:30 to 11 p.m.

READERS' SELECTIONS: "We had some of our best Dublin meals in **Rudyard's Restaurant and Wine Bar,** 15–16 Crown Alley (tel. 710846), where main courses such as mussels meunière and beefsteak and porter pie were surprisingly inexpensive" (T. Allen, Washington, D.C.). . . . "Our B&B hostess sent us to the restaurant downstairs at the **Carrick Hall Hotel,** 69 Orwell Rd., Rathgar, where we had an excellent meal of soup, main course, dessert and coffee for less than IR£5 ($6). We highly recommend it"(P. Shapiro, Wappinger Falls, N.Y.). . . . "The **Old Dublin Restaurant,** 90 Francis St., was a bit pricey, but a marvelous 'Big Splurge,' with delicious Russian and Scandinavian dishes prepared with all-fresh ingredients. It's in the Liberties, one of Dublin's oldest sections, and we had a meal and an evening long to be remembered" (S. Debnam, Norfolk, Va.).

THINGS TO SEE AND DO: Much of what you'll see in Dublin are the lines and wrinkles, blemishes and beauty spots left on her face by a long, rich, and colorful history. There were people living near the Liffey's hurdle bridge long before Vikings arrived in force in 841 to found a proper town. St. Patrick is said to have passed this way in 448; it is a fact there were several small churches and possibly there was a monastery. The Vikings, who had come as raiders, intermarried with the Irish and settled down to become merchants, traders, and craftsmen, but it wasn't until King Olaf was baptized shortly before his death in 979 that Christianity gained any sort of foothold. His son, Sitric, founded **Christ Church Cathedral** in 1038, one of three medieval buildings that have survived through the centuries. When Strongbow and his Normans captured Dublin in 1170, it was the beginning of another intercultural marriage, one sanctioned by King Henry II, who spent some time here in 1171 in a wicker palace that stood in present-day College Green. **St. Patrick's Cathedral,** the second medieval structure to survive, dates to 1190, and in 1192, King John authorized the building of **Dublin Castle,** the last of the city's medieval relics still standing.

There were few substantial changes in Dublin after that until the seventeenth century, and those magnificent Georgian buildings began to appear in the eighteenth century. The Victorian age arrived in the mid-1800s, leaving traces in railway stations, banks, pubs, markets, and hospitals, as well as some commercial buildings in the College Green vicinity. From 1916 to 1922, Dublin's face was scarred by the ravages of uprising, although careful rebuilding and restoration have erased most of the scar tissue. In the 1960s came the "office revolution" and the advent of characterless glass-and-concrete boxes to hail Ireland's new progressive era. Indeed, in a fit of "progressive" zeal, the grand old city came close to demolishing many of her finest legacies from all that history, until concerned citizens halted the destruction at an early stage so that today's visitor may happily browse through treasures of the past along with modern monstrosities.

All this is by way of illuminating your path as you explore the charms of this fascinating place and the people who live here.

Seeing the City

Before setting out to see Dublin, go by the Tourist Office at 14 Upper O'Connell St. and pick up their *Dublin, Ireland* brochure for 30p (36¢), which has a very good map of the inner city, as well as informative text on the major buildings, museums, etc., that you will want to see. There's also an illustrated walking tour guide titled *Tourist Trail* for 50p (60¢) that takes you along a signposted route (allow about three and a half hours) and tells you about the points of interest along the way. While you're there, take a look around the basement giftshop—it's one of the best you'll find anywhere in the country, with a wide selection of Irish crafts, souvenirs, books, etc.

Sightseeing Tours: If your time in Dublin is short, one of the best ways to make the most of it is by way of one of **CIE's half-day city tours** that leave from the central bus station on Store Street every weekday morning and afternoon and Sundays, April to November (three days a week during the months of March and November). Not only will you see the greatest number of Dublin landmarks in the shortest possible time, but you'll be treated as well to a very informative and witty narrative, with all sorts of anecdotes thrown in—guides all seem to be chosen for the express purpose of proving they are the epitome of the proverbial Irish talent with words. Fare is IR£6.50 ($7.80) for adults, half that for children, and you book in advance at the main CIE office, 59 O'Connell St. (across from the Tourist Office) or the CIE desk in the Tourist Office, at the central bus station on the day of travel. CIE also runs marvelous **day tours** to nearby scenic and historic spots such as Avondale and the Wicklow Hills, the North Dublin Coast and Malahide Castle, Glendalough and Avoca, etc., at prices that average IR£7.50 ($9) for adults, half-fare for children.

Dublin City Tours, 3 Wilton Pl., Baggot Street Bridge (tel. 786682/766887) also runs very good half-day city sightseeing tours for IR£8 ($9.60) and a full day of sightseeing at IR£14.50 ($17.40). Lunch isn't included in the fare, but you'll be given ample free time in the Grafton Street area for lunch on your own. There are also full-day tours to outlying sightseeing spots at IR£16.50 ($19.80). They'll give a 15% discount to our readers who mention the book when making reservations and show it when joining the tour, and they are the only tour operators who will pick you up and deliver you back to your hotel or a nearby designated point.

Ask at the Tourist Office about the two-hour walking tours conducted during summer months by members of the **Federation of Irish Guiding Interests of Georgian or Medieval Dublin** on two or three days of the week at a minimal charge of IR£1.50 ($1.80), or call Eileen Casey, Secretary, F.I.G.I., at 941251.

Horsedrawn Cabs: To those of us with romantic souls, Dublin streets (even when choked with today's automobile traffic) evoke strong images of horsedrawn carriages pulling up before Georgian mansions. And trust Dublin to humor us! Mr. **Paddy Sarsfield,** 5 Lower Kevin St. (tel. 755995), has resurrected those splendid old hansom cabs, lovingly restored them to their former glory and will clipclop us around the city. Your itinerary is yours to choose, and Mr. Sarsfield's charges are IR£6 ($7.20) an hour. Can't think of a better way to get to know this fascinating city!

Points of Interest

Dubliners will tell you that it takes years to take in all the city's treasures, and they're absolutely right. Let no one reading this book think they're going to "do" Dublin in a day or two! But we can cover a fair few of its highlights, and the following are my personal—and very subjective—recommendations on places not to miss.

One of the oldest and most beautiful of Dublin's buildings is **Christ Church Cathedral,** at the top of Lord Edward Street. Founded by King Sitric in 1038, it was originally a wooden structure, but was rebuilt in stone after the Norman invasion in 1169. Strongbow, who was instrumental in the rebuilding, lies here, and his effigy showing a child lying beside him is believed to be in memory of the son he slew when the boy turned back in the heat of battle. Four Irish high kings were knighted here by Richard II in 1394 when they pledged allegiance to that monarch, and in 1689 James II prayed for divine protection before marching off to the Battle of the Boyne, and a victorious King William came back to offer thanks for having prevailed. There are lovely architectural details and stonework in the nave, transepts, choir and chancel, and the crypt (the oldest section) is said to be one of the best of its kind in

Europe. It is open from Monday through Friday from 9:30 a.m. to 5 p.m. (sometimes closed between 12:45 and 2:15 p.m.), to 12:45 p.m. on Saturday, and only during holy services (11 a.m. and 3:30 p.m.) on Sundays. Take bus no. 21, 21A, 50, 50A, or 50B.

St. Patrick's Cathedral, Patrick Street, was founded in 1190, and over its varied history has served purposes as disparate as a university (from 1320 to 1465) and a stable for the mounts of Cromwell's troops in the 17th century. Its best known Dean (from 1713 to 1745) was Jonathan Swift, who wrote *Gulliver's Travels* and a host of sharp-tongued attacks on the humbuggery of his times. His tomb is in the south aisle, while his beloved "Stella" (Esther Johnson in real life) lies nearby. It had fallen into near ruin by 1860, when a member of the Guinness family financed its restoration to its present magnificent state. There's no admission, but visitors are invited (read that "requested") to leave a small donation to go towards upkeep. Hours are 9 a.m. to 6 p.m. (closed 12:30 to 1:30 p.m., November to February) Monday through Friday, to 4:30 p.m. on Saturday, and only during services on Sunday (11:15 a.m. and 3:30 p.m.). All services are ecumenical, and there are some weekday choral services also open to the public—check with the Tourist Board for exact days and hours. Take bus no. 50, 50A, 50B, or 56.

North of the Liffey, the square tower at **St. Michan's Church** on Church Street dates back to the 1096 Danish church which stood on this site, although the present structure is of 17th-century origin. Handel is said to have played its organ (perhaps when he was in Dublin to conduct the first performance of his *Messiah* in 1742). But it's the perfectly preserved bodies which have lain in its vaults for centuries with no sign of decomposition that draw many visitors. The Sheare Brothers, executed during the 1798 rebellion, rest here, and on my last visit it was a young Crusader and a 15th-century nun whose mummified bodies could be viewed. Hours are 10 a.m. to 12:45 p.m. and 2 to 4:45 p.m. during the week, to 12:45 p.m. on Saturday, and the vaults are not open to the public on Sunday. There's an admission of 80p (96¢) for adults, half that for children. Take bus no. 34 or 34A.

On College Green, **Trinity College** was founded by Elizabeth in 1592, but its oldest surviving buildings are the red-brick structures put up in the early 1700s. The striking West Front is worthy of note, as are the 1740 Printing House and the Dining Hall dating to 1760. It is, however, the Old Library that you should be sure not to miss, for it holds a priceless link with Ireland's antiquity, the magnificently illustrated *Book of Kells*. The book, which consists of the four gospels laboriously handwritten in Latin by monks and discovered in the monastery at Kells, has been bound in four separate volumes, two of which are displayed in glass cases. The lofty, vaulted Long Room, the exquisite beauty of the open pages and marble busts of famous Trinity graduates combine to create an awe-inspiring atmosphere you'll not soon forget. Pages are turned regularly to open a different page spread, and you may well find yourself returning for a second look. Other illustrated manuscripts are on display, as well as an ancient harp said to have accompanied Brian Boru into battle. Hours are 10 a.m. to 4:45 p.m. on weekdays, to 12:45 p.m. on Saturday, closed Sunday, and there's a small admission charge to view the book.

Just across College Green from Trinity, the **Bank of Ireland** building once was the seat of the Irish Parliament, and this is where the hated Act of Union was passed in 1800. An ailing Henry Grattan, whose statue now stands across the way, donned his worn Volunteer uniform and rose in these halls to bid an eloquent farewell to the independent Parliament. Today you can visit the House of Lords simply by asking directions from any of the Bank's uniformed attendants. Not so the House of Commons, however, for when the building was acquired by the Bank, it was on the condition that the lower house be demolished to avoid any possible coup d'état.

To touch more recent Irish history, take a look around the imposing **General Post Office** on O'Connell Street that was built in 1818. The massive granite building with its six fluted columns is where Padraic Pearse in 1916 gathered his Volunteers, hoisted the Irish Tricolour, and from its portico proclaimed to the Irish people and the world that Ireland would henceforth be an independent Republic. From the nearby Liffey, an English gunboat shelled the building, starting a fire that gutted its interior, now completely restored. Its central hall holds a statue of Ireland's ancient mythical warrior hero Cuchulain, who tied himself upright to a stake in order to fight a superior force to the death. A memorial to the men who fought here, its marble base is inscribed with the words of Pearse's Proclamation.

One of Dublin's more impressive sights is the north bank of the Liffey at night when floodlights illuminate the noble outlines of the 1791 **Customs House** on Customs Quay and the dignified, domed **Four Courts** building on Inns Quay. Both were burned-out shells after the 1921 Troubles, but both have been totally restored and are now in use for their original functions.

Dublin Castle occupies an elevated position west of Dame Street, just off Lord Edward Street, the site of an earlier Danish fortress. The only remaining portions of the Dublin Castle built between 1208 and 1220 are a bit of a curtain wall and two towers. You can get a pretty good idea of the original outline, however, from the **Upper Castle Yard** (disrespectfully dubbed "The Devil's Half-Acre" by Dubliners when this was the nerve center from which repressive British rule was administered for centuries). British Viceroys resided in the opulent **State Apartments** (now restored to their former elegance), but during World War I they were converted into a Red Cross hospital. It was from there that the prisoner James Connolly, patriot leader of the 1916 Uprising, was taken by stretcher to Kilmainham Jail to be executed, thus arousing international outrage and hastening the goal for which he gave his life. Today every President of Ireland is inaugurated in these splendid quarters. Guided tours are conducted Monday through Friday from 10 a.m. to 12:15 p.m. and 2 to 5 p.m. for a small charge. However, because they are sometimes closed to the public for official functions, it is best to check with the Tourist Office before going. You'll also want to see the **Church of the Most Holy Trinity** (formerly the Chapel Royal), as well as the memorial outside the main gate honoring those Irish killed here during Easter Week of 1916 and standing on the spot where heads of Irish kings once were displayed publicly on high spikes. Take bus no. 50, 50A, 50B, 56, 78, 78A, or 78B.

To retrace James Connolly's final journey, save a Sunday afternoon to travel out to **Kilmainham Jail Historical Museum,** within whose walls political prisoners languished, were tortured and killed, from 1796 until 1924 when the late president Eamon de Valera left as its final prisoner. Its rolls held such names as the Sheares Brothers, executed for their part in the Rebellion of 1798; Robert Emmet, who went from here to his death, proclaiming, "When my country takes her place among the nations of the earth, then, and not till then, let my epitaph be written!"; Charles Parnell, who directed Land League boycott strategy from within Kilmainham's walls; the Invincibles of 1883, five of whom lie buried here where they were hanged; scores of Volunteers who rose up in rebellion during Easter Week of 1916, 15 summarily shot, the others sentenced to life imprisonment and later pardoned; Eamon de Valera, who was imprisoned twice—once in 1916 and again in 1921 when he opposed the Treaty. It was Connolly and the 14 who died with him in May of 1916, however, whose sacrifice for Irish independence so fired their countrymen that the national will was united and, in the words of Yeats, "A terrible beauty" was born.

The old jail lay abandoned from the time of De Valera's exit until 1960, when a group of dedicated volunteers determined to restore it as a national shrine to Ireland's fight for freedom. Fittingly, it was President de Valera who opened the Museum at Easter, 1966. To walk along its corridors, through the exercise yard or into the Main Compound is a moving experience that lingers hauntingly in the memory. Volunteers conduct guided tours every Sunday from 3 to 5 p.m. and one day midweek during summer months (check with the Tourist Office for exact days and hours), and adult admission is a mere 40p (48¢), half that for children. Take bus no. 21, 78, 78A, 78B, or 79.

To visit the Parliament *(Dail Eireann)* that came into being when Ireland's long struggle finally brought liberty, go to **Leinster House** in Kildare Street. You'll have to be introduced by a member to gain admittance when the Dail (pronounced "Dawl") is in session; other times, hours are 10 a.m. to 12:30 p.m. and 2 to 4:30 p.m., Monday through Friday.

Museums and Art Galleries

Although currently undergoing major structural repairs slated for completion about 1987, the **National Museum** on Kildare Street (tel. 765521) should not be bypassed by any dedicated museum-hopper. True, some of its furniture and tapestry collections have been retired from public view until renovations are finished, but you can still stand and marvel at a host of archeological artifacts that chronicle Ireland's history from prehistoric times. Glass-enclosed burial mounds—one showing a skeleton and food vessel—bring new meaning to their counterparts you'll see scattered around the countryside. The eighth-century Tara Brooch with its delicate craftsmanship, as well as the beautiful Ardagh Chalice of heavy silver, are prime examples of Irish skills during the country's Bronze Age. Other collections include lovely samples of the lace for which Limerick and Carrickmacross are famous, Irish crystal, silver, and coins. An Arms Room holds, among other weapons, the crude pikes with which Irishmen went into battle from time immemorial (they were used as recently as the late 19th century by Fenians, and a few were carried into the General Post Office during the 1916 Uprising). Another room is dedicated solely to depicting the Uprising that finally brought freedom, and its collection includes letters written by its leaders, some composed as they awaited execution. A second building, entered from Merrion Street, holds natural history exhibits, and a third, on Merrion Row, is devoted to medieval Dublin, with Viking relics and other mementos of the Middle Ages on display. All are closed Monday, but open from 10 a.m. to 5 p.m. other days (including bank holidays), except Sunday, when hours are 2 to 5 p.m. Take bus no. 7A, 8, 10, 11, or 13.

The **National Gallery**, Merrion Square West (tel. 767571), is conveniently located in Leinster Lawn, and its collections include impressive works by Dutch masters, as well as ten major landscape paintings and portraits by Gainsborough, and canvasses by Rubens, Rembrandt, El Greco, Monet, Cézanne, and Degas. John Butler Yeats, perhaps Ireland's greatest modern portrait painter, is well represented, as are leading 18th- and 19th-century Irish artists. Portraits of Irish historical figures over the past three centuries are hung in the National Portrait Gallery. The young George Bernard Shaw spent much time browsing through the National Gallery and felt such a debt of gratitude for the education it afforded him that he bequeathed it a substantial monetary grant. The Gallery is open 10 a.m. to 6 p.m. weekdays (until 9 p.m. on Thursdays) and 2 to 5 p.m. on Sunday, with free guided tours every half-hour on Sundays. Closed Christmas Eve, Christmas Day, and Good Friday. There's also a cafeteria and a souvenir bookshop.

Near the top of O'Connell Street, the **Hugh Lane Municipal Gallery of Modern Art,** Parnell Square (tel. 741903), occupies a fine Georgian mansion which was once the residence of Lord Charlemont. A word of explanation is in order about the works you may find on view. Before his death by drowning on the *Lusitania* in 1915, and before Charlemont House was acquired as a permanent home for his paintings, Sir Hugh Lane lent his continental collection to the National Gallery in London. A codicil to his will, however, left the pictures to Dublin's Municipal Gallery, but lacked the two essential witnesses to his signature. After a long dispute, an agreement now has been reached to divide the 39 pictures into two groups, one to be housed in London, the other in Dublin, with exchanges to be made every five years. Among those you're likely to find in residence are works by Renoir, Corot, Monet, Daumier, and contemporary works by Irish artists. Hours are 9:30 a.m. to 6 p.m. Tuesday through Saturday and 11 a.m. to 5 p.m. on Sunday. There's an excellent downstairs restaurant (see "Where to Eat"), and just across the way is the beautiful **Garden of Remembrance,** dedicated in 1966 to those who died in the 1916 fight for liberty. Take bus no. 11, 12, 13, 16, 16A, 22, or 22A.

The **Irish Architectural Archive,** 63 Merrion Square (tel. 763430), while neither a museum nor an art gallery, will certainly intrigue anyone interested in Ireland's past. Since its establishment in 1976, the Archive has become the central information center of information on architecturally and historically significant Irish buildings from 1600 right up to the present. In addition to more than 30,000 pictures, the reference library holds a vast number of publications such as pamphlets, press cuttings, historical manuscripts, and engravings. While the emphasis is on architecture, as you would expect, all sorts of extraneous information can be gleaned from browsing through the box files of photos, many of which are fascinating shots of landscapes, period village street scenes, craftsmenlike thatchers and masons at work, a hunt meet at a country mansion, etc. Who knows, the cottage from which your ancestors left for America, long demolished, may show up in one of these old pictures! Pamphlets from the past also make good reading, while giving a unique insight to Ireland's social history. The Archive's collection is open to the public every weekday; check by telephone for hours the day you wish to visit.

The Guinness Brewery

A sightseeing attraction in a class by itself is the sprawling **Guinness Brewery,** set on 60 acres south of the Liffey. The largest brewery in Europe, Guinness exports more beer than any other company in the world. The rich, dark stout it has produced since 1759 is truly the "wine of Ireland," and you'll no doubt be a devout convert after your second pint (it is sometimes an acquired taste!). The tours which were once conducted around the brewery have been suspended indefinitely due to an extensive reconstruction program, but if you call in to the Visitors' Center (through the brewery's main gate in James St.) between 10 a.m. and 3 p.m. on a weekday, they'll be happy to treat you to a film about Guinness and a complimentary pint. Buses no. 21 and 78 from Fleet Street pass by the entrance.

Note: The old Guinness hop store in Rainsfort Street is currently being renovated and will, in due time, house shops and a restaurant—you may want to check on its progress when you're there.

Parks and the Zoo

Since 1690, **St. Stephen's Green,** at the top of Grafton Street, has been preserved as an open space to provide bucolic respite for Dubliners. Over the years, it has evolved into the beautifully planted park that today finds city residents and visitors alike strolling along its paths, enjoying a lunch break picnic style, and simply soaking up its rustic charm as the city's traffic swirls around its edges. Formal flowerbeds, the arched stone bridge crossing one end of the artificial lake, shaded pathways, and statuary placed in pockets of shrubbery make this a very special place. Gates are open from 8 a.m. until dark on weekdays, from 10 a.m. on Sundays.

The **National Botanic Gardens,** Botanic Rd., Glasnevin (tel. 374388), were founded in 1795 by the Royal Dublin Society to "increase and foster taste for practical and scientific botany." Spread out over 50 acres of an estate which once was the home of the poet Thomas Tickell, they are now under the direction of the Department of Agriculture and Fisheries, and in addition to exotic trees, shrubbery, and tropical plants there is an Economic Garden (for economic and poisonous plants), a vegetable garden, and a lawn garden. Just inside the gates, you'll find Thomas Moore's famous *Last Rose of Summer.* During summer months, hours are 9 a.m. to 6 p.m. (from 11 a.m. on Sunday), and in winter, they close at sunset. Greenhouses do not open until 2 p.m. on Sunday. Take bus no. 13, 19, 34, or 34A.

St. Anne's Park Rose Garden, Mount Prospect Ave., Clontarf, is one of the prettiest in the city, with climbers, florabunda, hybrid tea and old garden roses in profusion. In April and May, daffodils are in full bloom. Take bus no. 44A or 30.

The **Phoenix Park,** northwest of the city center, main entrance in Parkgate St. (tel. 213021), is one of the world's most beautiful, and is *always* referred to by Dubliners as "The" Phoenix Park. Within its nearly 2,000 acres are the residence of Ireland's President, that of the American Ambassador, the lovely **People's Gardens,** the **Zoological Gardens** and **Dublin Zoo,** and the **Phoenix Park Racecourse.** Its lofty trees shade all manner of humans during daylight hours and free-roaming herds of cattle and deer after dark.

The zoo is especially noted for breeding lions and other large cats, having bred the first lion cubs in captivity in 1857, but its fame also rests on the picturesque landscaping and gardens surrounding two natural lakes (alive with pelicans, flamingos, and scores of ornamental ducks and geese) and the spacious outdoor enclosures that house all manner of animals and birds. Youngsters will delight in the small **Children's Zoo** over in one corner, where they can take a pony ride, pet tame animals, and wish on the Wishing Seat. The glass-enclosed **cafeteria** provides light fare at inexpensive prices, and the **Lakeside Coffee Shop** has outdoor umbrella-table service. Adults pay a IR£2 ($2.40) admission, children from 3 to 14, IR£1 ($1.20), and children under 3 are admitted free. During summer months, hours are 9:30 a.m. to 6 p.m. on weekdays, from noon on Sunday. In winter, the zoo closes at sunset. Take bus no. 10, 14, 14A, 25, or 26.

In Search of Literary Greats

Ireland's greatest gift to the rest of the world may well be its writers, whose keen, sharp-witted, and uniquely phrased insights into the foibles of those who walk this earth are timeless and universal. From this sparsely populated little island have sprung an enormous proportion of civilization's greatest wordsmiths, and of them, a good many were born, lived, or died in Dublin. While some of the landmarks they left behind have disappeared and others have changed since they figured in their lives, the following will surely bring you closer to those whose legacy of such a wealth of words has prodded the minds and hearts of the rest of us.

The house at 7 Hoey's Court where **Jonathan Swift** was born is now gone, but it stood very near St. Patrick's Cathedral, where he was its most famous Dean, serving 32 years, and where he was laid to rest. Listen for his footsteps, too, at Trinity College, where he was a student. **Thomas Moore** also studied at Trinity, and you'll find his birthplace at 12 Aungier St. Both **George Bernard Shaw** and **Oscar Wilde** began their tumultuous lives in Dublin in the year 1854, Wilde at 21 Westland Row and Shaw at 33 Synge St. **W. B. Yeats's** birthplace was 5 Sandymount Ave., and 42 Fitzwilliam Square was his residence from 1928 to 1932.

James Joyce was born in Rathgar at 41 Brighton Sq. W., and from his self-imposed exile mapped the face of his native city in unremitting detail. The martello tower he occupied with Oliver St. John Gogarty in 1904 is now a Joyce museum (see Section 3 of this chapter), and his devoted followers can trace the Dublin meanderings of his Leopold Bloom as unerringly as if Joyce had written a guidebook rather than his *Ulysses* masterpiece. This is such an intriguing pastime for visitors that the Tourist Board has prepared a **Ulysses Map of Dublin** of the book's 18 episodes that is yours for a small charge.

Brendan Behan captured the heart and soul of modern Dublin in words that his countrymen sometimes agonized over but never denied. He was born in Dublin in 1921 and remained its irreverant, wayward son until the early end of his life in 1964, when the President of Ireland led a huge crowd to Glasnevin Cemetery for the interment. His spirit no doubt still roams the city streets, reveling in the things that have changed and those that have remained the same.

While not a literary landmark, the Moore Street market was well known to Behan and no doubt to many another Dublin writer. It's just behind the GPO, and to go along Henry Street, then turn into the lively commerce of Moore Street is to walk into a never-changing bit of the kaleidoscope of color that characterizes this city and kept its writers busy. From 10 a.m. to 5 p.m. on weekdays, fishmongers and greengrocers and vendors of a dozen other wares gather to haggle, gossip, and contemplate the vagaries of Dublin life. Not a literary landmark, but surely a haunt of those with a literary bent!

DUBLIN AFTER DARK: While you certainly wouldn't say that Dublin "swings" after dark, you *can*—just as certainly—say that it entertains. There's its internationally renowned **theater**, traditional Irish **music** in traditional Irish settings, **cabaret, dancing,** and, above all, the **pubs.**

The Pubs

Dublin pubs are, indeed, their own special kind of entertainment. It makes no difference if you wander into one known for its conversation ("crack," as the Irish say), its music, or its pint (actually, there probably isn't a pub in Dublin that won't tell you they "pull the best pint in the city"), you'll not walk out of any one of the above bored. As I have said before in these pages, the best possible beginning and/or end to a Dublin evening is the pubs.

If you're planning, however, on one of the "pub crawls" so often heard of on this side of the Atlantic, better gear up your strongest will to move from one to another: chances are *very* slim that you'll be able to walk out of the first one you enter—and very good that you'll settle in with the first pint as a newly appointed "regular," if only for that one night.

With more than 1000 pubs to choose from, every Dubliner you ask will come up with a different favorite (or list of favorites), and there probably won't be a clunker in the lot. The problem is to be selective, and in the section below I'll share with you the ones *I* have found most interesting. Whatever you do, however, don't confine yourself to *my* list—pop into the nearest establishment anywhere in the city you're overcome with a terrible thirst, and you'll likely come home raving about your own list of favorites. One last word, and it's for non-drinkers: Irish pubs are centers of sociability, where you can get happily soused or chat the night away just as happily with nothing stronger than soda.

Pub hours are from 10:30 a.m. to 11:30 p.m. in summer, 11 p.m. in winter, with "holy hour" closing in Dublin and Cork from 2:30 to 3:30 p.m. As this is written, there's talk among the governmental powers that be that the evening hours should be extended—check when you're there to see if they've reached any decision on that.

South of the Liffey: This is pub country, where I dare say you can't walk a block without having a choice of pubs for the evening. One much favored by the natives is the **Stag's Head,** tucked away in Dame Court. Getting there is a bit complicated, but easy if you leave College Green on the left side of Dame Street and in the middle of the second block keep your eyes glued to the sidewalk, where you'll find a stag's head set in mosaic right in the pavement. It fronts a small alleyway on the left and at its end you emerge right at this beautiful old pub that's been here since 1770. An interesting mix of ages, occupations, and character types drink here in the evenings (for young executive types, tourists, etc., come for the excellent pub lunch—see "Where to Eat").

The **Old Stand,** in Exchequer St., is named for the "old stand" at Lansdowne Road rugby ground, and it sometimes seems half the rugby players (past and present) have congregated in this popular pub. Celebrated athletes like Moss Kene, Phil Orr, and Ollie Campbell are familiar faces here, and the talk centers around sports 90% of the time. The clientele is made up of all ages and occupations, and around five in the afternoon, you'll find some of Dublin's most attractive younger set relaxing after a day of toiling in an inner-city office.

If you're a Brendan Behan devotee, you'll know about **McDaids,** 3 Harry St., the dark, high-ceilinged pub in which he claimed a corner for himself, his pint, and his typewriter. Patrick Kavanagh and Flann O'Brien are other literary lights who drank here, and the clientele is still very much of the written word and those doing the writing.

Neary's, 1 Chatham St., backs up to the Gaiety Theater's stage door, and both patrons and crack are many times centered around what's playing there, who's in the cast, and other things theatrical. You'll recognize Neary's by the two black sculptured bronze arms holding light globes at its entrance. Inside, decor is sort of neo-Edwardian, with a pink marble bar, brass gas lamps, mirrored walls, and lots of mahogany.

Doheny & Nesbitt, 5 Lower Baggot St., looks like a Dublin pub *should*— a great old wooden front with polished brass proclaiming the place a "Tea and Wine Merchant," high ceilings, mirrored partitions along the bar, iron and marble tables, and a snug. It's been here for more than 130 years, and no doubt has always enjoyed the popularity it does today, with Dubliners of every age and inclination claiming it as their "local," including the likes of journalists, politicians, artists, architects, etc., etc., etc. A great place for conversation and people watching, equally good at the front bar or back room.

O'Donoghue's, 15 Merrion Row, is not strictly a "singing pub," but it is seldom without music of one sort or another, provided, not on a planned basis but by the hordes of bearded, bejeaned, and instrument-wielding clientele who crowd in here to play traditional Irish music, blue-grass, country-and-western, or whatever on guitars, Uillean pipes, bones, spoons, and I don't-know-what-all else. It's a lively, fun-filled gathering place if you don't mind the crush. Or you could take the advice of readers Ann and Brian O'Connell, who wrote us that they've found Sundays after church (12:45 p.m. to 2 p.m.) to be the most uncrowded hours, the time when they could relax and enjoy the conversation and music without someone's elbow in their faces.

Toner's, at 139 Lower Baggot St., is the hangout of art students and other cultural types. The long mahogany bar in this venerable old pub that's been around more than a century and a half is set with partitions to provide a bit of privacy at the bar. W. B. Yeats drank here.

There are still traces of its greengrocer-cum-pub beginnings at **Kehoe's,** 9 South Ann St., right in the heart of Dublin's shopping area. Presided over by longtime manager Nicholas Thorpe, Kehoe's still has grocery bins in front, and the soft patina of time cloaks the wooden fixtures inside. A good place for an afternoon pint, as well as a place to meet Dubliners who have been coming here for years in the evening.

Mulligan's in Poolbeg Street ("within an ass's roar of the Liffey and the Port of Dublin," according to Dublin writer David Hanly), next door to the *Irish Press* offices, is, quite simply, a Dublin institution. Since 1782, it's pulled pints for the likes of dockers, journalists, and, in recent years, scores of students from nearby Trinity. Its front bar and four rooms ring with clubby conversation, especially around five in the afternoon, then it settles down a bit as the evening progresses. Lots of newspaper types can be found hanging out among the students.

The oldest drinking place in Ireland was licensed by Charles II in 1666. It's the **Brazen Head,** 20 Lower Bridge St., said to have got its name in memory of a curious redheaded beauty who stuck her head out a window during one or the other of Dublin's public disturbances and promptly lost it to an English sword. Be that as it may, this ancient pub sits at what used to be the only place you could cross the Liffey by bridge, and it's tucked away at the back of a courtyard down an arched alleyway on the west side of Bridge Street, and the entrance is easily overlooked. Low ceilings, brass lanterns, and ancient, uneven wooden floors are the same as when Robert Emmet lodged here while plotting his ill-fated uprising (his writing desk is pointed to with pride) and patriots like Wolfe Tone and Daniel O'Connell came in to drink.

James Joyce fans may want to look up **Davy Byrnes,** 21 Duke St., the "moral pub" of *Ulysses* hero Leopold Bloom. Well, it's been modernized right out of Joyce's day and into a tastefully sophisticated sort of cocktail lounge that one writer has called the closest thing Dublin has to a singles' bar. The 1890s wall murals are still here, and you can still get a very good pint, but these days there are likely to be more orders for mixed drinks than for the old stuff.

North of the Liffey: One of Dublin's very special pubs is over in the Phoenix Park area. **Ryan's,** 28 Parkgate St., is a real gem, and one largely undiscovered by tourists. I've heard Dubliners claim it is the finest pub in town, and they'll get no argument from me. It's a traditional place, with a mahogany bar in the center of the room, a high ceiling with a smoke-dimmed skylight, great mirrors, and *four* snugs. To quote David Hanly again—and there's no better pub authority in all of Dublin!—"the decibel level is usually murmurously pleasant, and the staff wear vests and fob watches and are ridiculously polite."

Kavanagh's, 1 Prospect Sq., Glasnevin, is just next to what was once the main gate to Glasnevin Cemetery. The pub has been there for a century and a half, and proprietor John Kavanagh is the eighth generation of his family to run the business. His fund of stories is endless, many of which concern the gravediggers who worked next door and who popped over to bang stones against the pub's wall, whereupon drinks were passed through an opening and placed on the poor man's shovel so he could get on with his work in a livelier state. (You can still see marks from those bangings on the wall outside.) For a long time, Kavanagh's did more than dispense liquid refreshment, and all sorts of household goods were once sold from all the drawers in the place. This is, as it has always been, a workingman's pub—sawdust on the floor, worn wooden booths and cubbyholes, a dart game or two, and the relaxed chatter of men who've finished an honest day's work.

You might call **Patrick Conway's,** 70 Parnell St., a theater pub, since it's just across the street from the Gate Theater, except that then you'd have to also call it a medical pub, since it is also across from the Rotunda Maternity Hospital. The fact is that you'll usually find a good mix of theater types and obstetricians welcoming friendly tourists like ourselves, along with a good many Dublin regulars. Some of my best pub conversations have been at Conway's, and the pub lunches are terrific (see "Where to Eat"). This claims to be Dublin's second oldest pub, dating from 1754, and while it's been modernized into comfort, there's much of the traditional wood, brass, and convivial atmosphere remaining. Take note of the back bar, a marvel of carved mahogany.

For sheer Victoriana, you can't beat the **Abbey Mooney,** 1 Lower Abbey St. You owe yourself at least one jar in this vast and splendid old pub, which is gleaming enough at eye level, with lots of brass and mahogany and stained glass. But look up to the high ceiling, and I can hear your gasp from here! Elaborate gilded garlands, cherubs, blossoms, and all manner of ornamentation form what is probably the most fanciful canopy in pubdom. The downstairs lounge is not quite so ornate, but both the O'Casey and Yeats lounges upstairs can almost hold their own. There's good pub grub (try the curries) at lunchtime and always a goodly crowd of theatergoers in the evening on their way to or from the nearby Abbey Theater.

Pubs With Music: You won't find a better ballad club in all of Ireland than the **Abbey Tavern** out in Howth, some nine miles north of Dublin on the peninsula that curves around to form the northern end of Dublin Bay. The village itself is a beauty, with cliff walks, narrow little winding streets and pathways, gorgeous sea views, Howth Castle gardens with a collection of over 2,000 rhododendrons, and some very good seafood restaurants. A day exploring this pretty place—perhaps with a boat trip out to Ireland's Eye (an uninhabited island just offshore) thrown in—topped off with dinner and music at the Abbey is just about as good an Irish day as you could hope for! The bar/restaurant is low-ceilinged, candlelit, and has a fireplace glowing on cool nights, making it an informal, cozy place to eat. The big hall out back is anything but cozy, until it fills with music-loving souls, as it does every night of the week. They've all come to hear the Abbey Singers, who are instrumentalists as well as vocalists, and the 8:30 to 11 p.m. show calls on all their talents as they run through a whole host of ballads you've heard all your life, then go on to some you'll never hear anywhere except on Irish soil. It's a grand show, and so popular that *you must reserve at least a day ahead,* more than that in summer months (tel. 322006). They do, however, hold back some seats which go on a first-come, first-served basis—but the lines can be *very* long during July and August and you shouldn't count on getting in via this route.

There's a IR£4 ($4.80) admission charge to the hall, and drinks are at regular bar prices (you're not obliged to order drinks, however). There's good bus and train service out to Howth—just be sure you leave the Abbey in time to catch the last one back to town.

In the city proper, north of the Liffey, **Slattery's** on Capel St., features traditional Irish music nightly during the summer and Sundays from 12:30 to 2 p.m. There's a small admission charge to their upstairs music lounge. South of the Liffey, you can find traditional music nightly and Sunday afternoons, plus jazz on Sunday nights, at **Foley's Lounge Bar,** Merrion Row.

Other Dublin pubs have singalong nights from time to time, so check newspapers and *What's on in Dublin* (available from the Tourist Office) when you're there.

Traditional Irish Music

It's sometimes hard to hear Irish music as it pours from the Irish heart in Ireland—with a very few exceptions, that's something you almost always have to stumble onto when the music and song is the totally unplanned, but irrepressible Irish spirit finding its own voice in its own environment. When you're in Dublin, however, that same joyous or melancholy or rebellious spirit in all its passionate glory is yours to share at **Culturlann na hEireann,** 32 Belgrave Sq., Monkstown (tel. 80029). There's some kind of traditional entertainment on there every night of the week, but to hear some of the best musicians in the country, go along on Friday, Saturday, and Sunday. Fiddlers fiddle, pipers pipe, whistle players whistle, dancers take to the floor, and singers lift their fine Irish voices in informal sessions that bear little resemblance to the staged performances mentioned above. Things get under way about 9 p.m. and carry on until 12:30 p.m., and you'll be every bit as welcome as if you'd stumbled onto the sort of unplanned session I mentioned above. There's an admission charge of IR£1.50 ($1.80).

The **Piper's Club** makes Saturday nights special, when the members of this popular Dublin institution hold forth during those same hours. Other nights, there's ceili dancing that will get you out on the floor and stage shows featuring step dancers and traditional music. Call to find out what's on when you're there, then hightail it out to Monkstown. If you call 800295, you can book an inexpensive dinner of traditional, homecooked Irish food in their kitchen/restaurant.

CIE runs a Traditional Irish Music Night tour to Culturlann na hEireann one night a week from mid-May through September for IR£7.50 ($9). Call 787777 for complete details and booking.

Comhaltas Ceoltoiri Eireann, the organization dedicated to preserving Irish culture in all its forms, sponsors all the above as well as some remarkable performing troupes of dancers, singers, and musicians who tour around the country during summer months. Keep an eye out for them as you travel, or inquire at local Tourist Offices. For IR£3.50 ($4.20), you'll be in for an authentic Irish treat!

Theater

Maybe you came to Ireland for the express purpose of experiencing Irish theater—many people do. If so, check Chapter III for details on the money-saving Theater-Go-Round discounts. Even if you didn't come just for that purpose, at least one of your Dublin nights should be spent at the **Abbey Theater,** Lower Abbey St. (tel. 744505). This is the national repertory company, born in 1898 when Augusta Lady Gregory, W. B. Yeats, and Edward Martyn determined to perform Irish plays with Irish casts to "show that Ireland is not the home of buffoonery and of easy sentiment, as it has been represented, but the home of an ancient idealism." And it did, indeed, provide a voice for such passionate writers as J. M. Synge and Sean O'Casey, sticking to its guns even when ultraconservative Irish audiences rioted at the showing of Synge's *Playboy of the Western World.* Siobhan McKenna, Cyril Cusack, Sara Allgood, and Barry Fitzgerald (who held down a full-time job, rehearsed at lunch, then rushed back for evening performances) are just a few of the stage talents who blossomed to stardom through their training and experience at the Abbey. The original Abbey was quite small, and when it burned in 1951, members of the company cheered because the government would then have to provide them with quarters not so cramped. And they did gain a modern, functional theater with the best in stage equipment—but it took 15 years for the government to get the job done, and all the while the company performed in a variety theater to stay alive.

The theater may be new and cast names sometimes unfamiliar, but the emphasis is still on Irish playwrights (contemporary and classic) and Irish actors, with an occasional import (Tennessee Williams' *The Glass Menagerie* played there in 1984). This is theater at its best, with the surprisingly low prices of IR£6 ($7.20), IR£7 ($8.40), and IR£8 ($9.60). Needless to say, the Abbey stays booked year round, and to avoid disappointment, you should write them directly a minimum of three weeks in advance to book the performances you want to see.

Downstairs at the Abbey, the small **Peacock Theater** hosts literary and poetry readings, experimental contemporary drama, and sometimes a retrospective of the classics. Ticket prices are the same as for the Abbey.

The **Gate Theater,** Parnell Sq. (tel. 744045), produces both Irish and international plays for six months of the year, with its resident company under the direction of the well-known Hilton Edwards. Tickets range from IR£4 ($4.80) to IR£7 ($8.40). The **Gaiety,** a long-time fixture on Dublin's legitimate theater scene, is closed as this is written, its future uncertain. Check when you're there to see if it's reopened. The **Project Arts Centre Theatre,** 39 East Essex St., often performs interesting and experimental contemporary works, with ticket prices of IR£4.50 ($5.40). Tickets for all theaters can be purchased at the box offices or through **Brown Thomas** (tel. 776861) and **Switzer's** (tel. 776821) department stores on Grafton St.

Concerts

The **National Concert Hall,** Earlsfort Terrace (tel. 711888), is a splendid auditorium and features first-rate musical events. The prestigious (and excellent!) RTE Concert Orchestra performs here regularly, as does the New Irish Chamber Orchestra. Visiting artists run the gamut from harpists to jazz stars. With tickets in the IR£4 ($4.80) to IR£7 ($8.40) range, this is superb entertainment at bargain-basement prices. Check with the Concert Hall or the Tourist Office to see what's on during your visit.

Cabaret

Cabaret in Dublin is served up with distinctly Irish seasonings—"Danny Boy" and "The Rose of Tralee" are favorites of the audiences (mostly visitors, but with more than a few Irish families in from the country), there's an Irish comic telling Irish jokes; pretty, fresh-faced colleens dancing, singing, playing the harp, etc.; at least one Irish tenor or baritone; and usually one or more of those captivating Irish youngsters in traditional dress to step a lively jig or reel or hornpipe. It's Irish entertainment on the light side. No purists, these—but they're loads of fun and the performances are usually well above average. Most are held in hotels, and you can opt for dinner and the show or come along for the show alone. Dinners feature Irish specialties such as potato soup, salmon, or steak, colcannon (cabbage and potatoes), and perhaps an Irish Mist soufflé for dessert (that's the exact menu at the Burlington Hotel, and others are very similar). If you come just for the show, the price includes two drinks.

A handy way to take in cabaret without having to drive is by booking with **Dublin City Tours,** 3 Wilton Pl., Baggot Street Bridge (tel. 786682), for their Nightlife Tour. They'll pick you up and deliver you back to your hotel, and if you mention this book when telephoning, then present it when you join the tour, they'll give you a 10% discount off prices that range from IR£12 ($14.40) to IR£25 ($30), depending on the show and whether you have dinner.

The most popular cabarets are those at **Jurys Hotel,** Ballsbridge (tel. 767511); the **Burlington Hotel,** Upper Leeson St. (tel. 605222); and the **Braemor Rooms** at the Country Club, Churchtown (tel. 988664). You must book ahead, which can be done directly with the hotels or through the Tourist Office.

Dancing

Dancing is the national pastime among Ireland's youth (from time immemorial, it's been the boy-meets-girl turf). Although Dublin's discos and nightspots are constantly changing, you'll always find a cluster along Lower Leeson Street (sometimes called "The Strip"), with admission charges of about IR£5 ($6) weeknights and IR£6 ($7.20) weekends. Some are fully licensed; others sell wine only. Main ballrooms for informal dancing (at lower admissions) are the **National Ballroom,** Parnell Sq. N. (tel. 746634), and the **Tara Ballroom,** D'Olier St. (tel. 712019).

READERS' SELECTIONS: "For a special evening in the Dublin area, we highly recommend either the regular restaurant or the cabaret at **Clontarf Castle.** We had a superb dinner in the tower dining room one evening and returned the next for the dinner and cabaret, which had good entertainment and which we enjoyed with more locals than tourists" (Harold and Mary Anne Ramsden, Anchorage, Alaska). . . . "The **Wexford Inn**, on Wexford St., offers the best in popular Irish ballads, with the Wolfe Tones, the Furey Brothers, the Dubliners, Dublin City Ramblers, and Paddy Reilly all performing there regularly. Owner Oliver Barden is a congenial host" (Frank McQueeney, Wayland, Mass.).

SPECIAL EVENTS: If you arrive in Dublin during one of these special events, you're in for a real treat—the entire city enters into the spirit of whatever is going on. You should check with the Irish Tourist Board about *specific* dates the year of your visit, and you should know that accommodations should be booked as far as possible in advance and will probably cost you a little more during these times when the city is packed out with Irish from around the country as well as international visitors.

In May of each year, the annual **Spring Show** action is concentrated in the Royal Dublin Society's show grounds in Ballsbridge. It's a grand exhibition of agriculture and industry, with prizes for sheep and cattle and pig champions, butter and cheese judgings, sheep dog trials, pony shows, jumping competitions, and even fashion shows. For the young fry, there are Punch & Judy shows, magic shows, and a babysitting crêche to free parents for a ramble around the grounds. All in all, the atmosphere is that of a major country fair, and it draws farm families from around the country, as well as more than a few from across the Channel. You can purchase an all-inclusive ticket for the five-day event, which went for IR£16 ($19.20) in 1984, or daily admissions which ran about IR£4.50 ($5.40) that same year.

The undisputed highlight of Ireland's social calendar each year comes with the **Dublin Horse Show** in August. For one glorious week, it draws a sophisticated international crowd, and the city dons its best duds to welcome them, with private and public parties scheduled around the goings on at the showgrounds of the Dublin Royal Society. There's much pomp and circumstance—and even more fun and frolic. As for the show itself, in what are acknowledged to be some of the finest jumping enclosures in the world, there are virtually nonstop jumping competitions; auctions net enormous sales figures for handsome horses with impeccable pedigrees; the Aga Khan Trophy competition raises the excitement level on Friday; and the whole thing winds up with the International Grand Prix of Ireland on Saturday. Side events include concerts by the Army bands, a beautiful floral display is the handiwork of the Royal Horticultural Society, and Irish arts and crafts exhibits are supplemented by folkdancing on the lawn. It's a great week to be in Dublin, and even one day at the showgrounds is bound to net you a score of new Irish friends. It is also probably the most heavily booked week for Dublin accommodations, so make your plans early. You can buy a ticket for all events for around IR£20 ($24), or a one-day general admission ticket for about IR£6 ($7.20). For a detailed program of events and ticket information, contact the Royal Dublin Society, P.O. Box 121, Ballsbridge, Dublin 4 (tel. 01-680645).

Theater lovers around the world look forward each year to the **Dublin Theatre Festival,** usually held the last week in September and the first week in October. Sadly, the Festival had to be cancelled in 1984, but I've been assured that there is every expectation it will be on again as usual in 1985. The two weeks are chock-a-block with drama, comedy, new plays, classics, experimental theater, mime, and musicals. And they're performed by topnotch casts from Europe, the Far East, America and, of course, Ireland. Every theater in the city participates, and the greatest problem is deciding which performance to attend on a given night. There's also a Festival Club, where members meet theater people on a social basis, and throughout the entire two weeks there are workshops and exhibitions around the city. Ticket prices are modest, from IR£5 ($6) to IR£10 ($12) per play, and they are usually available a few days before each performance. For full details on dates, schedules, and Festival Club membership, contact the Dublin Theatre Festival, 47 Nassau St., Dublin 2 (tel. 01-778439/778682).

One more reminder to make your plans early for any of these events, then book your accommodations and send a deposit to hold them.

SHOPPING: The Tourist Board issues an excellent free booklet called *Shopping in Dublin,* to help you find anything you could possibly want to buy in the city. It contains a very good center-city map, as well as a guide to sizes (many of which differ from those in America) and Customs regulations.

Speaking of Customs, you can mail gifts valued at IR£50 ($60) or less duty-free to any address outside Ireland, but no more than one per day can be mailed to the same address. Also, be sure to save your receipts for the Value Added Tax refund you'll receive on departure for all purchases you are taking out of the country.

A good place to begin your shopping—or just browse, for that matter—is the **Powerscourt Town House Centre,** Clarendon St. (look for the signpost on Grafton Street at Johnson's Court between Chatham and Wicklow Streets). If you just can't get excited about shopping centers, wait till you see this one! It's set in a 1774 mansion built by Lord Powerscourt, and the house and courtyard have been expertly renovated to accommodate small shops, wine bars, and restaurants. There's an Antiques Gallery, a Craftsman's Guild Gallery, high-fashion clothing shops, designer shoes and bags, and a hairdresser.

In Pearse Street, you'll find all manner of Irish craftsmen at work from 9:30 a.m. to 5 p.m., as well as a shop selling their products and a restaurant. Major department stores are **Brown Thomas** and **Switzer's,** on Grafton Street, and **Clery's** on O'Connell Street.

The **House of Ireland,** 37/38 Nassau St. (tel. 777473/777949) is a standout for finding anything from Waterford glass to Belleek, Wedgewood, Aynsley, and Royal Tara china to fine tweeds, special cashmeres, knitcrafts, linens, Celtic jewelry, pottery, blackthorn walking sticks, and a wide range of quality souvenir items. Look for the porcelain dolls by Owencraft of Ballyshannon, in handmade costumes that illustrate the social history of Ireland (Molly Malone, complete with wheelbarrow of cockles and mussels, flower vendor, countrywoman dressed for Fair day, emigrant, etc.). Good prices and outstanding service from a friendly staff, and they give a IR£10 ($12) discount on all purchases over IR£100 ($120). They'll mail or ship overseas. . . . The best place to buy smoked Irish salmon to take home is **McConnell and Nelson,** 38 Grafton St. (tel. 774344). Sean Nelson and his staff will seal it for travel, and prices are considerably below those at the airport duty-free shops. . . . **Patricia's,** Grafton Arcade, is run by Patricia York, a noted authority on heraldry, and has a good stock of heraldic items. . . . **Mullins of Dublin Ltd.,** Heraldic House, 36 Upper O'Connell St. (tel. 741133), also carries vast number of coats of arms emblazoned on a vast number of items. . . . Some of the most unusual replicas of antique Irish jewelry, copper, and wood handcrafts and other top-quality items with historical emphasis are at **Fergus O'Farrell,** 62 Dawson St. . . . **Colette Modes,** 66 S. Great Georges St., has one of the city's best collections of Donegal tweeds, cashmeres, knitwear, etc., and has frequent sales with good reductions. The staff here is especially helpful. . . . Tweed tailor-made jackets and suits for men are good value (last so long they're an investment rather than just a purchase) at **Kevin and Howlin,** 31 Nassau St. (at the bottom of Dawson St., facing Trinity College). Also a large range of ready-made men's clothing. . . . **Monaghan's,** Grafton Arcade, has our highest recommendation for Aran sweaters to fit all members of the family, as well as lambswool, cashmere, and Shetland sweaters and a good stock of menswear. They ship worldwide and offer a mail-order catalog. . . . **Blarney Creation Shops,** Creation Arcade, Duke St. (tel. 710068), is a branch of the famed Blarney Woollen Mills. They specialize in Irish sweaters, Pallas linen womenswear, and Donegal tweed suits and coats styled by leading Irish designers. . . . **Irish Cottage Industries,** 18 Dawson St., also has a good stock of tweeds and knitwear. . . . **Cleo,** 18 Kildare St. (across the street from the National Museum), specializes in designer woolens, as well as linens. . . . Break a shopping spree to get your hair done at **Paul Hair Studio,** Molesworth Pl. (tel. 762211/763824). . . . The best all-round music store in Dublin is **Waltons Musical Gallery,** 2/5 N. Frederick St. (at the top of O'Connell Street). Their stock of Irish traditional records and sheet music is tremendous, and they sell a complete line of musical instruments. . . . Book lovers can browse for hours at **Greene & Co.,** 16 Clare St. (tel. 762554), through two floors of new and secondhand books, or the rows of trays out front on the sidewalk. They'll hunt down scarce or out-of-print books at no charge, and the staff is both friendly and helpful. . . . **Parsons,** Baggot St. Bridge, is another traditional bookshop, with a large selection of books of Irish interest. . . . Inquire at the Tourist Office about the **Book Barrow Fair** held regularly in the Mansion House. About 30 booksellers come from all around the country to set up stalls for one day only, many selling old and rare volumes for bargain prices.

3. Around Counties Wicklow, Louth, Kildare, and Meath

Whether you elect to make your base right in Dublin or opt for accommodations in a more relaxed country atmosphere, you'll be no more than an hour's drive from most of the sightseeing riches of Counties Dublin, Wicklow, Louth, Kildare, and Meath. This region has been at the center of so much Irish history that it is literally so strewn with relics that it's hard to venture far without tripping over at least one.

ACCOMMODATIONS: For convenience, the following are listed by county. All are ideal bases for day trips into Dublin and sightseeing around the region.

Note: Prices shown below are those in effect in 1985—expect them to be higher in 1986.

County Wicklow

Hostels: You'll find hostels at **Glendaloch** (tel. 0404-5143) and **Aughrim** (tel. 0402-6102), as well as several other locations (consult the An Oige handbook for addresses).

Bed-and-Breakfast: See "Accommodations" in the foregoing section for an exceptional B&B on the waterfront in Bray.

Mrs. Patricia Hackett is hostess at **Croghan View,** Ballyellen, Inch, Arklow (tel. 0402-7323). This two-story house is set in a lovely country area just a half-mile off the Dublin/Rosslare Road just three miles from Arklow and is very near country pubs that encourage a singsong session at the drop of a note. The four bedrooms all have sinks, and there's central heating and ample parking. Rates are IR£8 ($9.60), with a 25% reduction for children. Open from Easter through September.

Thomond House, St. Patrick's Rd., Upper Wicklow (tel. 0404-2940), has splendid views of both the sea and the Wicklow Mountains. Mrs. Helen Gorman is the charming owner, and her four bedrooms all have sinks. One comes with a private bath and shower. Wicklow is just one-half mile away (St. Patrick's Road is just off the main Wicklow/Wexford Road, about one-half mile past the Catholic church). B&B rates are IR£8.50 ($10.20), with a 20% reduction for children. Central heating and private parking.

Ashdene, Avoca (tel. 0402-5327), is a modern, tastefully appointed house in a beautiful setting near the Avoca handweavers, and not far from Glendalough. Mrs. Jackie Burns has elicited many letters of praise from our readers for her friendly and thoughtful manner with guests. There are four bedrooms, all with sinks, and central heating. Rates are IR£8.50 ($10.20), and children get a 25% reduction. Open May through October.

County Louth

Hostels: There's a small **hostel at Port Oriel,** Clogherhead, Drogheda (tel. 041-22247), nine miles from Drogheda.

Bed-and-Breakfast: Just one mile from Drogheda, and convenient to Dublin Airport, **Harbour Villa,** Mornington Rd., Drogheda (tel. 041-7441), is a beautiful two-story home in its own grounds right on the River Boyne. There's a pretty sun lounge and private tennis courts. Only three of the four bedrooms have sinks, but all are handy to bath facilities. Mrs. Sheila Dwyer extends a warm welcome to Americans, and her rates for B&B are IR£10.50 ($12.60). Private car park.

County Kildare

Bed-and-Breakfast: Overlooking the famous Curragh Racecourse, **Dara Lodge,** Curragh Racecourse, Pollardstown, Curragh (tel. 045-21770), is a strikingly modern bungalow two and a half miles from Newbridge. Mrs. Joan McCann has six bedrooms, four with sinks, and her rates are IR£8.50 ($10.20), with 20% off for children. Central heating and private parking.

County Meath

Hostel: A small **hostel** is located at **Bridge of Boyne,** Hayes, Navan, Co. Meath (tel. 046-24119).

Bed-and-Breakfast: Mrs. Peggy Downey is your hostess at **Ardilaun,** 41 Beach Park, Laytown (tel. 041-27033). Her modern two-story home is set on its own grounds and is convenient to Dublin Airport. There are three bedrooms with sinks, one with private bath and shower. Central heating and private parking are also among the amenities. B&B costs IR£8.50

($10.20), and there's a one-third reduction for children. Open April to October.

READERS' SELECTIONS: "I recommend highly the home of **Mr. and Mrs. Malone,** Glen Gorse, St. Patrick's Rd., Wicklow (tel. 0404-3150). It is close to buses and trains and they will pick you up and deliver you back to the train. They also are full of information about the surrounding area" (Diann Castle, Calgary, Alberta, Canada). . . . "In beautiful Co. Wicklow, lovely hospitality from Mrs. May Caswell, **The Arbours,** Avoca (tel. 0402-5294). The house is set on a hill with a magnificent view of the countryside" (Don Craig, Danbury, Conn.). . . . "Mrs. M. Leavy, San Martino, **The Maudlins,** Trim, Co. Meath (tel. 046-31524), is on the edge of town. My substantial room with shared bathroom was quite inexpensive" (Leonard Wertheimer, Toronto, Canada).

WHERE TO EAT: There are good restaurants scattered throughout the Eastern Region. Most of those listed below feature the Special Tourist Menu, with prices of IR£5 ($6) to IR£7 ($8.40) for three-course meals. There is one Big Splurge, however, and I highly recommend it as the place to wind up a full day of sightseeing (but be sure to book ahead).

County Wicklow

A stop at the **Woodenbridge Hotel,** Woodenbridge (tel. 0402-5146/5219), is a must for me personally, whenever I'm anywhere near. The hotel was built in 1608, and there's a charming, neo-Tudor look to the stucco walls, overhead beams, and huge stone fireplace in the lounge. A lunchtime favorite of mine is boiled Wexford bacon with parsley sauce, which goes for IR£3.50 ($4.20), and other selections in the same price range are roast stuffed pork and applesauce, baked freshwater trout with herb stuffing, and roast ribs of beef with horseradish sauce—all come with two vegetables. Sandwiches are under IR£1 ($1.20). Dinners in the pretty dining room here are about IR£10 ($12) and are excellent. From May through September, there's a Special Tourist Menu. Hours are 12:30 to 2:30 p.m. and 7 to 9 p.m. Incidentally, this is where the late president Eamon de Valera came for his honeymoon, and you can make it an overnight stop for IR£15 ($18) single, IR£26 ($31.20) double.

The **Coffee Shop,** Fitzwilliam Sq., Wicklow (tel. 0404-2048), is a deli and restaurant specializing in home-cooked lunches. Soups, breads, cakes, scones, salads, and meats are all delicious and modestly priced. They will also fix picnic meals of filled rolls and sandwiches—a very good idea in this scenic county. The Special Tourist Menu is available year round, and a lunch from the à la carte menu will run around IR£4.50 ($5.40). Hours are noon to 5 p.m.

In Glendalough, the **Royal Hotel** (tel. 0404-5135) has bar food as well as a good, inexpensive à la carte menu. There are marvelous views of the river and mountains from the dining-room windows, a pleasant place to eat. A Special Tourist Menu is available from mid-March through October. Hours are 12:15 to 2:45 p.m. and 6 to 8:45 p.m.

County Louth

The **Buttery,** Rossnaree Hotel, Dublin Rd., Drogheda (tel. 041-7673), serves good bar food, or you can order from the à la carte menu or the Special Tourist Menu. À la carte lunches will run around IR£7 ($8.40), dinner from IR£11 ($13.20). Hours are 12:30 to 2 p.m. and 6 to 10:15 p.m.

County Kildare

O'Brien's Hillview House is a family-run restaurant at Prosperous, Naas (tel. 045-68252), where an à la carte lunch will run about IR£7 ($8.40), dinner about IR£10 ($12), unless you choose from the inexpensive Special Tourist Menu, available year round. Lunch is available from 12:30 to 2 p.m., dinner from 6 to 10 p.m.

County Meath

You can get just about anything from takeaways to steaks at **Monaghans Lounge**, Kells (tel. 046-40100). This is a pub-cum-health-club, with music on weekend nights during the summer. Lunch from the à la carte menu will average IR£4.50 ($5.40), dinner anywhere from IR£4.50 ($5.40) to IR£7.50 ($9), and the Special Tourist Menu is available year round. Hours are 12:30 to 2:30 p.m. and 6 to 9 p.m.

Big Splurge: If you're planning a day of sightseeing in the Boyne Valley (Trim, Newgrange, etc.), a great ending for the day is dinner at **Dunderry Lodge**, Dunderry, Navan (tel. 046-31671). Best call at least one day (more if possible) in advance, however, for this popular restaurant is packed out with Dubliners, who make the 45-minute drive for Catherine Healy's superb meals. The place itself, an old stone barn that Catherine and her husband, Nicholas, have converted to comfort but not to modernity, is loaded with charm, and if the weather is fine, you might eat outside in the rose-bordered courtyard. As for the menu, there's game in season, roast lamb, entrecôte steak with anchovy butter, salmon, and fresh fish from local waters. Vegetables are right out of the garden. In fact, freshness and a light hand with sauces and garnishes are the keynotes here. The wine cellar holds over 200 labels (Nicholas is on hand to help you select the one just right for your meal). A la carte prices run from IR£9 ($10.80) to IR£11 ($13.20), and there's a five-course table d'hôte dinner at IR£11 ($13.20). Hours are 7:30 to 9:30 p.m., Tuesday to Saturday, and it's closed one week at Christmas and Easter, as well as the last three weeks of August. Dunderry Lodge is actually about six miles from Navan, its entrance down a dirt lane—it's signposted, but to be safe, stop in the village and ask exact directions.

READER'S SELECTION: "We had a gorgeous meal at **Slane Castle**, a lovely stately home overlooking the River Boyne in Slane, Co. Meath (tel. 041-24207). Expensive, but certainly worth every cent" (C. Ives, Raleigh, N.C.).

THINGS TO SEE AND DO: Shades of James Joyce, King Billy, the High Kings of ancient Ireland, saints and monks—they all roamed the hills and valleys of the Eastern Region, and their haunts are there for you to visit. For detailed information on sightseeing, accommodations, and any other subjects, contact the **Eastern Regional Tourism Organization**, 1 Clarinda Park North, Dun Laoghaire (tel. 051-808571).

County Dublin

James Joyce Museum, Sandycove: Built during the Napoleonic Wars in the early 19th century, the martello tower that was home briefly in 1904 for James Joyce and Oliver St. John Gogarty is now a museum holding such Joyce memorabilia as personal letters and manuscripts, his walking stick and waistcoat, books, photographs, and other personal possessions. Lectures and poetry readings are held on the first floor, and there are marvelous sea views from the parapet. The tower is open Monday to Saturday from 10 a.m. to 1 p.m. and 2 to 5:15 p.m. May to September, and by appointment other months through the Eastern Regional Tourism Organization, 1 Clarinda Park North, Dun Laoghaire (tel. 051-808571). Admission charges are 50p (60¢) for adults, 40p (48¢) for students, and 30p (36¢) for children.

Malahide Castle, Malahide: This stately castellated residence was occupied until 1976 by the descendants of Lord Talbot de Malahide, its founder in 1180. Among the many historic happenings within its walls occurred on the morning in 1690 when some 14 Talbot cousins sat down to breakfast together before leaving to fight for King James in the Battle of the Boyne, a battle in which all lost their lives. Patrick Sarsfield and Oliver Plunkett were cousins of the Talbot family and visited the castle. Set in a 268-acre demesne whose formal gardens alone are worth a visit, the castle still retains traces of the original moat, and holds a rich collection of portraits of historical Irish figures as well as many fine examples of Irish period furniture. If all goes as planned, a special building will open in late 1984 with the **Fry Model Railway Museum,** the first of its kind in Ireland. On display will be model trains, trams, and railroad artifacts left by the late Cyril Fry. Hours from April through October are 10 a.m. to 5 p.m. Monday through Friday, 11 a.m. to 6 p.m. on Saturday, and 2 to 6 p.m. Sunday. The rest of the year, weekend and holiday hours are 2 to 5 p.m., with weekday hours the same as in summer months. Admission charges are IR£1.75 ($2.10) for adults, IR£1.10 ($1.32) for students and senior citizens, and 95p ($1.14) for children.

County Louth

Mellifont: To walk in the footsteps of monks who founded Ireland's first Cistercian monastery here on the banks of the Mattock River back in 1142 is to drink in the peacefulness of a setting that invites meditation. Their Chapter House and ruins of their cloister still remain from the structures built in the 13th century, but the foundations alone are left of the original building. There's no admission, and Mellifont is open year round.

Monasterboice: Muiredach's Cross stands a majestic 17 feet above this site which once held a large monastic community. It is universally recognized as the finest example of the sculptured high crosses of the 8th and 9th centuries, and the unknown master carver who created its many figures and ornamental designs used one piece of stone for this memorial to Muiredach, about whom we know only that he ordered the inscription on the shaft that asks for prayers on his behalf. Those dents in the base were left by immigrants who took chips of the cross with them as they crossed the seas to new homes. There is no charge to visit the small churchyard with its round tower.

County Meath

Tara: From the time that pagans worshiped here, the **Hill of Tara** has figured in Irish history and legend. It was here that the High Kings were seated, and there's a rock that legend says roared when a new king was found to be acceptable. Burial mounds here go back some 4,000 years, and there are earthworks and low walls of earth left from a fortification of the Iron Age. All else of Tara's regal trappings must be left to your imagination as you view this low hillside with the mind's eye and feel the mystical presence of pagan priests and ancient royalty.

Newgrange: Even older than the burial mounds at Tara, Newgrange was probably built by the first settlers who came to Ireland from the continent some 4,500 years ago. We know almost nothing about them, or what the ornamental spirals and other decorations at this impressive burial mound symbolized. We don't even know for whom the structure was built, whether holy men, chieftains, or kings. What we do know is that they were skilled builders, for the corbeled roof above the burial chamber has kept out the dampness of 40 centuries, and the 65-foot-long passage still serves quite well as an entry to the chamber, the stone at its entrance an enduring testament to prehistoric craftsmanship. Archeologists are constantly carrying out research at Newgrange in an effort to unravel such mysteries as the reason an opening above the doorway is so placed that the sun's rays reach the burial chamber only on the shortest day of the year, December 21, and then for exactly 17 minutes!

You can visit Newgrange daily from mid-June to the end of September from 10 a.m. to 7 p.m., and Tuesday to Saturday from 10 a.m. to 1 p.m. and 2 to 5 p.m. the rest of the year. There's a 70p (84¢) admission charge for adults, 20p (24¢) for students, children, and senior citizens.

Trim Castle, Trim: Ireland's largest castle built by Normans is in this pretty little village. From its tall, gray central tower you can see across the river to ruins of town walls dating from the 14th century. The site of an abbey which once held a statue of the Virgin credited with miracles is marked by what is called locally the Yellow Steeple. The castle's drawbridge tower once hosted England's Prince Hal, and its grounds have yielded up a mass grave of skeletons minus their heads who may have been the unfortunate (and unsuccessful) defenders of the stronghold against the forces of Cromwell.

County Wicklow

The **Wicklow Community Tourist Office** is in Market Square, Wicklow (tel. 0404-2904). There's also one in Arklow (tel. 0402-2484).

Powerscourt Demesne and Gardens, Enniskerry: The O'Tooles, Lords of Glencullen, once occupied a castle on the site of Powerscourt House, an impressive 18th-century mansion of hewn granite that was gutted by fire in 1974 and is no longer open to the public. From its perch on high ground with a view of Great Sugarloaf Mountain, however, magnificent Japanese and Italian gardens slope downwards, dotted with statuary and ornamental lakes. The 14,000-acre demesne, which straddles the River Dargle, holds rare shrubs, massive rhododendrons, and a deer park. Its most noted feature, however, is the Powerscourt Waterfall that tumbles 400 feet from a clifftop and is the highest waterfall in Ireland and Great Britian—it is at its most magnificent after a rainy spell. Outside the fortified tower stand two cannon from the Spanish Armada, and in the Armoury there's an excellent display of all manner of weapons—shields, pikes, bayonets, rifles, and some rather exotic examples from the Orient. A tea room and a giftshop featuring Irish goods are housed in the mansion's outbuildings. From Easter to October, the gardens are open every day from 10:30 a.m. to 5:30 p.m., and the waterfall (reached by its own gate, four miles from Enniskerry) is open all year from

10:30 a.m. to 8 p.m. Admission to the gardens and demesne is IR£2 ($2.40) for adults, IR£1 ($1.20) for children, with a small additional charge for the waterfall area.

In the town of Wicklow, there are traditional Irish music sessions one night a week during summer months at the **Boathouse.** Inquire at the Tourist Office for schedules.

Glendalough: "Valley of Two Lakes" is the literal translation of its name, and when St. Kevin came to this place of exquisite natural beauty, he found the solitude and spiritual atmosphere he was seeking. No visitor today can leave unaffected by that same peaceful atmosphere, which seems to cling to the hills and lakes and woods. For many years, St. Kevin lived here as a hermit, sleeping sometimes in a tree, sometimes in a small cleft in the rocks. When his sanctity and wisdom began to draw disciples to his side, a great school grew up that attracted thousands of students from all over Ireland, Great Britain, and the Continent. By the time of his death in 618 at an advanced age, the school had already become recognized as a great institution of learning.

Scattered around the shores of Glendalough's Upper and Lower Lake are ruins that trace the history of this mystical glen. There are relics of its great European influx, the Danish plunderers, the skirmishes between Wicklow chieftains, Anglo-Norman invaders, and of the burning in 1398 that brought its rich history to a close. On the south shore of the Upper Lake (and reached only by boat) stands the Church of the Rock (Tempall na Skellig), with St. Kevin's Bed (a tiny hollowed-out hole) to the east of the oratory and about 30 feet above the lake. The main group of ruins are just east of the Lower Lake and those farther east near the mouth of the valley, where the monastic city developed long after St. Kevin's death. The Tourist Office in Arklow or Bray can furnish a free pamphlet listing County Wicklow's antiquities and locations.

"Meeting of the Waters": About four miles south of Rathdrum, the Avonmore and Avonbeg rivers come together in an idyllic setting that inspired Thomas Moore's tribute:

> *There is not in the wide world a valley so sweet*
> *As the vale in whose bosom the bright waters meet.*

There's a flagstone path from the road down to the river banks, leading to a clearing which holds a bust of the poet, and the tree stump on which he sat while composing his famous lines is marked with a plaque.

Avoca: Not far from the junction of the two rivers, the little town of Avoca is where you'll find the oldest hand-weaving mill in Ireland. Do save time to stop by **Avoca Handweavers** (tel. 0402-5105), where second- and third-generation weavers man the mill that sits across a little bridge from the sales shop. The history of the mill is fascinating, and if you can find Jim Barry when he's not up to his neck filling orders, he can give you the account of how it has gone from near closing to its current humming state of good health. The patterns and weaves from this mill are marketed all over the world, and in the shop you'll find marvelous buys in bedspreads, cloaks, scarves, and a wide variety of other items, many fashioned by home workers from all over the country. Look for Dorothy Newman (who has been here nearly as long as Jim Barry). There's also another Avoca

Handweavers shop on the Dublin road in Kilmacanogue, where tweeds are transformed into finished products right on the premises. But for my money, the original mill is the place to visit.

There's a second meeting of the two rivers four miles south of Avoca at **Woodenbridge** (see "Where to Eat" for a good lunch stop), and right here I want to suggest that you detour from the major sightseeing route (on to **Arklow**) by turning onto the road signposted to **Aughrim** and **Tinahely.** First of all, it's a beautiful, scenic drive through the hills and vales of the Derry River Valley. But even more important, it's in Tinahely that you'll meet Dennis O'Brien, an Irish painter, gentleman, philosopher, and student of Irish history and the Irish people. When driving into town from Woodenbridge, just continue straight on past the square, and you'll see Dennis's sign on the left side of the little side street you enter from the square (if you have trouble finding him, just ask anyone). Here, in his home studio, he works and lives a lifestyle many people long for and few have the courage to pursue. Many of the necessities of life are acquired through a system of barter he has worked out, and his cash flow comes solely from the sale of paintings, hand-carved meerschaum pipes adorned with faces of legendary and historic Irish figures (look for one Dennis calls "Age and Youth," which shows a lovely young woman's face on one profile, and an aged crone's face on the other), blackthorn walking sticks with hand-carved handles, and a number of other items, all displayed in his family living room. He paints in a number of styles (some of which you'd swear were a couple of centuries old!), and his prices are quite reasonable. There's no charge at all for engaging and enlightening conversation you'll not soon forget.

The fishing village and seaside resort of **Arklow** is also where **Arklow Pottery** turns out lovely bone china as well as very good earthenware. Next to the pottery, there's a large sales room where you can purchase entire sets (not really too much lower than in other stores) or hunt through the lots of marked-down or discontinued items, all at bargain prices. If you're lucky enough to arrive for end-of-season sales, prices will be even lower.

READER'S SELECTION: "We visited one of Ireland's most impressive stately homes, **Russborough House,** in Blessington, Co. Wicklow (tel. 045-65239). It's open only on Sundays and bank holidays from Easter through October from 2:30 to 5:30 p.m., and Wednesdays and Saturdays in July and August. The main rooms are elegantly furnished, and the famous Beit art collection includes paintings by Rubens, Gainsborough, Vermeer, and many others. Lots of Irish silver, and interesting old Irish maps that date from 1592 to 1750" (C. Ives, Raleigh, N.C.).

Chapter V

WEXFORD, WATERFORD, AND THE SOUTHEAST

1. Introducing Counties Wexford, Waterford, Kilkenny, Carlow, and South Tipperary
2. Wexford
3. Waterford
4. Around the Southeast

THE SUNNY SOUTHEAST, THEY CALL IT—there are more sunny days along this part of Ireland's coast than anywhere else in the country. The Southeast is also one of the most scenic regions, with lush greenery, good beaches, seascapes from cliff drives, wild mountain country, and some of the country's best fishing in rivers and coastal waters. The richness of its counties prompted Cromwell and other invaders to confiscate much of the land for themselves, and it was from here that many Irish were banished "To Hell or Connaught." Two American presidents, John F. Kennedy (Co. Wexford) and Ronald Reagan (Co. Tipperary), have family roots in this beautiful region.

1. Introducing Counties Wexford, Waterford, Kilkenny, Carlow, and South Tipperary

County Wexford is pure charm, from the narrow old streets and lanes of Wexford Town to solid stone ruins of Norman castles to whitewashed farmhouses overlooking rolling fields and wooded pastures to thatched cottages to fishing villages to sandy beaches. Vikings came to build a town at the edge of a shallow harbor to use as a base for plundering excursions on land and at sea. And there they stayed until the first Norman forces to land in Ireland arrived on Wexford's coast in 1169 and settled in. And *they* stayed, in spite of uprisings followed by bloody massacres and a liberty-loving native populace that gave them little peace. Father Murphy, of legend and song, led a valiant band of rebels to Vinegar Hill near Enniscorthy in 1798, where for nearly a month the ill-fed and ill-armed patriots held out against the English king's forces. Down on the Hook Peninsula, a light to guide sailing ships has burned continuously for more than 1,500 years, winking across the water to Crook Castle on the Waterford side and giving rise to Cromwell's declaration that he would sail up the river by Hook or by Crook. Today's invaders are tourists such as you and me who find the now peaceful countryside a haven for sightseeing, sailing, fishing, and grand opera at the annual festival that draws international artists.

Say "Waterford" to most Americans and they'll promptly reply "glass." And certainly a visit to the Waterford Glass factory is a highlight of any visit. But in the old Norse town there are also fascinating reminders of Danes and Normans alike, with Reginald's Tower standing sentinel over the quays as it has since 1003. Fishing villages like Passage East and Dunmore East have changed little over the years. The coastal drive from Waterford to Dungarvan dips from clifftop to secluded bathing coves. Lismore's castle looms over a site once occupied by a great monastic community and the River Blackwater, a salmon fisherman's dream. Ardmore is a pleasant mixture of historic ruins and modern resort comforts. And at Ring, Irish is the language of everyday life.

Kilkenny's lovely pastoral landscape is dotted with Norman castles and keeps, while massive 13th-century Kilkenny Castle is filled with priceless art treasures, its old stables now occupied by designers and craftsmen of the Kilkenny Design Centre.

Normans also left their stamp (and their castles) on the face of tiny County Carlow, no doubt drawn by land as fertile and productive as it is beautiful and rivers that teem with fish. Historic Carlow town, on the River Barrow, is a pleasant, mostly industrial, town.

In South Tipperary, Cashel is dominated by the ruins of a medieval church and friary, their dramatic perch atop the lofty Rock of Cashel, adding to the awe with which visitors approach the site. Farther south is Cahir and its remarkably preserved castle. From mountain passes, breathtaking views overlook the Golden Vale, whose fertile pastures produce that wonderful butter, cream, and cheese.

2. Wexford

Wexford is a small, prosperous town with industry, agriculture and tourism happily blending into a relaxed atmosphere that makes it virtually impossible for the visitor to hurry through. Because of its shallow harbor, it was named *Waesfjord* ("The Harbor of the Mud Flats") by the Vikings, but it was the legendary Fir Bolgs who christened the River Slaney after their leader Slaigne.

Today, although very much in touch with the modern world, the town also displays with pride the many marks of its colorful past. Westgate and the wall at Rowe Street Church are relics of the Danish town wall later reinforced by the Normans. The sturdy bronze pikeman in the Bull Ring commemorates the bravery of those freedom-loving natives who stood—and fell—against tyranny in 1798.

Either Wexford or Waterford—a mere 40 miles apart—will serve as a base from which to explore this part of the Southeast region in easy day trips, and your decision may well rest on whether you prefer Wexford's small-town informality or Waterford's slightly (but ever so slightly!) more sophisticated big-town ambience (by no means, however, a big-city "bustle"). Whichever you choose, be sure not to neglect the other.

ORIENTATION: You can walk most of Wexford's streets in a half-hour or so, which means it has never seen fit to install a public transportation system. **Main Street**—so narrow you can very nearly stand in the middle and touch shops

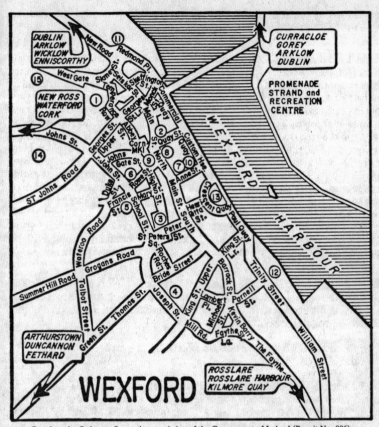

Based on the Ordnance Survey by permission of the Government of Ireland (Permit No. 906)

KEY TO THE NUMBERED REFERENCES ON OUR MAP OF WEXFORD: 1—Westgate Tower, Selskar Church, and Ruined Abbey; 2—The Bull Ring; 3—St. Patrick's Church and Graveyard; 4—Church of the Assumption; 5—Franciscan Church; 6—Church of the Immaculate Conception; 7—Presbyterian Church; 8—St. Iberius Church; 9—Methodist Church; 10—General Post Office; 11—Wexford North Railway Station and Local Bus Terminus; 12—Wexford South Railway Station; 13—Barry Memorial; 14—Municipal Buildings; 15—County Hall.

on either side with outstretched arms—runs parallel to the line of the quay, one block from the water, always alive with the buzz of friendly commerce. The aforementioned **Bull Ring** (scene of a Cromwellian massacre in 1649 that left 200 survivors of the 2,000 populace) is a wide intersection at the northern end of Main Street (its name comes from the fact that the cruel sport of bull-baiting was practiced here by the Norman aristocracy). The **Quay** runs for six blocks along the water's edge, with an inset semicircular **Crescent Quay** near the center facing a statue of Commodore John Barry (presented to the people of Wexford by the American government to honor this native son who became the "Father of the American Navy").

USEFUL INFORMATION: You'll find the **Tourist Information Office** at Crescent Quay (tel. 053-23111), open every day except Sunday from 9 a.m. to 6 p.m. (later in summer months). . . . The **train and bus depot** is at the north end of town at Redmond Place (tel. 053-22522). . . . **Private for-hire cars** are available in lieu of taxis. They meet most trains and buses and can be called to pick up fares at hotels and guesthouses. There's no standard rate and no meter, so you should agree on a fare when you engage a car. . . . **Car and passenger ferries** from Fishguard, Wales, and Le Havre, France, dock at Rosslare Harbour, 13 miles to the southeast, and CIE trains bring passengers into Wexford. . . . The **General Post Office** is in Anne Street, with hours of 9 a.m. to 5:30 p.m. every day except Sunday. . . . **Pubs and lounges** have hours of 10:30 a.m. to 11:30 p.m. (11 p.m. during the winter), every day except Sunday, when they're open noon to 2 p.m. and 4 to 10 p.m. . . . Current activities are detailed in the free booklet *Welcome to Wexford*, published by the Junior Chamber of Commerce from June to October and distributed by the Tourist Board, shops, and hotels. . . . Wexford's **telephone prefix** is 053.

ACCOMMODATIONS: In addition to the listings below in or on the outskirts of Wexford, the county is literally bursting with marvelous farmhouses within an easy driving distance of the town. You'll find our selections in Section 4 of this chapter, "Around the Southeast."

Note: Prices shown below are those in effect in 1985—expect them to be higher in 1986.

Bed-and-Breakfast: Mrs. Mary White, 11 High St. (tel. 053-23006), has been a favorite of our readers for several years. Her guesthouse located on one of Wexford's narrow old lanes (sometimes called McSwiney Street), Mrs. White is an enthusiastic hostess who offers both hospitality and good conversation. Her five bedrooms are comfortably furnished and all but one (next to the bathroom) have sinks. Tea and cookies appear regularly in the evening. B&B rates are IR£7.25 ($8.70), with a 25% reduction for children.

Mrs. O'Rourke, **Westgate House,** Westgate, Wexford (tel. 053-22794), has five comfortable rooms across from the rail and bus depot at the north end of town. Rates for bed-and-breakfast are IR£8.50 ($10.20), with a 25% discount for children.

Just two miles from town and about a half-mile down the Johnstown Castle road (off the Wexford/Rosslare Road), Mrs. Sarah Lee's **Rockcliffe,** Coolballow, Wexford (tel. 053-43130), is a pretty, modern home set high on an acre of landscaped grounds that feature huge, colorful roses in summer months. There are five nicely furnished and attractively decorated bedrooms, all with sinks and one with private shower. The Rosslare ferry is ten miles away, and Mrs. Lee is happy to fix an early breakfast for departing guests. B&B rates are IR£8.50 ($10.20), with a 20% reduction for children. There's central heat and private parking. Open Easter to October.

Farmhouse: Also two miles out from town, one mile off the Wexford/ Waterford Road (signposted), **Clonard House,** Clonard Great, Wexford (tel. 053-23141), is a lovely old 1783 Georgian house that was John Hayes's family home, and its 120 acres are still operated as a dairy farm. His pretty wife, Kathleen, and their three lovely offspring now offer warm Irish hospitality to visitors in bedrooms that are unusually spacious and nicely appointed, with bucolic farm views out every window (my favorite is the top-floor room under the eaves overlooking the century-old farmyard with its interesting outbuildings). Don't try to ascend to the fourth floor, even though there's a stairway leading up from the third—it seems Johnny's forefathers were just getting into adding that extra floor when they marched off to fight in the 1798 uprising and never came back; to this day, it hasn't been completed. Log fires and a piano make the lounge a friendly gathering place for guests, and Kathleen's evening meals are fast gaining a faithful following (a five-course meal with wine available, at IR£8—$9.60). B&B rates are IR£8.50 ($10.20), with youngsters paying half. Open April to October.

Guesthouse: At the north end of town, **Ryan's Riversfield,** Spawell Rd. (tel. 053-23172), sits in its own grounds, surrounded by spacious lawns. The nine rooms (all with showers) are both comfortable and attractive, and there's central heat and ample parking. A delightful sun porch and TV-piano lounge provide relaxation space, and in the dining room wine is available with meals. Rates for bed-and-breakfast are IR£9.50 ($11.40), one-third off for children.

Kay and Jim Whitty are the hospitable owners/managers of **Whitford House,** New Line Rd. (along the Duncannon Road), Wexford (tel. 053-22576/24673). The biggest surprise here is a full-sized, heated indoor swimming pool, unique as far as I know among Irish guesthouses! The 21 bedrooms in the two-story white guesthouse are all nicely done up, and ten have private toilet and shower, two have full baths. There's a large TV lounge, and in the dining room you can have an excellent high tea with wine, as well as a sumptuous full Irish breakfast with homemade bread. Soon to be completed is a public bar. Bed-and-breakfast rates are IR£11.50 ($13.80) single, IR£22 ($26.40) double, with a 50% reduction for children. Add IR£1.50 ($1.80) for private facilities.

READER'S SELECTION: "A little above the budget range, but a delightful place to base yourself in the Wexford area is the **Ferrycarrig Hotel,** Ferrycarrig Bridge (tel. 053-22999). It's just outside Wexford Town on the Wexford/Enniscorthy Road, right at the river Slaney's edge, with a river walk to the historic Norman Castle that rises above the bridge. Managers Paddy and Mary Hatton are the friendliest hosts you can imagine, and we found the rates to be extremely moderate for the high-quality rooms and service in this hotel. They also have package rates for three-day and one-week stays, which we will book next time" (S. Murdoch, New York, N.Y.).

WHERE TO EAT: At the south end of Main Street, **Tim's Tavern,** 51 S. Main St. (tel. 23861), dishes up some of the town's best pub grub at budget prices. Tim and Maureen Fogarty run the Tudor-style pub, which features exposed beams, whitewashed walls, and a thatch-roofed bar, and you'll find one or the other on hand whenever you stop by. All soups, meats, vegetables, and desserts are home-cooked, with portions more than ample. From noon to 2:30 p.m., Monday through Saturday, you can choose from a varied menu with everything from toasted sandwiches to open sandwiches of prawns, smoked or fresh salmon, or chicken to delicious salad plates of fresh or smoked salmon, prawns, or chicken at prices of IR£1.35 ($1.62) to IR£4.25 ($5.10). A hot, three-course lunch is IR£4.55 ($5.46). From July through October, evening meals are served from 6 to 8 p.m., with a 12-ounce sirloin steak, french fries, and vegetables priced at IR£6.95 ($8.34), plus a good selection of salad plates. The food is exceptional, but even better is the clientele, many of whom lead off a singsong at the slightest provocation, and others (including Tim, himself) who are only too eager to share their expertise at betting the horses at Wexford race meets or others around the country. This is a place you well could come to dinner and wind up staying until Tim sings out, "Time, gentlemen, please."

At the opposite end of Main Street, **The Bohemian Girl,** North Main St. (tel. 23596), is another Tudor-style pub. It's a homey place, with a loyal local following and Bar Catering Competition Awards proudly displayed. Soups and brown bread are homemade, and on hand are pâté and smoked salmon and other seafood. Lunch prices start at IR£2.50 ($3), dinners at IR£6 ($7.20), and snacks only are served Thursdays and Sundays.

By rights, I should list the **Oak Tavern,** Ferrycarrig, Wexford (tel. 22138), under a "Big Splurge" heading—that is, if you go for broke at dinner. However, this is such a special place that I heartily recommend you make the two-mile drive out the Wexford/Enniscorthy Road to indulge in a marvelous bar lunch of soup, sandwiches, seafood snacks, or pâté for under IR£5 ($6) if you're pinching the pennies, or a mouth-watering dinner for about IR£11 ($13.20) if the time for splurging has arrived. This old tavern has resided at the edge of the Slaney River for over a century and a half, and I must confess that I had a great fear it would disappear when a new bridge went up almost at its very entrance. John and Barbara Igoe, however, have not only kept the old place intact with not much more than a face scrubbing, but have added on an intimate little restaurant out back that fits right in with the tavern. It's in the two original front rooms, complete with open fire, piano, and lots of local faces, that you can indulge in bar food; or in fine weather, there's an outdoor terrace fashioned from a part of the old bridge, right at the water's edge. The charming **Ferry Restaurant** out back is lined with windows to take advantage of the river view, and also has an open fire as well as lovely tapestry upholstered seating. Specialties include a huge (10-ounce) grilled salmon steak with parsley butter, black or Dover sole on or off the bone, river trout poached in tomato provençale concasse, and John's pride and joy, the well-hung steak cooked over charcoal. Whatever your choice, this is one Big Splurge you won't regret! The Oak Tavern is open every day except Monday, and the Ferry Restaurant serves dinner from 7 to 10 p.m., with advance booking absolutely necessary.

Two miles outside the other side of Wexford, on the Rosslare Road, the **Farmer's Kitchen, Bar and Restaurant** is a fully licensed premises, and it is easily one of the nicest little restaurants in the Southeast. At lunch, salads and a daily special run about IR£3.95 ($4.74), and there's a full à la carte menu, as well as a quick-service grill menu, from 6 to 10 p.m. Dinner will average around IR£10 ($12).

The folks who publish *Inside Ireland* put me on to **Broom Cottage,** Drinagh, Wexford (24434), just down the road from the Farmer's Kitchen. Run by Teasie and John Devereux, it's a cozy restaurant in a charming, ivy-covered private home, with family knicknacks and lots of chintz in the small dining room. The Devereux children pitch in to help with table service, which adds to the homey feeling, and as for the food, it is, quite simply, superb! Everything is fresh and home-cooked, with seafood heading the list of specialties (plaice, trout, salmon, etc.), and pork, steak, and chicken are also on the menu. A full Irish breakfast is served from 6:30 to 10 a.m., IR£3.50 ($4.20), and high tea/dinner from 5:30 to 9:30 p.m. Dinner is priced at about IR£6 ($7.20) and it's best to reserve.

THINGS TO SEE AND DO: The very first thing you should do is stop in at the **Tourist Office** and pick up a copy of *South Wexford,* a marvelous illustrated booklet that's one of a series by Pat Mackey, an official of the Southeastern Regional Tourism Organization, who knows the region like the back of his hand and will bring each town, village, and country lane vividly alive for you. It's available at a small charge. You can also get this and others in the series at the Waterford Tourist Office.

See the Tourist Office staff, too, for information on how you can participate in local hunting, fishing, boating, golfing, horseback riding, and just about any other sport you can think of—you think of it, and Wexford's probably got it! As for swimming, there's a good beach at **Rosslare,** although the Irish Sea is not the warmest water you'll run across.

Go by the wide intersection at the north end of Main Street known as the **Bull Ring** and spend a few minutes reflecting on the bravery of the pikemen who are portrayed by the bronze statue there. Until Cromwell visited his wrath on the town in 1649, a great high cross stood here, and when Cromwell destroyed it, he slew some 300 people who knelt in prayer before it. The house in which he stayed in Wexford stood on the present-day site of Woolworth & Co.

Westgate Tower, at the northern edge of town near the rail and bus station, is the only surviving gateway of five in the old town walls, and is pretty well preserved. Nearby, **Salskar Abbey** stands on the site of an ancient pagan temple dedicated to Odin and a later Viking church. Henry II came here in 1172 to do penance for his murder of the devout Thomas à Becket.

On **Crescent Quay,** take a look at the **Commodore John Barry statue,** and if you pass through Ballysampson, Tagoat (some ten miles from Wexford), tip your hat to his birthplace. Homage is due this seafaring Irishman from Americans, since he is credited with founding our navy after being appointed by George Washington in 1797.

Berthed alongside the Quay is the lightship *Guillemot,* which has been converted into the **Wexford Maritime Museum.** If it's open, be sure to go aboard to see the many interesting seafaring items and models of famous ships which put into this harbor. Maintained solely by volunteers, the museum is a bit erratic in its hours.

Ask at the Tourist Office about what time and where to join the free **walking tour** conducted every summer evening by members of the **Old Wexford Society.** It's a labor of love for the dedicated group, and they'll point out such places as the birthplace of Oscar Wilde's mother next to the Bull Ring, the house in Cornmarket where poet Thomas Moore's mother lived, the house on North Main Street where the man who found the Northwest Passage, Robert McClure, was born, and many other historical spots. At the end of the tour, you'll look at Wexford with a different vision.

Some say that it was shipwrecked Cornish sailors who first brought **mumming** to Wexford. No matter how it arrived, however, it has survived, albeit with a decidedly Irish accent, down through the centuries, and it is unique to this county. The medieval folkdance with sword play was based on the Miracle Play triumph of good over evil, but today's mummers portray Irish patriots like Wolfe Tone and Robert Emmet. The three or four groups are composed of Wexford natives who have inherited their place in the ritualistic performances from family members going back several generations. They don't follow a regular schedule, but the Tourist Office will usually be able to tell you when the next appearance is likely to occur in one of the local pubs. If you can track one down, don't miss it.

Special Shopping Note

Joyces China Shop, 1 South Main St. (tel. 053-22212), is an excellent place to shop for Waterford glass, Belleek, heraldic crests, and high-quality Irish souvenirs. Murt Joyce, who has visited the States and has a special fondness for Yanks, has a large stock of such items, competitive prices, and frequent specials on even the pricier merchandise. Also on South Main Street, Sean Barker and his sister run **Barker China Shop,** with a large stock of gifts, china, and glassware. No charge at either shop for the friendly Irish service and conversation that will add immeasurably to the value of your purchases.

Wexford Pubs

The **Crown Bar** on Monck Street has been in the same family since it was established as a stagecoach inn in 1841, and Mrs. Fiona Kelly, its present proprietor, is usually on hand to welcome visitors and show them around the Crown's unique collection of ancient weapons. The two small back lounges hold racks and cases filled with dueling pistols and flintlocks, pikes from the 1798 Vinegar Hill seige, brass blunderbusses, powder horns, and Michael Collins' revolver, among many, many other historical items. The Crown has become internationally known through televised appearances in England, France, Finland, and at home in Ireland. Lest you think this is more museum, let me hasten to assure you it's one of the best drinking and talking pubs in these parts!

Stop in the **Cape of Good Hope** pub on North Main Street, where Con Macken (uncle of international horseshow jumping champion Eddie Macken) holds forth as publican, greengrocer, and undertaker. It may be the only place left in Ireland where you'll find all three occupations under the same roof.

There's always a good crack going at **Tim's Tavern,** 51 South Main St. (see "Where to Eat"), as well as sporadic singing nights. These folks are so good that they're sponsored by Guinness in the singing pub competitions during the Wexford Opera Festival. As yet they haven't won, but hope springs eternal and you'll find them in fine voice almost any night of the week.

Wexford Opera Festival

I can't wish anything happier for you than that you should arrive in town in October for the Wexford Opera Festival—it's 11 days of music and revelry, with international and homegrown companies presenting both standard favorites and less well known operas. Three are performed through each week, along with recitals, workshops, and a host of other related activities. And the whole town gets into the act, with events like the singing pub competitions mentioned above, spontaneous "recitals" by anyone with a song in his heart and a pint in his hand, and a general "welcome to the world" attitude on the part of every

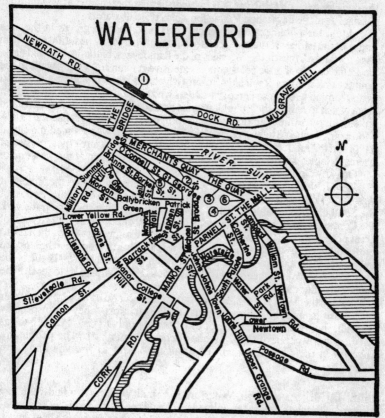

Based on the Ordnance Survey by permission of the Government of Ireland (Permit No. 906)

KEY TO THE NUMBERED REFERENCES ON OUR MAP OF WATERFORD: 1—Railway Station (north); 2—Bus Depot; 3—General Post Office; 4—City Hall; 5—Municipal Library, Art Gallery; 6—Reginald's Tower.

resident. For detailed information on dates, scheduled performances, and recitals, ticket prices and booking, contact: **Wexford Festival of Opera**, Theatre Royal, Wexford. Tickets vary from year to year, but run around IR£20 ($24) for operas and IR£3 ($3.60) for recitals.

3. Waterford

Just 40 miles from Wexford, Waterford is Ireland's fourth largest city as well as one of the country's most fascinating. Every phase of Irish history has left its traces here, and the fine harbor today is as alive with freighters to-ing and fro-ing along the broad River Suir (as wide here as the Thames at Westminster Bridge) as in the days when Viking longships plied its waters.

Prehistoric dolmens, promontory forts, and passage graves in the area speak of the earliest settlers; legends of valor and incredibly beautiful early Iron Age metalwork mirror the two sides of the flamboyant, battle-loving, and artistic Celtic clan of the Deise; the most extensive remains of Viking walls in the country and massive Reginald's Tower (which has stood intact for a thousand years) remind us of those fierce sea-raiders who came in 853 for a safe sea-haven from which to launch their plundering forays and stayed to become settlers and traders for over three hundred years; dozens of Norman towers like the "Half-Moon" in Stephen Street are legacies of the Normans, who claimed the city in 1170; and the modern Waterford Glass Factory, one of the city's most persistent claims to fame, is a descendant of the 1783 enterprise begun at the west end of the Quay by George and William Penrose.

The Irish call it Port Lairge ("Lairge's Landing-Place"); to the Vikings it was Vadrefjord; and always, this city on the Suir has been the main seaport of the Southeast. It remains so today, maintaining a thriving shipping trade with the Continent and England. King John of England dubbed it in 1210 "a pearl of great price." Its walls withstood a siege by Oliver Cromwell in 1649, then fell to one of his generals the next year. James II was loyally received when he stopped in Waterford en route to Kinsale after a crushing defeat at the 1690 Battle of the Boyne—and hot on his heels came the victorious King William III to receive the city's surrender on honorable terms.

As for the *people* of Waterford—an amiable blend of all who came over the centuries as settlers, conquerors, and/or artisans—they are especially warm in their welcome to those of us who come only to visit. As far back as 1586, it was written of them by one Richard Stanihurst, "The people are cheerful in their entertainment of strangers." And so you will find them today!

ORIENTATION: As cities go, Waterford is a small one, easy to find your way around, with shank's mare the only vehicle you'll need for a good day's sightseeing. Its focal point is the broad quay that runs along the Suir's south bank and is named simply **The Quay.** Distinctive **Reginald's Tower** is at one end, the **Clock Tower** is at near-center (an important landmark), and a bridge crossing the Suir is at the other. Narrow streets and lanes, as well as somewhat wider **Barronstrand Street,** lead off The Quay to the half-dozen or so streets in which are concentrated a great many of Waterford's sightseeing attractions, restaurants, pubs, and a few first-rate accommodations.

USEFUL INFORMATION: The **Irish Tourist Office** is at 41 The Quay (tel. 051-75788), open 9 a.m. to 6 p.m. every day during summer. This is one of the most helpful in the country, with facilities for booking accommodations, transportation, sightseeing—in short, as they say with pride, "anything that's bookable in Ireland." Accolades are due the staff in this efficient office for their friendly treatment of bewildered tourists in need of help. . . . At the northern end of the Suir Bridge, you'll find the **CIE bus and rail depot.** . . . **Taxis** man the rank at the rail and bus station, and you can telephone 75222 for a cab to pick you up anywhere in the city. . . . The **General Post Office** is on The Quay a few blocks from Reginald's Tower, and hours are 9 a.m. to 6:30 p.m. during the week, until 1 p.m. on Saturday, closed Sunday. . . . Waterford's **telephone prefix** is 051.

ACCOMMODATIONS: You won't have any trouble sticking to our budget in Waterford—affordable accommodations are plentiful in just about any section of the city and its environs you prefer.

Note: Prices shown below are those in effect in 1985—expect them to be higher in 1986.

Bed-and-Breakfast: Just off the Waterford/Cork Road (N25), **Annvill House,** The Orchard, Kingsmeadow, Waterford (tel. 051-73617), is a short walk from the Waterford Glass Factory. Alice (an officer in the Town & Country Homes Association) and Eammon O'Brien welcome you to their modern two-story home and are happy to arrange tours and help with any other holiday plans. The five guestrooms are bright, attractive, and comfortable, with built-in wardrobes and sinks. A most unusual feature of the large, airy dining room is a case holding two walking sticks made of Waterford Glass. There's central heat and off-the-street parking. B&B rates are IR£8.50 ($10.20), with a 10% reduction for children. Look for the Annvill signpost on N25 as you approach the glass factory.

Right in the heart of the city, **Mrs. Mary Ryan,** 7 Cathedral Sq. (tel. 051-76677), is the attractive hostess in a three-story home that faces Christchurch Cathedral. Just one block up from The Quay, the old house has been nicely renovated, and the five bedrooms afford views of either the cathedral and historic district or the hills across the River Suir. There's plenty of parking space on this quiet little street (a real bonus for a center-city location), and you can, in fact, leave the car parked most of the time, since a great many places are within easy walking distance and you can catch a bus out to the Waterford Glass Factory just a block away. Rates for bed-and-breakfast are IR£8.50 ($10.20).

Americans with an historic bent of mind will be drawn to **Derrynane House,** 19 The Mall (tel. 051-75179)—it was in this house that Thomas Francis Meagher was arrested by the British in 1852 and sent off to Tasmania, from whence he escaped and made his way to America, eventually rising to the rank of brigadier general in the Fighting 69th Brigade during the Civil War. The four-story house is of Georgian style, with a wide, gracious entry hall. There's a large family room with its own bathroom, and six others have sinks and are served by two shower rooms and two bathrooms. Eilish O'Sullivan presides over this historic house and maintains a homey TV lounge for her guests. B&B rates are IR£9 ($10.80).

On the north bank of the Suir in the Ferrybank section (about a mile from the center of town on the Waterford/New Ross Road), **Riverview House,** Ferrybank, Waterford (tel. 051-32785/32184) is a two-century-old country house surrounded by sloping lawns and gardens. Its hilltop perch affords marvelous views, and Mrs. Mullally has four large, colorfully decorated and comfortably furnished guestrooms. Plenty of parking space, and there's central heat. Rates are IR£8.50 ($10.20), half that for children.

Guesthouse: If you're driving into Waterford via the Rosslare Road, about two miles before you reach the city start looking for **Diamond Hill,** Slieverue, Waterford (tel. 051-32855/32254). It's a pretty, modern house set in lawns and gardens that have won the National Garden Award for guesthouses no less than four years. Its interior is as attractive as the exterior, with a nice lounge and beautifully decorated bedrooms featuring many built-ins and most with private shower/toilet. Mary and John Malone have won many devoted fans among our readers over the years, and now their charming daughter, Carmen, has joined them to run their excellent new restaurant (see "Where to Eat") as well as help with the guesthouse. The hospitable Malones take a real interest in their guests, and in good weather set out chairs in the sunny gardens for a bit of outdoor relaxation. Rates for bed-and-breakfast run IR£11 ($13.20) to IR£12.50 ($15). There's a private car park, and the house is centrally heated. A real winner!

Farmhouse: Another perennial favorite with our readers is **Foxmount Farm,** Halfway House, Waterford (tel. 051-74308). This 230-acre working farm is four miles out from town just off the Dunmore East Road (well signposted), and the elegant old home, dating from 1700, sits on a slight rise overlooking a verdant lawn edged with flowering shrubs, pastures and tilled acres. Margaret and David Kent are marvelous, caring hosts, always eager to accommodate their guests, whether by booking a glass factory tour, explaining the history of the region, or simply showing them around the farm. Children delight in riding Nellie, the obliging resident donkey (there are also a horse and pony) and exploring the farmyard. Other amenities include table tennis and a tennis court. The house is furnished with lovely antiques, and evening tea around a glowing fire in the drawing room is a special event. The five guestrooms are also furnished with antiques and all have sinks. Meals are superb, featuring all fresh ingredients and home baking (let Margaret know by noon if you want the evening meal). Central heat, and plenty of parking. Rates for bed-and-breakfast are IR£8.50 ($10.20), with the same charge for dinner, and there's a 25% reduction for children. Open April through September.

Hotel: Dooley's Hotel, The Quay (tel. 051-73531), is a bit above budget rates, but its central location, friendly staff, and general character may well tempt you to view this as a "little splurge." This was a leading 19th-century coaching inn, and the grandniece of the Dooley family still books in whenever she's in Waterford, even though for more than 40 years the hotel has been owned and managed by Mrs. June Darrer and her family. The staff are longtimers who cater to guests as if the hotel were their own. The lobby and lounge bar (see "Where to Eat") are warm with rich reds and greens, stained glass, oil paintings, and leather circular booths. The attractive restaurant offers low-cost Tourist Menu meals from May to October as well as excellent, more expensive lunches and dinners. Guestrooms vary, according to whether they're in the older section, with its odd-shaped rooms (some small and cozy, others large and full of interesting nooks), or the newer wing, where rooms are more standard, although still furnished in the traditional style in keeping with the hotel's character. Most rooms have private baths, and all have a radio, TV, and telephone. Rates begin at IR£21 ($25.20) single, IR£31 ($37.20) double and vary according to size, location, and season. Add a 10% service charge. Children under 10 stay free in parents' room.

READERS' SELECTIONS: "Mrs. Carroll, the hostess at **Roselda,** Cork Rd. (tel. 051-73922), really knocks herself out to see that guests enjoy themselves. She readily books visitors on the Waterford Glass Factory tour and is most helpful in steering people to interesting and scenic areas" (Sean and Shanna O'Hare, Oakland, Calif.). . . . "The clean, modern and inexpensive **San Michele,** Newtown Park (tel. 051-73632), overlooks the River Suir and has plenty of parking. Mrs. Pauline Heenan, the friendly lady who runs the San Michele, is full of information about things to see and do and places to eat in

Waterford" (James Nichols, Winona, Minn.). . . . "**Ashborne House,** New Ross Rd. (tel. 051-32037), is a lovely two-story modern farmhouse and our favorite place to stay in all of Ireland. Its gracious hostess, Mrs. Agnes Forrest, was happy to phone for reservations for the glass factory tours, to make a reservation at the hairdresser's, and to provide a relaxing cup of tea on a moment's notice. Six immaculate bedrooms are upstairs, grouped around an attractive lounge" (Dale Hilmer, Escondidio, Calif.).

WHERE TO EAT: Fitzgeralds, The Mall (tel. 74656), serves a wide selection of budget-priced plates and half of Waterford's young working crowd at lunch. More than just pub grub, Fitzgeralds serves hot dishes of a meat and two vegetables in portions ample enough to be the main meal of the day. Heaping plates of roast beef, ham, or chicken with a potato and two vegetables are features. If you're not that hungry, there's soup and sandwiches, cold salad plates, and something called a "blaa" (lettuce, meat, onion, and tomato on a small roll), found only in Waterford, that goes for under IR£1 ($1.20). It's a large, attractive pub/eatery run by the same Fitzgeralds of the Munster Bar (see "Pubs"). Hours are 12:30 to 2:30 p.m., Monday through Saturday, and prices run from IR£1.50 ($1.80) to IR£4 ($4.80).

    T. & H. Doolans, Georges St., is a century-and-a-half-old pub with much of its original decor and character still intact (see "Pubs") and a healthy local following for good pub lunches. Soup and sandwiches, salad plates, stews, and a variety of hot dishes are available from 12:30 to 2:30 p.m. at IR£1.50 ($1.80) to IR£4 ($4.80).

    At the **Reginald Bar,** just behind Reginald's Tower on The Mall, you can choose from soup and sandwiches, salad plates and hot dishes (meat plus two vegetables) for IR£1.50 ($1.80) to IR£4 ($4.80). At the **Reginald Grill Room,** a four-course lunch will run about IR£4.50 ($5.40).

    Very popular locally, the **Beer and Bite,** Blackfriars (turn up the hill at Woolworth's on Barronstrand St.). The two-level pub/restaurant serves sandwiches in the two-level bar section for under IR£1 ($1.20), and salads and snacks in the dining room on the lower level for IR£1 ($1.20) to IR£4 ($4.80).

    The attractive **Grill Room** at the Tower Hotel, The Mall (tel. 75801), serves continuously from 12:30 to 11 p.m., with inexpensive hot meat plates, cold salad plates, and a large à la carte menu. From 3 p.m. on, the inexpensive Tourist Menu is available.

    Such specialties as smoked salmon and brown bread are available in the pretty ground-floor bar of the **Granville Hotel,** The Quay, along with several tasty hot dishes, salad plates, and snacks. Hours are 12:30 to 2:30 p.m.

    Dooley's Hotel, The Quay (tel.73531), offers good bar food in its cozy bar/lounge for IR£1.50 ($1.80) to IR£4 ($4.80), as well as a three-course Business Person's Luncheon Special in the main dining room for IR£4 ($4.80) and the Tourist Menu from May through October. There are also excellent four-course lunches from the regular menu at prices of IR£5 ($6) to IR£6.50 ($7.80). A children's menu is priced at IR£2.50 ($3). This pretty dining room is also a good place for the evening meal, with prices running from IR£8 ($9.60) to IR£10.50 ($12.60). Hours are 12:30 to 2:30 p.m. and 5:30 to 9:30 p.m.

    Two Very Special Restaurants: Not really pricey enough to be labeled Big Splurges, but somewhat over our budget levels, the following two eateries are bargains in terms of value-for-money.

    The **Oak Room Restaurant** in the Munster Bar, Bailey's New St. (tel. 74656), is, in my humble opinion, one of the loveliest dining rooms in

Waterford. Dark wood paneling, an impressive fireplace, and a service bar of carved wood set the tone, and the Fitzgerald family's warm, personalized service and culinary expertise keep alive the traditions of the Munster when it was a coaching inn two centuries ago. Only the freshest locally grown produce, meats, and seafood are used in creating superb specialties of the house, which change according to what's available daily. Prices will run about IR£10 ($12) to IR£12 ($14.40) without wine (a good wine list is available at moderate prices), and hours are 6:30 to 9:30 p.m. every day except Sunday and Monday. Advance booking is a must during summer months because of its popularity with locals as well as visitors.

Two miles outside the city on the Rosslare Road, the **Diamond Hill** guesthouse (tel. 32254/32855—see "Accommodations") is another pretty place to dine. Pale-pink tablecloths and candles in silver holders add just the right touch of elegance, and Tiffany lamps compliment the colors. Carmen Malone oversees everything, and both service and the Cordon Bleu cuisine are exceptional. Salmon from the Blackwater and Barrow Rivers are featured, as are lamb and other locally grown meats and fish, along with garden-fresh vegetables. Dinner without wine will run from IR£7 ($8.40) to IR£12 ($14.40), and hours are 7 to 10 p.m. every day except Sunday. Again, advance booking is advisable.

THINGS TO SEE AND DO: The very *first* thing you should do is drop by the Tourist Office on The Quay to pick up two booklets that will bring this historic old town's streets alive with the ghosts of Celts, Vikings, and Normans. *Selected Walks Through Old Waterford* will send you prowling down narrow lanes and through impressive buildings to see the likes of **Christ Church Cathedral** (first established in 1050 by the same Reginald of "tower" fame), the French Church ruins, town walls, towers and castles. The second booklet, *Reginald's Tower and the Story of Waterford*, gives you a very complete (and entertaining) history of the massive tower that dates from 1003 and of Waterford from its very beginning. Both are written and illustrated by Pat Mackey, an official of the Tourist Board who knows and loves Waterford and the entire Southeastern Region. While you're at it, look for his *City and County Guide to Kilkenny*, as well, and if you haven't yet been to Wexford, this is the time to get Pat's excellent *South Wexford* guide, which will make your journey several times more enjoyable. The books are inexpensive and will become treasured souvenirs of your Irish holiday.

The Tourist Board will also book you for a tour of the **Waterford Glass Factory** (see below) and bring you up to date on what's going on in town during your stay (ask about the Waterford Arts Centre, which should be open by the time you read this) and advise you on **CIE day trips** around the area. As I said, go there *first*.

Reginald's Tower

At the end of The Quay which turns into The Mall, Reginald's Tower stands sentinel as it has for a thousand years, though today as a museum it guards gems from Waterford's historical treasures. When Reginald McIvor, the Danish ruler, built this stronghold, its 12-foot-thick walls stood right at the river's edge, and it was constructed so that entrance could only be gained from inside the city walls. In the centuries since, the tower has proved its worth as the strongest fortification on the River Suir, having resisted attack from all sides (even Cromwell failed to conquer it, although the bitterly cold winter may have had as much to do with his lifting an unsuccessful siege as did the tower's impregnability). And it has witnessed events of major significance in Ireland's history, such as the marriage in 1170 of Strongbow to Eva, Irish king MacMurrough's daughter, which marked the beginning of England's entanglement with Irish affairs. Today, you enter the fascinating museum through what was once the tower's dungeon (wherein the Sitrics met their end and Reginald and O'Faolain were imprisoned). On upper floors you'll find King John's mace and sword, along with many of the city's 30 royal charters. Interesting to Americans is the display on "Timbertoes," the wooden bridge across the Suir (now replaced with a modern structure) that was the work of Boston architect Samuel Cox in 1797. The following year, rebels who participated in the uprising of 1798 were hanged from its beams. There's also a bronze plate over which currency changed hands back in the 18th century—it's called simply the "Nail," and has entered our vocabulary through the expression "paying on the nail." The tower is open from 9:30 a.m. to 12:30 p.m. and 2 to 5:30 p.m. Monday through Friday (to 12:30 p.m. on Saturday) from mid-April to October. If you're in Waterford other months, ask at the City Hall (on The Mall) about winter hours. There's a small admission fee for adults, none for children.

The Waterford Glass Factory

You will surely not want to leave Waterford without a trip out to the plant where some of the world's finest crystal is fashioned into works of art, so before we talk about what you'll see, let me warn you that if you're not to be disappointed, you should book as far in advance as possible during summer months. The half-hour tours are one of Ireland's most popular attractions and only small groups are allowed through at a time. You can write directly to Waterford Glass Ltd., Kilbarry, Waterford, if you're sure of your dates, or you can arrange a booking through most Tourist Offices around the country. Many Waterford B&B hostesses will be glad to book it for you when you make your accommodations reservation. Tours are scheduled at 10:15, 11, and 11:45 a.m. and 1:45 and 2:30 p.m., and no children under 10 are permitted, although they may wait in the showroom and watch a 20-minute film on the factory. Also, the factory is usually closed the last week in July and the first two weeks in August for its annual holiday (this can vary, so best check).

The modern industrial complex is a far cry from the premises on The Quay in which George and William Penrose began the whole thing back in 1783, but the brilliance of the crystal (a 33% lead content elevates Waterford "glass" into the crystal category, which accounts for its fire and sparkle, as well as for the difficulty in blowing) and the artistry with which it is fashioned and cut have changed not one whit. Despite its early beginnings, Waterford Glass has not accumulated a two-century history: horrendous taxes on raw materials (not much change there, either!) back in 1851 closed its doors, and when the Irish government moved to open them again in 1947 it took five years to gather the necessary artisans and build a proper home for the industry. Some 30 master glass blowers, cutters, and engravers were brought from Europe and set to work training Irish apprentices, and in 1952, Waterford Glass was once more in production. Today, there's a staff of hundreds, all young Irishmen skilled in the exacting art and turning out 90,000 finished pieces of the beautiful crystal every week, of which about 70% is shipped to the U.S.

The tour begins in the blowing shed, where teams of three work swiftly and expertly with molten glass as it emerges fom the kiln, since in the space of three minutes it will become too hard to work. Once blown, the piece moves past checkers whose sole purpose is to spot even the slightest flaw—only two-thirds make it through this minute inspection, and they then go to the cutting shed, where teams of six (four qualified cutters and two apprentices) cut the 35 basic Waterford patterns into wineglasses, bowls, decanters, etc. Some 15% of the pieces fall by the wayside at this stage, since one cut even slightly out of line makes the piece a reject. The still-dull cut surfaces are dipped into a mixture of acids, followed by a bath in soapy water and a final rinse in white vinegar, by which time the characteristic fire and sparkle of Waterford glass shine forth in all their glory. Except for the acids, the Waterford people advise that you follow much this same procedure in keeping your own pieces gleaming, i.e., wash each piece separately in warm soapy water and rinse or rub with white vinegar, drying with one cloth, polishing with another. A bit of rice or coarse sand can be dropped into the soapy water and swirled around to clean the insides of decanters.

You'll end your tour at a showroom alive with dancing rays of light cast by finely cut pieces on display, but don't expect to purchase even one piece here. The plant sells only to retailers, and at uniform prices—it's the *dealers* who set price variations, so a little shopping around may net you a saving. And, while Waterford glass is far from a *budget* item, because of the Value Added Tax refund policy, your net price can be as much as 40 percent or more below that you would pay at home. A Waterford shop known internationally for its large stock of Waterford glass is **Joseph Knox Ltd.,** 3/4 Barronstrand St. (tel. 75307/72723).

WATERFORD AFTER DARK: On Saturday and Sunday nights, there's traditional Irish music (and a whale of a good time!) at the **Munster Bar,** Bailey's New Street behind Reginald's Tower. Call in around 9:30 or 10 p.m., when things should be just getting lively. Music is sometimes to be found in other Waterford pubs, but seldom on a regular basis, so check with the Tourist Office and in local papers.

The Pubs

You'd be hard pressed to find elsewhere the tasteful mix of antiquity and modern comfort that has been achieved at the **Reginald Bar,** on The Mall directly behind Reginald's Tower. Its antiquity is attested to by a plaque on the lefthand wall as you enter which bears the inscription "Built Circa A.D. 850 by Sitric the Dane." One of the original city walls, it has deep recesses which once served the Vikings as "sally ports," through which small boats were launched to "sally forth" along the river that back then was just outside. These days, the arched stone alcoves are fitted out with comfortable seating, and the only sallying forth that goes on is that of the attractive crowd that favors this lively pub. The peaked roof with its skylight and the modern fittings belie any image of musty reverence for history, and even such touches as gold and red Viking ships and a suit of polished armor have the look of today. For the most part, the Reginald is a pub for congenial mingling, but there's music from time to time, and on most Sunday afternoons between 12:30 and 2 p.m. there are jazz sessions by very good local musicians. Visiting instrumentalists who have their horn, guitar, etc., along are welcome to the local group.

Just down Bailey's New Street (which runs alongside Reginald's Tower), the **Munster Bar** is a cozy, wood-paneled, etched glass haven of conviviality, just as it has been for the past 200 years. It began life as a coaching inn, and the small room known as Peter's Bar (named for the Fitzgerald who took it over in the '50s) is a gathering place for some of Waterford's liveliest conversationalists. On cool evening, there's a coal fire in the small fireplace, reflecting off wall sconces and chandeliers of "old" Waterford glass (pre-1851). Peter's sons—Peter, Michael, and Tom—carry on their father's traditions of hospitality, and no matter which one is behind the bar, he'll see you're not long a stranger. On Saturday and Sunday nights, the large upstairs room rings to the strains of traditional music, and singsongs erupt spontaneously.

What was probably the stables for the old Munster Inn (with an entrance from The Mall) and more recently a dilapidated garage has been converted by the enterprising Fitzgerald sons into a pub larger than the Munster, but featuring handcrafted woodwork and Waterford glass fixtures in the same style. **Fitzgerald's** is mobbed at lunchtime (see "Where to Eat"), and evening finds it filled again with convival Waterford imbibers.

On Georges Street, you'll know **T. & H. Doolan's** by its Tudor-style front and frosted glass door. Inside, there's a wonderfully eclectic collection of old farm implements, whiskey jars, stone crock, mugs, copper jugs, and anything else the late Thomas Doolan took a fancy to hung from rough wooden beams or on the whitewashed walls. He was, of course, the "T" of the proprietorship, and if anything went amiss, blame promptly fell on the "H" of that partnership—and thereby hangs a tale. H. Doolan, it turns out, was purely a figment of T. Doolan's imagination, who came into being when Thomas was too long, T. and Tom too short, for the establishment's sign. The spirited characters of T. & H. still linger in this 150-year-old pub that was for many years a stagecoach stop, even though these days it's Stephen Boyle who oversees things. Conviviality reigns as always, whether you rest an elbow on the main bar or opt for the smaller lounge.

Gentlemen, leave your ladies behind when you head for **Thomas Maher's** pub in O'Connell Street! Surely one of a kind, this wonderful old pub that dates back to 1886 is presided over by one Thomas Maher, a small, white-haired, blue-eyed man who's been behind the bar some 54 years and knows his own mind when it comes to running his pub. "I don't want to see anyone too early, too late or too long," he declares and then sets opening hours of noon to 2 p.m., 3 to 5 p.m. and 7 to 9 p.m. "That way," he says, "there's not time for anyone to get too drunk, and between five and seven I get them home for their dinner." He brooks no swearing, no singing—and no ladies. With those rules in force, you may well ask, who comes? Crowds of devoted "regulars," *that's* who come. And well they might, for behind a traditional store front that has won many an award for its design there's an interior that has changed little, if at all, over the years. You may drink your pint in a glass stamped with a '20s or '30s date (since 1928, all pint glasses must bear a date stamp), and if there's no date at all, chances are it is one left from as far back as 1916. If you like, you can purchase spirits bottled by Mr. Maher himself. And what does the publican do between those short opening hours? He grows apples, potatoes, and vegetables, distributing any surplus among some of his widow-lady friends rather than selling them. He keeps one foot in the country, and one foot in town, which he says makes a nice balance, since "too many 'smart' drinkers can be wearying and too much country life makes for cobwebs." Mr. Maher and his pub are a Waterford institution you won't want to miss—if, that is, you're male.

Special Event

Wexford has its Opera Festival, but Waterford has its International Festival of Light Opera, a lighthearted gathering of amateur companies who converge on the city in September from Europe, Great Britain, the U.S., and all parts of Ireland. Each of the 16 nights of the festival there are performances of such musicals as *Brigadoon* and *Showboat,* all of amazingly high standards, and things wind up with the presentation of a beautiful Waterford Glass trophy. But light opera is not the only thing going on during those 16 days: there are singing pub competitions (with all pubs granted an extension of hours up to 1 a.m.) and a host of auxiliary activities, with a special Festival Office set up especially to see that you get to the competition, performance, or sporting event of your choice. You can book tickets in advance (advisable) by writing: Booking Office, International Festival of Light Opera, Waterford. Prices for individual performances are in the IR£2 ($2.40) to IR£5 ($6) range.

4. Around the Southeast

The Southeastern Region's counties Wexford, Waterford, Kilkenny, and South Tipperary are a veritable treasure trove of pleasures for tourists. Highlights will be listed below by county, and the nice thing is that you can base yourself almost anywhere in the region and be within easy day-trip distance of all of them.

ACCOMMODATIONS: Town and country B&Bs, farmhouses, and guesthouses of very high quality throughout the Southeast, and County Waterford has a gem of a self-catering complex in Dungarvan.

Note: Prices shown below are those in effect in 1985—expect them to be higher in 1986.

County Wexford

Hostel: Three cottages of the Coast Guard Station at Arthurstown, New Ross, are used for hostel accommodations.

Bed-and-Breakfast: Ivella, Rectory Rd., Enniscorthy (tel. 054-33475), is a modern house perched on a hillside abloom with colorful garden flowers. Miss Ann Heffernan has three attractive guestrooms, two with double and single beds to accommodate families, and one double room on the front of the house which overlooks a terrific view. Breakfast comes with homemade brown bread and jam, and Miss Heffernan, who is as bright and sparkling as her home, also serves guests fresh strawberries from her own garden, topped with generous dollops of fresh cream. B&B rates are IR£8 ($9.60).

About a mile and a half from New Ross, Mrs. Noreen Fallon's **Killarney House,** Newtowns Commons, New Ross (tel. 051-21062), has two things to make it highly recommendable: guestrooms are on the ground floor, a boon for those troubled by stairs, and there's a breakfast menu with several selections. Then, there's the peaceful country setting. All three bedrooms in this modern bungalow are equipped with sinks and electric blankets; there's a TV lounge for guests, central heating, and ample parking. Rates for bed-and-breakfast are IR£8 ($9.60), with a 50% reduction for children. Open May through September.

Farmhouses: Some 15 miles outside Wexford Town (to the west), the farming area around Foulksmills is fertile ground for farmhouse devotees.

There are no less than three outstanding places to stay amid rolling pastures, tilled field, and wooded countryside.

Mrs. Anne Redmond, of **Mill House**, Foulksmills (tel. 051-63683), opens her lovely old Georgian-style home to guests. Ivy-covered walls are the first hint of the traditional graciousness and hospitality to be found inside. The six bedrooms (four with sinks, the other two convenient to the bathroom) are all spacious, attractive, and furnished with many antique pieces. The water-powered mill that gives this place its name is a delight to adults and children alike, and Mrs. Redmond has set up croquet and clock golf for the young fry, as well as provide an appealing little donkey for their amusement. Children, she says, are especially welcome, since she grew up as an only child and always longed for a large family (a dream now realized through her 14 offspring!). It's that "family" feeling that makes Mill House so special—along with marvelous Irish breakfasts and evening meals that feature homemade cream soups and tons of fresh strawberries in season. Wooded walks are handy after one of those sumptuous meals; the Mullinderry River lures fishermen; and both golf and tennis facilities are close by. Bed-and-breakfast rates are IR£9 ($10.80), with a 25% reduction for children from 5 to 10, 50% for those under 5, and no charge for infants. Mrs. Redmond will be glad to send a brochure on request. Open from Easter to mid-September.

Mrs. Joan Crosbie's **Farmhouse**, Foulksmills (tel. 051-63616), is of 17th-century vintage, with a "newer" wing that only goes back to the 18th century. It's this part of the rambling, homey farmhouse that houses the ten comfortable guestrooms, all with sinks. There's central heating, and wood fires add a warmth of their own in both lounge and dining room. Mrs. Crosbie's sons, John and Jerry, are on hand to help manage the 150 acres, large herd of cattle, and a fair few thoroughbred horses. The horses can be hired by guests, and you don't have to miss a ride through this lovely countryside just because you've never sat on a horse, for John is happy to give lessons to beginners. Rates for bed-and-breakfast are IR£9 ($10.80); add dinner and the daily rate is IR£15 ($18); or if you decide to settle down for a whole week, B&B plus dinner will cost IR£100 ($120). There's a 20% discount for children, and Mrs. Crosbie welcomes guests from March through October.

Horetown House, Foulksmills (tel. 051-63633/63706), is an impressive Georgian manor house dating from 1698. The large main hall sets a tone of elegance, with marvelous old marble fireplaces carrying it one step further. All 12 guestrooms are spacious, and all but one have sinks. In the elegant drawing room, a piano and guitar are in residence as a constant invitation for spontaneous singsongs, just one facet of Horetown House hospitality that has earned it a reputation for relaxation and fun that makes it a favorite with Dubliners who come down for holidays. Vera and Theo Young and their family oversee things, with son David an accomplished horseman who gives qualified instruction for riding horses from their large stable of magnificent horses. There's an indoor ring, and cross-country riding is a joy. Special riding holidays are featured here (write for details and prices), and hourly lessons are available for short-term guests. As if all this were not enough, the Youngs have converted a centuries-old cellar into a charming restaurant (with whitewashed stone walls and a fireplace) that serves nothing but the freshest vegetables, meats, and fish at moderate prices (see "Where to Eat"). Rates for bed-and-breakfast are IR£10.50 ($12.60), with a 20% reduction for children. Closed from mid-January to March 1.

Just three miles outside Wexford Town, a half-mile off the main

Wexford/Rosslare Road, **Killiane Castle Farmhouse,** Drinagh, Wexford (tel. 053-22272), is John Mernagh's family home, which he and his lovely wife, Kathleen, now open to guests, who are assured of a warm welcome. It's hard to imagine a more romantic setting, with the farmhouse nestled next to a 13th-century Norman castle, huge old trees out front, and some 230 acres of pasture land creating an oasis of rural beauty. Inside, furnishings include many antiques, and on cool nights, there's a fire glowing in the lounge, even though the house is centrally heated. The 12 guestrooms are large and nicely furnished, most looking out to lovely views of the countryside, and one is a single (sometimes very hard to come by). The Mernaghs and their five lively young sons offer such warm hospitality and comfort for their guests that they won the Farmhouse of the Year Award for the Southeast in 1982. Rates for bed-and-breakfast are IR£9 ($10.80), with a 20% reduction for children (babysitting is available); for a terrific home-cooked evening meal, the tariff is also IR£9 ($10.80); a very good and ample high tea (steak and vegetables are a typical meal) costs IR£7.50 ($9). Open March through October. Booking as far in advance as possible is strongly advised at this popular farmhouse.

County Waterford

Hostel: There's a **hostel** at Glengarra, Lismore (tel. 058-54390). It's four miles from Lismore, about 43 miles from Waterford City.

Bed-and-Breakfast: On the outskirts of Dunmore East (seven miles from Waterford City), **Beechmont,** Dunmore East (tel. 051-83293), is a pretty country bungalow set on a hill overlooking the village and harbor. You approach through a well-kept acre of lawn and garden that presage what's inside. Mrs. Rita Power's bright and sparkling home is furnished with interesting antiques (you may want to take your impressive bedroom pieces home!) that create a homey, rather than stuffy atmosphere. The stone fireplace is a focal point in the lounge, whose windows look out to the garden. The three guestrooms (all with sinks) are as comfortable as they are attractive, and there's central heating. The two Power teenagers, William and Victoria, are great sailing and windsurfing fans and love to talk to guests about their favorite sports. B&B rates are IR£9 ($10.80), with a 25% discount for children, and there's central heating and a graveled car park. Open March through October.

In the seaside resort of Tramore, eight miles south of Waterford City, Mrs. Rita McGivney is the friendly hostess of **Rushmere House,** Tramore (tel. 051-81041). This century-old, three-story Georgian house is flanked by wide chimneys at each end and sits on a rise looking across Tramore Bay to Brownstown Head. The six guestrooms (three are family-size, with a double and two twins) are spacious, with high ceilings and tall windows. All have sinks, and only one does not face the bay. Mrs. McGivney is the soul of Irish hospitality and takes a real personal interest in her guests. Rates for bed-and-breakfast are IR£8.50 ($10.20), with a 25% reduction for children. There's central heating, and a large public car park just across the road. Open all year.

River View House, Cook St., Cappoquin (tel. 058-54073), is a real charmer. It's a three-story rambling house built by the Sisters of Mercy as an orphanage in the late 19th century, and under the loving direction of Evelyn and John Flynn, it has blossomed as one of the most unusual and hospitable lodgings in the country. The house itself is fascinating, with multiple stairways and corridors, a private dining room in what was once the chapel, two lounges (color TV in the more informal one back of the dining room), and a game room with pool tables, table tennis, darts and board games. Of the 21 rooms, my absolute favorites are the four on the top floor under the eaves, whose swing-out windows open up fantastic views of the town and the Blackwater River. All have sinks, and there are three singles, as well as a suite with one double bed, two twins, and a single and private bath. Outside, there's a small apple orchard set in a manicured lawn with benches for sitting in the sun and a play area with swings, swing balls, pitch-'n-putt, croquet, and a merry-go-round. As you can guess, children are very welcome here, and the four Flynn children—22-year-old Caroline, teenagers Paul and Sandra and 12-year-old Tracy—make certain that no River View guest, young or old, is neglected.

Personable Evelyn keeps her finger on the area's pulse and is always up to date on what's going on, the best fishing holes (the Blackwater is one of Ireland's best fishing rivers, and many River View guests return year after year for the sport), where entertainment may be found locally, etc., etc. If you're planning a day trip, she'll gladly pack a lunch and thermos bottle. Equally helpful, John will see that you have bait and fishing equipment if you decide on the spur of the moment to test your skill. Evening meals are very good, and tea and homemade scones (no charge) are a regular feature in the evening. The Flynns also provide self-catering facilities in a separate house which accommodates ten people, at a weekly rate (including linens, electricity, etc.) of IR£70 ($84). B&B rates are IR£7.50 ($9), and the weekly rate for full board is IR£60 ($72). Children get a 25% reduction. There's central heat and a paved car park. Open all year. You should book as far in advance as possible.

Jack and Eileen Landers, 2 Parks Rd., Lismore (tel. 058-54033), are positively habit forming! Since I first stayed in their shiny clean, attractive two-story home in 1973, I haven't missed a stay with them any year since. The house itself is bright, rooms are comfortable, and breakfasts are very good, but it is this pair who bring me back time and again. The teapot is ever on the ready, as is the sort of humor and fast-paced conversation that can only be Irish, and to say that guests are treated like family is a gross understatement. On the practical side, Jack and Eileen can point you to good eateries and special sightseeing in the area and take a special interest in seeing that your Lismore stay is a memorable one. There are three bedrooms, two doubles and one twin-bedded. Rates for bed-and-breakfast are IR£8 ($9.60), with a 25% reduction for children.

Farmhouses: The Castle, Millstreet, Cappagh (tel. Cappagh 49), incorporates into an attractive farmhouse an arched stone doorway and a few stone walls of a 350-year-old Irish castle. Joan and Emmet Nugent and their four children reign in this pleasant kingdom and extend warm, friendly hospitality to their guests. There are five bedrooms, all brightly furnished, all with sinks and electric blankets. Meals are a special treat, with Joan's fresh home-baked brown bread, lamb, and beef from the farm, salmon caught in local rivers, and vegetables straight from the farm fields. Guests are free to fish for trout right on the Nugents' land, and there's a pony for the young fry to ride. Located on the main Clonmel/Youghal road, the Castle is four miles north of the Dungarvan/Cappoquin road and is well signposted. Rates for bed-and-breakfast are IR£8 ($9.60), with 50% off for children. Dinner is IR£6.50 ($7.80).

Two and a half miles south of Dungarvan, just off the main Dungarvan/Youghal road, **Ballyguiry Farm**, Dungarvan (tel. 058-41194), is a lovely Georgian house dating from the 1880s and set in the foothills of the Drum Hills. Kathleen and Sean Kiely make guests feel right at home, as do their four charming children. They delight in helping plan sightseeing forays around the area and will even map out itineraries on an ordinance survey map for your use on day trips. The six guestrooms are exceptionally pretty, with floral wallpaper and coordinated pastel bedspreads. Two family suites have private baths and are suitable for parents and up to three children. There's a playground, hard tennis court, and a pony for children to pet and ride. B&B rates are IR£9.50 ($11.40), dinner (with farm-fresh ingredients) is IR£7.50 ($9), and high tea is IR£4 ($4.80). A week's stay with bed, breakfast, and dinner costs IR£100 ($120). Central heating, and electric blankets on all beds.

Guesthouse: In Cappoquin, the **Toby Jug**, Main St. (tel. 058-54317), is a favorite with anglers who come to fish the Blackwater River. Mr. and Mrs. Noonan are the cordial owner/managers, and their brochure bears the promise "we will do our very best to make you happy." There are ten bedrooms, all attractively decorated and comfortably furnished, some with private baths, all with hand basins, and there's a cozy TV lounge for guests. On the ground floor is the pretty dining room and popular public bar run by the Noonans' handsome red-haired son, John. Rates for bed-and-breakfast are IR£8 ($9.60) or IR£9 ($10.80) with private bath. For room, breakfast, and dinner, the charge is IR£16 ($19.20) and IR£17 ($20.40) per day or IR£90 ($108) and IR£97 ($116.40) per week. Add 10% service charge; 10% reduction for children.

Self-Catering: Set right at the edge of Dungarvan Bay, **Gold Coast Holiday Homes**, Ballinacourty, Dungarvan (tel. 058-42249), are some of the most attractive cottages available in the Southeastern Region. Arranged in a semicircle, each has its own garden area, and there's an outstanding restaurant and lounge bar on the premises, both very popular with locals. Each semi-detached, two-story cottage has a living/dining room with fireplace, fully equipped kitchen, two bedrooms on the ground floor and one upstairs, and bath. Bedrooms have built-in wardrobes and dressing tables and there's one double bed and four twins in each cottage. They're carpeted throughout, nicely furnished, and come complete with TV. Six people can be accommodated comfortably, and there's plenty of room to install an extra cot in the spacious upstairs bedroom. Weekly rates per cottage run from IR£90 ($108) to IR£240 ($288), depending on season. From October to May, there are attractive midweek and weekend rates available. Rates include all linens, with an extra charge for electricity.

County Kilkenny

Hostel: Sixteenth-century **Foulksrath Castle**, Jenkinstown (tel. 056-27674), provides hostel facilities eight miles from Kilkenny Town.

Bed-and-Breakfast: Nore Valley Villa, Inistioge (tel. 056-29418), is surrounded by scenic beauty. Located on the Rosslare/Kilkenny/Athlone road and overlooking the River Nore, this Georgian villa is hard by Woodstock Forest. It makes an ideal base for day trips to historical sites nearby. The three bedrooms all have handbasins, and there's central heat and plenty of parking space. B&B rates are IR£9 ($10.80), with 20% reduction for children.

Farmhouse: About a mile from the old Norman village of Ballyhale just off the main Waterford/Kilkenny road, **Kiltorcan House,** Ballyhale (tel. 056-28617), is a marvelous, 200-year-old Georgian manor house that Tom and Nellie Duggan have restored to its original charm and more than its original comfort. Furnishings are mostly lovely antique pieces, and some of the wallpaper has been duplicated from old Georgian wax blocks. The drawing room looks out onto ornamental gardens, while the dining room faces more garden walks. The 12 large bedrooms are beautifully decorated; some have private baths; and bathrooms feature heated towel racks. Guests tend to gather around a log fire in the cozy library of an evening and have been known to burst into song more than once in the congenial company of the Duggans. The Duggans and their six lively children breed horses (one has joined the ranks of the Queen's Guards in London), and riding instruction is available, as well as croquet and tennis. Rates for B&B are IR£9 ($10.80), with a 10% discount for children. Add IR£1 ($1.20) per day for private bath. For an illustrated brochure, write: Kiltorcan House, Ballyhale, Co. Kilkenny.

South Tipperary

Hostel: A lovely shooting lodge in scenic surroundings provides good hostel accommodations: **Ballydavid Wood House,** Glen of Aherlow (tel. 062-54148).

Bed-and-Breakfast: Mrs. Mary Quinn greets you at **Clonmore,** Cork/ Galbally Rd., Tipperary Town (tel. 062-51637). Her pretty bungalow sits in its own grounds, within sight of the Galtee mountains and a short walk from town. There are four bedrooms, all with handbasins, and the house has central heat. Plenty of parking. Bed-and-breakfast rates are IR£8.50 ($10.20), with 25% off for children.

Farmhouses: Parkstown House, Horse & Jockey, Co. Tipperary (tel. 0504-44315), is a 1770 Georgian manor house set in 200 acres of farmland eight miles north of Cashel. Its owner, the charming Mrs. Maher, has left her elegant touch all through the house, with gold velvet on the lovely seating grouped around the drawing room fireplace (made of fine Italian marble), matching wallpapers and fabrics, sprays of fresh flowers and glowing wood fires. Many of the beautiful antique furnishings (including hand-carved wardrobes and dressers in guest bedrooms) are heirlooms in Mr. Maher's family. There's a cozy library with a TV and comfortable leather chairs. All five guestrooms but one have handbasins, there are three hall bathrooms, and two rooms and a bath can be opened up as a family suite. Gracious is the word for house and hosts. Central heat. B&B rates are IR£12 ($14.40), IR£13 ($15.60) per person in the private suite, 20% reduction for children. Central heat.

To reach **Killoran House,** Moyne, Thurles (tel. 0504-45271), look for the signpost on your right as you drive from Kilkenny on the main Dublin/Cork road. When you turn off the highway, it's a five-mile drive to Peg and Ned Cambie's large Georgian house that dates from the 1600s.

This is Ned's family home, and among its antique furnishings are three stately grandfather clocks, two of which were crafted by his ancestors. There are five large bedrooms, comfortably furnished, with electric heaters in each. Log and peat fires glow in the drawing room. All meals feature farm-fresh ingredients. Killoran House sits in its own parklands, and just across the road is a round crenelated tower known as a "folly," which has an interesting history. Rates are IR£8 ($9.60) for bed-and-breakfast, with a 20% reduction for children. Dinner is IR£7.50 ($9).

READER'S SELECTIONS: *County Wexford:* "**Woodlands Farmhouse,** Ballynestragh, Gorey, Co. Wexford (tel. 0402-7125), run by Mrs. O'Sullivan, was the nicest lodging of our trip. Our room was spacious, clean and nicely decorated, and the farmhouse is quite comfortable, with a sitting room that includes a color TV and priceless antiques" (Joseph McGrath, Bridgeport, Conn.). . . . "We had such a wonderful visit at Mr. and Mrs. Gough's **Ballyorley House,** Boolavogue (tel. 054-66287), that we went out of our way to return there before flying on to the continent" (Marlene Carlen and Ilene Adler, Los Angeles, Calif.). . . . "Add to your list of super farm families Mrs. Breen, **Clone House,** Ferns (tel. 054-66113)" (R.J. Bunday, Emporia, Kansas). . . . "**Carrignee House,** Carrigbyrne, New Bawn (tel. 051-24310), is a lovely guesthouse on N25, convenient to J. F. Kennedy Park, Wexfod and New Rose. Mrs. French is a lovely and well informed hostess" (Mary M. Wentz, Suffern, N.Y.). . . . "We found **Ailsa Lodge,** Rosslare Harbout (tel. 053-33230), to be a lovely large Edwardian house, newly remodeled, that overlooks the sea" (Cora and Ray Smythe, Pointe Claire, Quebec, Canada). . . . "At **Mrs. O'Leay's Farm House,** Killilane, Kilrane (tel. 053-33134), the food and welcome were both excellent." (Michel Boilly, Ivry, France). . . . *County Waterford:* "We stayed with the Gough family at **Moat Farmhouse,** Faithlegg, Cheekpoint Rd., Waterford (tel. 051-82166), an 18th-century farmhouse in this family for generations. On the grounds is an earth fort called a Motte, surrounded by a moat. The Goughs are lovely and warm; the house is lovely and clean, clean, clean; and the food and hospitality are excellent (Bob and Joan Banks, Indianapolis, Ind.). . . . "Our stay near Waterford City at **Glencree,** The Sweep, Kilmeaden (tel. 051-84240), with Mrs. Rena Power and her family was a memorable experience. The home is beautiful, but best of all it's great to meet such a loving family" (Renee Reilly, Minneapolis, Minn.). . . . "The clean, beautiful home, Mrs. P. Croke's hospitality and delicious breakfasts at **Stella Maris,** Youghal Rd., Dungarvan (tel. 058-41727) will never be forgotten." (Mrs R. Vallejo, Calif.). . . . *County Kilkenny:* "We would like to add **Hillgrove,** Warrington, Kilkenny (tel. 056-22890), to your listings. Tony and Margaret Drennan are a delightful young couple with two small children and a lovely house" (Hilda Preston, Torrance, Calif.). . . . "**Lunar Lodge,** Bawnlusk, Cuffes Grange (tel. 056-29925), is run by the charming Mrs. Milne. There's an outdoor swimming pool and an unusual rose garden depicting Irish subjects" (Anne Reitman, Ft. Thomas, Ky.). . . . "**Brandon View House,** Graighamanagh (tel. 0503-24191), is the delightful farm home of Alice and Martin McCabe, where the meals were excellent and a fire always crackling when needed" (Irwin and Ellen Feldman, Erianger, Ky.). . . . "Miss Patricia Cantlon and her mother welcomed us at **Cullintra House,** Inistioge (tel. 051-23614). The place was lovely and comfortable, the food delicious, and the warm hospitality just great" (Mrs. M. Barnett, Ontario, Canada). . . . *County Tipperary:* "I want to recommend **Carrigeen Castle,** Cork Rd., Cahir, Co. Tipperary (tel. 052-41370). Staying in a castle is fun, and we had a bathroom the size of some of the guestrooms we've stayed in, but Mrs. Butler made the day." (Martha Mackin, Evanston, Ill.). . . . "Number one on my list is **Thornbrook House,** Kilkenny Rd., Cashel, Co. Tipperary (tel. 062-61480). The grounds are spacious, and my large room looked out to the Rock of Cashel. Mary Kennedy gives you a warm welcome" (Donna Mash, Newport Beach, Calif.). . . . "**Bansha House,** Bansha Tipperary (tel. 062-54194), is a lovely Georgian home with Mary Marnane its gracious hostess. She's a dear, and we made it a two-night stop" (Charles Fitzgerald, Beechhurst, N.Y.). . . . "Mrs. Foley's **Rathard Lodge,** Cashel (tel. 062-61052), is a farmhouse on the main road from Kilkenney. Tea and biscuits at night and plenty of pasture to roam around in" (Marilyn Bloomberg, Oakland, Calif.). . . . "**Mullinarinka,** Clonmel (tel. 052-21374), is a large manor house on some 100 acres. Mrs. Phelan is the hospitable hostess, and bedrooms are furnished in period pieces" (James Walsh, Lynbrook, N.Y.). . . . **"Hill Crest,** Powerstown Rd., Clonmel (tel. 052-21798), is a fine townhouse run by hospitable Mrs. O'Reilly" (Lance Ringel, Washington, D.C.).

WHERE TO EAT: One of the highlights of Irish dining is not so much a superb meal (which it is) as it is a superb experience on Ireland's only cruising restaurant. Then you can dine in a former bishop's palace in Cashel, enjoy fantastic home-cooked meals in a cozy Lismore pub, or watch the sun go down over Dungarvan Bay from the comfort of a first-rate waterfront dining room.

County Wexford

That marvelous cruising restaurant is the **New Ross Galley,** The Quay, New Ross (tel. 051-21723). Skipper Dick Fletcher conceived the idea several years ago, and now the *Galley* sets sail for lunches, afternoon teas, and dinners. Whichever cruise you select, you'll spend from two to four hours relaxing over delicious specialties created from locally grown produce, meats and fish in the comfortable, heated cruiser as you slide between the scenic banks of the rivers Barrow, Nore, or Suir. No canned music, no commentary—just the blissful comfort of good food, drink (the *Galley* is fully licensed), and conversation. If you're curious about the ancient stately homes, castles, and abbeys you glimpse along the shore, read the menu pages that give a detailed history of the area. There's seating for just 70, which makes for cozy intimacy, and the skipper is usually aboard in the role of gracious host.

In April and May and September and October, cruises depart Wednesday through Sunday from the Quay at New Ross at noon for a two-hour cruise featuring a terrific lunch (many times a smorgasbord buffet, so you can eat your fill) at an all-inclusive price of IR£10.50 ($12.60). During June, July, and August, there are daily departures. From June through August, there's a high tea two-hour cruise departing daily at 3 p.m., at a cost of IR£5 ($6). And if you want to go all out for a truly memorable evening, from April through September you can book for the three-hour dinner cruise that leaves every day at 7 p.m. (6 p.m. in September), at a cost of IR£14 ($16.80) to IR£18 ($21.60). From June through August, there are also afternoon and high tea cruises departing from Waterford, at prices of IR£5 ($6) to IR£9.50 ($11.40), but frequency can be uncertain, so best to check on days and times when you're there. It is possible on all the above to opt for the cruise only, at prices of IR£4 ($4.80) to IR£7 ($8.40). Booking is absolutely essential, especially during the high season. Call 051-21723 or book through the Wexford or Waterford Tourist Office. This, in my book, is a don't-miss!

The **Cellar Restaurant,** Horetown House, Foulksmills (tel. 051-63633/63706), is in the 300-year-old cellar of a marvelous Georgian mansion (see "Accommodations"). The thick stone walls, washed in pristine white, glowing fireplace, and wooden tables and chairs create a "back in time" atmosphere, and when your meal arrives, expertly prepared from only the freshest farm ingredients, sheer satisfaction sets in. There are hot and cold selections, and wine is available. Lunch, from 11 a.m. to 2 p.m., runs around IR£4.50 ($5.40); dinner, from 7 to 9 p.m., around IR£8 ($9.60). The Tourist Menu is offered from March through December. Closed Sunday evenings and Monday, and mid-January through February.

Elsewhere in County Wexford, you'll find the Tourist Menu offered at: **Jimmy's Steak & Seafood Restaurant,** Strand Rd., Rosslare (tel. 051-32151);

The Singing Kettle, Ardamine, Courtown Harbour (tel. 055-25151), on the coast; and **The Coach House,** 1 Main St., Gorey (tel. 055-21280).

County Waterford

Ballads and crubeen (boiled pigs' feet) hold center stage at **Rocketts Pub** on the coast road outside Tramore, but you'll also find such traditional favorites as colcannon (mashed potatoes and cabbage), spareribs, chicken, and stews, all at prices of IR£3.50 ($4.20) to IR£5 ($6).

In Dungarvan, the **Shamrock Restaurant,** O'Connell St. (tel. 058-42242), is a cozy, attractive restaurant upstairs (past the square on the Cappoquin route) that serves all three meals at prices which can only be called "bargain." It is one of the best values in the area, in fact, with the highest price on the menu being IR£5.50 ($6.60) for a T-bone steak with salad or vegetable. Other selections are buttered trout with two vegetables, chicken curry rice and roast stuffed chicken—all at IR£2.50 ($3) to IR£4 ($4.80). Burgers, quiche Lorraine, and a variety of other light meals go from IR£1.50 ($1.80) to IR£2 ($2.40). There's a full wine license, and hours are 9 a.m. to 10 p.m. with continuous service, making this a good place for an afternoon snack or one of their delicious and inexpensive (under IR£1) desserts and tea.

The **Gold Coast Restaurant,** Ballinacourty, Dungarvan (tel. 058-42249/42457), sits right at the water's edge on Dungarvan Bay. The glass-walled dining room is bright with blue, white, and red in tablecloths and napkins, and food here is exceptional, as well as very good value. Specialties are seafood dishes and locally grown meats and vegetables. Dinner will run around IR£7 ($8.40) without wine (the Gold Coast is fully licensed, and there's an attractive bar/lounge attached), lunch about IR£5 ($6). The Special Tourist Menu is available at both meals. Hours are 10 a.m. to 11 p.m., and it's very popular locally on weekends, so best book ahead.

Eammon's Place, Main St., Lismore, is also a tremendous value, with some of the best home cooking you'll find in Ireland. In this attractive bar and lounge, with its corner fireplace and three-legged iron pot for turf and wood, try Eammon Walsh's chicken liver pâté on Joan's homemade brown bread—scrumptuous! And if salmon is available, I guarantee you'll get portions so ample you'll be hard pressed to finish the plate. There are ham and chicken salad plates and a cold meat plate, and your bill will never go over IR£4.50 ($5.40). Food is served from noon to 9 p.m., and you'll be missing a real treat if you don't stop in at least once.

If it's tradition you're looking for, as well as good food, keep a lookout for the **Seanachie Restaurant and Pub,** Pulla, Ring, Dungarvan (tel. 058-46285), just off the main Dungarvan/Youghal road. It began life as a public house back in 1847, at the peak of the Great Famine, and a mass grave from those pitiful times is just next to the car park. These—happier—days, however, there's pub food in the rustic bar (with soup and brown bread hearty enough to be a full meal), and a marvelous menu in the restaurant that features such delicacies as Helvick Head turbot, lobster, and Blackwater salmon. A measure of the excellence here is the fact that the Seanachie has won numerous national awards for its food and restoration of the premises. À la carte prices in the restaurant begin at IR£5 ($6), with complete dinners starting at IR£8 ($9.60). In peak season, traditional music and dancing in the courtyard on Sunday afternoons are reminders that this was once the scene of crossroads dancing, when rural Irish gathered to dance away the shadows of oppression. Hours at the Seanachie are 11 a.m. to 11:30 p.m., with continuous food service. This is a good stop if you're driving from Dungarvan to Cork via Youghal.

County Kilkenny

The temptation is great to list **Kyteler's Inn,** Kieran St., Kilkenny (tel. 056-21064), as a sightseeing attraction, for the historic old building was once the home of Dame Alice Kyteler, a beautiful woman who grew rich by the successive deaths of her four husbands. When the Lord Justiciar of Ireland condemned her to death on charges of witchcraft, she was destined for a public whipping followed by burning at the stake. Dame Alice, however, took matters into her own hands and skipped town (nothing was ever heard of her again) and left her convicted accessories to go to the stake alone. When you enter this stolid stone house these days, it would behoove you to remember that within its walls were found a vast array of herbs, ointments, and other makings of magic spells. No magic potions in the food now, however, and a good lunch will run around IR£4 ($4.60), dinner from IR£7.50 ($9). There's a Tourist Menu at lunch (12:30 to 2:30 p.m.). Dinner hours are 6 to 9:45 p.m. Even if you don't make it for a meal here, do stop in for a drink and cast a leary eye at the "witchy" courtyard with its two wells that supplied Dame Alice with water to mix her deadly potions.

You'll also find the Tourist Menu offered in Kilkenny at the **Rose Hill Hotel,** College Rd. (tel. 056-62000); **Mulhall's Restaurant,** 6 High St. (tel. 056-21329); and the **Club House Hotel,** Patrick St. (tel. 056-21994).

South Tipperary

Not for budgeteers the main dining room at the **Cashel Palace Hotel,** Main St., Cashel. This elegant, first-class hotel is a Georgian palace, erected in 1730 for the archbishop of Cashel, and the elegant drawing room overlooks gardens and a breathtaking view of the Rock of Cashel. There are also marvelous works of art, both oils and colored engravings, in its public rooms and along the corridors. but, back to eating—down stone stairs, the flagstoned cellar holds the Derby Bar and the Bishop's Buttery, where you can hoist a pint before indulging in salad plates and hot dishes that run from IR£2 ($2.40) to IR£5 ($6).

In Tipperary Town, **The Brown Trout,** Abbey St., is one block off the main street. Rather plain in decor, its menu is composed of fresh local ingredients prepared expertly by Sean Buckley, who returned to Ireland after extensive training in leading restaurants on the Continent. The atmosphere and service are those of a typically friendly small Irish town, and your fellow diners are likely to be locals and traveling Irish who have favored this place consistently since it first opened its doors. Beef and lamb from Tipperary's renowned Golden Vale are specialties, as are fish dishes featuring fresh-caught specimens from local waters. Lunch will run around IR£5 ($6), dinner about IR£7 ($8.40).

The Tourist Menu is available at the **Royal Hotel,** Bridge, St., in Tipperary Town.

READER'S SELECTIONS: "One of the best dinners we had in Ireland was in the **Annestown House Restaurant** (tel. 051-96160), in the little town of Annestown on the beautiful coast drive from Waterford City to Dungarvan. This is a lovely old house overlooking the sea, and the food was great" (J. Noonan, New York, N.Y.). . . . "Our dinner at **Marlfield House,** Gorey, Co. Wexford (tel. 055-21124), was a Big Splurge in price, but oh, the quality! Everything was super fresh and super good. Just be sure to book ahead" (S. Ramsauer, Orangeburg, S.C.).

THINGS TO SEE AND DO: The Southeast is one of the most beautifully scenic regions of Ireland, with wooded mountains, rugged cliffs overlooking the sea, quaint fishing villages, Norman castles and, crowning them all, the massive Rock of Cashel. All sorts of sports are available: swimming, fishing, pony trekking and horseback riding, and hiking. It's a region to saunter through, savoring the sunshine, history and hospitality that are its trademarks.

County Wexford

In Enniscorthy, historic relics are displayed in a historic setting. The **Enniscorthy County Museum** is housed in a Norman castle built in 1172. It is said the Spenser wrote some of his epic *Faerie Queen* while living here. Cromwell gave it a battering, and it was on its way to becoming just another ruin until it was reconstructed in 1900. Today, its rooms hold items that figured in the lives of Irish country people in years past, as well as mementos of the tragic 1798 uprising and the 1916 rebellion which had a happier outcome. There's a country still in such good condition it could still be put to work turning out Ireland's brand of moonshine, poteen ("pot-sheen"). Other interesting items include the collection of rush lights—tight bundles of river rushes—that were the first torches in the country. There's a small admission to the museum, and hours are 10 a.m. to 6 p.m., June through September, and 2 to 5:30 p.m. all other months. This small, interesting museum is well worth a stop en route to Wexford.

Two miles outside Wexford town, **Ferrycarrig** is the site of the first Norman earthwork and castle in Ireland, and plans are presently afoot to develop a heritage park on the site. Work should be underway by the time you read this, so stop by the Oak Tavern at the foot of the bridge and make inquiries.

County Wexford has a very special sightseeing attraction in the **Saltee Islands,** four miles off the pretty little fishing village of **Kilmore Quay,** 14 miles south of Wexford Town, where local boatmen will take you out to the island after you've negotiated a fee (fishing trawlers will sometimes drop you off as they leave for the day's fishing and pick you up on the way home). A day on the Saltees can be soul-restoring even if you're not a birdwatcher, but if you qualify as the latter, you'll be treated to the sight of razorbills, kittiwakes, puffins, and thousand of gulls, along with hosts of seagoing species. It was in one of the Great Saltee's sea caves, incidentally, that the rebel leader of 1798, Begenal Havey, was captured and taken back to Wexford, where he was tortured and finally beheaded.

On your way to Kilmore Quay, you'll pass through **Kilmore Village,** a quaint little place with many traditional cottages crowned with roofs of thatch. Between the Village and the Quay, look for **Brandy Cross,** where you'll see a mound of little wooden crosses beside a certain bush. They've been put there by mourners on their way to the graveyard to bury a loved one—no one knows exactly why, but it's an ancient tradition.

Four miles southwest of Wexford Town on the road to Murrintown, the interesting **Irish Agricultural Museum** is on the grounds of **Johnstown Castle** in early 19th-century farm buildings. There's a reconstructed traditional kitchen and bedroom, as well as an extensive dairy display. Open Monday to Friday from 9 a.m. to 12:30 p.m. and 2:30 to 5 p.m., and on Sundays and public holidays, from 2 to 5 p.m. Small admission fee.

In 1848, when Patrick Kennedy left **Dunganstown** (near New Ross) for America, it was to escape the ravages of a devastating famine. He left behind a five-room thatched home set among stone farm buildings. A little more than a century later, his great-grandson, John Fitzgerald Kennedy, held the high office of President of the United States and returned to his ancestral home. The little thatched cottage had been replaced, but the outbuildings remained as they had been in his great-grandfather's time. Mrs. Ryan, a Kennedy by birth, and her daughter greeted the President and showed him around the place. Today, the **Kennedy homestead,** on a pleasant river road, is marked by a small plaque on an outside wall, and if you'd like to take a look (from the road, please—Mrs. Ryan does not open the house to the public), make the short detour en route from Wexford to New Ross.

About six miles from New Ross, the **John F. Kennedy Forest Park and Arboretum** is the tribute paid to the young slain president by the Irish Government and United States citizens of Irish origin. It was officially opened by the late President Eamon de Valera in 1968 and covers some 480 acres, of which more than 300 are set aside as the Arboretum. Already, there are more than 3,000 species of shrubs, and the number is expected to reach 6,000. In the Forest Garden, there are trees from all five continents of the world. There are lovely shaded walks throughout the Park, with shelters and convenient resting spots. If you follow the signposts to the top of Slieve Coillte, you'll be rewarded by a marvelous panorama of south Wexford and the splendid estuary of the rivers Barrow, Nore, and Suir. Be sure to stop by the reception center and see the explanatory display fashioned in beaten copper. No admission to the Park, and it's open from 10 a.m. to 5:30 p.m., April through September.

Take a drive down the **Hook Peninsula,** through historic and quaint old villages. The ruins of the Knights Templars foundation still stand at **Templetown;** Hook lighthouse is the oldest in Europe, built over seven centuries ago; near Fethard-on-Sea, at the now-buried town of **Bannow,** the Normans first landed in Ireland; at **Ballyhack,** catch the car ferry over to Passage East on the County Waterford side for ten minutes on the water to see these shores as they were seen by Viking and Norman invaders. The ferry runs continuously from 7:20 a.m. to 10 p.m. on weekdays, beginning at 9:30 a.m. on Sundays, from April through September, with the last departure at 8 p.m. during other months. One-way fare is IR£3 ($3.60), round-trip IR£4.50 ($5.40).

County Waterford

The nine miles from Waterford City to Dunmore East are picturesque and historic, and when you reach the little town perched above its historic harbor (mail ships used to put in here, as did smugglers, pirates and a variety of other characters), fine beaches and sheltered coves, you'll be tempted to stay a day or two for the fishing, swimming, sailing, and/or the good crack with some of the friendliest Irish in the country. You might lunch at the **Candlelight Inn,** the **Haven Hotel,** or the **Ocean Hotel,** or if it's a pint you're after, look for the **Strand Inn Pub,** where there's a small stone fireplace in the front room and good conversation in all three rooms. **The Butcher** is a pub in an old butcher shop and attracts mostly a youngish crowd. Spend some time on foot exploring the winding streets and going down to the quay to examine fishing and leisure boats, and when you're ready to get on with your journey, head for the coast drive to Tramore that winds along the clifftops with glimpses of the sea.

Tramore, eight miles south of Waterford City, is a popular seaside resort with good swimming and lots of recreational development. That giant of a statue you'll notice looking down on the bay from Great Newtown Head is known hereabouts as The Metal Man, and legend has it that any unmarried female who hops three times around its base on one foot will hop down the aisle within the next twelve months. Can't vouch for that, so I'll just pass it on. From Tramore, the coast road continues climbing and dipping among spectacular views through picturesque little towns until you reach **Dungarvan.** I've driven this route in bright sunshine (the best of times) and in lashing rain (the worst of times), and it never fails to delight and unveil yet another vista.

Ten miles from Dungarvan, the small town of **Cappoquin** sits in a sharp bend of the Blackwater River, whose waters yield up vast quantities of roach, dace, sea and brown trout, and salmon. Fishermen descend on Cappoquin in droves, year after year, to try their luck. However, even if you're not a fisherman, I'd like to tempt you to stop awhile in this quiet spot and learn something of the inner workings of all those "typical" Irish towns you've been passing through—this is a town I know well, and I'll share with you some of its daily life and some of the people who enrich it so. Let me suggest that you take time to meander (that's slower than stroll!) down the short Main Street, taking in some of the traditional shop fronts that have not, as yet, been gussied up. Call in to **Nellie Cliff's small craft shop** and let her tell you about the people who make the knits and pottery and Lord-only-knows-what-else you'll find heaped around in glorious confusion. Nellie can tell you more about the history of this region and the people who live here than you'd get from any book. Then saunter on down to **Mary Five's shop,** with its wooden front adorned with a sign announcing that she has "Jewelry, Fishing Tackle & Souvenirs" to sell inside. Mary is a charmer, but more than that, she carries in the small shop an amazing amount of Waterford Glass, Belleek, Royal Tara, watches, silverware, etc., all at competitive prices. Stop in the **Toby Jug** for a pint and a chat with handsome young redhead John Noonan and locals who happen to be in residence at the time. If, by then, you've begun to sink into the rhythm of this Irish town, it's time for a picnic. Still farther down Main Street, you'll come to **Maurice Kellerher's VG Supermarket,** which doesn't look a *bit* like the little greengrocer you'd imagine in a town like this, but resembles more the ones you left at home—until, that is, one of the pretty Irish lassies behind the counter smiles and inquires if you're having a good holiday. Pick up a bit of Irish cheese (cheddar from the West Waterford creamery, if you can get it), fruit, etc., and head back up Main Street and around the Allied Irish Bank corner (that's Cook Street, but nobody ever calls it that). Halfway down, you'll find **Mrs. Barron's bakery,** where you can pick up fresh baked loaves of brown, soda or white bread and mouthwatering pastries. There's been a member of the family baking here for over 200 years, and believe me, they've learned all the secrets of the trade. Now, take all your goodies out to **Glenshelane Park,** about a quarter mile outside town. Known locally as "The Glen," it's a shaded spot on the banks of a tumbling stream that flows beneath a charming old stone bridge with a hump in its middle, and there's a picnic table to spread your lunch. *Now,* if the peace of the ages doesn't descend on your head, there's no hope for you a'tall!

Four miles east of **Cappoquin,** in the foothills of the Knockmealdown Mountains, you'll find **Mount Mellary.** It's a monastic center for the Cistercian Order of the Strict Observance and was built over a century ago when the monks were banished from France. There's an impressive stone church and a cluster of other large stone buildings. The monks have turned a bare mountainside into productive fields and pastures, rising at 2 a.m. to do all their own work and retiring at 8 p.m. each evening. Until recently, they observed a strict rule of silence, with only the guestmaster permitted to speak. Visitors are welcomed here, and many Irish Catholics come to stay for several days in the peaceful retreat.

West of Cappoquin, the town of **Lismore** is just four miles away on the south bank of the Blackwater, with the majestic lines of a picture-perfect **castle** looming over town and river. King John had it built in 1185 on the site of St. Carthach's monastery of the 7th century. It was, for centuries, one of the most renowned of Ireland's distinguished learning institutions, and it became the target for Viking raids, as well as Norman and English conquest. It was here that Henry II came to accept homage from Irish chieftains, but the monastic community was finally destroyed by Raymond le Gros in 1173. There are those in Lismore who will tell you that the shades of murdered monks still roam the castle grounds in the dark of night. Sir Water Raleigh is listed among the castle's former owners, as is Richard Boyle, the Earl of Cork. Since 1753, however, it has been the Irish seat of the Dukes of Devonshire, one of whom married Lady Charlotte Boyle and thus acquired the property. Today, it is certainly among the most impressive still-lived-in castles in the country, and along with its mass of square towers, crenelated walls and great halls, there are comfortably furnished apartments. The people of Lismore recall with a special fondness the years that Fred Astaire's sister Adele lived here as a Duchess of Devonshire and was well loved in the town. The public is not admitted to the castle, but the beautifully tended gardens are open from 2 to 5 p.m. Tuesday through Friday, April through September, for a small admission charge. Just don't go wandering about in the dark of night!

Another Lismore link with history is the **Cathedral of St. Carthach.** Although it was rebuilt in 1633, there are 9th- and 11th-century grave slabs with inscriptions in Irish in the west wall of the nave. An altar tomb is dated 1557. About a mile east of the town on the "back road" to **Cappoquin,** is the great **Lis,** or earthen ring fort, from which the town took its name—not really a sightseeing attraction, but a pretty impressive high conical mound.

There are several scenic drives around the Cappoquin/Lismore area. One of the most breathtaking is that through a gap in the Knockmealdown Mountains known as **The Vee.** It's signposted from the outskirts of Lismore and climbs through mountainsides covered with heather to the V-shaped pass, with laybys that overlook sweeping views of Tipperary's Golden Vale, before descending to the little town of **Clogheen,** Co. Tipperary. Between the gap and Clogheen, keep a watch on the high side of the road for one of the most curious graves in the world, that of one Samuel Grubb, one-time owner of Castle Grace, who so loved his lands that he decreed he should be buried upright on the mountain slopes overlooking them. There's a small pathway leading up to the stone cairn that is his final resting place (if one can rest on his feet).

Then, there's the **Nire Valley** drive through the heart of the Comeragh Mountains among mountain peaks, wooded hillsides, and mountain pastures dotted with sheep and cattle. Turn off the Dungarvan/Cappoquin road onto the signposted **Clonmel** route—the road is well paved all the way. It is at **Ballymacarbry,** about halfway along the Nire Valley drive, that you'll find **Paddy Melody's Pony Trekking Center** (tel. 052-36147). Experienced rider or novice, you really should plan a stop here to explore this beautiful mountain country from horseback. Guide Ann McCarthy will see that you are seated correctly (even children are safe in her care); the horses are gentle and sure-footed; and there's a choice of paths from five to twelve miles, all through wooded mountainsides and bleaker slopes covered with gorse (or furze, as it is sometimes called locally) alongside rushing river waters and sparkling lakes. For those who absolutely refuse to sit a horse, there are jaunting cars. There are even longer treks available, as well as three- and four-day trekking holidays. For the two half-day rides, at 11:30 a.m. and 3:30 p.m., you'll pay IR£9 ($10.80), slightly more for the jaunting car. Especially in July and August, it is advisable to ring ahead and book for these popular treks. Plan enough time before or after your ride (or even if you just stop by the attached pub for a jar) to browse through Paddy's five scrapbooks in which enthusiastic riders have waxed poetic with comments, couplets, jingles, and epic poetry over the beauties of the Nire Valley.

Paddy (or anyone at Melody's) can direct you to a mountainside shrine to Irish patriots and leaders who met in March of 1923 in what is now known as the **Knockanaffrin Republican Cottage** ("The Cottage in the Glen of the Secrets") to talk in well-guarded secrecy of plans to bring about an end to the bloody Civil War. Standing in the simple whitewashed cottage, the ghosts of De Valera, Liam Lynch, and others rise up unbidden to remind you that it is in secluded locales such as this that so much of Irish history was forged.

Golfers will find good courses that welcome visitors at **Lismore Golf Club** (tel. Lismore 78) and **Dungarvan** (tel. 058-41605). **Swimmers** will delight in broad strands and calm waters at Tramore, Ardmore, and Clonea Strand (on the coast road between Dungarvan and Tramore).

County Kilkenny

The town of Kilkenny is virtually a sightseeing destination in itself—its narrow, winding streets and well-preserved structures make it perhaps the most perfect example in Ireland today of a medieval town, and Pat Mackey has produced a splendid little illustrated booklet entitled *A City and County Guide to Kilkenny* which outlines walking tours of the town, as well as suggested day trips in the surrounding area. It's available at the Tourist Office in Waterford.

Sometimes called the "Marble City" because of the fine limestone quarried hereabouts, its Irish name is *Cill Chainnigh,* or St. Canice's Church, a little monastery established here by the good saint in the 6th century on the grounds of the present **St. Canice's Cathedral** (the round tower dates back to the original settlement). But it was the Normans, and later the Anglo-Normans, who built up the dignified town as a trading center that enjoyed the protection of royalty up until the mid-14th century. It was in 1366 that the infamous "Statutes of Kilkenny" forbade any mingling of Anglo-Normans with the native Irish, and by the time Oliver Cromwell arrived in 1649, the city's population was pretty well demoralized, making it an easy matter for him to seize the town, stable horses in the cathedral, and smash its beautiful stained-glass windows, slaughter many residents and banish others to Connaught in order to confiscate their property. Despite all its turbulent history, Kilkenny has held on to a cultural tradition that makes it a natural site for one of the most respected crafts centers in Ireland today, the Kilkenny Design Workshops, housed in the one-time stables of Kilkenny Castle. More about that later.

For a look at the home of a prosperous Tudor merchant, visit the **Rothe House**, in Parliament Street, built in 1594 and now a museum and library. There's a small admission, and hours are 10:30 a.m. to 12:30 p.m. and 3 to 5 p.m. on weekdays, 3 to 5 p.m. on Sundays in the summer, Sundays only during winter months.

The impressive 13th-century **Kilkenny Castle** that dominates the town was the seat of the Butler family. It was built in 1391; Cromwell made a mess of it during his stopover; it was restored and continued to be used as a residence until 1935; and in 1967 the Marquess of Ormonde gave it to the people of Kilkenny, who turned it over to the state two years later. Now almost fully restored, and rich in artworks—there are miles of oil portraits—and elegant furnishings, it is open to the public for tours conducted by guides well versed in stories of the people who lived and visited here. If you are lucky enough to encounter Mick Mildowney, ask him about Black Tom, then get set to hear some rather outrageous tales. Daily tours in May and June are 10:30 a.m. to 12:45 p.m., July through September, 10 a.m. to 7 p.m., and there's a very small admission charge.

Created for the sole purpose of fostering good design in Irish industry, the **Kilkenny Design Workshops** are just across the street from the castle and occupy the former stables and coach houses. First-rate designers and craftspeople are provided equipment and work space to develop new designs of high standards for textiles, ceramics, glass, plastics, jewelery, and silver. Sadly, the workshops and crafts demonstrations are no longer open to the public, but there's a showroom where products based on these designs are for sale—a good place to do at least part of your shopping. Hours are 9 a.m. to 6 p.m. during the week, 10 a.m. to 6 p.m. on Saturday and Sunday.

Kytelers Inn, Kieran St., combines sightseeing with a pub-cum-restaurant (see "Where to Eat"), and is a don't-miss in Kilkenny. Two other pubs in which to put a terrible thirst to rest are **Tynan's,** John's Bridge (which won the "Best Pub in Ireland" award for its combination of polished brass, gleaming wood, etched glass, and interesting clientele), and the much plainer **Marble City Bar,** High St., a congenial spot since 1789 for the "meetin' o' the drinkers" that continues to thrive under the friendly eye of Laurence Langton.

Elsewhere in County Kilkenny, the quaint town of **Thomastown** sits at the head of the Nore Valley, and among its interesting and ancient ruins are the remains of the 13th-century church where there are fragments of a high cross and some badly weathered effigies. Three miles away, the **Kilfane church** ruins have an impressive medieval stone effigy of a crusader in full armour. Nearby **Jerpoint Abbey** dates back to 1158 and the riverside ruins contain many monuments and effigies, as well as sculptures of saints and knights.

A Kilkenny miscellany: From Tinacashel crossroad (two miles from the town of Urlingford), you can count no fewer than a dozen Anglo-Norman castles. In the town of **Knocktopher,** the Carmelite Priory garden holds a flat-topped Mass Stone which was used during the long years when Catholics were forbidden to practice their religion. If you pass through **Castlecomer,** spare a thought to native son John Walker (uncle of New York's famous mayor, Jimmy Walker) who, in 1899 invented the caterpillar track system which revolutionized so many phases of modern industry. And in **Rathosheen** townland (near the village of Johnstown), tradition says the Ring Fort is the final resting place of Ireland's legendary hero, Oisin.

South Tipperary

Soaring above the South Tipperary town of Cashel (*Caiseal,* or stone fort) is Ireland's most majestic historical landmark, the lofty **Rock of Cashel.** It stands 300 feet above the surrounding plains, and since time immemorial has been intimately connected with royalty and mysticism. Its summit encompasses a full two acres; its view is measured in miles. Ancient Celts worshiped here, and Irish kings built their palace on the sacred site. In the 5th century, the King of Munster erected a cashel, or stone fort, and it was there that St. Patrick came in the year 450 to preach to the current King of Munster, Aengus, using the humble shamrock as a symbol of the Christian trinity. Aengus (or, Angus) saw the light and with his family accepted baptism. Murtough O'Brien presented the Cashel of the Kings to the church in 1101, and in 1127, Cormac MacCarthaigh (McCarthy), King of Desmond, built the little chapel that is his namesake, a miniature gem of Romanesque style. In the years that followed, construction on a massive cathedral was begun; King Henry II came to receive homage from such Irish princes as Donal O'Brien, King of Thomond; Edward the Bruce held a Parliament here; the first Protestant service was held in the cathedral; it was burned in 1495, restored and damaged again by Cromwell's ruthless troops; and in 1748 the Archbishop of the day left it abandoned and unroofed because—or so the Irish say—his coach and four could not make it up the steep incline to its great west door.

Somehow, all the foregoing cannot *begin* to convey the awe-inspiring presence of the Rock. Its mystical sense of all the ages past and those yet to come can only be experienced as you follow the guided tour, then leave it to wander on your own among the ancient stones and ruins, climb to the top of the cathedral tower to wonder at Tipperary's Golden Vale plains, and gaze at the stone Cross of Cashel with a base that may have been a pre-Christian sacrificial altar. The tours are conducted from 10 a.m. to 7 p.m. June through September, and Tuesday through Saturday from 10 a.m. to 1 p.m. and 2 to 5 p.m., from 1 to 5 p.m. on Sunday. There's a small admission fee.

South of Cashel in the town of Cahir, a rocky islet in the River Suir has been the natural site of fortifications as far back as the third century, when the *Book of Lecan* reports that a fort here suffered utter destruction. Brian Boru maintained one of his residences here as High King of Ireland. The castle you see today on this ancient site was built by the Prince of Thomond, Conor O'Brien, in 1142, and was held by the Anglo-Norman Butlers until 1599, when the Earl of Essex captured it after a short siege. In 1650, it was surrendered to Cromwell without a single shot, and within its walls, the articles to end the long Cromwellian wars were signed in 1652. After years of neglect, the state took over in 1964, and it was opened to the public in 1971. Restored to near-original condition, **Cahir Castle** has figured in several motion pictures, but more importantly, with its residential apartments refurnished in authentic reproductions, it brings alive the life and times of all its centuries-old history. Guided tours are conducted during summer months, when there's a resident Tourist Office, and in winter, there's an informative caretaker on hand. During the summer, hours are 10 a.m. to 8 p.m.; in winter you make your own arrangements. Small admission fee.

Holycross Abbey is four miles south of Thurles (pronounced "Thurless") on the west bank of the River Suir. It was founded in 1168 and was a revered place of pilgrimage, since it held a particle of the True Cross preserved in a golden shrine set with precious stones which was presented to King Murtagh O'Brien, grandson of Brian Boru, in 1110. The shrine is now in the Ursuline Convent in Blackrock, Cork, but the Abbey still contains many interesting and religiously significant ruins, and Sunday pilgrimages still take place from May to September.

Elsewhere in South Tipperary, visit **Carrick-on-Suir,** where the Ormond Manor House is believed to be the birthplace of poor Anne Boleyn, and the town is for sure that of the Clancy Brothers and cyclist Sean Kelly. And look for signposts that will guide you through the scenic Glen of Aherlow drive. **Clonmel,** the County Town (in Irish, *Cluain Meala,* "Meadow of

Honey"), was a garrison town on the River Suir and the home of Charles Bianconi, a poor Italian who built up the first public transport system in Ireland with a coaching service based here.

READER'S SELECTIONS: "In the town of Kilkenny, you can tour the **Smithwick's Brewery** at 3 p.m., Monday through Friday. If you are not a beer lover, you will enjoy Smithwick's *(Author's Note:* pronounced "Smitticks" all over Ireland), as it is mild and not bitter. The brewery is across the street from the Rothe House" (Shirley Silverman, Glenview, Ill.). . . . "We visited **Nicholas Mosse Pottery,** Bennettsbridge, Co. Kilkenny, just south of Kilkenny Town. The pottery is fantastic, and we had an apprentice show us around. Mr. Mosse has sold to Bloomingdale's, among others in the U.S." (Sheila Noonan, Dallas, Tex.). . . . "We found two folk museums of real interest. The first is **Fethard Folk and Transport Museum,** Cashel Rd., Fethard (tel. 052-31516), about a 20-minute drive from the Rock of Cashel. The proprietors, Christopher and Margaret Mullins, live on the site and will open it at any time upon request. The second is **Bothan Scoir,** a 17th-century cottage museum, Upper Green, Cashel, just a ten-minute walk from the Rock. There are over 200 items in this restored laborer's cottage, which was opened in 1983 and has hours of 10 a.m. to 8 p.m. (S. McGraw, New York, N.Y.).

Chapter VI

CORK, KILLARNEY, AND THE SOUTHWEST

1. Introduction to the Southwest
2. Cork City
3. Killarney and Its Lakes
4. Around Counties Cork and Kerry

KILLARNEY AND THE BLARNEY STONE—they're both bound to be high on your "must see" list. And rightly so, for together they're a fair measure of the scenic beauty and the magic that make Ireland such a unique place. They are, however, little more than *hints* at the travel riches to be found in the Southwest, a region made up of two of the country's most important counties.

1. Introduction to the Southwest

The two large counties of Cork and Kerry contain what is virtually an embarrassment of natural splendors. Magnificent cliffs soar high above West Cork's rugged coastline. Majestic mountains with passes that open up breathtaking landscapes in County Kerry contrast with the mystical qualities of the Dingle Peninsula and its ghosts of ancient Celtic tribes and meditating monks. Fishermen put into Youghal Harbor as they have for centuries, while cargo ships still line up at Cork City docks. Along County Kerry's ragged, much indented coast, there are sweeping golden strands flecked with the foam of Atlantic breakers.

Cork City, Ireland's second largest, celebrates its 800th anniversary in 1985 and looks back on a history that has included involvement with every wave of population invasion, from Celts to Vikings to Normans to Cromwell's ruthless forces. Six miles away, Blarney Castle holds out the promise of silken phrases to those who will kiss its magic stone. Killarney is a testament to man's appreciation of nature's gifts; wooded Gougane Barra a testament to man's reaching out to his God in the midst of those gifts.

Scattered throughout all the above are quiet little villages peopled with strong characters and whimsical spirits. A Corkman is distinctive from other

Irish, and a *West* Corkman is unique unto himself! A Kerryman combines wit, independence, and pride in a special blend like no other in the country.

The Southwest is, then, a region to be explored as fully as time will permit and savored in memory the rest of your natural life.

2. Cork City

"Limerick was, Dublin is, and Cork shall be
The finest city of the three."

So says "The Old Prophecy" as quoted by Dean Hole in 1859. Well, never mind about *shall* be, any Corkman worth his salt will tell you that Cork *is*, and always has been, the finest city in Ireland! And with more than a little justification, I might add. This grand old city that native son and gifted actor Niall Tobin has described as "an intimate higgledy-piggledly assemblage of steps, slopes, steeples and bridges" is, to quote one visitor, "strewn like a bouquet along the valley."

Enough of quotes. Suffice it to say that for you and me, Cork is friendly, cosmopolitan without the pseudo-sophistication of some large cities, and fun to visit. Its great age (its charter was conferred in 1185) imbues Cork with an enormous pride which assumes the right to be quite comfortable with itself. As a native once assured me with a perfectly straight face, "Sure, it's only an accident of geography that Dublin is the capital of Ireland." Not that anyone really cares if it is the capital: to be Cork is quite enough.

Its ancient Irish name is *Corcaigh*, or "Marshy Place," and in this place of marshes Druids once held their religious rites in the dense woods of the southern hills that rose above it. Celtic tribes built forts and fought battles over territorial rights in the hills to the north. And in the seventh century, St. Finbar came to establish a monastery on a small island in the swamp, asserting that there would be "an abundance of wisdom continually in Cork."

Attracted by the religious foundation's riches, the Vikings arrived in the ninth century to plunder, then settle in as they had in other Irish locations. Normans took over in the twelfth century, fortified the city and proceeded to build great churches and abbeys. But it was the advent of Oliver Cromwell, who captured Cork in December of 1649, that settled the hash of natives in the district, for unlike Danes and Normans who had assimilated happily with the resident populace, those who came after Cromwell held in contempt everything that was Irish and imposed harsh penalties on any who attempted to live with them amicably. No doubt it is from the strangling repression of this period that present-day Corkmen date their fierce sense of independence and abhorrence of injustice. Nor did being on the losing side ever lessen their fighting spirit—for a few centuries, in fact, they consistently allied themselves with defeat, standing behind pretender-to-the-throne Perkin Warbeck, Charles I, and James II.

That the blood has never stopped flowing hot in their veins at any hint of injustice is clear from the fact that when their Lord Mayor, Terence MacSwiney, died after a 74-day hunger strike, his comrade-in-arms locked the door in St. George's where the Requiem Mass was to be held, opened his coffin, clothed his body in his I.R.A. Commandant uniform, and inscribed on his coffin "Murdered by the Foreigners in Brixton Prison, London, England, on October 25th, 1920, the Fourth Year of the Republic." Blissful in his ignorance, the Archbishop conducted the Mass never knowing the message of the inscription, which was in Irish.

For centuries, all that history slogged through acres of marshland, right up until the end of the 1700s. Vessels sailed up Patrick Street as late as 1760 (it was paved in 1791); in 1780, there was a canal down the center of the Grand Parade and a bridge where the Berwick Fountain now stands between Tuckey and Oliver Plunkett Streets.

Today, the streets in Cork are dry, and its citizens are reckoned to be among the ablest merchants and traders in Ireland. Still, they are a lively, cultural bunch, much attuned to the arts, and quick to welcome strangers. Theater, ballet, and one of Europe's best jazz festivals are highlights of each year, while street musicians carry on the tradition of ballad singers down through the ages and the old piper who once trod Winthrop Street wheezing out "An' De Vallee Lay Smilin' Afore Me."

ORIENTATION: Cork's city center is on an island in the River Lee, which can be confusing when you suddenly encounter the river you thought you'd just left behind. Some 16 bridges cross the Lee, and the city center's maze of one-way streets and narrow lanes can—and do!—confound the best drivers in the world. My best advice to drivers (based on *long* experience) is to make your way to your accommodation, park the car and leave it there. Public transportation (via lovely doubledecker buses and a good taxi service) is excellent and can take you virtually anywhere you wish to go. Besides, Cork is a great town for walking.

Another bit of advice: go by the Tourist Office and pick up one of their free city maps—it will save you a lot of grief in getting around Cork. Having said that, herewith is the basics of Cork orientation. The River Lee cuts across the city frome east to west, the hills bound it on the north and south. Major points of reference are **St. Patrick's Street** (universally called simply Patrick's Street) and the **Grand Parade.** Other main arteries are **Washington Street** (which becomes Western Road as it runs past University College and heads out towards Killarney); **South Mall,** from which you turn into Anglesea Street en route to both Kinsale (and the airport) and the Douglas Road; and **Glanmire Road,** leading out to Fota Park, Cobh, and the main Youghal/ Waterford road, with a turnoff to the Dublin road. Just across **St. Patrick's Bridge** at the foot of Patrick Street, a hill so steep you'll swear your car is going front over back leads to the Montenotte section, where the cream of Cork's merchant crop built great Georgian houses on the hillside overlooking the river.

USEFUL INFORMATION: The **Tourist Office** is centrally located at Tourist House, 42 Grand Parade (tel. 021-23251). Hours are 9 a.m. to 7 p.m. weekdays, 3 to 5 p.m. Sundays in July and August; 9:30 a.m. to 5:30 p.m. weekdays, 9:30 a.m. to 1 p.m. Saturdays other months. . . . The bus station is one block down from St. Patrick's Bridge on Parnell Place, and the railway station is on Lower Glamire Road. For all **CIE bus and rail** information, tel. 021-504422 . . . **Cork Airport** is four miles south of the city on the Kinsale road, with connections to England and the Continent, as well as Irish destinations. There's good, inexpensive public **bus** transportation into town . . . **Taxis** are stationed at the rank in the center of Patrick Street as well as at bus and railway stations and the airport, or you can telephone 961311 or 502211. They're metered, with a minimum fare of IR£1 ($1.20). . . . The **General Post Office** is in Oliver Plunkett Street, open 9 a.m. to 6 p.m. every day but Sunday . . . Current goings-on in Cork are reported in *Where to Go in Cork,* published weekly by the Junior Chamber of Commerce during summer months and available through the Tourist Office and most hotels. Also, check the *Cork Examiner*. . . . The **telephone prefix** for Cork is 021.

ACCOMMODATIONS: Some of Cork's best accommodations are in the Western Road area, very near University College. There's heavy truck traffic along this road, but those listed below are either on quiet side streets just off the Western Road or are set back from the street in their own grounds, so noise should not be a problem at any. While this area is within walking distance to the city center (a rather long walk, but with frequent bus service), other districts shown below are all convenient to bus lines running into town.

Note: Prices shown below are those in effect in 1985—expect them to be higher in 1986.

Western Road Area

Hostel: Hostel facilities at Nos. 1 and 2 Redclyffe, Western Rd. (tel. 021-432891), are rated "superior," and city bus no. 8 runs right past the door. While normal hostel hours are observed, you are allowed to drop off your luggage between noon and 5 p.m. during July and August.

Bed-and-Breakfast: St. Kilda, Western Rd. (tel. 021-23095), is the three-story home of the charming Pauline Hickey and her husband, Pat. Set back behind a low wall, with ample parking out front, the old-style house has recently been completely refurbished and redecorated. There's carpeting throughout, and the six bedrooms have built-in wardrobes. Most are doubles, but there's one small, cozy single. A piano in the lounge is frequently the focal point for guests in the evening. Bed-and-breakfast rates are IR£8.50 ($10.20). Take bus no. 5 or 8.

Farther out Western Road, **Laurels Guest House,** Western Rd. (tel. 021-431041), is a marvelous old Georgian house that dates back more than a century and is surrounded by grounds that allow ample parking. Laurels was once a home for the elderly, and because of this has such niceties as guestrooms and a dining room on the ground level, a boon for those with an aversion for stairs. Guestrooms are handsomely done up, and some feature antique beds and fireplaces (not in use, however, since there's central heating). The first floor's centerpiece is the wide entrance hall, stained-glass windows in the front door. The lounge, where guests gather to watch TV, has a lovely crystal chandelier and a magnificent sideboard. Hospitable Miss Davitt, who looks after it all, is a registered nurse, and serves her guests such healthful items as fat-free bacon and home-baked bread. You're welcome to use the ironing room. Rates for bed-and-breakfast are IR£8 ($9.60). No need to drive into town, since the no. 8 bus is just outside.

Very near Fitzgeralds Park and one block off the Western Road, **Roserie Villa,** 2 Roserie Villas, Mardyke (tel. 021-22958), is a four-story house presided over by Mrs. Nora Murray. The seven bedrooms all have hand basins and are a bit old-fashioned in furnishings, but all are very comfortable. There's a TV lounge, central heating, and good parking just across the road. Rates for bed-and-breakfast are IR£8.50 ($10.20), with a 20% reduction for children.

The street that turns up a hill just in front of the entrance to University College is Donovan's Road, and there are several B&Bs here that represent good value. **Askive House,** Donovan's Rd. (tel. 021-21475), is a three-story

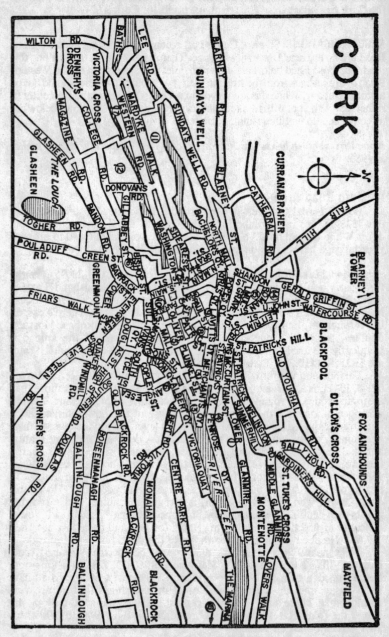

Based on the Ordnance Survey by permission of the Government of Ireland (Permit No. 906)

KEY TO THE NUMBERED REFERENCES ON OUR MAP OF CORK: 1—Glanmire Rd. Station; 3—Prov. Bus Depot; 4—Cross-Channel Boats; 5—General Post Office; 6—City Hall; 7—Court House; 8—Irish Tourist Office; 9—School of Art; 10—Public Library; 11—Park and Museum; 12—University College; 13—Custom House; 14—St. Mary's Cathedral; 15—Shandon Church; 16—St. Finbar's Cathedral, 17—Greyhound Track; 18—G.A.A. and Show Grounds.

gray terrace house, where Peggy and Ed O'Mahony have been welcoming guests for many years. Both are active in tourism activities and love to help visitors plan their time in Cork. Furnishings include many antique pieces, and crystal sparkles in the dining room, where you're given a choice of menus at breakfast and portions that are more than ample. Guestrooms are comfortably furnished, with shaver points at all hand basins. There's central heat, and good parking in the enclosed graveled car park out front. Rates are IR£6.85 ($8.22), with 25% off for children. Closed December and January.

Ashford House, Donovan's Rd. (tel. 021-263241), is right next door to Askive House. Charming Mairead Smythe and her husband, Jack, are hosts in the three-story house, where guestrooms are spacious and comfortably furnished. They also are eager to recommend places of interest as well as restaurants and entertainment centers. Rates, including a full Irish breakfast, are IR£6.85 ($8.22), with a 25% reduction for small fry. Closed January.

At the top of Donovan's Road, you'll find Connaught Avenue and **Ouvane House,** 2 Dunedin, Connaught Ave. (tel. 021-21822). Mrs. Maureen Vaughan makes guests very welcome, with a cuppa likely to appear whenever she thinks you have the need. The six bedrooms are unpretentious, comfortable, and homelike. There's central heat, and the lounge features a piano for guests' use. Rates are IR£7 ($8.40), with a 10% reduction for children.

Montenotte (Summerhill, St. Luke's) Area

Bed-and-Breakfast: Mrs. Leonard, at No. 2 Ardskeagh Villas, Gardiner's Hill, St. Luke's (tel. 021-501800), has an old-style home in this district that is convenient to the railway station and is within easy walking distance of the city center (although city bus lines are only a half-block away). There are six homey rooms, all with hand basins, and Mrs. Leonard is a friendly, hospitable hostess. Rates for bed-and-breakfast are IR£8.50 ($10.20), with 20% off for children. Open April through September.

In a quiet cul-de-sac overlooking the city and the river, **Mrs. Davitt,** 5 Sidneyville, Bellevue Park, St. Luke's (tel. 021-502070), has four bright, cheerful guestrooms. They all have hand basins, and some are spacious enough to accommodate families. There's ample parking, and city buses are nearby. Also near railway station. B&B rates are IR£7.50 ($9), with a 20% reduction for children.

Douglas Area

This area, southwest of the city center and very convenient to the airport, has excellent bus service into town (nos. 7, 7A, and 10). Mrs. Margaret Brett,

Monvana, Marble Hall Park, Douglas Rd. (tel. 021-25827), is surely one of Cork's most gracious hostesses. "We love the American guests," she says, and judging from our mail, American guests return the sentiment. This is an especially pretty place, set in a walled garden (whose colorful blooms and well-tended shrubs reflect Mr. Brett's loving care). You'll breakfast in a cheerful dining room that looks out to the garden and features a fireplace. There are three very attractive guestrooms, and furnishings include a writing desk in each. B&B rates are IR£7.50 ($9), high tea is IR£5 ($6), and the evening meal is IR£8 ($9.60). Open April through September.

Achill, South Douglas Rd. (tel. 021-966833), is a modern bungalow where warm, friendly hospitality is the order of the day. Mrs. Eileen Godsill, the attractive, energetic hostess, holds an office in the Town & Country Homes Association and goes out of her way to be helpful to guests. Husband Vincent is a walking-tour guide, assists in geological research, and is a prolific painter whose oils adorn Achill's walls as well as those in the office at Johnson & Perrott car hire, where he works. The three bedrooms (one is a single) all are nicely done up and have hand basins, and the window-lined conservatory is a relaxing late-afternoon retreat as it catches the sun. Rates for bed-and-breakfast are IR£8 ($9.60), high tea is IR£5 ($6), and there's a one-third reduction for children. Central heat and off-the-street parking. Open May through September.

Kinsale Road (Airport)

You'll need a car for these two, since they're about five miles out from the city center. Both offer good value in rural surroundings close to the airport.

Bed-and-Breakfast: Au Soleil, Lisfehill, Ballinhassig, Cork Airport/Kinsale Rd. (tel. 021-888208), is a new bungalow with three attractive bedrooms, all with hand basins. Helen Deasy is a sister to Noreen Raftery, whose Shalom you'll find listed in the Western Region (Co. Mayo), and the Irish tradition of hospitality certainly runs strong in this family. Helen and husband Des will make you feel right at home. B&B rates are IR£8 ($9.60), with a one-third reduction for children. Open April through September.

Set in a terraced garden, Mrs. Kathleen O'Mahony's **Fuchsia,** Adamstown, Ballinhassig, Co. Cork (tel. 021-888198), overlooks hedgerows bordering green fields. There are two twin rooms and one double-bedded, all with feather comforters and hand basins. The lounge, with a bay window affording splendid views, has tourist literature on this area, and Mr. and Mrs. O'Mahony delight in recommending points of interest. Breakfasts feature her homemade jam and bread, as well as the delicious local sausage. Rates for bed-and-breakfast are IR£8.25 ($9.90), with a 25% reduction for children, and the evening meal is available with advance notice. Central heat. Open March through October.

READERS' SELECTIONS: "Cork is possibly the nicest city from which to tour southern Ireland, and possibly the nicest B&B is that run by the hospitable Mrs. M. Barrett. The **Villa Ronan,** Glasheen Rd. (tel. 021-962459), is convenient to the city by the bus that stops just outside the door" (Rob Lehmann, Durham, N.C.). . . . "We stayed in a wonderful private home with **Mrs. Noonan,** 8 King's Terrace (tel. 021-53810), a few short walking minutes from the center of Cork. Mrs. Noonan is a marvelous lady and served excellent breakfasts complete with homemade bread. The room was great, too" (Judy and Mike Rothschild, Sherman Oaks, Calif.).

WHERE TO EAT: Cork has many good, inexpensive places to eat. One of my all-time favorites at lunch (or for a Big Splurge evening meal) is the **Oyster Tavern,** Market Lane, 56 St. Patrick's St. (tel. 227161). It's an old-world sort of place, with lots of wood, etched glass, old prints, and mirrors reflecting the centuries over which there's been a tavern here. The bar section is worth stopping by even if you don't eat. A bit complicated to find, the Oyster is signposted on the sidewalk on Patrick Street, which sign points you to Market Lane, leading into the block-long covered city market (worth a visit in itself before or after you eat). The à la carte lunch menu features the steaks and fish for which this place is famous, and you can put together a terrific lunch for about IR£4.50 ($5.40). Portions are so generous that this could well be your main meal of the day. Lunch hours are 12:30 to 2 p.m. every day except Sunday, and it's a good idea to book. For that Big Splurge dinner, come along from 6:30 to 9:30 p.m. and expect to pay around IR£12 ($14.40).

For less expensive but very good pub lunches, you can't do better than **Beecher's Inn,** Faulkners Lane (tel. 021-23144). Tucked away on this narrow old lane (enter from Emmet Place or Patrick Street), Beecher's also has the soft patina of time. The soft murmur of contented conversation fills the place as Cork regulars gather at lunchtime (12:30 to 2 p.m.). Seafood is a specialty, and a lunch of smoked salmon and brown bread washed down with a dark, creamy Guinness is memorable. There are hot plates and cold salads, none of which will run over IR£4 ($4.80).

De Lacy House, 74 Oliver Plunkett St. (tel. 20074), is large and lively, serving a good selection of hot plates and cold meats and salads for under IR£4 ($4.80) from 12:30 to 2:30 p.m. and 5:30 to 10 p.m. The Tourist Menu is offered from 12:45 to 7 p.m. Just one example of the good value here is a roast leg of lamb plate with two vegetables and potato for IR£3.50 ($4.20). Unusual for a grill bar and pub, De Lacy's accepts major credit cards. If you plan your evening meal here on any night Wednesday through Sunday, you might like to stick around for the traditional music sessions that get underway around 8:30 p.m. (see "Cork After Dark").

Shandon Tavern, 2/3 Lavitt's Quay (tel. 21807), offers a good lunch with table service from 12:30 to 2:30 p.m., but pub grub and snacks are available right up to closing time (11 p.m.). Snacks are in the neighborhood of IR£1 ($1.20), and lunch will run about IR£3 ($3.60).

In Queen's Oldcastle Shopping Centre, look for the **Periwinkle** (tel. 21199). As you'd expect, the specialty here is seafood, some of the freshest and best prepared you'll find in Cork. I especially like the seafood chowder, and there's a good seafood salad. There are always one or two non-seafood selections as well. It's self-service, and downstairs, you eat at the blond-wood counters, upstairs at tables overlooking the busy arcade. Prices can run anywhere from IR£2.50 ($3) to IR£8 ($9.60), and the Periwinkle is open every day except Sunday from 10 a.m. to 5 p.m., until 11 p.m. on Friday and Saturday.

The dependable O'Driscoll Brothers have brought their Dublin-based chain (see "Where to Eat," Chapter IV) to Cork with **Murph's** in the Savoy Centre, Patrick St. (tel. 54059). Specialties include steaks, fried chicken, seafood platters, scampi, and . . . well, the menu is virtually endless. If you've been hankering for a well-mixed martini, the full-service bar offers cocktails as well as traditional Irish drinks. Lunch prices range from IR£3 ($3.60) to IR£4 ($4.80); three-course set dinners from IR£7 ($8.40) to IR£9 ($10.80); and there's continuous service from noon to midnight, seven days a week.

Tung Sing Chinese Restaurant, 23A Patrick St. (tel. 24616/23793), offers excellent and inexpensive meals from noon to 12:30 a.m. weekdays; 1 p.m. to midnight on Sundays. Wine is available in this nice upstairs room.

You'll find the Special Tourist Menu at: **Henning's,** Market Lane off Patrick St. (tel. 506879); the **Metropole Hotel,** MacCurtain St. (tel. 508122); and **Upstairs Downstairs,** 102 Oliver Plunkett St. (tel. 24752).

Big Splurges

Over on the Montenotte section's lofty heights, the **Arbutus Lodge Hotel Restaurant** is known all over Ireland and the Continent for its legendary cuisine and exquisite service. The hotel was once an elegant townhouse, and the decor is that of subdued formality ("subdued" because the friendly service rescues it from "stuffy"). Large windows overlook the city below. Seafood, meats, and vegetables are the freshest—if your entree includes mushrooms, you may be sure they've been hand-gathered from the woods, not emptied from a can. Lunch in this very special place will run a minimum of IR£12 ($14.40), dinner about IR£20 ($24)—a Big Splurge, and very good value! If those prices are a bit steep for your budget, even in the Big Splurge department, the Gallery Bar at the Arbutus serves smoked salmon, delicious soups, for prices that average about IR£8 ($9.60). and seafood selections in the bar and a garden patio from 12:30 to 2:30 p.m. Restaurant hours are 1 to 3 p.m. and 7 to 9:30 p.m. Closed Sundays. Major credit cards are accepted. Best to book at both the Restaurant and Gallery Bar.

Also out the budget range, but an experience worth splurging for, is **Blackrock Castle** on the banks of the River Lee about two miles from the city center on the no. 2 city bus route. There's been a fortification here since 1605, but the marvelous stone concoction with crenelated towers and battlements that stands there now dates only back to 1830, when it was built to replace its predecessor which had been destroyed by fire. Its medieval past is preserved in rough stone walls, shields, swords, and other memorabilia, although restaurant furnishings are modern and very comfortable. The menu offers seafood, chicken, and meat specialties, and à la carte prices will run around IR£12 ($14.40). Hours are 7 to 10:30 p.m. every day except Monday, and major credit cards are welcomed.

READER'S SELECTIONS: "**Ruben's,** on Marlboro St., is cozy, convivial, and has good salad plates and other light fare at very inexpensive prices. The **Long Valley Pub** is very friendly and has good pub grub" (Rev. R. J. Goode, Eagle River, Wisc.).

THINGS TO SEE AND DO: Lucky you, if your trip to Ireland falls in 1985. That's the year Cork celebrates its 800th birthday, and it promises to be quite a celebration. As this is written, it is impossible to give you more than just an overview of some of the highlights—historical pageants, plays, musicals, art exhibitions, sporting competitions, street concerts, and other entertainments are just a few on the planning board thus far—but you can get full particulars by contacting **Cork 800,** Cork City Council, City Hall, Cork (tel. 966222). The people of Cork really know how to throw a party, and this one should be a right smasher!

One of Cork's chief charms is that it is so much a *walking* city, which is, of course, the best possible way to get around any city if you are to capture its true flavor and mingle with the people who give it life. My first recommendation, then, is to go by the **Tourist Office** and pick up their *Tourist Trail* guide to a signposted walking tour of Cork. It details a comprehensive route around the significant landmarks and tells you all about each one. Makes for a lovely day's ramble, with a stop whenever your fancy dictates for a jar, lunch or whatever.

From time to time, there are also free evening **guided walking tours** departing the Tourist Office two or three days a week during July and August. Inquire when you're there to see if they're on. For more personalized guided tours, contact Valerie Fleury, **Discover Cork,** Belmont, Douglas Rd., Cork (tel. 021-293873). She has put together half-day tours in and around Cork at fees of IR£10 ($12) to IR£12 ($14.40). Some of the more interesting that go outside the city are those to Blarney, followed by afternoon tea in a private home, Fota Park, and Kinsale. There's also a Kinsale trip, at a higher fee, that concludes with a 6-course evening meal followed by a visit to a traditional Irish pub.

The **Blarney Stone**—I *know* that's uppermost in your mind!—is six miles from Cork City, and another outstanding attraction, **Fota Park,** is nine miles away. You'll find them listed in "Around the Southwest," in order that this section may be devoted to those things in the immediate vicinity.

I can't really say that the **Coal Quay** (pronounce it "kay" in this instance) qualifies as a sightseeing attraction, but I *do* know that it's a place unique to Cork and one I drop by on every visit. You won't find it listed anywhere under that name—the signposts say Corn Market Street—but no one in town will know what you're asking for if you use any other. Right in the heart of the city, it's to the right (opposite the Grand Parade which curves off to the left) at the end of Patrick Street, and it's as grand a collection of hardy Irish countrywomen as you're likely to run across. From stalls, tables, carts, or cardboard boxes on the sidewalk, these shrewd, witty ladies hawk everything from secondhand clothes to fresh vegetables to old shoes to odd pieces of china to anything else they happen to have handy and can exchange for a "lop" or two ("lop" being, of course, a coin). I won't guarantee that you'll catch every nuance of conversation carried on in a language that's peculiar to this bunch, but I will guarantee that you'll catch a glimpse of genuine Irish folk life.

Not far from the Coal Quay, the red-brick **Crawford Art Gallery** on Emmet Place was built as the Custom House back in 1724 when ships unloaded where the sidewalk is now at the King's Dock. There's something almost homey about the big, rambling halls and exhibition rooms, and I've never been inside without encountering at least one art student diligently studying the masters. There are paintings and sculptures by modern Irish artists and an interesting collection of classical casts from the Vatican Galleries presented to Cork in 1818.

On Church Street, just off Shandon Street, **St. Ann's Church** is perhaps the most beloved of the city's many churches. What makes it so are the

> . . . bells of Shandon
> That sound so grand on
> The pleasant waters
> Of the river Lee.

immortalized by Francis Sylvester Mahony in his 1830s poem "The Bells of Shandon," penned under the name of Father Prout. Shandon takes its name from the Irish *sean dun,* meaning "old fort." The Protestant church is distinguished architecturally only by its red and white "pepper pot" steeple which houses the bells. Its 170-foot height is crowned by an 11-foot 3-inch weathervane in the shape of a salmon (the symbol of wisdom), and the clocks set in its four sides are known affectionately as the "four-faced liar," since no two of them ever show the same time. Climb the steeple's winding stairs to see the famous bells, and for a small charge you can follow numbers on the bell strings that will send "The Bells of St. Mary's" pealing out over the city. Father Prout, incidentally, lies below in the small churchyard.

Cork's birthplace is three blocks past the South Main Street Bridge, where **St. Finn Barre's Cathedral,** on Bishop's Street, marks the spot on which the venerable saint founded his monastery in 650. As it grew in stature as a seat of leaning, it became a mark of honor among Gaelic chieftains and Norman knights to be buried in its grounds. At the time of the Reformation, St. Finn Barre's became the seat of the bishopric of the Church of Ireland, as it is today. The French Gothic structure you see today was opening in 1870, and its great West Window is of particular note.

The magnificent **City Hall** on Albert Quay opened in 1936 to replace the one burned in 1920 during the War of Independence. This is where President Kennedy came to address an admiring throng during his visit in the 1960s.

Running parallel to the Western Road is **The Mardyke,** a mile-long, tree-shaded walk named after an Amsterdam walk called the "Meer Dyke" and bordered by **Fitzgerald Park,** where you'll find lovely landscaping, interesting sculptures, and a small museum.

For the best selection of Irish records, tapes, sheet music, books, and traditional musical instruments such as the tin whistle or bodhran, check **A. Shanahan & Co., Ltd.,** 53–54 Oliver Plunkett St. (tel. 21264). They're open Monday through Saturday from 9:30 a.m. to 5:30 p.m. and they have an excellent mail service.

A good many of the Irish books you browse through in bookshops around the country are published right here in Cork by **Mercier Press,** 4 Bridge St. Their inexpensive paperback editions are all by Irish writers on Irish subjects, fiction and nonfiction. These make good souvenirs as well as gifts.

During summer months, there are regular four-hour **harbor cruises** down the Lee. Hourly schedules vary, and they do not always run the same days every week, so check with the Tourist Office.

Golfers can hire clubs at the Cork Corporation-owned **Mahon Golf Course,** Mahon Peninsula, and if you have your own clubs, there are 18-hole courses at the **Douglas Golf Club,** Carr's Hill, Douglas, and **Monkstown Golf Club,** Monkstown.

Stop by the **Cork Craftsmans Guild** in the Savoy Centre on Patrick, where there's a good collection of Irish crafts.

This is a good place to enjoy one of Ireland's favorite spectator sports at the **Cork Greyhound Stadium** out on Western Road (tel. 43013). There's racing on Monday, Wednesday, and Saturday, starting at 8 p.m. Other nights, there are trial heats which you can attend at no charge (but no betting), but on race nights, admission is IR£1.50 ($1.80).

CORK AFTER DARK: The people of Cork devote themselves to commerce with great acumen during the workday, but when the shop doors close, you'll find them just as busy in pursuit of cultural pleasure, whether it be highbrow or lowbrow.

Theater

There's almost always something on at the **Cork Opera House** in Emmet Place. It could be first-rate drama, a musical review, a comedy, a concert, or an artist's recital. Ticket prices are in the IR£4 ($4.80) to IR£5 ($6) range.

For two months after Easter, four to six weeks in the summer, and again in the fall and winter, you'll find a resident company offering productions of outstanding quality at the **Everyman Playhouse,** Fr. Matthew St. (just off the South Mall, tel. 26287). Leading companies from Dublin, Belfast, Great Britain, and America often play here as well, and the standard is always high. A nice feature is the intermission coffee service, and if you'd like a chance to hobnob with the actors afterwards, drop in to Moore's Hotel around the corner, where a fair few can usually be found in the bar after the show. Ticket prices are under IR£ ($6), and there are reductions for Senior Citizens and students. On opening nights of all shows, and on Monday and Tuesday nights of the resident company performances, all seats sell for IR£1.50 ($1.80). Visa and Access cardholders can ring 23888 to book.

Ballet

The **Irish Ballet Company,** Emmet Place, has distinguished itself internationally since it was formed in 1973 with a nucleus of a dozen dancers. Its ranks have grown considerably, and now include dancers from Australia, South Africa, America, and Great Britain as well as Ireland. Classically trained, the troupe is equally at home with modern and Irish works. They're usually in Cork at the Cork Opera House in February, in Dublin at the Abbey in June, and in Killarney during some part of the summer. If you can catch them, don't miss a brilliant dance company, and you'll really be in luck if they're performing Joan Denise Moriarty's *Playboy of the Western World*, with music by the Chieftains.

Traditional Irish Entertainment

In the rear of the Tourist Office on the Grand Parade, the **Cork Entertainment Centre** puts on plays by Irish writers and traditional music nights several times a week during summer months. Occasionally, there's lunchtime theater as well. Check with the Tourist Office (tel. 23251), where you can buy tickets in advance, although they're also available at the door. Excellent entertainment at bargain prices.

De Lacy House, 74 Oliver Plunkett St. (tel. 20074) (see "Where to Eat"), has traditional music Wednesday through Sunday nights, and from time to time other forms of musical entertainment are offered on other nights.

The traditional music sessions at **An Bodhran** pub, 42 Oliver Plunkett St., are much more informal. The brick-walled century-and-a-half-old pub is a favorite with university students, most of whom take their traditional music quite seriously, while never losing that Irish twinkle of the eye. You'll usually find the ballads going Wednesday through Saturday nights, but you might drop in other nights to see what's doing.

THE PUBS OF CORK: Well, there is, according to some Cork experts, a pub for every 200 residents (including babes in arms): in a city populated by some 129,000 souls, that's a lot of pubs! You're just not likely to be seized by a terrible thirst without rescue close at hand, that's for certain. The pubs of Cork come in all sizes, styles, and decor and I have no doubt you'll find your own "local" during your stay. The following few are some I've found appealing, with convivial conversation usually on tap along with libations.

An Bodhran, 42 Plunkett St., has been renovated, but with a great deal of attention to its original character. It's a small, cozy place with brick walls, dim lights, low ceiling, lots of timbered beams and a lively clientele. It's a student hangout, but you'll usually find a mix of older types as well. Traditional music is loved here with all the fervor of a truly Irish heart (see above), as is stimulating conversation.

I first dropped in (literally) to **The Vineyard,** Market Lane (off Patrick St.), at the end of an exhausting afternoon of shopping. Things were pretty quiet except for a gaggle of Cork housewives, also exhausted for the same reason, who had sensibly decided there was nothing for it but a "drop" before heading off home to fix the dinner. It's an old, rambling place that dates back more than two centuries, but owner Tom Kiernan (the third generation of his family to run this place) has lightened it by installing a huge, high skylight in the center of the main bar. Rugby followers and players congregate in the Vineyard, where the crack leans a *lot* towards sports. Young, old, and in-between faces line up at the bar. It's a good pub in the evening, and can be a lifesaver in the late afternoon!

While I can't vouch for this personally, I have it on good authority (i.e, a kindred soul when it comes to pubs) that the **Mahon Tavern,** a small pub at the gates of Blackrock Castle, pulls a good pint and attracts a good clientele.

SPECIAL EVENTS: If you doubt that Cork is a party-loving town, just take a look at the festivals they put on every year. A festival in Cork, I might add, is a truly gala affair, with the entire city involved in the activities, and if you hit town in the middle of one, you're in for a treat. As this is written, firm dates are not available for 1985 and 1986, but the Tourist Board should be able to furnish them before you leave home.

My favorite of Cork's special events is the **Jazz International Festival,** usually in October. This is a *truly* international event, with some of the world's most outstanding musicians showing up for concerts held all around town, as well as impromptu jam sessions breaking out in pubs, B&B drawing rooms, and wherever two jazz devotees happen to meet. It's a joyous, free-spirited time.

In April or May, the **Cork International Choral & Folk Dance Festival** attracts top ranked performers from America, Great Britain, and the Continent. Come September, it's the **Cork Folk Festival.** Now, a word about a festival that may or may not come off—the **Cork Film Festival** for years enjoyed a worldwide reputation as a showcase for independent filmmakers, and it was the gala of galas in Cork. Sadly, it has been cancelled the last year or two, but when I was researching this book there was talk of reviving it, so it wouldn't hurt to make inquiries at the Tourist Board—and give a little nudge to St. Finbar to nudge the powers that be to bring it back.

As if all those festivals weren't enough, Cork also goes all out for the **Boat Show** in February, the **Summer Show** in June, the **Irish Assembly of Veteran/Vintage Motor Cycles** in September, and the **Cork 20 International Car Rally** in October! Pretty hard to miss a party, no matter *when* you come.

3. Killarney and Its Lakes

Its ancient Irish name is *Cill Airne* (Church of the Sloe); it was aptly described by the poet Moore as "Heaven's Reflex"; and *Irish Echo* columnist Joe Murphy has written, with awe akin to reverence, "Assuredly, he or she who has not seen Kerry or Killarney knows not the beauty of nature." The sheer perfection of that beauty has defied the best efforts of many a writer, poet, and artist to capture its essence, and your first glimpse of the lakes in their magnificent setting is certain to leave you wonderstruck. Nor will that wonder be dimished by repeated viewings, for the mercurial nature of this splendid landscape colors its grandeur with whimsical, ever-shifting nuances of sun and cloud and mist.

A broad valley holds the three main lakes, with Lough Leane (the Lower Lake) closest to Killarney and separated from the Middle Lake by Muckross Peninsula. It was on one of its 30 islands that dedicated monks faithfully recorded Irish history from the 11th to the 13th century in the Annals of Innisfallen. The Middle Lake covers 680 acres and holds four islands, and is connected to the small, narrow Upper Lake and its eight islands by a broad river called the Long Range. Each lake has several rivers flowing into it, and the River Laune connects them to the Atlantic. Their waters reflect the shim-

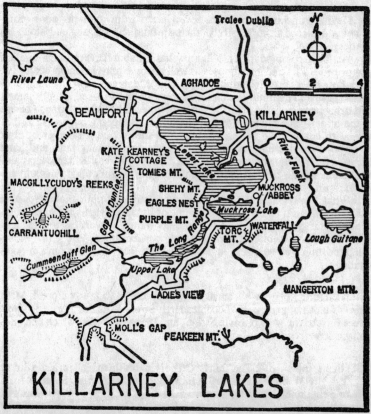

KILLARNEY LAKES

Based on the Ordnance Survey by permission of the Government of Ireland (Permit No. 906)

mering reflections of birch and oak and mountain ash and arbutus, while hovering over all are the peaks of some of Ireland's finest mountains: Macgillycuddy's Reeks, with Carrantuohill, the country's highest mountain at 3,414 feet; the Tomies; the Mangerton range; and Torc. As a Killarney jarvey once said to me, "'Tis a grand sight, one of God's blessings."

And what of Killarney? Well, it was a quiet little country market town until a visiting Englishman named Arthur Young "discovered" it in the 18th century and told the rest of the world about this natural beauty spot. Since then, of course, the rest of the world has arrived on Killarney's doorstep in droves, demanding accommodations, eateries, guides, entertainment, and a good deal more than a quiet little country market town could be expected to provide.

Right here, I'd like to dispel what seems to be a very popular myth about Killarney. It *is,* I grant you, more "commercial" than any other town in Ireland, but—and this is what I'd like to put to rest—if this is a "tourist trap," then the world could do with a few more like it! *Sure,* there are jarveys lined up ad infinitum, each hawking his own jaunting car ride. But no matter which car you climb aboard, you can do so in the sure knowledge that fees are carefully controlled (so you won't be "ripped off") and you'll hear at least one good story (like the one about the lad who plunged into the Devil's Punchbowl and was never heard from until his poor mother got a postcard from Australia asking would she please send along his clothes).

As for accommodations, Killarney has an abundance of high-quality, low-priced B&Bs and guesthouses as well as some pretty elegant luxury hotels whose prices are high but not exorbitant. Meals can be in any number of inexpensive and charming restaurants, in moderately priced establishments that bring near-gourmet dishes to table, or you can be as lavish as you please in the upper price range in one of the hotels. Shopping is good in Killarney, with competitive prices, well-stocked shops, and a number of craft workshops. As for entertainment, there are good singing pubs and hotel cabarets (and if your timing is right, the Killarney races). Killarney has also bred some of the best—and most entertaining—sightseeing guides in the world.

What I'm trying to get across is that you'll get your money's worth in Killarney. And, you'll get it from some of Ireland's friendliest, most ebullient citizens. From your landlady to your waiter or waitress to the clerk behind a shop counter to your jarvey or boatman, everyone seems delighted that you've come and can't *wait* to see that you have a good time.

ORIENTATION: Killarney is a small town, easy to find your way around. **Main Street** is its chief artery and becomes **High Street** at its northern end. **New Street** runs to the west of Main Street, and **Plunkett Street** (which becomes **College Street**) runs east.

USEFUL INFORMATION: The **Tourist Office** is in the Town Hall on Main Street (tel. 064-31633), open 9 a.m. to 7 p.m. weekdays, 3 to 5 p.m. Sundays from July to September, and 9:15 a.m. to 5:30 other months. . . . The **bus and train station** is off Railway Road (across from the Great Southern Hotel). For all **CIE information,** call 31067. . . . The **General Post Office** is on New

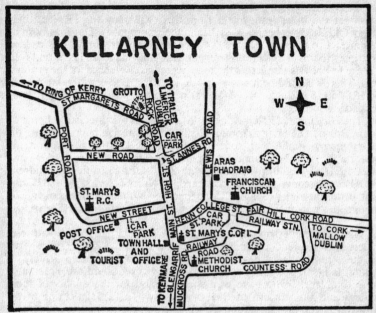

KILLARNEY TOWN

Based on the Ordnance Survey by permission of the Government of Ireland (Permit No. 906)

Street, with hours of 9 a.m. to 5:30 p.m. every day but Sunday. . . . **Taxi** ranks are at the railway station and in Main Street, and taxis are unmetered (tel. 31331 for hire). . . . There's no local bus service, but CIE runs several good day trips to nearby locations. . . . The *telephone* **prefix** for the area is 064.

ACCOMMODATIONS: As I said above, Killarney is fairly broken out with good, inexpensive places to stay—you'll even find two hotels listed, both of which are slightly above our budget range, but so slightly as to be acceptable, and both so centrally located I felt you should know about them. Some of the "Out of Town" places are within reasonable walking distance of town, though not with heavy luggage, and if you're coming by bus or train, those under the "In Town" heading will be most convenient.

Note: Prices shown below are those in effect in 1985—expect them to be higher in 1986.

In Town
Hostel: **Aghadoe House** (tel. 064-31240), Killarney's hostel, is one of the best in the country. An impressive brick mansion set on its own grounds, it's about three miles from the town center. It is absolutely necessary to book in advance during July and August, and because many hostelers are hikers as well, the wardens here (Mr. and Mrs. Claffey) ask that you be reminded that the mountains in the area can be quite dangerous and if you intend hiking or climbing them, you should be sure to notify the Claffeys of your intended route.
Bed-and-Breakfast: Bridie and Don Long, of **Wind-Way,** New Rd. (tel.

064-32835), are young, charming, and enthusiastic about helping their guests get the fullest enjoyment from their Killarney stay. Kojac, their shaggy Old English sheepdog, shares in their hospitality. Don was born in their attractive home, which they've decorated in pretty, bright colors. The three guestrooms are nicely done up, and the Linden House restaurant (see "Where to Eat") is just across the road, a great convenience for the evening meal. There's central heat and a private car park. Bed-and-breakfast rates are IR£7.50 ($9) single, IR£7 ($8.40) per person sharing. Highly recommended.

The **Hibernian,** 21 New St. (tel. 064-31258), is the three-story home of Maura Brosnan and her charming family. Mrs. Brosnan happily helps you book tours by jaunting car, coach, boat, or bike. The five guestrooms are comfortably furnished, and the location couldn't be more convenient. Rates are IR£7 ($8.40) per person, with a one-third discount for children.

Also very convenient, **The Orchard,** 65 New St. (tel. 064-31887), has eight bedrooms. Mrs. Joan O'Donoghue heads the friendly staff, all of whom take a personal interest in their guests. B&B rates are IR£7 ($8.40).

Guesthouses: Perhaps the most popular in-town guesthouse with our readers over the years is **Linden House,** New Rd. (tel. 064-31379). Set on this quiet residential street, just one block down from Main Street, its location is ideal, but much more appealing than location are Franz and Anne Knoblauch, who have won special praise for the quality of their lodgings and the warmth of their hospitality. There's something of an old-world small inn air about the three-story stucco house with many touches of wood, and bedrooms here are exceptionally comfortably and attractively appointed, all with private baths. There's central heat and one of the best moderate-priced restaurants in Killarney, with a large local following (see "Where to Eat"). Popular with traveling Irish as well as tourists, Linden House is one place you must be certain to book ahead. Rates are IR£9 ($10.80) for bed-and-breakfast, and there's a 25% reduction for children. Closed from mid-December to mid-January.

Danesfort Lodge, Muckross Rd. (tel. 064-32705), is less than ten minutes by foot from the center of town. Mrs. Juliette O'Sullivan took over the two-story cream-colored lodge in 1984 and has already begun to establish herself as a favored Killarney hostess. There are 15 guestrooms, all with hand basins, and some scheduled to have private baths. An excellent restaurant on the ground floor is moderately priced and open to the public (see "Where to Eat"). Bed-and-breakfast rates are IR£9 ($10.80), and there's a special reduced rate for families.

The **Gardens Guesthouse,** Countess Rd. (tel. 064-31147), is a charming place set in private grounds very convenient to the railway station and the town center. In the main two-story building, 20 bedrooms are nicely appointed, and all have private baths. A boon to many travelers, a dozen are on the ground floor. There's central heat and good parking. Rates are IR£10 ($12), sharing, with a 25% discount for children.

Hotels: The three-story lavender and white **Arbutus Hotel,** College St. (tel. 064-31037), once was favored by Franciscan monks when they came into town from their mountain meditations. For the past fifty years, it has been owned and operated by Pat Buckley's family, and both Pat and his wife, Norrie, continue the hospitality that's been handed down. There's an old-fashioned air about the place, enhanced by such touches as lots of etched glass and stained glass, a fireplace in the lounge, and an intimate lounge-bar presided over by the amiable Dennis, who's been here many years, as has his wife, Sheila. I am particularly fond of the cozy dining room. All 38 bedrooms have private baths, and the rate for bed-and-breakfast is IR£12.50, plus 10% service charge. A real bargain is the B&B plus dinner rate of IR£20 ($24), and the food is excellent. If you plan to use Killarney as a base for as long as a week, ask about special rates. *Note:* Connecting to the Arbutus is a low-priced, self-service restaurant called Pat's that offers very good value.

Owner Dermot O'Callaghan has recently refurbished the bar and restaurant of the small 14-room **Fáilté Hotel,** College St. (tel. 064-31893), to make it an extremely popular gathering place for both locals and tourists for good, inexpensive meals. Bedrooms are nicely done up and feature colorful Foxford blankets, even though there's central heating throughout. Bed-and-breakfast rates are IR£12.95 ($15.54) single, IR£21.40 ($25.68) double. Add 10% service charge.

Out of Town

Bed-and-breakfast: The large, modern bungalow that is **Alpine Heights,** Gap of Dunloe, Co. Kerry (tel. 064-44284), is the home of young, pretty Teresa Ferris and her family, which includes four engaging children. Less than a half-mile from the Gap of Dunloe, this pretty home, set behind white gateposts in a vibrantly green lawn, features guestrooms decorated in soft pastels, built-in wardrobes, a bright, sunny dining room, central heating, and superb views of green fields and lofty mountains. The family-orientated Mrs. Ferris keeps a crib on hand for visiting youngsters. B&B rates are IR£8 ($9.60), with a 30% discount for children. Open from Easter through October.

Shillelagh House, Knockasarnett, Aghadoe, Killarney (tel. 064-3198/ 33583), is a modern two-story home about a mile and a half from the town center. Mrs. Mary O'Connor is its gracious hostess. The pretty guestrooms have hand basins and quilted headboards for the beds. There's a lounge with TV, and full Irish breakfasts are served in the bright dining room. Rates for bed-and-breakfast are IR£8 ($9.60).

Farmhouse: Carriglea House, Muckross Rd. (tel. 064-31116), is a beautiful 200-year-old country home set on a rise overlooking the lakes a mile and a half from town. From the sweeping front lawn, approached by a tree-lined curving avenue, the view takes in the Lower Lake, Purple Mountain, Torc and Mangerton mountains. Marie and Michael Beasley own this working dairy farm and take great pleasure in helping guests plan their holiday time in Killarney. The lovely old centrally heated house has spacious rooms furnished with many antiques and tastefully decorated in restful colors. Particularly noteworthy is the dining room's chandelier of gold, blue, and pink porcelain. In addition to guestrooms in the main house, there are several in the adjoining coachhouse, whose entrance is paved with stone from Clare. One large coachhouse room has a bay window overlooking the front lawn. All guestrooms have hand basins, and some have private bath or shower. Rates for bed-and-breakfast are IR£8.50 ($10.20), with an additional IR£1.50 ($1.80) per person for rooms with private facilities.

Coolclogher House, off Muckross Rd. (tel. 064-31353), is another lovely old mansion (1737) set in green lawns. The Georgian residence has tall windows and spacious guestrooms (all with hand basins), and the hospitality of Mrs. Maura Lane Joynt has elicited many letters of warm recommendation from our readers. Rates for bed-and-breakfast are IR£8.50 ($10.20).

Guesthouse: Loch Lein, Fossa (tel. 064-31260), is three miles from town on the main Ring of Kerry road and is the domain of the delightful Kathleen Coffey. It is set in green lawns sloping down to the Lower Lake, and is approached via a country lane that's signposted on the main road just past the golf course (on your left as you approach from Killarney). The modern L-shaped guesthouse holds a dozen guestrooms that are exceptionally large and well furnished. All have hand basins and built-in closets and dresses, two have private baths, and four have private showers. Natural-wool bedspreads were woven in Kerry mills. There's a TV lounge with a fireplace and a bright, window-walled dining room. As attractive and sparkling as is the house, it is outshone by Mrs. Coffey, a small, pixie-like lady who is an accomplished conversationalist and storyteller. Her five sons and five daughters are all grown, but most live nearby and at least one is usually in attendance, as interested in guests' welfare as their mother. The family has been in this area for generations, giving the Coffeys a treasure trove of local legends they're only too happy to pass on to you, very special mementos of your Irish holiday. B&B rates are IR£8 ($9.60), with a 25% discount for children. There's a central heat and a graveled car park.

READERS' SELECTIONS: "**Dromin**, Lewis Rd., is the very lovely home of Mrs. Mary O'Driscoll Harman. It's only a short walk to the main street and has off-street parking" (E. Henritzy, New Orleans, La.). . . . "**Kathleen's Country House,** Tralee Rd. (tel. 064-32810), is just one mile from the town center and yet away from the bustle and noise. The beauty, charm, and comfort of the house is really an extension of Kathleen herself. She is everything anyone who visits Ireland expects to find in the Irish people" (Marci Harrington, Canton, Mass.). . . . "**Bridge View,** Mill Rd., is a quiet, clean, and comfortable small bungalow. Mrs. O'Shea is most pleasant and was kind enough to give us an early breakfast so we could be on the road early" (Gary Shaw, Rochester, N.Y.). . . . "The **White House Inn,** Lissivigeen Cross (tel. 064-32207), is a large, new home on a spacious lot with its own car park. Mrs. Doherty had a turf fire in the living room and had turned the heat on in our bedroom before we arrived on a damp, raw day" (Dick and Anne Connolly, Warwick, R.I.). . . . "Mrs. O'Connell's **St. Anthony's Villa,** Park Rd. (tel. 064-31534), is two minutes' drive from town, and Mrs. O'Connell is friendly, quiet-spoken and refined" (Edna McGlynn, Beverly, Mass.). . . . "The **Silver Spruce,** New Rd. (tel. 064-31376), is a modern, attractive and immaculate place, and both Mr. and Mrs. Sheehan take a personal interest in their guests" (Agnes Dunne, Manitowoc, Wisc.). . . . "We enjoyed staying at **Hilltop Villa,** Loreto Rd. (tel. 064-31084), with Mrs. Breda O'Sullivan. We had a spotless, comfortable room and the O'Sullivans were very helpful and friendly" (Mrs. Richard Danckert, Pittsfield, Mass.). . . . "Mrs. O'Donoghue, at **Cum A Ciste,** Cork Rd. (tel. 064-31271), is charming and helpful, and the modern house has central heating. Breakfast is served beautifully on bone china and silver" (Dr. J. M. King, Greenville, S.C.). . . . "**Mr. and Mrs. Brosnan,** Woodlawn Rd. (tel. 064-31328), couldn't have been friendlier. Their farmhouse is about a mile from town and the lovely rooms look out onto green fields" (Linda and John Penkalski, N. Arlington, N.J.). . . . "We heartily recommend the **Mystical Rose,** Woodlawn Rd. (tel. 064-31453). We had a good, clean room, a huge breakfast and most important, friendship" (Mrs. Stephen Aidlin, Brooklyn, N.Y.).

Note: Space does not permit full comments on the following, all of which have been enthusiastically endorsed by readers. Mrs. O'Meara's **Breffni,** Cork Rd. (tel. 064-31413); **Kilgrove** (tel. 064-31472), off Muckross Rd., the Dalys, owners; **Woodlands,** Ballydowney, Killarney (tel. 064-31467), Mrs. Evelyn Moynihan, hostess; St. Rita's Villa, Mill Rd. (tel. 064-31517), home of Mrs. Peggie Cronin: Mrs.

Dempsey's **Eagle House,** College St. (tel. 064-31351); Mrs. Noreen Landers' **Ardrinane,** Ballydowney, Killarney (tel. 064-31647). . . . Mrs. Mary Casey's **Direen House,** Tralee Rd. (tel. 064-31676).

WHERE TO EAT: Killarney's lake shores and mountain woods are perfect picnic spots, and you can pick up marvelous homemade breads (the German rye is delicious), rolls, sausage rolls, and a variety of mouthwatering pastries to take on an outing at the **Continental Pastries Shop,** Plunkett St. Herm Spôgler is Austrian born, and his culinary experience includes the post of pastry chef at two luxury hotels in Killarney. Dawn, his wife, shares the baking and running the small shop. All prices are under IR£1 ($1.20), unless, of course, you want to take away a whole pie or cake, in which case you'll pay IR£2 ($2.40) to IR£4 ($4.80).

The **Laurels** pub on Main Street serves terrific pub grub in old-style surroundings of low, beamed ceilings and rustic wooden tables. The food is good, the company congenial, and the crack stimulating.

The **Elite Restaurant,** High St. (tel. 32460), is a family-run little restaurant that is known in these parts for its very good food and low prices. It's one place you'll find Irish stew on the menu (you may have noticed it's uncommonly rare), priced at a mere IR£2.50 ($3). You'll also find several fish dishes, salads, grills (steak, pork, chicken), omelettes, curries, and beefburgers at IR£1.75 ($2.10) to IR£4.50 ($5.40). There's a daily lunch special for IR£2.50 ($3) from 12:30 to 3 p.m. The Elite is open from noon to 10 p.m., seven days a week.

The **Old Kentucky Restaurant and Bar,** New St. (tel. 31645), has a large menu of grills, salads, sandwiches, and snacks. There's also a children's menu and the Special Tourist Menu from noon to 3 p.m. Prices will run around IR£2.50 ($3) for lunch, IR£6 ($7.20) for dinner, and hours are 10 a.m. to 10 p.m., daily.

Both the bar and the restaurant at the **Fáilté Hotel,** College St. (tel. 31893), serve well-prepared food of high quality at very reasonable prices in an attractive setting. It is popular with the locals as well as visitors, and lunch will run around IR£3 ($3.60), dinner IR£7 ($8.40), and the Special Tourist Menu is offered from 6:30 to 8:30 p.m. Hours are 12:30 to 9:30 p.m.

The **Danesfort Lodge** restaurant, Muckross Rd. (tel. 32705) serves a fixed-price, home-cooked five-course dinner, with sirloin steak, fish, chicken, pork, and seafood selections, priced at IR£9 ($10.80). Hours are 6 to 9 p.m., seven days a week. There's a wine license, and they also serve luncheon and afternoon tea.

One of the best places in town for a delicious, home-cooked evening meal is **Linden House,** New Rd. (tel. 31379), described above under "Accommodations." Franz Knoblauch is German-born, married to the lovely Irish Anne, and together they have created a Bavarian-type dining room of exposed-brick and wooden booths. It's a cozy place, very popular with locals, and the menu is good, solid family fare. Son Peter supervises the spotless kitchen and insists on the freshest ingredients. Dinner will run about IR£8 ($9.60), and in July and August it's a good idea to book ahead—other months you'll usually have only a few minutes' wait at the most. Incidentally, residents are served a "House Special" menu at 6 p.m. at the reduced price of IR£6.50 ($7.80), and the restaurant is closed to nonresidents on Mondays and from November through mid-January. Highly recommended.

Another very special place to eat is **Foley's Steak & Seafood Restaurant,** 23 High St. (tel. 31217). This was a coaching inn many years ago, and there's an old-style air about the front bar lounge, where a fireplace adds to the coziness. The pretty back room is more formal, decorated with soft shades of rose and green. Carol and Denis Hartnett are the family team responsible for turning out superb meals with the highest standards. Seafood is a specialty, and Carol (who does the cooking) uses only the freshest fish. Denis cuts all their steaks and buys only Kerry mountain lamb, using nothing but centerline cuts. Actually, this is a full-service eatery, serving all three meals (breakfast from 8 a.m.), and bar food is available up to 7:30 p.m. Lunch prices run about IR£7.50 ($9), and main courses on the dinner menu are in the IR£7.50 ($9) to IR£10.50 ($12.60) range. The Tourist Menu is available from noon to 3 p.m. Dinner hours are 5 to 10:30 p.m., and there's a pianist on Friday, Saturday, and Sunday nights during the summer. Open seven days, and booking is advised in high season.

READER'S SELECTION: "The **Sugan Kitchen**, Michael Collins Place (tel. 33104), was by far the friendliest and warmest eating place we discovered. As Irish songs played in the background, hostess Margaret O'Shea made us feel like part of the family. The small dining room of just seven tables and country decor are homey, and traditional Irish and vegetarian portions are plentiful. To top it all off, our bill for two was well under IR£10 ($12). The Sugan Kitchen is truly an extraordinary dining discovery" (Cathy and Paul Monsees, Washington, D.C.).

THINGS TO SEE AND DO: Killarney's wealth of natural beauties can be a bit overwhelming as you face the prospect of trying to get around to see as many as you have time for. Not to worry, the jarveys and boatmen and coach tour people have it all worked out for you—their routes will take you to the high points, and although it is perfectly possible to wander around on your own, this is one time I highly recommend that you plan the budget around at least one or two of the guided tours, whether by jaunting car, boat, or CIE coach. Fares are reasonable, and the guides know and love the scenery through which they escort you, embellishing every spot with the folklore that will make the experience even more memorable. After you've done that, I recommend just as highly that you go back on your own to linger and savor all that beauty and contemplate the things your guide has shared with you. The two experiences make a soul-restoring combination.

Seeing the Lakes

By Jaunting Car: Uniform rates and routes are set each year for the season, and while the 1985 rates are not available as this is written, those listed are 1984 prices, which you can expect to rise by only a small amount, if at all. No need to stop by the Tourist Office to make arrangements—you'll be hassled by the long line of drivers down the street, and my advice is to look them all over and pick the Irish face and twinkling eye that tickles your fancy most. If you're strong-willed enough to hold out all the way to the last jaunting car, you're in for some entertaining conversation during the course of your "window shopping." In high season, it's a good idea to reserve your seat on the wonderfully colorful trap the evening before you plan to go.

If the budget can possibly be stretched to include the **all-day trip**, you'll go home with glorious memories worth far more than the IR£20 ($24) fare. The day begins about 10 a.m., when you hop into a jaunting car, tucking a woolly car rug around your knees if there's a chill in the air. Then, it's off at a trot through leafy scenery to **Kate Kearney's Cottage** (which is not the traditional thatched cottage you might expect from its name, but a giftshop and snack bar) at the mouth of the **Gap of Dunloe**. Next comes a transfer to either a pony's back (for experienced riders only) or a pony trap to make the six-mile trek through wild, silent walls of granite so awesome you'll speak in whispers, if at all. Along the way, there are still, mysterious lakes on either side, and it is in Black Lough that legend says the last snake in Ireland was drowned by the good St. Patrick—which explains, no doubt, why no fish have ever inhabited its depths. Lunch is a picnic at the end of the Gap (everyone brings his own) before meeting your boatman at the **Upper Lake**. The afternoon is a watery tour of all three lakes, ending when your boat docks at **Ross Castle**, where your jaunting car waits to return you to town about 5:30 p.m. A lovely day, and unrivaled by any other in my own travel experience.

Shorter tours (allow a half-day for most) take you through the Killarney Estate along the lake shores to **Muckross Abbey**, home to Franciscan monks from 1448 until Cromwell ordered it burned in 1652. There's time to wander around **Muckross House** and its gardens, then on to view the lovely **Torc waterfall** before returning to town. The 1984 charge was IR£16 ($19.20). For the same fare, you can choose the heights of **Aghadoe Hill** for a breathtaking view of mountains, lakes, and the town below. A church and round tower date back to the seventh century. The return to town is by way of the **Lower Lake** and **Ross Castle**. Various other routes are available at fares of IR£8 ($9.60) to IR£12 ($14.40).

By Boat: Killarney's boatmen are legendary for their skillful navigation of the lakes and their store of wondrous tales. Their numbers are also diminishing, but the Tourist Office can help you make arrangements for a day on the lakes with a party of four at fares that are set each year for the season. If you want to do the rowing yourself, rowboats and canoes are available at **Ross Castle** and **Muckross House** at about IR£10 per day for up to three people.

On Your Own: A delightful day can be spent biking along the **Lower Lake** and through the **National Park** (entrance just off Muckross Road) or along the lakeside paths in **Ross Castle Western Demesne** (there's a small admission charge). Cars are prohibited in both, and you'll feel very close to Mother Nature as you wheel along wooded paths, with stops to contemplate the timeless waters of the lake. Bicycles may be rented from **O'Callaghan's** in College Street, **O'Neill's** in Plunkett Street, and **Hearne's** in High Street.

If you're an experienced rider and fairly fit (important if you don't want to cart sore muscles around the rest of Ireland), horses are available for day treks from the **Killarney Riding School** in Ballydowney (tel. 31686). They may also be hired at the **Gap of Dunloe** for the two-hour ride to the top of the Gap and back, but as sure-footed as are these steeds, you want to be a good rider before attempting it. Hikers who prefer the exhilaration of walking over the Gap should allow a minimum of three hours.

Muckross House

Set in some 11,500 acres of parkland and surrounded by marvelously landscaped gardens, the Tudor-style Muckross House dates back to 1843, when it was built by Henry Arthur Herbert, a wealthy Kerry M.P. Americans bought it in 1911, and in 1932 the entire estate was presented as a gift to the Irish people.

Its upper floors hold some fascinating exhibits of maps, prints, and other documents, as well as a small wildlife and bird collection. Housed in its basement is a marvelous folk museum and craft shops that bring to vivid life the Kerry country lifestyle of a time long past. Exhibits include a country pub, printshop, dairy, carpentry shop, and weaving shop. You'll see craftsmen at work in some, and you can purchase their products in the giftshop. There's a light, airy teashop off the courtyard, a welcome respite for weary feet when you've toured the house and museum. There's no charge to wander about the park and gardens; adults pay IR£1 ($1.20), children half that, to tour the house and museum. It's open from 9 a.m. to 9 p.m. in July and August, various hours other times of the time —inquire at the Tourist Office.

Other Activities

You may **swim** in any of the lakes without charge, and you'll only need a license to **fish** for salmon—none needed to go after all those lovely brown trout. Donie Brosnan, at the **Handy Store** in Kenmare Place, is the man to fix you up with bait and up-to-the-minute information about the best fishing spots. There are two 18-hole, championship **golf** courses along the northern shore of the Lower Lake, and clubs, caddies, and caddy-cars are available at the clubhouse. Check with the Tourist Office or *The Kerryman* to see if anything is on at Fitzgerald Stadium on Lewis Road, the venue for Sunday **hurling and Gaelic football** matches. Killarney **horserace** meets occur in May and July, and it's worth juggling your schedule to catch them—the town assumes a "country fair" air.

You'll find the **Ring of Kerry** drive described in the next section of this chapter, "Around Counties Cork and Kerry," but, again, I strongly recommend that you stash the car and take a day off from driving to join one of the inexpensive coach tours. **CIE** (call 064-31067) has a day tour for IR£8 ($9.60), and Barry O'Connor, of **O'Connor's Auto Tours,** Adross Ross Rd. (tel. 064-31703), will give readers of this book a 12% discount on his mini-coach tour priced at IR£9 ($10.80). Tours of the Ring run daily from Easter to October, and you'll be collected at your accommodation in the morning and returned there in the evening. Be sure and mention the book when you book the tour and show it to the driver when he picks you up.

Crafts and Other Shopping

As I mentioned earlier in this section, Killarney is good shopping country. Also, in recent years several craft shops have opened in and near the town.

Crafts: Threads and Clay, College St. (tel. 33433), is a marvelous workshop run by John Joe and Mary Murphy. Located in an 18th-century granary down a little lane off College St. (look for the signpost), it holds a weaver's shed where you can watch the loom at work and a pottery. The shop sells products made on the premises as well as other interesting craft items and has a limited stock of Irish-interest books. They'll mail and insure any of your purchases. Hours are 9 a.m. to 6 p.m. Monday through Saturday. Students who present their I.D. card will be given a 5% discount.

At **Three Lakes Crystal,** 27–28 Plunkett St., you can watch Eddie Flavan, master glass cutter who trained in the Waterford Glass plant, and Aidan Scully as they hand-cut special designs (family crests, monograms, etc.) right in the shop's showroom. Every piece on sale has been cut right on the premises, and there are some real beauties. Hours are 9 a.m. to 5:30

p.m. every day except Sunday, and during summer months they open from 7 to 10 p.m.

The **Artist Gallery**, 5 Plunkett St. (tel. 32273), is the domain of Dublin-born Stephen Doyle. In addition to his interesting paintings, drawings, and graphics, there are lovely silk screen prints from the *Book of Kells*.

Vivid colors swirl in the heart of lovely paperweights, bowls, plates, ring holders, vases, and a host of other objects produced by **Kerry Glass Limited,** Fair Hill (tel. 32587). It's next to the Franciscan Friary opposite the Great Southern Hotel. The glassmakers work right in the showroom, and it is fascinating to watch them shape the liquid glass and apply the colors. The workshop is open 8 a.m. to 1 p.m. and 2 to 4 p.m. Monday through Friday. There's also a shop in College Street that sells seconds.

Shopping: Located just around the curve from the Town Hall and Tourist Office, **Tweeds & Crafts,** East Ave. Rd. (tel. 33306), carries a wide selection of high-quality tweed jackets and suits for men and women, cashmere jackets, handcut crystal, linen, Aran hand-knits, and a good many other items. The owner, personable young Geoff McCarthy, is usually on hand to assist you, but if he should be out when you call in, the staff is both friendly and helpful. Geoff also has a menswear shop, **Classic Menswear,** upstairs at 1 Main St. (tel. 33306), that carries outstanding values in Donegal tweed jackets, caps, and ties as well as leading brands of Irish, English, and Scottish knitwear.

Hilliards, Main St., is one of my favorite stores in the whole of Ireland. Maybe it's their huge stocks of Irish-made goods (over 3,000 pieces of Waterford glass, umpteen hundred pieces of Belleek and Royal Tara, Irish porcelain character figures like Paddy McGenty and the rose of Tralee for under IR£5, $6, and a whole host of other items) at terrific prices. But I suspect Hilliards has gained my affection because of the likes of Jim Cronin, the manager who always seems to be on hand to help with decisions, locate some special object, or simply give a little background information on something that has caught my interest. Ina Brosnan, in the glassware department, is of the same ilk, as are the rest of the staff in this busy shop—not surprising, since they are simply carrying on a tradition set back in 1846, when Hilliards first opened its doors. They'll ship and insure any purchases, and you can write for their mail-order catalog. Hours are 9 a.m. to 6 p.m., and in summer months, 7:30 to 10:30 p.m. Incidentally, if you've yearned to take home some of those lovely Irish lace curtains, there's a large drapery department here, managed by helpful Don Long.

KILLARNEY AFTER DARK: Killarney has two singing pubs to tempt your vocal chords. There's ballad singing and general hilarity in the back room of **The Laurels** pub from May to October, and letters pour in from our readers with enthusiastic endorsement of this liveliest of Killarney pubs. Go along about 9 p.m., when things are just tuning up. The larger and ever-so-slightly more subdued **Danny Mann** pub, on New St., installs ballad groups every night right through the year, and in summer, it's likely to be packed out with Yanks rendering heartfelt versions of such stock Irish exports as "Danny Boy" and "When Irish Eyes are Smiling." The action starts about 9:30 p.m., and if you're not ready to end the evening at 11:30 p.m., a posh new nightclub has been added to the pub, where things go on until 1:15 a.m.

During summer months, there's ceili dancing (set dancing you'll recognize as the ancestor of our square dancing) and traditional Irish music every night of the week. The **White Gates Inn Hotel,** on Muckross Rd., has a traditional music seisiun and singalong on Friday nights and other entertainment on Saturdays during the season (call 31164 to see what's on).

A Very Special Irish Folk Pageant

Top of my own list of favorite nighttime entertainment in the Killarney area is at least one performance of **Siamsa,** the **National Folk Theatre** troupe which is based in Tralee, but performs in the Great Southern Hotel annex during summer months as well as in their own **Siamsa Tire Theatre** in nearby Tralee. "Merrymaking" is the English translation of the Gaelic *siamsa,* and this is as merry a show as you'll come across, as it depicts through music, song, dance, and mime Irish country life of the past. In a stage setting of thatched cottage and farmyard, expert performers go about the business of thatching, churning, milking, harvesting, and other routine tasks that were the foundation of everyday life on the farm. It will no doubt surprise you, as it did me, to know that the troupe operates on a very limited budget, with just a handful of full-time performers and that most of those skilled actors, singers, and dancers give hours and hours of their time to perfect the show and travel with it on a strictly voluntary basis. It's an inspiring as well as fun-filled evening of entertainment and puts you in close touch with an Irish lifestyle that has been the foundation of the nation for centuries. Having seen siamsa, you'll know intimately the source of the irrepressible Irish spirit that charms us so. You can book for both Killarney and Tralee performances, at the Siamsa Tire Theatre, Tralee (tel. 066-23055), and tickets are under IR£5 ($6) for adults, less for children. This is a definite "don't miss."

Cabarets

Out at the **GlenEagle Hotel and Country Club** on Muckross Rd. (tel. 31870), there's inexpensive Irish entertainment every night except Sunday during summer months. Ballads, folk songs, traditional music and stories as only the Irish can tell them are on tap, with top-flight entertainers like the Wolfe Tones and Joe Dolan frequently on the bill. Admission is IR£6 ($7.20), and there's free shuttle bus service to the hotel from Kenmare Place between 8 p.m. and 1 a.m. There's dancing after the show until 1 a.m., or you might want to opt for the **Eagle's Nest,** a disco that often features jazz sessions or pub theater (small admission charge). A resident pianist and guitarist hold sway in the **Eagle's Whistle Lounge** (no cover charge), and they'll have you singing your heart out in a true Irish singalong.

"Irish Eyes Are Smiling," at the **Great Southern Hotel** (tel. 31262), opposite the railway station, is a polished cabaret entertainment that features Irish dancers, singers, and instrumentalists and a comic emcee. You can come either for dinner and the cabaret, for IR£17 ($20.40), or for the show alone, which costs IR£9 ($10.80).

Medieval Banquet

I'm going out on a more-than-shaky limb to tell you about a marvelous evening entertainment that first opened about midway in the 1984 summer season. That limb is unsteady simply because the future of the **Killarney Medieval Banquet** at the **Three Lakes Hotel** (tel. 31479) is uncertain as this is written.

However, it's such a good idea and so much fun that I wouldn't want you to miss it if it doesn't meet with an early demise. Sponsored on Wednesday nights by the Knights of Innisfallen, the banquet does not begin until every guest is garbed in the threads of Knighthood. Dubbed a Knight of Killarney for the evening, you then enjoy a sumptuous dinner and entertainment centered around the legends of Killarney. A nice idea is that any profits are to go to worthy causes in the locality. The 1984 price was IR£16 ($19.20), and the Tourist Office will be able to tell you if it lived through birth pangs for a second season.

SPECIAL EVENTS: For one week in mid-May, Celts from six countries converge on Killarney to celebrate and preserve their ancient ties during **Pan-Celtic Week.** There are interesting exhibits on display, and the week's schedule includes sports competitions, workshops, concerts, pipe band competitions, informal seisiuns, dancing, and a marvelous Cornish Pen Gwyn torchlight procession led by a black-robed, jaw-snapping horse's skull, with musicians of all nationalities hypnotizing sidewalk spectators with ancient dance rhythms that inevitably draw them into the procession. Admission prices are minimal, and many events are free. Check the Tourist Board "Calendar of Events" for exact dates in 1985 and 1986.

Killarney is an ideal base from which to be a part of one of Ireland's major annual events, the **Rose of Tralee International Festival.** Tralee is just 20 miles to the north, and you'll find details in the next section, "Around Counties Cork and Kerry."

4. Around Counties Cork and Kerry

ACCOMMODATIONS: Remember that prices shown below are those in effect in 1985—expect them to be higher in 1986.

County Cork
Hostel: There's a superior grade hostel in Summer Cove, Kinsale (tel. 021-72309). About a mile and a half out from Kinsale, the hostel has an extremely steep approach.

Bed-and-Breakfast: Donal and Philomena (Phil) Brooks open their Georgian home, **Avonmore House,** South Abbey, Youghal (tel. 024-2617), to guests, with eight nicely done up guestrooms and superb meals. Donal is a forester and has a keen interest in traditional Irish music. Avonmore is conveniently located in the main residential section of Youghal and is only a short walk from the beach. B&B rates are IR£8.50 ($10.20), with a 25% reduction for children. Dinner is IR£8 ($9.60).

The Lynch family will make you feel right at home at **The Gables,** Stoneview, Blarney (tel. 021-85330). This lovely period house is set in its own grounds and was once given to the parish priest by the owners of Blarney Castle. There are three attractive guestrooms, two with private facilities. Rates are IR£9 ($10.80) for bed-and-breakfast, with 25% off for children. Open April through October.

On the Blarney/Killarney road, you'll find **Glenview House,** Tower,

Blarney (tel. 021-85370). This two-story stone house has been charmingly renovated with due regard to retaining its original character. Partly because of its structure, one of the three guestrooms does not have a hand basin, though the bathroom is handy. Mr. and Mrs. Finbarr O'Brien take a personal interest in all their guests, and Mr. O'Brien is especially helpful to those tracing their Irish ancestors. Bed-and-breakfast rates are IR£7.50 ($9), with a 25% discount for children. Open April through September.

About a mile outside Kinsale, Mrs. Griffin's **Hillside House,** Camp Hill, Kinsale (tel. 021-72315), has sea views and a pleasant garden. Three of the four attractive bedrooms have washbasins. This is an especially nice place to stay if you prefer the country, but don't want to be too far from town. B&B rates are IR£8.50 ($10.20), with a 25% discount for children. Central heat and ample parking.

Shangri-la, Bantry (tel. 027-5244/50928), is a modern bungalow perched on a hill overlooking Bantry Bay. The glass-enclosed front porch affords gorgeous panoramic views of the Bay, and chairs are often set out on the beautifully landscaped lawn for guests to savor spectacular sunsets. Guestrooms are comfortably furnished and each is decorated around one color, which gives it its name of Blue Room, Pink Room, etc. Angela and Tony Muckley are gracious hosts who know the area well and love helping their guests plan their time here. Angela is a former president of the Town & Country Homes Association and is keenly interested in tourism. She is also known as a superior cook and her evening meals are memorable, with wine available. For breakfast, she many times offers guests a choice of the traditional Irish menu or pancakes or waffles (a nice change). Rates are IR&8.50 ($10.20) for bed-and-breakfast (20% reduction for children), IR£8.50 ($10.20) for the evening meal. There's central heating and a private car park.

Farmhouses: Lovely **Birch Hill House,** Grenagh, Blarney (tel. 021-886106), is a long-time favorite with our readers. The lovely century-old Victorian home sits on a wooded bluff, part of a 105-acre farm. Mrs. Dawson is the friendly hostess, who is as interesting as her plant-filled home. The six guestrooms have hand basins, and some are quite large. All are nicely decorated and comfortably furnished. There are wood fires downstairs, electric heaters in guestrooms. B&B rates are IR£8.50 ($10.20), and there's a 20% discount for children. Open mid-March through October.

Mrs. Fitzpatrick will welcome you to **Beechmount Farm,** Mallow (tel. 022-21764). The pretty Georgian house dates back to the 17th century and is partially furnished with antique pieces. Mrs. Fitzpatrick excels in the kitchen, and boasts that at Beechmount "you will never be cold or hungry." You'll sample her marvelous home baking at afternoon tea, which is served at no charge to guests. The 187 acres of green farm fields afford peaceful rural views, and the five simply furnished guestrooms feature electric blankets on all beds. Rates for B&B are IR£8.50 ($10.20), and dinner costs IR£8 ($9.60). Open June to September.

Guesthouses: Norma and Barry Twomey pride themselves on offering all the "traditional hospitality of a small inn" at **Whispering Pines Guesthouses,** Crosshaven (tel. 021-831448), a popular boating resort village some 13 miles south of Cork City. The two-story ultramodern guesthouse certainly offers every convenience you can imagine, and it's just across the road from the Owenabwee River and Crosshaven Harbour, with their pageantry of colorful sailboats. Guestrooms are beautifully decorated, have built-in wardrobes, a view of the river, and come with or without private baths. The dining room, with a fireplace for cool days, opens onto a patio, where breakfast is sometimes served in fine weather. In the lounge, large windows look out to the water, and a piano is on hand for guests (and Barry, when he can be prevailed upon to play). There are no less than 12 pubs in the village, an easy walk from Whispering Pines. Bed-and-breakfast rates are IR£12 ($14.40) to IR£15 ($18), and dinner (there's a wine license) is IR£12 ($14.40).

In the little village of Myrtleville, about 18 miles southwest of Cork City, a marvelous and quite extraordinary guesthouse perches atop a high cliff overlooking the sea. **Bunnyconnelan** (tel. 021-831237) was the holiday home built for a British diplomat back in 1830, but was not given its unusual name until a Scotsman bought it soon after World War II and christened it after his four daughters—Bunny, Connie, Nellie, and Ann. Now, it's in the capable hands of Pat and Sheila O'Brien. The view is spectacular, with Roches Point lighthouse blinking in the distance and award-winning gardens sloping down the cliffside. The ground floor holds an interesting bar/lounge which features stone fireplaces, beamed ceiling, and the most eclectic collection of decorations you can imagine, including bagpipies, barometers, a brass hunting horn and tartan drapes. Outside, umbrella tables dot a flag-paved patio. On weekend nights, this place is mobbed with people who've come down from Cork, often bringing their own music with them. The ground-floor dining room looks out to sea views through one wall of windows, and the meals are excellent, with seafood and steak starring on the moderately priced menu. Pub grub is available in the bar during the day. Upstairs, there are a dozen simply furnished rooms, most with that smashing view, that cost IR£10 ($12). Advance booking is absolutely essential in summer months.

Ard-na-Greine, in Schull (tel. 028-28181), is pricey enough to qualify as a Big Splurge and special enough to warrant kicking over budget traces. Set on a hill a mile to the west of town, its peaceful, bucolic views are a tonic for travel-weary souls. The English translation of its name is "Height of the Sun," and the gorgeous blooms in gardens and front lawns attest to the abundance of sunshine it enjoys. Frank and Rena O'Sullivan have created a haven of comfort and semi-sophistication in an old inn that dates back two centuries. The O'Sullivans have managed to retain much of the inn's original character while installing amenities that would do a big-city luxury hotel proud. The beamed-ceilinged, white-walled dining room has a fireplace on each end wall and features evening meals that draw large local crowds. There's an excellent wine list as well. A lovely stone-floored bar which is open to the public and a cozy, private guests' bar are also featured. All bedrooms are beautifully decorated, and all have private baths as well as tea and coffee makings. Rates, which include a full Irish breakfast, are from IR£20 ($24), and dinner (which must be booked ahead) runs IR£14.50 ($17.40). If you're planning to splurge on one special place, make it this one!

Hotels: In the little West Cork village of Leap, a night in the comfortable, old-fashioned **Leap Inn** (tel. 028-33307) is like taking a giant step back to a time when friendliness and gracious hospitality was the mark of all country inns. The same family has run this place since 1834, and today

Brian and Ann Sheahan continue the traditions of innkeeping that have grown with the years. Public rooms include a bar (which serves pub grub), lounge, and a pretty dining room, where a four-course dinner featuring fresh seafood runs about IR£8 ($9.60) and à la carte main courses are under IR£5 ($6). Upstairs, bedrooms are simply furnished but very comfortable. Only one of the ten has a private bath (no extra charge), and rates, which include a full Irish breakfast, are IR£8 ($9.60).

Another Big Splurge for your consideration. Set back from the road in spacious grounds, **Sea View House Hotel,** Ballylickey, Bantry (tel. 027-50073/50462), is a sparkling white three-story house built back in 1888. Miss Kathleen O'Sullivan, owner and manager, is known throughout Ireland for her hospitality, and her deft hand can be seen in every room, where antiques are not so much on display as placed for convenient use. Every room, in fact, fairly shouts "gracious." Sea View is also known for its excellent dining room, which has won several food awards, and its Sunday lunch is a great favorite with locals. Each bedroom is different in size and shape, and each is prettily decorated, and all have telephones. Most have private baths. Rates, which include private bath and full Irish breakfast, range from IR£18 ($21.60) to IR£20 ($24).

County Kerry

Hostel: There's a very nice **hostel** on the Dingle Peninsula at Ballyferriter, about ten miles from Dingle Town. Contact Dun Chaoin, Ballyferriter, Tralee (tel. 066-56121).

Bed-and-Breakfast: Some 13 miles east of Kenmare, **Sillerdane Lodge,** Coolnoohill, Kilgarvan (tel. Kilgarvan 59), offers a most unusual feature for an Irish B&B—a heated outdoor swimming pool! Set in a beautiful valley, the pretty bungalow has more than just that to offer, however, and perhaps its most appealing feature is the gracious Mrs. Joan McCarthy. This lovely lady takes a personal interest in all her guests and her home reflects her concern for their comfort. The bright dining room has huge windows to take advantage of gorgeous views, and bedrooms are beautifully decorated and spotless. All six have private bath and shower. Bed-and-breakfast rates are IR£8.50 ($10.20), with a 25% reduction for children. Central heat and plenty of room for parking. Closed two weeks in December.

On the outskirts of Kenmare, in a quiet street just off the main Kenmare/Ring of Kerry road, **Ardmore House,** Killarney Rd. (tel. 064-41406), is a modern one-story bungalow framed by a colorful rose garden. Toni and Tom Connor have four nice bedrooms, all with hand basins and three with private shower. Those on the front look out to the roses, and the back view is of peaceful green pastures, with mountains in the background. B&B rates are IR£7.50 ($9) without private facilities, IR£8 ($9.60) with, and children pay half. Central heat and plenty of parking space.

In Dingle, you'll get a very warm welcome from Mrs. Mary Leonard at **Dykegate House,** 8 Dykegate St. (tel. 066-51549). Conveniently located within walking distance of everything in town, the two-story house is rather plain but homey. Mrs. Leonard, a retired nurse, is the soul of hospitality and serves up one of the best breakfasts I've had in Ireland in a light and airy dining room. Guestrooms vary in size, but all are comfortably furnished. This has been a favorite of our readers for years, and after a personal stay, I heartily concur in their endorsements. Rates for bed-and-breakfast are IR£7.50 ($9), with 25% off for children.

Also conveniently located in the heart of town, **Mrs. Betty Hand,** Green St. (tel. 066-51538), has a large two-story home with four nicely appointed guestrooms. The friendliness of the Hand family is legendary, and they are always delighted to have American guests. There's central heat and a garden where guests are welcome to sit of a sunny afternoon. Rates for bed-and-breakfast are IR£7.50 ($9), with a 50% reduction for children.

In a breathtakingly beautiful setting high on a hill overlooking Slea Head and the Blasket Islands, **Slea Head House,** Dunquin, Tralee (no telephone), first opened as a guesthouse in the 1930s, when Mrs. Maureen O'Connell's grandmother took in students to teach them the Irish language. For many years now, Maureen and husband, Liam, have continued the tradition of warm, personal hospitality that began back then. A more gracious, witty, or fun-loving couple would be hard to find. Guestrooms are all different in size and shape, all are fitted out with plain but comfortable furnishings, and most have that smashing view. Bed-and-breakfast will cost you IR£7.50 ($9).

In Ballyferriter, on the Dingle Peninsula, Miss Bird O'Sullivan's **Cois Abhann** (pronounce it "Cush Owen," and it means by the side of the river), Emila, Ballyferriter (tel. 066-56301), is a pretty, modern bungalow with floor-to-ceiling windows to frame magnificent mountain views. The six guestrooms are all done in pastel colors and all have private bath and shower. There's a wine license, and Miss O'Sullivan is known for her fine dinners. B&B rates are IR£9 ($10.80), and dinner costs the same. There's central heat and plenty of parking space. Open March through October.

There are views of lofty Mount Brandon from all six guestrooms at **MacGearailt's Bungalow,** Bothar Bui, Ballydavid, Dingle (tel. 066-55142). The bright, modern bungalow is the home of Maura and Thomas Mac-Gearailt, who delight in welcoming guests and pointing out the splendors of the Dingle Peninsula. All bedrooms have private showers. Rates are IR£8.50 ($10.20) for bed-and-breakfast and the same for the evening meal, with 20% off for children. Central heat and parking. Open Easter through September.

A lovely modern bungalow named **Cliabhan** (it means "cradle," and is pronounced "clee-vaughn"), Dingle (tel. 066-51108), is about a ten-minute walk from Dingle Town. Ursula and Tommy Sheehy are marvelous hosts, with a seemingly inexhaustible knowledge of the Dingle Peninsula and a keen desire to share it with their guests. From the pleasant lounge and dining room, there are views of green pastures dotted with grazing sheep and the hazy shapes of mountains beyond the bay. There's an ancient Ogham stone in the field out back and a ring fort down in the pasture. All five of the guestrooms have private shower facilities, and two have bidets. Ursula is one of the few Irish hostesses to serve percolated coffee to Americans who've overdosed on tea. Bed-and-breakfast rates with this engaging couple are IR£7.50 ($9).

Rita and Geroiod Brosnan, of **Drom** (it means "hilly") **House,** Coumgaugh, Dingle (tel. 066-51134), are both Dingle Peninsula natives. Rita was born in a house just up the road, and Geroiod is Director of the West Kerry Co-op that has resurrected farming as a viable occupation hereabouts. Their hillside home sits amid sweeping mountain vistas, and the modern bungalow is nicely decorated throughout. There are three pastel-hued guestrooms, and all have private showers. B&B rates are

IR£8.50 ($10.20), with a 50% discount for children, for whom there is a playground.

Guesthouse: One of the prettiest guesthouses on the Dingle Peninsula is **Aisling,** Castlegregory (tel. 066-39134). The home of Dr. (retired) and Mrs. Healy, the two-story charmer is a mecca for visitors interested in Irish history and this unique region. The good doctor is an authority on both and delights in sharing his vast knowledge; both he and his wife, Helen, are also very helpful in directing their guests to good local eateries, craft workshops, etc. The house shines, with parquet floors, artistic arrangements of dried flowers, and examples of Irish pottery on display. The two upstairs bedrooms have washbasins, but share a bath, while two downstairs rooms off a patio have private baths. At breakfast, Mrs. Healy's justly famed brown scones star. Bed-and-breakfast rates are IR£10 ($12), with an additional charge of IR£1.50 ($1.80) for private facilities. Children are 15% off regular rates.

Farmhouses: Marino House, Reen, Kenmare (tel. 064-41154), has occupied one of Ireland's most scenic sites for over two centuries, a small, wooded finger of land extending out into Kenmare Bay. There's an old-fashioned air about the place, yet there's total modern comfort inside—an irresistible combination. Run by the O'Sullivans, Marino House has nine guestrooms in an extension, all with washbasins and central heating, and all comfortably furnished. Meals are served in a dining room overlooking the green lawn. Much patronized by regulars, this place gets booked out quickly from year to year, so best book as far in advance as possible. B&B rates are IR£8, dinner is the same, and there's a 20% reduction for children. Open May through September.

Entertaining, energetic, and above all gracious, Kitty and Pat Dineen, of **Hawthorn Farm,** Kilgarvan, Killarney (tel. Kilgarvan 26), wear many hats. There's Pat's fishing hat (salmon and trout from the nearby Roughty River are his prey), Kitty's chef's hat (her Christmas whiskey cake and traditional fruit cakes are known the world over), Pat's farmer's hat (for coaxing fresh vegetables from the 80 acres of land and tending the cows who supply milk and butter for the table), and a "congeniality" hat (if there is such a thing!) worn by both in greeting and caring for their guests. Their bright, modern farmhouse is set in a wildly beautiful mountain valley just 12 miles from Kenmare and the sea, on the Killarney road. There are six pretty bedrooms upstairs, three of them with private bath facilities, and downstairs are three additional bedrooms. Three are large enough to accommodate three to four occupants, and four to five persons fit comfortably in another. Kitty's meals are superb presentations of the freshest ingredients and feature her home-baked scones, wholemeal bread, and those famous cakes. Meals are served with china, linen, and silverware made in Ireland, as it only fitting in the home of two such enthusiastic Irish speakers and boosters of the country. Rates for bed-and-breakfast are IR£8.50 ($10.20), dinner is the same, and there's an additional IR£1 ($1.20) per-person charge for rooms with private baths. There's a 20% reduction for children. Incidentally, once a week, Kitty serves up a traditional Christmas dinner with all the trimmings. And, if you fall in love with her Christmas whiskey cake (every guest gets to try it), she does a thriving mail-order business. Open April through October. Central heating.

Two charming Irish sisters—Mrs. Leahy and Mrs. Cussen—redefine the meaning of "gentlewomen" as hostesses of **Mount Rivers,** Listowel (tel.

068-21494), an award-winning farmhouse on the outskirts of Listowel. Their two-story family home is a fascinating place, set high on a wooded hill overlooking the River Feale, with a small garden and graveled car park out front. Family photos, ornate relics of the Victorian Age, and souvenirs from around the world collected by a granduncle who went to sea crowd the lovely, old-fashioned parlor, where a fireplace glows on cool evenings and you're welcome to browse through scrapbooks and other family mementos. Meals are taken in the high-ceilinged dining room overlooking the front lawn. Upstairs bedrooms are of more-than-generous size and furnished with many interesting antiques. There's carpeting throughout, and washbasins in all guestrooms. Rates for bed-and-breakfast are IR£9 ($10.80), with a 25% reduction for children. A real charmer!

Hotel: There's a gem of an Irish country hotel on the Dingle Peninsula, and in many respects it is more a bed-and-breakfast place than a hotel. That's because of the informality and personal service you'll receive from Billy and Breege Granville at the **Ostan Granville,** Ballyferriter, Dingle (tel. 066-56116). *Ostan* is Irish for "hotel," but this 1838 Georgian house began life as a rectory, then was used by the Royal Irish Constabulary as a barracks until the 1920s, when it burned. That's when the Granville family took it over, restored it, and opened its doors to the public. There's an old-fashioned, homey look to the place, and its bar looks out to Mount Brandon, Ballydavid Head, Smerwick Harbour, and the Three Sisters—a wonderful place to bend an elbow before the fireplace while contemplating that sweeping view! Guestrooms are plain but comfortable. Some have private bath and shower, others only hand basins, but all have terrific views. A nice feather here is the attention given families with children; there's even a special tea each evening for the young fry, and babysitting is no problem at all. Meals are excellent and reasonably priced, with homemade soup and brown bread and fish straight from Dingle waters. Seasonal rates for bed-and-breakfast range from IR£9 ($10.80) to IR£12.50 ($15). Central heat and plenty of parking.

Self-Catering: Right at the tip of the Dingle Peninsula between the villages of Ballyferriter and Ferriters Cove and nestled into some of Ireland's most dramatic scenery, a cluster of sparkling white cottages surrounds the equally sparkling **Dun an Oir Hotel,** Ballyferriter, Dingle Peninsula (tel. 066-56133). All blend into the landscape, looking for all the world like another charming little fishing village. Surprisingly, Dun an Oir offers all the amenities of a modern luxury hotel without intruding on either the native environment or culture. Now, I'm not suggesting that budgeteers book into the hotel, where rates are IR£22 ($26.40) single and IR£37 ($44.40) double, but if you arrive with family or as many as five friends, the budget will be well served if you settle happily into one of the cottages. And, better still, you'll soon feel very much a part of this *Gaeltacht* (Irish-speaking) district, even if you find it utterly impossible to get your tongue around the musical but difficult language. That this is so is due largely to personable manager Matt Britton and his wife, Olive, who welcome locals as well as guests in the hotel's bar, lounge, and restaurant. In this isolated location, Dingle's residents flock to such a center of friendly conviviality. "Our guests love to hear the language spoken around them," Matt says, "and you'd be surprised how many are ordering drinks or meals in Irish by the time they leave."

In addition to their soft language, however, the natives bring along their music, and although the hotel provides traditional music and entertainment, it's not at all unusual to see a fiddle or tin whistle appear in the hands of someone just in to while away the evening. That makes for the kind of spontaneous good times that outshine any you might plan, and the stuffiest shirt is likely to find itself lustily joining in a singsong of old Irish ballads. A pint or two (or a splurge on one of Dun an Oir's superb seafood dinners) and an evening in such company is the perfect ending for a day of rambling through the unbelievable beauty nature has concentrated on the peninsula.

The self-catering complex surrounding the hotel has been planned with families in mind, and far from being a liability, children are cared for with affection. The play area holds swings, slides, climbers, and a variety of other equipment to keep them happily occupied. Even the swimming pool has a special toddlers' pool. For teenagers, there's a gamesroom, table tennis, and from time to time, a disco. Need a babysitter? Just give the hotel management a little notice and you're free for a night on your own.

Cottages come in two sizes: two-bedroom, which will accommodate four to five; and three-bedroom, which will sleep six comfortably. There's a fireplace in the living room, and for chilly nights, each bedroom has an electric heater. All kitchens are fully fitted out, with electric stoves for cooking. From May to September, there's a minimum seven-day stay (running from Saturday to Saturday); other months, the cottages are available at special midweek and weekend rates. Seasonal rates range from £165 ($198) to £325 ($390), a bargain on a per-person basis, and you'll be asked to send a deposit of £60 ($72) per week of booking to confirm your reservation (returnable if cancellation is received 21 days in advance). The balance is due three weeks in advance of your arrival.

READERS' SELECTIONS: "We stayed with Mrs. O'Regan and her family at **Sirocco**, Kinsale, Co. Cork (tel. 021-75129), in a modern house on a hill with a magnificent view of the surrounding far areas: We were charmed by the O'Regans and their five young children" (Sally Heaphy, Brooklyn, N.Y.). . . . "I had a wonderful stay with Miss Gretta Furlong at **Casa Della Rosa**, Carrigrohane, Co. Cork. Her hospitality and attention to detail made me feel right at home" (Phyllis Rosen, Rockville, Md.). . . . "John and Sheila O'Meara's **Sacre-Coeur House**, Mondaniel, Rathcormac, Fermoy, Co. Cork (tel. 025-36216), is one mile north of Rathcormac within sight of the Cork/Fermoy highway, on a county lane that winds through lush farmland. We enjoyed our stay here so much that we drove back down from Limerick before departing to see the O'Mearas and spend one last night here" (Mrs. Harold Hyde, Clemmons, N.C.). . . . "Mrs. Katherine O'Sullivan's **Sea View** farmhouse is located at Mountain Stage, Glenbeigh, Co. Kerry, which is west of Kilorglin, and has a commanding view of Dingle Bay. Katherine's meals are excellent, and she made us feel very much at home" (King Merendine, Fairfax, Va.). . . . "**Gap View Farm**, Firies, Killarney, Co. Kerry (tel. 066-64378), is a delightful place: great food, lovely rooms, three bathrooms for guests, and a genuine farmlike atmosphere. There's something very special about Mrs. Kearney—she spoils you for any place else!" (Jim and Lori Carrig, Buffalo, N.Y.). . . . "**Mrs. Griffin's** country farm house, Goulane, Castlegregory, Co. Kerry (tel. 066-39147), overlooks the bay, with a sandy beach. Our rooms were most comfortable, and there was that lovely smelling Irish soap at the sinks and plenty of large, clean towels. Mrs. Griffin is a delightful Irish mother of five and she shared with us many wonderful stories of life in the country" (Tracy Shepard, Ft. Lauderdale, Fla). . . . "Mrs. Josephine Grourke, **Burntwood House**, Listowel, Co. Kerry (tel. 068-21510), has a nice country home and serves a very good full Irish breakfast. We think your countrymen would enjoy staying with her" (G. Marle, London, England). . . . "One of our outstanding stays was at the warm and friendly farmhouse of **John and Mary Hanafin** in Beenbawn, Dingle. Their hospitality was exceptional, the food was terrific, and our room was extremely clean and tastefully decorated. The farmhouse overlooks the breathtaking view of Dingle harbor"(James J. Mulrennan, Londonderry, N.H.).

WHERE TO EAT: The vast wooded, mountain, and seaside area of Counties Cork and Kerry call out for picnics, and I urge you to stop at a greengrocer's for provisions and have at least one meal under the skies. There are also several outstanding eateries in this region.

County Cork

In Youghal, **Aherne's Pub and Seafood Bar,** 163 N. Main St. (tel. 024-2424), serves bar food of such quality that it has won the National Bar Food award for several years. Giant sandwiches cost IR£1.20 ($1.44). But pub grub is not its only distinction, for Captain Gerry Fitzgibbon, a retired Army officer, has also installed an outstanding full restaurant in this old pub and enhanced its decor with such touches as oil paintings, wood paneling, and soft lighting. Seafood dishes, such as mussels in garlic butter, take star billing, but beef, pork, and chicken dishes are equally well prepared. Except for bar food, prices in this attractive eatery will run slightly above budget, with lunch costing about IR£6 ($7.20) and dinner around IR£10 ($12). There is a Special Tourist Menu available, however, Tuesday through Friday. Restaurant hours are noon to 3 p.m. and 6:30 to 8 p.m. Major credit cards are accepted.

Bunnyconnelan, Myrtlesville (tel. 021-831237) (see "Accommodations" above), serves fresh seafood, expertly prepared, at moderate prices in a window-walled dining room overlooking the gardens and the sea. Steaks, lamb, chicken, and pork are also on the menu, and there's a good wine list. Dinner hours are 7:30 to 11 p.m., with prices in the IR£8 ($9.60) to IR£10 ($12) range, and there's a very good Sunday lunch from 12:30 to 2 p.m., priced at around IR£7 ($8.40).

The picturesque fishing town of Kinsale boasts many fine restaurants, many of gourmet quality. Among those I can personally recommend are: **Max's Wine Bar, The Vintage,** and **Man Friday.** There's superior pub grub in the cozy **Blue Haven Hotel bar lounge** (lamb stew, corned beef, and sometimes very good lasagne) at moderate to inexpensive prices.

In Bantry, look for **O'Connor's Seafood Restaurant** on the Square (tel. 027-50221). Young Matt and Ann O'Connor run the cozy pub and restaurant, and their seafood dishes are truly special (try mussels à la Guinness!). There's a wide selection of steaks, pork, lamb, and chicken for non-seafood lovers, and salads, sandwiches, shepherd's pie, and the like are on tap in the pub from 11:30 a.m. to early evening. Restaurant hours are 5:30 to 11:30 p.m. for full dinners, and 11:30 p.m. to 12:30 a.m. for light suppers. Main courses on the à la carte menu range from IR£6 ($7.20) to IR£9 ($10.80). Pub prices are lower.

Big Splurge: A few miles from Bantry, **Blairs Cove Restaurant,** Durrus (tel. 027-61127), is the loving creation of Phillippe and Sabine De Mey, who have converted the stone stables of a 250-year-old mansion overlooking Dunmanus Bay in West Cork into a casually elegant restaurant. In summer, meals are served on the covered terrace overlooking the courtyard. Specialties are fresh seafood, lamb, and beef grilled over a big oak log fire in the dining room, and there's an exceptionally good wine list. Candlelight and soft piano music complete the romantic setting. Dinners run from IR£12 ($14.40) to IR£15 ($18), plus 10% service charge, and advance booking is essential. Hours are 7 to 9:30 p.m., and it's closed Sunday and Monday.

County Kerry

In Kenmare, the **Purple Heather,** Henry St. (tel. 064-41016), serves both bistro food and full gourmet dinners in a setting best described as eccentric. There's lots of wood, copper, hanging wine bottles, and an assortment of other items. Lunch specialties include excellent omelets at IR£3.50 ($4.20), as well as salads and smoked salmon and mackerel, the latter two served with fresh brown bread, at prices ranging from IR£3.50 ($4.20) to IR£6 ($7.20). Marvelous full fish dinners, featuring such delicacies as Dover sole and salmon hollandaise, run about IR£9 ($10.80). Hours are 12:30 to 2:30 p.m. and 6 to 8:30 p.m., every day except Sunday, from Easter through October.

Slatts Bar and Restaurant (tel. 066-21161), in Tralee, serves fresh fish from Tralee Bay as well as a wide selection of steaks, pork, and lamb. Prices are in the IR£6 ($7.20) to IR£8 ($9.60) range, and a Special Tourist Menu is also available. Food service hours are noon to 2:30 p.m. and 5 p.m. to midnight, seven days a week, and there's entertainment in the bar nightly during summer months.

In Killorglin, Nick and Ann Foley have converted what was once a butchershop into a charming multilevel steak and seafood restaurant with exposed-stone walls, lots of dark wood, open fires, oil paintings, and comfortable seating with plush upholstering in shades of red and green. **Nick's Restaurant,** Lower Bridge St. (tel. 066-61233/61219), serves only the best meats, since Nick is himself a master butcher. Prime beef comes in enormous steaks that actually earn the accolade "melt in your mouth." Lobsters, crawfish, and oysters reside in the restaurant's fish tank until they are to be cooked, and other fish dishes feature only same-day catches. The soups, be they beef and vegetable, mussel or whatever, are thick and hearty with the unmistakable taste of "homemade." The menu is extensive, with ten starters and a choice from more than a dozen main courses, followed by a mouthwatering dessert trolley. But if you should have a yen for a special dish not listed—and if the makings are available—the Foleys are quite happy to prepare it for you. Lunch salads of ham, beef, or seafood are featured on the special pub menu at prices under IR£5 ($6), from noon to 5 p.m. À la carte prices range upwards from £9 ($10.80) for main courses. Nick's is open from noon to 10:30 p.m., seven days a week. Closed from Christmas Eve to New Year's Day.

Also in Killorglin, the **Old Forge,** Main St. (tel. 066-61231), is named for the huge forge, complete with bellows and anvil, which separates the pub and lounge. Home-cooked light meals are served in this atmospheric pub and eatery at prices of IR£1.50 ($1.80) to IR£3 ($3.60).

The **Bianconi Inn,** Killorglin (tel. 066-61146), serves very good meals in what was once an old coaching inn. Pub grub is available all day in the pub, and four-course dinners run about IR£12 ($14.40).

At **The Half Door,** John St., Dingle, Co. Kerry (tel. 066-51600), John and Celeste Slye can count more awards than we have space to list. Residents of Dingle are as fond of the place as visitors, always the sign of a good eatery, and one meal in the bright, informal dining room or the skylighted arbor room out back will add to their list of boosters. But before we get into the food, let me say something about the atmosphere here: it's as friendly, relaxed, and jovial a place as you'll find anywhere, which makes every lunch or dinner something of a special occasion. Of course, in the final analysis, it's the food that counts, and that's where all those awards come in. Celeste rules the kitchen, turning out mostly seafood dishes prepared with a marvelous simplicity that enhances their natural tastes. No need to worry about freshness—John has constructed huge tanks to hold several varieties until they're ready to pop into the pot, and others come right from Dingle's fishing fleet to the kitchen. I especially like the fresh side-salads that come with main courses. As for the wine list, it is extensive and of such excellence that it won the Woodford Bourne National Wine Award two years running. The Half Door is open from 12:30 to 2 p.m. for lunch, 6 to 9 p.m. for dinner, every day except Tuesday. A la carte prices begin at £9.50 ($11.40). Closed November to mid-March.

John and Stella Doyle have created one of the best restaurants in Dingle, **Doyle's Seafood Bar,** John St. (tel. 066-51174). The cozy old pub has rock walls, a flagstone floor, and a blackboard menu showing a selection of seafood from local fishing boats' same-day catch. You'll find John up front at the bar, while Stella reigns in the kitchen. In addition to salmon, lobster, oysters, and other shellfish, there's good homemade soup and Stella's freshly baked scones. Prices range from IR£5.50 ($6.60) to IR£7 ($8.40), and you can expect a wait in this small, popular place that doesn't take bookings (but that's no problem at all if you're ensconced at the friendly bar with other waitees). Don't plan to get there much after 7 p.m., however, to be sure of being seated. Hours are 12:30 to 2:15 p.m. and 6 to 9 p.m. Closed Sunday. Open mid-March to mid-November.

The **Armada Restaurant,** Strand St., Dingle (tel. 066-51505), is a pleasant, moderately priced eatery run by Mark and Ann Kerry (Ann does the cooking). Meals feature seafood and local meats, and there's also a good vegetarian salad on the menu. The Special Tourist Menu is also offered. Salads are IR£3.50 ($4.20), and main courses are in the IR£4.50 ($5.40) to IR£8.50 ($10.20) range. Lunch hours are 12:30 to 2:15 p.m., dinner 6 to 9 p.m. (10 p.m. in high season), seven days a week.

Also in Dingle, **An Cafe Liteartha** (tel. 066-51380) is a very special kind of place, with a bookshop stocked with an impressive array of Irish-interest publications and records out front, and an inexpensive restaurant in back that serves all three meals. Food is plain but very good, and prices range from IR£2.50 ($3) for breakfast to IR£4 ($4.80) for lunch to IR£5 ($6) for dinner. Hours are 9 a.m. to 7 p.m., closed Sundays except during June, July, and August.

READERS' SELECTIONS: "We had a very good meal at the **Restaurant Dock** (tel. 021-72732) in an old Irish cottage overlooking Kinsale Yacht Harbor, Co. Cork. Ton and Muriel Martens were marvelous hosts and the fish was fresh and well prepared" S. Caliri, Wayne, N.J.). . . . "The best food we had in Ireland was at Tony Fahy's **Rockvilla** in Kenmare, Co. Kerry. Somehow we managed to work our agenda around so that we had a second dinner with him—fantastic fresh seafood" (Margaret deCamp, Flourtown, Pa.). . . . "We discovered a delightful restaurant in Listowel, Co. Kerry. The **Spinning Wheel** is a spotlessly clean, friendly restaurant with excellent food and reasonable prices." (Al and Eileen O'Sullivan, Long Beach, N.Y.).

THINGS TO SEE AND DO: An entire book could be written about this varied region, with its magnificent scenery, relics of prehistory, and population of highly individualistic people. We'll hit the highlights, but do take time to explore on your own—this is "nook and cranny" country!

County Cork

Youghal: Be sure to allow time to linger in Youghal (it means "yew wood" and is pronounced "yawl"), the picturesque fishing harbor and seaside resort that has distinctive American connections. Movie buffs will be interested to know that this is where *Moby Dick* was filmed back in 1954, and there are still tales told in the town of Gregory Peck, the movie folks, and the giant white rubber whale that twice broke its moorings and drifted out to sea (local fishermen went to the rescue). More important in the annals of history, however, is the fact that this was where Sir Walter Raleigh took his first puff on a pipe of American tobacco and it was here that he put the first spud into Irish soil. So important do the Irish consider this last event that from June 30 to July 7, 1985, there's going to be a grand celebration of the 400th anniversary of that planting. There will be cookery demonstrations and competitions (centered, of course, around the lowly potato), a Sir Walter Raleigh playlet, an "official" potato cookbook, and such ancillary events as a sea angling competition and the official opening of the newly restored old town walls. Should be a fun time to hit town! If you miss the festivities, you can still see the Elizabethan house that sheltered the Englishman while he lived in Youghal. But first, go to the 18th-century **Clock Tower** in the center of town and pick up the *Tourist Trail* booklet from the Tourist Office there (take time to look through the small but interesting museum). The booklet features a walking tour of the town. You might plan to have lunch at **Aherne's** (see "Where to Eat" above), and you should definitely stop by the **Moby Dick pub** (which dates back to 1798) for a pint and some conversation with the locals who frequent the place. If you're lucky, owner Paddy Linehan will be on hand and you might prevail on him to break out the scrapbook that chronicles his many years as a publican and souvenirs of the *Moby Dick* crew who adopted the pub as its local during filming.

An aside: If, when traveling from Youghal to Cork City, you should find yourself in the little seaside village of **Ballycotton** (on the road from Midleton to Shanagarry), do stop in the bar at the two-centuries-old **Ballycotton Hotel**—it's an authentic Irish country bar, run by the friendly O'Sullivan family, and its decor has been described by fellow American writer J. Herbert Silverman as "vintage country classic."

Fota Island: Eight miles east of Cork City on the main Cork/Cobh road, Fota Island is a 790-acre estate that was once the property of the Earls of Barrymore. On the grounds are the **manor house,** a marvelous **wildlife park,** and an **arboretum** that is quite possibly the finest in the country. All in all, you can spend a fine morning or afternoon with the zebras, cheetahs, kangaroos, etc., and gape at the splendor with which the landed gentry used to surround themselves. There's a lakeside coffee shop, a children's playground, souvenir shop, and facilities for wheelchairs. It's open from April through September, and hours are 10 a.m. to 5:15 p.m. every day but Sunday, when it opens at 11 a.m. Admission to the wildlife park is IR£1.50 ($1.80), half that for children up to 12, and senior citizens and those under 3 go in free. There's an additional admission of IR£1 ($1.20) to tour the elegant manor house.

Blarney: Now, about that magical stone out at **Blarney Castle**—back in the 1830s, Father Prout wrote of it:

> There is a stone there
> That whoever kisses
> Oh! he never misses
> To grow eloquent.
> 'Tis he may clamber
> To a lady's chamber
> Or become a member
> Of Parliament.

All that blather about the stone started, it is said, when the first Queen Elizabeth tried to elicit the fealty of one Cormac MacCarthy, an Irish chieftain who was then Lord of Blarney. The silver-tongued MacCarthy smiled and flattered and nodded his head, all the while keeping firm hold on his *own* sovereignty until the Queen, in exasperation, is reputed to have exclaimed, "This is nothing but Blarney—what he says, he never means!" Which may be the first *recorded* instance of that lovely Irish talent for concealing a wily mind behind inoffensive words.

At any rate, if you would like to acquire a bit of Irish eloquence, Blarney Castle is six miles northwest of Cork (there's CIE bus service from Cork for non-drivers), and the Castle is open from 9 a.m. to 6 p.m. daily year round except for Christmas Eve and Christmas Day. Adults pay IR£1.20 ($1.44), children half that. Be warned, however, that kissing the stone involves having a guard hold your feet as you lie on your back, bend far back until you can reach the magic rock—and by the time you've gone through all those contortions, you'll have *earned* a silver tongue! Magic aside, however, the old castle ruin is well worth the trip in its own right, and there's a lovely sense of tranquility about the grounds filled with ancient trees. Dedicated shoppers may want to make the trek out from Cork for no other reason than to visit the **Blarney Woolen Mills** (tel. 021-85280), which dates from 1824 and today carry lovely Blarney Castle Knitwear and literally hundreds of high-quality Irish gift items. They're open seven days a week from 9 a.m. to 5:30 p.m., until 10 p.m. during summer months.

Kinsale: A scenic 18 miles south of Cork City, the fishing village of Kinsale has figured prominently in Ireland's history since it received its charter in 1333. Back in 1601, it looked as though the Irish might prevail against their English rulers when Don Juan d'Aguila arrived from Spain with a large force to assist the Irish rebels. Even though Mountjoy threw some 12,000 soldiers into a siege of the town, his position seemed doomed when Irish chieftains O'Donnell and O'Neill massed their forces behind the English, thus leaving them surrounded. History might well have been dramatically changed had it not been for an Irish soldier (reportedly in his cups) who let slip vital information to Mountjoy, enabling him to successfully rout both Irish and Spanish. South of town, you can visit the remains of **King James Fort,** the very one which housed the Spanish in 1601.

In **Summer Cove,** on the east side of the bay, there's quite a lot left of **Charles Fort,** English-built in 1677 and in constant use as late as the 1920s. It sits high on a clifftop, and the view of Kinsale Harbor is spectacular. (Summer Cove, incidentally, is where you'll find the popular **Bullman pub,** a hangout mostly for the younger generation, which gets quite lively at night.) You really should make the six-mile drive south to the **Old Head of Kinsale,** where a 12th-century **castle** sits in ruins atop high cliffs overlooking the spot where the *Lusitania* lies in its deep-water grave, sent there (along with some 1,500 souls) in 1915 by a German submarine.

Other Kinsale tag ends of history to look for include the town stocks (no longer used, of course, but kept on view as a reminder of the long-ago fate of lawbreakers). They're in **St. Multose Church,** whose congregation worships today in a structure erected in the 12th-century. A ruined 12th-century **Carmelite Friary** and 15th-century Desmond castle provide interesting poking around. One bit of interesting Kinsale miscellany: it is here that the town's womenfolk once wore the long, black hooded cape that's known as the **Kinsale Cloak**—you'll see it copied in rich fabrics to be used as an elegant evening cloak, but these days it is rare to see it on Kinsale streets.

If, by this time in your travels, you've become an Irish pub addict, there are two in Kinsale you won't want to miss. My personal favorite is the **Seanachai Pub** in Market Street. It's tucked away on a picture-post-card-pretty street, uses a second, phonetic spelling of its name (Shanakee), and is over 200 years old. Brothers Vincent and Gerard McCarthy, both musical, are genial hosts to resident locals who come in scores and warmly welcome all visitors. If time permits, I'll warrant you won't be able to go along to the Seanachai just *once*—it's as habit-forming as peanuts! In the two small front rooms, you'll find original old stone walls, open fires, and a marvelous painting of the legendary Irish storytellers for whom the pub is named. To those, the brothers McCarthy have added a larger back room by means of opening up equally old adjacent buildings, retaining stone walls and restoring ceiling beams and crumbling fireplaces. During summer months, there's music seven days a week. And that means traditional Irish music as well as the beloved singalong ballads which can seem a bit trite in other settings, but never in the Seanachai. Michael Buckley, the beloved All-Ireland accordion player, performs regularly, as do other local musicians who seem to enjoy the crack almost as much as the music. There's also dancing in the back room on weekends all through the summer, but absolutely *nothing* could draw yours truly from those front rooms where music and talk and the brown stuff flow easily until one of the McCarthys sings out "Time, gentlemen, please."

The second noteworthy pub is **The Spaniard,** an atmospheric converted stable where fishnets seem right at home in the horse-stall cubby holes. This is where you'll find a homogenous crowd of international sportsmen here for the world-famous shark fishing, guitar-toting students, and a fair smattering of local characters.

West Cork: You *can,* of course, make a beeline from Cork City to Killarney, and it'll be a scenic dash indeed. However, if it's humanly possible, try to take the long way around by swinging down through West Cork, an area of which it has been written, "West Cork is bigger than Ireland." Well, an hour or two of gazing at its wild, unspoiled and magnificent vistas of coast line, tiny villages, sheer cliffs, and miles and miles of emptiness will go a long way toward convincing you of the truth of that statement! The ghosts of Ireland past who roam this ruggedly beautiful region include that of independence fighter General Michael Collins, who was ambushed at a place called Beal na Blath in August of 1922 (there's a memorial marking the spot on the Dunmanway/Crookstown Road). And in **Castletownend,** surely the shades of two Victorian ladies named Edith Somerville and Violet Martin Ross still haunt the hallways and grounds of their beloved Drishane House, where together they wrote gently humorous tales of their Irish neighbors. The entire English-speaking world has chuckled over the misadventures recounted in their most famous work, *The Experiences of an Irish R.M.*, either in print or on the television screen.

Drive through Clonakilty (where Michael Collins was born), where castles dot the shores of the bay. Look for the **West Cork Craft Centre,** Leap (tel. 028-33217), where Claire Thompson and her husband have converted one room of their home overlooking Glandore Harbour into a showroom for locally made crafts. Claire will tell you about the talented people who produced the pottery, tweeds, glass objects, paintings, etc., and show you her own toys and crocheted collars. Incidentally, Claire asks that you just ring the bell if you find the door locked—she's only stepped into another part of the house and didn't hear you drive up. Stop for lunch or dinner or overnight at **Leap** (see "Accommodations" above). Don't miss **Baltimore,** with its ruined O'Driscoll castle brooding over the town from a high cliff and its tales of the horror in 1631 when Algerian pirates massacred all but 200 of the inhabitants and carried those off for a life of slavery in North Africa. Lovely **Sherkin Island,** with its ancient, ruined Franciscan abbey and peaceful, lonely coves, can be visited by motorboat from Baltimore during the summer—for schedules and rates, phone Mr. D. Sheehy, Baltimore 25. Pass through villages like **Ballydehob;** linger awhile at the picturesque fishing village of **Schull** and visit its waterfront; from Schull, travel the 18 miles to **Mizen Head** at land's end, through **Goleen,** with its sandy strand, **Crookhaven,** and around **Barley Cove;** return to Schull along Dunmanus Bay on the other side of **Mount Gabriel,** which rises 1,339 feet. It's a detour you'll long remember!

Bantry and Glengarriff: The little town of Bantry (named for an ancient Celtic chieftain) sits at the head of lovely Bantry Bay, surrounded by hills. The 21-mile-long inlet of the sea apparently had great appeal to the French, who twice (1689 and 1796) selected it for attempted naval invasions of Ireland. You'll see fishing boats tied up right at the foot of the town, and if you elect to stay over here, your B&B hostess will be able to arrange a day on the water to try your luck with Mr. M. J. Carroll, New St. During the summer, hour-and-a-half cruises of the bay take you past Whiddy Island and its oil terminal and castle ruins. For schedules and rates, contact Jim Minehan (tel. 027-50318).

Bantry House, on the southern outskirts of the town, sits in a magnificent demesne and is the ancestral home of the Earls of Bantry. Beautifully landscaped lawns and gardens slope downwards from the front of the Georgian mansion that looks out over the bay. Inside there is an impressive collection of European antiques, paintings, sculptures, and other items that caught the fancy of globetrotting earls over the centuries. A tearoom and a craft shop are open during summer months, and admission charges for the house are IR£2 ($2.40) for adults, IR£1 ($1.20) for students and senior citizens, and 50p (60¢) for children (under 6 free). There's no charge to visit the grounds.

There are lovely scenic drives and walks around Bantry, one of the most spectacular being to the top of Seskin Mountain, where there's a layby from which there are incredible views of Bantry Bay. The antiquity of the region's settlement is attested to by many stone circles, standing stones, and cairns dating to the Bronze Age.

If you're in Bantry in the evening, there's usually ballad singing and dancing at **Crowley's Bar** in the summer, and the **Bantry Bay Hotel** has ballad-singing sessions three nights a week.

Between Bantry and Glengarriff, on the edge of the little town of **Ballylickey,** nestled in a curve of the road (on the side nearest the sea), if you look carefully you'll see an unpretentious sign reading "Artist's Studio, Paintings of Irish Scenes." That modest sign is little indication of the fine paintings you'll find inside **Raymond Klee's studio** (tel. 027-50157) that adjoins his home. The Welsh-born artist has lived and worked all over the world and has won such coveted awards as those bestowed by the French Salon and the Fine Arts Guild (in England), but has chosen to settle in this beauty spot and devote his time and his art to depicting the very scenes that have won your own heart since you first put foot on Irish soil. His landscape canvases are remarkable in that they capture the elusive colors and sweeping majesty of Irish skies as well as the earthbound beauties most often painted by other artists. Sunsets over a dune-rimmed strand, storm skies which have fishermen scurrying to bring curraghs to safety ashore, and graceful configurations of sun-touched clouds are there to perpetuate your memories of those same scenes. Stone-enclosed fishing harbors and mountain stretches are other subjects, and hanging on the walls of his studio are portraits of that craggy Irish farmer and fisherman you were talking to just last night over a friendly pint. Surprisingly, prices run from just under £50 ($60) to just under £100 ($1.20), and there are sizes small enough to wrap securely and take back home easily, as well as larger canvases that might well become the focal point of a Stateside room. Whether you buy a painting or not, do stop by to see these marvelous works and chat with an interesting and talented artist.

Glengarriff is set in a beautiful, mountain-ringed cove on Bantry Bay, and it's worth a stop at some of the craft shops you'll see lining the streets. I've found good values here over the years, but none as good as those at **Donal Houlihan's Handcraft Shop,** Glengarriff (tel. 027-63038). The shop is on the corner just across from the road that turns up a hill to go to Killarney. and in addition to the small showroom out front, there's a large store out back up a little hill that carries lovely knitwear, mohair, cashmere, linen, and caps, gloves, and scarves. The most outstanding buys here, however, are the tweeds which Donal weaves in the shed back of the shop. You're welcome to step in to see the loom in action if your timing is right. Not only are his tweeds beautiful blends of soft Irish colors, but prices are some of the best in the country.

You're not likely to get out of Glengarriff without taking the boat trip out to **Garnish Island,** about a mile offshore—bold boatmen have been known to stop cars in mid-road to hawk the trip. As in Killarney, however, I urge you to listen to their good-humored pitch and let yourself be hawked. The lovely little island is a riot of subtropical plants in gorgeous bloom, and there's a landscaped Italian garden you shouldn't miss. George Bernard Shaw loved the place and wrote portions of **St. Joan** here. The cost is nominal, and both time and money are well spent.

Gougane Bara: One of the most beautiful spots in the country, Gougane Bara (which means "St. Finbar's Cleft"), is a still, dark, romantic lake a little northeast of the Pass of Keimaneigh (well signposted on the Macroom/ Glengarriff road). The River Lee rises here, and all around are deeply wooded mountains. St. Finbar founded a monastery here, supposedly on the small island connected by a causeway which now holds a tiny chapel (nothing remains of the good saint's 6th-century community) and eight small circular cells, dating to the early 1700s, as well as a modern chapel. Its isolation and connection with St. Finbar made this a natural refuge for Irish worshipers during Penal Law days when they were forbidden to hold Mass and turned to the out-of-doors for their services. Today, Gougane Bara is a national forest park, and there are signposted walks and drives through the wooded hills. There's a small admission charge per car to enter the park.

County Kerry

Festivals: For six days and nights in late August and early September, the competition is fierce to see which of the international beauties gathered in Tralee best fits the time-honored description ". . . lovely and fair as the rose of the summer." Now, understand, the **Rose of Tralee International Festival** is a far cry from a lot of other such competitions, which usually amount to little more than beauty pageants that take themselves quite seriously—*this* festival is one of lighthearted fun and frolic that entails parades, pipe bands, street entertainment, inter-festival singing competitions for the **Folk Festival of Ireland** (I ask you, where else but Ireland would you find two festivals in full sway at the same place at the same time!) and, *finally,* the crowning of the Rose. It's six days and nights of sheer merriment, and it's a grand time to be in County Kerry. If you'd like to be part of the fun (and who wouldn't?), there are usually several package deals that cover transportation and accommodation, details of which can be obtained from the General Secretary, **Festival of Kerry Office,** 5 Lower Castle St., Tralee, County Kerry. If you're making your own arrangements, be sure to do it well in advance, whether you plan to stay in Tralee or in Killarney, 20 miles to the south.

In mid-August, Killorglin lets its hair down in three days of what many Irish call sheer madness disguised under the name of the **Puck Fair.** It's been held every year since 1613, and things get off to a right rowdy start when a tremendous male (or puck) goat is hauled up to a high platform in the square and crowned as King of the Fair. What follows is a sort of carnival/country fair/free-for-all, with most pubs staying open around the clock, all sorts of street entertainment, and over on the green, some pretty serious horse and cattle trading. Just how all this began is a matter of dispute: some say a goat bleated to alert a shepherd boy of approaching enemy forces and he, in turn, alerted the town about impending attack, while those of a more prosaic turn of mind say it dates back to one ill-fated fair when only one goat was put up for sale. No matter its origins, it is traditionally a gathering place for the country's traveling people, who come to drive some hard bargains in the horse-swapping business, catch up with tinker gossip, and indulge in nonstop revelry.

The Ring of Kerry and the Dingle Peninsula: This famed scenic drive circles the broad Iveragh Peninsula. A good starting point is **Kenmare,** ending up at **Killorglin,** but you can just as easily travel in the opposite direction. To cover the 110 miles properly, you should allow an entire day—it simply is not "dashing through" territory, and you'll want plenty of time for stops along the way—a picnic, a pint, or a pub lunch. The same applies to its neighbor to the north, the Dingle Peninsula, and both are worthy of a day from your travel schedule. If, however, *two* full days are out of the question, my top recommendation has to go to Dingle, which has a character totally unique that in some mystical way seems to touch the soul.

The Ring of Kerry: From **Kenmare,** travel west along the Kenmare River, looking across to the Caha and Slieve Miskish Mountains on the opposite shore. The pretty little village of **Sneem** is the last resting place of Father Michael Walsh, who was parish priest here for 38 years in the 1800s and is immortalized as "Father O'Flynn" in an Irish ballad. Two miles to the south, **Parknasilla** is the site of an elegant hotel whose rock gardens and colorful subtropical blooms are worth a stop. The road then turns inland through wild and gorgeous scenery before coming back to the coast at **Castlecove.** This is another loitering spot, for about a mile and a half north of the road stands Straigue Fort, one of the country's best preserved stone forts built during the Iron Age. The circular stone walls, 13 feet wide and 18 feet high, have held over the centuries without benefit of mortar, and along their interior are several flights of stairs of near perfect construction.

Near **Caherdaniel,** Daniel O'Connell, "The Liberator," lived most of his political life at his beloved Derrynane House, now a museum open to the public year round. The **Pass of Coomakista** lifts you some 700 feet above sea level, with breathtaking views of the bay, the Skelligs, and the coastline. It was on **Skellig Michael,** a massive rocky hulk that rises 700 feet above the sea, that a colony of early Christian monks built a retreat of stone beehive huts. From the little villages of **Ballinskelligs** and **Cahirciveen,** there are boat trips out to the ruins in good weather, and you reach them after a climb of no less than 640 steps. The rocky islands that make up the Skelligs are also bird sanctuaries, and thousands of puffins and other seabirds are in residence. Near Cahirciveen, **Valentia Island** is joined to the mainland by a causeway. The island's Irish name is *Dairbhre,* "Place of Oaks," and it is from a romanticized pronunciation of the Irish *Beal Inse* (the name of a nearby sound) that "Valentia" evolved—not from the Spanish.

From Cahirciveen, you travel along the north coast of the peninsula through some of the Ring's most spectacular scenery, up a long valley to **Kells** at the edge of Dingle Bay, with the peaks of the Dingle Peninsula visible across the water, then up the steep sides of **Drung Hill** high above the Bay and on through **Mountain Stage** and down again to **Glenbeigh** at the foot of **Seefin Mountain.** At **Killorglin,** you can return to Killarney, or turn west for the Dingle Peninsula, passing through **Castlemaine** (home of Jack Duggan, "The Wild Colonial Boy").

The Dingle Peninsula: This is the most westerly point of land in Europe, its offshore **Blasket Islands** the "last parish before New York." Its beginnings are shrouded in the mists of prehistory, which left its marks scattered over the face of the Slieve Mish mountains, along its coves and rocky cliffs and in the legends that persist to this day. Its ancient Irish name is *An Daingean,* "the Fortress," and the remains of no less than seven earthen ring forts and two headland stone forts attest to the origin of that name. Its Glenagalt Valley translates as the "Valley of the Madmen," and is so called because as far back as the 12th century, mentally afflicted came to roam its wilds, drink the waters of Tobernagalt ("The Well of the Madmen"), eat the watercress that grew along the stream, and return home sound in mind and body after a few months. Mystical? Oh, yes. I sometimes feel the very essence of Celtic magic has been distilled into the air of the Dingle Peninsula. Or perhaps it is only the soft, lyrical accents of the Gaelic that is the everyday language here that makes it seem so.

Dingle Town is a busy little market town, with a boat-building industry right in the middle of things. Among the craftspeople who sell their wares in the town is silversmith Brian de Staic's small **Seodoir an Daingin** shop in

Green St. (tel. 066-51298), where he fashions an unusual silver necklace in the shape of an Ogham stone with your name inscribed in the strokes of that ancient language. There's bar food during the day and music on summer nights at the **O Gairbhi pub** and **Garvey's Pub,** both in Strand Street. But for a night of traditional music and song that comes from true family tradition, look for the red and white pub on Bridge Street with the name **UaFlaibeartaig,** which translates to O'Flaherty's. The late father of the present O'Flaherty clan was recognized as one of the country's best traditional musicians, and now son Fergus and daughter Maire raise instruments and voice each night surrounded by locals and visitors who've come to hear the best. It's a warm, informal gathering in a setting that's as traditional as the music, with the haphazard collection of pictures, posters, and other assorted items that has accumulated here as in almost any country pub in Ireland.

Driving west from town, **Ventry Harbour** was, according to legend, the scene of a fierce battle between the King of the World, Daire Doon, and the King of Ireland, Fionn MacCumhaill. Still farther west, **Dunbeg Fort** perches on a high promontory, its landward side surrounded by earthen trenches, and its 22-foot-thick wall riddled with an elaborate souterrain (inner passage). It's at the high cliffs of **Slea Head** that you get the most sweeping view of sheltered coves below and across the water the **Blakset Islands.** The last of their tiny population were moved to the mainland in 1953, when the fishing industry failed to provide a living wage and the government gave land grants for small farm holdings on the peninsula. Visitors from Springfield, Massachusetts, in the U.S. may feel a special bond to the people of the Blaskets, since many islanders emigrated and settled in that city. Boats go out from **Dunquin Harbor** on an intermittent basis during summer months, and an international student group has sporadically operated a guesthouse/hostel in one of the deserted houses on **Great Blasket.** If you're intrigued at the thought of staying overnight, call **Kruger's Pub** (066-56127) and make inquiries.

There are two very good potteries on the peninsula, the first of which is **Dunquin Pottery** on the road between Slea Head and Dunquin. Operated by Maureen and Eileen Daly, who worked for founder Jean Oldfield for many years, the pottery turns out hand-thrown, ovenproof stoneware in shades of sand and browns and blues. The reasonable prices range from IR£2.55 ($3.06) for a ramekin to IR£42.50 ($51) for a lovely coffee set. The small café at the pottery serves coffee from freshly ground beans, Irish porter cake, and other snacks.

At Ballyferriter, **Louis Mulcahy** operates a pottery studio/workshop, where he trains local potters in the production of many unusual items made from clay and finished with glazes developed in the workshop. There are the standard dinner sets, mugs, pitchers, and the like, but in addition, giant jugs and vases, unusual lamp bases and beautiful wall plaques are on display in the studio. Louis's distinctive designs set his work apart from any other. Visitors are welcome to visit the workshop and kiln, and prices are quite reasonable for the unusually high quality.

In the center of Ballyferriter, stop at the old school which houses **Seoda Chorca Dhuibhne,** "Treasures of the Dingle Peninsula." Ted Creedon, Development Officer of the exhibition, is usually on hand to expand on the story of Dingle's long history as illustrated by more than 200 photographs, artifacts, and text. You'll leave with more than a nodding acquaintance with the region's beehive huts, standing stones, mysterious graves, ring forts, and other relics.

Also in Ballyferriter, go by the **West Kerry Co-op** office and purchase their excellent illustrated guidebook, which outlines a driving tour. They can also book you into local lodgings if you've fallen under Dingle's mystical spell and can't bear to leave just yet. The office is open from 9 a.m. to 6 p.m., Monday through Friday. The story behind the Co-op is an inspiring one, which had its beginning in 1968, when young people were leaving in droves because much of the land was untillable, and there was great concern that the unique culture and heritage of the Gaelic-speaking region would wither and die. By banding together, 800 members of the farming community were able to import a special deep plowing machine to break up the layer of iron that lay just inches beneath the surface of their land and turn it into productive acres. They have now reclaimed more than 12,000 acres, established an experimental nursery, and are raising some 200 tons of tomatoes hydroponically. They've also taken an active part in upgrading tourist facilities, as well as expanding the summer school program that brings students to study Gaelic and live with local families who use the language in their everyday lives.

One of the peninsula's most astonishing relics is **Gallarus Oratory** between Dunquin and Ballyferriter. It's a marvelous specimen of early-Christian architecture. Built in an inverted boat shape, it has remained completely watertight for more than a thousand years, its stones perfectly fitted without benefit of any kind of mortar. Looks, also, for the Alphabet Stone in the church yard of **Cill Maolkeador,** an ancient ruined church. The pillar is carved with both the Roman alphabet and Ogham strokes.

At **Brandon Creek** (the traditional starting point of St. Brendan's voyage to the New World), stop in at **An Bother** (it means "The Road," and it sits right at the roadside), a pub that has for years been the gathering place of locals. It's a place to relax by the fire in the large lounge or sit at the bar in the small front room, with the constant flow of Gaelic conversation lulling you into a sense of the timelessness that is Dingle. It's mostly locals you'll meet here, and they welcome visitors warmly, breaking into English often enough to keep you from feeling excluded.

To reach the northern shores of the peninsula, take the **Connor Pass** road from Dingle Town over to **Castlegregory.** Views from the pass and along the coastal road from Castlegregory on into **Tralee** go from best to better with each curve in the road, an embarrassment of scenic splendors that has quickly exhausted the film supply of many a camera buff.

In the little town of **Camp,** turn off the main road and drive up to **James Ashe's Pub.** This is the Irish pub you dreamed of before you came to Ireland—smoke-darkened wood, low ceilings, a peat fire glowing on the hearth, and Irish faces at home in the pub their families have frequented for generations. Margaret Ashe or her son Thomas will likely be behind the bar. Back of the pub is a modern extension in which Peter and Elizabeth Coyle run the excellent **Ashe's Restaurant** (tel. 066-30133), where specialities always include fresh seafood, and the spring lamb with green peppercorns or pork escalope with brandied mushroom sauce are superb. Prices are moderate, main courses come with baked potato, vegetables, brown or garlic bread and a side salad, and the place is so popular at dinner you'd best ring ahead to book. There's bar food from 12:30 to 2:15 p.m., as well as an à la carte lunch menu from 1 to 2:15 p.m., and dinner hours are 6:30 to 9:30 p.m., seven days a week, Easter through September.

Shannon Car Ferry: If time is a factor—or, like me, you fancy a ferry ride any time one comes along—you can take the Shannon Car Ferry from

Tarbert over to **Killimer** instead of driving the long coastal road to **Limerick** (although it is a beautiful drive, with many good views of Shannon). The crossing takes 20 minutes, and from April to September, there are 30 sailings per day, beginning at 7 a.m. and ending at 9:30 p.m. (first sailing 9 a.m. on Sundays). From October through March, the last sailing is 7:30 p.m. For your car and all passengers, you'll pay IR£5 ($6) each way. Those on foot pay IR£1.50 ($1.80) each way.

Chapter VII

LIMERICK AND THE SHANNONSIDE

1. Introducing Shannonside
2. Shannon Airport
3. Limerick
4. Around Counties Limerick, Clare, and North Tipperary

ALL TOO OFTEN, VISITORS RUSH through the Shannonside region, perhaps because so many deplane at Shannon and they're off and away without realizing that so many of Ireland's treasures lie right at their point of entry. Yet it is quite possible, as I once did, to spend two full, happy weeks in Ireland and not go far beyond the boundaries of the area that has been dubbed Shannonside.

1. Introducing Shannonside

Limerick City is full of history, with fascinating sightseeing in and around town, from St. Mary's Cathedral to the Stone Age Centre at Lough Gur. As far as entertainment goes, there's theater and, of course, a choice of medieval banquets. In County Clare, from charming little seaside resorts like Kilkee day trips will take you to the lofty Cliffs of Moher, Knappogue Castle, and the intriguing Burren Display Centre that introduces that strange, lunar landscape. Northern Tipperary's Holy Cross Abbey is an enduring tribute to the dedication and devotion of early Christians and in Roscrea there's a beautiful home built within ancient castle walls.

There's much, much more in Shannonside, like the traditional music that lives so vigorously in generation after generation of County Clare fiddlers, whistle players, and pipers. And the crafts that flourish with such a flair in this part of the country. And the mighty River Shannon, with waters ideal for fishing, boating or just plain loafing.

With so many riches in such a small region, it would be a pity to make Limerick simply an overnight for first-day-in and last-day-out.

2. Shannon Airport

Chances are your first and last glimpses of Ireland will be from a plane arriving or departing Shannon Airport. It is, however, much more than a passing-through sort of airport. There's a **Tourist Information Desk** to help you book accommodations if you've arrived without them (I *implore* you not to in July or August!), to assist you with itineraries, and be as generally helpful as Tourist Offices all around the country. Here, too, you can book the medieval banquet you'd decided to forego but which grew irresistible on the flight over (look for the **Castle Tours** desk). **CIIE** has a tour desk, where you can find out about tours around the country and book, if you choose. There's a post office, a bank, and scads of car-rental desks (again, please *don't* arrive in high season without having booked a car in advance).

Budgeteers will find good, inexpensive food in the bright and attractive **Shannon Airport Grill.** It's self-service and offers a wide variety, from snacks to full meals, hot and cold.

The airport is in Co. Clare, some 15 miles west of Limerick, with good CIE service into town. **Buses** will drop you off at Ennis Road guesthouses (ask the driver when you get on) or take you to the bus terminal or any of the stops along O'Connell Street. If you're going from Limerick to the airport, there's a Shannon Airport bus stop on Henry Street, you can flag the bus down on Ennis Road, or you can catch it at the main bus terminal on Parnell Street. One-way fare is IR£2 ($2.40). **Taxi** fare will run around IR£10 ($12).

3. Limerick

Limerick gets its name from the Irish *Luimneach,* meaning "Bare Spot," and centuries ago, that's just what was here—a barren, hilly bit of land on an island. Today, you'll find a well-laid-out city with row after row of Georgian-style houses. In the intervening years, the site has been changed and molded by just about every group that has shaped the country's history. Because the island sat at the lowest ford of the Shannon, it is believed early Celts built an earthen fort at the island's highest point. Then came the Danes, in A.D. 831, to build a base from which to go aplundering. More than a century later, Brian Boru sent them packing, and installed the O'Briens as rulers. Next, it was the Normans, with their stout city walls and castles. Portions of their walls remain to this day, as does King John's Castle. They were the first to bridge the Shannon (at the spot now crossed by the 1838 Thomond Bridge). Native Irish, of course, had no place in that Anglo-Norman stronghold, but were exiled to the south side of the river, where they eventually built their own walls and called their area Irish Town.

It was in 1691 that William III's siege of Limerick (which had once been abandoned as the city's stubbornly brave defenders prevented any breach of their walls) ended with the signing of a treaty of honorable and reasonable terms. You can see the stone on which it was signed at one end of Thomond Bridge, where it is enshrined as a memorial to a treaty whose terms were never carried out by the British. Even now, Limerick is known as the "City of the Violated Treaty." During the 18th century, Limerick took on its present-day form, with stylish townhouses going up along broad avenues extending far beyond the old boundaries of Irish Town and English Town.

ORIENTATION: Limerick's main street is the three-quarters-of-a-mile-long **O'Connell Street,** which becomes **Patrick Street** at its northern end. The west-to-east road that leads to **Shannon Airport** is called **Ennis Road** west of the Shannon, **Sarsfield Street** at its western end in the city, and **William Street** at its eastern end. The major intersection of O'Connell and Sarsfield is the center of most of the city's business and shopping, and all city bus lines pass this junction.

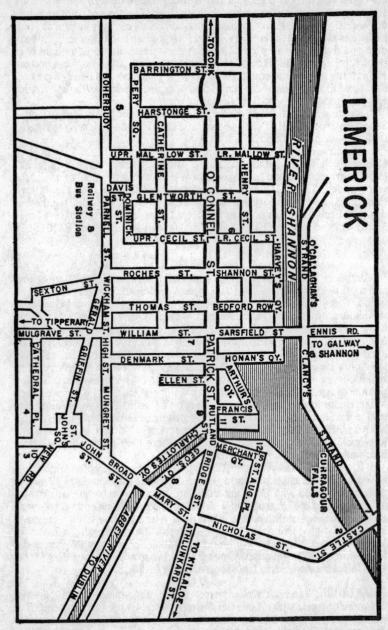

Based on the Ordnance Survey by permission of the Government of Ireland (Permit No. 906)

KEY TO THE NUMBERED REFERENCES ON OUR MAP OF LIMERICK: 1—Treaty Stone; 2—King John's Castle; 3—City Walls; 4—Statue of Patrick Sarsfield; 5—People's Park; 6—General Post Office; 7—Garda Station (Police); 8—Barrington's Hospital; 9—Town Hall; 10—St. John's Hospital; 11—Custom House; 12—Court House.

USEFUL INFORMATION: You'll find the **Tourist Office** (tel. 061-47522) in Michael Street in *The Granary,* a 1747 structure adjacent to the Dublin Road, overlooking the **Municipal Car Park** at Charlotte Quay, which has been beautifully converted into a tourism complex. Hours are 9 a.m. to 7 p.m. daily during summer months. . . . The **bus and railway station** is on Parnell Street on the southeast side of town, and the number to call for all CIE information is 48777. . . . **Taxi** ranks are at the railway station and at the corner of Thomas and Cecil Streets, just off O'Connell Street, and you can call 48844 or 46230 for a taxi. . . . The Limerick Junior Chamber of Commerce publishes a *Shannonside* entertainment guide weekly during summer months, which is available at most hotels as well as at the Tourist Office. . . . The **telephone prefix** for Limerick is 061.

ACCOMMODATIONS: The vast majority of good, inexpensive accommodations are located on Ennis Road, the road that connects Limerick to Shannon Airport. Many of those listed below are within easy walking distance to the city center, across the Shannon River. All, however, are on bus lines that provide frequent service.
Note: Prices shown below are those in effect in 1985—expect them to be higher in 1986.

Hostel: The **An Oige hostel** in Limerick is a large old Georgian house at 1 Pery Square (tel. 061-314672). Right in the heart of the city center, it is located on a public park, has a fully equipped kitchen and showers. Advance booking is advisable during summer months. From the railway station, take city bus no. 1.

Bed-and-Breakfast: Convenient is one word for **St. Mary's,** Clancey's Strand (tel. 061-55919)—the city center is only about four minutes away by foot. Mrs. Walsh's two-story home sits behind neat flowerbeds and rose trees, and there's a sun lounge for guests' use. The four guestrooms are comfortably furnished, and two connect to accommodate a family. There's a spacious dining room that also serves as a lounge, a small breakfast room, and off-street parking. Rates for bed-and-breakfast are IR£8 ($9.60).

Mrs. Joan McSweeney's **Trebor,** Ennis Rd. (tel. 061-54632), is only about a five-minute walk from the city center. There are three nice guestrooms, all with hand basins, and a TV lounge for guests. The centrally heated house also has parking facilities. Rates are IR£8.50 ($10.20) for bed-and-breakfast, with a 20% discount for children. Open March through October.

Aras Muire, 9 Coolraine Terrace (tel. 061-52118), is in a cul-de-sac just off Ennis Road and is the home of the gracious Mary Staunton. The four guestrooms are cheerful, with quilts on each bed. A piano in the TV lounge often serves as a focal point for musically inclined guests. Bed-and-breakfast rates are IR£8.50 ($10.20), with an additional IR£1 ($1.20) charge for baths.

Friendly Mrs. Power, of **Curraghgower,** Ennis Rd. (tel. 061-54716), makes visitors feel right at home in her three-story brick home. There are four guestrooms, all nicely decorated and comfortably furnished, and you'll breakfast with a view of the pretty back garden. B&B rates are IR£8.50 ($10.20), with a 10% discount for children. Central heat and off-street parking.

Carole O'Toole, **Glen Eagles,** 12 Vereker Gardens, Ennis Rd. (tel. 061-55521), is the sort of caring hostess who will pack you a lunch to take along on a day trip. The O'Tooles can also arrange for car hire and chauffeur-driven guided tours in the region. The two-story house, centrally heated, has four attractive guestrooms, all with hand basins, and there's a TV lounge and a pretty garden. Off-street parking. Rates for bed-and-breakfast are IR£8.50 ($10.20), with 20% off for children.

Bogside House, Ennis Rd. opposite Dunne's Store (tel. 061-52703), is the modern home of Carmel Beresford, and has been one of our most popular recommendations with readers. The four guestrooms are spacious and decorated in shades of brown and beige. Carmel will gladly book banquets and help you arrange transport to them. The house is centrally heated, and there's good off-street parking. Airport buses and city bus nos. 2 and 6 stop just outside the door. Rates are IR£11 ($13.20) single, and IR£9 ($10.80) *per person* sharing. There's a 10% reduction for children. Highly recommended.

The Misses Mary and Kathleen Collins, **St. Anthony's,** 8 Coolraine Terrace (tel. 061-52607), are delightful sisters first brought to our attention by a reader who wrote that "they really put themselves out to make a tourist's stay pleasant." The two-story house is their family home. It's neat as a pin and has a warm, homey atmosphere. Meals are served in a dining room overlooking a garden, and breakfast comes with homemade apricot and other fruit jams. The three guestrooms are comfortably furnished (one has three single beds) and have built-in wardrobes and washbasins. B&B rates are IR£8.50 ($10.20).

Guesthouses: Cloneen, Ennis Rd. (tel. 061-54461), is a lovely five-story guesthouse set back of a well-kept green lawn. Eva and David Tesky are warm, outgoing hosts, very knowledgeable about the Shannonside area, and always happy to help guests with holiday plans. The large guestrooms all have vanity units and many are furnished with period pieces. There are twins, doubles, and triples. Parking is in a paved car park out back. Rates are IR£11 ($13.20) single, IR£20 ($24) double, with a 25% reduction for children. So popular is this guesthouse that advance booking is essential during summer months.

Ballineen, Ennis Rd. (tel. 061-54285), a pretty, red-brick house approached by a long walkway bordered by a green lawn and rose beds, is the home of Mrs. Theresa Bourke. Rooms are a nice size and comfortably furnished, all with hand basins. The handsomely furnished dining room holds some lovely, hand-carved antiques. There's central heating, and parking is in a garage in the back. B&B rates are IR£10 ($12) single, IR£18 ($21.60) double.

READERS' SELECTIONS: "Please tell readers if they want a truly Big Splurge for not much more to try Fitzpatrick's **Shannon Shamrock Hotel** next to Bunratty. The restful surroundings and adjacent location to Bunratty and Shannon Airport are well worth the few extra dollars" (Mrs. Ted Moore, Claremore, Okla. . . . "I spent 13 days at **Boylans,** 22 David St. (tel. 061-48916), which is less than three minutes from the rail and bus terminal. Mrs. Teresa Boylan and family are the happiest and most accomodating people I have yet to meet, the rooms are immaculate and the breakfasts without comparison" (Evelyn Chorlton, Cambridge, Mass.). . . . **"Lisheen Guest House,** Coonagh, off Ennis Rd. (tel. 061-55393), is a truly lovely home. Mrs. Bridie O'Connell and her husband cannot do enough for guests, and since they are a little off Ennis Road, you feel you're in the country. All rooms have picture windows overlooking either the garden or fields of green and mountains. Beautiful atmosphere and extremely hospitable, warm and friendly people" (Marilyn and Charles Gelfenstein, Teaneck, N.J.). . . . "I cannot find enough praise for the home of Mrs. Feeney, **Della Strada House,** 136 Mayorstone Park (tel. 061-52300). Mrs. Feeney is so friendly one almost feels a part of the family" (James R. Banks, Mendota, Ill.). . . . "We stayed with Mrs. S. Roche at **St. Martins,** 4 Clanmorris Gardens, off the Ennis Rd. (tel. 061-55013). Our room was lovely, the breakfast superb and Mrs. Roche warm and friendly" (Lin Leblanc, Brighton, Mass.). . . . "The best B&B we found was Shannon View, Bunratty, Co. Clare (tel. 061-74056), just 4-1/2 miles from the airport. Mrs. Eileen Woulfe is a warm and charming lady who goes out of her way to accommodate guests. Her rooms are spotless and her breakfast is superb. We could not recommend a more delightful place to greet or bid farewell to lovely Ireland" (Barbara and George Finck, Santa Barbara, Ca).

WHERE TO EAT: The Tourist Office folks have done a superb job of restoring The Granary, Charlotte Quay, and one of the best things they did was to install the **Granary Tavern** (tel. 47266), retaining stone walls, vaulted ceilings, rough wood, and the general atmosphere of an old tavern. From May through September, the Tourist Menu is served from 12:30 to 2:30 p.m., and in the adjacent **Mariner Restaurant,** there's a more expensive selection—around IR£7 ($8.40)—during those hours and at night, a very good dinner that goes a good bit above the budget, but is very good value, at around IR£14 ($16.80). Specialties are seafood, stuffed duck, lamb and beef. In the tavern section, there's full ba r service, and even if you don't plan a meal here, do stop by and bend an elbow.

The **Chef's Gold Buffet,** Jurys Hotel, Ennis Rd. (tel. 55266), offers good value on weekdays from noon to 2:30 p.m. There's a wide range of cold meats and salads (with the chef's special dressing) served in the bar for under IR£5 ($6). For the evening meal, the **Coffee Dock** at Jurys gives good value in pleasant surroundings at abouty IR£8 ($9.60). Hours are 7 to 10:30 p.m. every day of the week. Both accept major credit cards if you want to conserve the cash.

The **Olde Tom Restaurant & Bar,** 19 Thomas St. (tel. 45961), is a delightful, family-run place in the city center. Irish food is featured, along with a nice selection of salads. Also, from 10:30 a.m. right through to 11:30 p.m., you can get bar food at the usual inexpensive prices. Lunch hours are 12:30 to 2:30 p.m., at under IR£5 ($6), and the evening meal is served from 6 to 11 p.m. at prices that average IR£8 ($9.60). Closed Sunday. Most major credit cards are accepted. **Note:** During summer months, there's ballad singing and dancing most nights (see "Limerick's Pubs" below).

The **Galleon Grillroom & Bistro,** 122 O'Connell St. (tel. 48358), is a busy, attractive little place run by the Lydon chain in Galway, and in addition to salads, burgers, chips, omelets, and grills at IR£3 ($3.60) to IR£5 ($6), the Tourist Menu is available from mid April through September. In the Bistro, specialties are pizza, crêpes, and lasagne, all priced well under IR£5 ($6). Hours are noon to 10 p.m., with continuous service (try to avoid regular lunch hours, when it gets pretty crowded). On Sunday, the Bistro is closed and the Grillroom opens at 5 p.m.

The plain, old-fashioned pub known as **Flannery's,** 20 Catherine St., at the corner of Cecil Street, serves pub grub and hot plates at the usual low pub prices.

Big Splurge: MacCloskey's at Bunratty House, Bunratty Co. Clare (tel. 74082), is a relative newcomer to the Shannonside, and it makes a smashing Big Splurge! Bunratty House (just back of the castle) is an elegant mansion that dates back more than a century and a half. Its living quarters have seen comings and goings which would probably fill a book, but it's a sure bet that its arched-ceiling cellar has never before seen the likes of MacCloskey's gourmet restaurant. Gerry and Marie MacCloskey left West Cork and their award-winning Courtyard restaurant in Schull to bring their expertise to Shannonside, and result is one of Ireland's most beautiful restaurants. The low ceilings and foot-and-a-half thick walls have been whitewashed to a pristine white as a background for delicate shades of pink and rose, which are punctuated by the deep blue of tall candles at each table. The mansion's original wine cellar has been retained, and behind its ironwork gates rests an excellent selection of good wines.

Main courses of the preset dinner change often to be sure that only the freshest produce, meats, and seafood are served. A typical five-course offering might include such starters as snails in garlic butter, selection of melon with kiwi fruit, or smoke salmon; cream of lettuce soup or salad with Stilton cheese dressing; main courses of sea trout with hollandaise sauce, rod-caught salmon baked with herbs, leeks and mushrooms, or black sole on the bone; fresh garden vegetables; and dessert of iced lemon and lime soufflé, rhubarb tart, or stuffed chocolate-covered pears. Amazingly, the price for such a feast comes to only £16 ($19.20).

Hours are 6:30 to 10 p.m. every night except Sunday and Monday. Highly recommended.

THINGS TO SEE AND DO: The very *first* thing to do is go by the **Tourist Office** in The Granary on Charlotte Quay (tel. 47522). This is one of the best in the country, and they're prepared to book accommodations for you, steer you to eateries, help plan sightseeing excursions, tell you about craft shops in the area, alert you about any special events, festivals, or evening entertainment currently on, and send you away loaded down with maps and brochures to make your time in Shannonside a joy. There's also a very good selection of Irish publications for sale in the office.

For sightseeing out of town, pick up the **CIE day trip** folder from the Tourist Office. There are some seventeen tours during summer months, and they go as far afield as Connemara to the north and the Ring of Kerry to the south. Eight other very good tours are operated by **Shannonway Tours,** Ennis Rd. (tel. 53066 or 53375), and they will reduce tour prices by 15% if you mention this book when booking and show it to the driver when you join the tour. For nightlife tours, the discount is 10%.

For an individual driver and guide, contact Liam Cahill, **Newmarket-on-**

Fergus, Co. Clare (tel. 061-71321). He's personable and knows the region well and is highly recommended.

In the City

Among the points of interest in the city, **St. Mary's Cathedral** ranks near the top. In the oldest part of the city, it was built in 1172 by Donal Mor O'Brien, the then King of Munster, on the site of his palace. It holds some intriguing antiquities, and the view from its bell tower is especially fine. There's no charge, and summer hours are 9 a.m. to 1 p.m. and 2:30 to 5:30 p.m. (in winter, it's only open in the mornings).

King John's Castle rises from the riverbank at one end of Thomond Bridge, and its 10-foot-thick walls include massive drum towers. The **Treaty Stone** is across the Shannon at the other end of the bridge.

At St. John's Square, the **Limerick Museum** exhibits artifacts from the **Lough Gur** area, as well as city charters, chains of office, the "nail" from the City Exchange on which merchants once struck their deals, currencies from periods in the city's history as far back as the Vikings, and a good deal more. It's free, and hours are 10 a.m. to 1 p.m. and 2:15 to 5 p.m., Tuesday through Saturday. Another interesting collection of ancient Irish metalwork, medieval bronzes, and enamels is in the **Hunt Museum,** at the National Institute for Higher Education, Plassey House (tel. 61511).

Limerick Lace

You're welcome to watch dedicated ladies making the famous and fine Limerick lace at the **Good Shepard Convent** on Clare Street (it's out the Dublin road, across from the People's Park) from 9:30 a.m. to 1 p.m. and 2 to 5 p.m., Monday through Friday. Painstakingly made on very fine Brussels net, the lace may slowly fade away in the next decade or so, since there are so few young women willing to devote the time and care to such intricate work. At the convent, you can purchase items ranging from lace handkerchiefs at about IR£35 ($42) to bridal veils at from IR£150 ($180) to IR£400 ($480).

Bunratty Castle and Folk Park

You can drive or take a bus (it's the Shannon Airport bus, which makes a stop here) out to Bunratty Castle, and you really should allow a full morning or afternoon for the excursion. The marvelously restored 15th-century castle was built for the O'Brien's, Earls of Thomond, and its restoration has included furnishings so complete the O'Briens who first lived here would feel right at home should their shades come back today. (That brings up a little aside: *officially,* Bunratty has no ghosts, but if you should chance to encounter a sad lady dressed in pink, or a soldier wearing a torn tunic and holding an empty scabbard, look quickly before they vanish—the lady threw herself into the courtyard upon learning that her lover had been killed the night before their wedding day, and from time to time they're spotted wandering the castle, though never together.) There are heavy carved-wood chests, woven tapestries, ornate wooden chairs, and pieces that look as though they have been here forever. You enter over the drawbridge into the vast, vaulted Great Hall, the center of castle life and where the tradition of entertaining guests with elaborate feasts is re-created these days with nightly medieval banquets (see below). Narrow, winding stone steps lead to upper floors where family life went on.

You can visit Bunratty Castle from 9:30 a.m. to 5:30 p.m. daily, year round, and admission is IR£3.50 ($4.20) for adults, IR£1.50 ($1.80) for children.

The charming and authentic cluster of homes, shops, and workshops from early Irish life on the castle grounds came about almost by accident when a centuries-old farmhouse was moved from the Shannon Airport to make way for a longer runway, and it became the nucleus of a collection of traditional buildings that include a blacksmith shop (with the smithy hard at work inside), a fisherman's cottage, a coastal cottage with its thatch firmly tied against Atlantic gales, and several craft shops. Each is a "working" exhibit, with a costumed "housewife" baking brown bread in a covered iron pot on the hearth, weavers at their looms, and everybody going about their daily chores. At one end of the park, a typical village street has been reconstructed, complete with post office, draper, tea room, and a tiny pub. All are occupied, and this is a good place to pick up gifts and souvenirs.

Also at Bunratty: You won't want to miss **Durty Nelly's** pub, even if you sip a nonalcoholic white lemonade. It's on a stone, arched bridge right at the entrance to Bunratty Castle grounds, and for centuries after it was built in 1620, it served the soldiers who were garrisoned there. Like the Earls of Thomond in the castle, those soldiers would feel perfectly at home in today's Durty Nellie's. The wooden chairs and benches are the same, peat still burns in the fireplaces, and some of the hodgepodge hanging on the walls and from the rafters look as though they were put there by one of the Earl's protectors and haven't been moved since. Even the pigeon cote has survived in one room of the loft, just as it was when it bred delicacies for the castle table. Durty Nellie's draws huge crowds: tourists, you'd surely expect, but the amazing thing is the large number of locals who love the place. It's a grand place for a pint, and there's good pub grub as well (I never go past without stopping for a toasted corned beef and cheese sandwich or soup and brown bread). After about 9 p.m., things get pretty lively, with music and singing, with even those drinking in the outside patio joining in.

On the other side of Bunratty Castle, just beyond Fitzpatrick's Shannon Shamrock Hotel, **Mike McGlynn Antiques,** Bunratty, Co. Clare (tel. 62011), has an interesting collection of antiques housed in an old-style thatched cottage. Mike and his brother have something to offer everyone from the dedicated antique hunter to those of us who would simply like to bring back home some of Ireland's antiquity. For me, it was an elegant teak walking stick which undoubtedly reached these shores by way of an Irish seafarer. For you, it might be a small bit of fine porcelain or some bit of ironwork. There are works of art, china, paintings, furniture, and a host of other larger items. They'll gladly insure and ship any purchase too large to tote home.

Limerick's Pubs

Sadly, a good many of the city's finest pubs have been modernized right out of their character, but **W. J. South's** (also known as the **Crescent Bar**), on the Crescent (that's where Daniel O'Connell's statue commands the center of O'Connell Street), holds on to the trappings of its age with a firm grip.

There's a long white marble bar up front, divided by wood and etched-glass partitions to give a bit of privacy. Faded tapestries hang on the wall opposite, and behind the bar there's an elaborate structure of mahogany, its arched niches farming old bottles and backed by mirrors speckled with age. Just back of the small front bar, a larger room is decidedly more casual, its walls displaying photos of rugby players (the Garyowen rugby team consider South's their "local." Still another room is behind this, with tapestries of hunting scenes illuminated by a skylight. The best pint in Limerick is said to be pulled here, and you'll hear a *lot* about rugby and other sports.

The "aged" look at **Flannery's,** 20 Catherine St. (at the corner of Cecil Street), comes from woodwork that once graced an old distillery, and according to Jerry Flannery, "there's still plenty of whisky salted in it." The pub itself is only a little more than 50 years old, but is has the comfortable atmosphere of a country pub, with a small snug at one end, and in the evening a core of regulars ever ready to converse with the visiting Yank, and at least one in the bunch who will hop right in to explain the game of rugby (this, too, is a sports pub) to the obviously ignorant. Flannery's also serves good pub grub at lunch.

My favorite of all Limerick pubs is neither aged nor particularly atmospheric, but it's very, very Irish. **Matt Fennessy's Pub,** New Street, Punches Cross, is the epitome of a neighborhood local, filled with convivial souls, a good pint pulled, and in general just the sort of place to pass a pleasant evening. A bit out from the city center, but easily reached via either a longish walk or a short bus ride, New Street turns off O'Connell (it's the intersection with Dan Ryan's Garage on one corner, Punches Pub on the opposite). Inside, there's an old-fashioned bar, a lounge, and a snug affectionately dubbed "The Senate" by regulars, since the affairs of the country are often debated and settled (sort of) within its walls. The clientele is almost all local, and they make Americans very welcome. Look for Mick Feerick behind the bar, one of Ireland's charmers. Incidentally, bar food is served from 12:30 to 2 p.m., should you find yourself in the neighborhood.

An old Georgian mansion is the setting for **Olde Tom's Pub** in Thomas Street. Quite different from those listed above, Olde Tom's has a flavor all its own (more of *this* age), and traditional Irish music and ballads liven things up during summer months.

LIMERICK AFTER DARK: From the Tourist Office, pick up the *What's On* booklet, which lists current goings on in Limerick and its environs, as well as a Calendar of Events published by the **Belltable Arts Centre,** 69 O'Connell St. (tel. 49866). The Belltable puts on very good concerts and plays at inexpensive prices. Also, The Royal George Hotel, West County Inn, and other hotels sometimes have "A Taste of Ireland" cabaret, with or without dinner, during summer months, with dates, times and prices listed in the *What's On* booklet (you can book through the Tourist Office or directly with the hotels). There's sometimes entertainment at King John's Castle; and Olde Tom's Pub, in Thomas Street, has ballad singing, traditional music, and dancing nightly during the summer.

The undisputed highlights of Limerick nighttime entertainment, however, are the medieval banquets in nearby Bunratty Castle and Knappogue Castle. Running a close second is the show at The Captain's Table in The Granary on Charlotte Quay. The banquets are Big-Splurge experiences I suggest you budget for before leaving home, and it's a good idea to book for them as far in advance as you can during summer months. If you're flying in and out of Shannon Airport, another good idea is to book one on your first night in Ireland, the other on your last.

Medieval Banquets

Bunratty Castle: Right here, I have to confess that for years I resisted the lure of the medieval banquet at Bunratty Castle, convinced of two things: that I'd spend the evening in the company of other tourists when I had come to Ireland to enjoy the company of the Irish; and that the whole show would be too "cute" to be wholesome. My second confession is that I was wrong, wrong, wrong, and that I've seldom missed attending one each trip since friends dragged me along a few years back. True, your fellow diners will almost surely be other tourists, but the great thing is that when you walk across the drawbridge into the Great Hall and are handed your first mug of hot mulled wine by a pretty, smiling Irish lass, the great good spirit of Irish fun takes over and Americans, French, German, Australians, Italians, and every other nationality represented lose their tourist trappings and become fellow conspirators in the evening's fantasy plot.

As for the show, *of course,* it's hokey—it's meant to be! Blarney may have originated down there in County Cork, but there's lots of it afoot in Bunratty, as fresh-faced, lovely Irish girls in period costumes come around to cover your front with a protective bib, story follows story and song follows song from the Ladies of the Castle and their male cohorts (a merry group of entertainers, indeed), and the stuffiest, most "touristy" type turns mellow in the sometimes hilarious struggle to get through a meal without benefit of cutlery. The talent on stage is first rate, and I defy you to keep a dry eye as the golden notes of an Irish harp wash over you in a massive room brought suddenly to a complete hush.

A typical banquet menu will begin with a cup of broth, followed by spare ribs, half a roast chicken (sometimes a hunk of well-done beef), salad, vegetables, homemade bread torn into ragged chunks, and a dessert just dripping with calories. To top it all off, you quaff a mug of mead (the traditional honey-based drink). You'll be given a knife, and after that it's you and your fingers, just as in the old days. Between each course, one little bit of stage business or another goes on, the most popular of which is the appointment of the evening's "Earl of Thomond" from among the guests, who reigns at the top of the long banquet table. His "duties" include banishing another one of the guests to the dungeon and addressing his assembled guests with as flowery a bit of oratory as he can manage. It's a memorable night—the Earls of Thomond should have such a good time under their own roof!

The cost for all this merriment is IR£21.50 ($25.80), and there are two banquets each night, at 6 and 9 p.m., year round. You should book before leaving home if at all possible, either through a travel agent or by writing The Reservations Manager, Shannon Castle Tours, Shannon Airport, Co. Clare, Ireland (tel. 061-61788). Should you arrive without a booking, any Tourist Office will try to get you a seat, or you can give the Reservations Manager a call to ask about an opening (sometimes there are cancellations). Just don't miss it!

Knappogue Castle: This massive 1467 stronghold is some 19 miles from Limerick City, which means you must have a car, since it is not served by local buses. The banquet at Knappogue Castle differs from that at Bunratty in that the group is smaller and more intimate and the entertainment tends to be somewhat less ribald, with sketches to bring to life myths and legends of Old Ireland and lots of song and dance. Many of my Irish friends prefer this to Bunratty (and there are usually a fair few Irish faces at the table), and in the best of all possible Irish holidays, you'd get to both. Prices, hours, and booking information is the same as for Bunratty, except that it runs from May through October only.

The Captain's Table

Entertainment of an entirely different ilk holds sway at The Captain's Table in The Granary on Charlotte Quay in Limerick City. In the restored 18th-century stone building, The Motley Crew treats you to the kind of song, dance, music, and merriment sailors looked for—and got—on shore leave in the 19th-century Port of Limerick. There are sea chanties, rousing tales of adventure on sea and land, traditional Irish music, and at the end a heartfelt rendition of Limerick's unofficial rugby song (which is sung spontaneously at many of the Gary-owen team games by fiercely loyal Limerick fans). Your dinner menu might include a starter of smoked mackerel with horseradish sauce, creamy vegetable soup, honey roast breasts of chicken or poached salmon, vegetables, potato and apple pie with fresh Irish cream. The all-inclusive price (including a free welcome drink) is IR£17.50 ($21), or you can come along for the show only (at 9 p.m.) for IR£5 ($6). The Motley Crew performs every night but Monday, from May through September, with dinner beginning at 8 p.m. Like the castle banquets, this should be booked in advance, which you can do from the U.S. by calling 1-800/645-7462 or contacting O'Shea Tours Ltd., 195 South Broadway, Hicksville, N.Y. 11801 (tel. 1-516/681-2223). In Ireland, call The Granary Tavern at 061-47266.

4. Around Counties Limerick, Clare, and North Tipperary

Within the Shannonside region, you can span Ireland's history from Stone Age relics around Lough Gur to Craggaunowen's Bronze Age lake dwelling and 15th-century castle to mementos of the 1800s in the Clare Heritage Centre. Traditional music thrives all through County Clare, and Mother Nature has turned up such wonders as the Aillwee Cave, the Cliffs of Moher and the rocky expanse of the Burren. For the visitor, it's a great convenience that all are concentrated in an area compact enough to be seen on day trips from one base.

ACCOMMODATIONS: Shannonside has an abundance of good, inexpensive accommodations scattered over the entire region.

Note: Prices shown below are those in effect in 1985—expect them to be higher in 1986.

County Limerick

Hostel: The county's only hostel is in Limerick (see above). See section following for very good hostel facilities in County Clare.

Bed-and-Breakfast: In the pretty little village of Adare, Mrs. Mary Dundon's **Abbey Villa**, Kildimo Rd., Adare (tel. 061-94113), has four nice guestrooms, all with hand basins and three with private shower. It's a modern bungalow in a scenic setting, and Mrs. Dundon is a member of the Town & Country Homes Association, keenly interested in all her guests. Bed-and-breakfast rates are IR£9 ($10.80), with a one-third discount for children. Central heat and plenty of parking.

Spa House, Castleconnell (tel. 061-377171), is a lovely 18th-century house about a half-mile from the village of Castleconnell, about seven miles from Limerick. It sits on the banks of the Shannon, and boats are available locally for fishing. Mrs. Helen Wilson has four bedrooms, all attractive and comfortable, and all with hand basins. There's central heat, plenty of parking, and marvelous scenic surroundings. Rates for bed-and-breakfast are IR£9 ($10.80), with 20% off for children. Open April through September.

Farmhouses: Cooleen House, Bruree (tel. Bruree 84), is the Georgian-style home of Mrs. Eileen McDonogh. Set on a working dairy farm overlooking the Maigue River, the house is beautifully furnished, and Mrs. McDonogh is the soul of charm. There's private fishing on the grounds for salmon and trout, and in the village of Bruree the De Valera museum was the late President's first shrine in the country. There are four attractive guestrooms with hand basins, there's central heat, and guests are welcome to relax in the garden. Rates for bed-and-breakfast are IR£9 ($10.80). A discount of 10% is offered for children.

Sisters Ann and Maureen O'Shea's **Roseville,** Kilbreedy East, Kilmallock (tel. Martinstown 9), is just off the main road to Cork/Tipperary/Dublin and to Lough Gur. The care the Misses O'Shea extend to their comfortable, homey farmhouse which won the Tourist Board's "Most Attractive and Well-Kept Farmhouse" award for several years spills over into the care and attention they give their guests. We've had nothing but praise from our readers for their graciousness. The house has central heating and four guestrooms with hand basins. B&B rates are IR£9 ($10.80), and there's a 10% discount for children.

County Clare

Hostel: There's a fine **hostel** in Mountshannon, Co. Clare (tel. Mountshannon 9). It's a large old residence with many of its original furnishings, and sits right on the shores of Lough Derg. Boats may be hired in the vicinity to go out to the island of *Inis Cealtra* (Holy Island), where there is a round tower and other ruins.

Bed-and-Breakfast: Kilkee is a small, quiet seaside resort, and Mrs. Mary Enright's **Aran House,** West End (tel. Kilkee 170), sits near the end of the curved bay, with a view of the cliffs across the water. Mrs. Enright is a warm, motherly sort who makes her guests feel right at home. Her buff-colored stucco house has twin bay windows in front and many antiques among its furnishings. There are six comfortable, homey guestrooms, and the two singles overlook a small garden and rocky cliffside. Bed-and-breakfast rates are IR£8.50 ($10.20), with a 25% discount for children.

Aran View House, Doolin (tel. 065-74061), is notable for two things: its gorgeous sea view of the Aran Islands, and its owner and hostess, Mrs. Chris Linnane. Chris, as she's known to all and sundry, is a warm, motherly lady about whom one reader wrote, "She's an amused, unobtrusive student of human nature, and what she doesn't know about the subject could be stored in a thimble!" She is, indeed, a sparkling lady whose guests tend to return again and again (in fact, two Irish traveling men who blamed Chris for their affliction of "Doolinitis," told me they arrange itineraries so as to spend three days with her every six weeks). The big two-story bluff-colored house sits high on a hill, and a window-walled lounge takes full advantage of the view. The eight attractive, homey guestrooms include three with private bath facilities and the others with hand basins—all have lovely views. One large room has three single beds, and there are two single rooms (sometimes very hard to find). Rates are IR£9 ($10.80) for bed-and-breakfast.

Leagard House, Miltown Malbay (tel. 065-84324), is set in quiet, rural surroundings and is an interesting, rambling one-story house that once was run as a nursing home by Ireland's President Hillary before he went into politics. Suzanne and John Hannon, the present owners, take a personal interest in all their guests, and John is happy to give advice on such important matters as getting to the right pub at the right time to hear some of County Clare's fine traditional musicians. Suzanne excels in the kitchen, and her meals have won such praise that they now accept dinner reservations for non-guests (there's a wine license, and dinners are superb, with a low IR£8—$9.60—price). The six guestrooms are all light and airy, and I especially was drawn to the two up front which open onto a small, glass-enclosed room. All look out on peaceful country scenes, and the dining room opens to a windowed porch. Rates for bed-and-breakfast are IR£9 ($10.80), with 50% off for children.

In Ennistymon, Joe and Mary McMahon have five homey guestrooms above **McMahon's Pub,** Church St. (tel. 065-71078). Joe is a cousin of a former Rhode Island governor, and Americans are given an especially warm welcome. Guestrooms are scattered about on several upstairs levels, and each has an individual size, shape, and character. Bed-and-breakfast costs IR£8.50 ($10.20), and Mary will cook an evening meal for the same price. Pub grub is available in the pub (along with good conversation with the locals who favor this place) at lunchtime.

Farmhouse: Tessies Fernhill Farmhouse, Doolin Rd., Lisdoonvarna (tel. 065-74040), is a marvelous old (200 years at least, according to Tess) farmhouse set on a hill overlooking fields and distant hills. It has twice won Best Farmhouse awards, and Tess Linnane, its owner, is a warm, enthusiastic hostess who takes great pleasure in making her guests feel at home. There's a large front lounge with picture windows looking out to the fields, and one guestroom on the ground floor is ideal for the handicapped. Upstairs bedrooms have kept the character of the house, some with wooden peaked or slanted ceilings. All are nicely furnished, and all have hand basins. Bed-and-breakfast rates are IR£8.50 ($10.20), and Tess serves a hearty Irish farm dinner for the same price. There's central heat and a paved car park.

Hotels: The **Smyth Village Hotel,** Feakle (tel. Feakle 2), is unique among Irish hotels. Located in the Rent-a-Cottage village of Feakle, the hotel is a sort of hotel/guesthouse, owned and operated by natives of the region, Mr. and Mrs. Con Smyth. The hotel consists of three connected two-story cottage-type buildings, and its bluff-top site overlooks the traditional cottages of the rental scheme. Hotel amenities include a full liquor license, tennis courts, a game room, and a dining room that is open to nonresidents for breakfast and dinner (lunch to guests only, if requested). Meals are served family-style, with no choice of menu, but with "the very best quality done in the simplest way" and with Mrs. Smyth's home-baked bread. There's an old-fashioned pub that draws local musicians as well as visitors from the rental cottages below. All twelve bedrooms have private baths and are nicely decorated. Rates for bed-and-breakfast are IR£9 ($10.80) per person sharing a room and IR£10 ($12) for singles, with a service charge of 10% and a one-third discount for children. Special rates are available for stays of three days or longer. Open March through October.

Hyland's Hotel, Ballyvaughan (tel. 065-77037), is a real charmer. Dating back to the early 18th century, the two-story hotel is now in the hands of the eighth generation of the Hyland family, and the personal atmosphere is evident the minute you walk through the front door. The comfortable, attractive residents' lounge has a fireplace glowing with turf, as does the public lounge on the premises where local musicians gather nightly and in impromptu sessions uphold the Co. Clare tradition of good music and good spirits. Dunguaire Castle is just 15 miles away, and the hotel will arrange for you to attend the medieval banquet there if you wish. Bedrooms differ in size, but are quite nicely decorated. Seasonal rates range from IR£16.50 ($19.80) to IR£18.50 ($22.20) single, IR£28 ($33.60) to IR£33 ($39.60) double.

County Tipperary

Bed-and-Breakfast: The **Country House,** Thurles Rd., Kilkeary, Nenagh (tel. 067-31193), is the modern bungalow home of Joan and Matt Kennedy. The family lounge, which guests are invited to share for TV or just visiting, has a peat-burning fireplace, and the house is set in scenic rural surroundings four miles out from Nenagh. Lough Derg is only about 20 minutes away. There are five nicely decorated guestrooms, all with hand basins and one with private bath and shower. B&B rates are IR£8.50 ($10.20), with one-third off for children. Steam heat and good parking.

Mrs. Mary Fallon, **Cregganbell,** Birr Rd., Roscrea (tel. 0505-21421), has four guestrooms with hand basins and private showers. All beds have electric blankets. This is a lovely modern bungalow on the outskirts of town, with river fishing nearby. Rates for bed-and-breakfast are IR£8.50 ($10.20), with a 20% reduction for children. Centrally heated, and plenty of parking.

Gortalougha House, Ballinderry, Terryglass (tel. Ballinderry 80), is a lovely, large period house set in 100 acres of woodland just 20 yards from the shores of Lough Derg. Bessie and Michael Wilkinson are the hosts here, and they have their own boat for hire if you care to try your luck with the pike for which the Lough is renowned. The Wilkinsons will provide a packed lunch for fishermen or daytrippers. There are five beautiful guestrooms, all with hand basins, and the house is centrally heated. Bed-and-breakfast rates are IR£12 ($14), with one-third discount for children.

READERS' SELECTIONS: "**Tullamore Farmhouse,** Kilshanny, Co. Clare (tel. Ennistymon 187), is on the Lisdoonvarna/Ennistymon road and is signposted on the main Lahinch-Cliffs of Moher road. There's a beautiful closed-in veranda looking out over the hills which serves as a lounge and TV room. The house is large, neat and attractive, and Eileen Carroll served an excellent high tea" (Leon and Harriet Reiter, Rockville,

Md.). . . . "I highly recommend **Carbery,** on Kilrush Rd., Ennis, Co. Clare (tel. 065-24046). Mrs. Pauline Roberts provides a breakfast that can't be beat, and the rooms are immaculately clean and tastefully decorated" (Kate and Stan Katz, Albany, N.Y.). . . . "We found the most hospitable family in our Ireland experiences to be Nuala and Jimmy Clancy, of **Kilcarregh farmhouse,** a couple of miles out of Kilfenora in Co. Clare. Nuala served us sandwiches, homemade fruit cake and tea soon after we arrived, and Jimmy played the accordion and tin whistle for us. He has won many prizes for his contributions to preserving the rich heritage of Irish folk music" (Dorothy Southall, La Fayette, Ky.). . . . "At Sixmilebridge, Co. Clare, **Riverview** is run by Tim and Martha Kearney. It is ideal for a first or last night's stay, since it is near Shannon Airport, and also for touring Co. Clare. Tim and Martha make you feel at home with coffee or tea always at hand" (Mrs. D. H. Weidenkeller, Santa Ana, Calif.). . . . **"Vaughn's Hotel** in Lisdoonvarna, Co. Clare, is a charming, spotless, 17-room haven in the center of this sweet little village. Irene Vaughn runs it and her husband runs the pub downstairs. No private baths, but very inexpensive rates" (Geraldine Levy, New York, N.Y.). . . . "Mrs. B. Barron's Newpark House, Ennis, Co. Clare (tel. 065-21233), is near Shannon, and is a Georgian house set in about 100 acres of farmland. Bernadette Barron was a charming hostess who waited up for us when our plane was delayed and greeted us with hot tea, sandwiches and cookies. The house is neat and clean, with a large entry hall, TV lounge and tall ceilings" (Richard R. Rogan, Burbank, CA). . . . "In Broadford, Co. Clare, Mr. and Mrs. Jim McGuire's The Lodge (tel. 061-73129) is a fine old hunting lodge set in a beautiful forest. We had a spotless double room with central heat and and hot-and -cold water, good food and outstanding hospitality and attention. The McGuires also serve an excellent three-course evening meal (wine, stout and ale are available). Jim is an expert angler and will gladly direct guests to the best spots for trout, salmon or pike in his lovely county of rivers and loughs" (Ian Nicolson, Queensland, Australia). . . . "The Avoca House, Cratloe, Co. Clare (tel. 061-97180 has bright, cheerful rooms with all facilities. Mrs. Mulcahy will give you efficient service at table and in looking after your bedroom. The house is just a mile-and-a-half from Bunratty Castle on the road to Limerick" (Kathleen Shreenan, Montreal, Quebec, Canada).

WHERE TO EAT: Picnic spots abound in the Shannonside area, as do country pubs serving inexpensive pub grub.

County Limerick

The **Cottage Restaurant,** Main St., Adare (tel. 94520), is a charming restaurant in a typical thatched cottage. Dinner prices (over IR£10—$12) are well beyond the budgeteer, but from May through September the Tourist Menu is available. Hours are 7 to 10 p.m.

You will also find the Tourist menu served from 12:30 to 2:15 p.m. year round at the lovely old **Dunraven Arms Hotel** in Adare (tel. 94209), as well as inexpensive bar food in the pretty lounge overlooking gardens.

In Kilmallock, the **Bulgaden Castle Restaurant** (tel. Kilmallock 209) is a delightful 18th-century tavern two miles east of town. Salads as well as hot lunches are under IR£5 ($6), and dinners featuring fresh seafood and local meats start at around IR£6 ($7.20). Hours are 12:20 to 10:30 p.m.

County Clare

The **Visitors Centre** at the Cliffs of Moher has a bright and cheerful self-service tea room offering inexpensive soups, sandwiches, and assorted snacks.

For a very special lunch in a setting of old-world charm, stop by the **Old Ground Hotel** in Ennis (tel. 28127). In its **Grill Room,** superb seafood, salads, omelets, and locally grown meats are served at prices of IR£5 ($6) to IR£9

($10.80). Hours are 12:30 to 2:15 p.m. Dinners here, featuring French cuisine and seafood, start at IR£12 ($14) and are served by candlelight in the hotel's pretty dining room.

Also in Ennis, **Brogans Restaurant and Bar** (tel. 28859/22480), serves bar food, as well as salads and hot or cold lunch plates for around IR£3.50 ($4.20) and grills in the evening in the same price ranges. Hours are 12:20 to 4 p.m. and 5 to 10:30 p.m. Soup and sandwiches are available in the bar continuously, beginning at 10:30 a.m.

In Doolin, alongside the Aille River you'll find **Bruach na hAille** ("Bank of the River"). Helen and John Browne serve marvelous seafood and local dishes in a restored country house with flagstone floors and whitewashed walls. The menu features everything from soup and salads to beef stewed in Guinness to fresh mackerel, salmon, and local shellfish and a limited range of foreign specialties. Wine is available by the glass, and prices run from IR£1 ($1.20) to IR£10 ($12). Hours are 1 to 4:30 p.m. and 6 to 9:30 p.m., and from June through September the Tourist Menu is offered. Open May through October. Highly recommended.

Claire's Restaurant, in Ballyvaughan, is the loving creation of Claire Walsh, a Dublin ex-patriot who moved here with her husband, Manus, several years ago. The tiny restaurant has whitewashed walls, wooden tables and chairs, and loads of charm. Claire does all the baking and most of the cooking, and the house specialties are lobster, baked crab, black sole, and shellfish such as oysters, mussels, and clams. A four-course dinner will cost IR£12.50 ($15), but you can order a full or partial meal from the à la carte menu and eat for much less. A Tourist Menu is also offered during summer months. Hours are 6 to 10 p.m., and it's closed Mondays.

North Tipperary

The dining room of the **Sail Inn Hotel,** Dromineer, Nenagh (tel. 067-24114/24175), specializes in pricey seafood dishes and French cuisine, but in the hotel's **Froggy's Café** during July and August, the Tourist Menu is available from 12:30 to 2 p.m.

Plain cooking, Irish style, is featured in the **Pathe Hotel,** Roscrea (tel. 0505-21301). In this family-run establishment, lunch costs about IR£4 ($4.80) and à la carte prices at dinner start at IR£6.50 ($7.80). Hours are noon to 3 p.m. and 6 to 10 p.m. The Tourist Menu is available from June through August.

You'll also find the Tourist Menu available from 12:30 to 2:30 p.m. in Thurles at the **Hayes Hotel,** Liberty Square (tel. 0504-22122), with many Irish dishes listed on the menu.

READERS' SELECTIONS: "Just as you enter Kilkee, Co. Clare, the **An Beal Bocht** (it means "the poor mouth") is at 5 Grattan St., and they serve an excellent soup-and-sandwich menu and apple tart with cream, all home cooked—the pie was right out of the oven. Virginia O'Dowd, one of the owners, sat with us and was genuinely hospitable, telling us where to find good Irish music, etc." (Mr. and Mrs. R. G. Keister, Scott DePot, W. Va.). . . . "We had a marvelous five-course meal, beautifully served by candlelight, with pretty china and silver, at **Mountcashel Castle Restaurant** in Co. Clare (tel. 061-72577). Our hosts, the Harringtons, were delightful, and we preferred our 'meal in a castle' to the medieval banquets" (Leila Morris, Columbus, Ga.). *Author's Note:* Mountcashel Castle is on the main Bunratty/Knappogue route, 2 miles north of Sixmilebridge. . . . "We especially enjoyed stopping in **Killilagh House,** a restaurant and craft shop in Doolin, Co. Clare (tel. 065-74183). The food was good, and there is a wine license" (S. Debnam, Virginia Beach, Va.). . . . "We especially enjoyed stopping in Killilagh House, a restaurant and craft shop in Doolin, Co. Clare (tel. 065-74183). The food was good, and there is a wine license. There's a peat fire in a cottage-like interior, and handcrafts hang about on the walls" (S. Debnam, Virginia Beach, VA).

THINGS TO SEE AND DO: Of which there are aplenty!

County Limerick

Tourist Offices are located at **Lough Gur Stone Age Centre,** Bruff (tel. 061-85186), open May through September, and the **Thatched Cottage and Craft Shop,** Main St., Adare (tel. 061-94255), open June to early September.

Lough Gur: Some 17 miles southeast of Limerick City, Lough Gur is one of Ireland's most important archeological sites, and thousands of Stone Age relics have been found in and around it. The lifestyle of those long-ago Irishmen comes vividly alive in the **Stone Age Centre** at Lough Gur (tel. 061-85186). It's designed in the style of Neolithic period dwellings, and inside there are replicas of many of the artifacts discovered in this area, as well as models of burial chambers, stone circles, and dolmens. An audiovisual show tells you what we know of Stone and Bronze Age men and their habits, and periodically, walking tours are conducted to some of the more important archeological sites. The Centre is open daily from 10 a.m. to 1 p.m. and 2 to 6 p.m., May through September (Sundays 2 to 6 p.m.). Admission is IR£2 ($2.40) for adults, half that for children.

Irish Dresden: The little town of Dromcollogher, southwest of Limerick City, is where you can visit the **Irish Dresden Ltd.** plant and shop (tel. Dromcollogher 30) Monday through Friday. Watch Exquisite Dresden figurines being made, then browse through their showroom.

Lough Derg and Killaloe: The 13-mile drive north of Limerick City to the charming little Lough Derg harbor village of Killaloe is delightful, and **St. Flannan's Cathedral** (12th century) is worth a visit to see the ornately carved Irish Romanesque doorway, Ogham stone (which also has Runic writings and a crude crucifix believed to be formed by a Viking who had converted to Christianity). Drive along the western shore of the lake to view magnificent scenery and ancient ruins on offshore islands. You're very welcome to **fish** or **swim** at no charge; **course fishing** is best at Plassy, and the Electricity Supply Board on O'Connell St. issues free permits to fish.

County Clare

Tourist Offices are at: **Bank Place,** Ennis (tel. 065-28366), open year round, and the **Cliffs of Moher Visitor Centre,** Liscannor (tel. 065-285/361), open March through October.

The **Craggaunowen Project:** One of the County Clare's most interesting sightseeing stops is the Craggaunowen (pronounce it "Crag-an-owen") Project near Quin. Craggaunowen Castle has an interesting display of medieval art objects, and in the lake a short walk away, there's a fascinating re-creation of a crannog, a lake dwelling of the Bronze Age inhabitants of

Ireland. The earthen ring fort on the grounds holds a reconstructed farmer's home of some fifteen centuries ago. For me—thrilled as I have been at Tim Severin's daring voyage across the Atlantic to retract St. Brendan's legendary route of A.D. 700—a highlight here is the glass shelter which has been constructed to house the tiny leather St. Brendan in which he made the voyage. The Project is open March through October from 9:30 a.m. to 5:30 p.m., with an admission fee of IR£2 ($2.40) for adults, half that for children.

Knappogue Castle: Also near Quin, Knappogue Castle (of the medieval banquets) is furnished in period pieces, somewhat more formally than Bunratty Castle. It's open daily from 9:30 a.m. to 5:30 p.m., with admission of IR£2 ($2.40) for adults, IR£1 ($1.20) for children.

Clare Heritage Centre: If your family roots are in Co. Clare, you'll want to visit the Clare Heritage Centre at Corofin, near Ennis (tel. 065-27632), where you'll find a genealogical research service, thousands of family records, and interesting exhibits portraying life in Co. Clare in ages past.

Ennis: The bustling market town of Ennis has many interesting historical buildings, and the Tourist Office (see above) can give you a walking tour guide through the more historic sections. Headquarters for traditional music, song, and dance is *Cois No hAbhna* (pronounced "Cush-na-how-na"), on Gort Road. Their shop has a large selection of records, tapes, and books on Irish traditional music, and they maintain a good schedule of happenings during summer months.

The Cliffs of Moher: Ireland's spectacular coastline really outdoes itself at the Cliffs of Moher near Liscannor. In Irish, they're named *Ailltreacha Mothair* ("The Cliffs of the Ruin"), and they stretch for five miles, rising at places to 700 feet. They're breathtaking and shouldn't be missed.

Loop Head Peninsula: A delightful day is one spent driving to seaside Kilkee with its curved bay and strand, then down the long finger of land that is the West Clare Peninsula to its end, where the Loop Head lighthouse holds solitary vigil. The coastline is one of clifftops, inlets and coves, sandy beaches, and a softly wild, unspoiled landscape. Along the way there are the ruins of forts, castles, and churches, and should you stop for a pint in a country pub, there are legends to be heard, like that of Kilstiffin Bank, a shoal that lies beneath the Shannon's waters. It was, so it is said hereabouts, at one time a part of the mainland, but was swept into the Shannon during a fierce storm in the 9th century, carrying people and their homes to a watery grave. But according to the older residents of this area, when sailing ships used to drop anchor off the Kisstiffin Bank, they'd be visited during the night by a small man from beneath the water who would climb the anchor cable and ask them to take up the anchor, for it had gone down his chimney. As you relax into the solitary beauty of the peninsula, you'll have no doubt at all about the truth in that story!

In the little Shannonside village of **Kilbaha** (*Cill Bheathach*, or "Birch Church"), the **Church of Moheen** holds a small wooden structure that is one of Ireland's most unusual testaments to the devotion of her people to their faith. It's a tiny three-sided chapel on wheels known as the Ark of Kilbaha which, during the years when English-imposed law forbad any landlord to permit a Catholic Mass to be held on his land, was hidden away during the week, but pulled down to the shore of Kilbaha Bay on Sundays and placed below the high-tide mark on land that belonged to no man. There Mass was said in safety, reverence, and peace. While you're in Kilbaha, look for **Jim Connolly's studio** (tel. Carrigholt 34). Jim lives and works in a thatched cottage, and his bronze sculptors are brilliant (the most noted is that of Eamon de Valera in Ennis). He's an interesting man to talk to, and while the bronzes are much too pricey and heavy to think of purchasing, he does have a ceramics shop with creative, inexpensive souvenirs. You might call before going, since he's often away.

Doolin: Doolin is a tiny coastal village that has gained international fame as a center for traditional Irish music. You'll find it in full sway most nights in **O'Connor's Pub,** a large, rustic place filled with musicians, singers, tellers of tales, students who may have hitchhiked across Europe to get here, and Yanks like us here to take it all in. There's regular boat service to the **Aran Islands** from here, only a 25-minute run, since Doolin is the closest point to the islands on the mainland. In fact, you'll sometimes meet Aran Islanders in O'Connor's of a Sunday night if the seas are calm. Boats leave from Doolin Pier daily, beginning at 10 a.m. during the summer, and the fare is IR£8 ($9.60). To book ahead (not usually necessary), call Lisdoonvarna 103.

The Pubs of County Clare: If there's one thing Co. Clare has, it's traditional music and good fiddlers, tin whistle players, bodhran players and pipers to play it. And their favorite venue by far is the local pub. The **Merriman Tavern,** in Scarriff, is an ancient place with a big ballad room that frequently hosts the likes of the Chieftains, with a small admission charge. The crowd in attendance is likely to include those cruising the Shannon who have pulled into Scarriff for the night, fishermen, and lots of locals.

On Friday nights, **Pat Donnlans,** in Kilkishen, rings with music. Other watering holes which regularly attract musicians are: **The Crab Tree** in Newmarket-on-Fergus; John Lynch's pub, **Do na ha** in Kilkee; **Hassets,** Quin; **John Minogues,** Tulla; **Lena Hanrahan,** Feakle; the **Smyth Village Hotel** in Feakle; and **Kennedy's Pub** in Puckane. The ancient **Crabtree Tavern,** Ballycar, Sixmilebridge, has ceili dancing and traditional music several nights a week during the summer.

The Burren: The northwestern hump of County Clare is a strange, barren moonscape with no apparent signs of life. This is the Burren *(An Bhoireann,* "The Stony District"). Those who walk its rocky hills, however, find that far from being sterile, it holds a wealth of tiny wildflowers, some of which are unique to this area. It was also inhabited in prehistoric times, and there are many dolmens, cairns, and ring forts left from that era. In Kilfenora, stop by the **Burren Display Centre** (tel. Kilfenora 30) to see an enlightening audiovisual presentation. A tea shop and craft shop are also on the premises, and hours are 10 a.m. to 6 p.m. from mid-March through October (to 7 p.m. June, July and August).

In the midst of the Burren, you'll find **Aillwee Cave** (tel. Ballyvaughan 36), a fascinating underground wonderland of magnificent stalactites. There's a tea room and craft shops on the premises.

In Ballyvaughan, stop by **Manus Walsh's Craft Workshop and Gallery** on the main Galway road. Manus's fascination with the Burren landscape is reflected in many of his paintings, and he also has a wide selection of enamelware of Celtic design, rings, necklaces, and wall hangings.

North Tipperary

Holy Cross Abbey: Four miles south of Thurles, Holy Cross Abbey was founded in 1180, and before it was restored in 1976, had lain roofless for more than two centuries. It is open to visitors daily from 9 a.m. to 8 p.m.

Roscrea: One of the finest collections of traditional Irish furniture is displayed in **Damer House,** a large Georgian residence actually built within the curtain walls of Roscrea Castle. In the castle yard, the **Roscrea Heritage Centre** displays local artifacts. Open every day but Tuesday and Wednesday from 2 to 6 p.m., mid-April through September, from 11 a.m. July and August.

Chapter VIII

GALWAY AND THE WESTERN REGION

1. Introducing the Western Region
2. Galway
3. Around Counties Galway and Mayo

THE WEST OF IRELAND. A simple phrase, yet one that conjures up an immediate and vivid image—brooding mountains; stony fields; windswept cliffs along a rugged coastline dotted with offshore islands; and air so heady that to breathe it is akin to drinking champagne. Oliver St. John Gogarty put it this way:

> There's something sleeping in my breast
> That wakens only in the West;
> There's something in the core of me
> That needs the West to set it free.

I. Introducing the Western Region

The Counties Galway and Mayo make up Ireland's Western Region, and within their boundaries lie such distinct geographic divisions as Connemara, the Aran islands, and Achill Island. Galway's landscape in the east is made up of flat, fertile plains that reach from Lough Derg and the Shannon Valley north to County Roscommon, while to the northwest, lumpy mountains push the mainland into a great elbow bent against the Atlantic. Lough Corrib stretches its 27 miles along an invisible line that marks the change, while Galway Town perches on the shores of romantic Galway Bay as a gateway to both areas.

Some 30 miles offshore, where Galway Bay empties into the sea, the Aran Islands are an outpost of rugged fishermen and their families who perpetuate a heritage of self-sufficiency and culture passed from generation to generation through the centuries. The walls of pre-Christian stone forts have endured the ravages of time to remind islanders of their "Celtic Twilight" origin. Round towers, oratories, and tiny churches tell of early Christians who spoke the musical Gaelic language, as do today's islanders. Menfolk still put out to sea in lightweight, tough little wood-and-canvas curraghs, as they have done over the ages, while their womenfolk spin and weave and knit the clothing that is so distinctly theirs. Visitors come by steamer or small aircraft, welcomed and entertained by natives who remain untouched by their foreign ways.

In Connemara, the serried Twelve Bens (sometimes called the Twelve Pins) look across a lake-filled valley at the misty peaks of the Maamturk range, and the jagged coastline is a solitary place of rocks and tiny hamlets and stark, silent beauty. This is a Gaeltacht area, where government grants make possible the survival of a language and the people who speak it. Among its rocky, untillable fields wander the spirits of Irishmen banished by Cromwell "to Hell or Connaught." Farther north, the long, narrow finger of Killary Harbour marks the County Mayo border.

Eastern County Mayo is also flat, and it was near Cong, on the Plain of Southern Moytura, that a prehistoric battle raged between Tuatha De Danann and the Firbolgs, ending in the first defeat of the latter, who declined in power afterwards until they were crushed forever seven years later in Sligo. Northeast of Cong is the small village of Knock, a shrine to the many visions reported here and a place of pilgrimage for thousands of Christians. Pilgrims gather on the last Sunday in July each year to walk barefoot in the steps of St. Patrick to the summit of Croagh Patrick on Clew Bay's southern shore. Connected to the mainland by a causeway, Achill Island presents a mountainous face to the sea, its feet ringed by golden sandy strands.

2. Galway

Galway owes its existence to a tragedy: Breasail, an ancient Celtic chieftain was so overwhelmed by grief when his daughter drowned in the River Corrib that he established a permanent camp on the riverbank. Located at the only point at which the river could be forded, the camp had become a tiny fishing village by the time the Normans arrived. The newcomers set about building a trading town utilizing the fine harbor, and in time a medieval town with fine houses and shops grew up, around which they built stout stone walls. Trade soon flourished between Galway, Spain, and France. Fourteen of the most prosperous merchant families became known early on as the "Tribes of Galway," and in 1984 when the city celebrated the 500th anniversary of its charter, there was a great "Gathering of the Tribes," with their descendants arriving from around the globe. During the mid-1800s, at the height of the Great Famine, the city was filled with starving men, women, and children who fought to board the infamous "coffin ships" to go to America and a new life.

Today, Galway is still a prosperous commercial center, proud of its university and welcoming visitors with open arms. Traces of its history abound: The Spanish Arch, a gateway of the old city walls; Lynch's Castle, a 14th-century townhouse that is now a branch of the Allied Irish Bank; tiny cobblestoned streets and lanes; and along the banks of the Corrib, the Long Walk, a much-loved waterside promenade for centuries.

ORIENTATION: The **River Corrib** flows through the heart of Galway, with the main shopping and business districts centered between the river and **Eyre Square** (where John F. Kennedy once addressed the citizens of Galway). To the west, along the shores of Galway Bay, the popular seaside resort of **Salthill** holds a concentration of the best inexpensive accommodations in the area. There's good bus service between Eyre Square and Salthill, with stops along the main Galway/Salthill road. The **Claddagh** (*An Cladach,* "the seashore") district is just across the river from the **Spanish Arch,** although its jumble of thatched cottages and narrow lanes has long since been replaced by neat Corporation houses laid out in neat rows. Only the lovely Claddagh ring (two hands clasping a heart surmounted by a crown) remains as the legacy of a people who once had their own manner of dress, dialect, customs—and even their own king—in this fishing village outside the walls of Old Galway.

USEFUL INFORMATION: The **Tourist Office** is in a modern building called Aras Fáilte just off the Great Southern Hotel side of Eyre Square (tel. 091-

63081). Hours are 9 a.m. to 6 p.m. During summer months, an office is open on the Promenade in Salthill. . . . The **bus and railway station** is at the rear of the Great Southern Hotel on Eyre Square. **CIE information** is available by calling 62141. . . . **Taxis** may be found at ranks around Eyre Square and the railway station; call 63777. . . . The **General Post Office** is in Eglinton Street, with hours of 9 a.m. to 6 p.m. on weekdays. . . . During July and August, the Junior Chamber of Commerce publishes a weekly booklet, *What's On in Galway and Salthill,* that's available from the Tourist Office and most hotels. . . . The **telephone prefix** for Galway is 091.

ACCOMMODATIONS: There are very few inexpensive lodgings in Galway proper, and Salthill, only a mile and a half away, is so convenient by bus or car that

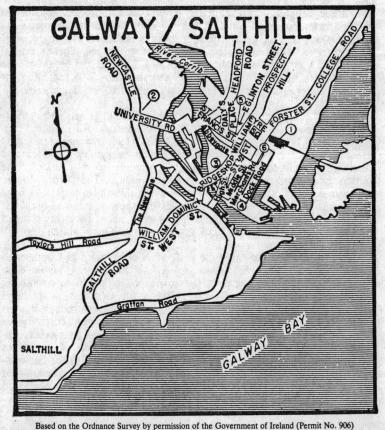

Based on the Ordnance Survey by permission of the Government of Ireland (Permit No. 906)

KEY TO THE NUMBERED REFERENCES ON OUR MAP OF GALWAY: 1—Railway Station, Bus Depot; 2—University College; 3—Church of St. Nicholas; 4—)Spanish Arch; 5—General Post Office; 6—Irish Tourist Office.

my best recommendation is to choose from the many superior accommodations listed in that area.

Note: Prices shown below are those in effect in 1985—expect them to be higher in 1986.

Hostels: The nearest **hostel** to Galway is 18 miles away in Kinvara. See Section 3 of this chapter for details.

Bed-and-Breakfast: Sailin, Gentian Hill, Upper Salthill (tel. 091-21676), is next door to a bird sanctuary on the shores of Galway Bay. The modern two-story house is home to Mary and Noel McLoughlin and their three delightful sons, and they extend an enthusiastic welcome to visitors, often joining them for bedtime cups of tea and conversation about Galway and the area. The four upstairs bedrooms are bright, airy, and attractive, with built-in hand basins and wardrobes. There's central heating and an enclosed car park. Rates for bed-and-breakfast are IR£8.50 ($10.20), dinner is the same, and there's a 50% reduction for children under 10. Open May through mid-October. Highly recommended.

One of the prettiest accommodations in Salthill is Mrs. Mary Geraghty's **Marless House,** 24 Seamount (off Threadneedle Rd.), Salthill (tel. 091-23931). A large two-story Georgian house, it sits in a quiet residential street on a rise overlooking Galway Bay. Inside, everything is spotless and beautifully furnished and decorated. The dining room overlooks the garden, where guests often sit on summer evenings. There's one double bedroom downstairs and five upstairs (one has three twin beds). All have hand basins, and three have private toilet and shower. Bed-and-breakfast rates are IR£8.50 ($10.20), dinner costs the same, and children are charged one-third less. Central heat and good parking. Open March through October.

A glowing fireplace takes the chill off cool evenings at Carmel and Tim O'Halloran's **Roncalli House,** 24 Whitestrand Ave., Lower Salthill (tel. 091-64159). Typical of the warm hospitality in this rambling two-story house overlooking Galway Bay is the fact that guests often wander in and out of Carmel's lovely modern kitchen as though it were their own home. There's a sunny front lounge and two outdoor patios for guests' use. There are two ground-floor bedrooms and four others upstairs, all with hand basins and built-in wardrobes; four of the rooms have private toilet and shower. Rates are IR£8.50 ($10.20) for bed-and-breakfast, the same for the evening meal, and there's a 20% reduction for children. Add IR£1 ($1.20) for private facilities. Central heat and good parking.

Cliff House: Inishmore, Aran Islands (tel. 099-61286), is a delightful place for an overnight stay on these offshore islands. Maura and David Dennis are hosts at the modern bungalow that perches on a site near Kilronan overlooking the sea and with sweeping views of the entire island. There are six attractive guestrooms with hand basins. B&B rates are IR£7.50 ($9), the evening meal (there's a wine license) is IR£7 ($8.40), and there's a 25% reduction for children.

Guesthouses: Kay and Pat Conroy are the cheerful, hospitable hosts at **Adare Guest House,** Fr. Griffin Place (tel. 091-62638), which is about halfway between the city center and Salthill. There's private parking out front, and in the lovely dining room, you'll eat from Royal Tara china. The three-story centrally heated house has ten guestrooms, all with built-in hand basins, and one with a private bath. B&B rates are IR£9.50 ($11.40), with an additional IR£1 ($1.20) for private facilities, and a 25% reduction for children.

Glendawn House, Upper Salthill (tel. 091-22872), sits right in the heart of Salthill, just off the coast road and adjacent to a bus stop. There are some 25 guestrooms, all with hand basins, all nicely decorated. Run by Mr. and Mrs. Mullaney, the low two-story building has an entrance hall paved with Connemara marble. Rates for B&B are IR£10 ($12), with a 25% reduction for children.

In northeastern Salthill, **Knockrea,** Lower Salthill (tel. 091-21794), sits in its own grounds and garden on a quiet street. The nine attractive guestrooms all have hand basins, and rates for bed-and-breakfast are IR£10 ($12), 10% less for children.

Hotel: The small (14 rooms) **Hotel Monterey,** Salthill (tel. 091-22563), is right in the middle of things, with good pubs and restaurants right at hand. Newly renovated and refurnished, the hotel has a large-function room in the rear, with entertainment from time to time, and a sizable parking area for guests. Rates for bed-and-breakfast are IR£9.50 ($11.40).

Self-Catering: Galway Bay Cottages, Barna, Co. Galway (tel. 091-69491), are on the main road leading out to Connemara. They feature townhouse-style cottages that sleep as many as seven, with completely furnished kitchens, turf-burning fireplaces and electric heating. There's good local bus service to Galway's city center, just 5 miles distant, and good views of Galway Bay. Rates range from IR£125 ($150) to IR£310 ($372) per week, depending on season, and electricity is extra. **Note:** These cottages can be booked in the U.S. through Round Tower Travel, 745 Fifth Ave., New York, NY 10151 (tel. 212-371-1064).

READERS' SELECTIONS: "The beach and good pubs are only about 3 minutes away from **The Inishmore House,** 109 Fr. Griffin Rd., Salthill, and Joe and Kay Stephens are very friendly hosts. Kay serves great homecooked meals, and the family room has a piano" (Paul Greenaway, Arlington, Mass.). . . . "**Loch-Lurgan House,** Ballymoneen, Barna Rd., Galway (tel. 091-22450), was the friendliest place we stayed. We came in from the rain at 3 p.m. and were treated to tea and cake and a peat fire" (Mr. and Mrs. Wm. Crowley, Yarkley, Pa.). . . . "We found the best B&B of our two-week tour of England, Wales, Scotland and Ireland to be Mrs. Sara Davy's **Ross House,** 14 Whitestrand Ave., Salthill (tel. 091-67431). Mrs. Davy was very helpful about points of interest, and the house was spotless" (Frances Johnson, Ridgewood, N.J.). . . . "After traveling along for five months, arriving at 39 Whitestrand Park, Salthill (tel. 091-68758), was like coming home! Mrs. Rushe and her family did their utmost to make me feel welcome—I had planned to stay only one day and spent a whole week" (Louise Frenkel, Johannesburg, South Africa). . . . "We found Stephen Dirrane's **Gilbert Cottage,** Oatquarter, Inishmore, Aran Islands (tel. 099-61146), the best place to stay on Inishmore. Mr. Dirrane spent 20 years working in New York restaurants and his food is excellent. Meals are also served to walkers-by" (Alison M. Conner, Olympia,

Wash.). . . . "On Inishmore, I stayed at **Bridget and Sonny Johnston-Hernon's manor house** in Kilmurvey (tel. 099-61218), and in the evenings enjoyed the company of the neighbors by a roaring fire. Bridget's meals are glorious" (Carol Smallenberg, Vancouver, B.C., Canada). . . . "For anyone who wants to stay in Galway and not have to go out to Salthill, I'd recommend **Mrs. Lydon's guesthouse,** 8 Lower Abbeygate St. (tel. 091-64914). Mrs. Lydon is a lovely woman who treated me like a houseguest, and her house is just three blocks from the train station and a half block from Lynch's Castle" (Sheila Roche, Chicago, Ill.).

WHERE TO EAT: Although these first two listings are not in Galway Town, they are not far away and are such favorites that residents often drive out for a meal. Either is a good stop en route between Galway and Limerick, and either warrants a special trip out from town.

Right on the main Galway/Limerick road, some ten miles south of Galway in Clarenbridge, **Paddy Burkes Oyster Inn** (tel. 86107) is a local institution. The old pub dates back three centuries, and beamed ceilings, wooden benches, copper and brass give the place a settled, comfortable feeling. It has been the hangout of such celebrities as John Huston, Paul Newman, and Burl Ives, to say nothing of half the population of Galway. Needless to say, oysters get star billing, and in fact, Paddy Burkes is headquarters for Galway's annual Oyster Festival. In addition to the succulent bivalves, the menu includes smoked salmon prawn cocktail, fish chowder, and fresh cockles and mussels in garlic sauce. For non-seafood lovers, there are cold and hot platters of chicken, ham, and beef. Prices range from IR£1.20 ($1.44) for hot, homemade apple pie with fresh cream to IR£8 ($9.60) for steak. A dozen oysters cost IR£6 ($7.20). Food is served continuously during pub hours.

About two miles farther out along the Galway/Limerick road, look for the signpost at Kilcolgan that directs you down a sideroad to **Moran's of the Weir** (tel. 86113). The two-hundred-year-old thatched pub is in the capable hands of the fifth generation of Morans to run the place, and at least a part of their success stems from the fact that oysters come straight from their own oyster beds close at hand. They're served with home-baked brown bread, as are smoked salmon, mussel soup, and other seafood items. Oysters go for IR£5.50 ($6.60) a dozen, smoked salmon plate for IR£4 ($4.80), and there's food service all through normal pub hours.

Also at Kilcolgan, **Raftery's Rest** (tel 86175) is right on the Galway road and serves really good pub food in a rustic country pub setting. More expensive lunches and dinners are available in the adjacent dining room.

There's also good pub grub at **The Tavern,** Eyre Square, in Galway Town. It's a large, woody place with lots of atmosphere and lots of lunchtime customers. The Mullarkey family run both the kitchen and bar.

Across the river from Eyre Square, you'll find bar food at **Flanagan's Corner Bar and Lounge,** Henry St. and William St. (tel. 63220). There's also a dart board and traditional and folk music Wednesday through Sunday.

LydonHouse, 5 Shop St. (tel. 64051), is an attractive, pleasant upstairs restaurant whose decor harks back to the days of Galway's thriving sea trade with Spain. White walls, wooden beams, heavy timber tables, touches of wrought iron and 12th- and 13th-century stone windows set the tone, and there are 14th-century family crests set into the walls. Surprisingly, prices are geared to budgeteers, with a four-course lunch costing only IR£4 ($4.80), a daily special priced at IR£3 ($3.60), and there's a "Kiddie Korner" menu for under IR£2 ($2.40). The Tourist Menu is served from April through September, and hours are 12:30 to 2:30 p.m. and 5:30 to 11 p.m. Incidentally, don't be discouraged if you arrive to find a long line—this is a large place and the line moves quickly.

In direct contrast to the restaurant, LydonHouse has developed a tastefully modern eatery on the ground floor named **Busy Bees.** A good selection of burgers come with Lydon's own sauce, and there are cold salad plates, pâté, and fresh-baked croissants. A good cold plate will cost around IR£2.50 ($3), and there's take-away service. Hours are 10 a.m. to 7 p.m. every day except Sunday.

Just off Eyre Square, the **Cellar Restaurant,** Williamsgate St. (tel. 65727), includes lasagne, seafood bouchée, and a wide variety of Irish meat dishes on its menu. The moderate prices range from IR£2.25 ($2.70) for the daily special to IR£3 ($3.60) for a three-course lunch to under IR£5 ($6) for a satisfying evening meal. The Tourist Menu is offered from mid-April through September. Hours are 12:30 to 2:30 p.m. and 5:30 to 9 p.m.

On Merchants Road, right next door to the Tourist Office, the **Vic Restaurant's** lunch menu is very good value, with plates of roast leg of pork, grilled chicken, beef stew, and filet of plaice (each served with vegetables) priced from IR£2.25 ($2.70) to IR£3 ($3.60). Hours are 12:30 to 2:30 p.m.

The small, cozy **Galleon Grill** on the coast road in Salthill (tel. 22963) is a member of the LydonHouse chain and carries out the Spanish theme in its decor. Prices range from IR£2.50 ($3) to IR£4 ($4.80) for a wide variety of hot plates, fish and chips, and burgers. Hours are noon to midnight, seven days a week.

In Barna (on the Spiddal road), the **Twelve Pins Restaurant** (tel. 69368) is an attractive place for lunch or dinner, with white stucco walls, low ceilings, lots of wood, and a small lounge area with a fire lit on cool evenings. There's a daily lunch special of steak, lamb, or chicken for IR£5 ($6) and salad plates of cold meats, smoked salmon, or prawns for about the same price. Dinner, with seafood specialties as well as steaks, veal, and roast duckling, will run between IR£8 ($9.60) and IR£11 ($13.20). Hours are 1 to 2:30 p.m. and 7 to 10 p.m. Fully licensed.

The **Salthill Hotel,** on the Promenade in Salthill (tel. 22711/22115), serves superb lunches and dinners at attractive prices in its pretty dining room. Run by the Murray family, the hotel features hot plates of fish, chicken, or beef, served with two vegetables and potato, for about IR£3.50 ($4.20) plus 10% service charge at lunch. Dinners of lamb, Irish veal, Galway Bay plaice, salmon, chicken, or turkey come with four courses at a set price of IR£10.50 ($12.60) plus 10% service charge, and there's a nightly special for IR£7.50 ($9), as well as an à la carte menu. Bar snacks are served all day, and restaurant hours are 12:30 to 2:30 p.m. and 7 to 10 p.m. In summer months, it's a good idea to book ahead. Fully licensed.

Big Splurge: Emer and John J. ("J.J." to all and sundry) Coppinger have converted space in old stone warehouses into the charming **Malt House Restaurant,** Olde Malte Arcade, High St. (tel. 67866). Amid stone walls and arches, they've created a bar area, a cozy cubbyhole lounge, and an attractive restaurant. The food has won all sorts of accolades, with such specialties as sirloin steak chasseur, peppered monkfish, scampi maison, scallops mornay, and veal Pompidour. They also serve homemade ice cream, and for a special treat order the Irish-coffee flavor. There's an excellent wine list, and a friendly, efficient staff. If the IR£14 ($16.80) plus 10% service charge set price for dinner is beyond your means, try to get by for lunch, which runs about IR£6.50 ($7.80), or sample the bar menu for less. Hours are 12:30 to 2 p.m. and 7 to 10 p.m. This popular place is packed at lunch, so come early or late. It's an absolute must to book for dinner.

THINGS TO SEE AND DO: To catch the full flavor of Galway's rich and colorful history, go by the Tourist Board and pick up their booklet, *Tourist Trail of Old Galway* (small charge), which will lead you along a signposted route through medieval streets with an informative and entertaining narrative filled with legends and anecdotes associated with places along your way.

In the City

Things to look for include the Civic Sword and Great Mace on display in the **Bank of Ireland** on Eyre Square. You'll want to see the **Spanish Arch** and the somewhat cramped **Galway City Museum** just beside it. Not only is the Museum filled with interesting artifacts, but its spiral staircase leads to a gallery that, in turn, leads to an open terrace from which there are great views of the city and harbor.

In **Market Street,** look for two interesting "marriage stones" set into the walls of houses there. The stones are carved with the coats of arms of two families united in marriage, and these two date from the early 1600s. Of even more interest is the **Lynch Memorial Window,** which immortalizes a legend that historians swear has no truth in it and most citizens of Galway swear just as vehemently is an event that added the word "lynch" to the English language. Be that as it may, the window points out that it was on this site (though not necessarily from this window) that Mayor James Lynch FitzStephen carried out a harsh sentence against his own son in 1493. The story goes that the Lord Mayor's 19-year-old son, Walter, was much enamored of a lovely girl named Agnes. He was also very good friends with a young Spanish lad, son of one of his father's Spanish friends, who had come to stay awhile in Galway. Good friends, that is, until Walter developed an acute case of jealousy when he thought the young Spaniard was courting Agnes. In a fit of rage, he murdered his friend, then filled with remorse turned himself in to the police. It was his own father who sat as magistrate and condemned the boy to death when he entered a plea of guilty. The town executioner, however, refused to perform his grisly duty, a tribute to the boy's local popularity, and the sorrowing father gave his son a last embrace and did the deed himself. From this tragic hanging—so the legend says—came the term "Lynch Law."

If you're a James Joyce fan, you'll find the girlhood home of his lady love, Nora Barnacle, in **Bowling Green**—it's the second house on the left as you enter the lane from Market Street.

For an inexpensive **day trip** around the region, check out the CIE Day Trip folder available at the Tourist Office or at the railway station, or call CIE at 62141. Also, there's a good, three-hour **cruise** of Lough Corrib aboard a waterbus, departing Woodquay in the midafternoon. For schedules, booking, and prices (moderate), check with the Tourist Office or call Salthill Rentals (tel. 22085, 22318, or 22307). Salthill Rentals can also arrange **deep-sea**

angling trips and **boat trips** on Galway Bay. They're open 9 a.m. to 7 p.m. every day during summer months.

The Aran Islands

Lying almost directly across the mouth of Galway Bay, the Aran Islands group consists of **Inishere** *(Inis Oirr,* "eastern island"), the smallest and nearest to the mainland (Doolin, Co. Clare is six miles away); **Inishmaan** *(Inis Meain,* "middle island"), three miles distant from each of the other two and three miles long by two miles wide; and **Inishmore** *(Inis Mor,* "big island"), seven sea miles from the Connemara coast, eight miles long and two and a half miles wide, with the only safe harbor suitable for steamer docking at **Kilronan,** its main village.

Life has been made easier on the islands with the introduction of electricity, modern plumbing, and regular sea and air service to the mainland. Still, much of the old customs and culture remains, and the hardy islanders are a breed apart, conditioned by generations who have braved the seas in their frail curraghs and laboriously built up the rocky soil with seaweed and sand in which to grow their meager crops. You'll debark at Kilronan pier on Inishmore, to be greeted by lines of jaunting cars for hire to explore the island, with a delightful and informative narratives by your driver/guide and a terrific vantage point from which to view the network of small stone fields marked off by meandering stone walls. You'll ride through the village and down the one main road that runs the length of the island past an ancient stone ring fort, ecclesiastical ruins, and tiny hamlets on the **Dun Aengus,** an 11-acre stone fort perched on a cliff some 300 feet above the sea. The jaunting-car fare runs about IR£8 ($9.60). There are bikes for rent as well, and if you're a walker, this is the country for it, with stops to chat a bit with an old man smoking his pipe in an open doorway or a housewife hurrying along a lane to the village. Although Gaelic is the everyday language, the courteous islanders will speak to you in English.

If you have a yen to visit Inishere or Inishmaan (where you're much more likely to see the traditional Aran style of dress than on Inishmore), ask any of the fishermen at the Kilronan pier and they'll arrange to take you over by curragh or other small boat. And if you're really taken with the islands, the Tourist Board lists several good accommodations, as well as the one you'll find listed under "Accommodations" above.

CIE operates regular service to the Aran Islands from the Galway docks, and you can book the day before at the railway station or the Tourist Office, or pay at the dockside kiosk. The round-trip fare in 1984 was IR£17 ($20.40), half that for children under 16. Inquire about their special family fares. It takes just over two-and-a-half hours for the trip, and the water can be choppy, so if you're not sure you're a good sailor, it pays to take Dramamine or some other motion-sickness remedy about 20 minutes before you embark. The CIE ferries dock only at Inishmore, but are met by curraghs from the other two islands to take off cargo. A shorter boat trip is that from **Rossaveal** (on the coastal road past Spiddal), which takes only 45 minutes and is run by **Aran Ferries.** The round-trip fare in 1984 was IR£12 ($14), half-fare for children, with special family and student fares. Book at the Galway Tourist Office or call 091-68904 (091-72273 after hours). You can fly out with **Aer Arann** (tel. 091-65110/65119) in a nine-seat, twin-engined aircraft from

Caranmore Airfield on the Monivea road four miles out from Galway. The round-trip fare is about IR£40 ($48), and you can also book through the Tourist Office.

GALWAY AFTER DARK: Be it a castle banquet, a night of theater, or a pint in a pub, you'll find plenty to do in Galway in the evening.

A Literary Banquet

Much more intimate than the medieval banquets at Bunratty and Knappogue, the **Banquet and Literary Evening at Dunguaire Castle** is certainly not a budget item, but it is special enough to warrant a Big Splurge from the most devoted budgeteer. The Castle is a small 16th-century keep, with banquet seating limited to 62. You'll learn its legend when you enter the reception hall and quaff a cup of mead as a pretty girl in medieval dress relates the story. In the upstairs banquet hall, you'll dine by candlelight on such delicacies as smoked salmon, baked guinea hen on rice, and sumptuous desserts, accompanied by a plentiful supply of wine. When dinner is over, your costumed waiters and waitresses repair to the stage and bring to vivid life Ireland's literary heroes and heroines through their stories, plays and poems.

Because attendance is so limited, this is one banquet you *must* book well in advance (through a travel agent before you leave home if possible, through the Galway Tourist Office, or the Tours Manager at Shannon Airport, tel. 061-61788/61444). There are two banquets each night from mid-May through September, at 6 and 9 p.m., and the all-inclusive price is IR£21.50 ($25.80). There's no parking space at the castle, so guests meet at Winles Hotel in Kinvara (17 miles south of Galway) fifteen minutes before banquet time to be taken to the castle by bus. A simpler way to go is to book with **CIE** for their tour which leaves from both Salthill Promenade and the railway station (tel. 091-62141).

Theater

Since 1928, Galway's **Taibhdhearc** ("thive-yark") Theatre, Middle St. (tel. 62024) has existed for the sole purpose of preserving Gaelic drama, and several nights a week during summer months they present a one-act play in Gaelic, with music, song, poetry, and dance both before and after the performance. Following the action is no problem, notwithstanding the language, and the musical program is simply spectacular, with step dancing that will leave you breathless, even as a spectator. This is where Siobhan McKenna began her training and career, and you'll see talent of much the same caliber on the stage almost any night. It's a very, very "Irish" entertainment, and very good value for money, as well, with tickets about IR£4 ($4.80). You can book through the Tourist Office or at the theater.

There's good drama, too, at the **Druid Theatre**, Chapel Lane (tel. 68617), where the resident professional company mounts productions like *The Beggars Opera*, avant-garde plays, and Anglo-Irish classics presented nightly year round. There are frequent lunchtime and late-night shows, and local newspapers usually publish the schedule. Tickets are in the IR£3.50 ($4.20) to IR£5.50 ($6.60) range, and you can book by telephone or at the theater.

Traditional Music

For the very best in traditional Irish music, check with the Tourist Board to see if your visit coincides with a Galway appearance of **Seisiun,** the troupe that tours the country during July and August.

In Galway, the **King's Head** pub, High St., has a large back room devoted to Irish music, with heavy emphasis on ballads and nightly performances during summer months. There's a small admission. **Flanagan's Corner Bar and Lounge,** Henry St. and William St. W. (tel. 63220), has traditional and folk music from Wednesday through Sunday nights, and they invite musicians to bring along their instruments and join in. The upstairs ballad room at the **Crane Bar** on Sea Rd. is often packed out, and the music here is very good. Galway's oldest family-run pub is **Rabbitt's,** 23 Forster St. (tel. 62215), just off Eyre Square. More locals than tourists, and a place for good conversation and conviviality.

In Salthill, it's **O'Connors Pub** or the **Sacre Coeur Hotel** bar for singing pubs, and in nearby Spiddal, **An Cruiscin Lan** pub is much favored by the locals. In all, you'll pay only for the pint, with no charge for music and song.

Between Salthill and Spiddal, the Teach Furbo is a hotel on the shores of Galway Bay that presents ballads in a large room just off the hotel entrance.

SPECIAL EVENTS: The Irish, of course, can come up with an instant party on an occasion no more auspicious than two friends happening to be in the same place at the same time. And if there's a *race meet,* the party often turns into a gala! The folks in Galway have, in fact, perfected their party-throwing skills to such an extent that it sometimes seems the entire country shuts down to travel up this way for the six-day **Race Week** in late July or early August. There's music everywhere, food stalls, private parties (to which strangers are often warmly welcomed), honest-to-goodness horse trading, and lots of activity at the track, where admission to the enclosures varies from IR£3 ($3.60) to IR£6 ($7.20). Because so many Irish descend on the town during that week, best book *way* ahead if you'll be arriving during the festivities.

The other "biggie" in Galway—and one which draws as many Irish as Race Week—is the **September Oyster Festival.** Actually, it's an international affair, with oyster-openers gathering from around the world to enter competitions for opening the most oysters in the shortest period of time. In a colorful ceremony, the Lord Mayor of Galway gets things underway by opening and eating the first oyster of the season. After that, it's two solid days (usually a weekend) of eating and drinking: oysters, salmon, prawns and almost anything else that comes from the sea are washed down with buckets of champagne or Guinness. The action centers around Moran's of the Weir, Paddy Burkes, and the Great Southern Hotel, and a ticket to all the scheduled partying is costly—around IR£85 ($102) for the two days—but since the entire town *becomes* a party, the general gaiety spills over into the streets and pubs at no cost at all. Again, advance booking is an absolute must. It's usually the third or fourth weekend in September, but you should check the Tourist Board's Calendar of Events.

To open the herring season in mid-August, there's a lovely **Blessing of the Sea** ceremony on the waters of Galway Bay. Fishing boats form a procession as they sail out of the harbor, and leading them is an entire boat load of priests who petition heaven for a good and profitable season.

SHOPPING: One of Ireland's best tweed shops is **Padraic O Maille's,** on Dominick St. (tel. 62696). There's a vast stock of gorgeous hand-woven tweeds by the yard to be tailored by the shop, as well as ready-made jackets, men's and ladies' suits, ladies' cashmere knits and tweed coats, scarves, Irish "paddy" hats, and much more. This is also a good place to shop for Aran hand-knit sweaters (O Maille's was, in fact, the first place ever to market them commercially). Prices are competitive, and the staff in this family-run store are among the most helpful and friendliest in the country, which probably accounts somewhat for their regular patronage by the likes of John Ford, John Wayne, Maureen O'Hara, and Peter Ustinov. There's another, smaller shop, in the Tourist Office building, but do go by the original store, to browse if nothing else.

Fallers, Williamsgate St. (tel. 61226), began as a jewelry shop back in 1879 and today carries a huge stock of crystal, silver, china porcelain, linen, jewelry, and quality souvenirs. Most of their very competitive prices include free delivery from Ireland, and if you purchase an item on which they must charge shipping, they'll send it by air across the Atlantic, then overland to your address, resulting in a substantial saving in postage. They do an international mail-order business, and you can write for their color catalog.

It's hard to know just what to call **Kenny's,** High St. (tel. 62739/61014/61021. It is, of course, just about the best bookshop and art gallery in the country—but it's also an institution! Begun back in the 1930s, the small bookshop has grown into a fascinating multilevel maze of rooms in ancient buildings lovingly restored by the Kenny family. There are marvelous works of Irish art, antiquarian maps and prints, old magazine issues, rare books on Irish subjects—and there are the Kennys. You'll nearly always find Mrs. Kenny behind the counter up front, and at least one of her sons on hand. They'll search for a specific book, and if necessary, mail it on to you in the U.S., and they even have their own bindery to wrap a prized edition in fine, hand-tooled covers. Periodically, they issue catalogs of Irish-interest publications, and many of the volumes in their stock come from private libraries they've purchased. Do go by to browse and look for that special Irish book to carry home, but be warned—this is not an easy shop to leave!

Students who present their I.D. card will receive a 10% discount at Evelyn Tully's **Just Looking** boutique in High Street. Evelyn stocks up-to-the-minute styles from leading Irish and European manufacturers, with racks and racks of fashionable dresses, knitwear, blouses, skirts, jackets, coats, and canvas and denim jeans. Prices are reasonable, and the staff is friendly and helpful.

On the outskirts of town, the **Galway Irish Crystal** factory, Merlin Park, Galway (tel. 091-57311), sells beautiful crystal at one-third off prices you'd pay in shops. In the showroom, it's a joy to watch Master Cutter John McNamara at work creating the very pieces displayed on shelves. John, who began cutting at age 13 and worked with Waterford Glass for twenty years, did the magnificent presentation pieces for both the Pope in 1979 and President Reagan in 1984. The showroom is open from 9 a.m. to 5 p.m. seven days a week, and John is on hand Monday through Friday.

You can tour the **Royal Tara China** factory and watch master craftsmen and women creating fine bone china. It's located off the Dublin road at Flannery's Motel, and tours are at 11 a.m. and 3 p.m., Monday through Friday.

The showroom and shop are open seven days a week from 9 a.m. to 6 p.m., and there's a full-service restaurant on the premises. Considerable savings on purchases here as compared to shops elsewhere.

On the Galway/Spiddal road, **Mairtin Standun,** Spiddal, Co. Galway (tel. 091-83108), grew from a small drapery and grocery shop into the large, bright store in which you can find very good bargains today. It's still very much a family business, but the stocks of Aran sweaters, tweed coats and jackets, glassware, china, souvenirs, and gifts is incredibly large. In the rear of the shop, there's a pleasant tearoom, a welcomed refuge for weary shoppers. Standun's is open from 9:30 a.m. to 6:30 p.m., Monday to Saturday, year round.

3. Around Counties Galway and Mayo

ACCOMMODATIONS: Whether you choose the short, direct route from Galway Town to Sligo via Tuam or the longer, coastal drive through Connemara's starkly beautiful landscape, you won't lack for excellent and inexpensive places to rest your head.
Note: Prices shown below are those in effect in 1985—expect them to be higher in 1986.

County Galway

Hostels: Superior hostel accommodations are available at **Inverin** (tel. 091-73154), some five miles from Rossaveal, and hostelers are eligible for reduced fares on the Aran Islands ferry. There's good, regular bus service to Galway, 19 miles away. The **Twelve Bens Youth Hostel,** Ben Lettery, Ballinafad (tel. Ballinafad, Co. Galway, 18), is set in mountains seven miles outside Clifden, and hikers are warned that climbing can be dangerous and should not be attempted without notifying the hostel warden of your intended route. Farther north, some 51 miles from Galway, there are very good hostel accommodations at **Rosroe,** Renvyle.

Bed-and-Breakfast: Most people pass right through the Burren, but a lovely place to spend a night or two in the middle of this unique area is **Teac Caoilte,** Galway Bay View, Geehy North, Duras, Kinvara, Co. Galway (tel. 091-37214). The modern bungalow is the home of Anne and Joseph Quilty and it looks out over the Burren on one side, across Galway Bay to Galway Town on the other. Mr. Quilty is an artist at the easel, and Mrs. Quilty is an artist in the kitchen, serving up superb meals. There's an excellent beach just down from the house, and the Quiltys enjoy steering guests to places of historical, botanical, and geological interest. The three guestrooms are all doubles, and all have hand basins. There's central heating, never a problem with parking, and the lounge features a lovely fireplace. Bed-and-breakfast rates are IR£8.50 ($10.20), dinner costs the same, and there's a 10% reduction for children. Open April through October.

On the Galway Bay coastal road, just a half-mile from Spiddal, Mrs. Vera Feeney's **Ardmore Country House,** Greenhill, Spiddal (tel. 091-83145), is a modern bungalow overlooking the Bay and the Aran Islands. The Cliffs of Moher are clearly visible on clear days and the panoramic view is framed by large windows in the lounge, or you can relax in the sun outside on the terrace with its rock garden. The six spacious guestrooms are attractively decorated all fitted out with hand basins and built-in wardrobes and vanities, and some with showers. The gracious Mrs. Feeney has thoughtfully provided washing and drying facilities to renew your travel-weary clothes. Evening meals are a specialty here (be sure and book by noon), and you're offered a choice of menu at breakfast. Rates for bed-and-breakfast are IR£8 ($9.60) and dinner is IR£8.50 ($10.20). Central heating and good parking. Open March through November.

Ben Baun House, Westport Rd., Clifden (tel. Clifden 220) sits on a hill some 50 yards from town. The comfortable modern bungalow looks out onto glorious mountain views, with spacious grounds around the house for taking the afternoon sun. Barbara and John Lydon welcome guests here and are always happy to help in planning day trips around the area, and provide an open fire in the cozy lounge to return to at the end of the day. The six guestrooms all are spotless and attractive, with hand basins and Donegal handwoven spreads and draperies. Two have private toilet and shower (no extra charge). Rates for B&B are IR£8.50 ($10.20), dinner is IR£7.50 ($9), and there's a 25% discount for children. Central heating and a paved car park out front. Open April through October.

Charming Mrs. Frances Tiernan's **Heather Lodge**, Westport Rd., Clifden (tel. Clifden 161), has magnificent views of a mountain lake and the Twelve Bens range, all framed by huge picture windows in the lounge, which also has a fireplace. The pretty modern bungalow is about a mile from town, set back from the road on a slight rise, and the eight lovely bedrooms all have hand basins and built-in wardrobes. One has a private shower, and another has both private toilet and shower (no extra charge). There are two on the ground floor, and one has three single beds. B&B rates are IR£8.50 ($10.20), with a 25% reduction for children. Central heating and car park; open April through September.

Farmhouse: Get set for a rave! Actually, two raves—one for **Knockferry Lodge**, Knockferry, Roscahill, Co. Galway (tel. 091-80122), and one for the delightful Des Moran who runs it. Set in a secluded spot on the shores of Lough Corrib, just 14 miles north of Galway Town, the lodge was originally occupied by the author of *Galway Bay,* Dr. Arthur Colohan. It was also Des's family home, to which he returned after several years in the hotel business in Europe to expand the house and establish a first-class accommodation with a superior cuisine. It is his own irrepressible personality which also added an element of fun that has attracted a loyal following of fishermen and relaxation-seekers who return again and again. There are turf fires in both of the large lounges, and there's a spacious dining room for outstanding meals (with such specialties as Corrib salmon, trout and pike, Viennese goulash, Connemara lamb and spiced beef, among others). A gameroom provides table tennis and bar billiards. Fishing boats are available for hire, and the lodge can supply bait (no charge for fishing except for salmon). Guestrooms are lovely, most with lake views. All have hand basins; several have private bath facilities; the Lake Room and Galway Bay Room both have private facilities and are furnished with antiques; and there's one huge room with four beds, wash basin, bidet, toilet, shower and bath. Bed-and-breakfast rates are IR£8.75 ($10.50), with additional charges for private facilities ranging from IR£1.50 ($1.80) to IR£4 ($4.80); 25% off for children. There's central heating, plenty of parking, and Des wants guests who have been here before to know that the "presence remains on the bridge"—newcomers should be sure to ask for the tall tale that goes with that statement!

Leckavrea View Farmhouse, Maam (tel. Cornamona 140), is the comfortable home of John and Breege Gavin, on the Maam/Cong road about two miles from Maam village, with marvelous views of Lough Corrib and a little island crowned by Castle Kirk ("Hen's Castle") just offshore. Fishing on the Lough is free (the Gavins have boats for hire), and if Castle Kirk intrigues you, John will (for a small fee) row you over to the island for a bit of exploring. In consideration for her guests who've come for peace and quiet, Breege keeps the TV in a separate lounge and usually keeps a fire glowing in the main lounge. Rates for bed-and-breakfast are IR£8 ($9.60), dinner is IR£7.50 ($9), with a 25% discount for children.

Big Splurge: If there is such a thing as casual elegance, **Ballynahinch Castle,** Ballinafad, Connemara, Co. Galway (tel. Clifden 135), has it. Set in lush woodlands at the base of Ben Lettry in the Twelve Bens mountain range, the impressive manor house overlooks the Owenmore River and is surrounded by lovely gardens. This was the ancestral home of the O'Flaherty chieftains, and in more recent years the sporting home of an Indian maharajah. There's excellent fishing on the grounds, with boats available for hire, and miles of walking or biking paths, with bicycles for hire. Log fires, oil paintings, and wall tapestries give a warm, comfortable air to the two beautifully furnished lounges, and the dining room overlooks the river and gardens. The Castle Pub is a favorite gathering place for residents of the locality, with traditional music on tap often during summer months. All twenty guestrooms have private baths, and some have fireplaces. Rates are seasonal, ranging from IR£18 ($21.60) to IR£26 ($31.20).

County Mayo

Hostel: Five miles from Westport, **Traenlaur Lodge,** Lough Feeagh, Newport (tel. 098-41358), overlooks a harbor on Lough Feeagh. **Maigh Mhuillinn,** Currane, Achill Sound, Westport (tel. 098-45280), sits on the mainland shore of Achill Sound, some 32 miles from Westport.

Bed-and-Breakfast: On the main Westport/Castlebar road, Mary and Joe Moran's **Lakeview House,** Westport Rd., Castlebar (tel. 094-22374), sits on spacious grounds, with a large, sloping lawn out front. This was Mary's family home, and both lounge (with fireplace) and dining room look out to green fields and rolling hills. Mary, whose warm personality bubbles with enthusiasm, bakes her own brown bread and scones and is always happy to share the recipe with guests (a frequent request). The four pretty guestrooms all have hand basins, and there's a twin-bedded room with private shower and a family-size room (two double beds) with private shower. Rates for bed-and-breakfast are IR£8 ($9.60), with an additional IR£1 ($1.20) for private facilities; 20% reduction for children. The evening meal is also IR£8 ($9.60). Central heating and a paved car park.

Shalom, Westport Rd., Castlebar (tel. 094-21471), is the home of Noreen Raftery, who has the fresh beauty of an Irish schoolgirl. She and Liam, who is a Garda, take a personal interest in their guests—as does Bruno, their gorgeous Collie dog. Conversation around the turf fire in their lounge has brought glowing letters from our readers, who have nothing but praise for the Rafterys. The three nice guestrooms all have hand basins and built-in wardrobes, and there's one family-sized room with a double and twin bed. B&B rates are IR£8 ($9.60), with a 25% reduction for children. Central heating and good parking. Open May to mid-October.

Rockmount, Achill Island (tel. 098-45272), is a modern bungalow convenient to the village and a bus stop. Mrs. Frances Masterson is the friendly, helpful hostess, who happily shares her knowledge of the island with guests, and the four Masterson youngsters are a delight. The four homey, comfortable guestrooms all have hand basins, and during my recent stay, other guests included natives who had come from other parts of the country to holiday here, making for lively Irish conversation. Rates for bed-and-breakfast are IR£7.50 ($9), with a 50% discount for children. Central heating and off-street parking.

Across the sound from Achill Island, **Teach Mweewillin,** Currane, Achill (tel. 098-455134), is a modern bungalow set on a hill overlooking sound and island. Mrs. Margo Cannon keeps a pony for children to ride, and gladly helps guests arrange fishing, sailing, or golf. There are four attractive guestrooms, all with hand basins. B&B rates are IR£8 ($9.60), with a 50% reduction for children. Central heating and parking; open Easter through September.

Mrs. Carmel Lydon, Cong (tel. Cong 53), is the gracious hostess in her large, modern house built in the Georgian style. Set on Lough Corrib (boats available for hire) and near Ashford Castle, the house has seven very attractive guestrooms, all with hand basins and one with private bath and shower. Bed-and-breakfast rates are IR£8.50 ($10.20); central heating and good parking; open May through September.

Farmhouses: A mile from Westport on the main Louisburgh road, **Rath-A-Rosa,** Rosbeg, Westport (tel. 098-25348), has magnificent views across a lawn bordered with flowers to a small cove and across Clew Bay to the mountains of Achill Island. Large picture windows in the modern bungalow's lounge frame the vista outside. Mrs. O'Brien, the lady of the house, is known far and wide for her cooking, using the freshest of ingredients and locally grown meats, with fish straight from local waters. Dinners are superb, and must be booked before noon. Breakfast often features just-caught mackerel along with Mrs. O'Brien's special mustard sauce. Mr. O'Brien, a fluent Gaelic speaker, is very much a part of the warm hospitality here, with witty and informative conversation his specialty. The six guestrooms all have hand basins, one has its own bathroom, and two come with showers and toilets. There's central heating and never a problem with parking. Rates for bed-and-breakfast are IR£9.50 ($11.40), and dinner costs the same. Open mid-March through October.

Seapoint House, Kilmeena, Westport (tel. 098-41254), has long been a favorite with our readers, and you'll know why when you arrive at the large two-story house in a beautiful, isolated setting on Clew Bay. Joe, Mary, and the O'Malley children will give you a real Irish welcome and make you a part of the family group around the open turf fire in the lounge. A small, sandy beach rings the inlet, and the O'Malleys have a boat available for guests' use. There's also a pony for children to ride. All nine guestrooms are nicely done up, all have hand basins, and five come with their own bath/shower/toilet (if you're booking ahead, do ask for a room with a view of the bay). The evening meal is a specialty (must be booked ahead), with home-produced, home-cooked fare—sauces, soups, brown soda bread, and scones are Mrs. O'Malley's specialties—and there's a more-than-generous breakfast, with a choice of menu. B&B rates are IR£9 ($10.80), with an additional IR£1 ($1.20) for private facilities; reduction for children is 20%. Central heating. Open April through October.

Mrs. Agnes Cronin's **Sea Call,** Carn, Belmullet (tel. Belmullet 47), sits on a dairy farm right at the sea's edge, and it houses the kind of warm, Irish hospitality that brings guests back year after year (as do Mrs. Cronin's apple tart and homemade brown bread). The two-story bungalow is centrally heated and has three homey guestrooms, all with hand basins. Rates here are IR£9 ($10.80) for bed-and-breakfast, the same for dinner, and you should book as far in advance as possible, since she's often filled with repeat guests.

Big Splurge: The **Hotel Synge,** Geesala, Balline (tel. Geesala 104), is one of those very special places you sometimes unexpectedly find in isolated spots. Set in the small seaside village of Geesala in northwest County Mayo, this is a thoroughly modern hotel, with picture windows looking out across rolling moorlands to the sea and distant mountains. Diners enjoy the same view in the Blue Pool restaurant, which features local seafood. The intimate "Man Bites Dog" Lounge (ask about the origin of its name!) specializes in a wide variety of mixed drinks, as well as the usual pint and nip, and is often filled with Irish-speaking locals mingling happily with hotel guests. Log fires take the chill off cool evenings and offer cozy gathering points. There are tennis courts on the premises, and the hotel provides transportation to nearby golf courses. Fisherpeople can fish from shore rocks or hire boats through the hotel (which can also provide bait and tackle and packed lunches). There are 32 luxury guestrooms, all with private baths and balconies, as well as telephones and radios. Seasonal rates are pricey for the budgeteer, but very good value at IR£19 ($22.80) to IR£26 ($31.20) single, IR£32 ($38.40) to IR£37 ($44.40) double. Special weekly and weekend rates are less. Highly recommended.

READERS' SELECTIONS: "Mrs. McDonagh's **Barickard House,** Headford, Co. Galway (tel. 093-21421), is about a quarter of a mile out of town on the Galway road. It's a beautiful farm, and we had a lovely room and excellent breakfast" (Jacqueline Hetman, El Cerrito, Calif.). . . . "Right outside Headford, Co. Galway, Mrs. Collins' **Mount Carmel** (tel. 093-21474), is excellent, and she's a good cook" (Ann and Brian O'Connell, McLean, Va.). . . . "Add to your list of super farm families, **Mrs. King,** Killany Harbour, near Leenane, Co. Galway (tel. Leenane 6). This is a most genuine, gracious and very devout Irish family. Don't miss Mrs. King's mother, a priceless—and very sharp—Irish grandmother" (Rev. R. J. Bunday, Emporia, Kans.). . . . "Mr. and Mrs. O'Neill made us at home in their beautiful country place, **Creeve,** Oughterard, Co. Galway (tel. 091-82210). Located on a private road bordering the lake, the place is a paradise for salmon and trout fishermen, and the O'Neills have their own boats for guests. Their breakfast is excellent, and the beds were the best we slept in" (Alice Leonard, Alexandria, Va.). . . . "A guesthouse called **Lakeland Portacarron,** Oughterard, Co. Galway, is run by the delightful Lal and Mary Faherty. It's a beautiful home on the lakeshore with several rooms with private baths. Mr. Faherty is a great source of information on trips, fishing—you name it" (Eleanor Jennings, Windsor, Conn.). . . . **"Nestor's Farmhouse,** Tuam, Co. Galway (tel. 093-23188), has excellent food and a quiet country setting" (Frank Norton, La Mesa, Calif.). . . . **"Rock Glen Country House Hotel,** Clifden, Connemara, Co. Galway (tel. Clifden 16), is without a doubt the most relaxing and cozy place that we've ever stayed in. John and Evangeline Roche are great people who go out of their way to create an atmosphere of warmth and friendliness. The entire place is immaculate, the food superb, and the environment gorgeous. Rates are a little above budget, but worth every pence!" (Erin and Neil Cronin, Windsor, Conn.). . . . "In Clifden, Co. Galway, I highly recommend the hospitality of Mrs. K. Morris and her son at **Ben View House,** Bridge St. (tel. Clifden 123). They make sure you're both comfortable and well fed" (Don Craig, Danbury, Conn.). . . . "Mrs. Catherine Fitzpatrick is a wonderful hostess at **Newtown** in Claremorris, Co. Mayo. We spent the evening visiting with the family and enjoyed every minute of our stay with this hospitable family in their lovely home" (Renee Reilly, Minneapolis, Minn.). . . . "Not far from Ashford Castle,

Hazelgrove, Drumshiel, Cong, Co. Mayo (tel. Cong 60), is run by Mrs. Ann Coakley, who is a friendly person with four modern, beautifully decorated bedrooms for rent" (Gay Griffin, Lauderhill, Fla.). . . . "We were so pleased with Kay O'Malley's friendliness and hospitality at **Riverbank House,** Louisburgh Rd., Westport, Co. Mayo (tel. 098-25719), that we stayed two nights instead of one" (Margaret and Donald Lawrence, New York, N.Y.). . . . "We came upon a cheerful, well-run guesthouse just as you enter Ballyhaunis, just two blocks from the main drag and about a five-minute ride from Knock. Mrs. Breeda Burke's sweetness and hospitality at her **Little Brook House,** Devlis, Ballyhaunis, Co. Mayo (tel. Ballyhaunis 151), made our stay memorable" (Frances Brennan, El Cerrito, Calif.).

Note: Other Co. Mayo recommendations by readers: Mrs. Evelyn O'Hara, **Riverside Guest House,** Charlestown (tel. Charlestown 500); **Mrs. Phil McGrath,** Kilbeg, Claremorris (tel. 094-71297); **Killadoon Beach Hotel,** Killadoon (west of Croagh Patrick); **Mrs. and Mrs. Chambers,** Loch Morchan (tel. 098-41221); Mrs. Sheridan, **Altamont House,** Ballinrobe Rd., Westport (tel. 098-25226); Mrs. M. Staunton, **Rock View,** Leenane road outside Westport; Mrs. O'Malley, **Windgates,** Rosbeg (near Westport).

WHERE TO EAT: Picnic spots abound in the wilds of Connemara and Achill Island, and country pubs often serve delicious, hearty bar food.

County Galway

The **Boluisce Seafood Bar,** Spiddal Village, Connemara (tel. 091-83286/83359), is a true "Irish" restaurant, piling your plate high with generous portions at moderate prices. You can choose anything from soup right up to lobster and other delicacies. A full dinner from the à la carte menu will run about IR£7 ($8.40). Hours are noon to 10 p.m.

On the coastal drive from Galway to Clifden, the **Hotel Carna** on the outskirts of the little village of Carna (the Clifden side) serves good bar food at inexpensive prices.

In Clifden, **O'Grady's Seafood Restaurant,** Market St. (tel. Clifden 110), is an attractive family-run restaurant that's been around a long time, earning an international reputation for their excellent seafood dishes. They have their own fishing boats, so you may be sure the fish you eat is not long out of Atlantic waters. On Saturday nights, there are candlelight dinners, and from Halloween to Easter, they feature game as well as seafood. Business lunches are served at moderate prices every day, and dinner will run about IR£8 ($9.60). The Tourist Menu is offered up to 2:30 p.m. Hours are 12:30 to 8 p.m. in winter, until 9:30 p.m. June, July, and August. Closed Sundays in winter.

On the outskirts of Clifden, **The Pantry,** Westport Rd., Clifden (tel. Clifden 281), is a large two-story white stucco building with black trim. Also family-run, its menu is extensive, offering a good variety of fish, fowl, beef, lamb, and pork. This is a relaxing, attractive place with friendly service, and it is fully licensed. Lunch will run about IR£5 ($6), dinner around IR£9 ($10.80), and they accept major credit cards. Hours are 1 to 4:30 p.m. and 6 to 10:30 p.m.

The **Doon Restaurant,** Moyard (tel. Moyard 21), is on the road from Clifden to Westport and it's a terrific place to stop for a super seafood lunch. It's a tiny place and very popular, so it might pay to call ahead and book. There's a wine license, and lunch will run about IR£7.50 ($9). Hours are 12:15 to 3 p.m., and they're closed from November to mid-April.

In Letterfrack, there's a good **tearoom,** where the fresh barm brack is outstanding, and the à la carte menu also includes soup, sandwiches, and sweets. The **Bards' Den Bar and Restaurant**, also in Letterfrack, is made cozy by open turf fires, and bar food is served from 10:30 a.m. to 7 p.m. year round (Irish stew, not always on bar menus, is very good here). During summer months, there's an à la carte dinner menu from 6 to 10 p.m. and there's often Irish music in the bar.

Des Moran's **Knockferry Lodge**, Knockferry, Rosscahill (tel. 091-80122)—see "Accommodations"—serves marvelous evening meals, but it is absolutely necessary to book ahead. You can look forward to such unusual offerings (for Ireland) as smoked pâté and gazpacho, and whatever Des has on the menu on a particular night, you may be sure it will be well prepared, fresh, and delicious. There's a wine license, and both the red and white vin ordinaire carafes are exceptional. Hours are 7 to 9 p.m., closed Sundays. Dinner will run about IR£9 ($10.80), and major credit cards are accepted.

In Tuam, the **Restauranat Cre Na Cille**, High St. (tel. 093-28232), specializes in seafood and game, in season. The family-run eatery has an extensive menu in its upstairs bar, and the Tourist Menu is offered from 12:30 to 2:30 p.m. From the à la carte menu, lunch will run about IR£5 ($6), dinner IR£8 ($9.60). Hours are 10:30 a.m. to 10:30 p.m. Fully licensed.

County Mayo

For an inexpensive lunch in elegant surroundings, go by the **Breaffy House Hotel** in Castlebar (tel. 094-22033), an impressive graystone edifice set in beautiful formal gardens and lawns. Its Mulberry Bar is a gracious room in the Tudor style, and a very good three-course businessman's lunch is served every day from 12:30 to 2:30 p.m., featuring the joint of the day and fresh vegetables, with smoked salmon or Irish stew frequently among other choices, all at prices of IR£3.50 ($4.20) to IR£4.50 ($5.40). If you can get a seat by the window, you'll be able to enjoy the beauty both inside and out.

On Achill Island, the **Amethyst Restaurant** in Keel (tel. Keel 4) is in an old-fashioned resort hotel. It's a large, comfortable room furnished with antiques and serviceable pieces that are merely old. There's a fireplace at one end, a peaked, beamed ceiling, oil paintings and prints of Achill scenes, and you dine to the accompaniment of classical music. The menu is quite extensive, with seafood featured (as you might imagine in this setting), but there are other specialties such as Tandoori chicken and several vegetarian selections. There's a wine license, and complete dinner prices range from IR£7 ($8.40) to IR£9 ($10.80). Lunches are in the IR£4 ($4.80) to IR£5 ($6) range. Hours are 9 a.m. to 9 p.m., and it's closed from October to April.

The **Asgard Tavern**, Westport Quay, Westport (tel. Westport 32), is a delightful nautical pub where owners Mary and Michael Cadden serve award-winning seafood dishes as well as bar snacks. If you're in Westport in the evening, you'll usually find traditional or folk music here. Pub grub is served from noon until early afternoon, and the restaurant serves dinner from 6:30 p.m. to 10 p.m. at prices that run around IR£11 ($13.20) from the à la carte menu. However, the Tourist Menu is available from 6:30 to 8 p.m., April through October. Major credit cards are accepted. Closed Mondays all year, and Sundays in the winter.

In Castlebar, **The Davitt Restaurant**, Rush St. (tel. 094-22233), has a good lunch menu at around IR£3 ($3.60). Dinner, featuring French and English dishes, goes for about IR£7 ($8.40). Hours are 12:30 to 10:30 p.m., closed Sundays.

Mulligan's Pub, James St., Claremorris (tel. 094-71792), serves full meals as well as pub grub. This traditional-style pub also offers the Tourist

Menu at both lunch and dinner. Lunch prices start IR£3 ($3.60), dinner at IR£5 ($6), and hours are 12:30 to 8 p.m. Bar hours are 10:30 a.m. to 11:30 p.m.

READER'S SELECTION: "**Ardmore House**, Westport, Co. Mayo, is a fine restaurant which has received culinary awards. It has an attractive atmosphere, good service, and excellent food—among the best we had in Ireland" (Margaret and Donald Lawrence, New York, N.Y.).

THINGS TO SEE AND DO: For the most part, it's the scenery that stars in the Western Region—the scenery and the host of ancient archeological sites that attest to just how long people have inhabited this lovely, but inhospitable, landscape.

County Galway

If time is a factor, you may want to drive through the heart of Connemara via Moycullen, Oughterard, and Recess to reach Clifden. Or you might follow this route through Moycullen and Oughterard as far as Maam Cross, then cut south to Screeb and west along the coast. If you choose this route, try to stop by the factory and showroom of **Celtic Crystal Ltd.** in Moycullen (tel. 091-85172). They specialize in the use of Celtic designs and motifs in their hand-cut crystal glassware, and they're open to the public every day from May to October from 9 a.m. to 6 p.m. Also in Moycullen, the **Connemara Marble Products** factory offers a tremendous stock of items made from polished marble, ranging from inexpensive souvenirs to moderately expensive items like bookends, clocks, etc. Prices are better here than in shops, and hours are 9 a.m. to 6 p.m. Monday through Saturday during summer months, five days only the rest of the year. Across the road, there's a tearoom serving tea, coffee, and cookies in a thatched cottage. Take a look, while you're there, at the good buys at Moycullen Crafts and Antiques.

A much more memorable Connemara experience is the **coastal drive** from Galway to Clifden, which will add perhaps as much as three hours to your travel time, but will leave photographs upon your heart to be examined and re-examined for years to come.

Connemara: The drive I strongly urge you to take runs along the coast from Galway to **Spiddal, Inverin, Costelloe, Carraroe, Screeb, Derryrush, Kilkieran, Carna, Glinsk,** and **Ballynahinch** (where a ruined castle keep on an island in Ballynahinch Lake is said to be where the Martin clan imprisoned their enemy captives). At Ballynahinch, you can join the main Galway/Clifden road for a quick run into **Clifden,** or continue to meander around the coastline through **Roundstone, Ballyconneely,** and **Ballinaboy** (look for the signposted memorial to Alcock and Brown, who landed near here on the first transatlantic flight in 1919—it's on a high hill with magnificent panoramic views) before reaching Clifden. (In Ballyconneely, look for Mrs. Nonie Walsh's **West Coast Handcrafts** shop.) It's a journey through silence and largely unpopulated spaces, through a landscape made beautiful by incredibly shifting light and shade and the starkness of rock-strewn fields and hills. Glimpses of sandy strands at the sea's edge and the tiny villages that dot your route add another dimension to the experience.

Pleasures are simple in Connemara, most often associated with the natural rhythms of country life. For a glimpse of some of these, keep your eyes open as you travel through for **turf** being cut and dried in the boglands from April through June, and especially along the coastal road you may see donkeys with loaded creels transporting the dried turf to be stacked against the winter's cold. **Sheep shearing** is done by hand, often within the roofless walls of ruined cottages, and if you come across sheep being herded through the fields in June and July, they're probably on their way to be shorn. Between Ballyconneely and Kilkieran, you can sometimes watch **seaweed** being harvested (done at the full and new moons for four hours only in the middle of the day). **Thatchers** are usually at work in September and October, and the biggest concentration of thatched cottages is between Ballyconneely and Roundstone and between Cleggan and the Clifden road by way of Claddaghduff. At Roundstone and Cleggan, small trawlers **fish** year round, with open lobster boats and currachs setting out only in summer months. The **Connemara Pony Show** in Clifden is held in August and buyers come from around the world to bid on the sturdy little animals; the town takes on a country fair look, with much revelry, handcraft demonstrations, etc. Sometimes spontaneous, there are "flapper races," in which children race Connemara ponies while families gather for a great day of eating and drinking in the out-of-doors. Little villages all along the coast hold frequent curragh races, a splendid sight if you're lucky enough to come across one. As I said, finding the when and where of the above is a matter of keeping your eyes open—and of a well-placed inquiry over a pint at the local pub.

One thing you won't want to miss in Clifden is the spectacular **Sky Drive,** a cliff road that forms a nine-mile circle around a peninsula and opens up vast seascapes. It's well signposted from Clifden. Boats are also available (through most accommodations) for **deep-sea fishing** for mackerel, blue shark, conger, cod, ling and many other varieties. Summer evenings bring **traditional music** in many of Clifden's hotel bars and pubs; check with the Tourist Office or your accommodation hostess.

Millar's Connemara Tweeds (tel. Clifden 32) has long been a Clifden landmark, with shop shelves filled with beautifully colored pure-wool lengths produced by weavers in the locality. A whole raft of other Irish-made craft items—glass, pottery, and other items—complete the downstairs displays, and when you ascend iron spiral stairs, there's a gorgeous display of Connemara scenes depicted by Irish painters. In a stone-walled wing of the shop, you can browse through Irish fashions in a setting that includes a turf fire on the stone hearth and furnishings such as an old spinning wheel. Patchwork quilts are beautifully executed and much sought after, thus not always available. In short, this is a happy hunting ground for almost anything Irish-made. Hours are 9 a.m. to 6 p.m. every day except Sunday.

Clifden is also the setting for week-long sessions of the **Irish School of Landscape Painting,** founded and conducted by master painter Kenneth Webb, now assisted by his daughter, Susan. Individual instruction is given, with emphasis on techniques to catch the shimmering Connemara light shadings. You can attend for the day only by paying a tuition, IR£15 ($18) in 1984, or for the week, with accommodations and two meals a day thrown in, for IR£75 ($210)—1984 prices. For details on dates and 1985/86 costs, contact: Miss C. Cryan, Blue Door Studio, 16 Prince of Wales Terrace, Ballsbridge, Dublin 4 (tel. 01-685548).

Letterfrack is where **Kylemore Abbey** sits in a picture-post-card setting of woodlands on the banks of Pollacappal Lough, its impressive façade reflected by the lake's mirror surface. The stone mansion dates from the

19th century, and is home to an order of teaching nuns. They have established a thriving pottery industry, and they welcome visitors to visit the shop. There's a tearoom for refreshment, and you can stroll the lovely grounds to your heart's content.

Just outside Letterfrack, **Connemara Handcrafts** (tel. Letterfrack 6), is one of the best craft shops in the country. Its displays feature items you will see in few other places, and each craft is given its own display space. There's even a good selection of Irish publications and records. The shopping is good, whether you're looking for inexpensive souvenirs and gifts of good quality or pricier works of art, jewelry, or crystal, and they'll gladly ship any purchases, thus saving the VAT. Upstairs, a tearoom overlooks the garden, where light lunches are available in addition to tea and snacks (such as homemade buttered barm brack, the traditional Irish fruitcake). From mid-March to June, hours are 9:30 a.m. to 6 p.m. weekdays and Saturdays; during June, July, and August, closing time is 7 p.m., and Sunday hours are 11 a.m. to 6 p.m. Closed November to mid-March.

On the Leenane/Maam Bridge road, look for **Griggins Lodge/Maam Valley Pottery**, Maam Valley, Co. Galway (tel. 091-71109). The well-stocked shop features hand-loomed ties, hats, scarves, wool knitwear, and a host of other items, all produced within roughly a 20-mile area of the shop. The pottery workroom is open to visitors, and it is fascinating to see the potters throwing the items displayed on shop shelves. Dublin escapees Ann and Dennis Kendrick are the helpful owner/operators.

From Leenane, you can continue northward to Westport, or turn east for a drive along the shores of Lough Corrib to Cong, just over the County Mayo line.

County Mayo

There are several good reasons to turn towards Cong—the magnificent ruins of an Augustinian Abbey, Ashford Castle, and the fact that it was in this locale that most of the film classic *The Quiet Man* was filmed.

Cong, Ashford Castle, and *The Quiet Man*: Cong is a picturesque little village where, in a phenomenon known as "The Rising of the Waters," the waters of Lough Mask, which go underground three miles to the north, come rushing to the surface to surge through the center of town before they dissipate into several streams that empty into Lough Corrib. At the edge of town, the **Royal Abbey of Cong** was built by Turlough Mor O'Connor, High King of Ireland, in 1120 on the site of an earlier 7th-century St. Fechin community. Considered to be one of the finest early-Christian architectural relics in the country, it is also the final resting place of Rory O'Connor, the last High King, who was buried here in 1198. You'll find **Ashford Castle** just outside Cong on the shores of Lough Corrib. The oldest part of the castle was built by the de Burgoes, an Anglo-Norman family, in 1228, and its keep is now a part of the impressive, slightly eccentric Ashford Castle Hotel, which also incorporates a French-chateau-style mansion of the Oranmore and Browne families built in the early 1700s and the additions made by Sir Benjamin Guinness in the mid-1800s (undertaken as much to provide employment for famine-starved natives as to improve the property). It's a marvelous, fairyland sort of concoction that makes a superb luxury hotel favored by international celebrities (President and Mrs. Reagan stayed here during their 1984 visit). No less marvelous are its grounds, with beautifully landscaped lawns sloping down to the island-dotted lake. While its rates are definitely out of reach for budgeteers, not so for a stroll through its elegant public rooms with massive fireplaces and wall-high oil paintings, or a drink in the **Dungeon Bar.** Not a penny charged to soak in all that luxurious beauty!

Now, about *The Quiet Man:* Successive generations of Americans have loved Ireland as a direct result of John Wayne's, Maureen O'Hara's and Barry Fitzgerald's antics as they romped through this film that has become a classic. So, I've done a little research, and if you want to track down some of the locales, look for these. (Also, if you can get a good crack going in one of Cong's pubs, there's bound to be a local there who remembers the filming and has tales to tell, like how some scenes had to be reshot many times because the inquisitive head of a local "extra" would be seen peering out from a hedge in the background.) Many of the exterior shots were taken on the grounds of Ashford Castle—the woodlands, the church, Squire Danaher's house and the salmon river with its arched bridge. The main village street scenes took place near the cross in the market square of Cong, and the nearby general store was transformed into Cohan's Bar for the picture. Over in front of the abbey, that pretty house you see at the side of the bridge was the Rev. Playfair's house. Many other locales, such as John Wayne's ancestral cottage (now a ruin near Maam Bridge) were shot on the hillsides of the Maam Valley in Co. Galway, and the village of Inishfree as seen from a distance at the very beginning of the film is actually a shot of Clifden, taken from the Sky Road. There, that should get you started—and one simple comment in a Cong pub will carry you a long way in the footsteps of *The Quiet Man.*

Immediately east of Cong towards Cross lies the Plain of Moytura, where you'll find the **Ballymagibbon Cairn.** Dating from about 3,000 B.C., the 60-foot-high, 129-yard circumference cairn was erected to commemorate a fierce prehistoric battle between the Firbolg and de Danann tribes. It seems that the Firbolgs carried the day during the early fighting, and that first evening each presented a stone and the head of a Danann to his king, who used the stones to build the cairn in honor of the grisly tribute. On a happier note, nearby Moytura House (privately owned and not open to the public) was once the home of Sir William Wilde and his wife, Speranza, parents of Oscar Wilde.

Ballintubber Abbey: The route north from Cong to Castlebar passes through the little town of Partry, four miles north of which you will find Ballintubber Abbey. It is the only church in the English-speaking world with a 7½-century history of uninterrupted services. What makes this all the more remarkable is that Mass has been said within its walls since 1216 despite years of religious suppression, two burnings and the assault of Cromwellian troops. At times during those centuries, it was necessary for supplicants to kneel before the altar in secret and under open skies when there was no roof. That it has now been completely restored is due almost solely to the devoted efforts of its pastor, Father Egan, who labored from 1963 to 1966 to push the project forward. The Abbey's doors are open every day and visitors are welcomed.

Knock: Twenty-five miles southeast of **Castlebar,** the little church in the village of Knock has become a shrine to which thousands of pilgrims come each year, for it was here that there were a number of apparitions during the 19th century.

Croagh Patrick and Westport: If your northward route from Connemara heads directly for Westport, I suggest you take the road that passes through stony, barren hillsides to **Louisburgh,** where **Clew Bay** opens before you. Between Louisburgh and Westport, the drive touches the Bay at several points, and on the other side of the road rises 2,510-feet-high Croagh Patrick, where St. Patrick is believed to have fasted for 40 days and modern-day pilgrims climb the stony paths in their bare feet in July for a 4 a.m. Mass at its top.

Westport House (tel. 098-25141) dates back to 1731, but it sits on the grounds of an earlier O'Malley castle, the dungeons of which are now visited by children who are happily "terrified" by the terrors that have been installed for their entertainment. The lovely old Georgian mansion house is a vitual museum of Irish memorabilia and craftsmanship, with a magnificent drawing room, two dining rooms (one large, one small), a long gallery, and a grand entrance hall. Up the marble staircase, four bedrooms hold such treasures as state robes and coronets and 200-year-old Chinese wallpaper.

Lord and Lady Altamont and their five daughters are in residence here, and over the years they have turned their estate into a stylish visitor attraction as a means of maintaining such an expensive operation. A full dozen shops feature quality Irish products, heraldic items, historic Irish scrolls, Irish art, fashion, gifts, and antiques. On the grounds, there's a marvelous children's zoo, a playground, tearoom, and boating and fishing on a lake and a river. **Connemara Horse Caravans** operate from the old stone stables, and there are self-catering holiday homes for rent, some right on the estate grounds. You can pick up a brochure detailing all these enterprises, or get one in advance by writing: Westport House Country Estate, Westport, Co. Mayo.

From mid-May to mid-September, the house and grounds are open daily from 2 to 5 p.m., with extended hours of 10:30 a.m. to 6 p.m. during June, July, and August. Adults pay IR£3 ($3.60) to visit the house only, an extra IR£1 ($1.20) to include the grounds; admission for children is IR£1 ($1.20) for the house and the same for the grounds. Parents who bring along more than two children are charged only for the first two—the others are admitted free.

Achill Island: Achill is Ireland's largest island, and its 57 square miles are connected to the mainland by a causeway that takes you into breathtakingly beautiful, unspoiled, and varied scenery. High cliffs overlook tiny villages of whitewashed cottages, golden beaches, and heathery boglands. The signposted **Atlantic Drive** is spectacular, and will whet your appetite to explore more of the island's well-surfaced roadways. This is a wild and at the same time profoundly peaceful place, peopled by friendly, hardy natives who welcome visitors warmly. In late May, the entire island is covered by such a profusion of rhododendrons that my bed-and-breakfast landlady smilingly told me, "every car that leaves will be loaded with those blooms, and we won't even miss them!" Achill has long been a favorite holiday spot for the Irish in other parts of the country, and there are good accommodations available in most of the beach villages. If time permits, I highly recommend an overnight stay on Achill (in summer, there's traditional music in many of the pubs), but if you can only spare a part of a day, this is one off-the-beaten-track place you really shouldn't miss.

READERS' SELECTIONS: "The **Belmullet Peninsula** and the **Inishkea Islands,** only 2½ miles off Co. Mayo's coast, are well worth a visit because of their wild beauty and fascinating history" (William Moynihan, Nashville, Tenn.). . . . "Angela Coen, of the **Spinning Wheel** shop in Gort, Co. Galway, is delightful, and her shop is excellent" (Margaret DeCamp, Flourtown, Pa.).

Chapter IX

SLIGO, DONEGAL, AND THE NORTHWEST

1. Introducing the Northwest
2. Sligo Town and Yeats Country
3. Donegal Town
4. Around Counties Sligo, Donegal, and Leitrim

THE NORTHWEST HOLDS SOME OF IRELAND'S most wondrous scenery—the sort of sea and mountains and far-flung vistas that shaped the poet Yeats's life and work. His words about this mystical, magical part of Ireland cannot, of course, be bested, and you will find yourself recalling them again and again as you travel the Northwest.

1. Introducing the Northwest

The three counties of the Northwestern region—Sligo, Donegal, and Leitrim—hold such a diversity of landscape wonders that an entire holiday could easily be spent within their boundaries.

It was County Sligo that nurtured Yeats, from boyhood stays in Magheraboy with his grandparents to the end of his life, when he was laid to rest in Drumcliffe Churchyard. His imagination was fired by local legends of ancient heroes and heroines who lived out their sagas in this part of Ireland and left the countryside strewn with mementos of their passing. Beautiful Lough Gill is where you'll find his *Isle of Inisfree,* and at Knocknarea's summit is the cairn where according to legend (and Yeats) "passionate Maeve is stony-still." All through the county are countless other cairns, dolmens, passage graves, and other prehistoric relics, bearing silent witness to the lives that so engaged the poet. Along the western part of the county are the Ox Mountains; the north holds high, flat-topped limestone hills like Benbulben; and for the pleasure-bent traveler, there's a fine beach at Strandhill, a golf course at Rosses Point, and good fishing in any number of rivers and lakes.

County Donegal sits at the very top of Ireland, its jagged coastline ringed by wide strands backed by steep cliffs, its inland mountains cut by deep valleys, and its countryside filled with antiquities and legends. In the rhythmic patterns of Donegal speech can be heard the distinctive cadence of

Ulster, and from Donegal cottages come some of the world's most beautiful hand-woven woolens. It is a county of vast uninhabited stretches, natives as rugged as the landscape in which they live, and an ancient culture kept alive in music, song and story.

Long and narrow, County Leitrim is split down the middle by Lough Allen, an extension of the Shannon. North of the lake, tall mountains stretch to the borders of County Sligo, while to the south, the countryside is dotted with lovely lakes. In Lough Scur, there are remnants of prehistoric lake dwellings, called crannogs. The harbor at Carrick-on-Shannon is alive with cruisers, and there's good fishing both here and in nearby lakes.

2. Sligo Town and Yeats Country

Sligo (*Sligeach,* "Shelly Place") grew up around a ford of the River Garavogue, which rises in Lough Gill and tumbles over swift rapids as it approaches its estuary. The town's strategic position gave it early prominence as a seaport, and as a religious center, it is the cathedral town of both a Catholic and Protestant diocese. For Yeats devotees and scholars, it offers a wealth of information and memorabilia, and all visitors will find a friendly welcome and accommodations that are friendly to the budget.

ORIENTATION: Sligo sits astraddle the **River Garavogue,** and the **Stephen Street Bridge** is a central point of reference. **O'Connell Street** runs south of the bridge and holds the major shopping and business district of the town. The beach resort of **Strandhill** is five miles to the west, **Rosses Point** five miles to the north, and there are several buses a day to each from the main bus station. **Magheraboy,** where Yeats spent many childhood summers, is a short distance from town to the southwest, and **Drumcliffe Churchyard** is five miles north of town.

USEFUL INFORMATION: You'll find the **Tourist Office** one block east of the Stephen Street bridge in Temple Street (tel. 071-61201), open 9 a.m. to 6 p.m. daily in summer. . . . The **bus and railway station** is just above Lord Edward Street on the western edge of town. For all **CIE information,** call 2151. . . . For **taxi** service, call 2596 or 3740; there's a taxi rank at the train station. There are preset fares to most points of interest, and cabs are not metered, so be sure to ask the fare. . . . The **General Post Office** is in Wine Street, west of the bridge, with hours of 9 a.m. to 5:30 p.m. weekdays, closed Sundays. . . . Most **shops** close all day on Monday. . . . The *Sligo Champion* carries notices of current goings on in town and the area. . . . The **telephone prefix** for Sligo is 071.

ACCOMMODATIONS: Accommodations listed here are in and around Sligo Town, all convenient bases for exploring Yeats Country.
Note: Prices shown below are those in effect in 1985—expect them to be higher in 1986.

Hostels: There is only one **hostel** in County Sligo—see Section 4 of this chapter for details.

Based on the Ordnance Survey by permission of the Government of Ireland (Permit No. 906)

KEY TO THE NUMBERED REFERENCES ON OUR MAP OF SLIGO: 1—Railway Station; 2—Gen. Post Office; 3—Town Hall; 4—Technical School; 5—Garda Station; 6—Courthouse & County Council Offices; 7—Sligo Abbey; 8—Catholic Cathedral; 9—Church of Ireland Cathedral; 10—Calry Church and Grammar School; 11—Presbyterian Church; 12—Dominican Church; 13—Methodist Church; 14—Tourist Office, County Library and Museum; 15 —Swimming Pool.

Bed-and-Breakfast: Near the railway and bus station, **Renate House,** Upper John St. (tel. 071-3014), is a small gabled house you'll recognize by its colorful windowbox blooms. Mrs. Hunt has five attractive guestrooms, all with hand basins, and she takes a personal interest in her guests. There's a pretty dining room, and color TV in the drawing room. Rates are IR£9 ($10.80), with 20% reduction for children. Central heating.

Mrs. Mary Whooley's **Ardenode,** Cartron Hill, Rosses Point Rd., Sligo (tel. 071-3570), is a sparkling bright two-story house filled with flowers from the pretty gardens outside. Decor in the five guestrooms includes bed-spreads and drapes that match floral wallpaper, and all have hand basins, built-in wardrobes, and full-length mirrors. The L-shaped dining room opens onto a pleasant patio out back. The centrally heated house is located in a peaceful cul-de-sac, and the widowed Mrs. Whooley and her three lovely children make guests feel right at home. Rates for bed-and-breakfast are IR£9 ($10.80), with a 20% discount for children.

Rathnashee (it means "Fort of the Fairies"), Donegal Rd. (tel. 071-3376), is the home of Tess and Sean Haughey, and it's the kind of place where guests often wind up sitting around the kitchen table for long conversations in which the Haugheys share their extensive knowledge of what to see in Sligo. They also have one of the best private libraries in Sligo, with all types of literature and poetry. The centrally heated modern bungalow is about two miles out from town, and there are four nice bedrooms, all with hand basins, and two with private bath and shower. B&B rates are IR£9 ($10.80), and there's good parking off the road.

Just off the Dublin/Galway road, **Aisling**, Cairns Hill, Sligo (tel. 071-5404), is a centrally heated modern bungalow overlooking Benbulben and Knocknare. The four guestrooms have hand basins and electric blankets. Mrs. Nan Faul is the charming hostess. Rates for bed-and-breakfast are IR£8.50 ($10.20).

Mrs. Nellie Cogan gives guests a warm welcome at **Mountain View,** Upper Pearse Rd. (tel. 071-3731). All four guestrooms have lovely views of Knocknarea and Benbulben, and the sea is only ten minutes away. Mrs. Cogan often ends the day over an evening cuppa and friendly chat with guests, giving helpful suggestions on where to go and what to do so that visitors won't miss out on anything in the area. Rates for B&B are IR£8 ($9.60).

Guesthouse: Fatima, 47 John St. (tel. 071-2463), is conveniently located within walking distance of the heart of Sligo Town. Mrs. Theresa Beirne has seven comfortable bedrooms, and provides off-street parking for guests. No evening meal is served, but good restaurants are just around the corner. Bed-and-breakfast rates are IR£9 ($10.80), with one-third off for children.

Farmhouses: Primrose Grange, Knocknarea, Sligo (tel. 071-62005), is the delightful home of Maisie and Ed Carter and their lovely children. Running the 1723 farmhouse as a guesthouse is very much a family affair, and the Carters make each guest feel like "family." The interesting old house served as the Sligo Grammar School until 1903, and there are now eight nicely decorated guestrooms, all with heat and hand basins. Maisie's meals are superb and served in a large, handsome dining room. Log fires are a regular occurrence in the equally large drawing room. The setting is gorgeous, some 350 feet up the southern side of Knocknarea Mountain, with views of Ballisodare Bay and marvelous walks just outside the front door (including one to the Neolithic-age passage grave that legend claims is Queen Maeve's last resting place). Rates for bed-and-breakfast are IR£10 ($12), with a 20% reduction for children. The marvelous dinners also are IR£10 ($12), and wine is available. Highly recommended.

Some seven miles from Sligo, **Castle Dargan House**, Ballygawley, Collooney, Co. Sligo (tel. 071-67127), sits on 200 acres of farmland. The comfortable old two-story house is covered with ivy out front, and the four guestrooms all come with hand basins and tiled fireplaces. The shower (which works very well, thank you) is the product of a bygone day and a real curiosity! Antiques are mixed with more modern pieces in the lounge, where an open log fire burns on chilly evenings. There's a large goldfish pond on the two acres of garden, and in addition to lawn tennis, coarse fishing is permitted in the farm's lake. The house has partial central heating. Both Mr. and Mrs. Hosie know the area well and their warm hospitality extends to helpful advice on sightseeing. Rates are IR£12 ($14) for bed-and-breakfast, with 25% off for children. Home-cooked dinners are also IR£12 ($14). Open Easter to October.

READERS' SELECTIONS: "**Westway** is a farmhouse accommodation run by Mrs. Mary McDonagh (tel. 071-73178) just outside Sligo. From the dining room of her spotless modern home, you can see the church steeple at Drumcliffe, where Yeats is buried, and our bedroom on the other side of the house had a gorgeous view of Benbulben. The warmth and generosity Mrs. McDonagh bestows on her guests are remarkable, even for the west of Ireland" (John Gormley, Baltimore, Md.). . . . "**Carrowkeel House** (tel. 071-2432) is a fairly new farmhouse about two miles from Sligo. Mrs. Hunter cannot be praised enough for her true Irish hospitality that makes one feel a part of the family" (Mrs. Gerti Elling, Mannheim, Germany). . . . "Mrs. Kearney, whose farmhouse **Avondale-Breeogue**, Knocknahur (tel. 071-78192), is four miles from Sligo, is a charming, thoughtful hostess, and her rooms are clean and very modern" (Mrs. John Rothwell, Rolling Hills, Calif.). . . . "Mrs. Rita Monaghan, at **Cedarville**, Mail Coach Rd. off Pearse Rd. (tel. 071-3080), won a major bread baking championship, and her spotless guesthouse is very homey and comfortable. She is one of the friendliest and kindest people I've ever met" (Mary Raleigh, Limerick, Ireland). . . . "I would like to recommend **Cillard** farmhouse, run by Mrs. Dillon (tel. 071-78201), for outstanding hospitality and the best breakfast we had on our trip. It is located in Carrowmore, only a five-minute walk from Sligo Riding Centre" (Sharlin McCabe, Houston, Tex.).

WHERE TO EAT: There are picnic tables scattered throughout lovely **Dooney Wood,** some four miles outside Sligo. Beside the car park, flat-topped Dooney Rock is where Yeats wrote of the fiddler playing. There are also car parks and picnic tables at **Carns,** setting of many cairns and giants' graves, a mile and a half from Sligo out the Holywell road, as well as **Deerpark,** on the old road to Manorhamilton.

Kate's Kitchen, 24 Market St. (tel. 3022), is a small delicatessen-cum-restaurant, with prices around IR£5 ($6) for a full meal. Hours are 9:30 a.m. to 6 p.m. every day but Sundays and bank holidays.

Bonne Chere, 45 High St. (tel. 2014), has been a favorite of Sligo families for years. It's a large room, with exposed beams and white arches, made cheerful by paintings of Yeats Country and potted plants. The menu features good, plain cooking, and there's a children's menu and a Tourist Menu. Prices run about IR£4 ($4.80) at lunch, around IR£8 ($9.60) at dinner. Hours are 12:30 to 3 p.m., with an à la carte menu from 3 to 10:30 p.m.

Beezies, 45 O'Connell St. (tel. 3031), is worth a visit, if only for a drink or a look around. The turn-of-the-century marble front bar, bar partitions of Tiffany glass and lamps with tulip-shaped shades, give a marvelous old-timey look to the place. In back, there are two large rooms in which inexpensive hot lunches are served.

Four miles southwest of Sligo, under Knocknarea, **Coolera House Pub-Restaurant** (tel. 68204/68177) serves an à la carte menu from 6:30 to 10 p.m., and a satisfying dinner should run no more than IR£8 ($9.60). During summer months, there's traditional music weeknights, dancing on Saturdays.

Big Splurge: Charles and Mary Cooper have, since 1978, built a reputation for their **Knockmuldowney Restaurant,** Glen Lodge, Culleenamore, Co. Sligo (tel. 68122), as one of Ireland's finest restaurants. Located five miles from Sligo Town at the foot of Knocknarea, the restaurant is in a Georgian country house in the midst of a small estate and lovely gardens. As much as possible, the Coopers use vegetables and fruits grown on their own grounds, and from neighboring farms they gather the freshest lamb, poultry, pork, beef, and game. Salmon, sea trout and other seafood come from the local Ballisodare fishery, some of which they smoke right at Knockmuldowney. The list of awards won by their outstanding creations is as long as your arm, and especially in summer months, advance booking is absolutely necessary. Needless to say, the atmosphere is one of relaxed elegance, and the table d'hôte dinner price of IR£10.50 ($12.60) makes this a Big Splurge for budgeteers and is extremely good value for the money. Hours are 7:30 to 10 p.m., Tuesday through Saturday. This restaurant has my highest recommendation.

(To reach Knockmuldowney, take the Sligo/Strandhill road and at Strandhill continue two and a half miles more on the Ballisodare road, where it's signposted.)

THINGS TO SEE AND DO: While many visitors come to Sligo and head straight out to those spots associated with Yeats, it would be a mistake not to see the highlights of the old town itself.

Sligo Town

To get the most out of a stay in Sligo Town, join one of the **walking tours** conducted without charge during July and August by young student guides who love the town and are intimately acquainted with such points of interest as St. John's Church, which was designed by the same architect as Leinster house, the seat of the Irish government in Dublin. Tours leave the Tourist Office at 11 a.m. and last an hour and fifteen minutes. (**Author's suggestion:** While there's no charge, it's perfectly in order to tip your enthusiastic young guide a minimum of IR£1 ($1.20). The Tourist Office also has an excellent booklet that outlines a signposted *Tourist Trail* do-it-yourself walking tour (a nice souvenir, even if you go along with the guided tour).

In Stephen Street, there's a good collection of Yeats' writings and unpublished letters in the **Yeats Memorial Museum,** which is part of the **Sligo County Museum.** The poet's Nobel Prize is also on display.

Sligo has always intrigued painters quite as much as writers, and the *poet* Yeats had no family monopoly on fascination with this countryside—his *painter* brother, Jack Yeats, sought to capture it on canvas. There's an excellent exhibition of his work in a gallery at the **Sligo Library.**

From the pier at the end of Doorly Park on the eastern side of town, **Gerry Sweeney** debarks for two-and-a-half-hour motorboat cruises of Lough Gill aboard the *Queen Maeve.* Gerry is quite a storyteller, and as the unofficial "Seannacaidhe of Lough Gill" will give you a full rundown on Dooney Rock, Innisfree, and Church and Cottage Islands as you pass them, plus a lot more on the folklore of the region. Tours leave the pier at noon and 3:30 p.m. during July and August, and the fare is IR£4 ($4.80). For detailed information and booking, call 2540. If you'd like to go out on the lake on your own, boats are available from **Peter Henry** at the pier (tel. 2530).

Rental bikes are available from **W. A. & A. F. Woods,** in Castle St. (tel.

2021); **Conway Bros.,** Wine St. (tel. 61240); and **Double R. Cycle Centre,** High St. (tel. 3536).

The local Irish Countrywoman's Association has rescued and restored **Dolly's Cottage,** in Strandhill, the last thatched house in Sligo. Dolly was a well-loved resident of the area, and now you can visit her home from 3 to 5 p.m. weekdays to see the dresser with its delph collection, a pouch bed with its patchwork quilt, spinning wheel and other authentic period furnishings. Handcrafted knit, wool, and leather items are on sale, as are sheepskin rugs and pottery. During summer months, country markets are held every Wednesday afternoon.

One of the most delightful ways I can think of to visit the beaches, Benbulben, Lissadell House, etc., is via horse and trap, and the **Moneygold Trekking and Horse Driving Centre,** Grange, Co. Sligo (tel. 071-63008), can arrange it for you. They also have a variety of other horse-related activities, such as pony trekking, fast beach rides, and weekly gymkhanas.

Yeats Country

One of the best ways to get an overall feeling for the country that so stirred the poet's soul is to take CIE's **Yeats Country Tour,** conducted on specific days during summer months. It's a nearly four-hour trip, with a very good commentary, and the low fare (about IR£4—$4.80) includes a visit to **Lissadell House,** where Countess Mankievicz (an important figure in the 1916 uprising) spent much of her childhood.

If you're rambling through Yeats Country on your own (which you might want to do even after taking the above conducted tour), go by the Tourist Office or a Sligo bookshop and pick up the excellent booklet *The Yeats Country,* which tells you which poems were written about which places. You'll also find those places associated with the great poet marked by simple signposts inscribed with the appropriate verses. One suggested route is to drive east along Lough Gill's northern shore to the **Holy Well,** a grotto where devout Catholics met during the years of the penal laws to celebrate Mass in secret. Its stone altar is more than 300 years old. Look out over the lake to the southeast and the small *Lake Isle of Innisfree.* From there, drive to **Glencar Lake** and leave your car to walk across the fields to **Glencar Falls,** where there are steps built up the left side of what Yeats called "pools among the rushes." As you return across the field, you can glimpse the little thatched cottage where Yeats called in for tea quite often as a young man. Just before you reach Sligo's town limits, you'll see the turnoff for **Drumcliffe** to the north. This is where Yeats lies "Under bare Benbulben's head," and his headstone bears the epitaph he composed for himself,

> Cast a cold eye
> On life, on death.
> Horseman, pass by!

Prehistoric Sligo

Scattered over the face of County Sligo are traces of the **prehistoric races** who lived here during three main periods: the Late Stone Age (Neolithic), 2500 to 2000 B.C.); the Bronze Age (2000 to 500 B.C.); and the Early Iron Age (500 B.C. to A.D. 500). The Tourist Office has a marvelously detailed leaflet, *Prehistoric Sligo,* that tells you where to find the most important of these court cairns, portal dolmens, passage graves, ring forts, and gallery graves. In the immediate vicinity of Sligo Town, you'll find **Carrowmore** (south of town near Ballysodare), a cemetery of about 65 megalithic tombs—one of the largest concentrations in Europe—in a one-mile-long, half-mile-wide area. And at the top of Knocknarea, there's the great **Misgaun Maeve,** an unopened cairn some 200 feet in diameter and about 80 feet high that archeologists believe covers a vast passage grave, but legend insists is the burial monument to Queen Maeve.

READER'S SUGGESTION: "Seven miles south of Sligo on road N4 is the **Innisfree Hand Cut Crystal** factory (at the bridge). This crystal is similar to Waterford, but about 40% cheaper and they specialize in limited editions. They also ship anywhere" (Charles Burgh, Pittsburgh, Pa.).

SLIGO AFTER DARK: It's fairly easy to find traditional music and ballads in Sligo pubs and those nearby. However, since the "schedule" for such happenings is often a *non*-schedule, best check with the Tourist Office when you're there about days of the week the following are likely to have music. Even if there's no music, you can bet on good conversation any night of the week in any of these pubs, and who knows *where* that could lead!

From time to time, the **Sancta Maria Hotel** in Strandhill (tel. 071-78113) has a "Gaelic Night," and when that happens, natives from all around flock to the hotel in the sure knowledge there'll be good musicians on hand and a lot of singing and reciting of poetry. Brush up on your own party piece and go along if you happen on one of these very special evenings (call the hotel or check with the Tourist Board—Thursdays used to be the nights for music, but it changes).

C.C.E. usually holds sessions on Tuesday nights at the **United Trade's Club** in Castle Street.

McLynn's Pub in Old Market Street frequently breaks out in song, almost always led by Donal McLynn, who carries on a tradition set by his late grandmother, who ran the pub for more than 30 years (the Ogham plaque by the doorway spells out "Granny" in the ancient script in her memory). The pub has the comfortable look of age, with a big hearth and lots of copper and old bar mirrors. The crowd tends to be on the young side, and you can usually count on ballads on Thursdays.

Another gathering place where the young come to mingle with farmers from the surrounding countryside as traditional music is passed from one generation to the next is **The Thatch,** in Ballisodare. The small cottage pub has a huge fireplace and church-pew seats in one of its two rooms, and kitchen furnishings in the other. There's usually music on Thursdays.

On the bridge at Drumcliffe, **The Yeats Tavern** has nightly musical goings on all year in a very popular, modern setting. It's out the Dublin road, about five miles from town.

At Rosses Point, **Bruen's Pub** (known locally as **"Austin Gillen's"**) is as nautical as Austin himself, filled with ship models, charts, and all sorts of other items related to the sea. Austin has a story to go with every one, and is a great one for the crack if you get him going.

Ellens, in Maugherow, dates back to the 1600s and is all you've ever thought a traditional Irish pub *should* be—music is on from time to time.

Not for music, but for a uniquely traditional Irish "local," where the crack is good and your company welcomed, is **Hargedon's** in O'Connell Street. It's over two centuries old and looks it, but as authentic as they come.

SPECIAL EVENTS: For two weeks every August (August 10–24, 1985) there's a glut activity in Sligo centered around the works of William Butler Yeats. That's when the **Yeats International Summer School** holds seminars, lectures, workshops, poetry readings, and drama for dedicated Yeats scholars. Afternoon tours are conducted, and evenings are filled with social and theatrical events. In 1984, tuition was IR£180 ($216), and the staff will help you find inexpensive accommodations. For full details, a brochure and application, write: Secretary, Yeats Society Inc., Hyde Bridge, Sligo, Ireland (tel. 071-2693).

If you happen into Sligo while the summer school is in session, you can attend many of the events by buying individual tickets.

The week following Easter is dedicated to the **Feiseanna,** with competitions in traditional music, dancing, singing, plays, and all sorts of other activities. It draws the Irish from all over the country, and the town is alive with festivities day and night.

3. Donegal Town

Where other Irish towns have a square right in the middle of town, Donegal (*Dun na nGall,* "the Fort of the Foreigners") has a wide triangular space they call The Diamond. It's the meeting place of three major roadways from Derry, west Donegal, and Sligo, and it points up Donegal Town's strategic location at the head of Donegal Bay and the mouth of the River Eske, a position of such importance that in ancient times the princes of Tir Chonaill (the O'Donnells) made this their chief seat. Red Hugh O'Donnell founded a Franciscan friary here in 1474, and when it was sacked in the 1600s and the monks were sent scurrying in fear of their lives, four went to Bundrowes for safety and set about compiling the scholarly *Annals of the Four Masters,* one of Ireland's most valuable sources of early church history. In The Diamond stands a 25-foot-high obelisk, inscribed with the names of the four monks at its base.

Today, Donegal Town is a friendly, thriving market town, famed for its woolens and as a touring base for the rest of this wildly beautiful county.

USEFUL INFORMATION: The **Tourist Office** is in Quay St. (tel. 073-21147), open May through September with hours of 10 a.m. to 6 p.m. . . . There's a bus pickup station on The Diamond for **CIE buses** with regular service to Derry, Dublin, Galway, Killybegs, Portnoo, and Belfast. . . . The **Post Office** is in Tir Conaill St. . . . Doherty's in Main Street has **bicycles** for rent. . . . **Shops** close early on Wednesdays. . . . Check with the Tourist Office for what's going on when you're in Donegal. The **telephone prefix** for Donegal is 073.

ACCOMMODATIONS: *Remember, prices listed below are those in effect in 1985 —expect them to be higher in 1986.*

Hostel: There's an excellent **hostel**—a former coastguard station—three miles outside Donegal Town (tel. Donegal 174).

Bed-and-Breakfast: Riverside House, Waterloo Place (tel. 073-21083), is just across the River Eske from Donegal Castle on a quiet residential terrace. The center of town is a quick walk away. Mrs. Kathleen Curristan and her pretty teenage daughter Eileen welcome guests here and have decorated the five nice guestrooms in cheerful colors. All have hand basins, and there's one large family room with a double and two twin beds. Even the bathroom is bright, with matching floral wallpaper and shower curtains. The lounge frames the river and castle view through wide front windows, and its piano is often in use by guests as well as the Curristans. Bed-and-breakfast rates are IR£8 ($9.60), with a 20% reduction for children, and Kathleen can furnish a good high tea for IR£6 ($7.20).

In a secluded woodland setting, Mrs. Pearl Timony's **Drumcliffe House,** Coast Rd., Donegal Town (tel. 073-21200), is a lovely old home that dates back some 300 years. Both the house and its antique furnishings are interesting, and meals feature Mrs. Timony's home baking. The four attractive guestrooms all have hand basins, and the house is centrally heated. Rates for bed and breakfast are IR£8.50 ($10.20).

Five miles outside Donegal Town, **Ardeevin,** Lough Eske, Barnesmore, Donegal (tel. 073-21790), sits on a rise overlooking Lough Eske and the Bluestack Mountains. There are four nice guestrooms, all with hand basins, and two have private bath with shower. Mrs. Mary McGinty is the charming hostess of the centrally heated dormer bungalow. B&B rates are IR£8.50 ($10.20), with a 20% reduction for children. Open April through October.

Hotel: You might have to call the **Hyland Central Hotel,** The Diamond (tel. 073-21027), a "Mini-Splurge"—it is a bit above our budget but has so much to recommend it represents the best rule of all budgeteering: value for money. This immaculately clean, family-run hotel is that rare combination of modern facilities with an old-fashioned, homey atmosphere. The dining room, overlooking the river, is lovely and serves moderate-priced meals (see "Where to Eat"). Rooms here are spacious and have a light, airy look and comfortable modern furnishings. All have private baths and color TV, and for a gorgeous view of Donegal Bay, ask for one on the back (the view in front is of The Diamond). Seasonal rates range from IR£17.50 ($21) to IR£22 ($26.40).

WHERE TO EAT: The best budget meals are at the **Hyland Central Hotel** on The Diamond (see above). There's an excellent lunch special (hot meat and vegetables and ample portions) at just IR£2.70 ($3.24) served in the comfortable lounge, and in the evening, a mini-dinner menu is priced at IR£6.50 ($7.80) and there's a full dinner menu that runs about IR£11 ($13.20). Evening meals are in the cream-colored dining room, which has wide windows along one wall, lots of dark wood trim and softly lighted, gold-framed oil paintings hung about.

Not much else to choose from, although there are scads of coffeeshops around The Diamond, all much the same except for decor.

THINGS TO SEE AND DO: Take a look at **Donegal Castle,** whose west tower dates from 1505, when Red Hugh O'Donnell rebuilt an earlier castle on the site and made this the chief O'Donnell stronghold. The rest was added by Sir

Basil Brooke in 1607 and features a mammoth Jacobean fireplace and windows and gables in the handsome house he built around the old tower. Tip your hat to the Four Masters Memorial, then examine the large mounted anchor by the bay—it's from a French ship, perhaps one of those bringing troops to fight with Wolfe Tone in 1798, and was salvaged from the sea by fishermen in the mid-1800s. South of town at the river's estuary, there are the interesting, but slight ruins of **Donegal Abbey.** Lough Eske is roughly five miles northeast of Donegal Town, with wooded shores and a backing of mountains.

Magee of Donegal, on The Diamond, is world-famous for its handwoven Donegal Tweed, and there's a weaving demonstration right in the store. Tours to the factory are organized from time to time, and you can inquire at the store for specific dates and hours. The store has a wide selection of quality clothing for men and women and a good variety of linens, knitwear, and other Irish products.

Another excellent place for tweeds is **Kathleen's,** in Manhattan Shopping Arcade. This is a branch of Kathleen Alcock's small **Mountcharles** shop that has been so popular with our readers for many years, and she carries hand-knits, mohair, and Irish linen items as well as a good stock of Belleek, Royal Tara, Waterford, and Cavan crystal, Connemara marble, and lovely hand-crocheted separates. As for tweeds, upstairs you'll find all the popular design names plus a line Kathleen designs and selects the tweeds for personally (they're shown under the "Combre" name), all outstanding styles. Kathleen worked in the States for a time and especially welcomes Americans to her two shops. She has an excellent mail service and accepts most major credit cards.

DONEGAL AFTER DARK: The St. John Bosco Centre has Bingo every Wednesday night and dancing some other evenings during summer months. Traditional music is on frequently at the **Talk of the Town** lounge. And Donegal has some good pubs, many of which have a "country" air about them, with the usual group of devoted regulars who'll be glad to welcome visiting Yanks.

4. Around Counties Sligo, Donegal, and Leitrim

ACCOMMODATIONS: *Remember, prices shown below are those in effect in 1985—expect them to be higher in 1986.*

County Sligo

Hostel: The only An Oige hostel in County Sligo is at the **E Vocational School,** Easkey (tel. Easkey 21). It is 26 miles from Sligo, 18 miles from Ballina, and is open only July and August.

Bed-and-Breakfast: Mrs. Mazie Rooney's modern bungalow, **Castletown House,** Drumcliffe, Co. Sligo (tel. 071-73204), is just off N15 Donegal road and is ideal for touring Yeats Country. The three bedrooms are comfortably furnished and all have hand basins, one has a private bath with shower. Bed-and-breakfast rates are IR£8 ($9.80), with a 30% reduction for children. Open March through October. Central heating.

To find **Sea Cove,** Kellystown, Knocknahur, Co. Sligo (tel. 071-78103), you follow neat, bright-blue signs off the Sligo–Strandhill main road. The winding little road goes all the way to the edge of Sligo Bay, then turns sharply to the right and follows the shoreline until you reach Sea Cove, which perches on a slight hill. The modern bungalow that looks out to the bay in front and Knocknarea in the back is the home of Mary and Vincent Banks, an attractive young couple who make guests feel right at home (the same sort of welcome is extended by Sam, the gorgeous family collie). There are wide picture windows in the lounge, the dining room and all four guestrooms so you may enjoy all those lovely views. Guestrooms are comfortably furnished and all have hand basins. Sea Cove is a bit isolated, but is so awash in scenic beauty and serene peacefulness that I find it soul-restoring. Rates are IR£8 ($9.60), and evening meals often feature fresh local salmon at only IR£5 ($6).

Two miles from Grange, Mrs. Mary Cadden welcomes you to **Cloonaghbawn,** Ballinful, Co. Sligo (tel. 071-73205). Set in a quiet, scenic location near Lissadell House and Ellen's Pub (traditional music), the centrally heated white bungalow has three nice guestrooms with hand basins. Rates are IR£8.50 ($10.20), with a 40% discount for children. Open April through October.

Our mail has been full of praise for Mrs. Maeve Walsh and her modern, centrally heated **Cruckawn,** Ballymote Rd., Tubbercurry, Co. Sligo (tel. 071-85188). Many readers write that they have returned to Cruckawn because of Mrs. Walsh's friendliness and helpfulness, and you'll understand why after staying in her relaxed, comfortable home. The two-story house is nicely decorated and has good views of the Ox Mountains. It sits on its own grounds, with a large garden and paved car park. Meals are superb, and there's a wine license. Guestrooms have built-in, bookshelf headboards and hand basins. Rates are IR£8.50 ($10.20), with a one-third discount for children.

Hotels: Out in Strandhill, the **Sancta Maria Hotel,** Strandhill, Co. Sligo (tel. 071-68113), is a small, old-fashioned country inn, with the sort of comfortable, homey air that only comes from caring hosts like Brigid and Nace O'Dowd. The attention at the Sancta Maria is very personal, and the O'Dowds will happily help you plan your travels around the area, fill you in on local stories to embellish your journey, and otherwise make your stay pure pleasure. The nine guestrooms are comfortably furnished, with built-in closets and hand basins, and there's central heating. The O'Dowds plan Gaelic Nights through the summer months, when there's always a complement of nearby locals to join in the singing and dancing. The hotel is also fully licensed. All in all, it's a pleasant, relaxed "home from home," not at all hotel-like! Seasonal rates range from IR£9 ($10.80) to IR£9.50 ($11.40) plus 10% service, with a 10% reduction for children. Open May through December.

The **Ocean View Hotel,** Strandhill, Co. Sligo (tel. 071-68115), is a gracious old house with a new extension. Knocknarea is at its back, the Atlantic at its front. Its lounge, large lounge bar, and lovely dining room are all nicely appointed, as are the eleven guestrooms, three of which have private baths. All are centrally heated and all have shaver points. Most look out to marvelous views. The Ocean View is run by Jean and Shay Burke, and Jean stars in the kitchen, using local produce, fish and shellfish to present fine meals. Rates range from IR£10.50 ($12.60) to IR£13.50

($16.20), and the private baths cost extra. There's a 25% reduction for children.

County Donegal

Hostels: There are several An Oige hostels around County Donegal, ranging from simple accommodations to superior facilities. Between Killybegs and Ardara, basic facilities are at **The Red House,** Carrick, Co. Donegal (no telephone); five miles from Dungloe, there's a good **hostel at Crohy Head,** Dungloe, Co. Donegal (tel. Dungloe 129); good facilities at **Youth Hostel,** Aranmore Island, Burtonport, Letterkenny, Co. Donegal (no phone), with regular ferry service between Burtonport and the island; near Glenveagh National Park, good **hostel at Erigal,** Dunlewy, Gweedore, Letterkenny, Co. Donegal (tel. Bunbeg 291); four miles from Downings, good facilities at **Youth Hostel,** Tra na Rosann, Downings, Co. Donegal (tel. Downings 42); on the shores of Lough Swilly, good facilities at **Youth Hostel,** Bunnaton, Glenvar, Co. Donegal (no phone); and on Tory Island (with irregular ferry service from Magheraroarty), basic facilities at **Youth Hostel,** Tory Island, Co. Donegal (no phone).

Bed-and-Breakfast: Mrs. Mary McGee's **Killeadan,** Bundoran Rd., Ballyshannon, Co. Donegal (tel. 072-65377), is a marvelous touring base one mile outside Ballyshannon and just four miles from the Belleek factory. The centrally heated bungalow has six lovely guestrooms with hand basins, and four have private bath with shower. Mary is an officer in the Town & Country Homes Association and keenly interested in all her guests. Bed-and-breakfast rates are IR£8.50 ($10.20), with a 25% reduction for children, and there's good parking. Open April through November.

Lismolin, Fintra Rd., Killybegs, Co. Donegal (tel. Killybegs 35), is the home of Mrs. Bernie Cahill and sits right at the edge of a beautiful forest area. The modern, centrally heated bungalow is tastefully decorated, with four nice guestrooms, all with hand basins and two with private shower. The friendly Mrs. Cahill has been lauded by our readers for her delicious breakfasts and homemade brown bread, as well as for her general helpfulness. B&B rates are IR£8.50 ($10.20), with a one-third discount for children.

Eileen and Ray Molloy are the delightful hosts at **Greenhaven,** Portnoo Rd., Ardara (tel. Ardara 29), which overlooks Loughross Bay and Slieve Tooey on the other side of the bay. There's a window-walled breakfast room open to the gorgeous view, and a large back garden. A modern extension holds seven comfortable guestrooms, all with hand basins, four with private bath and shower, and lovely, puffy eiderdown quilts on all beds. The Molloys are especially helpful in pointing their guests to the things to see and do in the area (visit local weavers, etc.). B&B rates are IR£8 ($9.60), half that for children. Dinners many times feature fresh, locally caught seafood, and are priced at IR£7.50 ($9). Open March through November.

Bay View House, Portnoo Rd., Ardara, Co. Donegal (tel. Ardara 45), also has magnificent views of Loughros Bay and the Owenea River. Located a half-mile outside town on the coast road, the centrally heated country home has a spacious lounge with picture windows and turf fires, and a large dining room, where dinners include traditional Irish dishes as well as fresh local fish. Marian and Charles Bennett are gracious, helpful hosts, and Charles (who plays traditional music in pubs with a local group) is Chairman of the Ardara Tourism Committee. Rates for bed-and-breakfast are IR£8 ($9.60), with a 25% reduction for children; dinner is IR£7.50 ($9).

Mrs. Rosleen Gill is the delightful, enthusiastic hostess at **Septora**, Convent Rd., Letterkenny, Co. Donegal (tel. 074-22330). Her attractive, centrally heated bungalow is set in a quiet cul-de-sac and has three nicely decorated bedrooms, with built-in wardrobes and hand basins. Goose-down comforters are on each bed, and Mrs. Gill even furnishes hand tissues in all guestrooms. Rates are IR£8.50 ($10.20), with 25% off for children. Open March through October.

The Manse, Ramelton, Co. Donegal (tel. Ramelton 47), is a lovely old (1760) Georgian house set in its own grounds on the shores of Lough Swilly. Mrs. Florence Scott has furnished it with interesting period pieces, and there's an extensive library and open fires before which to browse through the books that interest you. The four nice guestrooms all have hand basins, and rates for bed-and-breakfast are IR£9 ($10.80). Open from Easter to mid-September (later by special arrangement).

If you make it up to Malin Head, Ireland's most northerly point (which I strongly recommend if you can manage the time), **Mrs. Maire Doyle,** Barraicin, Malin Head, Co. Donegal (tel. Ballygorman 17), will welcome you to her modern bungalow twelve miles outside Malin village, overlooking the sea. There are three nice guestrooms, all with hand basins, and rates are IR£7.50 ($9), with 25% off for children. Open Easter through October.

Self-Catering: Ireland has many good self-catering cottages for visitors, but few with as breathtaking a location as the marvelous group known as the **Donegal Thatched Cottages** on Cruit Island, which sits just offshore (connected by a bridge) between Burtonport and Annagary. There are eight cottages, all traditional in design (with thatched roofs and turf-burning fireplaces as well as central heat), and all set on a sheltered clifftop with spectacular seascapes of Donegal's rugged coastline, with Aranmore and Owey Islands clearly visible. At the foot of the cliff, there's a lovely little half-moon of a beach, and at the other side of the cliff, a golden strand safe for swimming goes on for miles. The fishing, boating, and swimming around here are all superb—and it's a perfect place for just plain loafing! There are good local pubs and one very good restaurant nearby for those times you hanker for good company and good conversation (both in plentiful supply among the friendly locals). The cottages have been built and furnished with all Irish-made products, and while there's all the charm of bygone days in the decor, there are modern conveniences that would make any housewife of those days turn green with envy (like the automatic washer and dryer that are kept out of sight behind cabinet doors so as not to interfere with the traditional decor). Turf is furnished in generous quantities so you can indulge any penchant for the open hearth. Each cottage can sleep as many as seven adults comfortably, which makes the weekly rates fall easily within budget limits if you bring a full party. The seasonal rates range from IR£95 ($114) to IR£225 ($270), and can go as low as IR£70 ($84) for midweek and weekend stays from October through May. You can book into this very special place through the Tourist Office, Temple St., Sligo (tel. 071-61201), or by contacting the charming owners, Conor and Mary Ward, Rosses Point, Co. Sligo (tel. 071-77197). They'll be glad to send you a brochure with full details.

Big Splurge: Rathmullen Country House, Rathmullen, Co. Donegal (tel. 074-58117), sits amid spacious, landscaped grounds that slope down to Lough Swilly, and in the more than 20 years that Robin and Bob Wheeler have been in residence, it has become a beloved favorite with the Irish from all over the Republic, as well as nearby Northern Ireland. The marvelous old house dates back to the early 1800s, and the Wheelers have brought back a graciousness and charm that disappeared during the years of its rather checkered career. The soft glow of turf or log fires in drawing room and library lights furnishings that combine a tasteful mixture of period and comfortably overstuffed modern furnishings. The glass-enclosed dining pavilion looks out to award-winning gardens, and the cellar bar is a cozy spot for relaxed conviviality. Accommodations come in a wide range, from the large, almost luxuriously furnished guestrooms that look out to the Lough to plainer, somewhat smaller and less expensive rooms to 20 self-catering chalets a bit removed from the main house, but handy to safe swimming (completely furnished and, Robin assured me, "childproof" since they're a favorite with families). All guestrooms have hand basins, and most have private facilities with showers. The rate range is from IR£17 ($20.40) to IR£22 ($26.40), with special weekly rates available. Sumptuous dinners, for which chef Bob has earned an international reputation, are priced at IR£14.50 ($17.40). Rathmullen Country House is open from Easter through September, and advance booking for both accommodations and meals in this very popular place is absolutely essential. Most major credit cards are accepted. A special "Highly Recommended" to a Big Splurge that's cheap at the price!

County Leitrim

Hostels: There are no An Oige hostels located in County Leitrim.

Bed-and-Breakfast: Corbally Lodge, Dublin Rd., Carrick-on-Shannon, Co. Leitrim (tel. 078-20228), is about a mile and a half south of town, set on its own spacious grounds. The pretty modern bungalow is the Rowley family home, and they are gracious hosts indeed. Open turf fires are the cozy centerpiece for evening gatherings. There are four nice guestrooms, three of which have hand basins. Rates are IR£8 ($9.60) for bed-and-breakfast, and Corbally Lodge is open April through September. Central heat and good parking.

Farmhouse: Violet and Raymond Thomas are the warm, friendly hosts at **Riversdale,** Ballinamore, Co. Leitrim (tel. 078-44122). The large farmhouse sits amid peaceful rural scenery on 85 acres of dairy and sheep farming. There are open fires on cool evenings, and fishing right on the property. About a mile and a half south of Ballinamore, this centrally heated house has six attractive and comfortable guestrooms, all with hand basins. Dinners feature fresh produce, meats, and fish, and there's a wine license. Rates are IR£8.50 ($10.20) for bed-and-breakfast, with a one-third reduction for children; dinners cost IR£7.50 ($9). Open year round, but advance reservations are required from November through February.

READERS' SELECTIONS: "We stayed at **Lisadorn,** Strandhill, Co. Sligo (tel. 071-78210), with Lily and Paddy Diamond and were treated so grand we felt really special. They helped with suggestions of what to see and look for along the way" (Peggy Moran, Ft.

Wayne, Ind.). . . . "A wonderful cook, Mrs. Mary Ward, operates **Pinewood,** Straboy, Glenties, Co. Donegal (tel. Glenties 123). The Wards are a young couple, and Mary greets each guest with tea and scones when they arrive. Michael is a schoolteacher and familiar with historic and scenic sites all over Ireland, and Mary serves wonderful meals" (James M. Boyle). . . . In Ramelton, Co. Donegal, I stayed with Mrs. Anne Campbell in her guesthouse, **Ardeen.** It's immaculate, spacious, warm and friendly. She's a young, pixish woman with three bouncing, delightful children, and each of them, plus Mr. Campbell, went out of their way to make my stay pleasant and enjoyable" (Arthur Rubin, Bergenfield, N.J.). . . . "We really lucked out when we stayed in the thatched roof cottage on the farm of Teresa and Brian Kennedy, **Glenview,** Aughoo, Ballinamore, County Leitrim. There's B&B in the 17th-century farmhouse; a self-catering cottage lovingly furnished with cottage antiques, with a flag floor and open fire; and a comfortable self-contained apartment. But the greatest thing is the warm hospitality and friendliness of these caring people. This is the loveliest place we have found in our world travels." (Bb and Charlie Meyer, Springfield, Ill.). . . . "We stay at the **Sportsman Hotel** (tel. Mohil 12) every year and the hospitality and warmth of the owners, Mr. and Mrs. Richard Bayliss, is unsurpassed" (Margaret Gallagher, Mineola, N.Y.). . . . "We found Killybegs to be a convenient and charming base for exploring Donegal's rugged countryside and for shopping in the area's tweed and wool shops. We stayed at the **Conkay House** (tel. Killybegs 273), operated by Conal and Kay McGuinnes. It was recently built by Conal, and his wife, Kay, keeps the nicely furnished guesthouse impeccably clean" (Alfred McCallin, Canton, Ohio).

WHERE TO EAT: The Northwest is filled with spots Mother Nature seems to have designed especially for picnics. Stop on a mountainside, spread your lunch on a sandy strand, or head for the lovely **Ards Forest Park** two miles north of Creeslough in County Donegal on Sheephaven Bay, where tables face the beach.

County Sligo

In Rosses Point, **The Moorings** (tel. 071-77112) is a small, attractive seafood restaurant with vaguely Spanish decor. There are bar snacks in addition to an excellent à la carte dinner menu with prices of IR£7 ($9) to IR£14 ($16.80), the latter for lobster. Open noon to 2 p.m. and 7 to 10 p.m. every day except Sunday.

The **Traditional Restaurant/Lounge,** Teeling St., Tubbercurry (tel. 071-85111), is a restaurant plus a bar/lounge, and the service by owners Anne and Tommie Killoran is pleasant and personal. Antiques (like the old butter churns) carry out the traditional theme, and the menu is varied and the dishes well prepared. There are quick snacks as well as full meals, and prices are moderate. Lunch will run around IR£3.50 ($4.20), dinner about IR£7 ($9). They offer the Tourist Menu, and hours are 9 a.m. (they also serve a good breakfast) to 11:30 p.m. seven days a week.

The Tourist Menu is also available from mid-March to mid-November at **Rock House Hotel,** Lough Arrow, Ballindoon, Castlebaldwin (tel. 079-66073), from noon to 2:30 p.m. and 5:30 to 10 p.m.

County Donegal

In Gortahork, **McFaddens Hotel** (tel. 074-35267/35101) serves surprisingly good and varied meals in its dining room, specializing in fresh, local seafood like salmon, which comes with a beautifully done hollandaise sauce. Try the lemon mousse for dessert. Bar lunches are on tap from 1 to 2:15 p.m.

every day, and the à la carte menu, with entrees priced at IR£4 ($4.80) to IR£8 ($9.60), is served from 6 to 9 p.m.

The **Woodhill House Restaurant** in Ardara (tel. Ardara 12) is a country house in a beautiful setting, specializing in dishes that feature local produce and seafood at prices that start at IR£6 ($7.20). A Tourist Menu is offered from June through September. Hours are 6 to 10 p.m., and it's closed for the entire month of October.

In Ballyshannon, two choices: Good bar food (soup and sandwiches, mostly) at **Sweeney's White Horse Bar** in the lounge bar, which features an open fire, with hours from 10:30 a.m. to 11:30 p.m.; and **McIntyre's Restaurant** in Castle St. (tel. 072-65245), a family-run eatery offering the Tourist Menu as well as an à la carte selection ranging from about IR£4.50 ($5.40) at lunch, IR£6 ($7.20) at dinner. Open 10 a.m. to midnight.

Fitzgerald's Hotel, Bundoran (tel. 072-41336), also offers a Tourist Menu from June through August, and an excellent five-course dinner for IR£6.50 ($7.80) and up. Hours are 5:30 to 8:30 p.m. (Tourist Menu only offered up to 7:30 p.m.).

County Leitrim

The **Bush Hotel** in Carrick-on-Shannon (tel. 078-20014) is an excellent restaurant where the regular dinner will run about IR£7 ($9), and the Tourist Menu is available for less expensive lunches and dinners (lunch on the à la carte menu is IR£6—$7.20—and up). Lunch hours are 12:30 to 2:15 p.m.; dinner from 6 to 9 p.m. Closed mid-December to mid-January.

On the main Sligo/Dublin road, the **Breffni Inn,** Dromod (tel. Dromod 20), has a lovely lounge bar that serves homemade soup, sandwiches, and snacks at inexpensive prices.

THINGS TO SEE AND DO: The Northwest is not really a place to "do" as much as it's a region to be absorbed into your very soul, and that comes as naturally as breathing the clear, bracing air. There are special places you won't want to miss, but mostly you'll remember the sense of tuning in to a part of your inner self that all too often has been lost in the frenetic pace at which most of us gallop through modern life.

County Sligo

Even if archeology is not your primary interest, do pick up the Tourist Board pamphlet, *Prehistoric Sligo,* and stop by some of the fascinating megalithic monuments you'll pass as you travel through the county. There's a profound, inexplicable feeling of connection to ages past when you stand and gaze at these impressive mounds of stones carefully placed in meaningful patterns by human hands so long ago.

County Donegal

If your name happens to be O'Doherty (whether it's that spelling or has transformed over the centuries into Doherty or Dougherty), you'll want to know about a reunion being planned for this Donegal clan, with a three-week period of all sorts of hilarity—with a serious project or two thrown in for good measure—in June and July of 1985. For full details and help in making arrangements to attend, contact: Mr. Dennis Doyle, c/o Donegal/Leitrim/Sligo Regional Tourism Organization, Letterkenny, Co. Donegal (tel. 074-21160). Oh, to be an O'Doherty in 1985!

Base yourself at Donegal Town or Ardara to explore the splendors of southern Donegal, then take the main roadway that circles the northern part of the county. You'll want to plan at least one overnight stop—the jagged, cliff-filled coastline, rocky mountain pastures and breathtaking mountain passes that open a view that seems to go on to eternity can lead to an overload of the senses, and it's when you've reached saturation point that you'll welcome the warm and friendly company of the warm and friendly inhabitants of County Donegal.

Right around Donegal Town, the three-mile-long **Barnesmore Gap** is seven miles to the northeast, through wild, mountainy country that once harbored highwaymen. North of town, **Eglish Glen** cuts between the Bluestack Mountains and Banagher Hill, and farther along you'll find the "Grey Mare's Tail" waterfall in **Sruell Glen.** The good St. Patrick knew Donegal well, and he once fasted for 40 days on an island in isolated **Lough Derg,** where pilgrims still come faithfully to observe a three-day fast.

Due west of Donegal Town, in **Mountcharles,** stop by the little white shop with red trim that is **Gillespie Brothers.** Just meeting the Gillespies is a delight, but it can be profitable as well, for their tweed selections of suits and jackets, lap rugs, and blankets are exceptional (also sold by the length), and they also carry for the ladies a marvelous stock of hand-crocheted dresses, capes, and blouses. Prices are below most in other shops, and the brothers are happy to mail your purchases home.

At the western edge of Mountcharles, **Kathleen's** is Kathleen Alcock's original shop (see "Donegal Town") and occupies the ground floor of a terrace house on Main Street. The selection of fine giftware, tweeds, and hand-crocheted garments is much like that in the Donegal Town shop, except that the original designs are not carried here.

If you can manage to get to the picturesque little harbor town of **Killybegs** in the late afternoon, go down to the pier to watch the fishing fleet come in—it's a memorable experience, with seagulls swarming and screeching overhead and half the town gathered to greet the fishermen. Farther along, in **Kilcar,** look for **Studio Donegal,** where the fabulous misty tones of Donegal tweed come in jacket, skirt, or pants lengths, as well as ready-made garments from such Irish manufacturers as Brian Boru. They also carry a good selection of local crafts. There's a handweaving workshop next door, and a spacious tearoom serving home baking.

The drive to **Glencolumbkille** ("St. Colmcille's Glen"), through lonely mountain country with occasional glimpses of the sea, is a journey thorough history and a culture that has changed little since the days when (or so local legend insists) Bonnie Prince Charlie hid out in the Glen. The stony hills are dotted with more than 40 cairns, dolmens, souterrains, and other relics of a past that goes back as much as 5,000 years. At Glencolumbkille, there's one of the most authentic **Folk Village Museums** in the country, with three cottages built and furnished to bring to life three different eras stretching from 1700 to 1900. There are guided tours every hour on the hour, which explain the workings of each cottage. The home of a 1720 cotter is earthen-floored, and its open hearth has no chimney; by the 1820s, the cotter's home has a flagstone floor, chimney, and oil-lamp lighting (as well as, sad to relate, a tin trunk that would carry the immigrating family's treasures to "Amerikay"); and the 1920 cottage is very like many you'll have seen in your travels around today's Irish countryside. The courtyard around which the cottages are grouped holds such everyday items as a peat cart and fishing boat, with the large "famine pot" a somber reminder of famine days, when starving peasants lined up to be served a meager ration. A schoolhouse from a century ago and a country pub, or "sheebeen" (where the drink sold was illegal poteen, more often than not!), complete the village. There's a cottage craft shop and tearoom, where hot tea and scones are sold from June through September. The Folk Village has hours of 10 a.m. to 6 p.m. on weekdays from Easter to November, and 2 to 6 p.m. on Sundays.

Ardara has long been a center of the home-weaving industry, and its few streets are lined with shops selling tweeds at good prices. Two to look for are **John Jo Campbell's** and **Alan Given,** both on Main Street.

Heading north, the cliff and coastal scenery is heartstoppingly beautiful, with a haunting loneliness hovering over all. Drive through towns and villages with sonorous names like **Glenties** (Na Gleannta, "the valleys"), **Dongloe, Burtonport, Gweedore** (where there's always good traditional music), and **Dunfanaghy** (with a stop at **Mrs. Harley's Art Gallery,** which features Irish painter Tom Egginton's glowing landscape canvases and a huge stock of local crafts, and a detour around the clifftop Horn Head Drive). To the east, explore the shores of **Lough Swilly,** passing through historic **Rathmullen** and **Ramelton** and on to the cathedral town of **Letterkenny.** Drive on out to **Malin Head**—as far north as you can go on Ireland's mainland. Take time to go by the township of **Burt** three miles south of **Bridgend** and point your car (or walk) up the little road that leads to a great circular stone cashel known as **Grianan of Aileach** ("sun palace of Aileach"), once the royal seat of the O'Neills and a sacred meeting place for High Kings of Ireland. From its 800-foot-high summit, there are vast panoramic views of **Lough Swilly, Lough Foyle,** and the distant sea.

At some point in your Donegal rambles, switch off (from Gweedore or Letterkenny) to take in the deeply wooded reaches of **Glenveagh National Park** and its impressive castle. Set in the very heart of the Donegal highlands, between the Derryveagh and Glendowan mountain ranges, the park covers 25,000 acres of wilderness, with the castle and its magnificent gardens set like a jewel on the edge of Lough Veagh. At the main entrance near **Churchill Village,** the **Glebe Gallery** houses the art collection of noted painter Derek Hill, who has willed the property and the paintings to the nation.

County Leitrim

Dromahair (Druim Dha Eithiar, "The Ridge of the Two Air-Demons") is where a royal lady inadvertently set in motion the first Norman invasion of Ireland. It seems that back in the 12th century, Dervogilla, wife of Tiernan O'Rourke, eloped with the King of Leinster, who was promptly outlawed by his fellow chieftains. When he went to England's Henry II for assistance, the king gave his royal consent for any of his vassals who so chose to join up with the Irish king to win back his lost lands. When a bevy of barons from South Wales threw in with the Irish chieftain, they formed the group of Anglo-Normans who landed near Wexford in 1169. The ruins of the lady's residence, **Breffni Castle,** are found on the riverbank adjacent to the 1626 Old Hall, built by Sir William Villiers. On the other side of the river, there are ruins of the 1508 **Creevelea Abbey,** and the remains of an even older church nearby are thought to be those of one founded by St. Patrick when he spent some time here.

Carrick-on-Shannon (Cara Droma Ruisg, "The Weir of the Marshy Ridge") is a center for fishing and boating on the River Shannon.

READER'S SELECTIONS: "Just outside Ramelton on the road to Milford, I came across a wonderful craft shop owned by **Mrs. S. Browne,** Black's Glen. The Aran sweaters on display were knit by Mrs. Browne and her neighbors and she sells them at substantial savings. They're as beautiful ad well crafted as you'd find anywhere. There were lots of other interesting handcrafts in her shop also" (Arthur Rubin, Bergenfield, N.J.).

Chapter X

THE MIDLANDS

1. Introducing the Midlands
2. Around Counties Cavan, Laois, Longford, Monaghan, Offaly, Roscommon, and Westmeath

IRELAND'S MIDLAND COUNTIES are often called **Lakeland,** and indeed, the landscape is dotted with lakes. The Rivers Shannon and Erne glide between broad banks, spreading here and there into Lough Ree and Lough Sheelin.

1. Introducing the Midlands

This is the land of fishing, boating, and hunting, and in ancient days, it was the land of the lake dwellers, who built artificial islands called crannogs on which to raise their round huts, protected from enemy attack by the surrounding waters. At the geographical heart of the country, the great monastic community of Clonmacnois was settled near Athlone, withstood assaults by Vikings, Normans, and Cromwell, and has left us a rich heritage of Celtic crosses and round towers.

The great Irish poet Patrick Kavanagh was born in the Midlands, but "escaped" to live out most of his life in Dublin. Although he wrote of his birthplace, "O stoney grey soil of Monaghan, You burgled my bank of youth," there is something in the nearly flat, faintly rolling land of Ireland's innards that must nurture literary talent. Oliver Goldsmith spent much of his life here, and you can trace his footsteps, guided by the *Goldsmith Country* booklet published by the Tourist Board. The blind harper O'Carolan lies buried in County Roscommon. William Percy French was born in County Roscommon. County Longford was home to Maria Edgeworth, an 18th-century writer and angel of mercy during the famine years. Padraic Colum—poet, playwright, novelist, and essayist—was a product of County Longford, and chronicled the lives of its peasantry with an honest eye.

The **Lakeland Regional Tourist Office** is just off the Dublin road in Mullingar (tel. 044-48761), and the good folk there can furnish an amazing amount of literature to steer you to the treasures of the Midland counties.

2. Around Counties Cavan, Laois, Longford, Monaghan, Offaly, Roscommon, and Westmeath

ACCOMMODATIONS: Unfortunately, the Midlands Region does not have hostel facilities, but good bed-and-breakfast homes and farmhouses abound.

NOTE: Prices shown below are those in effect in 1985—expect them to be higher in 1986.

County Cavan

Bed-and-Breakfast: Gardens surround **Ker Maria,** Station Rd., Cootehill, Co. Cavan (tel. 049-52293), the pretty Georgian-style home of Mrs. Teresa Colhoun. Cootehill is just about midway between Donegal and Dublin, and Mrs. Colhoun has four nice guestrooms, all with hand basins and one with private bath and shower. Rates are IR£8.50 ($10.20), with a 20% reduction for children. Central heating and good parking. Open April to mid-October.

Self-Catering: One of the prettiest sites for getting away from it all in Ireland is Killykeen Forest Park in Co. Cavan, and the Forest and Wildlife Service has worked hand-in-glove with tourism people to develop a group of log-cabin units for holiday-makers. The beautifully wooded park also contains good fishing. For detailed information on facilities, rates, and booking, contact: Mr. Simon Tormey, Lakeland/Midland Regional Tourism Organization, Dublin Rd., Mullingar, Co. Westmeath (tel. 044-48761).

County Laois

Bed-and-Breakfast: In a pretty, wooded setting on the Portlaoise/Rosslare road, **Aspen,** Rock of Dunamase, Portlaoise, Co. Laois (tel. 0502-25405), is about four miles outside town. Mrs. Noreen Llewellyn is the gracious hostess in this pretty, centrally heated bungalow, and she has four attractive guestrooms with hand basins. There are lovely woodland walks just outside the door. Rates are IR£8.50 ($10.20), with a 20% discount for children.

County Longford

Bed-and-Breakfast: Mrs. Breege O'Donnell is a long-time favorite hostess with our readers. Her large two-story home, **Tivoli,** Dublin Rd., Longford (tel. 043-46898), is immaculate and well appointed, and her warm friendliness makes guests feel like members of her family. There are 11 guestrooms with hand basins (three also have private shower), and the house is centrally heated. Rates are IR£8.50 ($10.20), half that for children, and there's a car park.

County Monaghan

Bed-and-Breakfast: Surrounded by woods and nearby lakes, **Rose-Linn-Lodge,** Lurgans, Carrickmacross, Co. Monaghan (tel. 042-61035) is a centrally heated bungalow about a mile from Carrickmacross. Mrs. Rosaleen Haworth has three nice guestrooms with hand basins, and takes a personal interest in all her guests. B&B rates are IR£8.50 ($10.20), with 20% off for children. Open April through October.

County Offaly

Bed-and-Breakfast: Mrs. Margaret Soden's **St. Carthages,** Charleville Rd., Tullamore, Co. Offaly (tel. 0506-21216), is a half-mile out of town, set in pretty, landscaped grounds. The two-story Georgian-style house has four lovely guestrooms, nicely decorated and with hand basins, and three have private showers. Rates are IR£9.50 ($11.40), with a 25% reduction for children. Central heating and good parking.

County Roscommon

Bed-and-Breakfast: Hillside House, Doon, Corrigeenroe, Boyle, Co. Roscommon (tel. 079-66075), is the comfortable, slightly old-fashioned home of Mrs. Taylor. It's in a beautiful, scenic location with views of Lough Key and handy to the Forest Park. Of the six homey bedrooms, five have hand basins. Rates are IR£8.50 ($10.20), with 25% off for children. Central heating.

County Westmeath

Bed-and-Breakfast: Dympna and Sean Casey's modern split-level home, **Hilltop,** Delvin Rd., Rathconnell, Mullingar (tel. 044-48958), is in a beautiful setting two miles from Mullingar and adjacent to Lough Sheever. Dympna is an official of the Town & Country Homes Association and warmly interested in seeing that all her guests are comfortable and get the most from their holidays. All four guestrooms are nicely furnished, and all have private toilets and showers as well as hand basins. The rates are IR£8.50 ($10.20), and they are open from March through October.

Farmhouse: One of my favorite farmhouses in Ireland is **Woodlands Farm,** Streamstown, Co. Westmeath (tel. 0902-36114), some ten miles from Mullingar. Maybe it's because serenity sets in the moment you approach the rambling two-story by way of an avenue of aged trees which often shade grazing horses. More likely, it's the warm, friendly hospitality of Mary and Willy Maxwell and their attractive children that draws me back. The house itself is charming, with a 200-year-old section to which a wing was added about a century ago that is still called the "new" addition. Parlor windows look out onto wooded grounds, and a fire is lit most evenings when a tea tray is rolled into the gracious room, which is furnished with antiques. Breakfasts are truly special, featuring fresh milk from their own cows and Mary's home-baked bread. The house has central heating, and the six bedrooms include one cozy single. Donkeys and pet sheep are an added attraction, and guests are given the run of the farmyard and grounds. Rates are IR£8 ($9.60), with half off for children. Mary's delicious evening meals are IR£7 ($8.40). Open March through October. To find Woodlands, leave Mullingar via the Galway road, then take the road to Athlone; at

Streamstown, look for the sign near the school. If you get hopelessly lost, just stop and ask—the Maxwells are well known in the Streamstown area.

READERS' SELECTIONS: "All the Irish B&B hosts are unusually fine and lovable people, but Mrs. Bridie Casey is something special. Her **Padraig Villa**, Claskill, Screggan, Tullamore, Co. Offaly (tel. 0506-55962), is a modern two-story home surrounded by mature gardens and a private car park. There's pony riding for adults and children, and a welcoming cup of tea or coffee when you arrive. One of the four rooms has a bath and shower, and one has a shower" (Burton White, Harlingen, Tex.). . . . "We found Mr. and Mrs. Dolan to be gracious hosts in their lovely home, **Munsboro House,** Munsboro, Roscommon, Co. Roscommon (tel. 0903-6375). It's a Georgian guest-house about a mile and a half from town, with open fires and lovely bedrooms. We were served an excellent breakfast, and there's a wine license for evening meals" (Jean O'Brien, Lynchburg, Va.). . . . "We found a lovely, 200-year-old Georgian farm-house in its own grounds that were like a park. Marian and John Finucan-Clarke are the owners and gracious hosts at **Reynella House,** Bracklyn, Mullingar, Co. Westmeath (tel. 044-74134). There are log fires, a library and a games room, and the bedrooms all have hot and cold. Reynella House is eight miles from Mullingar on the main Delvin Road." (S. Gleason, New York, N.Y.).

WHERE TO EAT: Picnics are a joy in the Midland region, with woodlands and lake shores galore. Country pubs can also be a "discovery," although your best bet for pub grub is in any one of the little market towns you pass through.

County Cavan

In Butlersbridge, about four miles north of Cavan Town, the **Derragarra Inn** (tel. 049-31003/31205) sits by the side of the River Annalee. While it no longer provides accommodations, it has won just about every food award in the book, and its interior decor is a marvelous hodgepodge of items that range from old farm implements to exotic souvenirs owner John Clancey collected in his years of wandering the world. A three-course lunch here will run no more than IR£4.50 ($5.40), and the bar-food menu salads and sandwiches are less. There's an excellent fisherman's platter at IR£4.50. Take time to visit the riverside giftshop that specializes in Irish handcrafts, and as an added convenience, John has been appointed agent for a Bureau de Change, licensed by the Bank of Ireland and using bank rates of exchange to convert the currencies of a host of countries (including the U.S. and Canada and most of Europe) into Irish punts.

County Laois

In Portlaoise, **Eagan's Hostelry Inn,** 24 Main St., serves pub grub, with a hot buffet and a salad bar. Lunch will run about IR£3 ($3.60), and dinner around IR£8 ($9.60).

County Longford

The Tourist Menu is offered year round at the **Edgeworth Hotel,** Edgeworthstown, and both Irish and continental dishes are on the à la carte lunch and dinner menus, with lunch costing around IR£5 ($6) and dinner IR£7 ($8.40). Hours are 12:30 to 2:30 p.m. and 6:30 to 9 p.m.

County Monaghan

In Monaghan Town, look for **Sartos Bistro and Wine Bar** in Glaslough St. This is a modern restaurant where a good lunch will run about IR£4 ($4.80), dinner about IR£6 ($7.20). The Tourist Menu is also available. Hours are noon to 8 p.m.

County Offaly

Blazers Restaurant in Dooly's Hotel in Birr serves both the Tourist Menu and a nice à la carte selection. Lunch prices are in the IR£5 ($6) to IR£6 ($7.20) range, while dinner prices start at IR£8 ($9.60). Open 12:30 to 2:30 p.m. and 6 to 9 p.m.

County Roscommon

Combine sightseeing with lunching at the **Lakeshore Restaurant** in Lough Key Forest Park just outside Boyle. Picture windows overlook the boat basin, and you can choose from light meals (salads and sandwiches) or more substantial grills. Takeaways are available, and there's a wine license. The price range is IR£3 ($3.60) to IR£8 ($9.60). Open weekends only from Easter to May 1, daily from noon to 7 p.m. May to September.

In Boyle, the **Royal Hotel** on Bridge Street has a comfortable, family-run hotel dining room that serves a variety of good Irish-style meals, priced from IR£6 ($7.20) at lunch, IR£9 ($10.80) at dinner. The lower-priced Tourist Menu is available from 12:30 to 3 p.m.

County Westmeath

The **Gramby Restaurant,** 9 Dominic Street, in Mullingar is a cozy place, with open fires and friendly service. The food is good, honest fare well prepared, and moderate prices run about IR£3 ($3.60) for lunch, IR£8.50 ($10.20) for dinner on the à la carte menu, with the lower Tourist Menu available year round. Hours are 12:30 to 3 p.m. and 6 to 10 p.m.

THINGS TO SEE AND DO: Outdoors types will love the Midlands: **fishing** is excellent and free in most places; **hikers** and just plain **walkers** can tramp forest parks and lakeshores; there's **golf** in Mullingar and Athlone; and there are miles and miles of water for dedicated **boaters.** For **history buffs,** there are ecclesiastical ruins and stately homes.

County Cavan

Plan to spend some time in the 600 acres of **Killykeen Forest Park,** located between Killeshandra and Cavan Town. There's plenty to do: fishing, swimming, boating, shady nature trains and picnic sites, as well as a restaurant. Within its grounds you'll also find crannogs, ring forts, and the ruined **Lough Oughter Castle,** where in 1649 the great chieftain Owen Roe

O'Neil died (to this day some say he was poisoned by a treacherous hand).

County Laois

There's a perfectly preserved round tower at **Timahoe,** some five miles south of Stradbally (which has an interesting old car museum).

Nine miles south of Portlaoise, a **Cistercian abbey** was founded by Conor O'More in 1183 at Abbeyleix. The **de Vesci demesne,** adjoining the town, holds the tomb of Malachi O'More, a Laois chieftain. The grounds are open to the public during summer months.

County Longford

In **Edgeworthstown,** there's a small **museum** dedicated to the Edgeworth family, of whom the most notable members were Maria, English-born novelist and essayist who spent most of her life in Ireland and did much to relieve suffering during the worst famine years, and her father, an inventor and author. The town's historical museum is open during summer months.

County Monagan

Stop by the **St. Louis Lace Centre** (tel. 042-61247) in the charming little town of Carrickmacross. It's the convent high on a hill in which the good sisters sketch out original designs to be worked in the sheerest lawn appliqued to even sheerer net. The tiny, invisible handstitching is done in some 20 cottages by skillful and patient women, whose numbers are dwindling every year, with few young girls willing to learn the ancient art. The convent has a display room where you can purchase such items as collar-and-cuffs sets for IR£26 ($31.20) or go all out and invest in an heirloom wedding veil (IR£250 —$300—for the fingertip length, IR£350—$420—for a full cathedral length of three yards). These prices are considerably better than you'd find in the Shannon duty-free shop or Dublin's Brown Thomas. Whether or not you plan to shop, the convent is worth a visit to see the products of a fine art that is slowly disappearing. Hours are 10 a.m. to noon and 2 to 4 p.m. on weekdays; closed Saturday and Sunday.

County Offaly

The gardens at **Birr Castle** in the town of Birr (*Biorra,* "Spring Wells") are open to the public. The castle was a much besieged stronghold during the 16th and 17th centuries, and was later the seat of the Earls of Rosse. The third Earl had an observatory in the castle, where he designed a telescope that was, for some eighty years, the largest in the world.

One of Ireland's most holy sites is **Clonmacnois** (*Cluain Mic Nois,* "meadow of the son of Nos"), where St. Ciaran founded a monastery in 548. It was plundered by Irish chieftains, Vikings, and Anglo-Normans and finally gave up the ghost when Cromwell's forces desecrated it beyond restoration. Today, you'll find among its ruins a cathedral, eight churches, two round towers, the remains of a castle, more than 200 monumental slabs and three sculptured high crosses. There are guided tours during the summer months.

County Roscommon

Near Castlerea, **Clonalis House** dates from the 19th century and is furnished with Sheraton pieces and a collection of artifacts that includes O'Carolan's harp, rare glass and china, paintings, and Gaelic manuscripts. From May through June, it opens only on Saturday, Sunday, and Monday from 2 to 6 p.m.; in July and August, hours are 2 to 6 every day but Tuesday, and in September, weekend hours go back in effect.

In **Boyle,** the ruins of a 12th-century **Cistercian Abbey** are impressive, and if you'd like to see the interior, look up the caretaker whose home is just next door.

Two miles east of Boyle, visit the **Lough Key Forest Park.** It's one of the country's loveliest, and especially interesting are the Bog Gardens, with heathers and other small plants that grow well in peat.

Lovers of traditional Irish music may want to make a pilgrimage to **Kilronan,** where the revered blind harper, composer, and poet Turlough O'Carolan lies in a cemetery above whose arched gateway is inscribed: "Within this churchyard lie the remains of Carolan, the last of the Irish bards who departed this life 25 March, 1738. R.I.P."

County Westmeath

In **Athlone** (*Ath Luain,* "The Ford of Luan"), **King John's Castle,** which dates from the 13th century, is fascinating, and there's a museum within its walls. Athlone is where John McCormack, the famous Irish tenor, was born, and his birthplace is marked by a bronze plaque in the Bawn, off Mardyke Street.

Chapter XII

INTRODUCING NORTHERN IRELAND

1. The Practicalities
2. A Suggested Itinerary

YET ANOTHER FACE OF IRELAND lies across the border that marks the six-county province of Northern Ireland. Its green fields, cliff-studded and cove-indented coastline, forest-clad mountains and, above all, its hospitable inhabitants are reasons enough to cross that border. Beyond those, there are elements found *only* in the North that will add an extra, very special dimension to your Irish experience.

To begin with the obvious, this is where you'll find the famed Giant's Causeway—mighty Fionn MacCumhaill's rocky pathway across to Scotland —along with a curving stretch of green glens, secluded inlets, towering cliffs (two of which are connected in summer months by the ingenuous Carrick-a-Rede rope bridge high above a chasm between a salmon fishery island and the mainland), pleasant resort towns with safe beaches, and quiet, quaint little villages. So spectacular is the Antrim Coast that many of the 40,000 American visitors each year settle into this part of the province for their entire stay.

But what a pity to miss the gentler shoreline of Co. Down with its romantic Mountains of Mourne that sweep down to a sea replete with wide, curving strands fronted by charming holiday towns, and its firm claim on a good part of Saint Patrick's Irish sojourn, from his first footsteps on Irish soil to his last. Quiet little villages on the Ards Peninsula look across to Scotland (clearly visible in many places), and the countryside is dotted with Norman castles, forest parks beckoning the hiker, at least one windmill still whirling away at harvest time, Strangford Lough and palm-tree-bordered Carlingford Lough.

And who would want to miss Co. Fermanagh's Lough Erne and its 300-square-miles of boating or fishing amid exquisite scenery? Devenish Island with its ancient abbey and tower and White Island's mysterious Celtic stone figures, just two of the lough's 154 islands, entice the sightseer. Or Armagh's two cathedrals—one Protestant, one Catholic, and both named for Saint Patrick? Or the Sperrin Mountains of Co. Tyrone, as well as the unique folk park that so vividly depicts the rural lives of Irish immigrants on both sides of the

Atlantic? Or Derry's massive old city walls? Or—well, read on and you'll find a wealth of other scenic splendors spread throughout all six counties.

All that gorgeous scenery is not only a delight to the eye, but serves as well as a mighty spur to the imagination, for it has spawned a good many of Ireland's legends. It was in this part of Ireland that the brave Cuchulainn roamed and, singlehanded, guarded the border against the onslaught of Queen Maeve when she set out to capture the Brown Bull of Cooley. This was home territory for Fionn MacCumhaill (whom you may know as Finn McCool) and his faithful *Fianna* warriors. And the beautiful *Diedre o' the Sorrows* played out her life's tragedy within the borders of Ulster.

If the above mention of these heroes has set your mind soaring, let me recommend a marvelous little paperback on sale in most bookstores in Ireland: it's titled *Heroic Tales from the Ulster Cycle* and is published by O'Brien Educational Press (with offices at 20 Victoria Rd., Dublin 6).

And if the landscape and legends of Northern Ireland are magical, its people are no less so. Because of all that history related back in an early chapter of this book, the accents of the North will fall on your ears with the soft burr of Scotland, mingled with the clipped speech of native English and the lilting Irish brogue of the Republic. "Och, it's not a bad day at all," the Ulsterman will remark; to which his Republican neighbor will reply, "Sure, and isn't that God's truth." It's an enchanting mix, and don't be at all surprised if you find yourself ending sentences with the distinctive lift that characterizes so much of what you hear.

Along with their speech, these descendants of Great Britain's plantation era families have put into the mix strong elements of their cultures. Squash and cricket are sports you'll rarely find in the Republic, but they flourish above the border; the strains of traditional Irish music are interspersed with music of a distinctly British or Scottish flavor; Belfast's magnificent Opera House is as likely to plan an English drawing-room comedy as an Irish classic by O'Casey or Synge. And while Orangemen parade in great numbers and with great gusto on July 12th to celebrate their beloved King Billy's victory at the Battle of the Boyne, there is no less a festive air about Catholic parades and celebrations on the 15th of August, when the ancient Order of Hibernians take over to celebrate Lady Day.

Aha! you say, those two celebrations may be equally festive, but don't they reflect the politics and the *troubles* that make one hesitate to plan a trip to Northern Ireland? Sadly, I cannot answer an unqualified "No" to that question. As we go to press, the strife that has infected Northern Ireland since 1969 goes on, sometimes with long no-incident intervals, other times with headline-grabbing frequency. From time to time, there are signs that a peaceful solution may yet be found to the problems that beleaguer the province. The latest—and many believe most hopeful—is the All Ireland Forum Report of May 1984, which resulted from year-long meetings of leading political parties on both sides of the border and both sides of the political fence. Several alternative political resolutions were suggested, and approval of its recommendations came from governments around the world. But, again, I cannot tell you that an end is in sight for these tragic "troubles."

What I *can* tell you is that in those two decades, no tourist has come to any harm (a comforting thought!); the U.S. State Department has never issued a travel warning regarding Northern Ireland, as it does to destinations deemed unsafe to visit; that in all my own ramblings around Northern Ireland I have never felt endangered; and that the one guarantee I can unhesitatingly make is that the people of the province will welcome you warmly, delighted that you've come to visit.

That is not to say, of course, that you will be totally unaware of the tensions. Border checkpoints, posted guards at hotels and other public gathering places, and the occasional armed road patrol you meet on country roads all indicate that this is indeed a troubled area. However, body and purse searches of the past have, happily, almost disappeared and at most checkpoints you are passed quickly through with a polite wave. There *are* some very simple rules designed to ensure your safety—I'll tell you about those in detail later in this chapter—that will become automatic soon after your arrival.

In short, my best advice is: Don't miss this other—different—face of Ireland.

1. The Practicalities

THE CURRENCY: Northern Ireland's currency is that of Great Britain's, the pound sterling. As we go to press, the exchange rate against the American dollar is £1 = $1.40, and all prices quoted in these pages are based on that rate. In these uncertain days, exchange rates fluctuate with amazing frequency, so be sure to check the current situation when you come.

Americans will be well advised to buy pounds sterling with dollars rather than Irish punts, since the exchange rate is much more favorable—you can do that at banks in the Republic before you cross the border if it's more convenient. One caution, if you're arriving in the North on a weekend or bank holiday, be sure to buy pounds sterling before you come. And, of course, it is always best to change your currency at a bank rather than in department stores or hotels. In Belfast, the Thomas Cook office (11 Donegal Pl., Belfast 1) can also convert currency at the official rate.

The following table will give you an idea of how your dollars compare to the exchange rate quoted above:

£	$	£	$
1p	$ .01	£1.00	$1.40
5p	$ .07	£2.50	$3.50
25p	$ .35	£3.00	$4.20
50p	$ .70	£4.50	$6.30
75p	$1.05	£10.00	$14.00

ABOUT THOSE RULES AND REGULATIONS: There aren't that many, but you should know them in advance. The single most important regulation if you're driving is that concerning parking. When you see an area signposted "Control Zone," it means that cars must *not be left parked and unattended, even for a short time.* In those areas, it is felt that cars left empty (even if locked) are a security risk, and the regulation is strictly enforced. There will usually be a car park close at hand with an attendant on duty.

You'll also see some hotels, public offices, or shopping areas fenced off with security personnel on duty. Only rarely will you be stopped when entering these areas, and even then you'll be sent through with a courteous smile after a quick look at your purse or shopping bag.

When coming from the Republic, it is always advisable to enter through one of the approved checkpoints, which are clearly marked on tourist maps. You won't have to show your passport or produce a visa.

TOURIST INFORMATION: The **Northern Ireland Tourist Board** has offices at 27 locations around the Province, with helpful, friendly personnel anxious to help with any problem and make sure you see the highlights of their area. Tourist Offices are also at the Belfast International Airport and at Larne Harbour terminal. The main office is at River House, 48–52 High St., Belfast (tel. 0232-246609), with hours of 9 a.m. to 5:15 p.m. weekdays and 9 a.m. to noon on Saturday in the summer.

ACCOMMODATIONS: You'll find the same high standards for accommodations as in the Republic, with the Northern Ireland Tourist Board maintaining just as strict an inspection program as their counterpart to the south. Bed-and-breakfast homes, guesthouses, farmhouses, and moderately priced hotels are in generous supply, and it is generally not necessary to book in advance—you can meander around the Province pretty much at will without the worry of being stuck without a bed. A time-consuming idea is to come armed with the Tourist Board's directory, *All the Places to Stay,* which you can obtain for £1 ($1.40) by writing to Northern Ireland Tourist Board, River House, 48–52 High St., Belfast, Northern Ireland (tel. 0232-246609), or at any Tourist Office once you've arrived. There's also a helpful illustrated *Farm & Country Holidays* booklet with over 100 listings; *Town & Seaside House Holidays,* also illustrated and listing some 60 homes; and for campers, *Caravan & Camp Sites,* with more than 100 approved sites.

   Note: During off seasons (March to mid-June and mid-September to December), many Northern Ireland accommodations have special weekend and midweek packages. In 1984, for example, one guesthouse offered 2 nights bed-and-breakfast and one evening meal for only £12 ($16.80). If you plan to visit during those periods, write the Northern Ireland Tourist Board for their *Holiday Breakaways* booklet, which details all such specials in all six counties.

MEALS: The Tourist Board also publishes a directory of eateries, *Let's Eat Out in Northern Ireland,* that covers all price ranges, from pub grub to posh restaurants, in all six counties. A money-saver is the 6 p.m. high tea served in many hotels and some restaurants—portions are ample, and the menu usually includes eggs, sausage, ham, or fish and chips. High tea is less expensive than the regular dinner menu (which most often goes on at 7 p.m.). Best make reservations in the better hotel dining rooms and restaurants on weekends and holidays.

PUB HOURS: The last drinks are served in Northern Ireland pubs *promptly* at 11 p.m., although the doors don't close until 11:30 p.m. They open at 11 a.m. every day except Sunday, when they're closed (the only remedy for a terrible thirst on Sunday is to get yourself to a licensed restaurant or a hotel bar).

DRIVING: As in the Republic, driving is on the left. Northern Ireland has an excellent network of highways, with speed limits of 30 mph in town (unless a slower speed is posted), 60 mph on highways and country roads, and 70 mph on dual carriageways (divided highways). Traffic circles are called "round-abouts," and exits are well marked.

If you're driving a rental car from the Republic, you should check to see that the insurance covers your stay above the border—and the same, of course, applies if you're going the other way. In the North, the leading car-rental firms are **Avis, Hertz,** and **Godfrey Davis,** with offices in Belfast and at Belfast International Airport.

PUBLIC TRANSPORT: You can travel around the North quite easily and inexpensively using the very good rail and bus services. Day trips are also available to almost all sightseeing highlights. Northern Ireland Railways (NIR) has a seven-day, unlimited travel, **Rail Runabout pass** good April through October at a cost of £17 ($23.80) for adults, £8.50 ($11.90) for children. It's available at most railway stations. Primary rail service is from Belfast to Londonderry via Ballymena and Coleraine; Belfast to Bangor; and Belfast to Dublin (a 2½-hour trip). Information on all NIR services is available at the **Travel and Information Centre** in Belfast's Central Station, or by calling 0232-230301/230671. Good bus service will get you almost anywhere there's no train.

There are taxi ranks at the Belfast International Airport, harbor ports, and the principal rail and bus stations. For other taxi service, check the local telephone directory for numbers to call. Some of the black, London-style cabs are not metered, and you should agree on a fare to your destination when you start out.

SHOPPING: Prices are generally lower in Northern Ireland than in the Republic for such items as Belleek, hand-woven tweeds, crystal, and many other fine products. Folks from below the border, in fact, often make shopping forays to the six counties to take advantage of the price difference. Two shopping expeditions that can be enjoyable and profitable, but you should telephone ahead to make arrangements to visit, are **Belleek Pottery,** Belleek, County Fermanagh (tel. Belleek 501), and **Tyrone Crystal,** Dungannon, County Tyrone (tel. Dungannon 25335).

2. A Suggested Itinerary

The six counties of Northern Ireland are all good rambling country, and this section is by no means meant to be a rigid, not-to-be-deviated-from itinerary. It is, however, a convenient circular tour of the Province which will get you to most of the highlights. As in the Republic, you're sure to discover some places not mentioned in the county-by-county chapters which follow.

If you're coming from Donegal, the following route is recommended (and, of course, it can be reversed should your departure point be Belfast). From Londonderry, head north through Limavady and the Roe Valley to Coleraine and the Bann Valley. Then go on to Portrush and the Giant's Causeway. Bushmills distillery is a short detour south from this point. Drive on through Ballycastle and enter the Antrim Coast Road, which takes you through the Nine Glens of Antrim, Larne, and Carrickfergus to Belfast. Then it's south to Downpatrick (if time permits, cut east around the Ards Peninsula) and west to Armagh, Enniskillen, and Belleek. Outstanding sightseeing points in each county are listed in Chapter XIII.

Chapter XIII

BELFAST AND LONDONDERRY

1. Belfast
2. Londonderry

IN ANCIENT TIMES, Belfast was a fort set at a ford of the River Lagan (it's name in Irish is *Beal Feirste,* "Mouth of the Sandy Ford"). Around it a small village developed, and in the 17th century Protestant settlers from Scotland and parts of England moved in (and native villagers were moved out) by order of English rulers, thus establishing the character of the city that grew at a steady pace until the end of the 1700s, thanks in large part to a thriving linen industry. In 1791, Wolfe Tone founded the United Irish Society in Belfast to bring together Protestants and Catholics who chafed under the repressive Penal Laws, and in 1798 their efforts led to an uprising, one which was quickly squelched by English forces. The shipyard that was to contribute so much to the city's growth was opened in 1791, by the time the Industrial Revolution was in full bloom during the 19th century, both shipbuilding and the linen trade welcomed newer, more modern operating methods. Both prospered, and Belfast's population grew by leaps and bounds.

1. Belfast

The city today is a bustling, energetic center of industry, yet for the visitor it is easy to get around and holds many points of interest—most prominent of which has to be the good Queen Victoria, whose statue adorns Donegall Square and whose architectural style is in evidence all around the city.

ACCOMMODATIONS: The Queen's University area is a happy hunting ground for good bed-and-breakfast accommodations, and those listed outside the city are close enough to serve as a good base for exploring Belfast while enjoying the scenic countryside.

Note: Prices shown below are those in effect in 1985—expect them to be higher in 1986.

For Students and Other Academics: Queen's University of Belfast, 1 College Gardens, Belfast BT9 6BW (tel. 0232-665938/24133, ext. 3212), can provide basic accommodations with institutional-type furnishings to university students, postgraduates, faculty members, and other persons directly or

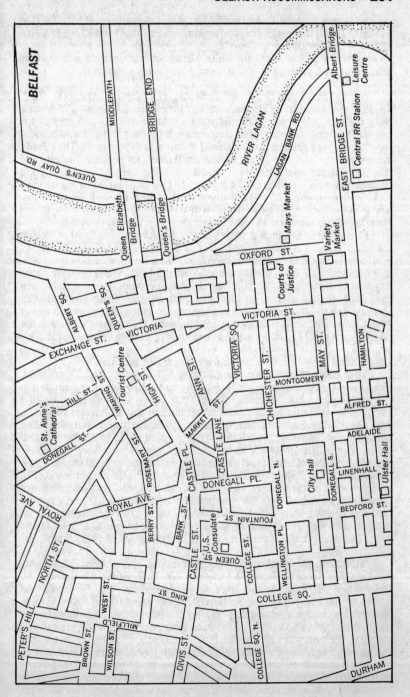

indirectly associated with university life. Rates range from £11 ($15.40) to £15.50 ($21.70) for singles (depending on bath facilities) and £27 ($37.80) to £29 ($40.60) for doubles. Plans are to upgrade all rooms to make them more attractive, but they are quite adequate and provide a university environment. Contact Mr. W. Hubert Armstrong, Administrator.

Bed-and-Breakfast: Liserin Guest House, 17 Eglantine Ave. (tel. 0232-660769), is set on a quiet street shaded by lime trees. It's about a 15-minute walk into the city center, and there's good bus service at the end of the block. The brick Victorian-style townhouse dates back to 1892, and original woodwork, high ceilings, and spacious rooms add to its charm. That charm comes in large part, too, from Mrs. Joan Walker, its gracious hostess, and she takes a personal interest in guests, serving evening tea and, upon request, a simple evening meal for about £6 ($8.40). The seven guestrooms include five singles, all attractively furnished and all with hand basins. Those in the back catch more sun than the ones in front, but all are light and cheerful. B&B rates are £9 ($12.60) single, £17 ($23.80) double.

Mrs. Angela Drumm, a native of Co. Meath who has lived in Belfast for many years, is the attractive and gracious hostess at **Camera House,** 44 Wellington Park (tel. 0232-660026/667856). This lovely guesthouse is just a few minutes' walk from the city center. The red-brick Victorian-style house has bay windows in the guest lounge and dining room, giving a light, airy look to both. All rooms, in fact, are quite bright. There are four with showers and toilet, seven with hand basin only, and of the eleven, four are single. Mrs. Drumm will furnish a light supper if you request it early in the day at a cost of £7 ($9.80). Bed-and-breakfast rates range from £16 ($22.40) single, £21 ($29.40) double for rooms with hand basins to £18.50 ($25.90) single, £26 ($36.40) double for those with private facilities.

Your enchantment with **The Cottage,** 377 Comber Rd., Dundonald, Co. Down (tel. Comber 878189), is likely to begin even as you drive into the parking area out back, for the driveway brings you into full view of a lovely lawn and colorful flowerbeds that beckon the traveler to sit awhile and enjoy such outdoors beauty. Once inside the traditional, sparkling white cottage, however, you'll be sorely tempted never to set foot outside again. Mrs. Elizabeth Muldoon has realized every cottage-lover's dream—she has lovingly retained (and even enhanced) all the original charm of the house and at the same time she installed every modern convenience. The living room is picture-pretty, as is the rustic dining area, and bedrooms are beautifully furnished with many antiques scattered about. Decor throughout is in keeping with a traditional country home. Just a short drive from Belfast, The Cottage is one of the most inviting accommodations in the area. Bed-and-breakfast rates are £8 ($11.20) single, £15 ($21) double.

Farmhouse: A comfortable old farmhouse that's been thoroughly modernized, **Greenlea Farm,** 48 Dunover Rd., Ballywalter, Co. Down (tel. Ballywalter 58218) looks out from its hilltop to the Ards Peninsula and across to the misty coast of Scotland and the Isle of Man. Mrs. Evelyn McIvor is its warm, friendly hostess who teaches crafts and enjoys sharing her considerable knowledge of the area with guests. Both the lounge and dining room have picture windows that frame the spectacular view, and the dining room holds lovely antique pieces, with lots of silver and crystal on display. Recreational amenities include tennis and bowling. Mrs. McIvor has one large family room with bunk beds for two children and a double for parents, as well as accommodations for singles and doubles. Her rates for bed-and-breakfast are £8 ($11.20) per person for one night only, £7 ($9.80) per person per night for longer stays, with a 25% reduction for children under 12 and 50% for those under 8. Senior citizens get a special £6 ($8.40) rate.

Self-Catering: The National Trust has two houses to rent by the week on the Ards Peninsula in the picturesque little fishing village of Kearney, Co. Down. There are lovely views of the Scottish coastline, the Isle of Man and the Mountains of Mourne, and bracing coastal walks are right outside the door. House No. 6 overlooks the sea and sleeps four, with a rental of £85 ($119), and No. 4, which will sleep six and also has good sea views, has a weekly rental of £100 ($140). These are high-season (July and August) weekly rates, and the houses are available at less during other months. For an illustrated booklet of these and other interesting self-catering cottages, write the National Trust, Holiday Cottage Bookings Secretary, Rowallane, Saintfield, Ballynahinch, Co. Down (tel. Saintfield 0238-510721).

WHERE TO EAT: From pub grub to elegant Big Splurges, you'll find meals to suit your mood and your pocketbook in Belfast. Pick up a copy of *Let's Eat Out* to supplement the selections below.

Catherine and Ronnie Craythorne have taken over a private railway station on the Belfast/Bangor line and converted it into one of this area's most charming restaurants, **The Carriage Restaurant,** Station Sq. Helen's Bay (tel. Helen's Bay 852841). A short and enjoyable ride from the city proper, the little stone building, with its rounded tower at one end, holds a small lounge near the entrance and intimate dining spaces which still retain the original station's interior divisions. There's a delightful informality about the place, yet it never descends to "casual," with lovely dinnerware, crystal, sparkling linen, and many other details attesting to the care and attention that will extend to the preparation and service of your meal.

The menu is varied and imaginative and changes frequently according to fresh ingredients available. A recent dinner offered such choices as sauteed brill with prawns and mushrooms, baked Dover sole with parsley butter, roast pheasant, roast suckling pig, and poached salmon with fennel and lemon sauce. À la carte prices for entrees are in the £7.50 ($10.50) to £8.50 ($11.90) range, and a 10% service charge is added to your bill. There's a set lunch at £7 ($10.50). The Carriage is not licensed, so bring your own wine. Hours are 12:30 to 2:15 p.m. and 7:30 to 11 p.m. Tuesday through Saturday, 12:30 to 2:15 p.m. on Sunday. Booking is absolutely essential.

Thompsons Restaurant, 47 Arthur St., Belfast, is one of those unobtrusive little places you sometimes—if you're very, very lucky—stumble across right in the heart of the city simply going about the business of supplying good food in ample portions at reasonable prices in a friendly, unpretentious setting. Because its front room is a pub, it might, in fact, be listed under the "Pub Grub" section below; but because its food goes so far beyond the usual, it warrants much more attention. Food service is in a room just beyond the bar, but you're likely to spend at least one drink's time out front waiting to be seated, for this is a popular place with Belfast natives who work in the inner city. Cordiality reigns, however, in both the pub and the restaurant sections, and any wait is bound to be a pleasant one. The extensive (and surprising) menu, concentrating mainly on such Irish offerings as seafood, steak, ham, and chicken, covers just about anything you could want, and far more than you could expect in this kind of eatery. There's plaice or sole poached with fresh prawns in cheese and wine sauce or in a mornay sauce or fried in bread crumbs with banana and chutney (as well as less exotic choices); scampi that comes in several forms (Newburg, provençale, grilled, or deep fried); fresh Irish trout baked or grilled; prime filet steaks (au poivre or tournedos Rossini); sirloin steaks; etc., etc., etc. À la carte prices for main courses range from £4 ($5.60) to £6 ($8.40), with omelets in the £2 ($2.80) to £3 ($4.20) range, and appetizers (from which I happily assembled an excellent lunch) running from under £1 ($1.40) to £3 ($4.20) for smoked salmon. All come with homemade Ulster wheaten bread and butter. Hours are 12:15 to 3:15 p.m. and 6 to 9:30 p.m. Monday through Saturday. As you may have guessed, this is a personal favorite and one I wouldn't want you to miss!

Good pub grub is to be found from noon to 2:30 p.m. at the following: the **Crown Liquor Saloon,** 46 Great Victoria St.; **White's Tavern,** Winecellar Entry; **Queen's Lounge,** 4/6 Queen's Arcade; **Kelly's Cellars,** 30 Bank St. (the oldest public house in Belfast); the **Bodega Bar,** 4 Callender St.; **Robinson's Bar,** 38 Great Victoria St.; **Fountain Tavern,** 16 Fountain St.; **Deer's Head,** 1/3 Lower Garfield St.; and on the outskirts of town, the **Shaftesbury Inn,** 739 Antrim Rd., and the **Homestead Inn,** 314 Hillhall Rd., Lisburn.

THINGS TO SEE AND DO: Your first stop should be the **Northern Ireland Tourist Board Information Office** in River House, 48 High St. (tel. 246609). They can give you brochures on sightseeing highlights, bus tours, day trips, and sports such as fishing, golf, cruising for Belfast and for all of Northern Ireland.

You can't miss the **City Hall,** a massive Portland stone building crowned with a copper dome in Donegall Square. It was ten years abuilding and its interior is elegant with Greek and Italian marble. The city's industrial history is traced in a large mural. If you don't recognize it otherwise, you'll know it by the bust of Queen Victoria out front (she was a guest of the city in 1846 and is much revered). A Great War Memorial sits on the west side, with a memorial sculpture to the *Titanic,* which was built in Belfast and went to the bottom in 1912.

Look for the **Albert Memorial** towards the river in High Street—it pays tribute, of course, to Queen Victoria's consort and is affectionately known as Belfast's "leaning tower" because it is slightly less than straight.

An interesting collection of stained glass, paintings, and sculptures—all dealing with Belfast's seafaring connections—is on display at the **Harbour Office** in Corporation Square. You can see it on weekdays from 9:30 a.m. to 4:30 p.m. if you call the Administration Officer at 234432, ext. 206, in advance.

On Lower Donegall Street, the **Belfast Cathedral** (St. Anne's) was built between 1899 and 1904. It has a particularly fine mosaic showing St. Patrick landing at Saul in A.D. 432, which you will find over the entrance to the Chapel of the Holy Spirit.

Bend an elbow at least once, or go by for a pub lunch, at the **Crown Liquor Saloon** on Great Victoria Street. It's a marvelous old Victorian pub, the ultimate in casual elegance with its carved woodwork, snugs lining one wall, flickering gaslights, and painted ceramic tiles. Some "chrome and mirror" addicts got their hands on it a few years back and nearly modernized the character out of it, but the National Trust came to the rescue and it is now back to its original state.

Try to get to a performance in the **Grand Opera House,** on Great Victoria Street. It's a marvel of rich, rococo eccentricity, with 24 gilt elephant heads separating boxes sporting canopies, Buddhas scattered about the draperies, and lots of gold and maroon. Closed from 1972 to 1981, it's been beautifully restored.

I don't know about you, but I am fascinated by happenings such as the **St. George's Variety Market,** a large, barny place with an entrance on May Street, where hordes of Belfast citizens congregate every Tuesday and Friday from 7 a.m. to 3 p.m. to rummage through stalls that have everything imaginable for sale. It's a terrific people-watching experience, and you just might pick up a totally unexpected—and different—gift or souvenir.

A morning or afternoon at the **Belfast Zoo** is a delight. It's out on Antrim Road in a mountain park with good views of the city and the lough. Open every day from 10 a.m. to 5 p.m.

Also out of town (about 8 miles), the **Ulster Folk Museum** on the Bangor Road is a trip back in Irish history. Its setting is 136 acres of the Cultra Manor estate, and the manor house serves as a museum, tearoom, and giftshop. Scattered around the grounds are cottages from all over rural Northern Ireland that have been transplanted from their original sites and authentically restored to re-create Irish country life of the past. It'll take you about half a day to walk the wooded grounds and browse through the farmhouse with its inside cow byre, forge, spade mill, weaver's house, flax scutching mill, and the 1790 church. It's a unique experience and one not to be missed. Weekday hours are 11 a.m. to 5 p.m., and on Sundays, 2 to 5 p.m. There's a small admission charge.

If your family is firmly rooted in Northern Ireland, the **Irish Genealogical Association,** 162a Kingsway, Dunmurry, Belfast BT17 9AD (tel. 0232-629595), will do advance research, assign someone to help you trace your Ulster connections during your visit, and can even arrange personalized tours for you to tread the ground of your ancestors.

2. Londonderry

There's the aura of the ages about Londonderry—in ancient times, it was known as *Doire Calgach* ("Calgach's Oak wood"), later simply as *Doire* ("Oak Grove"); then came St. Columba in A.D. 546 to found a monastic settlement which became *Cholomcille Doire* ("St. Columba's oakgrove"). Some ten centuries later, after years of seesaw battles to conquer it, King James succeeded in 1613 and promptly transferred it by charter to the City of London to be administered by The Honourable Irish Society, and its name became Londonderry. After all that, it is still affectionately called simply Derry by most of the Irish on both sides of the border.

Strong city walls 20 to 25 feet high and 14 to 37 feet high with seven gates went up soon after the Society took over things, and despite siege after siege, those walls are largely intact today. This old, walled section of modern-day Londonderry is west of the River Foyle, as are the main business and shopping districts, with ancient winding lanes and rows of charming Georgian and Victorian buildings. In the northeastern portion of the walls, Shipquay Gate is only two blocks from the river, and the historic old Guildhall with its turrets and tower clock is midway between river quays and this gate. Most of what you'll want to see will be within a short walk of these two points, including the bus station, Tourist Office, and inexpensive places to eat. Surrounding the original, walled city and across Craigavon Bridge (south of the Guildhall), modern Londonderry has sprouted along the river and hillsides, covering almost ten times the area that spawned it.

You'll find the **Tourist Office** in Foyle Street (tel. 269501), with hours of 9 a.m. to 5 p.m. weekdays and 10 a.m. to 6 p.m. Saturdays during July and August. The helpful staff will arrange accommodations (no charge) and walking tours, and provide sightseeing information for the city and its immediate vicinity.

The **railway station** is in Duke Street, Waterside (tel. 42228); the **Ulsterbus station** in Foyle Street (tel. 262261).

ACCOMMODATIONS: Most city center accommodations are well beyond the reach of budgeteers, but the Tourist Office can help you find nearby places within our price range.
Note: Prices shown below are those in effect in 1985—expect them to be higher in 1986.

Bed-and-Breakfast: In the city itself, Mrs. Eleonora Slevin operates **Clarence House**, 15 Northland Rd. (tel. 0504-265342), with singles, doubles, and one family room that sleeps up to four. Rates are £8 ($11.20) per person.

Florence House, 16 Northland Rd. (tel. 0504-68093), offers doubles and two family rooms. Mrs. McGinley is hostess here, and her rates for bed-and-breakfast are £8 ($11.20) per person.

Farmhouses: Friendly Mrs. Emma Craig presides over **Ballycarton Farm**, Bellarena, Limavady, Co. Londonderry (tel. Ballerena 50216), which is beautifully situated about 17 miles outside Londonderry in 50 acres of mountain and coastal scenery. The comfortably furnished guestrooms are all of ample size, many with good views. Mrs. Craig can arrange babysitting, and she doesn't mind travelers with dogs. Rates are £7 ($9.80), and the evening meal costs the same (with advance booking, Mrs. Craig will prepare dinner for nonresidents).

Bond's Glen House, 53 Bond's Glen Rd., Killaloo, Co. Londonderry (tel. Dunamanagh 253), is Mrs. Olive Rankin's 1840s farmhouse 11 miles from the city. There's a pony for guests to ride, and in the scenic surrounding countryside there's good fishing. One of the four nice guestrooms is a family room, and Mrs. Rankin will arrange babysitting. Rates are £7 ($9.80), and if you book for the evening meal at the same cost, Mrs. Rankin is willing to serve as late as 8 p.m., to allow you a full day of sightseeing.

Hotel: One of the nicest inexpensive hotels I've run across in Ireland is the **White Horse Inn,** 68 Clooney Rd., Londonderry (tel. 0504-860606). It's four miles outside town on the Limavady road, with good, frequent bus service into Londonderry. The owners of this modern, attractive hotel/ motel, Alwyn and Iris Kydd, have put into effect per-room pricing, which means your room costs the same whether you use it as a single or a double. Each room has tea-and-coffee-making equipment, direct-dial telephone, color TV, and an alarm clock. Attached to the hotel is a block of motel-like chalets with a fridge and cooking facilities. On the premises, you'll also find the Carousel Restaurant, Yesterdays grill room (see "Where to Eat"), and a sophisticated bar and lounge—with these complete facilities, the out-of-town location is no inconvenience at all, and the White Horse has my high recommendation (especially for two traveling together, when rates become budget). Rates begin at £18 ($25.20) for hotel rooms, and £22 ($30.80) for chalets.

WHERE TO EAT: The aforementioned **White Horse Inn** offers exceptional value with lunches that range from £2 ($2.80) to £4 ($5.60), and evening meals for under £8.50 ($11.90).

The **Parks Restaurant,** 31 Collon Lane, Shantallow (tel. 262712), is a fully licensed eatery that offers moderately priced light lunches and grills from 12:30 to 2:30 p.m. and a good à la carte menu from which a three-course evening meal will range from £5 ($7) to £10 ($14). Dinner hours are 7 to 10:30 p.m.

For pub grub between noon and 2:30 p.m., try the following: **Duffy's Tavern,** 17 Foyle St.; the **Anchor Inn,** 38 Ferryquay St.; and the **Duke Street Restaurant,** 90 Duke St.

THINGS TO SEE AND DO: The Tourist Office has a terrific folder, *Walk About Derry,* as well as loads of other background information on points of interest in the city.

One things you should *not* miss in Londonderry is a walk along the old **city walls.** They are the only unbroken city walls in the British Isles, and Londonderry was the last city in Europe to build protective wall fortifications. Check with the Tourist Office about days and times of their guided walking tours along the walls, and go along if you can—the narrative adds a lot to the city scene below and the landscape beyond. If you go on your own, enter at the Magazine Gate.

You can visit the imposing Gothic **Guildhall** on a tour with a guide (call the Superintendent, 65151). It dates from 1890, but had to be almost completely reconstructed after a terrible fire in 1908. Look for the window in the marble vestibule that depicts *The Relief of Derry*. The lovely stained-glass windows are the work of local artisans. The Guildhall is open Monday through Friday from 9 a.m. to 4 p.m.

St. Columb's Cathedral was built in the mid-1600s, but much of what you'll see today has been added since. One of its most important features is the memorial window showing the relief of the siege in 1689. You can visit any day between 9 a.m. and 12:30 p.m. and 2 and 5 p.m.

Outside the walls, take time to stroll down narrow little streets such as Albert and Nailor Row, both lined with interesting and quaint houses and buildings.

Londonderry is rich in traditional Irish music, with musicians from neighboring County Donegal often coming over to join in. Check with the Tourist Office, or go by the following pubs to see if and when there will be music: **Phoenix Bar,** Park Ave., Rosemount; **Gweedore Bar,** Waterloo St.; **Castle Bar,** Waterloo St.; **Andrew Cole,** Strand Rd.; **Dungloe Bar,** Waterloo St.; and the **Cutty Sark,** John St. Another hangout of traditional musicians is **The Quaver,** 31 Carlisle Rd., where its owner, young Doreen Rice, sells music and instruments (pick up a tin whistle for little or nothing—you'll be surprised how soon you'll be tootling a tune!).

Chapter XIII

AROUND NORTHERN IRELAND

1. County Antrim
2. County Armagh
3. County Down
4. County Fermanagh
5. County Londonderry
6. County Tyrone

1. County Antrim

ACCOMMODATIONS: My personal choice of accommodations in Co. Antrim is almost any of the friendly farmhouses, but there are two rather special hotels that definitely deserve consideration.
Note: Prices shown are those in effect in 1985—expect them to be higher in 1986.

Farmhouses: Mrs. Catherine Scally, 185 Torr Rd. (Cushendun 026-674-252) is a charming lady with a completely charming farmhouse very close to the Glens of Antrim. There's something homey and old-fashioned about the house and Mrs. Scally's hospitality, and the views from her hillside location are smashing. Rates are £8.50 ($11.90) for bed-and-breakfast, and you can choose your evening meal from an à la carte menu with prices of £5 ($7) to £8 ($11.20).

Ardnaree, 105 Dunluce Rd., White Rocks, Portrush BT56 8ND (tel. Portrush 0265-823407), overlooks the sea, with the hills of Donegal in the distance. A beautiful beach is just a few minutes' walk away, and there's a good golf course in the vicinity. The centrally heated modern bungalow is the home of Mrs. Elsie Rankin, who takes a personal interest in her guests. The attractive guestrooms include two on the ground floor, one with private toilet and shower and one large family room. Rates are £8 ($11.20).

Ben Neagh House, 11 Crumlin Rd., Crumlin BT29 4AD (tel. Crumlin 084-94-52271) has a grass tennis court and an indoor gameroom among its amenities. The Georgian-style farmhouse in its parklike setting is the home of Mr. and Mrs. Peel, who make their guests feel right at home. Rates for bed-and-breakfast are £9 ($12.60) single, £17 ($23.80) double.

Hotels: My top candidate for a Big Splurge (which really isn't all that big, dollarwise) is the **Londonderry Arms Hotel,** Carnlough (tel. 0574-

85255/85458/85459). It sits right across the road from Carnlough Harbour, and began life back in 1854 as a coaching inn. The O'Neill family has owned the pretty ivy-covered hotel since 1947, and Frank (the present O'Neill manager) continues the tradition of graciousness and home-style hospitality. There are beautiful antique furnishings scattered about, the tavern has a traditional decor, and the spacious lounge is warmed by a copper-hooded fireplace. Both the tavern and the lounge draw lots of locals, making a stop here even more interesting for us visitors. Guestrooms are beautifully done up, and hand-woven Avoca bedspreads are a nice touch. All have private bath, telephone, radio, and TV (upon request). The rather modest rates (for this type of accommodation) include a full Irish breakfast and run £16 ($22.40) single, £30 ($42) double from May through December, lower from January to May. Highly recommended, both for the high standards and for the O'Neills.

The **Bayview Hotel**, Portballintrae, Bushmills (tel. Bushmills 31453), is another small hotel whose hospitality and homey comfort seems to come from another era. It faces the seafront, and is a great favorite with locals, who regularly patronize both its Porthole Lounge Bar and Watch House Restaurant. In a brilliant concept of renovation, the hotel's owners have given all guestrooms a view of the curving bayfront, and all are nicely furnished and decorated. Bed-and-breakfast rates begin at £15 ($21) for singles, £28 ($39.20) for doubles.

WHERE TO EAT: When driving the Antrim Coast Road, plan to stop for lunch or dinner at the **Londonderry Arms Hotel** in Carnlough (see above). Meals are served in a dining room replete with period pieces, and if you can get a table in the front dining room, you'll have a view of the harbor as you dine. Lunch will run about £6 ($8.40), dinner about £9 ($12.60). If the budget simply won't stretch for those prices, just next door the **Glenbay Hotel's grillroom** serves excellent meals for under £5 ($7).

For pub grub, stop in Portballintrae at the **Bayview Hotel's Porthole Lounge Bar** and lunch with the locals.

In Portstewart, **O'Malley's Edgewater Hotel,** 88 Strand Rd. (tel. 026-5832224/5833688), serves excellent lunches and dinners in a glass-walled dining room overlooking the sea and a curving beach. Prices run about the same as the Londonderry Arms above.

In Portrush, **The Harbour Bar** is a good place for a before- or after-dinner libation. It sits on the wharf overlooking the boat-filled harbor, and it's mostly locals you'll find in the plain, old-style bar. Very Irish.

THINGS TO SEE AND DO: Co. Antrim has perhaps the largest concentration of sightseeing attractions of any of the six counties.

Americans will be interested to know that the following Presidents had Co. Antrim roots: Andrew Jackson's parents came from Carrickfergus; Andrew Johnson's grandfather was from Larne; Chester Arthur's father was born near Ballymena; Grover Cleveland's grandfather was a Co. Antrim merchant; William McKinley's great-great grandfather emigrated from Conagher near Ballymoney; and Theodore Roosevelt's maternal ancestors were from Larne. Quite an impressive score for one county!

In **Carrickfergus,** there's another American connection: Commander John Paul Jones stood offshore just below Carrickfergus Castle in 1778 in the *Ranger* and mounted an attack on the British *Drake* that ended with his capture of the larger vessel. The massive castle dates from the late 12th and early 13th centuries, there's an interesting museum inside featuring mementos of the Irish Hussars, the Inniskillin Dragoons, and the North Irish Horse regiments. Hours are 10 a.m. to 1 p.m. and 2 to 6 p.m., Monday through Saturday. In the summer, it's open Sundays from 2 to 6 p.m. You might want to inquire about medieval banquets in the Castle—their future is uncertain as we go to press, but they could be fun in such an impressive setting.

Driving north from Carrickfergus, you'll pass through—and slowly, please, so you won't miss one whit of some pretty gorgeous scenery—the nine **Glens of Antrim,** which open to the sea.

The **Giant's Causeway,** east of Portrush, is much more impressive when you walk its basalt columns (there are some 37,000!) than any photograph can possibly convey. How they came to be packed so tightly together that they form a sort of bridge from the shoreline out into the sea, submerge and then surface on the Hebrides island of Staffa, is a matter of conjecture. Scientists will tell you unequivocally that they're the result of a massive volcanic eruption about 60 million years ago, when molten lava cooled and formed into geometric shapes. But, after all, what do *they* know—as far as the *Irish* are concerned, the causeway would still be above water all the way across had it not been for a ferocious tiff between the Ulster giant, Finn MacCoul and his Scottish counterpart, Finn Gall. You see, it was the Ulsterman who built the causeway in the first place, and when he went home to rest up a bit from his labors, the wily Scotsman tripped across, club in hand, to catch his foe unawares. Now, *Mrs.* McCoul was busy at the hearth with the dinner, and when Finn Gall burst into her kitchen and demanded to know if the sleeping giant were her husband, she—in a master stroke of quick thinking—assured him, "Ooh, no, sor, 'tis only ma wee babe." Well, the very thought of what the father of such a gigantic babe must be like put such a fright into the Scotsman that he hightailed it back across the water, destroying the causeway behind him to keep Finn MacCoul in Ireland where he belonged. Choose your own version (I, personally, favor the giants!), but don't miss a stop by this curiosity. It's free, and there's even a minibus (with a very small fare) down to the bottom of the cliff for those who don't care to make the short walk.

If you happen along the Antrim Coast Drive between May and September, stop about 8 kilometers northwest of Ballycastle to take a look at the **Carrick-a-Rede Rope Bridge.** It's strung across a 25-yard chasm to connect two clifftops that are separated by seas too treacherous to be crossed any other way. If you're not the fainthearted type, you'll not be charged to cross over the wooden planks as you grip the wire handrails. There's a roadside car park from which you walk to the bridge.

Just east of Portrush, look for a rocky headland crowned by the great lump of ruined **Dunluce Castle.** Some say its name means "mermaid's fort," and they might well be right—there's a deep cave that penetrates the rock on which the castle sits at the sea's edge. There are too many tales and legends surrounding Dunluce to recount here, but you can read them in the official guide available at the entrance. From April through September, you can visit the castle between the hours of 10 a.m. and 1 p.m. and 2 and 7 p.m. Tuesday through Saturday, from 2 to 7 p.m. on Sunday. During other months, closing time is 4 p.m.

A short detour off the coast road will take you to the village of Bushmills and the oldest licensed distillery in the world. The **Old Bushmills Distillery** is a fascinating place, and still turning out "the wine of the country" after all these centuries (people in Northern Ireland will urge you to try Black Bush—

do!). To see a marvelous exhibition of its history and follow a guided tour through the distilling process, book with one of the free tours every Monday through Thursday morning and afternoon or Friday morning. There are sometimes schedule changes, however, so it's best to ring ahead to make sure (tel. Bushmills 31521).

The farmhouse from which President Chester Arthur's father left for America in 1816 is at **Dreen,** near Cullybackey, Ballymena, and the white-washed thatched cottage is worth a drive through beautiful countryside to meet the delightful people who maintain it for visitors like you and me. They'll greet you any day except Friday from April through September from 2 to 6 p.m.

In the town of **Antrim,** look for the perfectly preserved round tower that is 49 feet around and over 90 feet tall.

If you're an island lover, you will want to reserve an overnight to spend on **Rathlin Island,** a rugged outpost off the Antrim coast that is Ireland's largest inhabited island. It has a fascinating history, and can only be reached via the mail boat that makes one trip a day, leaving Ballycastle Harbour about 11 a.m. and not returning to the mainland until 9 a.m. the following day. The 50-minute open motorboat trip costs £3 ($4.20) round trip. The island's only accommodation is the **Rathlin Guest House,** The Quay, Rathlin, Co. Antrim (tel. Rathlin 71217/71216), run by Mrs. Kay McCurdy. Bed-and-breakfast rates are £6.50 ($9.10), with the evening meal costing £5 ($7). There are marvelous cliff walks, magnificent views of Ireland's northern coast, and the fun of topping off the day at the one pub in the company of some of the 100 inhabitants.

2. County Armagh

ACCOMMODATIONS: For bed-and-breakfast accommodations in Northern Ireland's smallest county, try **Mary and Michael Murphy's guesthouse,** 63 Drumcairn Rd., Armagh (tel. Armagh 0861/525074). It's about a mile and a half from town, set on 16 pleasant rural acres. The modern bungalow is centrally heated, and all the attractive guestrooms are on the ground level, all have hand basins. Mary can arrange for a babysitter. Rates are £9 ($12.60) single, £16 ($22.40) double.

Farmhouse: In Portadown, **Redbrick House,** Corbrackey La. Portadown BT62 1PQ (tel. Portadown 0762-335268), is three miles out of town, and Mrs. Moreen Stephenson, the accommodating hostess, will arrange to meet first-time visitors with enough advance notice. The centrally heated modern bungalow counts one large family room among its nice guestrooms, all of which are on the ground floor. Rates are £7.50 ($10.50) single, £14 ($19.60) double.

WHERE TO EAT: In Armagh Town, the **Archway,** 5 Hartford Pl., has inexpensive set lunches as well as pastries and light snacks. Hours are 10 a.m. to 5 p.m. Tuesday through Saturday. **Spider's Rest,** 2 Scotch St., serves sandwiches from 12:30 to 2:30 p.m. every day except Sundays. Excellent evening meals are available at the **Ulster Inn Gallery,** 147 Railway St. (tel. Armagh 0861-522103), with à la carte prices for a three-course meal running from £10 ($14) to £15 ($21). Hours are 7 to 9:45 p.m., and it's fully licensed.

In Portadown, look for inexpensive lunches at **Allen's Coffee House,** West St., and the **Crown Bar,** Woodhouse St.

THINGS TO SEE AND DO: The town of Armagh is Northern Ireland's most interesting cathedral town, with imposing edifices of both the Catholic and Protestant faiths facing each other from their respective hilltops. According to a tablet on the north side of the **Church of Ireland cathedral** (which was restored in the 18th and 19th centuries), this is the final resting place of Brian Boru. Red hats of every cardinal archbishop of Armagh and medallions for each of Ireland's saints are part of what you'll find in the Gothic-style **Catholic cathedral,** which dates from the mid-1800s.

On **The Mall** in Armagh Town, there's a fine small **museum** that holds an exceptionally good collection of prehistoric relics, historical costumes, and natural-history exhibits as well as an art gallery. It's free, and hours are 10 a.m. to 1 p.m. and 2 to 5 p.m., Monday through Saturday. Also on The Mall is **The Royal Irish Fusiliers Regimental Museum,** housed in The Sovereign's House and open weekdays from 10 a.m. to 12:30 p.m. and 2 to 4:30 p.m.

About two miles outside Newry on the Newtownhamilton road, there's an interesting 18th-century thatched manor house. **Derrymore House** is reputed to be the setting for the Act of Union between Great Britain and Ireland, and you can go through the house by calling ahead (Saintfield 510721) for an appointment.

3. County Down

ACCOMMODATIONS: During summer months, many accommodations in Co. Down offer special-interest (fishing, golf, etc.) "Super Summer Saver" midweek and weekend rates. For details, write Recreation/Tourist Department, Down District Council, Strangford Rd., Downpatrick, Co. Down (tel. Downpatrick 4331).

In addition to the Co. Down accommodations listed in Chapter XII, the farmhouses below are highly recommended.
Note: Prices listed below are those in effect in 1985—expect them to be higher in 1986.

Farmhouses: You know that traditional Irish farmhouse you've pictured in your mind all the time you were planning your trip? Whitewashed stables and outbuildings grouped around a courtyard along with an old-style farmhouse opening onto the courtyard? Well, **Ivybank Farm,** Maghera, Newcastle (tel. Newcastle 22450), exactly fits your fantasy! What's more, Mr. and Mrs. Hart, the warmly gracious owners, will go well beyond anything you could have imagined in the way of Irish hospitality. You'll begin to fall under their spell when you first drive up to the well-cared-for farmyard and see the front garden with seating for proper enjoyment of a smashing view of the Mountains of Mourne. Across the road, a rose trellis leads to another hillside garden where guests also enjoy getting the late afternoon sun. Inside, the house is nicely appointed and neat as a pin, and guestrooms have terrific views, floral wallpaper, and pretty bedspreads. To top it all off, Mrs. Hart has a well-deserved local reputation for her outstanding cooking. Rates at Ivybank are £8 ($11.20), and only £6 ($8.40) for a superb, four-course evening meal (book before noon).

Historic **Mourne Hall,** 76 Kilbroney Rd., Rostrevor (tel. 069-37-38389), has been a haven for several notable figures of Northern Ireland's history, and it offers the same hospitality to today's travelers. The imposing Georgian house is set in a 12-acre wooded estate and furnished throughout with period pieces. Mrs. Leitch, its gracious hostess, is chairman of the Farm & Country Holidays Association and both she and Mr. Leitch take a personal interest in every guest. There are three twin-bedded rooms and one single; all have hand basins; and all look out to lovely rural views. Ask Mr. Leitch about the ancient cemetery just across the way. Mourne Hall is open May through October, and rates are £12 ($16.80) single, £19 ($26.60) double. It is essential to book ahead at this popular country home.

Hotel: In the pleasant seaside resort of Kilkeel, the **Kilmorey Arms Hotel,** Greencastle St., Kilkeel (tel. Kilkeel 62220/62801), is a delightful small inn, with the sort of homey atmosphere that draws Irish families back year after year. Its attractive public rooms are much favored by people in the town, and you're likely to find Miss Hopper, the friendly manageress, scurrying around attending to last-minute details for a local wedding dinner or some other function. There's a nice cocktail lounge, and the flag-floored public bar is full of character, both from its relic-hung walls and from the faces passing the time of day at the bar (if you're just passing through Kilkeel, do stop by this interesting bar for a pint). There are 14 nice bedrooms, all with private baths. Rates are £13 ($18.20) single, £24 ($33.60) double.

Self Catering: The National Trust has three interesting self-catering premises in Co. Down in addition to those listed in Chapter XII in Kearney. For full descriptions and rates, send for their illustrated directory at the address shown in Chapter XII.

WHERE TO EAT: Rea's, 78 Market St., Downpatrick (tel. 2017), is one of my personal favorites among Northern Ireland eateries. First of all, it's an old-style place, with two small front rooms crammed full of an eclectic collection of old objects (like the pottery bottle that was once used to hold Guinness, a marble for its stopper). Secondly, it always has the contented hum of a good crowd—many of them obviously regulars—enjoying good company and good food. Best of all, the food is just great and prices are moderate. For example, the highest price on the lunch menu is £2.50 ($3.50), and for that you have a choice of beef, ham, or roast chicken with stuffing served with potatoes (boiled, roast, or french fried) and fresh vegetables. The snack menu features toasted sandwiches, pizza, soup, and roll, etc., for under £1 ($1.40). For heartier evening meals (Wednesday through Saturday), entrees like chicken in a whiskey and cream sauce, lambs kidneys with mushrooms and red wine, or sirloin steak peppered and served with garlic butter range in price from £6 ($8.40) to £7.50 ($10.50), all served with potatoes and vegetables. There's a more modern dining room back of those character-filled front rooms, and an almost-formal dining room upstairs (fireplace, gilt mirrors, etc.). Lunch is served from noon to 3 p.m. Monday through Saturday; dinner from 6:30 to 9:30 p.m. Wednesday through Saturday. In case you didn't guess, Rea's is highly recommended!

Just offshore (connected by a causeway) on Skettrick Island, **Whiterock,** Co. Down, Daft Eddies (tel. 541615), serves an excellent cold buffet lunch from 12:45 to 2 p.m. Monday through Saturday, through September, with such specialties as chicken in plum sauce and honey-and-lemon pork for around £5 ($7). From Tuesday through Saturday, dinners feature seafood, local meats, etc., at prices of £10 ($14) and up from 7:30 to 9:30 p.m.

For superior pub grub, stop in the **Primrose Bar**, 30 Main St., Ballynahinch. They're known locally for their steak casseroles and open-faced prawn sandwiches. Other offerings include fresh trout, salmon, and a variety of salads. There's always a nice fire blazing, and as a Northern Ireland friend assured me, "The crack is always good." Hours are 11:30 a.m. to 11 p.m., Monday through Saturday.

In the little town of Hillsborough (a perfect example of an Ulster plantation town), the **Watershed Restaurant,** 10 Ballynahinch St. (tel. 683555/ 683544), is a beautiful, restful sort of eatery, decorated in soft pastels. An excellent four-course table d'hôte lunch priced at £6 ($8.40) features entrees of poached smoked trout with prawn sauce, fresh cod scampi-style, and roast turkey and ham. Dinners, with specialties like pheasant in brandy sauce, run anywhere from £10 ($14) to £15 ($21). Hours are noon to 3 p.m. and 6 to 10 p.m., Monday through Saturday, and it's a good idea to book.

THINGS TO SEE AND DO: Co. Down has been immortalized by William Percy French for its Mountains of Mourne which "sweep down to the sea." One of the places you can best see that sweep is the resort town of **Newcastle,** which curves around a gorgeous bay with a wide, golden strand. (A little trivia item: actress Greer Garson was born in Castlewellen.)

A delightful Co. Down exploration takes in the **Ards Peninsula,** 23 miles of unspoiled countryside dotted with picture-postcard villages, windmills, and ancient ring forts. Drive out to the little 19th-century village of **Kearney** and you drive back through the centuries. There's a car ferry that crosses from **Portaferry** to **Strongford** in about four minutes and lets you look straight out to sea (if, that is, you look quick enough).

St. Patrick's first stone church is thought to have been erected on the site of the present-day **Down Cathedral** in Downpatrick, and a stone in the churchyard purports to be his gravestone, as well as those of St. Brigid and St. Columba. The fact that those assertions are a matter of much dispute does little to dispel the sense of the continuity of the centuries when you stand on the peaceful hillside site—certainly it would take a heart of stone not to believe that they could be true!

The **Newry Arts Centre Museum,** 1a Bank Parade (tel. Newry 61244), features exhibitions of ancient archeological items, folk art, and pottery as well as touring exhibitions of interest. There's no admission charge, and hours are 11 a.m. to 4:30 p.m. Monday through Friday.

Near Strangford Village, **Castle Ward** is a fascinating house that's a sort of architectural hodgepodge, part pseudo-Gothic and part classical. The estate, administered by the National Trust, sits on the shores of Strangford Lough and includes formal gardens, a Victorian laundry and theater in the stableyard, and a sawmill. A tearoom is open in the stableyard from April through September. The house is open from April through September every day but Friday for a small admission; grounds are open to the public without charge from dawn to sunset daily year round.

Bang in the middle of Co. Down, **Ballynahinch** might have been the setting for a dramatic change in the course of Irish history had not the 7,000 United Irishmen (led by a linen draper from Lisburn named Henry Munroe) been roundly defeated in their battle to take the town. The bloody battle raged the length of Ballynahinch's broad main street until, in the end, the Royal Forces were the victors. Munroe was executed, as was a young Presbyterian girl named Betsy Gray, who had seized an old, rusty sword, mounted a horse, and joined in the fray. It was a last, desperate stand for the United Irishmen, and you might give a tip of the hat to their memory as you pass through.

4. County Fermanagh

ACCOMMODATIONS: *Note: Prices listed below are those in effect in 1985—expect them to be higher in 1986.*

Bed-and-Breakfast: In the town of Enniskillen, Mrs. Acheson's **Erindale Guest House**, 15 Sligo Rd. (tel. Enniskillen 3279), has two double rooms and two family rooms in a centrally heated home that overlooks the town. Rates are £8 ($11.20) single, £15 ($21) double.

Farmhouse: About 20 miles from Enniskillen and 12 miles from good beaches, **Manville House,** Aughnablaney, Letter (tel. Kesh 036-56-31668), is the centrally heated, lakeside home of Mrs. Pearl Graham. There are marvelous views of Lough Erne and the Sligo Mountains, and there's good fishing right at hand. All the well-appointed guestrooms have hand basins. Rates for bed-and-breakfast are £8 ($11.20). To reach Manville House, take A47 from Kesh and turn right at the signpost for Letter.

Self-Catering: The **Carlton Cottages,** Belleek, Co. Fermanagh (tel. Belleek 282), are well-planned three-bedroom cottages set in wooded grounds on the banks of the River Erne. It's hard to imagine a more beautiful setting, and each cottage is fitted with twin beds, bath and shower, fully equipped kitchen, and a large lounge with an open-hearth fireplace. Patios doors open to the outside, and guests have full use of the facilities of the Hotel Carlton. Seasonal rates range from £110 ($154) to £180 ($252) per week, and there are special weekend rates available. Highly recommended.

WHERE TO EAT: In Enniskillen, the **Crow's Nest,** 12 High St. (tel. 22865), covers just about all your needs: there's morning coffee, snacks available all day, lunches of sandwiches, hamburgers, and salads, and a good à la carte menu for evening meals, all at inexpensive and moderate prices. Hours are 10 a.m. to 10 p.m., Monday through Saturday.

The **Encore Steak House,** Main St., Ballinamallard (tel. Ballinamallard 606), is just a short drive from Enniskillen, and a real find. There's an air of intimacy in the beautifully appointed, two-centuries-old building, and partners Cyril Evans and Roger Davis present an excellent menu that features steak (what else!), scampi, plaice, trout and other seafood as well as a very good beef curry. The wine list is as fine as the menu, and for after dinner, you can choose from an array of liqueur coffees—Irish, Russian, Caribbean, French, etc., etc. Table d'hôte dinner prices run from £8 ($11.20) to £10 ($14), and hours are 5 to 11 p.m. Definitely worth a detour to have dinner here.

In Bellanaleck, **The Sheelin** (tel. Florencecourt 232) is a small, picturesque house, and dining there is like eating with friends in a family dining room. Open from 10 a.m. to 9:30 p.m. Mondays through Saturdays, and 1:30 to 6:30 p.m. on Sundays, the Sheelin offers morning coffee, lunches, afternoon teas (all at moderate prices) and, once a week, usually Saturdays, gourmet dinners (pricey).

THINGS TO SEE AND DO: The **River Erne** and its **Upper and Lower Loughs** are tourist centers for Co. Fermanagh. The river and the loughs are dotted with interesting and historical islands, and a holiday cruising their waters is a very special experience. You can book a variety of watery accommodations in Enniskillen, and the **Lakeland Visitor Centre,** Shore Rd., Enniskillen (tel. Enniskillen 0365-23110), publishes a detailed *Holidays Afloat and Ashore* booklet with illustrations of many of the cruisers available.

To learn more about this fascinating part of Northern Ireland (some of the mountainy country around the loughs is quite mysterious and wild, and there are historic monastic ruins on many of the islands), go by the Visitor Centre and browse through the mountain of literature they can provide to help you plan an itinerary. If possible, try to get on the water, even if only for a brief time.

In Enniskillen, the **Royal Inniskilling Fusiliers Regimental Museum and the County Museum** are in the **Castle Keep,** Castle Barracks (tel. Enniskillen 3911). The castle keep dates from the 16th century, was built by the Maguires, and was remodeled in the 18th century. The Regimental Museum features battle trophies of the Dragoons and Fusiliers from the Napoleonic Wars, arms, and a host of colorful uniforms. In the County Museum, the history of the county is traced through archeological relics from the Middle Stone Age to the end of the early Christian period. Hours are 10 a.m. to 12:30 p.m. and 2 to 4:30 p.m., April through October, and there's a small admission.

On the shores of Lough Coole, about a mile and a half southeast of Enniskillen, **Castle Coole** is a splendid neoclassical mansion set in its own park land. As this is written, extensive renovations are being carried out, but check when you're there to see if they've been completed. Normally, the house is open from April through September every day except Friday from 2 to 6 p.m.

Another stately home worth a visit is **Florence Court,** about eight miles southwest of Enniskillen. The three-story 18th-century mansion has pavilions on each side, connected to the house by open, arched walkways. The woodland setting is as romantic as the house, with a landscaped "pleasure garden." Open 2 to 6 p.m. every day except Friday, April through September.

Telephone ahead to arrange a guided tour of the **Belleek** chinaware factory (tel. Belleek 501). It's not only interesting, but fun—the skilled workers always welcome a bit of a chat with visitors.

5. County Londonderry

See Chapter XII for the city of Londonderry. You may also want to go by the **Ballarena Smokery** in Limavady (tel. Limavady 481), where fish are smoked by traditional methods. It's a good place to buy oak-smoked fish for a picnic farther along the road. The smokery is open Monday through Friday 10 a.m. to 6 p.m., and the shop is also open on Saturdays.

6. County Tyrone

ACCOMMODATIONS: *Note: Prices listed below are those in effect in 1985—expect them to be higher in 1986.*

Bed-and-Breakfast: The **Grange,** 15 Grange Rd., Ballygawley BT70 (tel. Ballygawley 066-253-266), is a charming little cottage that dates back to 1720, but has been thoroughly modernized, even to central heating. Mrs. Lyttle is hostess here, and her attractive guestrooms (one is a family room) all have hand basins. Rates are £7.50 ($10.50) single, £14 ($19.60) double.

Farmhouse: Set on a 150-acre farm, **Greenmount Lodge,** 58 Greenmount Rd., Gortaclare, Omagh BT79 0YE (tel. Fintona 0662-841325), is a large two-story farmhouse with nicely appointed guestrooms. Mrs. Frances Reid, the friendly hostess, is a superb cook and evening meals are a delight. Bed-and-breakfast rates are £9 ($12.60) single, £16 ($22.40) double.

Hotel: Convenience, comfort, and a friendly, accommodating staff make **The Royal Arms Hotel,** Main St., Omagh, Co. Tyrone (tel. 0662-2119), an ideal base. Family owned and operated, it exudes a homey warmth, and there's an old-world charm about its Tavern Lounge and the adjoining dining room. There's also an attractive lounge, a coffeeshop, and residents' gameroom. All 21 bedrooms are nicely appointed and comfortably furnished, and all have telephone, TV, radio, and private bath. Rates for bed-and-breakfast start at £14 ($19.60) single, £25.50 ($35.70) double.

Self-Catering: Four miles west of Cookstown (about 50 miles from Belfast), the National Trust has a fine little traditional cottage for weekly rental. **Wellbrook Cottage** is beside a water-powered beetling mill on the Ballinderry River. The cottage sleeps four, with a bedroom that has two single beds and a pull-out bed/settee in the sitting room. It's a charming house, and weekly rates range from £50 ($70) to £90 ($126), depending on season. For full details and an illustrated directory of National Trust properties, contact: The National Trust, Holiday Cottage Bookings Secretary, Rowallane, Saintfield, Ballynahinch, Co. Down (tel. Saintfield 0238-510721).

WHERE TO EAT: In Omagh, the **Mellon Country Inn,** 134 Beltany Rd. (tel. Newtownstewart 06626-61224), is only a mile from the Ulster-American Folk Park and offers inexpensive meals all through the day. Morning coffee is served from 11:30 a.m. to 12:30 p.m., a ploughman's lunch and grills from 12:30 to 2:30 p.m., and an extensive à la carte menu from 6 to 9:30 p.m. The food is good, and prices reasonable.

THINGS TO SEE AND DO: The **Ulster-American Folk Park** is an outdoor museum which has as its main theme the history of 18th- and 19th-century emigration from Ulster to North America. Their life in rural Ulster and in the New World is re-created through exhibits that include the ancestral home of the Mellon family of Pittsburgh, whose forefathers were from Ulster and who endowed the folk park. There's a pioneer farm and gallery exhibitions. Hours are 11 a.m. to 6:30 p.m. daily, and there's a small admission charge.

Chapter XIV

THE ABC'S OF IRELAND

ALTHOUGH MUCH OF THE INFORMATION listed below is also contained in the foregoing chapters, we hope this will serve as a quick-reference when you need to know the nitty-gritty of traveling in Ireland.

AMERICAN EMBASSIES: In the Republic, the American Embassy is in Dublin, at 42 Elgin Rd. (tel. 01-688777). In Northern Ireland, it's the U.S. Consulate General, Queen's House, Queen's St., Belfast BT1 (tel. Belfast 228239).

AMERICAN EXPRESS: You'll find the American Express office at 116 Grafton St. (tel. 01-772874), with a full range of services, including accepting mail for members. The same is true of the Northern Ireland office, which is located at Hamilton Travel, 23 Waring St. (tel. Belfast 230321).

BANKING HOURS: Banks close for the lunch hour all over the country, and observe weekday opening hours of 10 a.m. to 12:30 p.m. and 1:30 to 3 p.m. They're closed Saturday, Sunday, and bank holidays. Airport banks are open every day except Christmas from 7:30 a.m. to 11 p.m.

ELECTRIC CURRENT: Ireland's current is A.C. 220 volts, so if you must bring small appliances (like hairdryers), you should also pack a voltage converter and a variety of plug adapters (you'd be *amazed* how many different-shaped plugs and outlets there are!). Electric shavers using 110 volts should present no problem, since there will be shaver points in virtually every accommodation.

EMERGENCIES: Throughout the country, the number to call for police, ambulance, firemen, or any other type of emergency assistance is 999.

HAIRDRESSING: There are branches of the excellent **Peter Mark** salons throughout the country, with Dublin addresses at 74 Grafton St. (tel. 714399), 36 Grafton St. (tel. 715000) and 11a Upper O'Connell St. (tel. 745580/9). They specialize in international standards of cutting and styling, as well as all regular salon services. Men will find barbershop prices moderate to inexpensive by American standards.

HOLIDAYS: In the Republic, national holidays fall on: January 1, New Year's Day; March 17, St. Patrick's Day; Good Friday, Easter Monday; the first Monday in June; the first Monday in August; the last Monday in October; Christmas Day and December 26, St. Stephen's Day. The whole country shuts down for these days (well, shops and banks, anyway). Northern Ireland observes the same holiday schedule, with the exception that the August bank holiday is replaced by the first Monday in September and the Battle of the Boyne is celebrated on July 12. Also, some towns observe an "Early Closing Day," with shops closing at 1 p.m.; since the day of the week varies from community to community, be sure to inquire if you have shopping to do.

MAIL DELIVERY: General Delivery in Ireland is known as **Poste Restante,** and it is received at the General Post Office, O'Connell St., Dublin, and the GPO in other large cities around the country. Hours for pickup of mail in Dublin are 8 a.m. to 8 p.m. Monday through Saturday and 9 a.m. to 8 p.m. on Sunday; in other locations, it's 9 a.m. to 5:30 p.m. Monday through Friday. Mail will be held a maximum of two months.

MEDICAL ATTENTION: Medical facilities in Ireland are excellent (in fact, I plan *always* to be sick only when I'm on Irish soil!). If you need a doctor, dentist, or hospital service, the first source of information should be your accommodations hostess or someone on the local scene. Failing that, the **Irish Medical Association,** 10 Fitzwilliam Pl., Dublin (tel. 01-762550) can put you in touch with local medical help.

PHOTOGRAPHIC SUPPLIES: Film of most types is readily available in Ireland, even in small towns (usually at the chemist's outside large cities), and Dublin, Cork, and Limerick have good camera shops. You'll find film more costly than at home, however, and as a young American told me with great earnestness, "In Ireland, you're going to need about three times the film you thought you would —there's another good shot around every bend in the road!" So, keep that in mind and save money by coming prepared.

POLICE: Garda Siochana, "protector of the peace," is the Gaelic name for the Irish police force, and they're familiarly known as Garda (if there's just one), and Gardai ("gard-ee," collectively). Except for special detachments, they're unarmed, and they wear dark-blue uniforms. In Northern Ireland, the police are known as the Royal Ulster Constabulary.

POSTAGE: In the Republic, airmail postage to the U.S. for letters is 44p (53¢) for the first half ounce, 10p (12¢) for each additional half ounce. The less expensive air letters (available from post offices) cost 30p (36¢) per letter. Postcards require postage of 26p (31¢). Street mailboxes are painted green. In Northern

Ireland, United Kingdom postal rates apply, and their street mailboxes are painted red.

RESTROOMS: Even the smallest Irish town usually has public restrooms, as do most hotels, department stores, pubs, restaurants, and theaters—gas (petrol) stations do not. A helpful tip: some public toilets are not as well equipped as they might be, and it's a good idea to carry paper tissues in your handbag for emergencies. Restrooms are usually marked with the Gaelic **Mna** (women) and **Fir** (men).

STUDENT DISCOUNTS: Any student traveling to Ireland should bring an **International Student Identity Card.** You must, however, arm yourself with this valuable document *before you leave home*. The cost in 1984 was $8, and you can obtain your card through **CIEE** (the **Council on International Educational Exchange), 205 E. 42nd St.**, New York, NY 10017 (tel. 1/212/661-1414). The **Irish Student Travel Service (USIT),** 7 Anglesea St., Dublin (tel. 01-778117), is the place to go for discount transportation tickets and information on other student reductions. There are USIT offices in several other locations around the country (see Chapter I). For student exchange arrangements and home stays in Ireland, pick up a copy of the *Discover Young Ireland* booklet from any Tourist Office.

TAXIS: You'll find taxi ranks at bus and railway stations, airports, ferry ports, major hotels, and along the main street of some cities. Don't expect to be able to hail them on the street, but the telephone directory will list numbers to call under the heading "Taxi-cab Ranks and Shelters." In rural areas, if there is taxi service available, *everybody* knows the number!

TELEGRAMS: No Western Union—telegrams are sent through the post office, and even if regular postal services are not available on weekends, there is usually telegraph service for several hours on Saturday and Sunday (call the local telephone operator for specific information).

TELEPHONES: Well, they're better than they *used* to be—but still a far cry from the service you're probably accustomed to at home. It can be an adventure to make a call in Ireland, and I must confess to a certain amount of enjoyment if it happens to entail a bit of conversation with the helpful (and witty) operators. Coinboxes use 2p and 5p coins, and you should have an ample supply if you're making a toll call.

TIME: A good part of the charm of the Irish is due to their almost total disregard for time (the monster that drives the rest of us to distraction). They firmly believe that "When God made time, he made plenty of it," yet in my experience, after spending several months there each year, everything seems to get attended to in *good* time, even though many times not in the time *I* had in mind! Be that as it may, Ireland's official time is Greenwich Mean Time in winter and Summer Time (Daylight Savings) from April to October. Summer days are brilliantly light (or mistily light, depending on the whimsical showers) until 10:30 or 11 p.m., while in winter darkness descends as early as 4 p.m.

TIPPING: There really is no hard-and-fast rule for tipping in Ireland—the tradition of no tipping at all still clings to some rural areas and in some social situations (such as pubs, where you *never* tip the man behind the stick), but in most cases the waitress, taxi driver, or anyone else rendering a service will accept your tip with courteous appreciation. As a general rule, you'd want to tip porters carrying bags, waitresses, car-park attendants, hairdressers, and barbers. As for amount, observe the 10% to 15% rule, with one exception—your *minimum* tip should be 50p, whether or not a percentage of the bill amounts to that much. Actually, whether you tip or not, it's the sincere "thank you" that the Irish value most.

TRANSPORTATION: The **Eurailpass** is good for unlimited rail travel in Ireland and on the Continent (but not in Great Britain or Northern Ireland), as well as on Irish Continental Lines ferries between Ireland and France. It can also be used on Ireland's Expressway Bus Network. They're available to any non-European resident, and should be bought before you leave home. Costs for 1985 are: $260 for 15 days, $330 for 21 days, $410 for one month, $560 for two months, and $680 for six months. Those between the ages of 14 and 26 are eligible for the **Eurail Youthpass,** which costs $290 for one month, $370 for two. Purchase through travel agents or write: Trains, P.O. Box M, Staten Island, NY 10305 (tel. 1/212/586-0091). If you're not using a Eurailpass, CIE will sell you a money-saving **Rambler Pass** for unlimited travel on rail or bus. Prices in 1984 were: IR£63 ($75.60) for 15 days, IR£43 ($51.60) for 8 days. A combination rail and bus Rambler Pass cost: IR£78 ($93.60) for 15 days, IR£54 ($64.80) for 8 days. Students are eligible for the **Youth Student Pass** (see Chapter I). All passes are available from mainline railway stations in Ireland, or you may purchase them through travel agents in the States or CIE Tours International, 590 Fifth Ave., New York, NY 10036 (tel. 1/212/944-8828). Northern Ireland Railways has a 7-day, unlimited travel **Rail Runabout pass** good April through October at a cost of £17 ($23.80) for adults, £8.50 ($11.90) for children. It's available at most railway stations.

WEATHER FORECAST: The weather in Ireland is fickle, and must give forecasters fits—you can, however, get their best judgment and a report on weather conditions at the moment for the country as a whole by calling 01-743320, and for the Dublin area forecast, the number is 01-1199.

YOUTH HOSTELS: There are 54 hostels around the Republic, ranging from basic facilities to simple-but-adequate to a good deal more than adequate. They're available to members of the **International Youth Hostel Association,** and the Irish hostel association (**An Oige**) issues a comprehensive handbook of the country's hostels, rules and regulations, charges, etc. You can pick up a copy from their Dublin headquarters at 39 Mountjoy Sq. (tel. 01-745734) or by writing for one before you leave home. In Northern Ireland, contact the **Youth Hostel Association of Northern Ireland,** 56 Bradbury Pl. (tel. 0232-224733).

Chapter XV

P.S.—MORE BIG SPLURGES

YES, THIS *IS* A BOOK ABOUT BUDGET TRAVEL. And, yes, budget travel in Ireland *is* a fun way to go. But, as I have also said earlier in this book, you will find the same Irish friendliness and charm in large, luxury establishments as in the bed-and-breakfast homes and farmhouses so dear to our budgeteering hearts. And which of us has not yearned, at one time or another, to indulge a penchant for—as the Irish would say—"upmarket" accommodations, or to be pampered over dinners in posh restaurants.

So, for those of you who may have won the Irish Sweepstakes, inherited a fortune, or simply saved enough to forget the budget (be it for only a day or for your entire trip), I'm adding this postscript of additional places in which your "splurge" dollars will buy as good value in the upper range as your budget dollars will in our foregoing recommendations. Together with those listed in earlier chapters, they should provide you a luxury pad in just about any region in Ireland. All this is organized first by region, and then by county or city within this chapter.

As you read through the following, bear in mind that in many cases (though not all, by any means), we're talking not just Big Splurge, but BIG Splurge!

THE EASTERN REGION
(COUNTIES DUBLIN, WICKLOW, LOUTH, KILDARE AND MEATH)

1. County Dublin

ACCOMMODATIONS: The Westbury Hotel, Grafton St., Dublin 2 (tel. 01-791122), is not only Dublin's newest luxury hotel, but it's one of the city's most convenient. Tucked away just off Grafton Street right in the heart of the city center, it is also without doubt one of the most beautiful. Its white marble entrance leads into a lower foyer carpeted in pale pink, and that same Navan/Youghal carpet leads up a sweeping staircase of cream marble and brass to the upper foyer, lobby, dining room and other public spaces. Soft shades of peach, lots of marble, walnut panels, peach silk wall coverings, oil paintings, valuable artifacts, wing-back Chinese Chippendale chairs mixed companionably with modern furniture—all tastefully combined to create an atmosphere of spacious elegance. The upper foyer Terrace provides soft music throughout the evening and for afternoon tea; the Russell Room's peach-and-mint-green decor is the setting for fine dining; the Seafood Restaurant Bar features shellfish from Dublin Bay; and the Polo Bar is hung wall-to-wall with hunting prints.

Guest rooms and suites all are furnished in mahogany and brass, have canopies over beds, marble bathrooms, built-in hair dryers and bathrobes for guests. They're also among the most spacious I've encountered in Ireland, and there are even some suites with jacuzzis. Rates start at IR£65 ($78) single, IR£80 ($96) double, plus 15% service charge.

For many international travelers, the **Shelbourne Hotel**, St. Stephen's Green (tel. 01-766471) is synonymous with Dublin. The lovely old red-and-white brick hotel has been an Irish "home" for heads of state, entertainment celebrities, and literary lights (Thackery praised it highly in his account of an 1843 visit) from the time it opened its doors in 1824. Its lobby and Horseshoe Bar continue to be among the city's most popular gathering spots for Dubliners as well as visitors. There's an Old-World elegance and graciousness about the public rooms, and its haute cuisine restaurant is just the place for one of those "pampered" dinners. A major refurbishing has just been completed, putting a new gleam to guestrooms whose furnishings differ in decor from period pieces to the poshest modern. As you would expect in such an establishment, each comes complete with TV, radio, telephone, and private bath. Rates for such luxury range from IR£75 ($90) to IR£90 ($108) single, IR£85 ($102) to IR£125 ($150) double, with a one-third reduction for children and a 15% service charge. For a superb view of St. Stephen's Green, ask for a room on the front.

Buswell's Hotel, 25 Molesworth St., Dublin (tel. 01-764013) is a Dublin institution. Over the years, Buswell's has hosted such Irish notables as Sir Roger Casement and Eamon de Valera. Located just up from the Dail, it offers center-city convenience, superb accommodations at reasonable rates and a dining room/pub lunch/drinking clientele liberally sprinkled with politicians, leading Dublin businessmen and colorful personalities. And small wonder, for since 1925, the hotel has been owned and operated by the Duff family with the sort of personal involvement which has led to possibly the lowest staff turnover in the city and an enviable guestlist of "regulars" who return year after year. More and more conferences are being held here, also, with the addition of several attractive meeting rooms.

Georgian elegance surrounds you in the lobby, the Leinster Room Restaurant and the Georgian Bar, while the Tudor-style Molesworth Cellar Bar offers conviviality along with excellent lunch and evening snack selections. As for guestrooms, all 70 come equipped with private bath and shower, tea/coffee makers, hair dryers, direct-dial telephones, radios and color TV. Best of all, few are a "standard" size and shape, and each is individually decorated —there are quaint, old-fashioned rooms up under the eaves and others which are brightly modern. Rates run IR£36 ($43.20) single, IR£50 ($60) double, and IR£56 ($67.20) triple, with special winter weekend offers at considerable discounts.

A great favorite with Americans is **Jury's Hotel**, Pembroke Road, Ballsbridge (tel. 01-605000). It's very near the American Embassy, and a long walk or short bus ride from the city center. While in many respects its exterior resembles luxury hotels around the world (not much character to the straight up-and-down concrete-and-glass structure), inside there are delightful touches of a distinctive Irish flavor, such as the Dubliner Bar in the lobby (which serves an excellent, moderately priced lunch). A glass-roofed pavilion holds lounges, a sunken bar, indoor/outdoor pool and a quality seafood restaurant. Jury's Embassy dining room is a favorite for lunch and dinner among the city's businessmen and diplomats, and its Coffee Dock Grill serves moderately priced meals and snacks (as well as wine) 23-hours a day (5 to 6 a.m. is when it's closed). And during summer months, its huge ballroom is the setting for Jury's Irish Cabaret, one of the longest running in the country. Every conceivable convenience for travelers has been provided, with a car rental desk, airline desk, same-day laundry and dry cleaning, beauty salon, barber shop, boutique and newsstand.

Prints of Old Dublin are hung in the beautifully appointed guestrooms, which all have direct-dial telephones, TV, radio and private bath. There's a comfortable and attractive seating area in each, and fresh fruit greets each new guest. Rates: IR£65 ($78) to IR£70 ($84) single, IR£75 ($90) to IR£80 ($96) double, with a one-third discount for children from 4 to 12 and no charge for those under 4. Service charge is 12½%.

Also in the embassy area, the **Berkeley Court,** Landsdowne Road, Ballsbridge (tel. 01-601711) sits in four acres of beautifully landscaped grounds. Pampering begins the minute you drive up to its awning-covered car porch, where you're protected from inclement weather by an enclosure. The elegant lobby features marble pillars, a fountain, wall hangings, impressive antique pieces that include an 18th-century Kingwood marquetry bombo commode, lots of plants, and luxurious Youghal carpeting. There's a lovely lobby bar replete with wood paneling, etched glass panels and cane-backed chairs, and a gourmet, international cuisine restaurant done in the formal, Louis XIV style. Guestrooms are a bit on the small side, but nicely appointed and decorated, with half-canopies over the beds. TVs come with remote controls to be operated from bed, and telephones are all direct-dial. Needless to say, each has its own private bath. Rates begin at IR£65 ($78) single, IR£80 ($96) double, with one-third off for children, and a 15% service charge.

RESTAURANTS: First of all, review the Big Splurges recommended in Chapter IV. These will provide a wider choice for luxury dining.

The **Lord Edward,** 23 Christchurch Place (tel. 752557), has already been recommended as an exceptionally good pub grub source. But for a memorable seafood lunch or dinner, make your way to the small upstairs restaurant, with a stop at the middle-floor bar where you imbibe before a glowing fireplace in a white-stucco-walled room with beamed ceiling. The cozy, bay-windowed dining room one floor above is a haven of soft lights, velvet chairs and intimacy, with seating for only 36 diners. Relaxed elegance is the tone, with expert service and a menu that can offer as many as eight different prawn dishes and main courses you'll know are the freshest possible, since the knowledgeable and caring proprietors make shopping forays twice daily —once for lunch and again for dinner. There's a wide range of specialty coffees, including Calypso (with Tia Maria), Cossack (with vodka) and one of Dublin's best Irish Coffees. Lunch hours are 12:30 to 2:30 p.m. Monday through Friday, dinner from 6 to 10:45 p.m. Monday through Saturday. For a five-course dinner, count on spending about IR£25 ($30) without wine. You can raise or lower that estimate from the extensive a la carte menu, but reservations are a must in the popular and highly recommended eatery. Closed Sundays.

If it's sophisticated French cuisine you yearn for, head for **Le Coq Hardi,** 35 Pembroke Road, Ballsbridge (tel. 689070), where owner-chef John Howard features a blend of Haute, Bourgeois and Nouvelle Cuisine. In the warm, inviting atmosphere of a Georgian house, surrounded by a decor of rosewood and brass, you can choose from such specialties as Dover sole stuffed with lobster, prawns, and mushrooms in hollandaise sauce and double cream, bread-crumbed and deep fried; les coquilles aux fruits de mer thermidor (a marvelous creation of fresh seafoods poached in white wine with shallots and parsley) and a good selection of veal, chicken and beef. The star of the menu is undoubtedly the Coq Hardi (what else!), a mouthwatering breast of chicken stuffed with mashed potato, mushrooms and secret seasonings, wrapped in bacon, baked and flamed with Irish whiskey at your table. This sort of culinary expertise has won the restaurant several well-deserved awards. With seating for only 45, this is another place that advance booking is absolutely essential. Lunch is served from 12:30 to 2:30 p.m., dinner from 7:30 to 11 p.m. The table d'hote lunch runs IR£12 ($14.40), a four-course, a la carte dinner will average IR£25 ($30) without wine, and there's a 12½% service charge. It's closed the first two weeks in August, Saturdays for lunch, Sundays and bank holidays.

Out in Howth, set right on the edge of Dublin Bay in the old harbormaster's house, the **King Sitric,** East Pier, Howth Harbour (tel. 32535 or 326729) is one of the best seafood restaurants in the country. The owner/managers, Joan and Aidan McManus personally oversee the entire operation, with Joan very much in evidence in the dining room, and Aidan (whose background includes extensive training on the continent) negotiating seafood purchases directly from the trawlers that put into the harbor. The decor is Georgian, with antique chairs and sofas in the charming two-room lounge, and candlelight and crystal chandeliers softly illuminating antique prints hung in the four dining rooms. As for the menu, it all depends on the season. Your best course is to ask the waiter about the day's catch, and from time to time you can expect to see dishes featuring salmon, bass, plaice, turbot, brill, scallops, prawns and lobster (with more exotic fish depending on just what the trawlers have snared that day). There's a set dinner at IR£15.50 ($18.50), and an a la carte menu with prices from IR£7.50 ($9) to IR£12 ($14.40). Hours are 6:30 to 11:30 p.m., Monday through Saturday. Closed Sundays. Be sure to book ahead.

South of the city, the freshest of seafood is also a specialty of the **Restaurant na Mara,** Marine Road, Dun Laoghaire (tel. 806767). It's an attractive place with an interesting history that began as the result of a seafood festival a few years back when the Great Southern Hotel was requested to cater a seafood menu in the buffet room of the old railway station. The success of that short-term venture was so great that the Great Southern set about a transformation of the Victorian-style room with its high, vaulted ceiling. Using the softness of salmon-pink walls, turf-brown carpeting and candlelight, the managers have created a relaxing and inviting restaurant that serves only seasonal seafood dishes, with creative cooking turning out such specialties as the popular poached sole filets in white-wine sauce with prawns. Lobster comes in several guises, and the dessert in my own humble opinion is an elegant flambe crepe that serves two. Lunch is from 1 to 2:30 p.m., with a set, four-course seafood lunch at IR£10 ($12) and up; dinner hours are 7 to 10:30 p.m., with a la carte prices from IR£9 ($10.80) to IR£14 ($16.80). Closed Sunday, Monday, Christmas and Easter. About 90% of their business comes from locals who eat here regularly, so best to reserve.

2. County Wicklow

ACCOMMODATIONS: Just 28 miles from Dublin, **Hunter's Hotel,** Rathnew, Co. Wicklow (tel. 0404-4106) is a lovely old coaching inn situated on the banks of the River Vartry. Its beautifully landscaped gardens have won awards, and they're the perfect place to relax in the late afternoon or early evening. In fine weather, pre-lunch and pre-dinner drinks, as well as afternoon tea, are served in these serene outdoor surroundings. The restaurant is superb (see below) and much patronized by locals and Dubliners. Mrs. Maureen Gelletlie is the fifth generation of her family to own and manage Hunter's, and she takes great pride in seeing to the personal comfort of all guests. There are only seventeen guestrooms, all charmingly decorated in country-house style, and some come with private baths. Rates (wihch include breakfast) are IR£17 ($20.40) per person, single or double, with a 25% reduction for children and a 10% service charge.

The **Woodenbridge Hotel,** Vale of Avoca, Arklow, Co. Wicklow (tel. 0402-5146/5219) was built as an inn back in 1608 and its doors have been open to travelers ever since. Perched on a hill overlooking some of Wicklow's most beautiful countryside, the two-story wooden structure has a comfortable, Old World air. There's a bar/lounge with whitewashed, stucco walls, overhead beams, a huge stone fireplace and tankards hung above the corner bar, and an old-fashioned dining room that looks out over that gorgeous view of green rolling hills and mountains. Owners Jim and Briget Hogan are all that you'd expect of traditional innkeepers, projecting a warm, friendly hospitality that explains the popularity of the place. There are only a dozen guestrooms, which vary in size and shape. Most have private baths, and furnishings are plain, but comfortable. It was in one of the large front bedrooms that the late Eamon de Valera came for his honeymoon—easy to understand when you step inside this old, assured country residence where serenity is enlivened with an Irish twinkle and the "crack" in the lounge sparkles with Irish wit.

The hotel's location makes it an ideal base for exploring Avoca's pottery works and woolen mill, Glendalough, the meeting of the waters and County Wicklow's other attractions. The Hogans will arrange for guests to fish in the adjacent river, and there's riding and pony trekking nearby as well as one of the most scenic golf courses in Ireland just 200 yards from the hotel. In the large function room that has been added back of the lounge (with a careful eye to the hotel's original character), there's frequent entertainment, usually including traditional Irish music and dancing. High-season rates (including breakfast) begin at IR£16 ($19.20) single, IR£26 ($31.20) double.

RESTAURANTS: In Wicklow Town, the **Old Rectory Country House** (tel. 0404-2048) is an 1870s, Georgian-style rectory that has blossomed as one of County Wicklow's premiere eateries under the loving guidance of Paul and Linda Saunders. Set in its own gardens on the edge of town, the house exudes tranquil elegance, with spacious public rooms, high ceilings and cheerful log fires. Dinner is served by candlelight, with Linda in the kitchen and Paul attending to the very personal service in the lovely dining room. Fresh seafoods and local produce and meats are the basis of the gourmet menu, and there's a good wine list. There's a table d'hôte dinner for IR£17 ($20.40), and an à la carte menu with selections from IR£15 ($18) to IR£20 ($24). From Sunday to Thursday, there's only one seating, at 7:30 p.m.; on Friday and Saturday, hours are 7:30 to 9 p.m.; and advance booking is absolutely essential. Accommodations are also available in bright, attractive guestrooms with private baths and telephone, at rates of IR£23 ($27.60) per person for bed and breakfast.

Hunter's Hotel, Rathnew (tel. 0404-4106), recommended above, is a terrific place for a Big Splurge meal, with lunch served from 1 to 3 p.m., dinner from 7:30 to 9:30 p.m., and afternoon tea in between. Vegetables come straight from the hotel's own garden, seafood is freshly caught and roasts, steaks and other meats are locally grown. Service is the pampering kind. Lunch runs about IR£8 ($9.60), afternoon tea is IR£4 ($4.80) and dinner will cost about IR£16 ($19.20), and there's a 10% service charge. Be sure to book ahead.

3. County Louth

ACCOMMODATIONS: Set in 130 wooded acres and surrounded by green lawns, **Ballymascanlon House Hotel,** Dundalk, Co. Louth (tel. 042-71124) has twice won awards for its lovely gardens. The peaked-gabled old country mansion has high ceilings and spacious rooms in the original house, and there's a modern extension with more standardized guestrooms. A sports center that includes a heated indoor swimming pool, sauna, solarium, gym, children's playground and squash and tennis courts make it an all-round, self-contained resort, with golf and the seaside nearby. All 36 guestrooms have telephones and private baths and are attractively decorated. Its location just about at mid-way on the main Dublin/Belfast road makes this a convenient stopping point. Seasonal rates range from IR£21.50 ($25.80) to IR£23 ($27.60).

4. County Kildare

RESTAURANTS: Set in a Georgian style country house, the dining room at **Curryhills House,** Prosperous, Naas, Co. Kildare (tel. 045-68150) is the pride and joy of owner/managers Bridie and Bill Travers. Decor is Tudor, and cuisine features gourmet dishes prepared from local, fresh ingredients. On Fridays, there's traditional Irish music, and on Saturdays you're invited to an old-fashioned sing-along. Hours are 12:30 to 2 p.m. for lunch, 6:30 to 11 p.m. for dinner; lunch prices begin at IR£8 ($9.60), dinner prices at IR£13 ($15.60). Closed Sunday.

John Doyle's Schoolhouse Restaurant, Castledermot, Co. Kildare (tel. 0503-44282) is a small, cozy place for a relaxed, beautifully prepared Big Splurge dinner. John is always on hand to see that both service and meals are perfection, and the menu strikes a nice balance, with offerings of seafood, beef, chicken and seasonal specialties. All ingredients are of the highest standards. From April to October, dinner begins at 6:30 p.m.; at 7:30 p.m. other months, and it's closed Sundays and Mondays. There's a table d'hôte dinner at IR£15 ($18), and à la carte prices begin at IR£12 ($14.40). There's seating for only 40, so best book ahead.

THE SOUTHEAST
(COUNTIES WEXFORD, WATERFORD, KILKENNY, CARLOW, AND SOUTH TIPPERARY)

1. County Wexford

ACCOMMODATIONS: Marlfield House, Gorey, Co. Wexford (tel. 055-21124/ 21572) was once the home of the Earl of Courtown. Surrounded by some 35 acres of wooded countryside and landscaped gardens, the stately Regency house is filled with antiques, gilt-framed mirrors and crystal chandeliers. Log fires in the public rooms add a gracious note of warmth, and a lovely curved staircase sweeps up to elegantly decorated and furnished guestrooms. Wall-papers, draperies and bedspreads are all coordinated, antiques are used lavishly, and all eleven rooms have private baths. Mary and Ray Bowe, the charming owners who have brought the old home back to its former glory, go out of their way to see that guests are catered to. There's an excellent restaurant (see below). Rates, which include a full Irish breakfast, are IR£23 ($27.60) to IR£27 ($32.40), and only children over the age of six are accepted.

The **Ferrycarrig Hotel**, Ferrycarrig Bridge, P.O. Box 11, Wexford (tel. 053-22999), was described by one reviewer as "a modern lump of concrete," and I'd have to go along with that description except for several things that make it quite exceptional (as, indeed, that reviewer went on to do).

First of all, it is situated just across the Ferrycarrig Bridge on the Enniscorthy side of the Slaney Estuary, and although it is very close to a main thoroughfare, it is nestled right down on the riverbank, out of sight and sound of traffic, with green lawns that give it a true country setting. Then, there's that terrific view of the river and the scores of sailing and fishing boats busily pursuing pleasure or profit. Not only that, but every single room faces the river with broad picture windows to take advantage of those river views. And best of all, I'd have to count personable Paddy and Mary Hatton, who run the hotel (Mary's in charge of the kitchen and dining room) with the sort of hospitality you expect in Ireland, but not in a modern hotel. Add to all those reasons for staying at the Ferrycarrig the fact that Wexford is just two miles away, and they make this an ideal touring base for the Wexford area.

Actually, an outstanding sightseeing attraction is almost at the doorstep of the hotel. A wooded river walk from the hotel grounds leads (in about three minutes) to a ruined tower perched atop a craggy cliff at the northern edge of the bridge which crosses the Slaney. Some historians claim this is all that remains of the first Anglo-Norman castle erected in Ireland, although others dispute that. No matter, it's certainly ancient (all agree it dates at least to the 15th century), and the short climb up to the tower rewards you with unbounded admiration for its builders as well as a superb overview of the Slaney rushing through a narrow gorge below. There's also a unique Wexford Heritage Park under construction on the south side of the river, although at this writing it is impossible to say when that will be completed.

As for the hotel, bedrooms are all attractively furnished, with comfortable chairs arranged to add living room comfort. All have private bath. There's a cozy bar, and the Sandpiper Restaurant (a favorite with locals as well as guests) specializes in the freshest of local seafood, meats and vegetables.

Rates for bed and breakfast are £22 ($26.40) single; £30 ($36) to £37

($44.40) double, depending on season (high rates apply during Wexford Festival as well as July and August). Special weekend and package rates are available. Children under 10 sharing a room with parents stay free. Send a £20 ($24) deposit to confirm all bookings. Open Easter through October.

RESTAURANTS: If you can't manage to *stay* in **Malfield House** (see above), do try to have at least one Big Splurge meal there. Mary Bowe is known for her expertise with seafoods, although any choice from the menu will consist of home grown or locally produced ingredients prepared with a gourmet cook's touch. The restaurant is set in a Victorian-style conservatory, with sweeping views of the lawns and gardens. It's altogether charming and the epitome of luxury dining. Lunch is served from 1 to 2:30 p.m., with prices beginning at IR£9 ($10.80); dinner hours are 7:30 to 9:30 p.m., at prices of IR£17.50 ($21) and up. Closed from mid-December to mid-January. Reservations essential.

2. County Waterford

ACCOMMODATIONS: The **Granville Hotel,** The Quay, Waterford, Co. Waterford (tel. 051-55111) has figured in Waterford's history since it was built during the reign of George III as a gracious residence for the Quan family. A daughter of that family gave birth to Thomas Francis Meagher in 1823 in the room now named for him. He grew up to become a close friend of Daniel O'Connell; be sentenced to death for his part in the Young Ireland rising of 1848; be banished by transportation for life when the death sentence was commuted; escape to America in 1852; form the famous "Fighting 69th" Irish Brigade during America's Civil War; and become Acting Governor of Montana. During its years as Commins' Hotel, Parnell always stayed here when in Waterford and he delivered one of his last speeches from the hotel windows.

In 1980, Ann and Liam Cusack bought the old hotel and set about transforming it into the Grade A hostelry that today attracts visitors drawn by its luxury accommodations, gracious decor and central location, as well as its friendly and efficient staff. Public rooms reflect the gleam of polished wood, warm red carpets, and crystal chandeliers. The bar is a favorite Waterford meeting place and lunch spot; the Bianconi Grill offers an extensive menu; and the Sword Restaurant serves up elegance with fine cuisine. As for guestrooms, they're all attractively decorated, and all have bath/shower, direct-dial telephones, color TV and radio. Family rooms even include baby-listening devices. Rates begin at £27 ($32.40) single, £53 ($63.60) double. All service charges and VAT are included, and there are special weekend rates available.

The **Tower Hotel,** The Mall, Waterford, Co. Waterford (tel. 051-75801), just across from the 11th century Reginald's Tower, has been a mainstay of Waterford hotels for years. Recent renovations, however, have made it even more desirable as a Waterford base. It combines the best of the old (Waterford glass chandeliers in the lobby and dining room, as well as beautiful, dainty Waterford glass sconces in the dining room) with the best of modern conveniences, and all in a convenient location for shopping and sightseeing, with more-than-adequate parking facilities (an important factor in Waterford!).

The bar, with its dark green upholstery and carpeting, lots of mahogany, opaque globe lighting and inviting "snug" seating areas; the dining room done in shades of rose and green; the Grill Room with its moderately priced menu and comfortable fittings; and guestrooms brightly decorated and comfortably furnished; all go into a mix that makes this one of the city's most popular places to stay. It is a particular favorite of tour groups, and yet you're just as likely to find a local wedding party (as I did recently) as bus loads of visiting tourists. Rates range from IR£22 ($26.44) to IR£27 ($32.40) single, IR£35 ($42) to IR£44 ($52.80) double, depending on season.

In the little town of Lismore, **Ballyrafter House,** Lismore, Co. Waterford (tel. 058-54002) is a rambling country house set high on a hill overlooking the Blackwater River and wooded countryside. It's a gracious old house, with a wide entrance hall, a wood-paneled lounge with comfortable sofas and padded booths to invite relaxed conversation over drinks, and a lovely dining room with antique furnishings, sparkling linens and a bay window overlooking the garden. Thoroughbred horses graze on the sloping pasture beyond the sloping front lawn, and off to one side soar the turrets of Lismore Castle, the picturebook seat of the Duke of Devonshire, one of the few castles in Ireland that has been used continuously as a residence since its construction by King John in 1185. At one time it was passed to Sir Walter Raleigh as a reward for some pretty dastardly deeds on behalf of the English crown, but the Devonshire dukes have been in residence since 1763. Across a pretty stone bridge, the charming town of Lismore is just a half-mile away, and the famous Vee road across the Knockmealdown Mountains is just a short drive away. James and Nancy Willoughby welcome guests warmly and take a personal interest in their comfort.

Decor in the 14 guestrooms is simple, but attractive, and all have handbasins, some have private baths. Single rooms are a bit on the small side, but doubles are quite spacious. Rates for bed and breakfast are IR£18 ($21.60) single, IR£33 ($39.60) double, with private bath (lower rates without). Dinners are exceptionally good and run about IR£12 ($14.40). Ballyrafter House is very popular, which makes advance booking for both accommodations and meals a necessity.

3. County Kilkenny

ACCOMMODATIONS: On the outskirts of town, set in spacious grounds, the **Rose Hill Hotel,** College/Callan Road, Kilkenny, Co. Kilkenny (tel. 056-62000) is a two-story, red and white country house to which a modern extension has been added. The public rooms reflect the character of the original home, with gracious furnishings, high ceilings and tall windows. Elsewhere, every conceivable modern convenience has been added to make this a truly luxury establishment. There are 60 top standard guestrooms with private bath, color TV, video films, radio tea-and-coffee making facilities, and even wall safes. A health and leisure center holds a heated swimming pool, hot tub, gym, saunas and tennis courts. A restaurant and a coffee shop complete the amenities. Rates (which include breakfast) are IR£24 ($28.80) single, IR£39 ($46.80) double, with a 20% reduction for children and a 10% service charge.

4. South Tipperary

ACCOMMODATIONS: When sightseeing takes you to Cashel and its famous Rock, you couldn't do better than to book into the **Dundrum House Hotel,** Dundrum, Cashel, Co. Tipperary (tel. 062-71116/-71409). This magnificent

Georgian Mansion dates from the 18th century and sits on over 100 acres of scenic countryside. There are some thirty handsome guestrooms, and Mary and Austin Crowe are proud of the fact that they have installed an elevator to upper floors and otherwise cater to handicapped or disabled travelers. All guestrooms have private baths and telephones. There's also an excellent dining room with superb cuisine and a good wine list. Rates, including breakfast, are IR£17 ($20.40) to IR£20 ($24) single, IR£32 ($38.40) to IR£35 ($42) double, with a one-third reduction for children and a 10% service charge.

THE SOUTHERN REGION
(COUNTIES CORK AND KERRY)

1. County Cork

ACCOMMODATIONS: In Chapter VI, you'll find an enthusiastic endorsement of **Arbutus Lodge,** Montenotte, Cork, Co. Cork (tel. 021-501237) as a Big Splurge place to eat. Now, let me add my heartfelt recommendation of this special place as a Big Splurge accommodation. The elegant 1802 townhouse overlooking Cork City is surrounded by gardens, features a surprising and excellent collection of the works of modern Irish artists, and holds only 20 guestrooms, each of which is beautifully and individually decorated and furnished. Owner/Manager Declan Ryan personally oversees the comfort of his guests, and a stay at Arbutus is much like a visit in a private home. Guestrooms overlook either the garden or the city (the cityscape is stunning!). Rates, which include breakfast, are IR£33 ($39.60) per person, single or double.

Ashbourne House Hotel, Glounthaune, Co. Cork (tel. 021-953319), is a lovely hotel overlooking the River Lee and just ten minutes from Cork City (on the Waterford road). With all the Old World charm of a country home (which indeed is how it began life), and surrounded by gardens which include trees and shrubs from Kew Gardens and magnolias, flame trees, eucalyptus and camellias from around the world, Ashbourne was originally known as Harmony Lodge because of the songfests conducted daily by vast numbers of wild birds attracted to the botanical setting.

Inside, the residents' lounge and public bar are paneled in glowing walnut and feature open fires on cool days. The Fisherman's Kitchen restaurant is a light, airy garden room replete with white furnishings and masses of flowers. Bedrooms are brightly decorated in a country style and come with bath/shower, direct-dial telephone, television and video. There's a heated swimming pool, sauna, two tennis courts and nearby facilities for golf, fishing, riding and croquet. During summer months, there's entertainment (in 1984 it was jazz on Thursday nights) in the bar or lounge. Its location makes Ashbourne an ideal touring base for day trips from which you can return in the evenings to beautiful, relaxed accommodations in an idyllic setting. Rates begin at IR£30 ($36) single, IR£44 ($52.80) double; dinners are in the IR£14 ($16.80) to IR£18 ($21.60) range.

Marian and Brendan Long hvae taken a lovely old 1791 mansion set high on a hill overlooking the Lee and Blackrock Castle and transformed it into a luxurious guesthouse just a four-minute drive from the city center. You'll fall in love with **Lotamore House,** Tivoli, Cork City, Co. Cork (tel. 021-822344), from the moment you enter the wide central hall with its elaborate ceiling or climb the magnificent staircase which features a large stained glass window on the landing.

The spacious bedrooms are tastefully decorated in brown and beige tones set off by mahogany furnishings (which include a comfortable armchair in each room). All 20 have private bath/shower, telephone, and color TV. Rates for bed and a full Irish breakfast are IR£18 ($21.60) single, IR£30 ($36) double. The Longs don't serve dinner, but Lotamore is just next door to an excellent restaurant and within easy driving distance of several others.

Set in a 500-acre farmland estate, **Longueville House,** Longueville, Mallow, Co. Cork (tel. 022-27176), is three miles west of Mallow, overlooking the Blackwater River valley. Off in the distance are visible the ruins of 16th-century Dromaneen Castle, ancestral home of owner Michael O'Callaghan, and on the front lawn, rows of huge oaks are planted in the same formation as French and English troops at the Battle of Waterloo. There's significance in both these views, for the castle was forfeited to Cromwell in 1641 by an O'Callaghan and the land only repurchased by Michael's father (who served in the Irish Senate some 30 years) in 1938, thus reclaiming his family heritage and passing it along to Michael and his charming wife, Jane. The battle-line oaks were planted when the land and house were in English hands.

The handsome 1720 Georgian mansion sports a wide entrance hall whose walls are hung with O'Callaghan portraits, and a lounge that is surely one of the loveliest in the country, with plush, soft gold armchairs pulled up to face the carved fireplace and a beautifully detailed stucco ceiling. The lounge bar is Victorian in style, with wine-red upholstery, and in the gourmet restaurant (see below), portraits of every Republic of Ireland president dub it the President's Room. All twenty guestrooms are attractively furnished, and all have private baths. There's trout and salmon fishing in the Blackwater right on the estate, and free golf three miles away. A decided bonus to those of a literary bent is the excellent library. Rates for bed and breakfast are IR£25 ($30) single, IR£48 ($57.60) double, and there are weekly rates available. Open from Easter to mid-October. Note: children are not encouraged as guests, since Longueville House is essentially an adult retreat.

At **Assolas Country House,** Kanturk, Co. Cork (tel. 029-50015), you're only about an hour's drive (through scenic and historic countryside) from Killarney to the west and Cork to the east. The 17th-century Queen Anne-style house is set in 100 acres of parkland, and its flower gardens have won more than one award. Towering old trees and green lawns lead down to the edge of the Blackwater River (where guests fish free). Inside the wide front doors, there are spacious public rooms with a traditional country house decor and open fires, a large rumpus room with stone fireplace, and upstairs guestrooms come in a variety of sizes and shapes, all done up in country fabrics and colors. There's a comfortable, relaxed air about the place that is the direct result of Eleanor and Hugh Bourke's gracious hospitality. Dining is superb (the restaurant is recognized internationally—see below), and in addition to fishing, guests have access to tennis, boating and croquet. Rates for bed and breakfast range from IR£17.50 ($21) to IR£25 ($30), with a 25% reduction for children and a 10% service charge. Open from mid-April through September.

RESTAURANTS: See above for a full description of **Longueville House,** Mallow (tel. 022-27156). Its President's Room restaurant is one of the best in the country, and even if you're only passing through this part of the Southern Region, you'll be in for a very special treat if you ring ahead to book a meal here. Meals are served in the stately Georgian dining room under the gaze of Ireland's presidents since it became a Republic and beneath an ornate plaster ceiling adorned with the delicate work of an Italian artist. In fine weather, the Victorian conservatory, with its massed greenery, white ironwork and glorious views of the garden, is open to diners, as well. As for the food, it's won just about every award and international recognition going, as well it should. Cordon Bleu trained Jane O'Callaghan oversees the preparation of gourmet selections that utilize produce grown in their own fields, as well as their own lamb and fish fresh from waters that flow through Longueville estate. Mallard and venison are featured in season, and the wine list includes wines produced from Michael's own vineyards (among the first—and few—in Ireland). Dinner will run about IR£17 ($20.40), and the restaurant is fully licensed. Dinner hours are 7 to 9 p.m. (closed to non-residents Sunday and Monday), Easter to mid-October, and you must have reservations.

Assolas Country House (see above), Kanturk (tel. 029-50015), is another good choice for a Big Splurge meal in the Southern Region. The dining room is a real gem, with Queen Anne period furnishings, Dresden china, mahogany tables and comfortable lounge for before- or after-dinner drinks. The paté maison is homemade, and the menu always features home-grown fresh vegetables, often salmon fresh from the Blackwater. The Irish coffee is excellent, and there's a good, extensive wine list. The set dinner price is IR£18.50 ($16.20), plus a 10% service charge, and it's served from 7:30 p.m. every day but Sunday, from mid-April through September. Again, you must book ahead.

2. County Kerry

ACCOMMODATIONS: Hotel Ard-na-Sidhe, Caragh Lake, Killorglin, Co. Kerry (tel. Caragh Lake 5) is a real find for those who value a scenic, tranquil holiday base. You may find it hard to believe that this grand red sandstone Victorian mansion was built more than a century-and-a-half ago by one Lady O'Connell as a private guesthouse! And the Lady certainly knew how to accommodate guests, a tradition which has not eroded over the years that have seen the magnificent structure perched above the shores of Caragh Lake evolve into a professional guetshouse that combines traditional elegance with all the amenities of a modern luxury hotel.

It should be pointed out that the hotel's location is a bit isolated, and I can only echo what the management, itself, tries to impress on prospective guests: Ard-na-Sidhe (which means height of the fairies) is strictly for those who enjoy a quiet holiday—wooded walks, fishing (boats and guides are available) and reading or other such pursuits are the main activities here. Personally, I can't think of a more beautiful spot for a retreat with loved ones —or better yet, for a honeymoon! However, I should also add that Killarney is only 17 miles away for those whose tastes are a bit more lively. Also, golf links are only 3 miles away and all the sporting facilities of Hotel Dunloe Castle and Hotel Europe (under the same ownership) are free to all guests here.

Spacious public rooms are decorated in soft tones of blues and browns and beige, furnished with antiques and feature open fireplaces. The dining room is an intimate and restful setting for fine dining. As for bedrooms, they're a far cry from your standard hotel room—no two are the same size or shape; there are some without bath; and views are either of the lake or the beautifully landscaped gardens. A short distance from the main house, there's a modern block where rooms and suites are more uniform and of a different character than in the older building. Per room rates range from IR£18 ($21.60) for a single room without bath to IR£32 ($38.40) for a single with bath (garden view; lake view costs more) to IR£30 ($36) for a double without bath to IR£40 ($48) for a double with garden view. Rates include a full Irish breakfast; all taxes and service charges. Open May to September.

Dun an Oir Hotel, Ballyferriter, Dingle Peninsula, Co. Kerry (tel. 066-56133) has been described in Chapter VI for its self-catering facilities, and I'll not repeat here its full description. Suffice it to say that, situated right at the tip of the Dingle Peninsula between the villages of Ballyferriter and Ferriters Cove and nestled into some of Ireland's most dramatic scenery, the hotel the Dun an Oir offers all the amenities of a modern luxury hotel without intruding on either the native environment or culture. Personable manager Matt Britton, welcomes locals as well as guests in the hotel's bar, lounge and restaurant, making it a warm, convivial social center on the Peninsula. The hotel's public areas are attractively decorated with native motifs, and guestrooms all have private baths, telephones, TV and windows looking out to that gorgeous scenery. There's a 9-hole golf course, heated swimming pool and hard-surface tennis court on the premises, as well as a lovely sandy beach in front of the hotel. Rates begin at IR£22 ($26.40) single, IR£37 ($44.40) double; children under 10 stay free in parents' rooms; and there's a 12½% service charge. Open May through September.

SHANNONSIDE
(COUNTIES CLARE, LIMERICK, AND NORTH TIPPERARY)

1. County Clare

ACCOMMODATIONS: If I could treat myself to only one Big Splurge accommodation in Ireland, I wouldn't have to give the decision even one moment's thought—it would be **Dromoland Castle,** Newmarket-on-Fergus, Co. Clare (tel. 061-71144). It is the perfect castle hotel, a fantasy come true. Dromoland was home to the royal O'Brien clan, later declared Barons of Inchiquin by King Henry VIII, from the 1570s right up to 1962 when the 16th Baron of Inchiquin sold it to an American financier who thought he was buying a summer home for himself. Instead, Bernard McDonough decided to completely rebuild and redecorate the interior as a luxury hotel—in so doing, he never lost sight of its feeling of "home" and went to great pains and expense to see that it was retained. Today, when you enter the grounds through impressive tower gates, wind your way through a velvet-smooth golf course, then pass beneath the dignified old grey castle's turrets through massive carved doors, you may be totally unprepared for the warmth and total charm which greet you in such a baronial setting. Royal it most certainly is, but from the informal friendliness of its staff to the country coziness of its pretty guestrooms, Dromoland exudes the spirit of a luxury home-away-from-home.

From the high, dark green walls of a wide central hall, huge gold-framed paintings of O'Briens and their royal friends gaze down on thick carpets, wonderfully comfortable armchairs arranged in intimate groupings and a large fireplace with its welcoming wood-and-turf fire. You'll sign in with a goose-quill pen, then luxuriate behind picture windows that frame magnificent views of the exquisitely groomed 1500-acre estate. There's a natural lake for boating, a winding river for fishing, an old-fashioned garden to explore and wooded walks beneath ancient trees. There's that nine-hole golf course, a putting green, tennis courts, and facilities for horseback riding and duck shooting.

Indoors, the sumptuous scarlet-and-gold dining room serves up one of the best Irish breakfasts in the country as well as a continental dinner cuisine featuring the freshest in native seafoods, lamb and beef. The small, paneled bar (once the Baron's library) has entertainment most nights, and Dromoland's gift shop is outstanding in both selection and value. Bedrooms are beautifully decorated in bright colors and flowery prints, have private bath, telephones, commodious closets and those wonderful views.

Just eight miles from Shannon Airport, Dromoland makes an ideal base for sightseeing, medieval banqueting, and touring a great deal of the west of Ireland. Singles start at IR£64 ($76.80), doubles at IR£80 ($96) and vary according to size and location. Rates include VAT and there's no service charge; a one-third deduction for children. Open April through October.

Its location alone would qualify **Fitzpatrick's Shannon Shamrock Hotel,** Bunratty, Co. Clare (tel. 061-61177), as a Big Splurge—five miles from Shannon Airport, nine miles from Limerick, and just next door to Bunratty Castle. The Folk Park, the medieval banquet, and Durty Nellie's are all just a short walk away, and there's courtesy coach service to the airport upon request as well as to Limerick twice daily. There's much more than location, however, to recommend this lovely hotel. It's a sister to Fitzpatrick's Castle Hotel in Killiney (see Chapter IV), and while the two bear no outward resemblance, they are both looked over with the same personal care and attention by the Fitzpatrick family. The exceptionally efficient and friendly staff reflects that same sort of personal concern.

The **Shannon Shamrock,** a low, rambling stone building, exudes low-key informality in a setting of pure luxury. The stone-floor lobby leads into a large lounge whose focal point is a huge stone fireplace (ablaze on cool evenings). Comfortable seating arranged for intimate groupings make this an inviting place to have morning coffee, afternoon tea or late-night drinks. The pretty cocktail bar, with dark blue velvet upholstering, skylights and lots of dark wood and green plants, has music Wednesday through Sunday during summer months. Shades of soft green and rose dominate the dining room. There's an indoor heated swimming pool and a sauna on the premises and plenty of parking space.

All 110 guestrooms come with private bath, radio, TV and telephone. Decor and furnishings are outstanding in all, but for a sumptuous break from the rigors of travel, treat yourself to a stay in one of the beautiful and spacious River Suites—velvet chair and sofa coverings, king-size beds, and windows with a view are featured in bed/sitting rooms for two, separate bedroom and bed/sitting room for four.

Depending on season, rates range from IR£32 ($38.40) to IR£42 ($50.40) for singles; IR£44 ($52.80) to IR£60 ($72) for doubles; IR£49 ($58.80) to IR£63 ($75.60) for family rooms. River Suites for two are IR£60 ($72) and IR£68 ($81.60); IR£99 ($118.80) to IR£110 ($132) for four. Service charge is 10%.

The **Old Ground Hotel,** Ennis, Co. Clare (tel. 065-21127), is an ivy-covered, two-story brick building set behind an iron fence in spacious grounds right in the heart of Ennis, just 12 miles north of Shannon Airport. It is known for its happy blend of Old World elegance and charm with modern comfort and efficiency. Its interior is an intriguing mixture of contemporary and period decor and furnishings, with a luxurious restaurant in the traditional manner (see Chapter VII for description) and open fires when there's a chill in the air, and guestrooms furnished with the latest in guest conveniences. For example, in addition to private bath, direct-dial telephone, and color TV, each room also has facilities for making tea or coffee. Some are decorated pretty much as standard hotel rooms are around the world; others have such Victorian touches as occasional tables with delicately curved legs, gold-framed mirrors, touches of old brass on chests, and mini-chandeliers. All have handwoven Donegal bedspreads. The Celtic Bar, with its tweed-bottomed chairs and tables of teak inset with woven rushwork, is a relaxing meeting place for locals as well as guests. The Old Ground is a Trust Houses Forte property, assuring the highest standards in service as well as amenities. It's also a very convenient base for exploring the glories of Shannonside. Rates, which include a full Irish breakfast, are IR£41 ($49.20) single, IR£56 ($57.20) double, with a one-third reduction for children.

RESTAURANTS: See Chapter VII for Big Splurge recommendations of restaurants and castle banquets—those listed are absolute top value-for-money in the Shannonside region.

2. County Limerick

On the edge of what has been called Ireland's prettiest village, **Dunraven Arms Hotel,** Adare, Co. Limerick (tel. 061-94209) is a two-story, traditional-style, gold-colored hotel that has the look of an old-time inn. Indeed, that small-inn type hospitality greets you at the door and never diminishes throughout your stay. There's the pleasant glow of being a welcomed guest in a comfortable, country-style hostelry where friendliness and courtesy are outstanding. The spacious lounge bar overlooks pretty gardens and offers excellent bar lunches at inexpensive rates, and the dining room features French cuisine, using fresh ingredients from local farms. Comfortable, traditional furnishings add a homey touch. Both public rooms and guestrooms are attractively done up in country prints, and all guestrooms have private baths and telephones. This is where Princess Grace and Prince Rainier stayed during their 1963 visit. Not only is this a great sightseeing base—only 10 miles from Limerick, 16 from Bunratty Castle, 25 from Shannon Airport, 61 from Killarney and 60 from Cork—but there are fishing, horseback riding and golf close at hand. Rates, which include breakfast, start at IR£30 ($36) single, IR£43 ($51.60) double during high season, lower other months. There's a 50% discount for children and a 12½% service charge.

THE WESTERN REGION
(COUNTIES GALWAY AND MAYO)

1. County Galway

ACCOMMODATIONS: Set in fifty acres of gardens and woodland walks at the head of Cashel Bay among the jagged peaks and rocky headlands of Connemara, **Cashel House Hotel,** Cashel Bay, Connemara, Co. Galway (tel. Cashel 9, Co. Galway 9), has a delightful country house atmosphere. Among the notables who have chosen to come here for holidays were General and Madame Charles de Gaulle in 1969, who turned out to be enthusiastic boosters of the warm Irish hospitality shown by owners Kay and Dermot McEvilly. The stylish 19th-century house blends antique pieces with comfortable modern furnishings, and the cozy bar is the setting for many a friendly crack at the end of a day of sightseeing. The pretty dining room overlooks the gardens, and crackling peat and log fires add to the hominess of this utterly charming place. The dining room, which is open to non-residents as well as guests, enjoys a countrywide reputation for its fine food (see below). The McEvillys are happy to arrange trout and salmon fishing for their guests, as well as horseback riding and picnic itineraries. And there is all of Connemara to be explored.

There are thirty guestrooms, all with private baths, heated towel racks and superb views. Nine have sitting areas that transform them into small suites. Rates, including breakfast, are IR£20 ($24) to IR£26 ($31.20), with a 12½% service charge. Open March through October, and reservations may be made in the U.S. by calling 800/223-6764; in N.Y. State, 800/522-5568; in N.Y. City, 212/758-4375.

Guests at **Currarevagh House,** Oughterard, Co. Galway (tel. 091-82313) often feel as if they're visiting in a private home, as indeed they are, for this is the family home of the present owner, Harry Hodgson, who manages the small inn with his lovely wife, June. The mid-19th-century country house sits in 150 wooded acres on the shores of Lough Corrib, and the Hodgsons provide boats and ghillies (guides) if you wish for some of the best trout fishing in the country. There's a tennis court on the grounds, golf and horseback riding close by. Furnishings and decor carry out the relaxed informality of the place, and spacious guestrooms look out to splendid views. Rates, including breakfast, are IR£22 ($26.40) per person, plus a 10% service charge. A marvelous country dinner will run about IR£13 ($15.60). Open Easter to early October.

Also conveniently located for Connemara sightseeing, the **Oughterard House Hotel,** Oughterard, Co. Galway (tel. 091-82207/82161) is a two-centuries-old country mansion surrounded by 14 acres of lawns, gardens and venerable beech trees. Moira and Patrick Higgins make their guests feel right at home, with hospitality much the same as that of old-time innkeepers. Decor is casual and comfortable, and pleasant tranquility reigns supreme. The beamed ceiling dining room has a cozy charm, and the large downstairs bar looks out onto the garden. Dinners feature traditional Irish and classic French dishes, with a good wine list. There's central heating, as well as open turf fires. The Owneriff River runs through a craggy gorge just across the road, creating small rapids where salmon are seen jumping their way upstream in season. Game fishing is free in Lough Corrib, a short distance away, and golf is also nearby.

Guestrooms vary in style and size depending on whether they're in the original house or an extended wing, but all are comfortably furnished and have private bathrooms and telephones. There's an elevator and wheelchair facilities. Rates, including a full Irish breakfast, start at IR£30 ($36).

A former shooting lodge, **Rock Glen Country House,** Clifden, Connemara, Co. Galway (tel. Clifden 16) is beautifully situated about a mile-and-a-half out the Roundstone/Ballyconneely road from Clifden. Its low, rambling profile belies the spaciousness inside, where a large, lovely drawing room sets a gracious and informal tone. There's also a cozy bar and a dining room which features excellent meals prepared by the friendly owner/manager, John Roche. All thirty-one bedrooms have private baths, and fifteen of them are on the ground floor (a boon to the handicapped and those of us who tote around tons of luggage!). Rates, which include a hearty Irish breakfast, range from IR£16 ($19.20) to IR£18 ($21.60) per person, with a one-third reduction for children and a 12½% service charge.

Right in the middle of the ruggedly beautiful Connemara region, **Rosleague Manor Country House**, Letterfrack, Co. Galway (tel. Moyard 7), overlooks Ballinakill Bay. The fine old Georgian mansion has the high ceilings, tall windows and spacious rooms typical of this style, and its furnishings include many fine period pieces and works of art. Open turf fires complement the central heating. Anne and Patrick Foyle are the friendly owners who run the small hotel with special regard for guests comfort and enjoyment of the area, giving it a distinctly "family" flavor. Bedrooms all have private baths and are nicely decorated and furnished. Rates range from IR£20 ($24) to IR£23 ($27.60) per person, with a 20% reduction for children and a 10% service charge. Open from Easter through October.

RESTAURANTS: Cashel House (tel. Cashel, Co. Galway, 9), recommended above as a Big Splurge accommodation, is also one of Ireland's best places to splurge on a memorable meal. The pretty, cheerful dining room overlooks colorful gardens, and meals here are simple, but beautifully prepared, with Irish seafood and lamb high on the list of menu specialties. Traditional dishes such as boiled bacon and cabbage appear from time to time, as well, and Cashel House serves salmon caught and smoked in the area. There's a good wine list, and dinner will run around IR£16 ($19.20). From March through October, lunch hours are 1 to 2 p.m. (with an à la carte menu), and dinner is at 7:30 p.m. Advance booking is absolutely essential.

About six miles from Clifden on the Westport road, you'll find **Crocnaraw**, Moyard, Connemara (tel. Moyard 9), a lovely Georgian country house set in 20 acres of gardens and farmland. Its dining room features a stone fireplace, and one paneled wall adds to its relaxed warmth. Mrs. Joan Fretwell, the owner, gathers vegetables, salad makings, fruit, butter and eggs from her own lands, insisting on the utmost in freshness. Using just-caught ingredients, she makes an excellent bouquet of seafood (lobster, plaice, crab, salmon and turbot) that is a favorite of regulars. This is a good stop for either lunch or dinner, with set prices of IR£9 ($10.80) and IR£13 ($15.60). Hours are 1 to 2:30 p.m. and 8 to 10 p.m., every day except Sunday and Monday. It's a good idea to book ahead.

2. County Mayo

ACCOMMODATIONS: Ashford Castle, Cong, Co. Mayo (tel. 094-22644) is the stuff of which dreams are made—at least, for Americans with nary a castle to call their own. In 1984, it was the place President and Mrs. Reagan chose to stay during their Irish visit. The grey stone pile, with its towers and turrets, sprawls across great green lawns that slope down to Lough Corrib, surrounded by 500 acres of woodlands and landscaped grounds (including a nine-hole golf course). The original castle was built here in 1228, and those surrounding acres have seen plenty of military action in their day. A member of the Guinness family, however, changed things in the 19th century, when he erected two large wings in the style of a French chateau, and today's modernized castle hotel is a delightful blending of the two.

A medieval touch greets you in the reception hall, where suits of armor and coats of arms line the walls. A truly magnificent staircase sweeps upward, and huge, gilt-framed oil paintings add to the opulence. There is nothing overpoweringly formal about Ashford Castle, however, and the guest lounge is downright inviting (not quite small enough to call cozy), with thick carpeting and comfortable seating and a huge, baronial fireplace just to remind you that it began life as a noble abode. The downstairs lounge bar has a distinctly modern feel, even though it is fitted out as a dungeon, and the palatial dining room is worthy of a Big Splurge in anyone's book (see below). Guestrooms have all been modernized, with not a hint of medieval beginnings, but with contemporary furnishings and decor to cater to guests' comfort—even the bathrooms are carpeted! All have gorgeous views of lake, river or gardens, with such luxurious touches as bedside panel controls for radio and lights.

Sports people will find some of the country's best fishing right on the grounds, and hunters come from all over Europe to stalk pheasant, snipe and duck during winter months. Sightseers find this an ideal base for exploring the west of Ireland.

Rates begin at IR£45 ($54) single, IR£78 ($93.60) double; and if you want to go all out in your splurging, there are weekly rates available. Closed February and March.

Breaffy House Hotel, Castlebar, Co. Mayo (tel. 094-22033), also has a regal air, and is one of the most beautiful stone mansion houses in Ireland. The large gabled house sits in 60 parklike acres, and under the management of Gerry Walshe manages to infuse warmth and charm into a setting that is nothing less than baronial. There's enough to do right on the grounds to keep you entertained—lake fishing, pony trekking, shooting in season, tree-lined walks, and even a nine-hole pitch-and-putt course. For more sedentary types (or the final retreat for sportsmen after all that activity), there's a Tudor-style lounge bar with wooden rafter, pewter dishes and hanging lanterns, and another more in the style of an urban cocktail lounge, with big armchairs, a fireplace and a TV. Meals are so superb that I'm going to recommend the dining room as a Big Splurge (see below), and breakfasts (included in the rates) are outstanding, with grilled kippers, sausages or bacon, homemade brown bread, black pudding and even doughnuts!

As for guestrooms, they reflect the very personal attention given to guests' needs, with such extras as facilities for making tea or coffee, hot water bottles (though there's central heating and not much need for them), mending kits, writing desks, and conveniently placed hooks for bathrobes. Decor is pastel, walls are paneled, and views are lovely. All, of course, have private baths. Rates are IR£27 ($32.40) per person sharing (singles pay a supplement of IR£4 ($4.80), with no service charge, and a one-third discount for children. There are good special rates for stays of three to seven nights.

More a country mansion than a true castle, **Mount Falcon Castle Country House,** Ballina, Co. Mayo (tel. 096-21174) is a place of quiet tranquility, set in wooded grounds not far from lovely deserted beaches. Fishermen can choose between the River Moy, Lough Conn or the sea; other sports-minded guests will find golf, pony trekking and horseback riding close by and a tennis court on the grounds; a games room will keep you occupied indoors. The lovely gabled house has spacious rooms, high ceilings and log fires. Best of all, it has the friendly management of Mrs. Aldridge, who takes a personal interest in all guests and is especially proud of meals that come to her table with vegetables, fruit, milk and cream straight from her own gardens. The attractive guestrooms have private baths. Rates for bed and breakfast are

IR£26 ($31.20) per person, with a 50% reduction for children four to ten, no charge for those under four. Closed Christmas week, February and March.

RESTAURANTS: If you're not going to go all out and stay in **Ashford Castle,** Cong (tel. 094-22644), see above, let me suggest that you book in for dinner in a dining room that is splendid to look at and where service matches the elegance of the setting. It's a large room (seats 200), with sparkling crystal chandeliers, Doric pillars and tall Gothic windows overlooking the lake. Dinners are flawlessly prepared, often with fish fresh from the waters outside, and you'll find such specialties as poached turbot with hollandaise sauce, escalope de veau Tipperary, and beef Stroganoff among menu selections. There's a large dessert and cheese menu to finish things off. There's an à la carte menu, but the best value is the set dinner at IR£22 ($26.40). One thing more: even with its large capacity, the dining room is not prepared for drop-ins, so be sure to book ahead.

I can recommend a Big Splurge meal at **Breaffy House,** Castlebar (tel. 094-22033) with equal enthusiasm (see above for full description). The lovely dining room is modern in decor, but made intimate by soft lighting and thick carpeting. A measure of the care taken with all meals is the fact that everything is cooked to order, making this a place to relax and dine at a leisurely pace (allow at least twenty minutes for your order to arrive). The menu selection is quite extensive, with such regional specialties as seafood, pork, lamb and beef, as well as curried prawns, chicken Maryland, and several French dishes. Aylesbury duckling with orange sauce comes crackly crisp. You can dine à la carte or opt for the set dinner that starts at IR£12 ($14.40), and hours are 7 to 9 p.m., seven days a week.

The Northwestern Region
(Counties Sligo, Donegal, and Leitrim)

1. County Sligo

ACCOMMODATIONS: **Coopershill Country House,** Riverstown, Co. Sligo (tel. 071-65108), is a great stone Georgian family mansion built back in 1774 amid more than 500 acres of woodlands and pastures grazed by sheep and cattle. The graciousness of its original era are reflected in the large rooms, high ceilings and beautiful furnishings, as well as the charming manner of its owner/hostess, Mrs. Joan O'Hara. There are only five bedrooms, but all are special, with private bathrooms and most with either four-poster or canopy beds. There's fishing for pike and perch on the river that flows through the grounds (Mrs. O'Hara has a small boat available to guests), and beautiful beaches are close by. Rates, which include breakfast, are IR£18 ($21.60) per person, with a 10% service charge. Open from Easter to mid-October.

When you head for Yeats Country, consider treating yourself to Big Splurge accommodations at **Ballincar House Hotel,** Rosses Point Rd., Sligo (tel. 071-5362). Helen O'Brien is the friendly hostess at this small hotel (only 20 bedrooms) located about midway between Sligo Town and Rosses Point. Once a comfortable country home, the hotel is surrounded by mature gardens, and the sports-minded will find a leisure complex that includes a sauna, tennis court and squash courts. Golfers are close to the Rosses Point course, and there's safe swimming at the Rosses Point beach. Bedrooms all are nicely appointed and have private baths, and the dining room serves award-winning meals in a lovely setting. Rates, including breakfast, range from IR£20 ($24) to IR£25 ($30) per person, depending on season, with a 15% reduction for children and a 10% service charge.

2. County Donegal

ACCOMMODATIONS: You'll find Rathmullen House, my personal first choice for a County Donegal Big Splurge, fully described in Chapter IX.

Up near County Donegal's spectacular Bloody Forelands, the **Ostan Gweedore,** Bunbeg, Co. Donegal (tel. Bunbeg 85/86) is a modern hotel perched on a small hill that gives it a gorgeous view of miles and miles of sandy beaches and offshore islands. Charles Boyle manages it for his family, and among the amenities they provide are a health complex, tennis courts, golf and fishing. All rooms have private baths and picture windows to take advantage of the views, and the dining room is outstanding, featuring local seafoods. Rates for bed and breakfast are IR£26 ($31.20) single, IR£37 ($44.40) double, with a 25% discount for children and no service charge. Open mid-April through September.

In one of the most beautiful settings in County Donegal—on Donegal Bay, midway between Connemara and the Donegal highlands—the **Sand House Hotel,** Rossnowlagh, Co. Donegal (tel. 072-65777), is a modern, three-story hotel that looks out onto a two-mile crescent beach to the front and a nine-hole golf course to the back. So modern is the hotel in appearance that I was somewhat surprised to learn that it was once a fishing lodge—its expansion and metamorphic expansion is undoubtedly due to the indefatiguable Mary Britton, the charming manageress. The attractive pub is often filled with enthusiastic surfers, since the Sand House has its own surf club (surfboards are furnished at no charge for guests), and its theme is fittingly nautical. It is also the setting for weekend ballad sessions. Another pleasant lounge features a stained glass wall and scenes of Ireland executed in beaten copper. Antique pieces are scattered throughout public areas. Fresh seafood shares menu honors with continental and traditional Irish selections. Guestrooms are nicely done in warm earth tones, all with private baths, and those in front have smashing sea views. Rates for bed and breakfast are in the IR£23 ($27.60) to IR£32 ($38.40) range for singles, IR£40 ($48) to IR£50 ($60) double, with a service charge of 10%. There's a one-third reduction for children during July and August, 50% in May, June and September. Closed October to Easter.

3. County Leitrim

ACCOMMODATIONS: Only about 12 miles outside Sligo Town, **Drumlease Glebe House,** Dromahair, Co. Leitrim (tel. Sligo 071-74141), is situated near the River Bonet amid green lawns and wooded grounds. The Georgian house, presided over by Barbara and Patrick Verner, has all the elegance of a bygone era, but adds the rather surprising modern touch of a 40-foot outdoor swimming pool. Fishing on Lough Melvin can be on your own, or in the care of ghillies (guides) provided by the Verners, who also supply boats and tackle. In winter months, there's good shooting. Although the house has central heating, cheerful log fires create another kind of warmth, and you'll find this a truly relaxing atmosphere. Guestrooms are beautifully appointed, and dinners are by candlelight, accompanied by good wines and ended with a selection of Irish cheeses. Rates for bed and breakfast start at IR£19 ($22.80), with a 12½% service charge, and there are family rates available. Open all year except for Christmas week.

The Midlands
(Counties Cavan, Laois, Longford, Offaly Monaghan, Roscommon, and Westmeath)

1. County Monaghan

ACCOMMODATIONS: The family-owned and operated **Nuremore Hotel,** Carrickmacross, Co. Monaghan (tel. 042-61438) is only about 50 miles from Dublin, and its 100 acres of surrounding woodlands, green lawns, gardens, and smooth golf course provide a restful country setting for sightseeing in either the Midlands or the Eastern Regions. There's also an indoor heated swimming pool, a spa pool, snooker room, sauna and squash court, as well as good fishing in the hotel's own lakes. The thoroughly modern guestrooms all have private baths, TV, video and telephone, and there's an excellent restaurant. Rates, which include breakfast, range from IR£25 ($30) to IR£30 ($36) for single, IR40 ($48) to IR45 ($54) double, with a 25% reduction for children.

Northern Ireland
(Counties Antrim, Londonderry, Down, Armagh, Tyrone, and Fermanagh)

1. County Antrim

ACCOMMODATIONS: A magnificent former Bishop's Palace, set in its own wooded park, the **Culloden Hotel,** Craigavad, Belfast, Co. Antrim (tel. Holywood 5223), is a delightful and luxurious respite from the city's bustle, even though it's just a short drive from the center of activity. Public rooms are elegant, with lots of wood paneling, chandeliers and antique furnishings. Guestrooms, done in modern style, come with private bathrooms, lovely furnishings, facilities for tea and coffee and beautiful views of the landscaped grounds. The restaurants are excellent, and during summer months there's often entertainment at night. Bed-and-breakfast rates are £54 ($75.60) single, £72 ($100.80) double—truly a Big Splurge, but worth every cent!

The **Dunadry Inn,** Dunadry, Co. Antrim (tel. Templepatrick 32474) is farther out from Belfast city center (15 miles), but handy to the airport (4 miles) and to the town of Antrim (3 miles). It's an ideal touring base and a restful and interesting place to end sightseeing days. Because of its out-of-town location the Dunadry offers a unique car-hire service that allows you to pick up and drop off your car there, and they'll pick you up and deliver you back to the airport. The hotel's name translates to "The Middle Fort," since it was the center of three fortifications between Tara and Dunseverick. Over its long history, it's been a paper mill and a linen mill, surrounded by a village of some 20 cottages (a site now covered by the inn, whose restaurant is built right over the old mill stream). The Copper Bar is a striking, two-story baronial hall with a fireplace at one end, exposed wooden rafters and a wood-railed mezzanine leading off to second-story guestrooms. The copper-hooded bar offers a good buffet lunch and draws a convivial group of late-night drinkers. At one side of the courtyard, there's a two-feet-wide stone wall left from the old mill. There's good fishing (free to guests) in the river. All guestrooms are luxuriously furnished, have private baths, color TV, radio and direct-dial telephones—many have French windows that open to the garden or courtyard. Bedspreads are of locally woven tweeds. Rates begin at £29 ($40.60) single, £48 ($67.20) double. An especially good value is the weekend rate of £40 ($56) per person for a weekend, including two nights (sharing), full breakfasts, Saturday dinner-dance and Sunday lunch.

For an inner-city luxury hotel in a quiet, residential setting, you couldn't do better than the **Wellington Park Hotel**, 21 Malone Rd., Belfast (tel. 0232-661232). Situated in the Queen's University area, it's a less than a ten-minute walk to the city center and is one of Belfast's most sophisticated hostelries. Public rooms feature contemporary Irish paintings and sculpture, and there's an attractive lounge bar as well as an excellent restaurant serving both à la carte and table d'hôte meals. Guestrooms all have private baths, color TV, radio, direct-dial telephones and coffee-and-tea-making facilities. Rates begin at £33 ($46.20) single, £52 ($72.80) double.

Along the Antrim Coast, there's a charming, old-style hotel in the little town of Portsteward. **O'Malley's Edgewater Hotel**, 88 Strand Rd., Portsteward (tel. 026-583224/583688), keeps a wood fire glowing in the small, homey lobby. In the lounge and dining room, big windows look out to the sea—ending the day snuggled into one of the comfortable lounge chairs, drink in hand, looking out over the strand is one of my most pleasant memories of a recent Northern Ireland visit. A mini-leisure center holds a sauna, sun bed and Jacuzzi. On the staircase leading up to second-floor guestrooms, a stained glass window on the landing lends an old-fashioned look. Guestrooms come with private bath, TV, radio and telephone—some have sea views. Rates for bed and breakfast are £18.50 ($25.90) single, £34 ($47.60) double during summer months, lower the rest of the year. There's a one-third reduction for children.

See also the recommendation in Chapter XIII for Londonderry Arms Hotel, Carnlough, Co. Antrim—another personal favorite.

2. County Londonderry

ACCOMMODATIONS: Set in its own grounds at the edge of town, the **Everglades Hotel**, Prehen Rd., Londonderry BT47 2PA (tel. 0504-46722), is one of Northern Ireland's leading luxury hotels, and you're likely to find a fair sprinkling of locals in the bar and restaurant on any given day. Guestrooms are attractively furnished with cane chairs, tables and beds and have private bath, color TV, in-house movies, radio, direct-dial telephone, and facilities for tea and coffee. There's an inviting cocktail lounge, the Buttery Bar for quick meals, snacks or drinks, and the lovely Seminole Restaurant for excellent full-meal service. Rates begin at £27 ($37.80) for singles, £37 ($51.80) for doubles.

3. County Down

ACCOMMODATIONS: At the **Slieve Donard Hotel,** Newcastle, Co. Down (tel. Newcastle 23681), you can look across Dundrum Bay to where the Mountains of Mourne sweep down to the sea and walk along the four-mile curving sandy strand to their very feet. You can also live out any latent Victorian fantasies in the turreted, red-brick hotel set in its acres of green lawn. When it was built, back in 1897, there were coal fires in every bath. These days, every modern convenience is incorporated into public and guestrooms, somehow leaving intact a genteel atmosphere that evokes an era of sweeping long skirts and frockcoated gentlemen. Front rooms overlooking the sea are especially nice, and I am particularly fond of Nos. 103 and 104, both singles with curved windows and the bath up a short flight of steps (a perfect retreat for the single traveler). The Dogs Head pub and restaurant at the entrance gates is a whitewashed gate lodge serving food at moderate prices, and the hotel's main dining room excells in fresh seafood creations. Rates begin at £24 ($33.60) single, £37 ($51.80) double during summer months (lower other times), and it's a good idea to book ahead in this popular hostelry.

FROMMER/PASMANTIER PUBLISHERS   Date_____
1230 AVE. OF THE AMERICAS, NEW YORK, NY 10020

Friends, please send me the books checked below:

$-A-DAY GUIDES
(In-depth guides to low-cost tourist accommodations and facilities.)

☐ Europe on $25 a Day....................	$10.95
☐ Australia on $25 a Day.................	$9.95
☐ England and Scotland on $25 a Day.....	$9.95
☐ Greece on $25 a Day...................	$9.95
☐ Hawaii on $35 a Day...................	$9.95
☐ India on $15 & $25 a Day..............	$9.95
☐ Ireland on $25 a Day..................	$9.95
☐ Israel on $30 & $35 a Day.............	$9.95
☐ Mexico on $20 a Day..................	$9.95
☐ New Zealand on $20 & $25 a Day.......	$9.95
☐ New York on $35 a Day................	$8.95
☐ Scandinavia on $35 a Day.............	$9.95
☐ South America on $25 a Day...........	$8.95
☐ Spain and Morocco (plus the Canary Is.) on $35 a Day.....	$9.95
☐ Washington, D.C. on $35 a Day........	$8.95

DOLLARWISE GUIDES
(Guides to accommodations and facilities from budget to deluxe, with emphasis on the medium-priced.)

☐ Austria & Hungary	$10.95	☐ Cruises (incl. Alaska, Carib, Mex, Hawaii, Panama, Canada, & US)	$10.95
☐ Egypt.........................	$9.95	☐ California & Las Vegas	$9.95
☐ England & Scotland	$10.95	☐ Florida.......................	$9.95
☐ France........................	$10.95	☐ New England...................	$9.95
☐ Germany......................	$9.95	☐ Northwest....................	$10.95
☐ Italy.........................	$10.95	☐ Southeast & New Orleans...........	$9.95
☐ Portugal (incl. Madeira & the Azores) .	$9.95	☐ Southwest....................	$10.95
☐ Switzerland & Liechtenstein	$9.95		
☐ Canada	$10.95		
☐ Caribbean (incl. Bermuda & the Bahamas)	$10.95		

THE ARTHUR FROMMER GUIDES
(Pocket-size guides to tourist accommodations and facilities in all price ranges.)

☐ Amsterdam/Holland	$4.95	☐ Mexico City/Acapulco	$4.95
☐ Athens.......................	$4.95	☐ Montreal/Quebec City	$4.95
☐ Atlantic City/Cape May	$4.95	☐ New Orleans...................	$4.95
☐ Boston.......................	$4.95	☐ New York.....................	$4.95
☐ Dublin/Ireland	$4.95	☐ Orlando/Disney World/EPCOT	$4.95
☐ Hawaii	$4.95	☐ Paris	$4.95
☐ Las Vegas	$4.95	☐ Philadelphia...................	$4.95
☐ Lisbon/Madrid/Costa del Sol.........	$4.95	☐ Rome	$4.95
☐ London	$4.95	☐ San Francisco	$4.95
☐ Los Angeles	$4.95	☐ Washington, D.C.	$4.95

SPECIAL EDITIONS

☐ How to Beat the High Cost of Travel ...	$4.95	☐ Marilyn Wood's Wonderful Weekends.. (NY, Conn, Mass, RI, Vt, NJ, Pa)	$9.95
☐ New York Urban Athlete (NYC sports guide for jocks & novices)	$9.95	☐ Museums in New York	$8.95
☐ Where to Stay USA (Accommodations from $3 to $25 a night)	$8.95	☐ Guide for the Disabled Traveler	$10.95
		☐ Bed & Breakfast-No. America........	$7.95
☐ Fast 'n' Easy Phrase Book (Fr/Sp/Ger/Ital. in *one* vol.)	$6.95		

In U.S. include $1 post. & hdlg. for 1st book; 25¢ ea. add'l. book. Outside U.S. $2 and 50¢ respectively.

Enclosed is my check or money order for $_____

NAME_____

ADDRESS_____

CITY_____   STATE_____ ZIP_____